The Therapeutic Powers of Play

The Therapeutic Powers of Play

Comparing Theories and Practice

Edited by
Athena A. Drewes and Edward Franc Hudspeth

BLOOMSBURY ACADEMIC
NEW YORK • LONDON • OXFORD • NEW DELHI • SYDNEY

BLOOMSBURY ACADEMIC
Bloomsbury Publishing Inc, 1359 Broadway, New York, NY 10018, USA
Bloomsbury Publishing Plc, 50 Bedford Square, London, WC1B 3DP, UK
Bloomsbury Publishing Ireland, 29 Earlsfort Terrace, Dublin 2, D02 AY28, Ireland

BLOOMSBURY, BLOOMSBURY ACADEMIC and the Diana logo are trademarks of Bloomsbury Publishing Plc

First published in the United States of America 2025

Cover design: Dustin Watson
Cover image © istock/Yana Tatevosian; istock/pialhovik

A catalog record for this book is available from the Library of Congress.

ISBN: HB: 979-8-216-27761-3
PB: 979-8-216-27760-6
ePDF: 979-8-216-27763-7
eBook: 979-8-216-27764-4

Typeset by Deanta Global Publishing Services, Chennai, India
Printed and bound in the United States of America

For product safety related questions contact productsafety@bloomsbury.com.

To find out more about our authors and books visit www.bloomsbury.com and sign up for our newsletters.

This book is dedicated to my son, Seth Andrew Bridges, whose zest for life and adventure, through his lifelong love and career of acting and stunt work, has taught me about the true meaning of the therapeutic powers of play!—Athena A. Drewes

This book is dedicated to those who taught me about play therapy and all those I've taught play therapy. Each has challenged me to know more and pass along play therapy knowledge and traditions.—Edward Franc Hudspeth

Contents

Figures and Photos

Preface

In Memoriam

Part 1 Chapter 5

Part 1 Chapter 6

Part 2 Chapter 1

Part 3 Chapter 3

Part 3 Chapter 4

Part 3 Chapter 7

Tables

Part 1 Chapter 3

Part 1 Chapter 7

Part 2 Chapter 7

Part 2 Chapter 8

Part 3 Chapter 5

Part 3 Chapter 6

Part 4

About the Contributors

Ann Beckley-Forest, LCSW-R, RPT-S, is a licensed Clinical Social Worker, Registered Play Therapy Supervisor, and Approved Provider of play therapy education. She is EMDR Approved Consultant and Trainer in private practice in Buffalo, NY, and specializes in trauma and play therapy for children, teens, and adults. She is also a clinical consultant and trainer for play therapy, trauma, and EMDR.

Staci Born, EdD, LMFT, RPT-S, is the founder of The Blue Couch, specializing in therapeutic treatment for children and families. With over fifteen years of experience, she is a Licensed Marriage and Family Therapist in Minnesota and South Dakota, and a Registered Play Therapist Supervisor, focusing on play therapy, complex trauma, and early childhood mental health. An international speaker and author, Dr. Born has contributed to numerous publications and served on editorial boards for major journals.

Sherri Cauthen, LCSW, RPT-S, IECMH-C, is Clinical Director of the Horowitz-Zusman Center in Atlanta, Georgia, trained under Dr. Terry Kottman. She combines Adlerian principles with innovative play therapy techniques to help children and families address challenges and build resilience. Sherri focuses on strengthening family dynamics by promoting encouragement, connection, and shared goals through interactive interventions like collaborative problem-solving activities and creative expression.

Gloria M. Cockerill, LCSW, PMH-C, CATP, CCTP, CFTP, Registered Play Therapist-Supervisor is a Certified Theraplay® Practitioner, Supervisor, and Trainer and previously served as the Training Director at The Theraplay Institute. She has worked as a Field Consultant at the University of Chicago's Crown Family School of Social Work, Policy, and Practice and as Adjunct Faculty member at the University of Illinois at Chicago's Jane Addams College of Social Work. For over twenty years, she has practiced extensively with children, adolescents, and families impacted by trauma, attachment disruptions, and a broad range of social, emotional, and behavioral challenges in a variety of settings.

Janet A. Courtney, PhD, RPT-S, is founder of FirstPlay Therapy and author of the books, *Infant Play Therapy: Foundation, Models Programs and Practice*, and *Healing Child and Family Trauma through Expressive and Play Therapies*, and *Touch in Child Counseling and Play Therapy*. She is former Chair of the APT Ethics and Practice Committee and former president of the Florida Association for Play Therapy. She is in Private Practice at Developmental Play & Attachment Therapies, Inc., Boynton Beach, Florida.

Athena A. Drewes, PsyD, MA, MS Ed, RPT-S, Founder and President Emeritus of the New York Association for Play Therapy; Former director of the Association for Play Therapy; Lifetime Achievement Award from NYAPT and the Association for Play Therapy. Semi-retired, Private Practice, Ocala, Florida.

Ken Gardner, M.Sc., R.Psych (CPT-S) is a Clinical Psychologist and a Certified Play Therapy Supervisor. He is a past executive board member of the Canadian Association for Play Therapy and has been a clinical practitioner for over thirty years. Ken has presented nationally and internationally on a wide range of topics related to the Play Therapy Dimensions Model and play-based interventions. Calgary, Alberta, Canada.

Paris Goodyear-Brown, MSSW, LCSW, RPT-S, and Approved EMDR Consultant, is the creator of TraumaPlay™, the executive director of the TraumaPlay Institute, the Clinical Director of Nurture House, and an adjunct instructor of Psychiatric Mental Health at Vanderbilt University. She is a TED Talk speaker, a master clinician, a thought leader in the fields of child trauma and play therapy globally, has received the APT award for Play Therapy Promotion and Education, and served as the Executive Director of the Lipscomb Play Therapy and Expressive Arts Center. She is on the board of TNAPT and has written over twenty chapters and articles as well as twelve books, including *Trauma and Play Therapy, Parents as Partners in Child Therapy, Big Behaviors in Small Containers.*, and her newest edited volume, *Polyvagal Power in the Playroom*. Paris delights in serving traumatized children and families locally, loves to travel with her family, and finds great joy in equipping child trauma therapists all over the world.

Robert Jason Grant, EdD, LPC, RPT-S, is the creator of AutPlay® Therapy. He is a therapist, supervisor, and consultant who utilizes several years of advanced training and his own lived neurodivergent experience to provide affirming services to children and their families. He is an international trainer, keynote presenter and multi-published author of several articles and books. Private Practice, Springfield, Missouri.

Elizabeth Kjellstrand Hartwig, PhD, LMFT-S, LPC-S, RPT-S™, is a professor in the Professional Counseling Program at Texas State University. She is the founder and director of the Texas State University Animal-Assisted Counseling Academy. Her research interests include solution-focused play therapy, animal-assisted counseling, and sand tray therapy.

Edward (Franc) Hudspeth, PhD, NCC, LPC-S, ACS, RPT-S, RPh is Coordinator and Clinical Associate Professor in the EdS in Counselor Education-Play Therapy Emphasis, in the School of Education, at the University of Mississippi. He received his PhD in Counselor Education and Supervision in 2009 and has been a Registered Pharmacist since 1989 and a Licensed Professional Counselor since 2004.

Terry Kottman, PhD, LMFT, RPT-S, developed Adlerian play therapy, an approach to working with children, families, and adults that combines the ideas and techniques of

Individual Psychology and play therapy. She founded the League of Extraordinary Adlerian Play Therapists, a training program for Adlerian play therapists.

John Paul "JP" Lilly, LCSW (deceased), Sierra Counseling Associates, Inc., Provo, Utah.

Yung-Wei Dennis Lin, PhD, NCC, associate professor in the Counselor Education Department at the University of Iowa, has extensive experience in research, has served as editorial board member for multiple professional journals, and was the chair of the research committee of APT.

Rachel McRoberts, PhD, LPC/MHSP, ACS, RPT-S is an award-winning Jungian-oriented counselor, play therapist, supervisor, educator, and researcher. She is a member of the core faculty at the University of the Cumberlands and is the author of *Jungian Counseling & Play Therapy: Classical Theory for the Digital Age.*

Clair Mellenthin, LCSW, RPT-S, is a sought-after supervisor, international speaker, and renowned play therapist. Clair is the author of the best-selling books *Attachment Centered Play Therapy*; *Play Therapy: Proven Strategies for Childhood Disorders*, and many more. In addition to being an experienced play therapist and professor, she frequently appears on local and national media as an expert on children and family issues.

Annie Monaco, LCSW-R, RPT-S, is co-founder of Playful EMDR, an online hub for training and consultation, and co-editor and contributor of chapters for EMDR with Children in the Play Therapy Room, including her specialty in dissociation in children and teens.

Sarah Moran, LMFT, RPT-S, Child and Family Therapist, AAMFT Approved Supervisor Candidate, Olympia, Washington.

Julie Nash, PhD, RPT-S, is a clinical psychologist and owner of Riverside Psychological Associates, LLC, where she provides continuing education training and consultation for play therapists and supervisors.

Judi Parson, PhD, MA in Play Therapy, M HthSc, GDip Paeds, GCHE, BN, RN, Discipline Lead and Senior Lecturer in Play Therapy at Deakin University, Geelong, Australia.

Mary Anne Peabody, EdD, LCSW, RPT-S, is a professor at the University of Southern Maine where she teaches undergraduate courses on play and graduate courses in play therapy. Throughout her career, she has remained active with the Association for Play Therapy, serving as a past Board Director and currently serving as the chair of the APT Foundation Board and an editorial advisory board member for the International Journal of Play Therapy. Dr. Peabody presents internationally on a range of topics, including play pedagogy in higher education, feedback practices in play therapy supervision, and the methodology of Seriously Therapeutic Play with LEGO®.

Kristi Perryman is an associate professor of Counseling at the University of Arkansas. She is an LPC-S, RPT-S, and CCPT-S. Her experience includes working as a special education teacher, an elementary and middle school counselor, and as a counselor in private practice. She is in her second term serving on the governing board for the Association for Play Therapy.

Lisa Remey, Med, LPC-S, NCC, IPT-CST, RPT-S, is a Certified FirstPlay Practitioner, past president of the Texas Association for Play Therapy, and owner of Bluebonnet Play Therapy with over twenty-five years of experience. She specializes in working with infants through adolescence, using play as a transformative tool for emotional healing and development. Lisa is also a passionate trainer, empowering mental health professionals with her extensive knowledge and expertise.

Bridgette Mitchell Sanders, PsyD, LCSW, RPT-S, is a licensed therapist and Registered Play Therapist-Supervisor in Los Angeles, California. Having trained and supervised play therapists, students, and licensed therapists for twenty years, Dr. Sanders is passionate about teaching play therapy theory and supporting play therapists to identify and embrace their theoretical orientation.

Jessica Stone, PhD, RPT-S, is a clinical psychologist, registered play therapist-supervisor, and pioneer in integrating technology into play therapy. She is the creator of Digital Play Therapy™, founder of the MHVR-International Coalition, and a sought-after author, speaker, and trainer. Dr. Stone specializes in innovative approaches to mental health and therapeutic engagement.

Renee Turner, PhD, LPC-S, RPT-S™, is the owner of the Expressive Therapies Institute, PLLC, with a private practice in San Antonio, Texas. She is a contributing faculty member at Walden University and a past president of the Texas Association for Play Therapy.

Dana Wyss, PhD, LMFT, ATR-BC, RPT, is a licensed marriage and family therapist, board-certified clinical art therapist, registered play therapist, and co-author of *The Invisible String Workbook* and *Hope and The Winds of Grief Workbook*. Her doctorate in expressive therapies has led her to create programs integrating art, music, poetry, and animal-assisted therapy in clients' healing processes and staff's self-care. Dr. Wyss resides in Southern California, where she is a clinical training specialist, owns a small private practice, and loves to create art.

Lorri Yasenik, PhD, RPT-S, CPT-S, is the director of the Rocky Mountain Play Therapy Institute (RMPTI) in Canmore, Alberta, Canada, and the Co-director of the International Centre for Children and Family Law (ICCFL) in Australia. Lorri is a Registered and Certified Supervisor of Child Psychotherapy and Play Therapy and delivers approved play therapy training programs nationally and internationally in the areas of child and play therapy, play therapy supervision, and child-inclusive practice in the family law sectors. She has an Honorary Fellowship at Deakin University in Geelong, Australia.

Anqi Yu is currently a doctoral student in the Counselor Education and Supervision Program at the University of Iowa. Her research interests include the development of international counseling students, qualitative methods, and instructional design in counselor education.

Karlie Lynn Zaban, MA, LPC-A, is a Licensed Professional Counselor-Associate in Connecticut and Pennsylvania. She received her MA in Clinical Mental Health Counseling from Sacred Heart University in 2023. Karlie's area of clinical focus lies in supporting LGBTQ+ clients and survivors of trauma. She is also certified in EMDR Basic Training. Private Practice, Hope & Meaning Counseling.

About the Editors

Athena A. Drewes, PsyD, MA, MS Ed, RPT-S, is a licensed psychologist, certified school psychologist, registered play therapist and play therapist supervisor, and noted author and co-editor of over thirteen books on play therapy, including *The Therapeutic Powers of Play: 20 Core Agents of Change* (with Charles Schaefer, 2014) and *Supervision Can be Playful. Second Edition* (with Jodi A. Mullen, 2024, Rowman and Littlefield). She has produced a video demonstrating her Prescriptive Integrative Play Therapy approach through the American Psychological Association Children and Adolescents Series IX. She has a long and prestigious career as a passionate play therapist with over forty-five years of clinical experience in working with children and adolescents with complex trauma and sexual abuse in schools, residential treatment, and foster care settings.

Dr. Drewes has supervised colleagues and doctoral psychology interns for over forty years in play therapy, encouraging and assisting many in becoming registered play therapists and registered play therapist-supervisors. She was formerly director of clinical training and the director of the American Psychological Association Accredited Doctoral Psychology Internship Program at Astor Services for Children and Families, Rhinebeck, NY. She served sixteen years as president of the New York Association for Play Therapy and six years as director of the Association for Play Therapy and has served, and continues to serve, in leadership roles on many APT committees. She was adjunct professor of Play Therapy at the graduate level for fifteen years for Sage College, Western Connecticut University and Marist College. She founded the New York Association for Play Therapy and was awarded the permanent honorary status of Founder and President Emeritus of the New York Association for Play Therapy.

Dr. Drewes was honored with the Lifetime Achievement Awards from the New York Association for Play Therapy and the National Association for Play Therapy (2024). She also received the American Red Cross of Greater NY Leadership Award for Disaster Mental Health Leadership, the Psi Chi Florence Denmark Graduate Research Award, and an Empire State Challenger Scholarship. She has been active with the Red Cross, the Disaster Mental Health Institute of SUNY New Paltz, USAID, and the United Nations and has been responsible for the creation of internationally used manuals and training devoted to helping children and families deal with post-disasters, wars, and trauma.

Dr. Drewes serves on the editorial boards of the *Australian Journal of Rural Health, International Journal of Play Therapy, Journal of Child and Adolescent Trauma, Journal of Child Sexual Abuse, Journal of Family Violence, Journal of Religion and Spirituality,* among others.

Dr. Drewes received her master's in Clinical Psychology from New York University, New York, NY, in 1977; her master's in education from Pace University in 1990; and her doctor of psychology, specializing in clinical and school psychology, from Pace University, New York, NY, in 1992. She received her Registered Play Therapist and Supervisor credential in 1994.

She is currently semi-retired in Ocala, Florida and is a volunteer Guardian ad Litem (court-appointed special advocate for foster care children) and received the Guardian ad Litem Volunteer of the Year Award, 2023. She has a private practice focusing on supervision on the national and international level, consultation, and national and international training. She continues to be actively involved in writing articles, book chapters and edited books on play therapy along with being a much sought-after international (across four continents) and national presenter.

Edward Franc Hudspeth, PhD, NCC, LPC-S, ACS, RPT-S, RPh, is Coordinator and Clinical Associate Professor in the EdS in Counselor Education-Play Therapy Emphasis, in the School of Education, at the University of Mississippi. He was the editor of *International Journal of Play Therapy* for ten years and the *Journal of Counselor Preparation and Supervision* for four years. He is currently coeditor of the *Journal of Military and Government Counseling* as well as an editorial board member for the *Journal of Creativity in Mental Health, The Professional Counselor, and Journal of Counseling Research and Practice.*

He received his PhD, in Counselor Education and Supervision, from the University of Mississippi in 2009. He has been a registered pharmacist since 1989, a Mississippi licensed professional counselor since 2004, an Arkansas licensed professional counselor since 2015, registered play therapist supervisor, and a nationally approved clinical supervisor since 2007.

He is a member of multiple national associations and has served in multiple leadership roles and on many committees for the Association for Play Therapy, the Association for Creativity in Counseling, and the Military and Government Counseling Association. He has also served in various roles for the Mississippi and Arkansas Associations for Play Therapy.

Franc received the Association for Play Therapy's National Service Award in 2012 and 2015, the Arkansas Counseling Association's Blair Olson Professional Service Award in 2014, Henderson State University's, Teacher's College Faculty Excellence Award for Service in 2016, the North Atlantic Region of the Association for Counselor Education and Supervision's Marijane Falls Counselor Educator of the Year Award in 2018, the Military and Government Counseling Association's Outstanding Organization Support Award in 2022, and the Association for Play Therapy's President's Award in 2022.

His writing and research interests include trauma's impact on brain development, psychopharmacology, neuroscience influences on counseling, counselors' military cultural competency, and play therapy applications to attachment disorders. He has written numerous book chapters and journal articles spanning these topics.

Foreword

Judi Parson

I couldn't believe it, on Charlie Schaefer's birthday, the 15th of November, I was offered a gift—to write a foreword for *The Therapeutic Powers of Play: Comparing Theories and Practice*. Thank you, Athena Drewes and Franc Hudspeth, you piqued my interest right away with the structure and a contents list, which showcases the collective wisdom of leading colleagues in the field. I was genuinely impressed because this book arrives at a pivotal moment in the evolution of play therapy. It offers both emerging and established practitioners an invaluable resource to deepen their understanding of the therapeutic powers of play and their application across diverse theoretical frameworks. I can foresee both students and teachers delving into theories and practices together to advance professional applications.

Children's play serves as a language bridge that connects a child's inner world to their external environment, where the play therapist patiently observes, listens, and attunes to the child's unique voice. In play therapy, children build connections, express themselves, process experiences, and find healing in ways that words alone often cannot. And just as Loris Malaguzzi (1996) states in his poem, "the child is made up of a hundred languages, . . . a hundred ways of thinking, of playing, of speaking" there are also hundreds of therapists witnessing and responding to the hundred ways of addressing the child's symbolic expressions and psychosocial and emotional needs through play. Therefore, we need a transformative framework to navigate the multitude of theories, concepts, and approaches for engaging children in therapy. And the therapeutic powers of play provide this framework for play therapists.

This book goes beyond surface-level interventions to shine a light on the deeper therapeutic process, providing a pathway to explore the therapeutic powers of play across various theories and clinical practice modalities. The editors and contributors have crafted an exceptional exploration of theory, neuroscience, and practice. The book's structure—beginning with foundational concepts and advancing to comparative theoretical applications and integrative approaches—is both comprehensive and accessible. The inclusion of case studies grounds theoretical discussions in practical, authentic examples, making the ideas easier to apply directly in clinical work.

As I explored chapters on foundational theories like Psychoanalytic, Adlerian, and Gestalt play therapies, among others, I was delighted to see the rich theoretical diversity and the unifying thread of the therapeutic powers of play. Whether exploring the Play Therapy Dimensions Model, neuroscientific theory, or case conceptualization, the authors highlight how the core principles of play therapy transcend disciplinary boundaries, offering hope and healing to children and families around the world.

I encourage you to journey through these pages with curiosity and an open mind. Whether you are a clinician, educator, or researcher, this book will inspire new ways to integrate the therapeutic powers of play into your work. I hope it will challenge you to think critically about how theory informs practice and how practice, in turn, advances the field.

Play Therapy is all about creating a safe space for children to express, explore, and reshape their inner worlds, fostering resilience and psychosocial health and wellbeing. As you read through the chapters, I encourage you to think about how the ideas shared here could shape the future of play therapy and positively impact the lives of the children we work with.

I am confident that *The Therapeutic Powers of Play: Comparing Theories and Practice* will leave an enduring mark on our profession and the countless lives it touches.

Associate Professor Judi Parson, PhD,
Play Therapy Discipline Lead,
Deakin University, Australia.

Reference

Malaguzzi, L. (1996). *The hundred languages of children: The Reggio Emilia approach to early childhood education.* Ablex Publishing Corporation.

Preface

There are no texts similar to this one. Unlike previous play therapy texts, which focus on seminal play therapy theories or the therapeutic powers of play (TPoP), this text presents them in unison. Each chapter, in Parts II and III, applies them to the case of Herman, allowing readers to see them as a golden thread linking initial conceptualization to planning a play therapy course of action to application. As such, and as a reader, whether you are a play therapist-in-training, credentialed play therapist, play therapy supervisor, or play therapy trainer/educator, this text is a valuable and comprehensive resource for any play therapy practice. The conceptualization of this text began as a conversation in October 2022. In 2023, the full scope of the book was established, and in 2024, the authors wrote chapters. The end product fills a gap, positioning the TPoP alongside (in unison) seminal play therapy theories so that play therapy practitioners can see that no play therapy theory operates in isolation: each relies on the TPoP as change agents.

In 2019, the Association for Play Therapy (APT) published a series of short articles in their *Play Therapy* magazine, which linked seminal play therapy theories to the therapeutic powers of play (APT, 2019). Each is available on APT's website under the Membership, Publications tab. Though these articles addressed some of the aspects we address in this text, there was no application piece.

Play has long been recognized as a fundamental component of child development, providing children with the means of expression and understanding (Hendricks, 2020). For decades, the therapeutic benefits of play have garnered increasing attention in psychological and medical research. In therapeutic settings, play transcends its obvious role, becoming a powerful tool for healing and emotional expression (Kohrt et al., 2020). Play has been shown to possess significant therapeutic potential across various stages of life (Whitebread et al., 2017). From alleviating stress and anxiety to enhancing cognitive function and social skills, the therapeutic application of play continues to be explored and validated (Kaizar & Alordiah, 2023).

Play therapy, as a therapeutic approach, relies on play for communication and expression. Rooted in the understanding that children process and express emotions differently than adults, play therapy provides an opportunity for children to externalize thoughts and feelings, helping them make sense of complex experiences in a safe, structured environment (Shrinivasa et al., 2018). Play therapy stands as a testament to the profound impact of play in therapeutic settings, offering a unique avenue for emotional expression, healing, and growth among individuals, particularly children and adolescents (Koukourikos et al., 2021). Play therapy is defined by the Association for Play Therapy (APT) as "the systematic use of a theoretical model to establish an interpersonal process wherein trained play therapists use the therapeutic powers of play to help clients prevent or resolve psychosocial difficulties and achieve optimal growth and development." (APT, 2001).

The TPoP refer to the specific change agents in which play initiates, facilitates, or strengthens their therapeutic effect. These play powers act as *mediators* that positively influence the desired change in the client (Drewes & Schaefer, 2016). In other words, play actually helps produce the change and is not just a *medium* for applying other change agents, nor does it just *moderate* the strength or direction of the therapeutic change. The therapeutic powers of play (TPoP) are akin to a universal translator in that they have the ability to surpass verbal communication barriers, helping to provide a safe and structured environment where clients can explore and make sense of their inner and outer worlds. They are core features of play therapy that go unmatched.

Based upon a review of the literature and the clinical experiences of play therapists, Schaefer (2016) identified twenty core therapeutic powers of play. Among these powers are change agents that improve a client's attachment formation, self-expression, emotion regulation, resiliency, self-esteem, and stress management, among other areas (Drewes & Schaefer, 2016). These change agents are extensively written about in *The Therapeutic Powers of Play: 20 Core Agents of Change* (Schaefer & Drewes, 2014). This book has become a gold standard for learning about these change agents and how they manifest in various settings and with a variety of diagnoses.

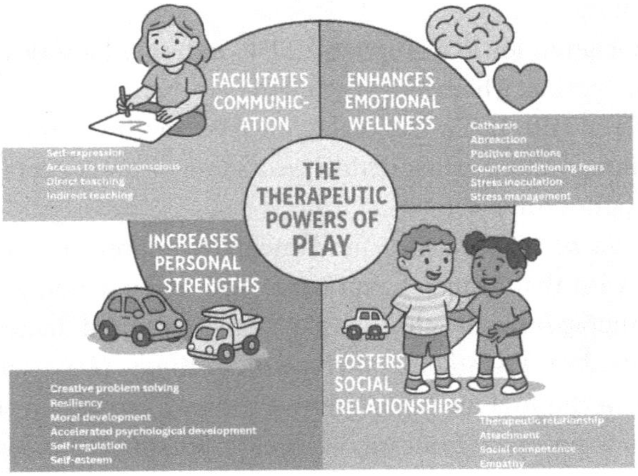

The above graphic was created by Judi Parson (as cited in Peabody & Schaefer, 2019) to help visualize and conceptualize the overall categories and specifically where the twenty core agents of change fall. Broad categories of the therapeutic powers are: (1) Facilitates Communication, which lists the agents of change: self-expression, access to the unconscious, direct, and indirect teaching; (2) Fosters Emotional Wellness, with catharsis, abreaction, positive emotions, counter-conditioning fears, stress inoculation, and stress management as agents of change. Under (3) Enhances Relationships, the core agents of change are the therapeutic relationship, attachment, social competence, and empathy; and under (4) Increases Personal Strengths, the core agents of change are creative problem solving, resiliency, moral development, accelerated psychological development, self-regulation, and self-esteem. Not all of the core agents of change may be affecting change within a specific theory or method of treatment. So, the therapist needs to prescriptively select which agents of change would be needed to facilitate the treatment process and address the treatment plan.

Through the efforts and advocacy of the late Dr. Charles Schaefer, the therapeutic powers of play have been incorporated into the Association for Play Therapy's (APT) requirements for training to become registered in one of their several credentials as a play therapist (RPT, RPT-S, SBPT) as well as to incorporate TPoP into any submission of conference proposals and subsequent presentations.

APT also requires training in learning about seminal and historically significant theories. APT recognizes three major branches as seminal theories to the field of play therapy: Cognitive Behavioral, Humanistic and Psychodynamic. They recognize ten historically significant theories to the field of play therapy:

1. Adlerian
2. Child-Centered
3. Cognitive-Behavioral
4. Developmental (Viola Brody)
5. Ecosystemic
6. Filial—although not a theory, this approach is historically significant.
7. Gestalt
8. Jungian
9. Object-Relations
10. Theraplay—although not a theory, this approach is historically significant.

However, some play therapists have not been trained in nor have a solid theoretical foundation for case conceptualization, and it has also become apparent to these editors that many play therapists do not have a full understanding of what the therapeutic power of play is, how it interplays with theory, and how the change agent operates, as well as how to utilize these change agents in creating treatment plans and conducting therapy. Consequently, we felt in order for research to further study the impact of TPoP and for clinicians to have a firm footing in theory as well as understanding of the implementation of the TPoP, this book needed to be born! As a way of extending the work of Dr. Schaefer, we felt that by taking one case study and examining it through different seminal and historically significant theoretical lenses, readers would be able to better understand the theoretical underpinnings of their treatment approach and further apply their understanding to their casework. In addition, we felt it important to have the therapeutic powers of play highlighted through various current models and settings in order to offer the broadest lens for application.

For purposes of consistency and continuity across chapters, each chapter author in Parts II and III was required to include an abstract, introduction, delineate the underlying philosophy of their theory, the personality theory involved within their theoretical framework and method, and what the model of psychopathology was, if any. The authors were to conceptualize their treatment goals, along with the role of the therapist, caregivers, and collaterals, and supply any relevant research/empirical support. For each part, a single case study was supplied with which each author would respond. They would approach the case study through the lens of the therapeutic powers of play by identifying which therapeutic powers were employed in treatment, as well as cultural/diversity/inclusion considerations, the actual case formulation for how treatment would occur through their theoretical lens and/or model, and challenges in implementation. References and any supportive materials were to be added.

This book is, therefore, divided into three major parts. Part I addresses understanding the therapeutic powers of play in the broadest spectrum. Eight chapters focus on defining what the therapeutic power of play is and provide an overview of the TPoP, with additional chapters helping readers understand what a theory is and how to select one for practice; the interplay of neuroscience and the TPoP; how to conceptualize cases from a theoretical and TPoP lens, along with relevant research and empirical support so far on TPoP. Two chapters focus on the transtheoretical model of supervision and on using the Dimensions model to think through application.

Part II deals with comparing theoretical approaches through the lens of TPoP. Eight theories are focused on, each presenting their foundation utilizing a single case study for comparison (see Appendix for case study of Herman) and then how the case would be treated using their theoretical lens. The case of Herman was purposely created with a broad range of complex traumas, cultural and gender issues, and attachment and behavioral issues that would allow for a wide range of interpretation, focus and treatment approach. The seminal and historically significant theories presented include psychoanalytic play therapy, child-centered play therapy, gestalt play therapy, attachment theory and Theraplay, Jungian analytical play therapy, Adlerian play therapy, cognitive-behavioral play therapy, and solution-focused play therapy.

Part III delves into integrative approaches and various current models of treatment in comparison utilizing the case study of Herman through the lens of the TPoP. The seven chapters in this part include Prescriptive play therapy, AutPlay, First Play, Trauma Play, Digital Play Therapy, EMDR and play therapy, and Attachment Play Therapy. Each chapter author delineates their theoretical base and how they would approach the treatment of the case study utilizing their model through the TPoP.

Part IV gives readers closing thoughts and a detailed summary overview of the book's highlights around the TPoP and its applications.

But the work doesn't end here! There is future research and direction needed in exploring the therapeutic powers of play that go beyond the scope of this volume! Here are some thoughts.

Future Directions

Many prominent psychotherapists have called for a shift in psychotherapy training from an emphasis on broad theories of psychotherapy to a focus on therapeutic change mechanisms. Two main reasons a greater understanding of change agents is of vital importance to play therapists and other clinicians are (Drewes & Schaefer, 2014):

1. It should improve clinical effectiveness by facilitating a more targeted and efficient treatment delivery through "prescriptive matching," that is, the matching of curative factor(s) in play to the underlying cause(s) of a disorder (Shirk & Russell, 1996).

In this regard, Kazdin (2001) proposed that the first step in treatment planning is the identification of the core cognitive, affective, and behavioral forces involved in the development and maintenance of a particular clinical problem, for example, insecure attachment. Once the primary origin(s) of a disorder are uncovered through a comprehensive assessment, specific therapeutic powers can be applied that are designed to elicit change in the factors causing and/or maintaining the disorder.

2. It should encourage the development of a broad repertoire of change agents that transcend adherence to a single theory model (Goldfried & Wolfe, 1998).

   In our opinion, one needs the full arsenal of the therapeutic powers of play to effectively and efficiently overcome the many forces of psychopathology. In addition to expanded instruction and training on the importance and application of the causal mechanisms in play therapy, we need to substantially expand process research studies on play therapy so as to further identify and validate the specific therapeutic powers of play. We believe these change mechanisms are the essence, the "heart and soul" of play therapy and, as such, deserve much greater attention by play therapists and researchers (Drewes & Schaefer, 2014).

Potential of Neuroscience and Play Modules

- So much more can be done to explore and investigate:
  Changes in brain activation patterns during play.
  Especially, changes in brain activation occur when affect, either as actual feeling states or as emotionally laden words, is expressed.
- The therapeutic powers of play in the use of protocols to facilitate pretend, imaginative play.
  For example, Hoffman (2016) found children engaged in watching and modeling, which increased facilitative play
- Exploring play protocols
  - For use with various medical conditions, a study by Witt and colleagues (2023) in Sweden and Germany found children with cancer who participated in six to eight play sessions experienced significant improvements in: child reported communication, emotional and psychosocial well-being, and self-efficacy in the care situation.
  - Studying the effectiveness of modeling, reflecting, and summarizing with children who need more scaffolding to play.
  - Studying pretend play interventions. For example, Doernberg and colleagues (2021) found cognitive skills improved significantly in an in-person pretend play intervention study group compared with a waitlist group of ASD children. There were generalization effects with improvements in emotional understanding, more imagination, better coping with negative affect, and less internalization of

symptoms. The mediator agent of change was coping flexibility, and symbolic play facilitated a social-emotional context.

Development and Use of Play Scales

Russ (2014) found in several studies with elementary school children that three to five play sessions increased imagination, organization of the story, and affect expression. Russ's Pretend Play Affect in Play Scale (APS and APS-P) (Russ, 2014) taps correlates of pretend play: divergent thinking tasks, creativity rating of stories, teacher ratings of imagination, coping, and thinking of solutions, emotion regulation, emotion expression in daily life, and emotional understanding. Over forty longitudinal validity studies found that pretend play predicted divergent thinking at a seven-year follow-up (Russ, 2014) and that play was a protective and beneficial factor independent of IQ. Also, the mediator factor between play and the reduction of internalizing symptoms was coping flexibility (behavioral strategies).

What Have We Learned from Play Research (Russ, 2014)

- We can measure the processes in pretend play and use changes in play for the evaluation of the effectiveness of therapy.
- We can improve play skills with a play training protocol (becoming more imaginative and expressive in play).
- There are transfer effects to correlates of play.
- Pretend play reflects many different cognitive and affective processes.
- Different processes may have different developmental trajectories.
- Different processes have different mechanisms of change (such as developing a narrative around trauma that may work differently than slowly expressing fears about a situation and becoming desensitized).

It is our hope that by the end of this volume, readers will have a comprehensive understanding of what a theory is, what the core theories used in play therapy see as their foundation so they can identify with and utilize one or more of them, and how the therapeutic powers of play are conceptualized and utilized in treatment planning and treatment approaches in their practice. Finally, we especially hope that readers will be spurred on to conduct more research to further our understanding of the therapeutic powers of play and the agents of change in play therapy treatment.

Athena A. Drewes

Edward Franc Hudspeth

References

Association for Play Therapy. (2001). Play therapy. *Association for Play Therapy Newsletter, 20*, 20.

Association for Play Therapy. (2019). Back to basics. *Play Therapy, 14*(3), 1–52.

Doernberg, E. A., Russ, S. W., & Dimitropoulos, A. (2021). Believing in make-believe: Efficacy of a pretend play intervention for school-aged children with high-functioning autism spectrum disorder. *Journal of Autism and Developmental Disorders, 51*(2), 576–88.

Drewes, A. A., & Schaefer, C. E. (2014). Introduction: How play therapy causes therapeutic change. In C. E. Schaefer & A. A. Drewes (Eds.), *The therapeutic powers of play: 20 core agents of change* (pp. 1–7). Wiley.

Drewes, A. A., & Schaefer, C. E. (2016). The therapeutic powers of play. In K. J. O'Connor, C. E. Schaefer, & L. D. Braverman (Eds.), *Handbook of play therapy* (pp. 35–60). Wiley.

Goldfried, M. R., & Wolfe, B. E. (1998). Toward a more clinically valid approach to therapy research. *Journal of Consulting and Clinical Psychology, 66*(1), 143–50. https://doi.org/10.1037/0022-006X.66.1.143.

Hendricks, T. S. (2020). Play studies: A brief history. *American Journal of Play, 12*(2), 112–55. https://www.museumofplay.org/app/uploads/2022/01/AJP-12-2-Article2-Play-Studies.pdf.

Hoffmann, J. D. (2016). Intervening without interfering: Supporting the imaginative play of elementary school girls. *The International Journal of Creativity & Problem Solving, 26*(1), 85–105.

Kaizar, V. O., & Alordiah, C. O. (2023). Understanding the role of play in promoting cognitive, social, and emotional development in school children: Implications for counsellors and evaluators. *University of Delta Journal of Contemporary Studies in Education, 2*(1), 138–52. https://www.researchgate.net/publication/374419878_UNDERSTANDING_THE_ROLE_OF_PLAY_IN_PROMOTING_COGNITIVE_SOCIAL_AND_EMOTIONAL_DEVELOPMENT_IN_SCHOOL_CHILDREN_IMPLICATIONS_FOR_COUNSELLORS_AND_EVALUATORS.

Kazdin, A. E. (2001). Bridging the enormous gaps of theory with therapy, research, and practice. *Journal of Clinical Child Psychology, 30*, 59–66.

Kohrt, B. A., Ottman, K., Panter-Brick, C., Konner, M., & Patel, V. (2020). Why we heal: The evolution of psychological healing and implications for global mental health. *Clinical Psychology Review, 82*, 101920. PMID: 33126037. https://doi:10.1016/j.cpr.2020.101920.

Koukourikos, K., Tsaloglidou, A., Tzeha, L., Iliadis, C., Frantzana, A., Katsimbeli, A., & Kourkouta, L. (2021). An overview of play therapy. *Materia Sociomedica: Journal of the Academy of Medical Sciences of Bosnia and Herzegovina, 33*(4), 293–7. PMID: 35210953; PMCID: PMC8812369. https://doi:10.5455/msm.2021.33.293-297.

Peabody, M. A., & Schaefer, C. E. (2019). The therapeutic powers of play: The heart and soul of play therapy. *Play Therapy, 14*(3), 4–6.

Russ. (2014). *Pretend play in childhood, foundation for adult creativity*. APA Books.

Schaefer, C. E., & Drewes, A. A. (2016). *The therapeutic powers of play: 20 core agents of change*. Wiley & Sons.

Shirk, S. R., & Russell, R. L. (1996). *Change processes in child psychotherapy. Revitalizing treatment and research*. Guilford Press.

Shrinivasa, B., Bukhari, M., Ragesh, G., & Hamza, A. (2018). Therapeutic intervention for children through play: An overview. *Archives of Mental Health, 19*(2), 82–9. https://doi:10.4103/AMH.AMH_34_18.

Whitebread, D., Neale, D., Jensen, H., Liu, C., Solis, S. L., Hopkins, E., Hirsh-Pasek, K., & Zosh, J. M. (2017). *The role of play in children's development: A review of the evidence* (research summary). The LEGO Foundation, DK.

Witt, S., Quitmann, J., Höglund, A. T., Russ, S., Kaman, A., Escherich, G., & Frygner-Holm, S. (2023). Effects of a pretend play intervention on health-related quality of life in children with cancer: A Swedish–German study. *Journal of Pediatric Hematology/Oncology Nursing, 40*(3), 158–69.

In Memoriam

Charles E. Schaefer

November 15, 1933–September 19, 2020

Dr. Charles E. Schaefer was a dear friend, colleague, and collaborator, with our friendship spanning over twenty-four years. He began his play therapy journey back in 1976 when he authored *Therapeutic Use of Child's Play*. Since then, he has authored and co-authored over

100 research articles and 83 professional play therapy and psychology books. He is best known as the "father of play therapy," having co-founded the Association for Play Therapy in 1982, which now has almost 8,000 members. He served in 1982 on the Association for Play Therapy Board of Directors until he was given the honorary title of APT Director Emeritus in 1996, as well as the distinguished APT Service Award. In 2006, APT bestowed upon him the honor of Play Therapy Lifetime Achievement Award.

Charlie, as friends and I called him, was passionate about play and play therapy, especially the therapeutic powers of play. It was through his pursuit to find and further delineate the agents of change in play therapy that our collaborative book, *The Therapeutic Powers of Play: 20 Agents of Change*, was born. The concept of play as a healing power and its components was embraced by the Association for Play Therapy as a gold standard to be incorporated into conference proposals, training workshops, and training criteria for registered play therapist credentials.

It was Charlie's hope that research and additional writings would help to refine what the agents of change in play therapy were and take his concept to even higher levels. We were about to embark on a second edition of *The Therapeutic Powers of Play* when he passed away. This book is, therefore, an extension of that dream.

We are indebted to Charlie for his visionary leadership in creating the Association for Play Therapy, along with his strong advocacy for play and his never-ending passion for its therapeutic powers. I am honored to have known him and cherish many fond memories of debates we had around prescriptive versus integrative play therapy, fifteen years of collaboration at Wroxton College in Wroxton, England (the overseas campus of Fairleigh Dickinson University in New Jersey) with his small group think tank, the International Play Therapy Study Group, our ping pong competitions, and all of our joint book projects. I miss him, but his legacy lives on through this book. —Athena A. Drewes

Below is the obituary that was written about him and his life:

> Dr. Charles E. Schaefer, a world-renowned psychologist, died suddenly of a stroke on September 19th. Dr. Schaefer, who was 86, spent his life advancing the field of child psychology. Most notably, he pioneered the technique of play therapy, through which children express difficult feelings and experiences by playing them out with the coaching of a supportive therapist. Dr. Schaefer's work has helped thousands of children throughout the world process difficult life events and gain relief from mental health disorders. Dr. Schaefer's other areas of specialty included parent training and positive psychology.
>
> Dr. Schaefer, sometimes referred to as "the father of play therapy," was Professor Emeritus of Psychology at Fairleigh Dickinson University in Teaneck, New Jersey, where, for many years, he was also Director of the University's Center for Psychological Services. The University honored him with the Distinguished Faculty Award for Research and Scholarship in 1994. He was the co-founder and Director Emeritus of the Association for Play Therapy, located in Fresno, California. He was the founder of the International Play Therapy Study Group, which meets annually in countries throughout the world. He was a frequent presenter at national and international child psychology conferences, a presenter on nationally televised programs including the Oprah Winfrey Show, and a mentor to many clinicians and academics.

A prolific author and researcher, he was the author/editor of more than 100 academic articles and 60 books. His academic books include *Foundations of Play Therapy* and *Play Diagnosis and Assessment*. His books for general audiences include *How to Help Children with Common Problems*, *Toilet Training Without Tears*, and *Raising Baby Right*, named by Child Magazine as its 1992 Book of the Year.

Dr. Schaefer earned a Bachelor of Arts degree from Fairfield University and a Ph.D. in Clinical Psychology from Fordham University. He began in the field by serving as the Director of Psychological Services at The Children's Village in Dobbs Ferry, New York.

Profoundly gentle, unfailingly kind, deeply thoughtful, and always funny, Dr. Schaefer will be deeply missed by everyone who knew him. He is survived by his loving children, Karine and Eric, by his grandchildren James and Allison, daughter-in-law Irene Ma, and by his siblings Lawrence Schaefer and Elizabeth Schaefer. He is preceded in death by his wife of 52 years, Anne Weldon Schaefer, who died in March, and by his siblings William Schaefer and Marie Schaefer.

Part I

Understanding the Therapeutic Powers of Play

1

What Is a Therapeutic Power of Play?

Athena A. Drewes

Chapter Outline

Numerous reviews of play therapy outcome research have shown that play therapy is effective, with effect sizes ranging from medium to large (Griffin & Parson, 2023; Shrinivasa, Bukhari, Ragesh, & Hamza, 2018). The question remains, however, *why* and *how* does play therapy work? It is necessary to study the mechanism of change and the therapeutic powers of play underlying play therapy to understand the specific forces that cause therapeutic improvement in a client. This chapter will examine what the therapeutic power of play is and its application.

Therapeutic Factors

Therapeutic powers of play (TPoP) are "core agents of change" inherent in all play therapy approaches practiced worldwide (Drewes & Schaefer, 2014, p. 1; Griffin & Parson, 2023). These factors are the actual mechanisms that effect change in clients (Yalom, 2005; O'Connor,

2023). They represent a middle level of abstraction between general theories and concrete techniques. Theories, such as humanistic, psychodynamic, and cognitive-behavioral, comprise the highest level of abstraction. They offer a framework for understanding the origin and treatment of problematic behaviors and often a philosophical view on the nature of human life. Therapeutic factors, the middle level of abstraction, refer to specific clinical strategies, for example, catharsis, counter-conditioning, and contingency management, for obtaining the desired change in a client's dysfunctional behavior. Techniques, the lowest level of abstraction, are observable clinical procedures designed to implement the therapeutic factors, for example, sand play, role-playing with puppets, and storytelling. Therapeutic factors have been given various names, for example, "therapeutic powers," "change mechanisms," "mediators of change," "causal factors," and "principles of therapeutic action" (Shirk & Karver, 2003). These terms have been used interchangeably to refer to the same concept, that is, the overt and covert activities that various theoretical systems use to produce change in a client. A therapeutic power may be a thought, for example, insight; a feeling, for example, a positive affect; or a behavior, for example, role play. What they have in common is that they all act to produce a positive change in the client's presenting problem.

Therapeutic powers transcend culture, language, age, and gender. They are considered to be "specific" factors versus "common" factors in psychotherapy (Barron & Kenny, 1986). Specific factors refer to causal agents of change specific to a particular therapeutic approach. Common factors, on the other hand, refer to change agents common to all theoretical orientations, for example, a supportive relationship and the instillation of hope.

The therapeutic powers of play refer to the specific change agents in which play initiates, facilitates, or strengthens its therapeutic effect. These play powers act as *mediators* that positively influence the desired change in the client (Barron & Kenny, 1986). In other words, play actually helps produce the change and is not just a *medium* for applying other change agents, nor does it just *moderate* the strength or direction of the therapeutic change.

Research

Initially, the literature on therapeutic powers was largely anecdotal and consisted of clinicians describing the change principles they found effective in treatment. Corsini & Rosenberg (1955) are considered the first to offer a taxonomy of therapeutic factors in psychotherapy. They reviewed the group psychotherapy literature for observations reflecting change mechanisms and compiled a list of nine factors. Irving Yalom (2005) expanded the list to eleven factors that he described in his classic group psychotherapy text. In accord with his belief that group members are the major source of change for group members, his factors included "universality" (realization that you are not alone and others are struggling with the same problem), "vicarious learning" (client improves in response to the observation of another group member's experience), "catharsis" (release of pent-up feelings in the group), and "interpersonal learning" (learning from personal interactions with other clients in the group).

While the change mechanisms of play and play therapy are not fully researched, Singer and Singer (1990) see play as reinforcing when it allows expression of positive affect and appropriate control of negative affect. Research has found that developing a coherent narrative is central to the structured techniques that Gaensbauer and Siegal (1995) used with toddlers who had experienced traumatic events. These researchers believed that the mechanisms of change when play was used by younger children were similar to the mechanisms of change in older children with PTSD.

Russ (2003) also has identified, through a review of the literature, the following therapeutic powers and cognitive and affective processes, which empirical research has validated: fantasy/make-believe, symbolism, organization, divergent thinking, expression of emotion, expression of affect themes, enjoyment of play and cognitive integration, emotion regulation, and modulation of affect. Further Russ and Lee (2021) concluded from the empirical literature (Russ, 2003) that play relates to or facilitates: problem solving that requires insight ability, flexibility in problem solving, divergent thinking ability, the ability to think of alternative coping strategies in coping with daily problems, experiencing positive emotion, the ability to think about affect themes (positive and negative), the ability to understand the emotions of others and take the perspective of another, and aspects of general adjustment.

Based upon a review of the literature and the clinical experiences of play therapists, Schaefer (1999) identified twenty core therapeutic powers of play. Among these powers are change agents that improve a client's attachment formation, self-expression, emotion regulation, resiliency, self-esteem, and stress management, among other areas.

Transtheoretical Model of Play Therapy

The therapeutic powers of play transcend particular models of play therapy by defining treatment in terms of cross-cutting principles of therapeutic change (Castonguay & Beutler, 2005; Kaxdin & Nock, 2003). While some play therapists will be interested primarily in the narrow band of change agents underlying their preferred theory, for example, cognitive-behavioral play therapy, a growing number of play therapists will seek to understand and apply all of the multiple change agents in play therapy.

By adopting a transtheoretical orientation (Prochaska, 1995), play therapists avoid becoming locked into a single theory that they then must apply to all clients in a "one size fits all" manner. Clearly, no single theoretical approach has proven strong enough to resolve all the diverse presenting problems of clients. Indeed, empirical research has supported the "differential therapeutics" concept that certain change agents are more effective for specific disorders than other agents (Siev & Chambless, 2007).

Transtheoretical play therapy entails selecting and adding to your repertoire the best change agents from among all the major theories of play therapy. Among the underlying premises of this eclectic, transtheoretical approach to psychotherapy are the following:

1. Each of the major theories of play therapy has practical change agents that can increase one's clinical effectiveness (Prochaska, 1995).
2. The more therapeutic powers of play in your repertoire, the better able you will be to *eclectically* select the one(s) with the best empirical support for treating a particular disorder (Schaefer, 2011).
3. With multiple change agents at your disposal, you can implement an evidence-based treatment plan that *prescriptively* tailors your play intervention to meet the individual needs and preferences of a client as well as your own skills and judgment (Schaefer, 2001).
4. Therapists who possess multiple change agents can *integrate* several of them to strengthen the impact of a play intervention when the client's psychopathology is complex, multi-determined, and/or long-lasting.

Major Therapeutic Powers of Play

Facilitates Communication

Self-Expression

The ability to communicate is one of the most powerful tools we possess. In therapy, it allows clients to express their conscious/unconscious ideas and emotions, and therapists to impart their knowledge and wisdom to clients. Play is the most universal of all languages and is used as a form of expression by people of all ages in every country across the world (Griffin & Parson, 2023).

Self-expression as a therapeutic factor in play therapy and in facilitating healing in children has been written about by numerous noted clinicians (Axline, 1969; Badenoch, 2008; Landreth, 2012; Piaget, 1951; Schaefer, 1993; Terr, 1981). Providing a safe and open relationship where children lead the play activates areas of the limbic system (Badenoch, 2008). Once this system is activated, the release of dopamine provides a sense of enjoyment, focus, and the drive to complete tasks. In the presence of supportive adults, children can find access to this system quickly (Badenoch, 2008). Further, the circuits of the middle prefrontal area and emotions of the limbic system balance and eventually help the child to develop the capacity for self-regulation (Badenoch, 2008).

Among the reasons client self-expression is therapeutic are: it promotes a deeper awareness of one's disturbing thoughts, feelings, and conflicts it allows for the validation and normalization of one's thoughts and feelings, as well as the correction of erroneous beliefs, and it strengthens one's sense of self.

The features of play that facilitate self-expression by the client are as follows:

1. Natural Language. Characteristically, young children do not have the vocabulary or abstract thinking ability to verbally express their inner world. However, they can readily express their thoughts, feelings, and wishes through their natural medium of expression—play.

2. Talking in the Third Person. Pretend play allows children to "talk in the third person", that is, have dolls, puppets, and make-believe characters express or act out for them the thoughts, feelings, and behaviors that are too difficult or threatening to express directly.
3. "As if" Not Real Life Quality. Since make-believe play is apart from real life, you can express emotions, drives, and thoughts in play that you would not do in real life. Play presents clients with plausible deniability concerning upsetting material; that is, it permits clients to suspend and, if necessary, disavow its reality. After all, it's just pretend or a game (Levy, 2008).
4. Ineffable. At times, we cannot express inner states well in words, but we may be able to depict them better in one of the creative arts, such as drawing, dance, or play creations.
5. Engrossment. The intense affective involvement that is typical of play tends to result in the overcoming of self-consciousness. As a result, a child is more likely to inadvertently express things that would ordinarily not be expressed. In the safe, enjoyable environment of the playroom, children are likely to let their guard down and reveal their inner selves, both in words and in play activities.
6. Doing While Talking. Often, doing something like playing allows a child a level of ease that facilitates talking.

Applications. Almost all schools of play therapy value and seek to activate the self-expressive power of play. This change mechanism is extensively used with children who are pre-verbal or relatively non-verbal, such as shy or selectively mute children, and children unable or unwilling to talk about issues or trauma.

Access to the Unconscious

Play facilitates access to emotional centers of the brain, allowing implicit memories to be accessed and reorganized (Griffin & Parson, 2023; Schaefer & Drewes, 2014; Swan & Bratton, 2021).

According to Elkind (1981), "play work" is a parallel mental process and serves as the royal road to the child's unconscious. Interpretation by the play therapist is often needed to decipher the hidden meaning and give insight into unconscious mental processes.

In both play work and dream work, one primarily bypasses the censorship of the superego by the defense mechanisms of projection, displacement, symbolization, sublimation, and fantasy compensation.

Projection. Projection is a process in which one attributes unacceptable parts of oneself, that is, thoughts, feelings, impulses, to individuals or play objects. This can be done in either a conscious or unconscious manner. It is a way of believing that certain characteristics belong to someone or something else rather than taking responsibility for them.

Displacement. Displacement in the playroom involves taking out frustrations, feelings, and impulses on play objects that are less threatening. Displacement of aggression is a common example of this defense mechanism.

Symbolization. Symbolization means using a concrete thing to represent an abstract concept, for example, a skeleton to represent death, a volcano to represent feelings ready to explode.

The process of symbolization enables one to establish meaningful connections between different realms of experience based on proximity and likeness. Symbols allow us to express that which is inexpressible in words.

Sublimation. Sublimation is a defense mechanism that allows one to channel libidinal drives, both aggressive and sexual impulses, into socially acceptable activities, for example, art, sports. Cap guns, use of swords, or throwing clay can help sublimate aggressive impulses into socially acceptable play activities.

Fantasy Compensation. When one's needs, impulses, and wishes are unfulfilled, one tries in one way or another to obtain satisfaction through the defense mechanism of fantasy gratification, for example, pretend play, movies, and books.

Applications. This healing power is a major change mechanism in psychoanalytic play therapy. It is best applied when unresolved conflicts from earlier in life are negatively impacting the client's current functioning.

Direct Teaching

Play encapsulates a person's attention, increasing their ability to learn skills through the play partner providing explicit instruction and modeling (Griffin & Parson, 2023; Schaefer & Drewes, 2014).

In direct teaching, the therapist imparts knowledge or skills through such strategies as instruction, modeling, guided practice, scaffolding, and positive reinforcement. When we make learning fun and enjoyable, we increase children's motivation to spend time and effort in learning. When this happens, changes in the chemical balance in the blood have been found to boost the production of neurotransmitters needed for alertness and memory.

Apart from increasing the motivation to learn, the special qualities of play that foster learning by direct teaching include:

1. Captures attention. Toys and play materials attract and hold a child's attention with their colorful and novel appearance. Only after you have a child attending and listening to you can you teach your lesson.
2. Sensory Input. Young children think and learn primarily through their senses, not by abstract thought. The more senses used in the learning process, such as through 3-D play objects, the more information is retained.
3. Safe Environment. In the safe environment of the playroom, there is no evaluation or fear of failure, so the child can ask questions and take risks during the learning process.
4. Active Involvement. Children tend to actively explore, become involved, and often get deeply engrossed in play activities. Active, self-initiated learning is more effective than just passively listening to instructions.

5. Consolidates Skills. In addition to learning new things, play allows children to practice behaviors they have always known over and over again. Thus, play can consolidate skill development through repetitive practice. In a similar manner, play helps children learn social skills, assertiveness, and anger control skills through frequent rehearsals without fear of consequences for making a mistake.
6. Learn by example. Toys, such as stuffed animals, dolls, and puppets, can demonstrate and model the adaptive behavior the therapist wants the child to learn.

Indirect Teaching

Play allows clients to process information implicitly through stories, metaphors, and pictures. Engaging in play offers a transitional space for learning between parent and child (Griffin & Parson, 2023; Schaefer & Drewes, 2014; Swan & Bratton, 2021).

Storytelling is a universal and enduring way to teach children adaptive behaviors by arousing emotions and offering solutions. Play therapists read books or create individualized stories to indirectly teach children a life lesson or solution to their problems, and that helps to distance themselves from painful themes and reduce defensiveness by bypassing the censorship of the ego/superego. They can read or hear about others who have overcome problems similar to their own, giving them the opportunity to apply what they have learned from the stories to their own real-life situations.

Applications. The teaching power of play is a primary change mechanism in cognitive-behavioral play therapy. It is best applied when the client presents with a knowledge or skill deficit that is impeding the development of social or emotional skills. Anger control training and social skills training are examples.

Fosters Emotional Wellness

Catharsis

Play can facilitate a release of emotional tension or negative affect (e.g., anger and sadness) (Griffin & Parson, 2023; Schaefer & Drewes, 2014; Yasenik, 2021).

Catharsis involves the release of pent-up negative affect, such as anger or sadness. It is regarded by many as a major mechanism of change in psychotherapy. Catharsis is believed to produce therapeutic change by not only discharging deeply felt emotions that are stored up, but also by increasing one's conscious awareness and control of them. By deliberately expressing a strong emotion, one is likely to experience power over it. A shift from an external locus to an internal locus of control can then occur.

Also, catharsis allows one the satisfaction of completing some or all of a previously restrained or interrupted sequence of self-expression. In the safety of the playroom, one can verbally or physically express that which would have occurred as a natural reaction to some upsetting experience had the expression not been thwarted at the moment (Nichols & Efran, 1985). This termination of "unfinished business" prevents future emotional arousal.

The Role of Play. Play contributes to the effectiveness of catharsis in several ways:

1. The playroom provides a safe and supportive environment to vent negative affect.
2. Symbolic play expression provides a sufficient psychological distance from experiencing painful affect. Physical play activities, such as pounding clay, allow the release of both physical tension and negative affect.
3. The positive feelings aroused in play (power, fun) help to balance the negative emotions that are released.

Applications. Cathartic release is intended for situations where stress has triggered strong negative affect that the client has been unable or unwilling to express and release.

Abreaction

Clients can reexperience traumatic events through play, facilitating graded exposure to the trauma (Griffin & Parson, 2023; Schaefer & Drewes, 2014; Yasenik, 2021). Abreaction gives children a sense of power over the event.

1. Active Control and Mastery. Children actively control the playing out of a trauma event that has been experienced passively. They can change the ending of the re-experiencing to one of mastery of the trauma, which results in a cognitive restructuring of the experience.
2. Piecemeal Assimilation by Repetition. Children will typically reenact the trauma over and over again in their play so that there is a slow healing process through repetition. Freud termed this process of habituation—the repetition compulsion.
3. By playing out the trauma in the form of a story, the child can form a coherent narrative from the often-fragmented memories elicited by the trauma and place it within a larger context. The concrete play materials facilitate the remembrance of vivid sensory details of the trauma, which tend to be stored in the right hemisphere of the brain.
4. Pretend play can allow children enough psychological distance from the reenacted trauma so that they are not overwhelmed by the accompanying negative affect.
5. The positive effects resulting from the play can help to balance any negative emotions felt by the child.
6. Abreaction in the playroom offers an opportunity for a "corrective emotional experience." According to Alexander and French (1980), children after a trauma need not only a cathartic release of negative affect, but also a corrective emotional experience that can be obtained from the acceptance and empathic response of a therapist to their painful re-experience.

Applications. Abreactive play is intended to help children master the negative impact of child abuse, natural disasters, and other specific traumatic experiences.

Positive Emotions

Play allows clients to experience positive affect, broadening their repertoire of thoughts and actions, and motivating them to continue playing (Griffin & Parson, 2023; Schaefer & Drewes, 2014; Yasenik, 2021).

It is well known that people at play experience a number of positive emotions, including joy, excitement, interest, flow, and delight. Studies have confirmed that children at play exhibit more positive affect expressions than those not at play (Moore & Russ, 2008).

Counteracts Negative Emotions

Positive feelings provide a balance to the preponderance of negative emotions that we experience during stressful times. They produce a feeling of relief and respite from the weight of negative emotions. The most natural way to experience positive emotions is through play.

Contributes to Creative Problem-Solving.

The "Broaden-and-Build" theory of positive emotions (Fredrickson, 1998) posits that when people have a momentary experience of positive emotion, they widen the array of possible thoughts that come to mind. In this open state of mind, they feel the urge to contemplate new ideas, develop alternative solutions to problems, reinterpret their situation, and initiate new courses of action to resolve difficulties.

Counter-conditioning of Fears

Counter-conditioning refers to the systematic desensitization, reduction, or extinction of an undesirable response to a fear-producing situation or stimulus, for example, fears/phobias, through the introduction of a more desirable, often incompatible, response, such as relaxing, eating, and playing. Through the repeated gradual exposure and pairing of a historically fearful or anxiety-provoking stimulus with an incompatible counter-response of positive affect in play, the fear response is reduced (Griffin & Parson, 2023; Schaefer & Drewes, 2014; Yasenik, 2021). "In vitro" desensitization is used to overcome imagined threats, for example, monsters, while "in vivo" desensitization refers to real-life threats, for example, spiders.

Stress Inoculation

Play allows clients to mentally rehearse future stressors, manage difficult emotions that arise, and develop coping strategies (Griffin & Parson, 2023; Schaefer & Drewes, 2014: Yasenik, 2021). Stress inoculation power of play is intended to help clients prepare, in advance, for how to handle stressful events successfully and with an appropriate, that is, moderate, amount of anticipatory anxiety. This is based on the idea that a therapist is inoculating or preparing a client to become resistant to the effects of stressors in a manner similar to how a vaccination works to make patients resistant to the effects of a particular disease (Meichenbaum, 1993).

The Role of Play. Toys related to the upcoming stressful event, e.g., medical toys for a planned medical procedure, are presented. Then the therapist plays out with the play objects exactly what will happen to the child in real life. Questions from the child are answered honestly. This play rehearsal is repeated until the experience becomes predictable and normalized. The concrete, multi-sensory toys and play actions help the child better understand the event. Also, by taking an active role in playing out the stressful event, the child can gain a sense of power and control over the stressor that in real life is uncontrollable.

The elements of the play rehearsal that fortify the child to handle future stressors are:

1. The strange experience becomes familiar and predictable, and thus less scary.
2. The child learns and practices coping skills for dealing with the stressor.
3. The fun and enjoyment of this play rehearsal acts to reduce the activation of negative emotions during the play.

Applications. Stress inoculation play can help children prepare for many common stressful events, including, starting school, undergoing medical procedures, the birth of a sibling, divorce, and natural disasters.

Stress Management

Play allows clients to develop stress management skills by decreasing levels of cortisol, providing opportunities to self-soothe, use humor, and be exposed to stress (Griffin & Parson, 2023; Schaefer & Drewes, 2014; Yasenik, 2021).

Play can be an excellent antidote to stress because it allows working through the stresses encountered and emerging with a stronger self-concept and renewed optimism about the future.

The Role of Play. There are numerous ways play can serve as "stress-busters" for children, including:

Humor Therapy. Fun and laughter are powerful antidotes to stress reactions. Over the past forty years, empirical studies on laughter have documented its effectiveness in reducing stress reactions (Borcherdt, 2002; Galloway & Cropley, 1999). It produces *physical benefits*, such as lowering blood pressure and boosting the immune system by decreasing stress hormones and increasing both immune cells and infection-fighting antibodies.

Psychological benefits result from laughter triggering the release of endorphins—the body's natural "feel good" chemicals which elevate mood and promote an overall sense of well-being. Humor can help to "distance" oneself from threatening experiences by taking them less seriously, thereby reducing emotional reactions to the stressors.

Self-soothing play helps during times of stress using sensory materials, such as, water, clay, sand, paints, or cuddling with security objects, such as a teddy bear. Along with *fantasy escape*, pretend play and gameplay can provide a temporary escape from the stresses and pressures of real life.

Enhances Social Relationships

Therapeutic Relationship and Attachment

The therapeutic relationship and alliance are considered to be the most important ingredients in successful therapy (Griffin & Parson, 2023, Kazdin et al., 1990). Without the establishment of a helping relationship, no technique or strategy is likely to be effective. Meta-analytic studies (Swan & Bratton, 2021) have confirmed that the therapeutic relationship is related to positive outcomes across diverse types and models of child treatment. The characteristics of the therapist that are frequently listed as desirable for the formation of a therapeutic relationship are warmth, caring, understanding, acceptance, respect, and trust. The therapist often takes on the role of a secondary attachment figure, helping the child whose initial attachment with a significant parent or caregiver has been disrupted or negatively impacted to regain trust and connection.

The Role of Play. There are several unique qualities of play that help build a helping relationship:

1). The positive effects triggered by play are conjunctive emotions that connect us with other people. A mutually enjoyable activity like play creates a "pleasure bond" between two people that strengthens the relationship. The excitement sparked by play can enliven and energize a relationship.

3). By smiling and laughing, you give a signal to a child that you are fun to be with, friendly and safe to be around, and you are viewed as more trustworthy, caring, and approachable.

4). When children laugh with an adult, they feel they are on a level playing field with the adult and that they are in an egalitarian rather than hierarchical relationship.

Social Competence

Our sense of self includes roles, attributes, behaviors, and associations that we consider most important about ourselves. Self psychologists (Kohut, 1971) believe that the outcome of healthy development is a cohesive and integrated sense of self.

Role of Play. A sense of self in young children is largely developed in the field of play. Free from reality constraints, play provides them an opportunity for self-definition; to reveal what they choose to do and who they choose to be, to integrate right and left brain functioning, and primary and secondary process thinking. Through non-directive play, children have the *freedom* to think for themselves, to make their own decisions, and to solve their own problems. By mirroring responses, the play therapist further promotes the child's self-awareness.

In play, children's *imagination* can play out different possible selves, which is the beginning of self-creation. Children can access *primary process thinking,* i.e. concrete, emotion-laden, symbolic, and drive-dominated thought, and become aware of their "forgotten self."

Empathy

Empathy refers to the ability to take the perspective of others and imagine what they are thinking and feeling. The ability to empathize is an important part of social and emotional development, improving the quality of social relationships and promoting altruistic behaviors. The effects of a lack of empathy can be seen in wars, crime, inequality, prejudice, and antisocial behaviors.

The determinants of empathy include both internal, neurological factors and external, environmental factors. A key to understanding how empathy is fostered neurologically is the action of mirror neurons. Discovered in primates in the 1990s, mirror neurons are a set of neurons in the premotor area of the brain that are activated not only when performing an action oneself but also while observing someone else perform that action (Iacoboni et al., 2005). Mirror neurons can be activated in the child through the empathic responding and play of the therapist.

The Role of Play. In regard to external influences on the skill of empathy, play fosters the development of empathy in children in numerous ways, particularly through the empathic attunement of the therapist in responses, along with role-playing and storytelling.

Role Play. Role play occurs when you transform yourself in pretend play to be a person or object other than yourself. Role playing promotes perspective taking—imagining the thoughts and feelings of others—which in turn promotes the development of empathic and altruistic behaviors.

Storytelling. It is well known that stories facilitate children's understanding of the thoughts, feelings, and motives of others. Thus, by listening to stories, children develop empathy and compassion for others. According to Manney (2008), it is the imaginative act of the listener/reader translating the words on the page into thoughts and feelings, enabling them to see the world through the characters' eyes and feel their feelings.

Clinical Applications: Children who present with deficits in empathy could profit from this therapeutic power of play, including children displaying non-adaptive expression of anger, and conduct disorder, for example, bullying.

Increases Personal Strengths

Creative Problem Solving

Play and playfulness facilitate the use of divergent and flexible thinking, which are associated with increased creativity (Kronengold, 2021; Griffin & Parson, 2023; Schaefer & Drewes,

2014). Since in play the process is more important than the end product, children can freely and without fear of consequences come up with novel combinations and discoveries that can aid them in solving their own problems and social problems (Shrinivasa et al., 2018).

Resiliency

Play allows children to experience a new perspective of themselves and their environment, which requires them to build resilience in order to adapt and cope (Kronengold, 2021; Griffin & Parson, 2023; Schaefer & Drewes, 2014). Resilience (Latin: resilio = I bounce back) can be defined broadly as those skills, attributes, and abilities that enable individuals to adapt successfully to hardships, difficulties, and challenges (Alvord & Grados, 2005). Resilient children have been found to have high self-efficacy, strong interpersonal skills, above-average intelligence, and good problem-solving skills (Masten, 2001).

Role of Play. Play behaviors promote resilience in several ways:

1. *Flexibility.* Resiliency requires the ability to think flexibly and creatively rather than rigidly in response to changing situational demands, especially stressful encounters. Play functions to increase the versatility of cognitive and emotional responses to unexpected events, which can involve danger, where there is a sudden loss of control. In the safe environment of play, confronting dangerous situations gives the opportunity to experiment with a variety of novel and possible adaptive responses.
2. *Positive Emotions.* Resiliency is also fostered by the many positive emotions one experiences in play. This builds up an inner well of good feelings that can be drawn upon to cope with the negative emotions triggered by daily life stresses.
3. *Humor.* The emotions of mirth and delight that are aroused by humor are particularly helpful because they are incompatible with feelings of stress. A sense of humor has been identified as one of the attributes of protective factors in resilient youth.

Clinical Applications. Play to build resilience is particularly appropriate for children living in "at-risk" environments, such as poverty, crime, war, homelessness, terrorism, abuse, and recurrent natural disasters.

Moral Development

Play offers a developmentally appropriate method for children to explore and develop their moral compass and social conscience, including respect and acceptance of others, self-control, responsibility, and empathy (Kronengold, 2021; Griffin & Parson, 2023; Schaefer & Drewes, 2014).

Moral development can be fostered in children through *gameplay.* Piaget (1997/1932) argued that children's spontaneous rule-making in gameplay (e.g., in deciding what is fair to all players in a game) provides a crucially important experience in the development of mature moral judgment. Such peer group experiences help the child to move away from the earlier stages of morality based on authority (rules are seen as external, constraining forces arbitrarily imposed and enforced by powerful adult authority figures) to the concept of a morality based on the principles of mutual cooperation and consent among equals. Also, according to Vygotsky's (1978) theory, as children follow rules in the context of play, they are developing an understanding of social norms and expectations and learning to act against their egocentric impulses.

In gameplay, children learn about fairness, equality, justice, creating and following rules, respecting oral contracts, understanding the motivations of others, adopting their perspectives, considering their needs, and taking action against wrongdoers—things that help children develop a sense of morality and ethical behavior.

Clinical Applications. Poor moral reasoning is a basis for the development of antisocial behavior in children. Thus, children and adolescents referred for various forms of conduct disorder could benefit from this healing power of play.

Accelerated Psychological Development

Play allows individuals to develop cognitive, linguistic, social, and emotional skills at their highest potential through scaffolding by a more advanced player (Kronengold, 2021; Griffin & Parson, 2023, Schaefer & Drewes, 2014). Through modeling and scaffolding play, a child's development can be enhanced and accelerated. Also, due to the stifling impact of trauma on development, constricting emotional and mental energy and even physiological growth, play helps in the release of pent-up psychic energy and development.

The role of Play. Once you make accomplishing a developmental task a thing of fun and delight, children are motivated to attend to and persevere at the task.

Applications. The power of play to boost development is apt to be effective with children with developmental delays in language, cognition, and social-emotional development. In particular, playful interactions have been successfully used (Carter, 2011) to accelerate the development of neuro-divergent children on the autism spectrum and those having experienced trauma.

Self-regulation

Self-control refers to the ability to control one's thoughts, feelings, impulses, and behaviors. It has been found to be positively related to both social and academic competence in children. On the other hand, problems with self-control are linked with the etiology and maintenance of a broad array of childhood psychosocial problems including crime and drug use (Strayhorn, 2002).

Role of Play. Preschoolers who play more often or in more complex ways score higher on various measures of self-regulation (Fantuzzo et al., 2004). There are several types of play behaviors that promote the development of self-control:

1. *Pretend play.* Pretend play involves the use of make-believe and symbolism. Imaginative play by young children tends to result in their being less impulsive and aggressive (Singer & Singer, 1990). Rather than acting out their impulses, they can, in pretend play, express them symbolically. They can also engage in private speech, self-talk, about what they are doing and how they are feeling. This aids self-awareness and emotional regulation.
2. *Socio-dramatic Play.* This collaborative dramatic play involves sustained, elaborate imaginary play where children make a plan, stay in character (i.e., doctor, teacher), and act out that alternate world for an extended period of time. In socio-dramatic play, you have to subordinate yourself to the role you are acting in, which means often acting against your own impulses and wishes.
3. *GamePlay.* Games like Simple Simon, Red Light/Green Light, and Statue help children develop control over their impulses and motor responses. Strategy games like chess and checkers strengthen children's executive functioning, i.e., their ability to stop and think, plan ahead, consider alternate moves, and anticipate the consequences of their moves.
4. *Self-soothing Play.* The ability to relax is an important way to cope with stress. The use of sand, water, and clay play, finger painting, guided imagery, the use of stuffed animals and squishy balls, along with deep breathing techniques, facilitates relaxation.
5. *Rough and Tumble Play.* The time-limited release of aggression and negative emotions through the use of stomping on bubble wrap, throwing clay against the wall, hitting an inflated object, jumping rope, and running around the room can help release pent-up energy and result in a calming effect.

Clinical Applications. Children most in need of the self-regulation power of play include those with difficulty controlling their thoughts, for example, Obsessive-Compulsive Disorder; their attention, for example, ADHD; their impulses, for example, sexual behavior problems; and their behavior, for example, oppositional-defiant disorder.

Self-esteem

The term self-esteem is used to describe a person's overall sense of self-worth or personal value. Self-esteem can involve a variety of beliefs about one's self, such as an appraisal of one's capabilities, competence, achievements, and attractiveness to others. Play boosts children's self-esteem through the enhancement of their sense of power/control, competence, and self-efficacy.

Power/Control. One of the biggest needs for children at every stage of development is the sense of personal power and control. Most children feel very little power over what happens in their lives. As a result, they may fight for control by engaging in power struggles or by acting out aggressively, or resign themselves to a role of dependent helplessness.

Role of Play. Play is one aspect of their lives where children can feel in control. They determine what and how to play and can be powerful giants towering over the miniature play objects. Free play provides children with the opportunity to control body actions, ideas, objects, and relationships, and is structured only by their own interests and imagination.

Specific examples of empowerment play are: (1) playing with toys associated with extraordinary strength or abilities, for example, superheroes, dinosaurs, dragons, fairies, witches, goblins; (2) playing with aggressive play objects such as swords or guns; (3) rough-and-tumble play; (4) changing the rules in gameplay; and (5) playing a role such as doctor, teacher, or firefighter.

Clinical Applications. Children feeling overwhelmed by powerful forces in nature, for example, hurricanes, earthquakes, by powerful adults, for example, authoritarian or abusive caretakers, by powerful peers, for example, bullies, or by other environmental stressors could benefit from play activities where they are in complete control. Additionally, hospitalized children and children with chronic illness can use play to balance out the lack of control over their lives.

Helping children regain a sense of mastery or control is the primary curative factor. Fantasy play (be it revenge, rescue, or nurturing) allows children to change the story so that they become empowered and strong enough to overcome feelings of helplessness and lack of autonomy. In doing so, they regain their sense of control.

Practical Application

A prescriptive approach is best utilized when thinking about your client's needs, where they currently are, and what symptoms and goals you are addressing out of your case conceptualization in your treatment plan, which drives the therapeutic powers of play you are addressing. Are your clients dealing with *cognitive processes, emotional processes,* or *interpersonal processes,* or perhaps all of these at one time or at various stages in the treatment?

Cognitive processes involve learning adaptive or compensatory cognitive skills, such as social skills; the reorganization of the meaning of experiences; and the gaining of increased self-awareness (Shirk & Russell, 1996; O'Connor, 2010). Examples include children struggling with a trauma that has impacted their worldview, thus creating cognitive distortions and misconceptions, or neurodivergent children who lack knowledge of friendship skills and how to respond in socially acceptable ways, or children with executive functioning difficulties due to attention deficit hyperactive disorder.

In these types of cases, the therapist might focus on change agents involving the direct and indirect teaching of skills such as social and problem-solving skills, or teaching compensatory or adaptive skills, along with ways to increase a client's cognitive development, self-esteem, and resiliency (O'Connor, 2010). Therapeutic powers that would best help with cognitive processes might include: Direct Teaching, Indirect Teaching, Creative Problem Solving, Accelerated Development, Self-Esteem, and Resilience.

If the client does not seem to display an ability to develop insight and needs help in reorganizing the meaning of their experiences (cognitive distortions and misattributions) and modifying assumptions and expectations that might be brought to the session (seen in the content of the play, symbolically or from direct verbalizations), the clinician might want to also focus on: Self-Expression and Access to the Unconscious.

Clients may display difficulty in the area of *emotional processes* (Shirk & Russell, 1996; O'Connor, 2010). More specifically, deficits in feelings identification, emotional expression, discharge of negative emotions, and integration of emotions. This may be due to a variety of causes ranging from trauma (sexual abuse, physical abuse, domestic violence) to systemic and biological issues. In these cases, the therapist would want to look at helping with affect regulation through the cathartic release of feelings, which results in mastery or control; teaching the client how to recognize, as well as be aware of, name, and talk about their own feelings and those of others; the integration of their feelings and personal emotional experience; and the development of coping strategies or psychological defenses that would avoid emotional dysregulation (O'Connor, 2010). Therapeutic powers that would assist in the treatment of maladaptive emotional processes would include: catharsis, abreaction, stress inoculation, stress management, positive emotions, and empathy.

If the client, perhaps as a result of trauma or other situational issues, develops specific fears and phobias, the therapist would want to be sure to include the therapeutic power of counter-conditioning of fears.

Clients may show deficits in *interpersonal processes* (Shirk & Russell, 1996; O'Connor, 2010) and need treatment designed to foster positive relationships. Attachment difficulties may be present due to prolonged separations from parents due to hospitalizations/ placements, or due to parental neglect, abuse, disengagement, or loss. Through the therapeutic relationship, the client is able to utilize the play therapist as a secondary attachment figure to work through past negative experiences and develop an alternative relationship of trust and connection. Difficulties with peer relationships and forming friendships might necessitate treatment that offers social-emotional support as well as supportive scaffolding in bolstering the client's functioning in the environment (school, after-school activities, engaging parents) (O'Connor, 2010).

Therapeutic powers that impact such social difficulties include: Direct Teaching, Attachment, Therapeutic Relationship, Positive Peer Relationships, Moral Development, and Creative Problem-Solving.

Summary

The principle underlying the therapeutic powers of play is that it is the play itself that is the source of change. It is not the medium of play, techniques, approaches, or the moderator/ therapist by which change occurs. This is an important distinction, and its transtheoretical approach is at the heart of how play therapy is defined.

References

Alexander, F., & French, T. (1980). *Psychoanalytic theory.* University of Nebraska Press.

Alvord, M., & Grados, J. (2005). Enhancing resilience in children; A proactive approach. *Professional Psychology: Research and Practice, 36*(3), 238–45.

Axline, V. (1969). *Play therapy* (Revised Edition). Ballantine.

Badenoch, B. (2008). *Being a brain wise therapist: A practical guide to interpersonal neurobiology.* W.W. Norton & Co.

Barron, R., & Kenny, D. (1986). The moderator-mediator variable distinction in social psychological research: Conceptual, strategic, and statistical considerations. *Journal of Personality &Social Psychology, 5,* 1173–82.

Borcherdt, B. (2002). Humor and its contribution to mental health. *Journal of Rational-Emotive & Cognitive-Behavioral Therapy, 26,* 247–57.

Carter, A. S. (2011). A randomized controlled trial of Hanen's "More Than Words" in toddlers with early autism symptoms. *Journal of Child Psychology and Psychiatry, 42,* 1–13.

Castonguay, L., & Beutler, L. E. (2005). *Principles of therapeutic change that work.* Oxford University Press.

Corsini, R., & Rosenberg, B. (1955). Mechanisms of group psychotherapy: Process and dynamics. *Journal of Abnormal and Social Psychology, 51,* 406–11.

Drewes, A. A., & Schaefer, C. E. (2014). Introduction: How play therapy causes therapeutic Change. In C. E. Schaefer & A. A. Drewes (Eds.), *The therapeutic powers of play: 20 core agents of change* (pp. 1–7). Wiley.

Elkind, D. (1981). *Children & adolescents.* Oxford University Press.

Fantuzzo, J., Sekino, Y., & Cohen, H. (2004). An examination of the contributions of interactive peer play to salient classroom competencies for urban head start children. *Psychology in the Schools, 14*(3), 323–36.

Fredrickson, B. (1998). What good are positive emotions? *Review of General Psychology, 2,* 300–19.

Gaensbauer, T.J. & Siegal, C.H. (1995). Therapeutic approaches to postraumatic stress disorder in infants and toddlers. *Infant Mental Health Journal,* 16(4), 292–305.

Galloway, G., & Cropley, A. (1999). Benefits of humor for mental health: Empirical findings and directions for further research. *Journal of Humor Research, 30,* 301–14.

Griffin, L., & Parson, J. (2023). Evidencing the therapeutic powers of play to understand the mechanism of change in filial therapy. *International Journal of Play Therapy, 32*(2), 107–21.

Iacoboni, M., Molnar-Szakacs, I., Gallese, V., Buccino, G., Mazziotta, J., & Rizzolatti, G. (2005). Predicting the future: Mirror neurons reflect the intentions of others. *PLOS Biology,* March, *3*(3), 1.

Kazdin, A., & Nock, M. (2003). Delineating mechanisms of change in child and adolescent therapy: Methodological issues and research recommendations. *Journal of Child Psychology and Psychiatry, 44*(8), 1116–29.

Kazdin, A., Siegel, T., & Bass, D. (1990). Drawing on clinical practice to inform research on child and adolescent psychotherapy: Survey of practitioners. *Professional Psychology: Research and Practice, 21,* 189–98.

Kohut, H. (1971). *The analysis of self.* International University Press.

Kronengold, H. (2021). An hour at Le Mans: Increasing strength and resilience through play. In E. Prendiville & J. Parson (Eds.), *Clinical applications of the therapeutic powers of play: Case studies in child and adolescent psychotherapy* (pp. 159–67). Taylor & Francis Group.
Landreth, G. L. (2012). *Play Therapy: The art of the relationship*. Routledge.
Levy, A. J. (2008). The therapeutic action of play. *Clinical Social Work Journal, 36*, 281–91.
Manney, P. (2008). Empathy in the time of technology: How storytelling is the key to empathy. *Journal of Evolution & Technology, 19*(1), September.
Masten, A. (2001). Ordinary magic: Resilience processes in development. *American Psychologist, 56*, 227–38.
Meichenbaum, D. (1993). *Stress inoculation training* (2nd ed.). Pergamon Press.
Moore, M., & Russ, S. (2008). Follow-up of a pretend play intervention: Effects on play, creativity, and emotional processes in children. *Creativity Research Journal, 20*(4), 427–36.
Nichols, M. & Efran, J. (1985). Catharsis in psychotherapy. *Psychotherapy, 22*, 46–58.
O'Connor, K. (2010). *Beyond the power of play: Using therapeutic change processes in play therapy*. Presented at the Association for Play Therapy conference, Louisville, KY.
O'Connor, K. (2023, October 13). *Therapeutic change processes: An integrative approach to optimizing play therapy outcomes* [Conference session]. Association for Play Therapy International Conference, The Westin Rancho Mirage, Palm Springs, CA, United States.
Piaget, J. (1951). *Play, dreams, & imitation in childhood*. Heinemann.
Piaget, J. (1997/1932). *The moral judgment of the child*. Harcourt.
Prochaska, J. O. (1995). An eclectic and integrative approach: Transtheoretical therapy. In A. S. Gurman & S. B. Messer (Eds.), *Essential psychotherapies: Theory and practice* (pp. 403–40). Guilford Press.
Russ, S. W. (2003). *Play in child development and psychotherapy: Toward empirically supported practice*. Lawrence Erlbaum Associates.
Russ, S. W. & Lee, A. W. (2021). Pretend play and creativity. In Creativity and innovation (pp. 133–49). Routledge.
Schaefer, C. E. (1993). *The therapeutic powers of play*. Jason Aronson.
Schaefer, C. E. (1999). Curative factors in play therapy. *Journal of Professional Counseling, 14*, 7–16.
Schaefer, C. E. (2001). Prescriptive play therapy. *International Journal of Play Therapy, 10*(2), 57–73.
Schaefer, C. E. (2011). Prescriptive play therapy. In C. E. Schaefer (Ed.), *Foundations of play therapy* (pp. 365–78). Wiley.
Schaefer, C. E., & Drewes, A. A. (2014). *The therapeutic powers of play: 20 core agents of change* (pp. 365–78). Wiley.
Shirk, S. R., & Karver, M. (2003). Prediction of treatment outcome from relationship variables in child and adolescent therapy: A meta-analytic review. *Journal of Consulting and Clinical Psychology, 71*, 452–64.
Shirk, S. R., & Russell, R. L. (1996). *Change processes in child psychotherapy*. Guilford Press.
Shrinivasa, B., Bukhari, M., Ragesh, G., & Hamza, A. (2018). Therapeutic intervention for children through play: An overview. *Archives of Mental Health, 18*(19), 82–9.
Siev, J., & Chambless, D. (2007). Specificity of treatment effects: Cognitive therapy and relaxation for generalized anxiety and panic disorders. *Journal of Consulting & Clinical Psychology, 75*, 513–27.
Singer, D. G., & Singer, J. L. (1990). *The house of make-believe*. Harvard University Press.

Strayhorn, J. (2002). Self-control: Theory and research. *Journal of the American Academy of Child & Adolescent Psychiatry, 41*(1), 7–16.

Swan, A., & Bratton, S. (2021). Alex plays his unspeakable story: Facilitating communication. In E. Prendiville & J. Parson (Eds.), *Clinical applications of the therapeutic powers of play: Case studies in child and adolescent psychotherapy* (pp. 117–28). Taylor & Francis Group.

Terr, L. C. (1981). "Forbidden games": Post-traumatic child's play. *Journal of the American Academy of Child Psychiatry, 20*(4), 741–60.

Yalom, I. D. (2005). *The theory & practice of group psychotherapy* (5th ed.). Basic Books.

Yasenik, L (2021). Polly meets maddie: Fostering emotional wellness. In E. Prendiville & J. Parson (Eds.), *Clinical applications of the therapeutic powers of play: Case studies in child and adolescent psychotherapy* (pp. 129–44). Taylor & Francis Group.

Vygotsky, L. (1978). *Mind in society*. Havard University Press.

2

The Therapeutic Powers of Play Overview

Julie Nash

The therapeutic powers of play were originally conceptualized by Dr. Charles Schaefer, who was always interested in why play therapy works (Schaefer, 1979). His early work in the field of play therapy education included a focus on not just teaching which techniques were effective for various presenting issues, but also in exploring a diversity of theoretical understanding, historical perspectives, and digging deep into the "how" and "why" of play therapy effectiveness while encouraging ongoing research into the same. Knowing, understanding, and utilizing a theoretical approach to play therapy is critical, as is using techniques or interventions to achieve treatment goals. But why does play therapy work—what is it about play that actually causes change for a client in a therapeutic setting—this was the question Dr. Schaefer focused on for over forty years (e.g., Schaefer, 1979, 1999; Schaefer & Drewes, 2014; Peabody & Schaefer, 2019). Labeling these change agents the therapeutic powers of play, he called them the "heart and soul of play therapy" (Schaefer & Drewes, 2014, p. 4).

The concept of therapeutic powers in therapy as a whole is not new. Also called curative factors, therapeutic factors, agents of change, mechanisms of change, and many other names, the idea of what exactly leads to therapeutic change and improvement for clients has been studied since the beginning of organized psychological theories and therapeutic interventions. For example, Sigmund Freud spoke about insight as a curative factor, specifically in relation to interpretations and transference (Slipp, 1982). Carl Rogers wrote from a humanistic perspective about attributes of the therapist that were necessary for therapeutic change in the client, including genuineness, warmth, and respect (Rogers, 1957). Freud, Rogers, and other leading theorists discussed curative factors in light of their own theoretical orientations and interventions. In 1972, Bergin and Strupp described ten therapeutic factors that existed across theoretical perspectives. Yalom (1985) then identified ten change mechanisms specific to group psychotherapy. Inspired by Yalom's work, Schaefer first applied this investigation to causal factors in play therapy in 1993, when he identified fourteen therapeutic powers of play (Schaefer, 2019). He later expanded this list to twenty-five curative factors in 1999, and his last compilation included twenty therapeutic powers of play in 2014 (Schaefer & Drewes, 2014).

Of note is that Schaefer, along with others like Bergin and Strupp, discussed the concept of curative factors as transtheoretical. That is, the understanding of each theoretical orientation includes a discussion of what causes therapeutic change for clients based on views of child development, the development and maintenance of psychopathology, and so on. These changes are often considered specific to the theory. For example, Rogers' ideas about genuineness, warmth, and unconditional positive regard or respect are necessary and sufficient concepts for therapeutic change from a humanistic psychotherapy perspective. Freud's idea of a client developing insight for therapeutic growth is an essential concept for psychoanalytic psychotherapy. Rogerian psychotherapists are not likely to cite insight as a core condition for therapeutic change, just as Freudian psychotherapists are not likely to cite genuineness, warmth, or unconditional positive regard by the therapist as necessary and sufficient for growth! The introduction of the therapeutic powers of play removed these potential limitations in case conceptualization and treatment and encouraged a more prescriptive approach to play therapy.

In suggesting a prescriptive approach to play therapy and utilization of the therapeutic powers of play, Schaefer suggested that a play therapist could encourage the most effective form of play therapy for each client by prescriptively matching the needs of the client and presenting concerns with specific therapeutic powers of play to promote effective play therapy treatment. The application of the therapeutic powers answers the "how" portion of Gordon Paul's question: "*What* treatment, by *whom*, is most effective for *this* individual, with *that* specific problem, with *which* set of circumstances, and *how* does it come about?" (Paul, 1967, as cited in Kaduson, Schaefer, and Cangelosi, 2020). Thus, treatment plans are determined for each individual client through intake and assessment, taking into account the needs of the client, etiology of their psychopathology, and understanding of their circumstances and systems. The therapeutic powers of play that should be activated, facilitated, or utilized in play therapy are determined through analysis of this information as well as empirically supported treatments for any specific presentations.

The therapeutic factors that Bergin and Strupp (1972) identified that transcend theoretical orientation include counterconditioning, extinction, cognitive learning, reward and punishment, transfer and generalization, imitation and identification, persuasion, empathy, warmth, and interpretation. The presence of one or more of these therapeutic factors in psychotherapy sessions leads to therapeutic growth for the client regardless of the theoretical orientation of the therapist. In Yalom's observance of therapeutic factors present within group psychotherapy, he identified acceptance, altruism, catharsis, guidance, instillation of hope, interpersonal learning, self-disclosure, self-understanding, universality, and vicarious learning as the ten primary change mechanisms (Yalom, 1985).

Schaefer's (1993) original list of fourteen therapeutic powers of play was developed following exhaustive studies of the published play therapy and related literature. This list included overcoming resistance, communication, competence, creative thinking, catharsis, abreaction, role play, fantasy/visualization, metaphoric teaching, attachment formation, relationship enhancement, positive emotion, mastering developmental fears, and game play. While describing these therapeutic powers, Schaefer defined a therapeutic factor as "an element of play that contributes to a positive outcome" (Schaefer, 1993, p. 5), specifying that therapeutic factors in play therapy are elements of the play process that result in clinical improvement in a client's presentation. Each therapeutic factor, or therapeutic power of play, is linked to a specific beneficial outcome and therapeutic improvement for the client. While the therapeutic factors are often practically intertwined, explanations of them are typically distinct for ease of discussion. In this original list, overcoming resistance via play was linked to working alliance, and communication was linked to understanding. The therapeutic factor of competence led to self-esteem, while creative thinking led to innovative solutions to problems. Catharsis was linked to emotional release, while abreaction was linked to adjustment to trauma. Role-play as a therapeutic factor led to practice and the acquisition of new behaviors and empathy, while fantasy/visualization led to fantasy compensation. The therapeutic power of metaphoric teaching is linked to the outcome of insight, and attachment formation leads to overall improved attachment. Relationship enhancement through play was linked to three beneficial outcomes: self-actualization, self-esteem, and closeness to others. Finally, positive emotion was linked to the beneficial outcome of ego boost, mastering developmental fears was linked to growth and development, and the therapeutic factor of game play led to ego strength and socialization.

In a 1999 publication entitled "Curative Factors in Play Therapy," Schaefer adapted this list to include self-expression, access to the unconscious, facilitates learning, metaphorical insight, abreaction, catharsis, sublimation, alliance formation, attachment, relationship enhancement, moral judgment, stress inoculation, counterconditioning, power/control, competence, self-control, creative problem solving, fantasy compensation, reality testing, empathy, behavioral rehearsal, accelerated development, sense of self, physical health, and distraction. These twenty-five curative factors were determined through a review of research and clinical experiences, and Schaefer offered the twenty-five as an introductory step in compiling therapeutic powers even though it was his second published list. He encouraged further research and practice to determine which powers were consistently observed and facilitated through play therapy, and ongoing editing of the "general map" (Schaefer, 1999, p. 13) that these twenty-five therapeutic powers of play could provide.

Schaefer later organized his list of therapeutic powers of play into categories by beneficial outcomes and adapted his list based on the growing field of clinical experience and empirical findings within play and play therapy research (Schaefer & Drewes, 2014). At this point in time, literature had been published by psychologist Alan Kazdin calling for identification of the forces at play in the development and maintenance of specific clinical problems (2001) as well as specifying mechanisms of change within child and adolescent research (Kazdin & Nock, 2003), which were some of the first publications to focus on the need for research into the why and how regarding treatment outcomes. Matthew Nock later furthered this literature by underscoring the importance of understanding and utilizing change mechanisms in psychotherapy to help bring order to psychotherapy, highlighting the effective parts of treatment, and eliminating ineffective or inefficient aspects of treatment (Nock, 2007).

The underlying understanding here is that while specific treatments can be empirically validated or supported for specific psychological conditions, there continues to be a need to understand why and how psychological treatment itself works, so that the why and how change occurs can be understood and then isolated and applied to individual case presentations. This allows for the development of better clinicians and research that targets change agents (Schaefer & Drewes, 2014). Specific to play therapy, understanding the therapeutic powers of play shows that engagement in play itself facilitates active forces within play that lead to changes in behavior (Schaefer & Drewes, 2014), as well as changes in the ability to communicate, emotional wellness, interpersonal skills, and social relationships, and increases in personal strengths. These therapeutic outcomes provide the categorization of the current list of twenty therapeutic powers of play.

The current list of therapeutic powers of play consists of four categories, which help organize the twenty therapeutic powers of play by beneficial outcome: facilitates communication, fosters emotional wellness, enhances social relationships, and increases personal strengths. Within the category of facilitating communication are the therapeutic powers of self-expression, access to the unconscious, direct teaching, and indirect teaching. The category of fosters emotional wellness includes the therapeutic powers of catharsis, abreaction, positive emotions, counterconditioning fears, stress inoculation, and stress management. Within the category of enhancing social relationships are the therapeutic powers of the therapeutic relationship, attachment, social competence, and empathy. The final category of increased personal strengths includes the therapeutic powers of creative problem solving, resiliency, moral development, accelerated psychological development, self-regulation, and self-esteem.

When looking at the current list of therapeutic powers of play, there are again direct links between elements in the play process (the therapeutic powers of play) and positive clinical outcomes. The self-expression power of play promotes clients' ability to express themselves, especially when dealing with limited vocabularies and abstract thinking abilities, with a goal of increased understanding of self and others. The access to the unconscious power of play works to help clients develop insight with the guidance of a play therapist. The direct teaching power of play is based on the concept that play-based activities provide the best learning environment, while the indirect teaching power of play allows for the abstract to become concrete through play (Schaefer, 2019).

Within the category of therapeutic powers of play that foster emotional wellness, abreaction encourages mastery of traumatic events and subsequent emotional reactions. Catharsis in play allows for the release and cognitive awareness of restrained emotions, which leads to an increased ability to control feelings. The therapeutic power of positive emotions provides more opportunities to experience positive emotions and restore a client's sense of well-being. The counterconditioning of fears through the power of play involves playful exposure to fear-inducing stimuli, thus encouraging a powerful antidote to fear and anxiety. Activating the stress inoculation power of play allows clients to practice new skills to deal with upcoming stressors in a fun and playful way, while utilizing the stress management power of play helps clients reduce the physical and emotional impacts of current stressors (Schaefer, 2019).

In looking at the therapeutic powers of play that enhance social relationships, facilitating the therapeutic relationship power of play encourages the development of a positive and healthy therapeutic alliance, which is essential for effective play therapy. Facilitating the attachment power of play helps a client experience positive emotional bonds, which strengthen attachment relationships across the lifespan. Utilizing the therapeutic power of social competence helps clients to establish and maintain satisfying relationships, while utilizing the therapeutic power of empathy in play therapy helps them understand other people's feelings and experiences, thus enhancing their ability to connect with others (Schaefer, 2019).

Finally, the therapeutic powers of play that work to increase a client's personal strengths lead to the development of divergent thinking, as is seen through the therapeutic power of creative problem-solving. With the resiliency therapeutic power of play, clients develop skills to handle unexpected events in a playful way, utilizing positive emotions and humor to buffer stress. As the moral development power of play is activated, clients develop an understanding of the purpose of rules and norms in society, thus improving their ability to interact with others. Utilizing the power of accelerated psychological development leads to therapeutic benefits, as significant learning can happen during play that is beyond a child's current developmental stage. Play helps children develop perseverance and self-control through the therapeutic power of self-regulation, thus helping them resist distraction and refrain from engaging in behaviors they should not do. The therapeutic power of self-esteem is activated in play therapy to help strengthen self-efficacy, feelings of competence, and augment a sense of personal power and control (Schaefer, 2019).

From a historical perspective, the field of therapeutic factors has continued to grow, develop, and further educate clinicians about the specific forces within psychotherapy that lead to change in individual clients. From continued observation, identification, and discussion of therapeutic factors in individual and group psychotherapy (e.g., Kivlighan & Holmes, 2004; Holmes & Kivlighan, 2000) to development of an empirically based scale to assess therapeutic factors (Lese & MacNair-Semands, 2000), researchers will continue to seek answers to why psychotherapy is effective. This study is important because it allows clinicians to understand how to provide the most effective and efficient courses of treatment for their clients.

Within play therapy, there has been growth in clinical applications of the therapeutic powers of play (e.g., Prendiville & Parson, 2021) and global utilization of the therapeutic powers of play. Models to identify and implement the most effective treatment courses based on therapeutic factors and change processes within play and play therapy are gaining traction (e.g., O'Connor, 2023; Nash, 2024). The therapeutic powers of play currently endure as the guiding forces within play and play therapy that contribute to positive clinical outcomes. Continuing to gain insight into the specific therapeutic powers of play in various domains and providing ways to integrate this knowledge into treatment planning and provision will provide ongoing development and utilization of this vital aspect of play therapy.

References

Bergin, A. E., & Strupp, H. H. (1972). *Changing frontiers in the science of psychotherapy*. Aldine.

Holmes, S. E., & Kivlighan Jr, D. M. (2000). Comparison of therapeutic factors in group and individual treatment processes. *Journal of counseling psychology, 47*(4), 478. https://psycnet.apa.org/doi/10.1037/0022-0167.47.4.478.

Kaduson, H. G., Schaefer, C. E., & Cangelosi, D. (2020). Basic principles and core practices of prescriptive play therapy. In H. G. Kaduson, D. Cangelosi, & C. E. Schaefer (Eds.), *Prescriptive play therapy: Tailoring interventions for specific childhood problems* (pp. 3–13). The Guilford Press.

Kazdin, A. E. (2001). Bridging the enormous gaps of theory with therapy, research, and practice. *Journal of Clinical Child Psychology, 30*(1), 59–66. https://doi.org/10.1207/S15374424JCCP3001_7.

Kazdin, A. E., & Nock, M. K. (2003). Delineating mechanisms of change in child and adolescent therapy: Methodological issues and research recommendations. *Journal of Child Psychology and Psychiatry, 44*(8), 1116–29. https://doi.org/10.1111/1469-7610.00195.

Kivlighan, D. M., & Holmes, S. E. (2004). The importance of therapeutic factors: A typology of therapeutic factors studies. In J. L. DeLucia-Waack, D. A. Gerrity, C. R. Kalodner, & M. T. Riva (Eds.), *Handbook of group counseling and psychotherapy* (pp. 23–36). SAGE Publications.

Lese, K. P., & MacNair-Semands, R. R. (2000). The therapeutic factors inventory: Development of a scale. *Group, 24*(4), 303–17.

Nash, J. B. (2024). *Nature-based play therapy: A prescriptive approach to integrating the therapeutic powers of nature and play*. Routledge.

Nock, M. K. (2007). Conceptual and design essentials for evaluating mechanisms of change. *Alcoholism: Clinical and Experimental Research, 31*(s3), 4s–12s. https://doi.org/10.1111/j.1530-0277.2007.00488.x.

O'Connor, K. (2023, October 13). *Therapeutic change processes: An integrative approach to optimizing play therapy outcomes* [Conference session]. Association for Play Therapy International Conference, The Westin Rancho Mirage, Palm Springs, CA, United States.

Peabody, M. A., & Schaefer, C. E. (2019). The therapeutic powers of play: The heart and soul of play therapy. *Play Therapy, 14*(3), 4–6.

Prendiville, E., & Parson, J. A. (2021). *Clinical applications of the therapeutic powers of play: Case studies in child and adolescent psychotherapy*. Routledge.

Rogers, C. R. (1957). The necessary and sufficient conditions of the therapeutic personality change. *Journal of Consulting Psychology, 21*(2), 95–103.

Schaefer, C. E. (1993). *The therapeutic powers of play*. Jason Aronson, Inc.

Schaefer, C. E. (1999). Curative factors in play therapy. *The Journal for the Professional Counselor, 14*(1), 7–16.

Schaefer, C. E. (2019). *The therapeutic powers of play* [Online course]. The Play Therapy Training Institute, New Jersey. https://the-play-therapy-training-institute.teachable.com/p/the-therapeutic-powers-of-play.

Schaefer, C. E. (Ed.). (1979). *The therapeutic use of child's play*. Jason Aronson, Inc.

Schaefer, C. E., & Drewes, A. A. (2014). Introduction: How play therapy causes therapeutic change. In C. E. Schaefer & A. A. Drewes (Eds.), *The therapeutic powers of play: 20 core agents of change, (pp. 1–7).* John Wiley & Sons, Inc.

Slipp, S. (1982). *Curative factors in dynamic psychotherapy*. McGraw-Hill.

Yalom, I. D. (1985). *The theory and practice of group psychotherapy*. Basic Books.

3

Developing a Theoretical Orientation and Play Therapy Identity

Bridgette Mitchell Sanders

Chapter Outline

Picture it Minneapolis, Minnesota. It was a Wednesday or Thursday evening at the 2017 Association for Play Therapy (APT) International Play Therapy Conference. I sat down at the bar in the conference hotel and inadvertently found myself sitting next to the co-founder of *the* Association for Play Therapy, Dr. Kevin O'Connor. I am typically quite shy, but that fateful evening, I could not resist taking a moment to ask such a respected member of the play therapy profession some burning questions. Mustering up courage, I asked Dr. O'Connor about his assertion that play therapists first become grounded in one theoretical approach before integrating additional theoretical approaches into their work (O'Connor et al., 2016). To my shock and awe, Dr. O'Connor slowly turned to me and said, "I didn't say that. What I *actually* said was" (K. O'Connor, personal communication, October 2017). About an hour of focused conversation about play therapy theory, the selection of a theoretical orientation, and eclecticism versus the single theory approach ensued. Our conversation ultimately turned to our commiserate caution for play therapists leaning toward interventions and moving away from allowing theory to guide their practice. That was a defining moment in my play therapy career—a hallmark conversation which cemented what I knew then, and what I know to be true now. Play therapy theory is a cornerstone of good play therapy practice.

Play Therapy Theory and Theoretical Orientation

A knowledge base grounded in play therapy theory is a hallmark of a well-trained play therapist (Grant et al., 2021). This assertion is consistent with APT Best Practices (APT, 2022) and aligns with APT credentialing standards (APT, 2023a). APT requires play therapists to select and study one seminal and/or one historically significant play therapy theory during their credential training. However, what is the difference between a seminal and a historically significant play therapy theory? How does one decide which play therapy theory to select and orient themselves toward? Moreover, what are the steps to selecting a play therapy theory that is consistent with one's worldview, cultural beliefs, and personal and professional values? This chapter aims to answer these questions and offer a developmental framework to assist in the identification and selection of a play therapy theoretical orientation that will guide and support the development of your identity as a play therapist.

Play Therapy Theory

In 1997, the APT board of directors defined play therapy as "the systematic use of a theoretical model to establish an interpersonal process wherein trained play therapists use the therapeutic powers of play to help clients prevent or resolve psychosocial difficulties and achieve optimal growth and development" (p. 7). According to this definition, play therapy has five keystone components: (1) Play therapy is grounded in a theoretical model; (2) Play therapy involves an interpersonal process; (3) Play therapy employs a play therapist trained in the practice of play therapy; (4) Play therapy activates the therapeutic powers of play; and (5) Play therapy helps clients prevent or resolve psychosocial difficulties and achieve optimal growth and development. One cannot practice play therapy without using a theory in an intentional and systematic way to guide one's thinking and behavior.

Seminal and Historically Significant Play Therapy Theories

APT play therapy credential requirements include requisite training in a seminal and/or a historically significant play therapy theory (APT, 2023b). In the play therapy profession, seminal play therapy theories "are from the three major schools of thought. They are deemed original and influential theories from which historically significant theories have originated. They represent the foundational work that has been used to develop future theories and models" (APT, 2023b, p. 20). Seminal play therapy theories are called such due to their significance in establishing groundbreaking, original ideas that influenced the development of later theories and models. APT recognizes three seminal play therapy theories: psychoanalytic, humanistic, and cognitive-behavioral (APT, 2023a) from three major schools of thought. In contrast, historically significant play therapy theories "have roots in seminal theories and are considered landmark works in the field of psychotherapy. They are a second layer of theoretical richness from which third-generation theories and models may be emerging" (APT, 2023b, p. 3). There are ten identified historically significant play therapy theories and approaches recognized by APT (2023a): (1) Adlerian, (2) Child-centered, (3) Cognitive-behavioral, (4) Developmental (Viola Brody), (5) Ecosystemic, (6) Filial—although not a theory, this approach is historically significant, (7) Gestalt, (8) Jungian analytical, (9) Object-relations, and (10) Theraplay®—a play therapy approach based on attachment theories (p. 8). Additional play therapy theories continue to emerge from the seminal and historically significant play therapy theories, some of which will be addressed in other chapters within this publication.

Play therapy theory is "A set of interrelated ideas and principles that provide a broad theoretical framework for understanding how experiences affect children, how psychopathology develops, and how to remedy it through play interactions" (Peabody & Schaefer, 2016). The bulk of APT's play therapy credential requirement is dedicated to the study of play therapy theory. Of the 150 hours of play therapy-specific instruction required to become a credentialed play therapist, 37 percent of the credential requirements or fifty-five instructional hours, are allocated to learning seminal and/or historically significant play therapy theories (APT, 2023a). A minimum of twenty-five hours must be dedicated to the exclusive study of one play therapy theory. APT's definition of play therapy, as well as its credential standards, underscores the central and important role play therapy theory occupies in the professional development of a play therapist.

Theoretical Orientation

A theoretical orientation sets the stage for translating play therapy theory into clinical practice (Strupp, 1955). According to Poznanski and McLennan (1995), a theoretical orientation provides mental health professionals with a theory-based framework for:

- Generating hypothesis about a client's experience and behavior
  (*This is why the client thinks, feels, behaves the way that they do*)
- Formulating a rationale for specific treatment interventions
  (*This intervention will address that issue*)
- Evaluating the ongoing therapeutic process
  (*Is treatment progressing according to a and b?*) (p. 412)

One's theoretical orientation offers an organized framework for providing play therapy with intention. Your theoretical orientation may be rooted in one primary play therapy theory, or you may choose to combine one or more theories in an integrative or eclectic approach. One may also follow a prescriptive play therapy approach where one selects a combination of "whatever works" from a range of play therapy theories to meet a client's individual needs (Peabody & Schaefer, 2016). Whether embracing a singular, integrative, eclectic, or prescriptive play therapy theory approach, developing a theoretical orientation is a developmental process that requires discipline, training, and time (Halbur & Halbur, 2019); It is a step beyond the learning process. In essence, you are purposefully allowing your thinking, behavior, and therapeutic choices as a play therapist to be shaped and guided by the roadmap embedded in your theory or theories of choice.

Transforming Theory into Theoretical Orientation

The process of selecting a theoretical orientation is a complex and ever-changing process (Petko et al., 2016). How one selects a theoretical orientation over another may be influenced by several factors including one's personal beliefs about theory (Howatt, 2000); cognitive style (Barrio Minton & Myers, 2008); personality style (Boswell et al., 2009; Ivanovic, 2011); religious beliefs (Bilgrave & Deluty, 1998; 2002); and personal belief system (Fear & Woolfe, 1999; Rønnestad & Skovholt, 1993). One's profession, gender, and years of clinical experience play a role in selecting one's theoretical orientation (Ogunfowora & Drapeau, 2008). Bitar et al. (2007) further identified ten factors that influence the development of a theoretical orientation: (1) personality, (2) personal philosophy, (3) family of origin, (4) their own therapy, (5) marriage, (6) undergraduate courses, (7) graduate training, (8) clients, (9) professional development, and (10) clinical sophistication. While the research on the factors contributing to developing a theoretical orientation is mixed and sometimes conflicting, it is likely that multiple personal and professional factors influence the selection of a play therapy theoretical orientation (Halbur & Halbur, 2019; Southern & Devlin, 2010). Because selecting a theoretical orientation may be a complicated and multifaceted process (Buckman & Barker, 2010; Freeman et al., 2007), it may be helpful to lean on a model that uses multiple personal and professional factors to guide play therapists through the process of selecting a theoretical orientation.

Intentional Theory Selection (ITS) Model

The Intentional Theory Selection (ITS) model (Habur & Habur, 2019) offers a developmental framework that can help play therapists identify and select a theoretical orientation. The ITS model not only incorporates research-based factors that influence theory selection but also encourages selecting a theoretical orientation that reflects one's personal values, cultural beliefs, and life experiences. The ITS model has four key components: (1) Develop your life philosophy; (2) Explore a school of thought; (3) Select your theory or theories; and (4) Adopt goals and techniques (Habur & Habur, 2019).

Develop Your Life Philosophy

The ITS model begins with exploring and understanding one's life philosophy; a broad concept that includes awareness of how you view yourself, others, and the world around you (Halbur & Halbur, 2019). Because our theoretical orientation serves as a reflection of who we are and the values and beliefs that we ascribe to (Prescod et al., 2020) understanding our life philosophy is the first step to translating theory into practice. Your schema of the world is at the center of who you are, influences your actions and decision-making, and is ultimately what gives your life meaning (Petko et al., 2016). We human beings are also products of our culture, ethnicity, gender, family experiences, education, sexual orientation, socioeconomic background, and religion/spirituality. Our life philosophy is an accumulation of our past life and future events yet to be experienced; it is uniquely our own, yet a product of multiple influences and interactions with our environment.

Self-reflection and introspection help facilitate awareness of our life philosophy. Spend time journaling or taking personal inventory of what you believe your life philosophy to be. Mindfully explore your personal values, cultural beliefs, spiritual and religious views, and your core values, and so on to deepen self-awareness of your core beliefs. Personality inventories are helpful tools that will support you in gaining insight into your personality characteristics and worldview. While research on the connection between personality factors and theory selection is mixed (Freeman et al., 2007; Weinrach, 2006) personality factors are a key component of one's life philosophy. When you better understand yourself, you will be better able to select a play therapy theory that not only serves your clients in intentional ways (Howatt, 2000; Ivanovic, 2011) but also complements who you are as a unique individual that occupies a unique space in the world (Petko et al., 2016).

Explore Schools of Thought

After identifying your life philosophy, the next step of the ITS model is to examine the major schools of thought (Halbur & Halbur, 2019). Before settling on a play therapy theory, it is helpful to first develop a working knowledge of the larger schools of thought that inspire theory. There is some debate about how many psychological theories have developed; however, major schools of thought generally include: (1) Psychodynamic, (2) Behavioral, (3) Humanistic, (4) Pragmatic, (5) Constructivist, and (6) Family Approaches (Corsini & Wedding, 2008; Halbur & Halbur, 2019; Ivey et. al., 2007; O'Connor et al., 2016). Within the play therapy profession, the seminal play therapy theories (previously referenced) represent the psychoanalytic, humanistic, and cognitive-behavioral schools of thought (APT, 2023a). While each major school holds distinct assumptions regarding human nature, how pathology develops, the role of the practitioner, the path to healing, and so on, there may also be similarities between them that make the job of choosing one school over the other challenging. This initial examination of theory only requires that you understand the basic assumptions of each school (Halbur & Halbur, 2019). The goal is to empower yourself to identify the schools of thought that align with your life philosophy and the core of who you are.

After gathering information about the major schools of thought, summarize the information into a chart (see Table 3.1). Feel free to adapt the chart to meet your individual needs. After completing the chart, use a 1–5 Likert scale (1 = strongly disagree; 2 = disagree; 3 = neutral; 4 = agree; 5 = strongly agree) to rate how closely you agree with each school's theoretical assumptions. Add the Likert scale ratings across the rows and place the total in the final column.

Use the results of your Likert scale ratings to rank the major schools of thought from highest to lowest. The two or three schools of thought that you rank the highest are likely those that most closely match your life philosophy. After identifying your life philosophy and having a general understanding of the major schools of thought, you will be ready to begin exploring potential play therapy theory or theories.

Select Your Theory or Theories

The third step of the ITS model will assist you in identifying a play therapy theory or theories that align with your life philosophy and identified school(s) of thought. This process begins with comparing and contrasting theories within the schools of thought that you identified in the previous step. There are self-report rating scales designed to assist with this process. A commonly used scale is the Selective Theory Sorter-Revised (STS-R). While not specific to play therapy theory, the STS-R was developed to help practitioners discover which researched theories they might endorse (Ghazali et al., 2018). It is based on a literature review of the underlying assumptions and beliefs comprising major psychological theories (Corey, 2004; Doyle, 1998; Ivey & Ivey, 1999; Jackson & Thompson, 1971). The STS-R, and similar rating scales are not validated diagnostic assessments but rather a means for self-exploration. Theory sorters are designed to offer you information on which theories' views on pathology, the treatment process, treatment modalities, and theoretical preferences most parallel your own views (Halbur & Halbur, 2019). Because these theory sorters are not necessarily play therapy specific, you may have to invest some time thinking about which of the identified theories align with the play therapy theories you are interested in.

Play Therapy Specific Theories

Play therapy is grounded in the fields of psychology, play, and child development (Ray, 2011). As such, there are potentially hundreds of interrelated theories representing these fields. However, the available list of play therapy theories and approaches is not unlimited. According to APT (2023a) Credentialing Standards:

> In order to preserve and strengthen the credentialing program, APT wishes to distinguish seminal theories and historically significant theories that were derived from them, which

Table 3.1 Comparing Major Schools of Thought

	Assumption 1		Assumption 2		Assumption 3		Assumption 4		Summary	
	Human Nature	**Rating**	**Pathology Development**	**Rating**	**Practitioner Role**	**Rating**	**Path to Healing**	**Rating**	**Total**	**Ranking**
School 1										
School 2										
School 3										

> have had a lasting impact and have stood the test of time, from newer theories or approaches that have emerged in more recent years and have not yet proven their significance, though they may at some point with more time and empirical evidence. (p. 7)

APT has endorsed three seminal theories and ten historically significant theories to offer a guide to the identification and selection of a play therapy theory that is grounded in research, peer-reviewed, and/or has made significant time-tested contributions to the play therapy profession (APT, 2023a). In addition to the APT-recognized seminal and historically significant play therapy theories, there is a growing number of burgeoning play therapy models; some of which are highlighted in subsequent chapters. To sort through the plethora of play therapy theories, it may be helpful to compare their corresponding philosophy, therapist role, goals, and common techniques (see Table 3.2). Feel free to adapt the chart to meet your individual needs.

Follow the same steps that were used to identify a major school of thought. After using a 1–5 Likert scale to rate your agreement with the tenets of each play therapy theory, summarize the scores and rank the theories from highest to lowest. The two or three play therapy theories you rank the highest are likely those that most closely match your life philosophy. If you have broad theoretical interests, multiple perspectives about human nature, and the role of play and play therapy in the healing process, you may have identified more than two or three play therapy theories. Trust the process; identifying a theoretical orientation is a developmental process that takes time to sort out.

Adopt Goals and Techniques

The final step in the ITS model is to select goals and techniques that are aligned with your identified theoretical orientation (Halbur & Halbur, 2019). Your identity as a play therapist includes embracing an array of tools and techniques for your play therapy toolbox. However, your play therapy goals and techniques must align with your theoretical orientation; it will make you accountable to ensure that your play therapy work is congruent with the underlying theory or theories guiding your practice. As your preference for a play therapy theory or theories emerges, you may begin to feel increased confidence in your play therapy work with clients due to the structure and direction that a theoretical orientation provides (Buckman & Barker, 2010).

Conclusion

While on the road to developing your theoretical orientation and identity as a play therapist, it is important to remain open to both personal and professional growth and change. Halbur & Halbur (2019) stated, "(i)f traveled successfully, the road to development begins with self-reflection and ends with application" (p. 14). Knowing *who* you are as a play therapist is as important as knowing *what* to do. As Dr. O'Connor and I ended our

Table 3.2 Comparing Play Therapy Theories

	Philosophy	Rating	Therapist Role	Rating	Goals	Rating	Common Techniques	Rating	Total	Rank
Theory 1										
Theory 2										
Theory 3										
Theory 4										

conversation that evening at the APT conference, we discussed our increasing observation that developing play therapists are tempted to seek out interventions and techniques before being firmly grounded in a theoretical orientation. Naturally, one wants to know what to do and how they can help. However, play therapists must remember that *we* are the greatest instrument of change. The self, and the therapeutic use of self, is the most effective tool a play therapist possesses and the primary tool to facilitate change (Dewane, 2006; McTighe, 2010; Reupert, 2007). Play therapy techniques are useful, but how one supports the client and follows up with the client before, during, and after the technique is guided by the play therapist's underlying theory. Play therapy always has and will remain rooted and grounded in the power of the therapeutic relationship and bolstered by the therapeutic powers of play (Schaefer & Drewes, 2014).

References

Association for Play Therapy. (1997). A definition of play therapy. *The Association for Play Therapy Newsletter, 16*(1), 7.

Association for Play Therapy. (2022). *Play therapy best practices: Clinical, professional, and ethical issues.* https://cdn.ymaws.com/www.a4pt.org/resource/resmgr/publications/best_practices.pdf.

Association for Play Therapy. (2023a). *Credentialing standards for the registered play therapist. APT professional credentialing program.* https://cdn.ymaws.com/www.a4pt.org/resource/resmgr/credentials/standards_&_applications/rpt_standards.pdf.

Association for Play Therapy. (2023b). *Glossary of terms. Professional credentialing program. Approved center and approved provider programs.* https://cdn.ymaws.com/www.a4pt.org/resource/resmgr/credentials/terms.pdf.

Barrio Minton, C. E., & Myers, J. E. (2008). Cognitive style and theoretical orientation: Factors affecting intervention style interest and use. *Journal of Mental Health Counseling, 30*, 330–44. https://doi.org/org/10.17744/mehc.30.4.5626315033866460.

Bilgrave, D. P., & Deluty, R. H. (1998). Religious beliefs and therapeutic orientations of clinical and counseling psychologists. *Journal for the Scientific Study of Religion, 37*, 329–49. https://doi.org/10.2307/1387532.

Bilgrave, D. P., & Deluty, R. H. (2002). Religious beliefs and political ideologies as predictors of psychotherapeutic orientations of clinical and counseling psychologists. *Psychotherapy: Theory, Research, Practice, Training, 39*, 245–60. https://doi.org/10.1037/0033-3204.39.3.245.

Bitar, G. W., Bean, R. A., & Bermudez, M. (2007). Influences and processes in theoretical orientation development: A grounded theory pilot study. *The American Journal of Family Therapy, 35(2)*, 109–21.

Boswell, J. F., Casonguay, L. G., & Pincus, A. L. (2009). Trainee theoretical orientation: Profiles and potential predictors. *Journal of Psychotherapy Integration, 19*, 291–312. https://doi.org/10.1037/a0017068.

Buckman, J. R., & Barker, C. (2010). Therapeutic orientation preferences in trainee clinical psychologists: Personality or training? *Psychotherapy Research, 20*, 247–58. https://doi.org/10.1080/10503300903352693.

Corey, G. (2004). *Theory and practice of counseling and psychotherapy* (5th ed.). Wadsworth.

Corsini, R. & Wedding, D. (2008). *Current psychotherapies* (8th ed.). Thomas Higher Education.

Dewane, C. J. (2006). Use of self: A primer revisited. *Clinical Social Work Journal, 34*(4), 543–58.

Doyle, R. E. (1998). *Essential skills and strategies in the helping process*. Brooks/Cole.

Fear, R., & Woolfe, R. (1999). The personal and professional development of the counselor: The relationship between personal philosophy and theoretical orientation. *Counseling Psychology Quarterly, 12*, 253–62. https://doi.org/10.1080/09515079908254095.

Freeman, M. S., Hayes, G., Kuch, T. H., & Taub, G. (2007). Personality: A predictor of theoretical orientation of students enrolled in a counseling theories course. *Counselor Education & Supervision, 46*, 254–65. https://doi.org/10.1002/j.1556-6978.2007.tb00030.x.

Ghazali, N., Wan Jaafar, W. M., & Anuara, A. (2018). Supervision outcomes as predictor to the supervisory relationship and supervision contextual factors: Study on the internship trainee counsellors. MATEC Web of Conferences, 150, 05073. https://doi.org/10.1051/matecconf/201815005073.

Grant, R. J., Stone, J., & Mellenthin, C. (Eds.). (2021). *Play therapy theories and perspectives: A collection of thoughts in the field*. Routledge.

Halbur, D. A., & Halbur, L. V. (2019). *Developing your theoretical orientation in counseling and psychotherapy* (4th ed.). Pearson.

Howatt, W. A. (2000). *The human services counseling toolbox: Theory, development, technique, and resources*. Thompson Learning.

Ivanovic, M. (2011). *Theoretical orientation and personality of the therapist: A graduate student sample*. The Chicago School of Professional Psychology. ProQuest Dissertations and Theses, 105. Retrieved from http://ezproxy.net.ucf.edu/login?url=http://search.proquest.com/docview/860133929?accountid=10003. (860133929).

Ivey, A. E., & Ivey, M. B. (1999). *Intentional interviewing and counseling: Facilitating client development in a multicultural society*. Wadsworth.

Ivey, A. E., Ivey, M. B., D'Andrea, M., & Simek-Morgan, L. (2007). *Counseling and psychotherapy: A multicultural perspective* (6th ed.). Pearson.

Jackson, M., & Thompson, C. L. (1971). Effective counselors: Characteristics and attitudes. *Journal of Counseling Psychology, 18*(3), 249–54.

McTighe, J. P. (2010). Teaching the use of self through the process of clinical supervision. *Clinical Social Work Journal, 39*(3), 301–7.

O'Connor, K. (2011). Ecosystemic play therapy. In C. E. Schefer (Ed.), *Foundations of play therapy* (2nd ed., pp. 253–72). Wiley.

O'Connor, K. J., Schaefer, C. E., & Braverman, L. D. (Eds.). (2016). *Handbook of play therapy* (2nd ed.). Wiley.

Ogunfowora, B., & Drapeau, M. (2008). Comparing counseling and clinical psychology practitioners: Similarities and differences on theoretical orientations revisited. *International Journal of Advanced Counselling, 30*(2), 93–103.

Peabody, M. A., & Schaefer, C. E. (2016). Towards semantic clarity in play therapy. *International Journal of Play Therapy, 25*(4), 197.

Petko, J. T., Kendrick, E., & Young, M. E. (2016). Selecting a theory of counseling: What influences a counseling student to choose?. *Universal Journal of Psychology, 4*(6), 285–91.

Prescod, D. J., Zeligman, M., Greene, J. H., & Kristopher, G. H., (2020). Navigating the therapeutic waters: How counselors develop and utilize their theoretical orientation. *Journal of Counselor Practice, 11*(1), 55–84. https://doi.org/10.22229/ntt1112020.

Poznanski, J. J., & McLennan, J. (1995). Conceptualizing and measuring counselors' theoretical orientation. *Journal of Counseling Psychology, 42*, 411–22.

Ray, D. (2011). *Advanced play therapy: Essential conditions, knowledge, and skills for child practice*. Taylor & Francis.

Reupert, A. (2007). Social worker's use of self. *Clinical Social Work Journal, 35*(2), 107–16.

Rønnestad, M. H., & Skovholt, T. M. (1993). Supervision of beginning and advanced students of counseling and psychotherapy. *Journal of Counseling and Development, 71*, 396–405. https://doi.org/10.1002/j.1556-6676.1993.tb02655.x.

Schaefer, C. E., & Drewes, A. A. (Eds.). (2014). *The therapeutic powers of play: 20 core agents of change* (2nd ed.). Wiley.

Southern, S., & Devlin, J. (2010). Theory development: A bridge between practice and research. *The Family Journal: Counseling and Therapy for Couples and Families, 18*(1), 84–7.

Strupp, H. H. (1955). An objective comparison of Rogerian and psychoanalytic techniques. *Journal of counseling psychology, 19*, 1–7.

Weinrach, S. G. (2006). Selecting a counseling theory while scratching your head: A rational-emotive therapist's personal journey. *Journal of Rational-Emotive & Cognitive-Behavior Therapy, 24*, 155–67. https://doi.org/10.1007/s10942-006-0042-1.

4

The Neuroscience of Theories, Play, and Therapeutic Powers of Play

Edward Franc Hudspeth and Karlie Lynn Zabin

Chapter Outline

Introduction

The overarching goal of this chapter is to highlight how neuroscience interplays with the 20 core change agents (viz., the therapeutic powers of play [TPoP]), play, and theoretical approaches. We do this specifically focused on play therapy, knowing that the play in play therapy is the source of change. This task, if examined thoroughly, would be a book in and of itself. While doing the research for this chapter, hundreds of references were found. Some references led to direct evidence, while others provided indirect evidence that could be extrapolated/inferred. The basic notes for this chapter totaled nearly 60 pages. To conceptualize the immensity of the information, think about the possible neuroscience aspects of each of the 20 TPoP and their four categories. Then, add to these the possible neuroscience aspects of all of the elements that make a seminal play therapy theory a fully viable theory. Finally, add the possible neuroscience aspects of play. The outcome of this and all the interplays between them should look like a growing word cloud. Therefore, to describe this content in practical, usable terms would be long and overwhelming.

Neuroscience is intriguing. It captivates the minds of readers, researchers, and practitioners. Neuroscience adds a level of descriptiveness that typical assessments cannot. A search of the internet will yield various definitions of neuroscience ranging from "the scientific study of the nervous system and brain" (Cambridge Dictionary, 2024) to more detailed definition such as the one offered by Mitra (2023) "Neuroscience is a subject matter which is multidisciplinary and not only combines anatomy, physiology, molecular biology, cytology, developmental biology, computer science but also mathematical modeling" (p. 1).

Whether it is the brain structural knowledge, the physiological knowledge, or the neurochemical knowledge that neuroscience research illuminates, all together, the information provides valuable insight into many aspects of human experience. Across multiple disciplines, neuroscience research has examined a multitude of topics. The resulting information feeds back into these disciplines and increases awareness of how the brain and nervous system work, how they are involved in complex issues, and eventually sparks investigation into possible solutions. Among these disciplines, the many branches of mental health have grasped neuroscience concepts and applied them to case conceptualization, diagnostics, treatment planning, and intervention development. Many specializations within the mental health branches have embraced neuroscience research as a new dimension of understanding.

Play therapists are just one of the groups of specialized practitioners who value neuroscience research. Though some may not be able to articulate all of the ways neuroscience research has impacted their practice, it is plausible to think that all could name some of the influences. Play therapists are well-versed in developmental theory, trained from at least one theoretical philosophy, and know the therapeutic power(s) of play. Each year, at the Association for Play Therapy's conference, many workshops include neuroscience principles. Now in its thirty-fourth year of publication, the *International Journal of Play Therapy* (IJPT) has included fifty-nine articles that describe aspects of neuroscience research or cite neuroscience research when utilized to explain some aspect of play therapy. Countless book chapters in play therapy texts have used neuroscience research to describe how play therapy works. To name a few, Gaskill and Perry (2014) wrote about the neurobiological power of play, Hudspeth and Mathews (2016) wrote about neuroscience, play therapy, and the neurobiologically informed play therapist, and Gaskill and Brown (2025) wrote about how neuroscience informs play therapy theory and practice.

Now, in this chapter, we add to play therapy neuroscience writing. In the pages that follow, we use neuroscience terms to describe some of the necessary components of a theoretical approach, play, and the TPoP.

Theoretical Approaches

For a theory to be a fully functioning, viable theory, it must include and address some basic components. At a minimum, these include (a) a conceptualization of personality development, (b) the development of psychopathology, (c) the role of the therapeutic relationship, and (d) how change occurs. In the next sections, these components are described in neuroscience terms.

Conceptualization of Personality Development

In 1937, Gordon Allport described personality traits as "neuropsychological systems with the purpose of making a variety of stimuli functionally equivalent, in order to trigger a consistent and meaningful response." The neuropsychological systems in our brains intake the stream of information from a given stimulus and make sense of how to respond. Those individual differences in behavior and response among people can be attributed to the fact that every neuropsychological system is different. In addition, due to each brain's unique physical structure, functional neuroanatomy will be impacted as a result (Gordon et al., 2017). A key component of personality is the consistency and stability of traits over an individual's lifespan, meaning that certain trait characteristics should elicit similar responses to similar stimuli for an extended period of time. This is true for psychopathologies such as personality disorders, depression, anxiety, and more. Research has produced information to better shape our understanding of the neural foundations for the personality traits of neuroticism, novelty-seeking, and extraversion.

DeYoung (2010) wrote, "A person cannot be understood without understanding their brain." Personality neuroscience is a young field seeking to explore an in-depth picture of how personality functions and the neural principles behind it. This often starts with both genetic and environmental influences, taking into consideration the interaction between the two. According to Polderman et al. (2015), genetic influences can account for 49 percent of our personality traits, which implies the other half can be attributed to their environment.

Development of Psychopathology

Psychopathology cannot be described in a single section within a book chapter. Each of the diagnostic categories, within Section II of the *Diagnostic and Statistical Manual of Mental Disorders, Fifth Edition, Text Revision* (DSM-5-TR; American Psychiatric Association [APA], 2022) is a cluster of symptoms that lead to the diagnosis of a psychopathology. In the *DSM-5-TR*, each diagnostic category chapter contains introductory pages that describe the neurobiological underpinnings of the diagnoses within the category. There are few similarities in neurobiological aspects across all the researched and accepted diagnoses. At best, one could say that psychopathology is related to dysfunctions in brain regions, brain structures, and neurotransmitter systems, which lead to varying levels of impairment across cognitive, behavioral, social, and cultural domains.

The Role of the Therapeutic Relationship

Describing the neuroscience aspects of the therapeutic relationship, as it exists within play therapy, would include how the brain processes social interactions and how these interactions, particularly in the context of play therapy, can promote healing and change. The therapeutic relationship itself has been described as having an impact on brain function, emotional regulation, and psychological well-being (Malhotra & Sahoo, 2017). Some of the neuroscience aspects of note, related to the therapeutic relationship, include:

1. **The Brain and Attachment:** Therapeutic relationships mirror secure attachment experiences. Brain regions involved include (a) the ventral striatum and reward processing (Fisher, 2004; Takiguchi et al., 2015), (b) the amygdala and emotion regulation (Gaffrey et al., 2021), and (c) the prefrontal cortex and cognitive regulation (Sahin et al., 2023; Siegel, 2007).
2. **Empathetic Understanding and Mirror Neurons:** When play therapists model empathy, the clients' mirror neuron systems foster a deeper sense of understanding and emotional connection (Praszkier, 2016; Rizzolatti & Craighero, 2004).
3. **The Brain and the Therapeutic Alliance:** Positive therapeutic relationships (a) promote neuroplasticity (Davidson & McEwen, 2012; Sened et al., 2022) and (b) lead to greater integration between the prefrontal cortex and the limbic system (Cammisuli & Castelnuovo, 2023; Kovner et al., 2019; Schore, 2003).
4. **The Parasympathetic Nervous System:** The development of a safe, supportive, and calm environment during play therapy is necessary to facilitate healing. Safety engages the parasympathetic nervous system via the vagus nerve, leading to relaxation, emotional regulation, and social engagement, which allows for emotional processing and integration (Duarte & Pinto-Gouveia, 2017; Geller & Porges, 2014; Porges, 2011).

How Psychological Change Occurs

The neuroscience of psychological change involves complex interactions between brain structures, neural networks, neurotransmitters, genetics, and environmental factors. In this section, we refer to psychological change because it encompasses improvements in behavior, emotion regulation, and cognition, and can occur through many mechanisms. These include:

1. **Psychological Change and Brain Structures:** Specific brain regions are critical for various aspects of psychological change. These include: (a) the prefrontal cortex (PFC), which plays a central role in higher-order cognitive functions such as decision-making, self-regulation, and executive control. PFC levels of activity are linked to improvements in emotional regulation and cognitive flexibility (Friedman & Robbins, 2022; Ochsner & Gross, 2005), (b) the amygdala, which is involved in generating and processing emotions. Changes in amygdala activity are observed in individuals who undergo therapy (Alexander et al., 2021; Gee et al., 2013; Shin & Liberzon, 2010), and (c) the hippocampus, which has been studied in relation to its encoding and retrieval of memories and is crucial for emotional regulation. Functional as well as structural changes in the hippocampus, are associated with psychological changes (Bremner, 2006; Laurita & Spreng, 2017; Maguire & Mullally, 2013).
2. **Psychological Change and Neuroplasticity:** Neuroplasticity refers to the brain's ability to reorganize itself by forming neural connections across the lifespan.

Specifically involved are (a) synaptic plasticity by which the strength of connections between neuron synapses changes (Applebaum et al., 2023; Bliss & Collingridge, 1993) and (b) cortical plasticity by which the brain can rewire itself after injury or in response to environmental changes [Pascual-Leone et al., 2005; Price & Duman, 2020; Voss et al., 2017].

3. **Psychological Change and Neurogenesis:** Neurogenesis, the process of generating new neurons, occurs predominantly in the hippocampus in adults. The generation of new neurons is critical for learning, memory, regulation of emotional responses, and resilience. Specifically involved is hippocampal neurogenesis: The hippocampus is connected to emotional regulation and memory formation. Stress and depression have been known to inhibit neurogenesis, while antidepressants and exercise have been shown to promote it (Gould et al., 1997; Schoenfeld & Cameron, 2015; Wu et al., 2021).
4. **Psychological Change and Neurotransmitter Systems:** Neurotransmitter systems are fundamental to psychological change. Some of the neurotransmitters involved include: (a) serotonin, which is involved in mood regulation. Serotonergic pathways are important in social behavior and emotional processing (Fischer & Ullsperger, 2017; Kanen et al., 2021; Mann, 2003) and (b) dopamine, which is involved in reward processing, motivation, and learning. Therapeutic interventions that increase dopamine activity often lead to elevation of mood and increased motivation (Alexander et al., 2021; Papalini et al., 2020; Pizzagalli, 2014).

Developmental and Neurobiological Aspects of Play

The purpose and benefits of play have been the source of investigation than nearly a century. The works of Freud (1958), Piaget (1932, 1951), and Vygotsky (1976) set the stage for much of what would be examined in later research. Though Freud, Piaget, and Vygotsky did not conduct neuroscience research, their early work identified developmental constructs that would later be explored in neuroscience research. Recent research has advanced our understanding of the neurobiology of play, highlighting its evolutionary importance, developmental role, and underlying neural mechanisms.

From an evolutionary perspective, play and play behaviors are believed to have adaptive functions that promote social skills, enhance cognitive abilities, and facilitate motor development (Burghardt, 2014; Gray, 2019; Lillard, 2015).

From a developmental perspective, play is paramount for the maturation of cognitive and social skills (Pellis et al., 2014). Pellis et al. (2014) proposed that play contributes to the development of neural circuits involved in emotional regulation and social competence, which are important for adaptive behavior later in life. The plasticity of developing brains allows for the incorporation of experiences during play into lasting neural connections, shaping behavioral responses and social interactions (Baarendse et al., 2013; Bell et al., 2010; Siviy et al., 2011).

Finally, from a neurobiological perspective, studies utilizing neuroimaging have identified specific neural circuits associated with play behavior. For instance, the mesocorticolimbic dopamine system, which includes projections from the ventral tegmental area to the nucleus accumbens and prefrontal cortex, is activated during play, suggesting its role in motivation and reward processing (Alcaro et al., 2007; Salamone & Correa, 2012). The cerebellum, known for its involvement in motor coordination, also plays a significant role in coordinating the physical aspects of play (Rudolph et al., 2023; Salman & Tsai, 2016). Alos, neurochemicals such as dopamine, serotonin, and endorphins play crucial roles in modulating the motivation and reward aspects of play behavior. Dopamine, for instance, is implicated in the reinforcement of play activities, promoting continued engagement and learning (Manduca et al., 2016). Serotonin is involved in mood regulation and social behavior, influencing the frequency and intensity of play interactions (Salvan et al., 2023; Trezza et al., 2010).

The Neurobiology of Play from a Therapeutic Perspective

Generally, play can be described as a natural activity that children engage in for enjoyment, learning, and social development. Play includes various forms, such as physical play, imaginative play, and symbolic play, and is an essential part of child development (Bergen, 2009; Lillard et al., 2013). Play helps children explore their world, develop cognitive and social skills, and practice problem-solving in a safe and engaging environment (Annet, 2024; Ginsburg, 2007; Whitebread, 2017; Whitebread et al., 2017).

Therapeutic implications of play are well established throughout research, and understanding the neurobiology of play has implications that bolster the therapeutic value of play. For instance, play therapy, which often utilizes play activities to promote emotional healing and behavioral adjustment in children, uses the neurobiological mechanisms underlying play to facilitate therapeutic outcomes. Disruptions in play behavior have been linked to neurodevelopmental disorders such as autism spectrum disorder, emphasizing the importance of studying play from a neurobiological perspective to better understand and treat these disorders.

Play has been shown to be a buffer against the adverse effects of stress, providing a coping mechanism for stress and anxiety. Play reduces cortisol levels, helping to mitigate the long-term effects of chronic stress on the brain, particularly in regions like the hippocampus and amygdala that are critical for emotional regulation (Aamodt & Wang, 2012; Shonkoff et al., 2012; Wang & Aamodt, 2012).

Therapeutic Powers of Play as Core Agents of Change

In Chapter 1 of this text, readers learned about the TPoP and learned the history of the TPoP in Chapter 2. Chapter 1 thoroughly described each of the twenty TPoP as well as provided examples for application. The TPoP are core agents of change inherent in all play therapy approaches practiced worldwide (Drewes & Schaefer, 2014, p. 1). Drewes (2025) positions them as "a middle level of abstraction between general theories and concrete techniques," with theoretical orientations as the highest level of abstraction and specific techniques as the lowest level of abstraction (Drewes, 2025). The TPoP "refer to the specific targeted aspects within treatment in which play initiates, facilitates, or strengthens the therapeutic effect" (Drewes & Schaefer, 2015, p. 36).

When play is the source of change, the TPoP, acting as agents of change, can be understood via their mediation effects on communication, emotional wellness, social relationships, and personal strengths. Within a neuroscience frame, though not directly identified in research, if research is extrapolated/inferred, these agents of change likely have an impact on neural development, stress regulation, and cognitive functioning (Cantor et al., 2018; Siviy, 2016), because play as the source of change is present. Therapeutically, and especially with children, the play in play therapy promotes neuroplasticity, emotional regulation, and social cognition by engaging key brain areas such as the prefrontal cortex, limbic system, and the mirror neuron system (Ginsburg, 2007; Liu et al., 2017).

Summary

In 2010, the *American Journal of Play* published a special issue on the science of play, which included a series of articles about research related to play. Then, ten years later, in 2020, the *International Journal of Play* (not to be confused with the *International Journal of Play Therapy*) published a special issue about the neuroscience of play. This issue covered numerous topics connecting neuroscience to play. In 2016, as a celebration of the *IJPT*'s twenty-fifth anniversary, a special issue was published entitled Integrating Neuroscience and Play Therapy, which highlighted the implications of neuroscience research when applied across play therapy. These special issues, along with the many other articles cited within this section, demonstrate the desire for neuroscience researchers to understand as much about play and play therapy as possible. Eventually, from hard science, practical applications develop. Though many of these journal articles provide noteworthy information, likewise, many do not provide practical information that can be routinely applied in practice. The information they provide often confirms some of our hunches, but it will take further research to develop realistic, practical applications.

Neuroscience aspects that can be connected to theoretical approaches, play, and the therapeutic powers of play, though limited in some areas, highlight how neuroscience research adds a level of understanding not accomplished by any other research. At the least, what was provided in the chapter should provide insight into the connections between theoretical approaches, play, and the therapeutic powers of play. If possible, it should also spur new thought, discussion, and potentially ideas and methods for adding to the research.

References

Aamodt, S., & Wang, S. (2012). *Welcome to your child's brain: How the mind grows from conception to college*. Bloomsbury.

Alcaro, A., Huber, R., & Panksepp, J. (2007). Behavioral functions of the mesolimbic dopaminergic system: An affective neuroethological perspective. *Brain Research Reviews, 56*(2), 283–321. PMID: 17905440; PMCID: PMC2238694. https://doi:10.1016/j.brainresrev.2007.07.014.

Alexander, R., Aragón, O. R., Bookwala, J., Cherbuin, N., Gatt, J. M., Kahrilas, I. J., Kästner, N., Lawrence, A., Lowe, L., Morrison, R. G., Mueller, S. C., Nusslock, R., Papadelis, C., Polnaszek, K. L., Richter, S. H., Silton, R. L., & Styliadis, C. (2021). The neuroscience of positive emotions and affect: Implications for cultivating happiness and wellbeing. *Neuroscience and Biobehavioral Reviews, 121*, 220–49. https://doi.org/10.1016/j.neubiorev.2020.12.002.

Allport, G. W. (1937). *Personality: A psychological interpretation*. H. Holt and Co. Retrieved from http://archive.org/details/personalitypsych00allprich.

American Psychiatric Association. (2022). *Diagnostic and statistical manual of mental disorders* (5th ed., Text revision). American Psychiatric Publishing Inc.

Annet, K. A. (2024). The role of okay in early childhood education: Balancing fun and learning. *Eurasian Experimental Journal of Arts and Management, 5*(3), 31–5. https://www.researchgate.net/publication/383551094_The_Role_of_Play_in_Early_Childhood_Education_Balancing_Fun_and_Learning.

Appelbaum, L. G., Shenasa, M. A., Stolz, L., & Zafiris, D. (2023). Synaptic plasticity and mental health: Methods, challenges and opportunities. *Neuropsychopharmacology, 48*, 113–20. https://doi.org/10.1038/s41386-022-01370-w.

Baarendse, P. J., Counotte, D. S., O'Donnell, P., & Vanderschuren, L. J. (2013). Early social experience is critical for the development of cognitive control and dopamine modulation of prefrontal cortex function. *Neuropsychopharmacology, 38*(8), 1485–94. PMID: 23403694; PMCID: PMC3682143. https://doi:10.1038/npp.2013.47.

Bell, H. C., Pellis, S. M., & Kolb, B. (2010). Juvenile peer play experience and the development of the orbitofrontal and medial prefrontal cortices. *Behavioural Brain Research, 207*(1), 7–13. PMID: 19786051. https://doi:10.1016/j.bbr.2009.09.029.

Bergen, D. (2009). Play as the learning medium for future scientists, mathematicians, and engineers. *American Journal of Play, 1*(4), 413–28.

Bliss, T. V., & Collingridge, G. L. (1993). A synaptic model of memory: Long-term potentiation in the hippocampus. *Nature, 361*(6407), 31–9. https://doi.org/10.1038/361031a0.

Bremner, J. D. (2006). Stress and brain atrophy. *CNS & Neurological Disorders-Drug Targets, 5*(5), 3–13. https://doi:10.2174/187152706778559309.

Burghardt, G. H. (2014). A brief glimpse at the long evolutionary history of play. *Animal Behavior and Cognition, 1*(2), 90–8. https://doi:10.12966/abc.05.01.2014.

Cammisuli, D. M., & Castelnuovo, G. (2023). Neuroscience-based psychotherapy: A position paper. *Frontiers in Psychology, 14*, 1101044. PMID: 36860785; PMCID: PMC9968886. https://doi:10.3389/fpsyg.2023.1101044.

Cantor, P., Osher, D., Berg, J., Steyer, L., & Rose, T. (2018). Malleability, plasticity, and individuality: How children learn and develop in context *Applied Developmental Science, 23*(4), 307–37. https://doi.org/10.1080/10888691.2017.1398649.

Davidson, R. J., & McEwen, B. S. (2012). Social influences on neuroplasticity: Stress and interventions to promote well-being. *Nature Neuroscience, 15*(5), 689–95. https://doi.org/10.1038/nn.3093.

DeYoung, C. G. (2010). Personality neuroscience and the biology of traits. *Social and Personality Psychology Compass, 4*(12), 1165–80. https://doi.org/10.1111/j.1751-9004.2010.00327.x.

Drewes, A. A. (2025). What is a therapeutic power of play? In A. A. Drewes & E. F. Hudspeth (Eds.), *The therapeutic powers of play: Comparing theories and practice* (pp. 3–22). Rowman & Littlefield.

Drewes, A. A., & Schaefer, C. E. (2015). The therapeutic powers of play. In K. J. O'Conor, C. E. Schaefer, & L. D. Braverman (Eds.), *Handbook of play therapy* (2nd ed., pp. 35–60). John Wiley & Sons Inc.

Duarte, J., & Pinto-Gouveia, J. (2017). Positive affect and parasympathetic activity: Evidence for a quadratic relationship between feeling safe and content and heart rate variability. *Psychiatry Research, 257*, 284–9. https://doi.org/10.1016/j.psychres.2017.07.077.

Fischer, A. G., & Ullsperger, M. (2017). An update on the role of serotonin and its interplay with dopamine for reward. *Frontiers in Human Neuroscience, 11*, 484. PMID: 29075184; PMCID: PMC5641585. https://doi:10.3389/fnhum.2017.00484.

Fisher, H. E. (2004). *Why we love: The nature and chemistry of romantic love.* Holt Paperbacks.

Freud, S. (1958). *On creativity and the unconscious.* Harper.

Friedman, N. P., & Robbins, T. W. (2022). The role of prefrontal cortex in cognitive control and executive function. *Neuropsychopharmacology, 47*, 72–89. https://doi.org/10.1038/s41386-021-01132-0.

Gaffrey, M. S., Barch, D. M., Luby, J. L., & Petersen, S. E. (2021). Amygdala functional connectivity Is associated with emotion regulation and amygdala reactivity in 4- to 6-year-olds. *Journal of the American Academy of Child Adolescent Psychiatry, 60*(1), 176–85. PMID: 32119912; PMCID: PMC7483219. https://doi:10.1016/j.jaac.2020.01.024.

Gaskill, R. L., & Brown, J. (2025). Neuroscience informs play therapy theory and practice. In D. A. Crenshaw, A. L. Stewart, & D. C. Ray (Eds.), *Play therapy: Theory, research, and practice* (2nd ed., pp. 270–82). The Guilford Press.

Gaskill, R. L., & Perry, B. D. (2014). The neurobiological power of play: Using the neurosequential model of therapeutics to guide play in the healing process. In C. A. Malchiodi & D. A. Crenshaw (Eds.), *Creative arts and play therapy for attachment problems* (pp. 178–94). The Guilford Press.

Gee, D. G., Humphreys, K. L., Flannery, J., Goff, B., Telzer, E. H., Shapiro, M., Hare, T. A. Bookheimer, S. Y., & Tottenham, N. (2013). A developmental shift from positive to negative connectivity in human amygdala–prefrontal circuitry. *Journal of Neuroscience, 33*(10), 4584–93. https://doi:10.1523/JNEUROSCI.3446-12.2013.

Geller, S. M., & Porges, S. W. (2014). Therapeutic presence: Neurophysiological mechanisms mediating feeling safe in therapeutic relationships. *Journal of Psychotherapy Integration, 24*(3), 178–92. https://doi.org/10.1037/a0037511.

Ginsburg, K. R. (2007). The importance of play in promoting healthy child development and maintaining strong parent-child bonds. *Pediatrics, 119*(1), 182–91. https://doi:10.1542/peds.2006-2697.

Gordon, E. M., Laumann, T. O., Gilmore, A. W., Newbold, D. J., Greene, D. J., Berg, J. J., Ortega, M., Hoyt-Drazen, C., Gratton, C., Sun, H., Hampton, J. M., Coalson, R. S., Nguyen, A. L., McDermott, K. B., Shimony, J. S., Snyder, A. Z., Schlaggar, B. L., Petersen, S. E., Nelson, S. M., & Dosenbach, N. U. F. (2017). Precision functional mapping of individual human brains. *Neuron, 95*(4), 791–807.e7. https://doi.org/10.1016/j.neuron.2017.07.011.

Gould, E., McEwen, B. S., Tanapat, P., & Galea, L. A. M. (1997). Neurogenesis in the dentate gyrus of the adult tree shrew is regulated by psychosocial stress and NMDA receptor activation. *The Journal of Neuroscience, 17*(7), 2492–8.

Gray, P. (2019). Evolutionary functions of play: Practice, resilience, innovation, and cooperation. In P. K. Smith & J. Roopnarine (Eds.), *The Cambridge handbook of play: Developmental and disciplinary perspectives* (pp. 84–102). Cambridge University Press.

Hudspeth, E. F., & Matthews, K. (2016). Neuroscience and play therapy: The neurobiologically-informed play therapist. In K. J. O'Connor, C. E. Schaefer, & L. D. Braverman (Eds.), *Handbook of play therapy* (2nd ed., pp. 583–97). John Wiley & Sons, Inc.

Kanen, J. W., Arntz, F. E., Yellowlees, R., Cardinal, R. N., Price, A., Christmas, D. M., Apergis-Schoute, A. M., Sahakian, B. J., & Robbins, T. W. (2021). Serotonin depletion amplifies distinct human social emotions as a function of individual differences in personality. *Translational Psychiatry, 11*, 81. https://doi.org/10.1038/s41398-020-00880-9.

Kovner, R., Oler, J. A., & Kalin, N. H. (2019). Cortico-limbic interactions mediate adaptive and maladaptive responses relevant to psychopathology. *American Journal of Psychiatry, 176*(12), 987–99. PMID: 31787014; PMCID: PMC7014786. https://doi:10.1176/appi.ajp.2019.19101064.

Laurita, A. C., & Spreng, R. N. (2017). The hippocampus and social cognition. In D. E. Hannula & M. C. Duff (Eds.), *The hippocampus from cells to systems: Structure, connectivity, and functional contributions to memory and flexible cognition* (pp. 537–58). Springer International Publishing AG. https://doi.org/10.1007/978-3-319-50406-3_17.

Lillard, A. S. (2015). The development of play. In L. S. Liben, U. Müller, & R. M. Lerner (Eds.), *Handbook of child psychology and developmental science: Cognitive processes* (7th ed., Vol. 2, pp. 425–68). Wiley. https://doi.org/10.1002/9781118963418.childpsy211.

Lillard, A. S., Lerner, M. D., Hopkins, E. J., Dore, R. A., Smith, E. D., & Palmquist, C. M. (2013). The impact of pretend play on children's development: A review of the evidence. *Psychological Bulletin, 139*(1), 1–34. https://doi.org/10.1037/a0029321.

Liu, C., Solis, S. L., Jensen, H., Hopkins, E. J., Neale, D., Zosh, J. M., Hirsh-Pasek, K., & Whitebread, D. (2017). *Neuroscience and learning through play: A review of the evidence* (research summary). The LEGO Foundation, DK.

Malhotra, S., & Sahoo, S. (2017). Rebuilding the brain with psychotherapy. *Indian Journal of Psychiatry, 59*(4), 411–19. PMID: 29497182; PMCID: PMC5806319. https://doi:10.4103/0019–5545.217299.

Maguire, E. A., & Mullally, S. L. (2013). The hippocampus: A manifesto for change. *Journal of Experimental Psychology: General, 142*(4), 1180–9. https://doi.org/10.1037/a0033650.

Manduca, A., Servadio, M., Damsteegt, R., Campolongo, P., Vanderschuren, L. J., & Trezza, V. (2016). Dopaminergic neurotransmission in the nucleus accumbens modulates social play behavior in rats. *Neuropsychopharmacology, 41*, 2215–23. https://doi.org/10.1038/npp.2016.22.

Mann, J. J. (2003). Neurobiology of suicidal behaviour. *Nature Reviews Neuroscience, 4*(10), 819–28. https://doi:10.1038/nrn1220.

Mitra, M. (2023). Neuroscience and its applications. *Neurology & Neurotherapy, 8*(1), 1–8. https://doi:10.23880/nnoaj-16000175.

Neuroscience. (2024). In *Cambridge Dictionary.org*. Retrieved June 16, 2024, from https://dictionary.cambridge.org/us/dictionary/english/neuroscience.

Ochsner, K. N., & Gross, J. J. (2005). The cognitive control of emotion. *Trends in Cognitive Sciences, 9*(5), 242–9. https://doi:10.1016/j.tics.2005.03.010.

Papalini, S., Beckers, T., & Vervliet, B. (2020). Dopamine: From prediction error to psychotherapy. *Translational Psychiatry, 10*, 164. https://doi.org/10.1038/s41398-020-0814-x.

Pascual-Leone, A., Amedi, A., Fregni, F., & Merabet, L. B. (2005). The plastic human brain cortex. *Annual Review of Neuroscience, 28*, 377–401. PMID: 16022601. https://doi:10.1146/annurev.neuro.27.070203.144216.

Pellis, S. M., Pellis, V. C., & Himmler, B. T. (2014). How play makes for a more adaptable brain: A comparative and neural perspective. *American Journal of Play, 7*(1), 73–98.

Piaget, J. (1932). *The moral judgment of the child*. The Free Press.

Piaget, J. (1951). *Play, dreams, and imitation in childhood*. Routledge.

Pizzagalli, D. A. (2014). Depression, stress, and anhedonia: Toward a synthesis and integrated model. *Annual Review of Clinical Psychology, 10*, 393–423. https://doi:10.1146/annurev-clinpsy-032813-153724.

Polderman, T. J., Benyamin, B., de Leeuw, C. A., Sullivan, P. F., van Bochoven, A., Visscher, P. M., & Posthuma, D. (2015). Meta-analysis of the heritability of human traits based on fifty years of twin studies. *Nature Genetics, 47*(7), 702–9. PMID: 25985137. https://doi:10.1038/ng.3285.

Porges, S. W. (2011). *The polyvagal theory: Neurophysiological foundations of emotions, attachment, communication, and self-regulation*. W. W. Norton & Company.

Praszkier, R. (2016). Empathy, mirror neurons and SYNC. *Mind & Society, 15*(1), 1–25. https://doi.org/10.1007/s11299-014-0160-x.

Price, R. B., & Duman, R. (2020). Neuroplasticity in cognitive and psychological mechanisms of depression: An integrative model. *Molecular Psychiatry, 25*(3), 530–43. PMID: 31801966; PMCID: PMC7047599. https://doi:10.1038/s41380-019-0615-x.

Rizzolatti, G., & Craighero, L. (2004). The mirror-neuron system. *Annual Review of Neuroscience, 27*, 169–92. PMID: 15217330. https://doi:10.1146/annurev.neuro.27.070203.144230.

Rudolph, S., Badura, A., Lutzu, S., Pathak, S. S., Thieme, A., Verpeut, J. L., Wagner, M. J., Yang, Y. M., & Fioravante, D. (2023). Cognitive-affective functions of the cerebellum. *Journal of Neuroscience, 43*(45), 7554–64. PMID: 37940582; PMCID: PMC10634583. https://doi:10.1523/JNEUROSCI.1451-23.2023.

Sahin, N. H., Tasso, A. F., & Guler, M. (2023). Attachment and emotional regulation: Examining the role of prefrontal cortex functions, executive functions, and mindfulness in their relationship. *Cognitive Processing, 24*, 619–31. https://doi.org/10.1007/s10339-023-01144-2.

Salamone, J. D., & Correa, M. (2012). The mysterious motivational functions of mesolimbic dopamine. *Neuron, 76*(3), 470–85. PMID: 23141060; PMCID: PMC4450094. https://doi:10.1016/j.neuron.2012.10.021.

Salman. M. S., & Tsai, P. (2016). The role of the pediatric cerebellum in motor functions, cognition, and behavior: A clinical perspective. *Neuroimaging Clinics of North America, 26*(3), 317–29. PMID: 27423796; PMCID: PMC4948592. https://doi:10.1016/j.nic.2016.03.003.

Salvan, P., Fonseca, M., Winkler, A. M. Beauchamp, A., Lerch, J. P., & Johansen-Berg, H. (2023). Serotonin regulation of behavior via large-scale neuromodulation of serotonin receptor networks. *Nature Neuroscience, 26,* 53–63. https://doi.org/10.1038/s41593-022-01213-3.

Schaefer, C. E., & Drewes, A. A. (2014). *The therapeutic powers of play: 20 core agents of change* (2nd ed.). Wiley.

Schoenfeld, T. J., & Cameron, H. A. (2015). Adult neurogenesis and mental illness. *Neuropsychopharmacology, 40*(1), 113–28. PMID: 25178407; PMCID: PMC4262910. https://doi:10.1038/npp.2014.230.

Schore, A. N. (2003). *Affect regulation and the repair of the self.* W. W. Norton & Company.

Sened, H., Zilcha-Mano, S., & Shamay-Tsoory, S. (2022). Inter-brain plasticity as a biological mechanism of change in psychotherapy: A review and integrative model. *Frontiers in Human Neuroscience, 16*, 955238. https://doi.org/10.3389/fnhum.2022.955238.

Shonkoff, J. P., Garner, A. S., The Committee on Psychosocial Aspects of Child and Family Health, Committee on Early Childhood, Adoption, and Dependent Care, and Section on Developmental and Behavioral Pediatrics, Siegel, B. S., Dobbins, M. I., Earls, M. F., Garner, A. S., McGuinn, L., Pascoe, J., & Wood, D. L. (2012). The lifelong effects of early childhood adversity and toxic stress. *Pediatrics, 129*(1), e232–46. https://doi.org/10.1542/peds.2011-2663.

Siegel, D. J. (2007). *The mindful brain: Reflection and attunement in the cultivation of well-being*. W. W. Norton & Company.

Siviy, S. M. (2016). A brain motivated to play: Insights into the neurobiology of playfulness. *Behaviour, 53*(6–7), 819–44. PMID: 29056751; PMCID: PMC5646690.https://doi:10.1163/1568539X-00003349.

Siviy, S. M., Crawford, C. A., Akopian, G., & Walsh, J. P. (2011). Dysfunctional play and dopamine physiology in the Fischer 344 rat. *Behavioural Brain Research, 220*(2), 294–304. PMID: 21335036; PMCID: PMC3081852. https://doi:10.1016/j.bbr.2011.02.009.

Takiguchi, S., Fujisawa, T. X., Mizushima, S., Saito, D. N., Okamoto, Y., Shimada, K., Koizumi, M., Kumazaki, H., Jung, M., Kosaka, H., Hiratani, M., Ohshima, Y., Teicher, M. H., & Tomoda, A. (2015). Ventral striatum dysfunction in children and adolescents with reactive attachment disorder: Functional MRI study. *The British Journal of Psychiatry Open, 1*(2), 121–8. PMID: 27703736; PMCID: PMC4995568. https://doi:10.1192/bjpo.bp.115.001586.

Trezza, V., Baarendse, P. J. J., & Vanderschuren, L. J. M. J. (2010). The pleasures of play: Pharmacological insights into social reward mechanisms. *Trends in Pharmacological Sciences, 31*(10), 463–9. https://doi.org/10.1016/j.tips.2010.06.008.

Voss, P., Thomas, M. E., Cisneros-Franco, J. M., & de Villers-Sidani, É. (2017). Dynamic brains and the changing rules of neuroplasticity: Implications for learning and recovery. *Frontiers in Psychology, 8,* 1657. PMID: 29085312; PMCID: PMC5649212. https://doi:10.3389/fpsyg.2017.01657.

Vygotsky, L. (1976). Play and its role in the mental development of the child. In J. S. Bruner, A. Jolly, & K. Sylva (Eds.), *Play: Its role in development and evolution* (pp. 76–99). Basic Books.

Wang, S., & Aamodt, S. (2012). Play, stress, and the learning brain. *Cerebrum, 12*. PMID: 23447798; PMCID: PMC3574776.

Whitebread, D. (2017). Free play and children's mental health. *Lancet Child & Adolescent Health, 1*(3), 167–9. PMID: 30169163. https://doi:10.1016/S2352-4642(17)30092-5.

Whitebread, D., Neale, D., Jensen, H., Liu, C., Solis, S. L., Hopkins, E., Hirsh-Pasek, K., & Zosh, J. M. (2017). *The role of play in children's development: A review of the evidence* (research summary). The LEGO Foundation, DK.

Wu, Z., Xiao, L., Wang, H., & Wang, G. (2021). Neurogenic hypothesis of positive psychology in stress-induced depression: Adult hippocampal neurogenesis, neuroinflammation, and stress resilience. *International Immunopharmacology, 97*, 107653. https://doi.org/10.1016/j.intimp.2021.107653.

5

Bringing the Therapeutic Powers of Play into Focus Using the Play Therapy Dimensions Model®

Lorri Yasenik and Ken Gardner

Chapter Outline

The Play Therapy Dimensions Model™ (PTDM) (Yasenik & Gardner, 2004, 2012, 2019, 2024) helps Play Therapists case conceptualize. It provides a visual representation upon which to situate therapeutic use of self along the continuum dimensions of *directiveness* and *consciousness*. The two continuums cross and form four quadrants, and this is where the practitioner can not only identify how directively or consciously they are working with a child client but also name the theoretical approach utilized. Play therapists must consider what approach to use, for which child, and when to stay or shift from one approach to another. Play therapists are trained in the use of at least nine seminal play therapy theories (Association for Play Therapy, 2019) leading the play therapist to consider a variety of factors for working with children and families. The complexities continue as each theory comes with its own language, ways of understanding a presenting issue, and ways of being with clients. This is a lot to consider and hold onto without a graphic aid such as the Play Therapy Dimensions diagram.

During the process of answering core play therapy clinical questions such as "What? When? Where? Why? and How?" play therapists must also identify the Therapeutic Powers of Play (TPoP, Schaefer & Drewes, 2014). In what ways are the four main therapeutic powers: *Communication, Emotion Regulation, Relationship Enhancement,* and *Personal Strengths* identified and represented in play therapy session(s), and how does the play therapist conceptualize and discuss the TPoP? It is proposed that the PTDM diagram can also be used to visually anchor an observed TPoP and support the discussion of the interaction between the play therapist, child client, and TPoP. This makes way for integrative thinking, as the play therapist is required to examine multiple factors that impact the therapy process. This chapter introduces four key concepts to deepen case discussions of TPoP: (1) Therapeutic potency, (2) Timing, (3) Entry point(s), and (4) Facilitation. As a way to organize and bring the TPoP into focus, the PTDM is briefly explained and brought to life by describing how to use the four quadrants to track a number of therapeutic factors, including the TPoP. The goal is to provide a way to visually track the fluid movements of the therapist and client; the interaction of which is critical to understanding the play therapy process.

The Play Therapy Dimensions Model® and the Therapeutic Powers of Play

How do these two concepts go together? Firstly, the reader is invited to take a closer look at the PTDM diagram (Figure 5.1). The four quadrants provide an organizing structure that allows the therapist to identify levels of directiveness and the degrees of consciousness represented in the play and actions taken by the therapist. Although it is possible that a therapist may represent work in all four quadrants in a single session or across several sessions, there is no prescribed order. Some theories of play therapy more naturally fall primarily within one or two quadrants, such as Child Centered Play Therapy™ (Quadrant

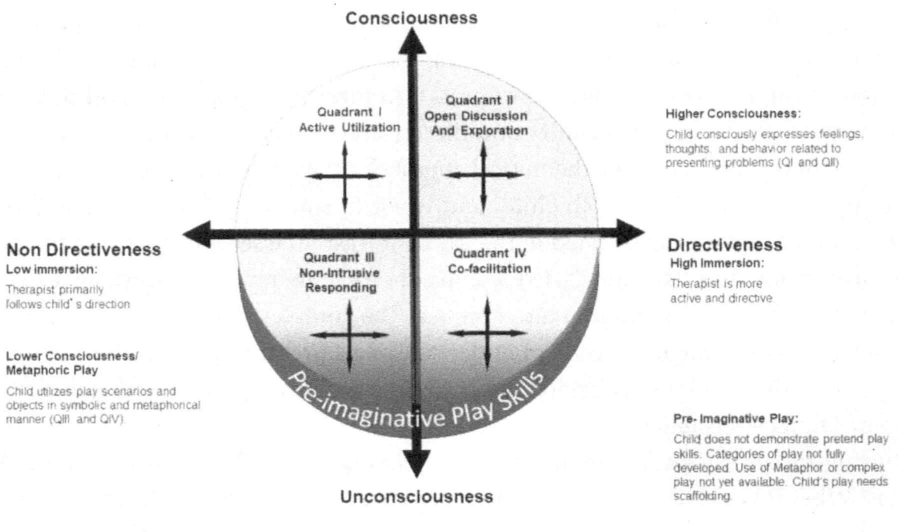

Figure 5.1 Full Play Therapy Dimensions Model® Diagram. From Yasenik & Gardner (2024, p. 48), Play Therapy Dimensions Model: New Insights for Integrative Play Therapists. Reproduced with permission of the Licensor through PLSclear.

III) or Cognitive Behavioral Play Therapy (Quadrant II), and therapists may be observed working in QIII or QII. The quadrants are identified by the intersection of the two primary dimensions (consciousness and directiveness), versus being tied to specific play therapy models. When thinking of various play therapy theories, some have more inherently prescribed directive actions and goals utilizing higher consciousness and directiveness than others. Movement within a quadrant, as reflected by the crisscrossed arrows in each quadrant, may be subtle yet significant, and movement between quadrants may either be therapist facilitated or child led.

We begin our discussion with the newly added addition at the bottom of the PTDM Diagram "the cradle of all play-based activity" (Yasenik & Gardner, 2024). There would be no imaginative play without the cumulative development of discrete play skills that come together to form what we so casually refer to as "play." If a child is observed as lacking one or more play skills or "a category of play," the play therapist's use of self is purposeful in assisting a child to scaffold the skill(s). This is a bottom-up model whereby the play therapist must understand play from the "melting pot of abilities" (Stagnitti, Wadley, & Sheppard, 2012) which includes narrative, cognition and metacognition, social competence, problem-solving, divergent thinking, understanding context, self-regulation, creativity, language, metacommunication, and emotional understanding. In the lower part of the diagram, play therapists may be observed as first following a child's lead to discover the child's special interests (lower Quadrant III, Non-Intrusive Responding). The play therapist then utilizes the child's interests (i.e., objects that make noise or a particular toy set such as dinosaurs) to scaffold the child's play in a more directive manner while staying in the field of play (lower Quadrant IV, Co-facilitation).

The therapist would engage in purposeful lead-follow-lead activities with a child who demonstrates limited play skills. The rise of consciousness and self-awareness is just forming at this stage, and that is why the practitioner would be seen working in the bottom shaded area. This is a pre-contemplative stage of the therapeutic powers of play where the therapist and child engage with play objects together in varied ways to increase the use of toys as tools for incrementally complex play-based communication.

Quadrant I: Active Utilization: Positioned in the upper left corner of Figure 5.1, Quadrant I, Active Utilization is represented by those therapists who believe in the intermittent importance of making interpretive reflections to assist the child in gaining insight and self-understanding. The name Active Utilization is derived from the point that through following the child's lead, the therapist *utilizes* the symbolic or metaphorical play initiated by the child to make interpretive reflections. Therapist activity in this quadrant is typically brief and does not generally lead to exiting a play scenario into a direct discussion. When an interpretive comment is made, a child may acknowledge the comment and add something to it, but more often, the child returns to or stays in the play. When viewed according to the diagram, movement briefly occurs upward from Quadrant III when the therapist provides an interpretation about what is occurring metaphorically, an example being "The dragon is lonely and wishes to be back with his parents." An interpretation of the dragon is offered even though the child did not directly state that the dragon was lonely or wanted to be with his parents. The goal of offering interpretations is to facilitate processing and to deepen the play. The Play Therapy Dimension Model identifies three levels of interpretation: (1) Reflective interpretations that are embedded in the child's current play actions, (2) Linking interpretations that link play-based themes and actions, and (3) Bridging interpretations that serve to mobilize internal resources by highlighting the significance of play actions to the child's life story (Yasenik & Gardner, 2004, 2012, 2019, 2024). Interpretations may lead to the TPoP: *access to the unconscious*, as bringing a comment forward offers a potential invitation of meaning that the child, if ready, may consider.

Quadrant II Open Discussion and Exploration is located in the upper right corner of Figure 5.1. Positioned on the right-hand side of the directiveness dimension, therapist activity in this quadrant would be observed as initiating and/or structuring an activity that contributes to conscious processing of the child's presenting issues. Whether it is the use of a board game, a structured drawing activity, or a role-play re-enactment, bringing an issue to a moderate to high degree of consciousness is present. Therapists often choose to work in this quadrant when a child is in need of greater structure to facilitate self-expression and self-understanding. In terms of the TPoP (Schaefer & Drewes, 2014), both *direct and indirect teaching* may be observed in this quadrant.

Quadrant III: Non-intrusive Responding: As the name implies, a therapist working in Quadrant III is responsive to the child's play actions and verbalizations by tracking non-verbal behaviors, reflecting feelings, and restating content. The non-directive play therapy approaches (Child Centered Play Therapy™ and Humanistic Play Therapy, etc.) tend to be situated in this quadrant. The child leads the play, and the therapist does not attempt to interpret or bring metaphorical play themes to conscious awareness. Most therapists working in this quadrant emphasize the inner resources of the child to process troublesome issues or experiences through the play. Overall, the play is viewed as having intrinsic value and, from a phenomenological perspective, a deeper understanding of the child's worldview occurs. The TPoP accessed here could include powers that fall under Increasing Personal Strengths such as *self-regulation*, *development of self-esteem*, *creative problem-solving* and *resiliency building*.

Quadrant IV: Co-facilitation: The degree of immersion of the therapist in play differentiates this quadrant from Quadrant III. Occurring below the mid-point of the consciousness continuum, play actions are at a symbolic or metaphorical level. Instead of the child solely leading the play, the therapist purposefully makes use of their role/character and knowledge of the presenting problem to elaborate the play. Typically, the therapist has first observed and tracked a number of themes or sequences in the play to understand the child's symbolic communication and then through a character or role, tests a hypothesis and elaborates the play by inserting comments, actions, or soft interpretations. This, of course, means some level of direction is provided by the therapist, but not at the expense of the flow and reciprocal nature of play. For example, after observing what a child is communicating through a character, the therapist may test a hypothesis about what the child is symbolically representing by introducing a helper character to bring forward the possibility of accessing external resources. Alternatively, the therapist might select two characters whose conversation parallels the child's inner conflict or exemplifies inner resources currently blocked. Once shared or introduced, the child will then decide, in play, how to respond. A primary goal of working in this quadrant is to offer new opportunities for the child to express, process, and differentiate emotions and experiences. Work in this quadrant supports many TPoP, such as *fostering positive emotions, empathy building, therapeutic relationship enhancement, catharsis, and stress inoculation*, to name a few.

Four Concepts that Guide Case Conceptualization and Applications of TPoP

It is sometimes said that the "art" of the therapist lies in attuning to the specific needs of the individual client at any one time (Finlay, 2016). Our drive to understand how the therapeutic powers of play can be accessed and applied at specific points in therapy takes us into the realm of demystifying the "art" of therapy by exploring the underlying nature and application of these change mechanisms.

Therapeutic Potency

Therapeutic potency in psychotherapy can be viewed from a constructive, growth-oriented vantage point (Gilchrist, 1976). As Play Therapists we often rely on symbolic or metaphorical expressions in play to conceptualize potential shifts or growth in the child's sense of self or worldview. From this perspective, the manner in which Mills and Crowley (2014) conceptualize therapeutic potency is important to consider as they emphasize that it is accessed through the power of the metaphor, is reflected in changes in how the child thinks or feels about something, and can have a transformational power or outcome.

In discussing the case of Sammy, an eight-year-old boy subjected to bullying experiences at school, a supervisee indicated she was surprised that he didn't say anything after she made an interpretive reflection regarding the motivation behind a character's actions, by stating that the character appeared "mean" and "like a bully." The supervisee correctly noted that this type of reflection, as is sometimes done in Jungian analytical approaches (Lily & Heiko, 2019), representes a shift from Quadrant III, Non-Intrusive Responding, to Quadrant I, Active Utilization. The supervisee questioned whether Sammy was highly defended or simply not ready to consciously process these issues. She hoped to bring the matter to higher levels of consciousness to assist Sammy in directly expressing feelings about his experiences. In conceptualizing this interaction, the supervisor asked the supervisee to consider what happened next. As it turned out, a few minutes later, Sammy briefly introduced a character that "complained" about an "unfair and hurtful" experience. This was a very brief play scenario, initially missed by the supervisee. Further exploration revealed that the "complaint" was made with heightened emotionality. Although in the play the bully character persisted in its actions, this moment likely represented a shift in how Sammy *thought or felt* about his experiences. The supervisor also pointed out that the supervisee's reflections likely supported the child to stay with, or possibly elaborate, their symbolic communications. Next, the supervisor explored various decision-making parameters for assessing the TPoP of self-expression, by either remaining in Quadrant III, versus periodic use of interpretive reflections, representative of Quadrant I, Active Utilization.

Timing

Is *timing* everything? No, but we believe it helps distinguish practitioners who are skilled in their application of play-based strategies. The advanced practitioner is not only able to identify which underlying TPoP might be accessed through a specific strategy or technique but also able to gauge the timing for introducing a specific technique.

Returning to the case of Sammy, later in the therapy process, the therapist invited Sammy to set up a scene to explore different ways of responding to the "mean kids" on the playground. This represents movement toward Quadrant II, Open Discussion and Exploration. Here, the TPoP of direct teaching might be accessed through problem-solving strategies, along with the TPoP of stress management. From an Adlerian perspective (Kottman & Meany-Walen, 2015), a collaborative process of brainstorming and role-play re-enactment might help Sammy develop new strategies and gain insight into underlying feelings evoked in these situations. The manner in which the therapist frames the invitation for Sammy to enter this play is, of course, important. However, it is critically important that the therapist considers Sammy's readiness and capacity to engage in higher levels of discussions that are closer to consciousness.

Ultimately, it is the child who sets the speed limit. Movement between or within a quadrant can evoke a defensive or distancing response from the child when poorly timed. Accordingly, the *timing* of a TPoP should be considered in regard to the stage of therapy, along with in-session indicators or cues arising from the child, including verbalizations and symbolic communications. The child's readiness to move toward higher levels of consciousness or, alternatively, a need to remain at a lower level (in the metaphor), should be actively monitored.

Entry Points

Bradley walked into the playroom, picked up two swords and threw one to the play therapist, Jennifer. An *entry point* is identified in this instance. If we were to freeze the video, Bradley has spontaneously directed an invitation to play. Jennifer takes the sword and has a decision to make. She can wait for further instructions from Bradley (working in Quadrant III, Non-Intrusive Responding) or she could enter the play with an idea in mind based on previous sessions with Bradley (Co-facilitation, Quadrant IV). What therapeutic power has been initiated? The swordplay may be fostering emotional wellness as Bradley uses the objects to express his anger in a cathartic manner. The model of play therapy she is utilizing will influence Jennifer's responses.

Several play therapy theories, such as Psychoanalytic, Jungian, Child-Centered, and Gestalt, emphasize the role of symbolic play in accessing the child's unconscious. Quadrant

III, Non-Intrusive Responding, is very familiar to the child-centered play therapist, where safety and trust in the therapeutic relationship are seen as offering a non-threatening window to the child's inner world (Swan & Bratton, 2021). The *entry point* here is essentially the invitation for the child to take the lead and decide which objects and play scenarios to access. In child-centered or child-led play therapy, the therapist trusts that the child will, often unconsciously, choose when and how the therapist may be invited to enter their inner world.

Gestalt play therapists recognize the importance of unconscious regressive play as a means for the child to express needs that underlie the presenting concern (Oaklander, 1997). The Gestalt play therapist might make use of the child's metaphorical expressions in Quadrant III to set the stage for a structured activity such as a projective drawing. This indicates a shift toward Quadrant IV, Co-facilitation, as it is the therapist who provides an invitation for a structured drawing activity. Subsequent to the completion of the drawing, the Gestalt therapist might inquire about the drawing, initially keeping this at a symbolic/metaphorical level. As the inquiry progresses, the therapist might invite the child to make meaning between underlying dynamics in their drawing and here-and-now experiences, representing movement to Quadrant II, Open Discussion and Exploration. Notably, the *entry point* for the projective drawing came from unconscious material arising from the child's initial play. This represents the TPoP domain of facilitating communication (access to the unconscious).

Entry points can either be planned invitations or occur spontaneously. One's theoretical stance or model, as well as understanding of the child and the stage of therapy, influence the manner in which a TPoP is accessed.

Facilitation

We often advise supervisees to keep in mind that once you are "in the play," either at the invitation of the child or through accessing a suitable entry point, you should "remain in the play" but be prepared to monitor one's use of self. *Facilitation* may be conceptualized in terms of two levels: (1) Awareness of thematic elements, in relation to the referral issue and the child's context, and (2) Awareness of the degree of therapist immersion in the play.

After several sessions of swordplay, Jennifer noticed that Bradley moved from energetic, cathartic expressions and was beginning to represent themes of power and control. Jennifer's reflections on her use of self over the last few sessions suggested that she was moderately immersed in terms of her physical and emotional use of self. Bradley's response was judged to be positive as he not only stayed with the play, but the play began to deepen with Bradly showing new thematic elements in play, such as trickery, versus repetitive back-and-forth fighting without reference to characters. As Bradley was fully leading or directing the play, Jennifer correctly identified that the play was primarily centered in Quadrant III, Non-intrusive Responding. Keeping in mind the broader context for Bradley (i.e., feeling isolated from peers due to learning difficulties), Jennifer *facilitated* the process by assuming the role of a less powerful, vulnerable character, giving voice to Bradley's situation, representing movement toward Quadrant IV, Co-facilitation.

For instance, Jennifer stated that she didn't know how to fight very well because no one taught her how to use swords. Initially, Bradley's response was unsympathetic, and he remained in a position of power. Over time, and after seeking direction from Bradley through the whispering technique (i.e., "What should my character do/say?"), Jennifer *facilitated* elements of competence, representing the TPoP of increasing personal strengths.

Combined, these brief vignettes help illustrate the complex decision-making that underlies the "art" of therapy previously mentioned. In the end, the play therapist's ability to effectively facilitate the child's trust and involvement in the process will directly impact the potency of a TPoP.

References

Association for Play Therapy. (2019). Seminal theories of play therapy. *Play Therapy Magazine, 14*(3), 12–42.

Finlay, L. (2016). *Relational integrative psychotherapy: Engaging process and theory in practice.* Wiley.

Gilchrist, A. A. (1976). Potency in psychotherapy. *Australian and New Zealand Journal of Psychiatry, 10*(2), 191–200. https://doi.org/10.3109/00048677609159499.

Lily, J. P., & Heiko, R. (2019). Jungian analytical play therapy. *Play Therapy, 14*(3), 41.

Kottman, T., & Meany-Walen, K. (2015). *Partners in play: An Adlerian approach to play therapy* (3rd ed.). American Counseling Association.

Mills J. C., & Crowley, R. J. (2014). *Therapeutic metaphors for children and the child within.* Wiley Routledge.

Oaklander, V. (1997). The therapeutic process with children and adolescents. *Gestalt Review, 1*(4), 292–317.

Schaefer C. E., & Drewes, A. A. (2014). *The therapeutic powers of play: 20 core agents of change* (2nd ed.). Wiley.

Stagnitti, K., Wadley, C., & Sheppard, L. (2012). Impact of the learn to play program on play, social competence and language for children aged 5–8 years who attend a specialist school. *Australian Occupational Therapy Journal, 59*(4), 302–11

Swan, A. M., & Bratton, S. (2021). Alex plays his unspeakable story: Facilitating communication. In E. Prendiville & J. Parson (Eds.), *Clinical applications of the therapeutic powers of play* (pp. 117–28) Routledge.

Yasenik L., & Gardner, K. (2004). *Play therapy dimensions model: A decision-making guide for integrative play therapists* (1st ed.). Rocky Mountain Play Therapy Institute.

Yasenik, L., & Gardner, K. (2012). *Play therapy dimensions model: A decision-making guide for integrative play therapists* (2nd ed.). Jessica Kingsley Publishing.

Yasenik, L., & Gardner, K. (2019). Turning points and understanding the development of self through play therapy. In L. Yasenik & K. Gardner (Eds.), *Turning points in play therapy and the emergence of self: Applications of the play therapy dimensions model* (pp. 15–42). Jessica Kingsley Publishers.

Yasenik, L., & Gardner, K. (2024). *Play therapy dimensions model: New Insights for integrative play therapists* (3rd ed.). Jessica Kingsley Publishing.

6

Case Conceptualization from a Theoretical and Therapeutic Powers of Play Lens

Mary Anne Peabody

Chapter Outline

Case conceptualization is a complex cognitive process vital to efficient and effective mental health treatment. Considered an essential clinical competency (Dudley et al., 2011), case conceptualization has been referred to as the "backbone of therapy" (Christon et al., 2015, p. 37), as the "critical link" in treatment decisions (John & Segal, 2015, p. 1) and as the "bridge" that connects assessment and treatment with clinical outcomes (Sperry & Sperry, 2020a, p. 2). Despite the widely acknowledged importance of case conceptualization, it is often taught cursorily in the education of mental health practitioners, resulting in it being one of the more challenging competencies for both trainees and experienced practitioners (Sperry & Sperry, 2020a).

While multiple definitions of case conceptualization exist, Samantha John and Daniel Segal's (2015) definition is most fitting for this chapter, as it states:

> Case conceptualization is the clinician's collective understanding of the client's problems as viewed through a particular theoretical orientation; as defined by the biological, psychological, and social contexts of the client; and as supported by a body of research and practice that links a set of co-occurring symptoms to a diagnosis and, ultimately, a treatment plan. (p. 1)

Conducting case conceptualization through a theoretical lens will influence and shape the thinking of the therapist as they gather, organize, and synthesize multiple pieces of client information into a well-developed client story. Building upon the recognition that therapists should operate from a theoretical basis, in this chapter, I explore how the therapeutic powers of play (TPoP) (Schaefer & Drewes, 2014) can be integrated with the theoretical orientation of the play therapist during case conceptualization. As definitions of the TPoP appear elsewhere in this volume, this chapter focuses on how weaving theory-driven practice with the TPoP offers the play therapist a solid guiding framework at all stages of thinking, sense-making, and action. It is the weaving of theory with the TPoP during the case conceptualization process that helps distinguish the unique services of a play therapist from other mental health practitioners.

For our purposes, two related definitions of the TPoP are utilized. First, the TPoP are the specific change agents in which play initiates, facilitates, or strengthens their therapeutic effect (Drewes & Schaefer, 2014, p. 1). Second, they are the mechanisms in play that actually produce the desired change in a client's dysfunctional thoughts, feelings, and/or behaviors (Peabody & Schaefer, 2019, p. 5).

Complexity: Sequential, Fluid, and Iterative

It is acknowledged that case conceptualization in mental health is a complex task (Sperry & Sperry, 2020b). I propose that this complexity increases exponentially when providing play therapy to children and families. Children are complex human beings whose behaviors are multiply determined. Children often present with complex comorbid conditions requiring the therapist to gather a range of information to holistically understand the child developmentally, culturally, socially, cognitively, and neurobiologically. Case conceptualization with children considers the reality that they live in and are influenced by multiple systems, including families, schools, peer groups, and neighborhoods. The multicultural aspect of case conceptualization is critically important with families because culture may influence parenting style, developmental expectations, beliefs, values, and specific attitudes regarding mental health treatment (Winters et al., 2007).

While the steps involved in case conceptualization are often thought of as preceding treatment planning, upon closer examination, case conceptualization should be considered as a sequential, yet fluid and iterative process that provides structure at every point in the treatment process. Skilled play therapists will revisit and reassess their case conceptualizations throughout treatment, remaining responsive to the changing situations that inevitably emerge in the lives of clients. To illustrate this point, two recent books have focused on treatment planning as a key component in the case conceptualization play therapy process.

Homeyer & Bennett (2023) used a documentation, parent consultation, and treatment planning lens situated across several theoretical play therapy models to illustrate the process from initial inquiry to the termination summary (Homeyer & Bennett, 2023). In addition, Wonders & Affee's (2024) text on treatment planning gathered expert play therapists to share conceptualization wisdom, integrating a theory-driven perspective, an allied family stance, and the necessity of behaviorally measurable goals and treatment plans (Wonders & Affee, 2024). Both volumes are welcome additions to the play therapy literature to aid contemporary therapists in the components of case conceptualization, including treatment planning and ethical documentation (Homeyer & Bennett, 2023; Wonders & Affee, 2024).

Given treatment planning is a significant part of case conceptualization, Athena Drewes (2024) captured the importance of theory-driven conceptualization when she stated: Writing treatment plans and conceptualizing them from a theoretical framework is not an easy task, and it requires nuance and takes practice, support, and guidance (Wonders & Affee, 2024, p. xiv). It is often in the context of supervision or consultation where the opportunities for guidance, support, and practice in case conceptualization take place (Yasenik & Gardner, 2023).

Woven Constructs

Let us back up by examining the definition of play therapy from the Association for Play Therapy (2024a) which states: *Play therapy is the systematic use of a theoretical model to establish an interpersonal process wherein trained play therapists use the therapeutic powers of play to help clients prevent or resolve psychosocial difficulties and achieve optimal growth and development.* Embedded in the definition are two key elements: *The systematic use of a theoretical model* and the *use of the therapeutic powers of play.*

The Association for Play Therapy (2024b) has identified ten seminal and historically relevant play therapy theories from which the play therapist should choose to operate. Most play therapy seminal theories and approaches regard case conceptualization implicitly throughout their frameworks; however, some position it more explicitly. Ecosystemic theory (O'Connor & Ammen, 2013), Adlerian play therapy (Kottman & Meany-Whalen, 2016), Cognitive-Behavioral play therapy (Knell, 2011), and Child-Centered play therapy (Landreth, 2012) seem to weave case conceptualization, throughout their respective theories, albeit each differently, offering various tools and numerous case examples.

Next, while the TPoP are part of the Association for Play Therapy definition, they are additionally noted in the competencies for becoming credentialed as a play therapist and in the proposal process for approved professional development training (APT, 2024 a, c, d). At the global level, the International Consortium of Play Therapy Associations (ICPTA) (2024) distinguishes "Theoretical knowledge informing Play Therapy" prominently in their education-based clinical competencies, identifying both knowledge of the therapeutic powers of play and broad theoretical knowledge in this domain. It is important to note, that while global and national knowledge of theory and the therapeutic powers of play are identified as

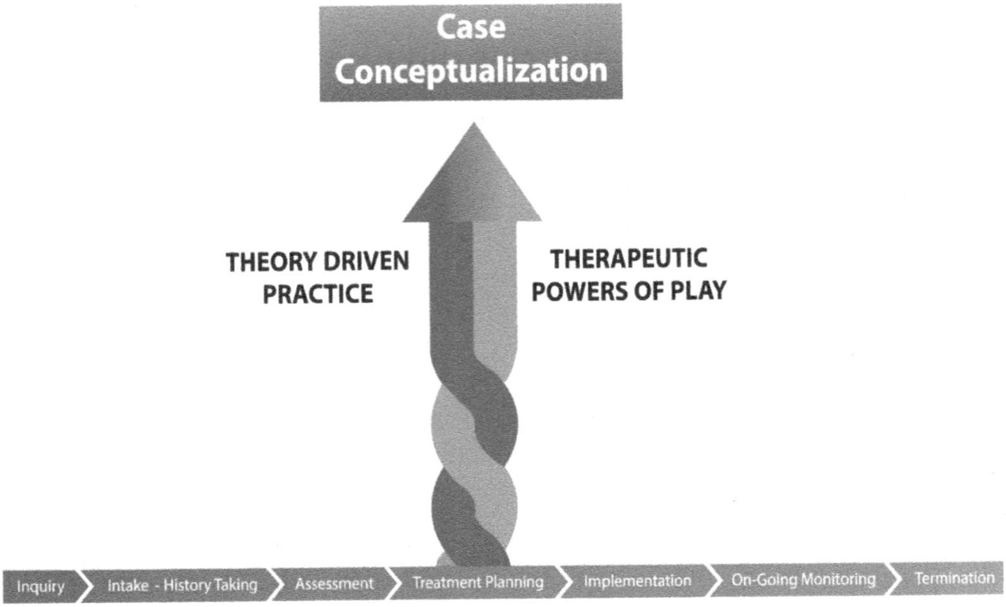

Figure 6.1 Case Conceptualization Weaving.

play therapist competency areas (APT, 2024d; ICPTA, 2024), possessing knowledge of a theory and putting it into practice are distinct and separate competencies. While theoretical knowledge may guarantee that you understand the fundamental concepts and how something works, the ability to apply it in practice is what sets great practitioners apart.

Likewise, simply knowing the therapeutic powers of play does not guarantee the application of the specific powers to meet the unique needs of the specific child client, at the right time. To that end, I now discuss theory-driven practice and the potential application of the TPoP separately, which in one sense may imply their separability, however, they are very interrelated and can be woven together throughout the case conceptualization process.

Theory in Case Conceptualization

With case conceptualization, our theories influence what information the play therapist might seek during history-taking or initial parental interviews, and conversely what they are not asking (John & Segal, 2015). Theories influence the kind and type of formal and informal assessments being selected. For example, theory can influence whether a therapist would include formal behavioral assessments such as the Child Behavioral Checklist (CBCL) (Achenbach & Rescorla, 2001) or choose assessments that focus on the relational interactions between caregivers and children, such as the Marschak Interaction Method (MIM) assessment (Lindaman et al., 2000) or a family play therapy observation and assessment (Gil, 2015). If a therapist is driven by a theory that includes a developmental play perspective, then an assessment such as the extended play-based developmental assessment

(Gil, 2011) or the child-initiated pretend play assessment (CHIPPA) that measures a child's play capacity (Stagnitti, 2021a) might be administered. Guided by theory, a play therapist may consider collecting additional information to explore the family's play history (Nash, 2023) or the role of technology (Altvater, 2021; Homeyer & Bennett, 2023; Nash, 2023).

Theories have a significant impact on how therapists perceive the root causes of a child's distress or concern. Moreover, they determine the frequency of parental involvement, the playroom's layout, the therapist's immersion in the child's play, and whether they will interpret the play. If play therapists practice purposefully, proactively, and systematically from their theory-driven lens, they are better able to conceptualize and communicate the direction of the treatment with others.

A Pre-condition

Being play-informed contributes to and strengthens one's case conceptualization skill set. Therefore, understanding play is a precondition to understanding the TPoP (Drewes & Schaefer, 2016: Schaefer & Drewes, 2014). Play has specific characteristics, functions, traits, and styles (Homeyer & Bennett, 2023; Nash, 2023; Ray, 2015; Schaefer & O'Connor, 1983) which all impact the child's capacity to play (Stagnitti, 2021b; Yasenik & Gardner, 2023). Play therapists need to start with an initial understanding of play and play capacity to fully understand how to use play therapeutically (Nash, 2023; O'Connor, 2016; Stagnitti, 2021b; Yasenik & Gardner, 2023).

Play therapists will most likely see children whose play capacity is limited due to a lack of opportunities for imaginative play, biological makeup, or trauma-based experiences. Many aspects of play therapy require imaginative play skills, and yet, not all children may be developmentally at the imaginative play level (Stagnitti, 2021b; Yasenik & Gardner, 2014.) Play therapists should be able to recognize, assess, and support child clients in their play profiles by seeking additional training or referring to other professionals as needed.

Therefore, it is essential to give equal attention to both play and the therapeutic process to ensure the success of therapy, as each holds equal importance. It is imperative to honor and understand both therapeutic change processes and the importance of play and how the latter informs the first. If a play therapist only focuses on the TPOP without a foundational understanding of play and a child's play capacity, they may diminish the overall treatment process.

Therapeutic Powers and Play in Case Conceptualization

In the beginning stages of data collection and assessment, the therapist has obtained multiple layers of information informed by parents or collateral supports and has made numerous observations of the child and family. All this information must now be synthesized and narrowed to pinpoint the underlying causes of the child's distress. Consideration of where symptoms originated, and how and why they are maintained, allows the play therapist to create hypotheses helpful in creating individualized goals and a treatment plan to meet the goals.

Depending on the individual child, the therapist merges their hypotheses of what they believe is happening in the child's experiences based on their theoretical perspective (the why) with what can be tangibly done in the play session to address the issue (the how) (Nash, 2023, p. 111). Armed with knowledge of the specific empirical play therapy research matched with the core needs of the child and family; knowledge of what specific therapeutic play powers will most likely impact or resolve the client's presenting problem; and the therapist's own experience and training all contribute to creating goals for an individualized treatment plan (Kaduson et al., 2020).

Weaving theory with the TPoP, the play therapist can then consider for each goal which of the four main domains of the TPoP match the child's profile and needs. Do the goals belong in: facilitates communication; increases personal strengths; fosters emotional wellness; or enhances social relationships? Given the nature of these broad domains, there will certainly be some goals that overlap into more than one category.

Next, the play therapist would identify which of the potential twenty TPoP under the four main categories might be utilized and through what play delivery modality (individual, group, or family), as well as specific interventions or techniques. For example, for a child displaying frustration and emotional meltdowns, the therapist might identify the TPoP domains and specific powers, identified in italics, such as: facilitating communication (e.g., *self-expression*) and fostering emotional wellness (*direct teaching*). The therapist has a range of possible play choices to access, such as individual puppet play, sand tray, doll play, or group work using directive games. Given play is the natural form of expression for children (Landreth, 2012), and the fact that the therapeutic powers are transtheoretical, the powers may occur naturally in a spontaneous manner or be guided by the purposeful choices and responses of the play therapist (Nash, 2023).

Some play therapists operating from a singular or preferred theory, may be interested in a narrower range of change mechanisms inherent in play. For example, a child-centered play therapist would focus on self-expression and relationship-enhancing powers and would not select the "direct teaching" power with a child client, as direct teaching does not align with child-centered theoretical tenets. Their approach would focus on the powers of therapeutic relationship, self-expression, empathy, or attachment. The skills would involve facilitative statements and, in some circumstances, enlarging the meaning of the play (Ray, 2011; Ray & Landreth, 2015) based on evidence-based knowledge and research.

A more integrative or prescriptive play therapist might consider a wider range of therapeutic change agents to guide their clinical decision-making by selecting interventions based on differential therapeutics and evidence-based practice knowledge (Kaduson et al., 2020). Differential therapeutics means that some approaches and interventions work better for different presenting concerns (Nash, 2023, p. 93). Fortunately, the research on play therapy's effectiveness for various populations continues to grow (Evidence-Based Child

Therapy, 2024; Bratton et al., 2005) and is available to all play therapists to stay current in the research-based literature.

An example of the weaving ability within a structured case conceptualization model is exemplified by play therapist, Julie Nash (2021). By connecting play characteristics, theoretical tenets, and the TPoP for each individualized child client, the therapist can systematically create a treatment plan with a focus on the powerful change mechanisms built into the treatment process. This model helps the play therapist determine which interventions are best suited for the client given their strengths, needs, and circumstances by seeking to answer the following questions:

1. Given that this presenting concern is likely occurring because of (hypothesis based on theoretical tenets), the fact that play is (characteristic) leads to initiation or facilitation of (therapeutic powers), which will lead to (desired outcome).
2. Given that we want to achieve (desired outcome), how would we do that by utilizing (this specific therapeutic power) and (this/these play characteristics)? (Nash, 2021, p. 28).

The therapist engages in this cognitive process guided by their theoretical beliefs and an understanding of the potencies inherent in the TPoP to start, accelerate, maintain, or bolster a therapeutic effect. This type of intentionality in case conceptualization helps not only bring structure to the case conceptualization treatment planning process but also to filter parts of the data that may not be relevant at this specific time, with this specific client.

Conclusion

Case conceptualization is a complex endeavor that has a central role in planning, guiding, and executing efficient and effective play therapy treatment. Strong case conceptualization skills are what separates the skilled play therapist from the beginner. Yet, mastering case conceptualization does not occur by chance, instead, it requires intentionality and a structured approach best accomplished in clinical supervision or consultation where support, practice, guidance, and feedback can be given (Caspar et al., 2004; Nash, 2023; Sperry & Sperry, 2020a; Yasenik & Gardner, 2023). Because play therapists are ethically responsible for delivering effective interventions (Bratton & Swan, 2017), creating time and space for the complex and nuanced thinking necessary for sound case conceptualization is an ethical imperative. Having strong case conceptualization skills allows the therapist to experience a sense of confidence in their work (Hill, 2005), which can be communicated to the child, the family, and collateral supports.

In addition to supervision and consultation, practitioners can deepen their case conceptualization knowledge base through reading case studies. By reading case conceptualization case studies, readers are allowed to step inside the "thinking" process of play therapists as they put their theory-driven practice stance into operation to guide treatment decisions that include specific therapeutic play change mechanisms. Numerous play therapy books or guides are available that showcase case conceptualization case studies of advanced practitioners (Baggerly & Drewes, 2023; Kottman & Meany-Whalen, 2016; Nash, 2023; O'Connor & Ammen, 2013; Prendiville & Parson, 2023; Pliske et al.,2021; VanFleet, 2024; Yasenik & Gardner, 2023).

Yes, case conceptualization is complex, but as play therapists we are used to the complexities inherent in the mental health treatment of children and families. Complexity can be viewed as a challenge or as an opportunity. Armed with strong case conceptualization processes, decision-making tools, and support, a play therapist can engage in the nuanced complexities of case conceptualization with self-confidence, knowing their clinical decisions are based on identified competencies recognized by the field of play therapy. Our clients deserve play therapists who understand and apply theoretical intention with the therapeutic powers of play to guide their clinical decisions.

References

Achenbach, T. M., & Rescorla, L. A. (2001). *Child behavior checklist for Ages 6–18 (CBCL/6–18, ASEBA CBCL/6–18)* [Database record]. American Psychological Association Psychological Tests. http://doilorg/10.1037/t47452-000.

Altvater, R. A. (2021). The culture of technology and play therapy. In E. Gil & A. A. Drewes (Eds.), *Cultural issues in play therapy* (2nd ed., pp. 172–90). Guilford Press.

Association for Play Therapy. (2024a). *Definition of play therapy.* https://www.a4pt.org/page/WhyPlayTherapy.

Association for Play Therapy. (2024b). *Seminal & historically significant play therapy theories.* https://www.a4pt.org/page/Publications?&hhsearchterms=%22seminal+and+theories%22.

Association for Play Therapy. (2024c). *Therapeutic powers of play.* https://www.a4pt.org/page/Publications?&hhsearchterms=%22seminal+and+theories%22.

Association for Play Therapy. (2024d). *Competencies.* https://www.a4pt.org/page/CredentialsInfo?&hhsearchterms=%22competencies%22.

Baggerly, J. N., & Drewes, A. A. (Eds.). (2023). *Contemporary case studies in clinical mental health for children and adolescents.* Rowman & Littlefield.

Bratton, S. C., & Swan, A. (2017). Status of play therapy research. In R. L. Steen (Ed.), *Emerging research in play therapy, child counseling and consultation* (pp. 1–19). IGA Global.

Bratton, S. C., Ray, D., Rhine, T., & Jones, L. (2005). The efficacy of play therapy with children: A meta-analytic review of treatment outcomes. *Professional Psychology: Research and Practice, 36*(4), 376–90. https://doi.org/10.1037/0735–7028.36.4.376.

Caspar, F., Berger, T., & Hautle, I. (2004). The right view of your patient: A computer assisted, individualized module for psychotherapy training. *Psychotherapy: Theory, Research, Practice, Training, 41*(2), 125–35. http://dx.doi.org/10.1037/0033 3204.41.2.125.

Christon, L. M., McLeod, B. D., & Jensen-Doss, A. (2015). Evidence-based assessment meets evidence-based treatment: An approach to science-informed case conceptualization. *Cognitive and Behavioral Practice, 22*(1), 36–48. https://doi.org/10.1016/j.cbpra.2013.12.004.

Dudley, R., Kuyken, W., & Padesky, C. A. (2011). Disorder specific and trans-diagnostic case conceptualization. *Clinical Psychology Review, 31*(2), 213–24. https://doi.org/10.1016/j.cpr.2010.07.005.

Drewes, A. A. (2024). Foreword. In L. L. Wonders & M. L. Affee (Eds.), *Play therapy treatment planning with children and families: A guide for mental health professionals,* (pp. 13–14). Routledge.

Drewes, A., & Schaefer, C. E. (2014). *The therapeutic powers of play: 20 core agents of change* (2nd ed.). John Wiley.

Drewes, A., & Schaefer, C. E. (2016). The therapeutic powers of play. In K. O'Connor, C. E. Schaefer, & L. Braverman (Eds.), *Handbook of play therapy* (3rd ed., pp. 35–60). Wiley.

Evidence based child therapy. (2024). https://evidencebasedchildtherapy.com/.

Gil, E. (2011). *The extended play-based developmental assessment.* Self Esteem Shop.

Gil, E. (2015). *Play in family therapy* (2nd ed.). Guilford.

Hill, C. E. (2005). Therapist techniques, client involvement, and the therapeutic relationship: Inextricably intertwined in the therapy process. *Psychotherapy: Theory, Research, Practice, Training, 42*(4), 431–42. https://doi.org/10.1037/0033-3204.42.4.431.

Homeyer, L. E., & Bennett, M. M. (2023). *The guide to play therapy documentation and parent consultation.* Routledge. https://doi.org/10.4324/9781003258766-2.

International Consortium of Play Therapy Associations. (2024). *Play therapy education competencies and standards of practice.* https://www.ic-pta.com/standards.

John, S., & Segal, D. L. (2015). Case conceptualization. In R. L. Cautin & S. O. Lilienfeild (Eds.), *The encyclopedia of clinical psychology* (1st ed., pp. 1–4). Wiley & Sons. https://doi.org/10.1002/9781118625392.webecp106.

Kaduson, H. G., Schaefer, C. E., & Cangelosi, D. (2020). Basic principles and core practices of prescriptive play therapy. In H. G. Kaduson, D. Cangelosi, & C. E. Schaefer (Eds.), *Prescriptive play therapy: Tailoring interventions for specific childhood problems* (pp. 3–13). Guilford Press.

Knell, S. (2011). Cognitive-behavioral play therapy. In C. E. Schaefer (Ed.), *Foundations of play therapy* (2nd ed., pp. 313–28). John Wiley.

Kottman, T., & Meany-Whalen, K. (2016). *Partners in play: An Adlerian approach to play therapy* (3rd ed.). American Counseling Association.

Landreth, G. L. (2012). *Play therapy: The art of the relationship* (3rd ed.). Brunner-Routledge.

Lindaman, S. L., Booth, P. B., & Chambers, C. L. (2000). Assessing parent–child interactions with the Marschak Interaction Method (MIM). In K. Gitlin-Weiner, A. Sandgrund, & C. Schaefer (Eds.), *Play diagnosis and assessment* (2nd ed., pp. 371–400). Wiley & Sons.

Nash, J. B. (2023). *Nature-based play therapy: A prescriptive approach to integrating the therapeutic powers of nature and play.* Routledge.

Nash, J. B. (2021). Utilizing the therapeutic powers of play to create change. *PlayTherapy, 16*(4), 26–9.

O'Conner, K. J. (2016). Ecosystemic play therapy. In K. J. O'Connor, C. E. Schaefer, & L. D. Braverman (Eds.), *Handbook of play therapy* (2nd ed., pp. 195–226). Wiley.

O'Connor, K. J., & Ammen, S. (2013). *Play therapy treatment planning and interventions: The Ecosystemic model and workbook* (2nd ed.). Academic Press.

Peabody, M. A., & Schaefer, C. E. (2019). The therapeutic powers of play: The heart and soul of play therapy. *PlayTherapy, 14*(3), 4–6.

Pliske, M. M., Stauffer, S. D., & Werner-Lin, A. (2021). Healing from adverse childhood experiences through therapeutic powers of play: "I can do it with my hands". *International Journal of Play Therapy, 30*(4), 244–58. https://doi.org/10.1037/pla0000166.

Prendiville, E., & Parson, J. A. (2023). *Clinical applications of the therapeutic powers of play: Case studies in child and adolescent psychotherapy*. Routledge.

Ray, D. (2011). *Advanced play therapy: Essential conditions, knowledge, and skills for child practice*. Routledge.

Ray, D. (Ed.). (2015). *A therapist's guide to child development: The extraordinary normal years*. Routledge.

Ray, D., & Landreth, G. L. (2015). Child centered play therapy. In D. Crenshaw & A. Stewart (Eds.). *Play therapy: A comprehensive guide to theory and practice* (pp. 3–16). Guilford.

Schaefer, C. E., & Drewes, A. A. (2014). *The therapeutic powers of play: 20 core agents of change* (2nd ed.). John Wiley.

Schaefer, C. E, & O'Connor, K. J. (1983). Major approaches to play therapy: Advances and innovations. In C. E. Schaefer & K. J. O'Connor (Eds.), *The handbook of play therapy* (1st ed., pp. 1–10). Wiley & Sons.

Sperry, L., & Sperry, J. (2020a). *Case conceptualization: Mastering this competency with ease and confidence* (2nd ed.). Routledge.

Sperry, L., & Sperry, J. (2020b). *Case conceptualization: Key to highly effective counseling. Counseling today*. American Counseling Association. https://ct.counseling.org/2020/12/case-conceptualization-key-to-highly-effective-counseling/.

Stagnitti, K. (2021a). *Learn to play therapy: Principles, process and practical activities* (2nd ed.). Learn to Play.

Stagnitti, K. (2021b). Learning to play. In E. Prendiville & J. A. Parson (Eds.), *Clinical applications of the therapeutic powers of play: Case studies in child and adolescent psychotherapy* (pp. 87–98). Routledge.

VanFleet, R. (2024). Case conceptualization guide for professionals working with children and families. https://risevanfleet.com/case-formulation-guide-for-professionals-working-with-children-and-families/.

Winters, N. C., Hanson, G., & Stoyanova, V. (2007). The case formulation in child and adolescent psychiatry. *Child and Adolescent Psychiatric Clinics of North America, 16*, 111–32.

Wonders, L. L., & Affee, M. L. (2024). *Play therapy treatment planning with children and families: A guide for mental health professionals*. Routledge.

Yasenik, L., & Gardner, K. (2014). *The consciousness dimension in play therapy: Sharpening the play therapist's focus and skills. Play Therapy Today* (pp. 29–46). Routledge.

Yasenik, L., & Gardner, K. (2023). *Play therapy Dimensions Model™: New insights for the integrative play therapist* (3rd ed.). Jessica Kingsley Publishers.

7

Research and Empirical Support

Yung-Wei Dennis Lin and Anqi Yu

Chapter Outline

The use of play as a therapeutic approach has been well researched in the history of play literature. Since late nineteenth century, pioneer researchers (e.g., G. Stanley Hall, Hermine Hug-Hellmuth, Melanie Klein, Anna Freud, Virginia Axline, etc.) have published their observational findings regarding the significance of play in child development and the therapeutic use of play in child psychotherapy (Landreth, 2024). These early observational studies served as an essential foundation for later researchers to further investigate the therapeutic effect of play in child therapy. The first experimental study examining the effect of play in child psychotherapy was in mid-twentieth century (Dulsky, 1942). Since then, researchers have published hundreds of studies to provide research evidence for the benefits of the therapeutic use of play through methodologies such as meta-analysis, randomized controlled trials (RCTs), quasi-experimental designs, and single-case designs. In this chapter, we will provide a brief summary of the research and empirical support for the effectiveness of the therapeutic power of play. Particularly, we will address the research evidence based on the following categories: research in play therapy, research in play-based caregiver training, and research in other therapeutic uses of play.

Research in Play Therapy

The majority of empirical studies in the literature that investigate the effectiveness of the therapeutic use of play are in play therapy. To date, there have been six meta-analytic

Table 7.1 Meta-Analytic Studies

Meta-Analyses	# of Studies	Focuses	Collection Years	Child Mean Age (years)	# of Participants	Effect Size (*ES*)
Leblanc & Ritchie (2001)	42	PT in general	1947–1996	7.8	Not reported	0.66
Bratton et al. (2005)	93	PT in general	1953–2000	7.0	3,248	0.80
Lin & Bratton (2015)	52	CCPT	1995–2010	6.7	1,848	0.47
Ray et al. (2015)	23	School-based CCPT	1975–2011	4–13	1,106	0.21–0.38
Jensen et al. (2017)	100	PT in general; outcome measures	1953–2010	Not reported	Not reported	0.44
Parker et al. (2021)	23	CCPT; child behavioral problems	2000–2017	6.0	908	0.34–0.48

studies synthesizing controlled outcome studies that examined the treatment effects of play therapy. These meta-analytic studies have provided ample and solid empirical support for the effects of play therapy on a variety of presenting problems among children across age and ethnicity groups. The following table presents a brief summary of the main findings from these meta-analytic studies.

These meta-analytic studies not only provide thorough reviews of play therapy empirical research but also strong research evidence for the effectiveness of play therapy. It should be noted that the effect sizes reported in these meta-analyses are Cohen's d effect sizes, which should be interpreted as the number of standard deviations of difference between the mean scores of two groups (usually experimental and control groups). For example, the effect size of 0.47 in Lin and Bratton (2015) means that before and after CCPT, the experimental group demonstrated an improvement that was 0.47 standard deviations better than the control or comparison group. Also, some meta-analytic researchers utilized both pre- and post-treatment data, while others preferred to use only post-treatment data, which might result in different magnitudes of the effect sizes reported in these meta-analyses. Despite the discrepancies among the effect size values, they all indicated statistically significant treatment effects for CCPT. In addition to the overall treatment effect, the researchers in these meta-analyses further suggested that the play therapy effect may be highly associated with several important factors, such as child age, parent involvement, child ethnicity, and outcome measures.

The aforementioned meta-analyses provide clear summaries for the controlled outcome studies published or conducted until 2017. Since 2018, there have been eleven more individual experimental and quasi-experimental studies published. These more updated studies continue to expand empirical evidence for the treatment effect of different play therapy approaches on a variety of child populations and presenting concerns or issues. For example, researchers using RCT designs continued reporting medium to large treatment effects for CCPT, in either individual or group format, on improving children's social-emotional competencies, empathy, and self-regulation (Blalock, Lindo, & Ray, 2019;

Wilson & Ray, 2018), and on the same outcomes among African American children (Taylor & Ray, 2021). The benefits of CCPT have also been found with children with autistic symptoms and attention-deficit/hyperactivity disorder (ADHD). Schottelkorb, Swan, and Ogawa (2020) published their pilot study based on an RCT design and suggested a large treatment effect of CCPT in reducing externalizing behavioral problems, attention problems, and aggressive behaviors among children with autism spectrum disorder after receiving twenty-four thirty-minute CCPT sessions across six weeks. Wong and colleagues (2025) also conducted a RCT study (N = 17) focusing on the effect of CCPT on children with ADHD symptoms. In their findings, the twelve children who received CCPT over twelve weeks demonstrated significant improvement in their behavioral problems, particularly social behaviors, thought problems, anxiety/depression, and externalizing behaviors, as well as neuropsychological performance. Ray and colleagues (2022) conducted a RCT study (N = 112) exploring the effect of CCPT on children with adverse childhood experiences (ACEs). Across six weeks of CCPT (10–16 sessions), children in the experimental group improved significantly in their self-regulation, social competence, empathy, and total behaviors compared to children in the control group who did not receive CCPT.

In addition to CCPT research, Obiweluozo and colleagues (2021) conducted a large-scale cluster randomized trial study (N = 176) investigating the effectiveness of cognitive-behavioral play therapy (CBPT) with school children in Nigeria suffering from stuttering (aged between 6–16). Their findings suggested CBPT as an effective intervention for reducing social anxiety among children with stuttering symptoms. Similarly, Egbe and colleagues (2023) utilized a RCT design (N = 122) to examine the effect of CBPT on pre-adolescent and adolescent students with speech impairments. They reported a medium to large treatment effect of CBPT in decreasing social anxiety and improving social behaviors among students with speech impairments. In a small-scale RCT study (N = 24), Ashori and Shamsi (2023) explored the effect of Adlerian play therapy (AdPT) with deaf high school students. Their findings suggested a large treatment effect of AdPT in improving alexithymia symptoms and decreasing social isolation among deaf students.

Single case research designs have drawn play therapy researchers' attention since 2007 because of their feasibility and increasing methodological rigor. Pester, Lenz, and Dell'Aquila (2019) conducted a meta-analysis reviewing nine single case studies on CCPT between 2015 and 2017. These nine studies together included forty-three total child participants and 65 total effect sizes. Their findings suggested a moderate treatment effect of CCPT on reducing children's externalizing and internalizing symptoms as well as improving social skills. In addition to the synthesized findings from this meta-analysis, there are other single case studies in the play therapy literature providing research support for both CCPT and AdPT across a variety of child populations, including children with Adverse Childhood Experiences (ACEs), children with ADHD, children with autism spectrum disorder, early elementary school children, at-risk preschool students, and Caucasian boys in kindergarten. Overall, these single case studies suggested a promising treatment effect of play therapy in decreasing disruptive and externalizing behaviors (Schoonover & Perryman, 2023; Dillman Tylor et al., 2021; Phipps & Post, 2020; Swank et al., 2017; Stutey et al., 2017), anxiety (Swan, Kaff, & Haas, 2019), and perfectionism (Akay & Bratton, 2017), and improving social skills (Meany-Walen & Teeling, 2016) as well as on-task behavior (Swank & Smith-Adcock, 2018; Dillman Taylor et al., 2019).

Research in Play-based Caregiver Training

Since Bernard Guerney and Louise Buerney developed filial therapy in the 1960s, play therapists have recognized the therapeutic power of play facilitated by caregivers. Researchers have also conducted numerous empirical studies providing rich research evidence for play-based caregiver training models, such as filial therapy or child-parent relationship therapy (CPRT), parent-child interaction therapy (PCIT), and child-teacher relationship training (CTRT). Allen (2020) conducted a meta-analysis summarizing twenty-three individual outcome studies on CPRT between 1995 and 2015. By examining pre- to post-treatment changes among 333 parents who received CPRT in these 23 studies, the meta-analytic results suggested a moderate treatment effect of CPRT on reducing parental stress and improving child behavioral problems. While comparing with parents who did not receive CPRT in the 19 studies (n = 292), the 309 parents who received CPRT also demonstrated significantly greater changes prior to and after the CPRT, which also suggested a moderate treatment effect of CPRT on the same outcomes.

Since 2015, there have been several more empirical studies exploring CPRT effects with a variety of populations. For example, Tal, Tal, and Green (2018) investigated CPRT effects with families that experienced child sexual abuse from perpetrators outside of the family. Their findings based on fifty-one parents suggested promising CPRT effects on reducing their parental stress and compassion fatigue and improving their children's internalizing and externalizing behavioral symptoms. Opiola and Bratton (2018) conducted a RCT study on CPRT with forty-nine adoptive families. Their results revealed very large treatment effects of CPRT on reducing stress in the parent-child relationship, improving children's problematic behaviors, and enhancing parents' empathy while interacting with their children. In addition, Ebrahimi and colleagues (2019) conducted another RCT study on CPRT with thirty-two parents whose children suffered from cancer. Although their sample size was not large, their findings suggested promising CPRT effects on reducing parents' depression, anxiety, and parental stress as well as decreasing their children's depression. The benefits of CPRT have also been researched with parents suffering from hearing loss. Ashori and Karimnejad (2021) in their randomized controlled trial study explored the effect of CPRT with thirty mothers with hearing loss. Particularly, their findings suggested the CPRT effect on improving the child-parent relationship through increasing closeness and decreasing conflict and dependency. In another recent RCT study with thirty-eight mothers who suffered from domestic violence witnessed and whose children witnessed it (Gunaydin & Zincir, 2024), the findings suggested promising benefits of CPRT on reducing parental stress within the parent-child relationship and children's behavioral problems among families impacted by domestic violence.

Filial therapy has been applied to teachers in school settings since 2000, and this approach was later modified as child-teacher relationship training (CTRT). Although there has not been any meta-analysis conducted for CTRT, many of the CTRT outcome studies have been reviewed and included in CCPT meta-analytic studies (i.e., Jenson et al., 2017; Lin & Bratton, 2015; Parker et al., 2021). There have been several recent CTRT studies that have not been included in these meta-analyses. For example, Gonzales-Ball and Bratton's (2019) randomized controlled outcome study provided promising evidence for the CTRT effect on reducing children's disruptive behaviors. Post and colleagues (2020) conducted a quasi-experimental study with forty-six elementary school teachers to explore the CTRT training effects. Their findings suggested a medium training effect on enhancing teachers' attitudes about trauma-informed care, a medium to large training effect on improving teachers' child-centered attitude, knowledge, and skills, and a very large training effect on enhancing teachers' ability to demonstrate child-centered skills in their classrooms. In addition, Coggins and Carnes-Holt (2021) conducted an RCT study exploring the CTRT effect with young children in Head Start programs. Although the sample size was small, they reported a moderate to large CTRT training effect on reducing children's behavioral problems.

Parent-Child Interaction Therapy also has extensive research supporting its effectiveness. The following table provides a brief summary of eight meta-analytic studies that specifically explored the treatment effect of PCIT modalities.

Table 7.2 Parent-Child Interaction Therapy Meta-Analytic Studies

Meta-Analyses	# of Studies	Focuses	Collection Years	Child Mean Age (years)	# of Child Participants	Effect Size
Ward, Theule, & Cheung (2016)	12 (9)	Child disruptive behavior disorders	1991–2010	3.2–5	372	1.65 (1.39)
Kennedy et al. (2016)	6	Future physical abuse	1999–2012	5.3	571	0.31–0.52
Thomas et al. (2017)	23	Externalizing behavioral symptoms	1995–2016	1.5–15	1,144	0.87
Valero-Aguayo et al. (2021)	100	Child behavioral problems	1991–2020	1–13	6,252	0.87–1.40
Phillips & Mychailyszyn (2021)	15	Child anxiety	2005–2021	2–9.75	370	0.96
Phillips & Mychailyszyn (2023)	29	Preschool children	1992–2020	1–4.9	908	0.76–2.00
Phillips et al. (2024)	9	Children with ADHD	2009–present	2–7	280	0.44–2.15
Zhang, Wang, & Li (2024)	11	Maltreated children	1999–2021	5.18	1,069	0.30–7.28

Ward, Theule, and Cheung (2016) conducted the first meta-analysis exploring the overall effect of PCIT on children with disruptive behavioral disorders (DBDs) across twelve studies. All the children in these twelve studies who and their parents received PCIT improved their DBD symptoms by 1.65 *SDs*, and the children in nine of the twelve studies who and their parents received PCIT improved their DBD symptoms by 1.39 *SDs* when compared with the children who did not. Kennedy and colleagues (2016) also conducted a meta-analysis exploring the effect of PCIT on reducing future child abuse. Two of the six collected studies examined the PCIT effect on reducing physical abuse recurrence, and the meta-analytic results revealed a moderate effect (*ES* = 0.52). Four of the six collected studies examined PCIT effect on reducing parenting stress, and the meta-analytic results revealed a small but statistically significant effect (*ES* = 0.35). Five of the six collected studies examined PCIT effect on reducing child abuse potential, and the meta-analytic results revealed a non-significant effect (*ES* = 0.31). Another meta-analysis synthesizing twenty-three PCIT studies indicated a large treatment effect (*ES* = 0.87) on reducing children's externalizing behavioral symptoms (Thommas et al., 2017).

Valero-Aguayo and colleagues (2021) conducted the largest meta-analysis that synthesized findings from 100 PCIT studies between 1991 and 2020. Within the 100 studies, 39 studies compared PCIT with at least one control group, and 35 studies utilized single group designs comparing pre- and post-treatment data. The thirty-nine studies comparing PCIT with control groups generated an overall large treatment effect (*ES* = 0.87), and the participants in the thirty-five studies using single group designs demonstrated a significantly large improvement of 1.40 *SD*s before and after PCIT. In the same year, Phillips and Mychailyszyn (2021) conducted a meta-analytic study specifically exploring the effect of PCIT on reducing children's anxiety. Based on the fifteen collected studies, the children in the experimental group demonstrated a significant reduction in their anxiety by 0.96 *SDs* after they and their parents received PCIT, while the children in the control group only reduced their anxiety by 0.40 *SDs* across the same period of time without PCIT treatment. Phillips and Mychailyszyn (2023) conducted another meta-analysis comparing the effects with younger (12–24 months) and older (25–59 months) preschool children. Based on the twenty-nine studies collected in their meta-analysis, their results indicated that preschool children demonstrated large to very large amounts of improvement in their externalizing (*ES* = 1.10) and internalizing (*ES* = 0.76) behavioral concerns before and after participating in PCIT. The parents of those preschool children also showed a large decrease in their parenting-related distress (*ES* = 0.80) and an extremely large increase in their positive parenting behaviors (*ES* = 2.00). In addition, the analysis results revealed no significant differences in these outcomes between younger and older preschool children groups, indicating similar effectiveness of PCIT across two to five years old preschoolers. More recently, two more meta-analytic studies were published. Phillips and colleagues' (2024) meta-analysis specifically aimed to explore PCIT effects on families with young children with ADHD. Their findings indicated significant PCIT effects on improving children's externalizing behavioral symptoms, ADHD symptoms, as well as parental stress and parenting behaviors. Zhang, Wang, and Li (2024) conducted a meta-analysis to synthesize eleven individual studies that examined PCIT effects on maltreated families. They reported an extremely large PCIT effect on improving parenting skills (*ES* = 6.85–7.28), large effect on reducing parenting stress (*ES* = 0.94), a large to very large effect on improving children's externalizing behavioral concerns (*ES* = 0.63–1.91), and small effect on reducing child abuse potential.

Research in Medical Therapeutic Uses of Play

The use of play-related activities and tools is also widely used in medical settings. Researchers across countries have attempted to explore the benefits of play during medical treatment in reducing children's fear, anxiety, and negative emotions, and improving relationships and collaboration with healthcare professionals (Godino-Ianez et al., 2020). For example, "Teddy Bear Hospital" is a medical pretend play where children bring their soft toys and act as parents to their "sick" babies in a hospital play setting. The "Teddy Bear Hospital" has been confirmed to have positive effects on reducing children's anxiety and fear related to healthcare settings (Rashid et al., 2021). Researchers also reported the treatment effect of virtual reality computer games in reducing depressive symptoms among Hong Kong Chinese children who were hospitalized due to cancer (Li et al., 2011). In addition, unstructured play activities with toys have been proven to be an effective approach in reducing anxiety for children in the pediatric unit hospitalized for at least three days in Turkey (Ai-Yateem & Rossiter, 2017). Different types of play, such as doll therapy with school-aged children undergoing day surgery (William Li et al., 2007) and unstructured play with young children with Leukaemia (Gariepy & Howe, 2003) have also been examined in healthcare research.

Conclusion

The research evidence that supports the therapeutic power of play has been well documented in the literature. Particularly, the therapeutic power of play can be used by not only trained play therapists but also caregivers such as parents in home settings, teachers in school settings, and medical personnel in hospital settings. There have been more and more studies examining the therapeutic power of play conducted by international researchers outside of the United States. We believe such a positive trend will greatly enrich the play research literature. We also observe that the current literature still shows the need for more research on play therapy approaches based on theoretical orientations other than CCPT, on using therapeutic play with culturally diverse families and children, and on therapeutic play utilized by different professionals in a variety of settings that directly serve children in need.

References

Akay, S., & Bratton, S. (2017). The effects of Adlerian play therapy on maladaptive perfectionism and anxiety in children: A single case design. *International Journal of Play Therapy, 26*(2), 96–110. https://doi.org/10.1037/pla0000043.

Allen, B. (2020). Child-parent relationship therapy for externalizing problems: A meta-analysis and methodological critique. *Evidence-Based Practice in Child and Adolescent Mental Health, 5*(4), 426–36. https://doi.org/10.1080/23794925.2020.1784054.

Al-Yateem, N., & Rossiter, R. C. (2017). Unstructured play for anxiety in pediatric inpatient care. *Journal for Specialists in Pediatric Nursing, 22*(1), e12166. https://doi.org/10.1111/jspn.12166.

Ashori, M., & Karimnejad, R. (2021). The effect of filial therapy on the interaction of deaf mothers with their hearing children. *International Journal of Play Therapy, 30*(3), 195–205. https://doi.org/10.1037/pla0000161.

Ashori, M., & Shamsi, A. (2023). The effect of Adlerian play therapy on the alexithymia and social isolation of deaf students. *International Journal of Play Therapy, 32*(1), 10–21. https://doi.org/10.1037/pla0000192.

Blalock, S. M., Lindo, N., & Ray, D. C. (2019). Individual and group child-centered play therapy: Impact on social-emotional competencies. *Journal of Counseling & Development, 97*(3), 238–49. https://doi.org/10.1002/jcad.12264.

Bratton, S. C., Ray, D., Rhine, T., & Jones, L. (2005). The efficacy of play therapy with children: A meta-analytic review of treatment outcomes. *Professional Psychology, Research and Practice, 36*(4), 376–90. https://doi.org/10.1037/0735–7028.36.4.376.

Coggins, K., & Carnes-Holt, K. (2021). The efficacy of child-teacher relationship training as an early childhood mental health intervention in Head Start programs. *International Journal of Play Therapy, 30*(2), 112–24. https://doi.org/10.1037/pla0000154.

Dillman Taylor, D., Meany-Walen, K. K., Nelson, K. M., & Gungor, A. (2019). Investigating group Adlerian play therapy for children with disruptive behaviors: A single-case research design. *International Journal of Play Therapy, 28*(3), 168–82. https://doi.org/10.1037/pla0000094.

Dillman Taylor, D., Purswell, K., Cornett, N., & Bratton, S. C. (2021). Effects of child-centered play therapy (CCPT) on disruptive behavior of at-risk preschool children in Head Start. *International Journal of Play Therapy, 30*(2), 86–97. https://doi.org/10.1037/pla0000125.

Dulsky, S. G. (1942). Affect and intellect: An experimental study. *The Journal of General Psychology, 27*(2), 199–220. https://doi.org/10.1080/00221309.1942.10544409.

Ebrahimi, E., Mirzaie, H., Saeidi Borujeni, M., Zahed, G., Akbarzadeh Baghban, A., & Mirzakhani, N. (2019). The effect of filial therapy on depressive symptoms of children with cancer and their mother's depression, anxiety, and stress: A randomized controlled trial. *Asian Pacific Journal of Cancer Prevention, 20*(10), 2935–41. https://doi.org/10.31557/APJCP.2019.20.10.2935.

Egbe, C. I., Ugwuanyi, L. T., Ede, M. O., Agbigwe, I. B., Onuorah, A. R., Okon, O. E., & Ugwu, J. C. (2023). Cognitive behavioural play therapy for social anxiety disorders (SADs) in children with speech impairments. *Journal of Rational-Emotive & Cognitive-Behavior Therapy, 41*(1), 24–44. https://doi.org/10.1007/s10942-022-00442-6.

Godino-Iáñez, M. J., Martos-Cabrera, M. B., Suleiman-Martos, N., Gómez-Urquiza, J. L., Vargas-Román, K., Membrive-Jiménez, M. J., & Albendín-García, L. (2020). Play therapy as an intervention in hospitalized children: A systematic review. *Healthcare, 8*(3), Article 3. https://doi.org/10.3390/healthcare8030239.

Gariepy, N. & Howe, N. (2003). The therapeutic power of play: Examining the play of young children with leukaemia. *Child: care, health and development, 29*(6), 523–537.

Gonzales-Ball, T. L., & Bratton, S. C. (2019). Child-teacher relationship training as a head start early mental health intervention for children exhibiting disruptive behavior. *International Journal of Play Therapy, 28*(1), 44–56. https://doi.org/10.1037/pla0000081.

Günaydin, Y., & Zincir, H. (2024). The effect of child–parent relationship therapy-based play support on parental stress and acceptance, and child behaviours in children who witness domestic violence: Randomized controlled study. *Australian and New Zealand Journal of Family Therapy, 45*(3), 336–48. https://doi.org/10.1002/anzf.1579.

Jensen, S. A., Biesen, J. N., & Graham, E. R. (2017). A meta-analytic review of play therapy with emphasis on outcome measures. *Professional Psychology, Research and Practice, 48*(5), 390–400. https://doi.org/10.1037/pro0000148.

Kennedy, S. C., Kim, J. S., Tripodi, S. J., Brown, S. M., & Gowdy, G. (2016). Does parent–child interaction therapy reduce future physical abuse? A meta-analysis. *Research on Social Work Practice, 26*(2), 147–56. https://doi.org/10.1177/1049731514543024.

Landreth, G. L. (2024). *Play therapy: The art of the relationship* (4th ed.). Routledge.

Leblanc, M., & Ritchie, M. (2001). A meta-analysis of play therapy outcomes. *Counselling Psychology Quarterly, 14*(2), 149–163. https://doi.org/10.1080/09515070110059142.

Li, W. H., Chung, J. O., & Ho, E. K. (2011). The effectiveness of therapeutic play, using virtual reality computer games, in promoting the psychological well-being of children hospitalised with cancer. *Journal of Clinical Nursing, 20*(15–16), 2135–43. https://doi.org/10.1111/j.1365-2702.2011.03733.x.

Lin, Y.-W., & Bratton, S. C. (2015). A meta-analytic review of child-centered play therapy approaches. *Journal of Counseling and Development, 93*(1), 45–58. https://doi.org/10.1002/j.1556-6676.2015.00180.x.

Meany-Walen, K. K., & Teeling, S. (2016). Adlerian play therapy with students with externalizing behaviors and poor social skills. *International Journal of Play Therapy, 25*(2), 64–77. https://doi.org/10.1037/pla0000022.

Obiweluozo, P. E., Ede, M. O., Onwurah, C. N., Uzodinma, U. E., Dike, I. C., & Ejiofor, J. N. (2021). Impact of cognitive behavioural play therapy on social anxiety among school children with stuttering deficit: A cluster randomised trial with three months follow-up. *Medicine, 100*(19), e24350. https://doi.org/10.1097/MD.0000000000024350.

Opiola, K. K., & Bratton, S. C. (2018). The efficacy of child parent relationship therapy for adoptive families: A replication study. *Journal of Counseling & Development, 96*(2), 155–66. https://doi.org/10.1002/jcad.12189.

Parker, M. M., Hunnicutt Hollenbaugh, K. M., & Kelly, C. T. (2021). Exploring the impact of child-centered play therapy for children exhibiting behavioral problems: A meta-analysis. *International Journal of Play Therapy, 30*(4), 259–71. https://doi.org/10.1037/pla0000128.

Pester, D., Lenz, A. S., & Dell'Aquila, J. (2019). Meta-analysis of single-case evaluations of child-centered play therapy for treating mental health symptoms. *International Journal of Play Therapy, 28*(3), 144–56. https://doi.org/10.1037/pla0000098.

Phillips, S., & Mychailyszyn, M. (2021). A review of Parent-Child Interaction Therapy (PCIT): Applications for youth anxiety. *Children and Youth Services Review, 125*, 105986. https://doi.org/10.1016/j.childyouth.2021.105986.

Phillips, S. T., & Mychailyszyn, M. P. (2023). Parent-child interaction therapy for preschool aged youth: A meta-analysis of developmental specificity. *Child & Youth Care Forum, 52*(2), 267–84. https://doi.org/10.1007/s10566-022-09694-w.

Phillips, S. T., Druskin, L. R., Mychailyszyn, M. P., Victory, E., Aman, E., & McNeil, C. B. (2024). The efficacy of parent–child interaction therapy (PCIT) for youth with attention-deficit/hyperactivity disorder (ADHD): A meta-analysis. *Child Psychiatry and Human Development*. https://doi.org/10.1007/s10578-024-01678-2.

Phipps, C. B., & Post, P. B. (2020). The effect of child-centered play therapy on the externalizing behaviors of low-income male preschoolers: A single-case design study. *International Journal of Play Therapy, 29*(2), 74–85. https://doi.org/10.1037/pla0000115.

Post, P. B., Grybush, A. L., Flowers, C., & Elmadani, A. (2020). Impact of child-teacher relationship training on teacher attitudes and classroom behaviors. *International Journal of Play Therapy, 29*(3), 119–30. https://doi.org/10.1037/pla0000118.

Rashid, A. A., Cheong, A. T., Hisham, R., Shamsuddin, N. H., & Roslan, D. (2021). Effectiveness of pretend medical play in improving children's health outcomes and well-being: A systematic review. *BMJ Open, 11*(1), e041506. https://doi.org/10.1136/bmjopen-2020-041506.

Ray, D. C., Armstrong, S. A., Balkin, R. S., & Jayne, K. M. (2015). Child-centered play therapy in the schools: Review and meta-analysis. *Psychology in the Schools, 52*(2), 107–23. https://doi.org/10.1002/pits.21798.

Ray, D. C., Burgin, E., Gutierrez, D., Ceballos, P., & Lindo, N. (2022). Child-centered play therapy and adverse childhood experiences: A randomized controlled trial. *Journal of Counseling & Development, 100*(2), 134–45. https://doi.org/10.1002/jcad.12412.

Schoonover, T., & Perryman, K. (2023). Child-centered play therapy and adverse childhood experiences: A single-case research design. *Journal of Child and Adolescent Counseling, 9*(1), 1–20. https://doi.org/10.1080/23727810.2022.2138045.

Schottelkorb, A. A., Swan, K. L., & Ogawa, Y. (2020). Intensive child-centered play therapy for children on the autism spectrum: A pilot study. *Journal of Counseling & Development, 98*(1), 63–73. https://doi.org/10.1002/jcad.12300.

Stutey, D. M., Dunn, M., Shelnut, J., & Ryan, J. B. (2017). Impact of Adlerian play therapy on externalizing behaviors of at-risk preschoolers. *International Journal of Play Therapy, 26*(4), 196–206. https://doi.org/10.1037/pla0000055.

Swan, K. L., Kaff, M., & Haas, S. (2019). Effectiveness of group play therapy on problematic behaviors and symptoms of anxiety of preschool children. *The Journal for Specialists in Group Work, 44*(2), 82–98. https://doi.org/10.1080/01933922.2019.1599478.

Swank, J. M., Cheung, C., Prikhidko, A., & Su, Y.-W. (2017). Nature-based child-centered group play therapy and behavioral concerns: A single-case design. *International Journal of Play Therapy, 26*(1), 47–57. https://doi.org/10.1037/pla0000031.

Swank, J. M., & Smith-Adcock, S. (2018). On-task behavior of children with attention-deficit/hyperactivity disorder: Examining treatment effectiveness of play therapy interventions. *International Journal of Play Therapy, 27*(4), 187–97. https://doi.org/10.1037/pla0000084.

Tal, R., Tal, K., & Green, O. (2018). Child-parent relationship therapy with extra-familial abused children. *Journal of Child Sexual Abuse, 27*(4), 386–402. https://doi.org/10.1080/10538712.2018.1451420.

Taylor, L., & Ray, D. C. (2021). Child-centered play therapy and social–emotional competencies of African American children: A randomized controlled trial. *International Journal of Play Therapy*, *30*(2), 74–85. https://doi.org/10.1037/pla0000152.

Thomas, R., Abell, B., Webb, H. J., Avdagic, E., & Zimmer-Gembeck, M. J. (2017). Parent-child interaction therapy: A meta-analysis. *Pediatrics (Evanston)*, *140*(3). https://doi.org/10.1542/peds.2017-0352.

Valero-Aguayo, L., Rodríguez-Bocanegra, M., Ferro-García, R., & Ascanio-Velasco, L. (2021). Meta-analysis of the efficacy and effectiveness of parent child interaction therapy (Pcit) for child behaviour problems. *Psicothema*, *33*(4), 544–55. https://doi.org/10.7334/psicothema2021.70.

Ward, M. A., Theule, J., & Cheung, K. (2016). Parent–child interaction therapy for child disruptive behaviour disorders: A meta-analysis. *Child & Youth Care Forum*, *45*(5), 675–90. https://doi.org/10.1007/s10566-016-9350-5.

William Li, H. C., Lopez, V., & Lee, T. L. I. (2007). Effects of preoperative therapeutic play on outcomes of school-age children undergoing day surgery. *Research in Nursing & Health*, *30*(3), 320–32. https://doi.org/10.1002/nur.20191.

Wilson, B. J. & Ray, D. (2018). Child-centered play therarapy: Aggression, empathy and self-regulation. *Journal of counseling and development*, *96*(4), 399–409.

Wong, F. K., Leung, V. W., Chong, W. W., Hung, J. H., Wong, F., Leung, C., & Tsang, A. K. T. (2025). Capacity-building program for parents of children with SEN: A randomized controlled trial. *Research on Social Work Practice*, *35*(4), 358–371.

Zhang, H., Wang, W., & Li, Z. (2024). Effectiveness of parent–child interaction therapy for maltreated families: A meta-analysis of randomized controlled trials. *Trauma, Violence, & Abuse*, *25*(4), 2689–702. https://doi.org/10.1177/15248380231222041.

8

Play Therapy Supervision in Flux

Navigating Supervisee Change and Growth through the Transtheoretical Model of Clinical Supervision

Staci Born

Chapter Outline

Supervision is the foundation of effective and competent play therapy skill practice and therapist development (Longest, 2023). Quality play therapy supervision is informed by clinical supervision frameworks and purposeful integration of play therapy theory and techniques (Hudspeth, 2015). As standards for the development, education, and supervision of play therapists continue to evolve, play therapy supervision has become acknowledged as a specialized area of play therapy practice (Born et al., 2023). The APT Best Practices (2022) document provides some guidance on the provision of supervision in play therapy and defines supervision as:

> A formal professional clinical role which is recognized and defined by the relevant state law and professional guidelines of the supervisee's professional organization and/or APT. The intent is that the supervision time will be documented and reported to a third party so that

it can be applied toward professional licensure, registration and/or certification. As such, the supervisor maintains liability for the supervisee's clinical work. (p. 15)

Supervisors serve as gatekeepers of the play therapy profession. In this role, supervisors monitor, intervene, and verify that play therapy professionals possess and apply the necessary knowledge, adhere to ethical standards, and demonstrate competence in their field (Bernard & Goodyear, 2019).

While the Association for Play Therapy has continued to improve its requirements for those earning and maintaining their credentials, there is a widespread absence of consistency among the foundational clinical training, licensure, and supervision across different mental health disciplines (Baker, 2023; Falender, 2018). This lack of consistency creates a challenge for supervisors and the field of play therapy as a whole. There is an opportunity for play therapist supervisors to enhance the integrity and practice of play therapy supervision so as to raise the standard and quality of therapeutic support available to our youngest community members.

The Transtheoretical Model of Supervision provides more than a framework for practicing supervision (Aten et al., 2008); it provides a philosophy that change is ongoing, dynamic, and cyclical (Prochaska & DiClemente, 1983). This chapter will provide an overview of the Transtheoretical Model of Supervision and apply this model to play therapy supervision. Before introducing the Transtheoretical Model of Supervision, an overview of the Transtheoretical Model of Change will be reviewed. The chapter will conclude by providing examples of playful and expressive interventions to support supervisee transition between stages within the Transtheoretical Model.

Transtheoretical Model of Change

The Transtheoretical Model of Change (TMC) is a theoretical framework developed by Prochaska and DiClemente in the late 1970s and early 1980s to understand how individuals change behavior (Prochaska & DiClemente, 1983). The model, which has been widely used in health psychology and addiction counseling, asserts that change occurs gradually and through a series of stages as opposed to abruptly. Prochaska et al. (1982), developed TMC based on the assumption that the content of therapy changes based on the client (history, environment, personality, etc.), which will guide the focus of therapy more than the therapist's theoretical orientation. Additionally, the client serves as the content expert of their lives while the therapist serves as the expert on the processes that can support change (Prochaska et al., 1982). Prochaska and DiClemente (1983) identified stages that both precede and follow change:

1. Precontemplation: At this stage, individuals are not considering changing their behavior and may not even recognize that there is a need for change.
2. Contemplation: In this stage, individuals start to recognize that there is a problem and consider the possibility of making a change sometime in the future.

3. Preparation: During this stage, individuals intend to take action to change their behavior in the near future. They may start taking small steps toward change.
4. Action: This stage involves actively modifying behavior to bring about the desired change. Individuals put effort into changing their habits and take steps to overcome obstacles.
5. Maintenance: Once individuals have successfully changed their behavior, they enter the maintenance stage, where they work to prevent relapse and consolidate the gains they've made.

(Prochaska & DiClemente, 1983)

Movement through the stages is not linear; at any stage, an individual may regress to an earlier stage. In addition, moving from one stage to the next involves processes of change, discussed later in this chapter (Freyer, et al. 2006).

Transtheoretical Model of Clinical Supervision

Aten et al. (2008) introduced the Transtheoretical Model of Clinical Supervision (TMCS) by translating and adapting the Transtheoretical Model of Change (Prochaska & DiClemente, 1982, 1983, 1986; Prochaska & Norcross, 2007). TMCS asserts nine assumptions:

1. No one model of supervision can fully grasp the complexities inherent in the supervision process (Gilbert & Evans, 2001). Supervisee needs ought to drive the supervisor's selection and utilization of a variety of supervision techniques and modalities (Aten et al., 2008; Watkins & Scaturo, 2013).
2. Supervisees experience varying degrees of apprehension, motivation, and anxiety about their performance and competence (Aten et al., 2008; Bernard & Goodyear, 2014; Ellis et al., 2015; Stoltenberg & McNeill, 2010).
3. TMCS can support the overall professional growth and development of supervisees, and it can also be applied to address specific supervisee challenges or deficiencies.
4. Supervisees have varying degrees of openness and ability to grow (Aten et al., Stoltenberg & McNeill, 2010).
5. Assessment of supervisee needs is essential and requires individualization of supervisory interventions to supervisee needs (Axelsson et al., 2023; Watkins & Scaturo, 2013). Supervisors will be most effective when they are able to accurately evaluate a supervisee's needs utilizing the stage of change and then employing a corresponding intervention (Aten et al., 2008).
6. Applying TMCS, supervisors and supervisees will navigate clinical and supervisory encounters with greater complexity as their experiences advance and their supervisory alliance strengthens (Aten et al., 2008).

7. TMCS differs from psychotherapy-based models of supervision because it utilizes supervision constructs, techniques, and interventions from a variety of approaches (Aten et al., 2008).
8. TMCS allows for greater identification and tools necessary for flexible integration of diverse client and supervisee needs (Aten et al., 2008).
9. The advantages of this model are enhanced by supervisor experience, as a more advanced supervisor is better equipped to develop complex, integrative, and personalized approaches to supervision (Aten et al., 2008).

TMCS includes six Supervisee Stages of Change (SSC) used to support supervisors' conceptualization of supervisee needs and provide a model for intervening to support those needs at both the macro-level (play therapist development and knowledge) and micro-level (use of play therapy skills and interventions). While presented in a linear fashion, like TMC, it is understood that change is not a linear process but a cyclical process (Aten et al., 2008; Freyer et al., 2006).

The first SSC is Precontemplation, where supervisees may not recognize the potential for change, perceive change as unattainable, or exhibit resistance to the concept of change. While the supervisee is unaware, others may be very aware of the potential areas of needed growth. Precontemplative supervisees may react defensively if an adequate supervisory alliance has not been formed (Aten et al., 2008).

The second SSC is Contemplation. During this stage, supervisees acknowledge the need for change but may feel uncertain about how to initiate or fully commit to the process of change. This awareness of a professional deficit, but uncertainty about how to proceed, can foster feelings of anxiety, self-doubt, and stress (Turnbull, 2000). A key role for a supervisor is to acknowledge and normalize these feelings and offer support in considering the pros and cons associated with the potential change, too (Aten et al., 2008).

The next stage of SSC is Preparation. The hallmark of the Preparation stage is the awareness of the area in need of growth and an active intention to change. Some supervisees may even begin making small changes that precede larger shifts in behavior (Aten et al., 2008). Time in this stage is often short, as supervisees either quickly progress to Action or regress (Turnbull, 2000). During this stage of change, it is important to provide the supervisee with the time and space to establish goals that will result in small behavioral changes that lead to greater changes (Lehrman-Waterman & Ladany, 2001).

The fourth stage of change is the Action stage, where supervisees' desire for growth propels them into taking concerted action. This Action stage also requires supervisees to re-experience self-doubt, anxiety, and distress as they apply and implement new knowledge, skills, and interventions (Aten et al., 2008). Pearson (2004) cautions supervisors to monitor this growth, remain supportive and accessible, and not to assume too quickly that supervisees have attained competence.

In the fifth supervisee stage of change, the Maintenance stage, supervisees have begun to reap the benefits of their efforts and have started to gain confidence as they experience fewer setbacks. Effort is still required to sustain their area of change. Supervisors can assist supervisees in this stage by encouraging their forward progress, promoting the integration of developmental shifts, and fostering ongoing development (Aten et al., 2008). Integration of new skillsExperiential Processes and building on positive change is critical to prevent regression.

The final stage, Termination stage, is not meant to imply that supervision is complete or no longer needed. Instead, this stage marks the achievement of increased competency, acquisition of new skills, correction of problematic behavior, or a progression to a new developmental stage (Aten et al., 2008). Supervisees at this stage may assume a more solidified professional identity, use new skills and knowledge more fluidly and automatically, and can observe a greater therapeutic effect (Turnbull, 2000). This stage provides an excellent time for reflection on professional goals, development, and the supervisory relationship.

Supervisor Processes of Change

Individuals proceed from one stage of change to the next via defined processes of change (Freyer et al., 2006). Aten et al. (2008) adapted these processes of change to supervision, calling them the Supervisor Processes of Change. Utilizing the ten Supervisor Processes of Change (SPC) (Aten et al., 2008) described here, play therapist supervisors can support supervisees with experiential and/or behavioral interventions intended to facilitate a supervisee's movement from one SSC to the next.

A "process" describes *why* a pattern or change has evolved; a mechanism details *how* a process creates change. Important to play therapy, Schaefer & Peabody (2016) articulated that the "therapeutic powers of play are the mechanisms in play that actually produce the desired change [process] in a client's dysfunctional thoughts, feelings, and/or behaviors." A firm understanding of the therapeutic powers of play and how play creates therapeutic change may be more important than a supervisee's knowledge of play therapy theories, models, or techniques (Peabody & Schaefer, 2019). It is imperative for play therapist supervisors to support supervisees' awareness and application of the therapeutic powers of play to facilitate client change. Similarly, play therapist supervisors can utilize the therapeutic powers of play as a mechanism to support supervisee change.

Akin to a therapeutic relationship, a supervisory alliance allows for the formation of safety in the expression and exploration of professional and personal topics that can advance or impede therapeutic work. Play, as an expressive modality, allows for content to surface in the absence of intellectual defenses or resistances that may be known or unknown to the supervisor or supervisee. Like play therapy for children, SPCs can support supervisees in learning to manage emotional and behavioral challenges that hinder supervisee development by facilitating communication, fostering emotional wellness, enhancing social relationships, and increasing personal strengths (Schaefer & Drewes, 2014). Emphatically, supervision interventions are most effective when employed within the felt safety of a supportive supervisory alliance where supervisees can safely express challenges, receive and give feedback, and learn new ways of considering client cases and professional behaviors (Aten et al., 2008).

Experiential Processes

The Supervisor Processes for Change (SPC) includes five experiential processes that promote supervisee thinking and experiencing (Aten et al., 2008; Freyer et al., 2006). Experiential processes can be used across supervisee development; however, they may be most useful for novice play therapy supervisees.

The first experiential process is Consciousness Raising. Supervisors' use of purposeful questions can help the supervisee clarify meaning or identify alternative responses. This reflection enhances the supervisee's ability to conceptualize and treat clients in a more skilled manner (Aten et al., 2008). Examples of play therapy supervisory questions can be wide and may include: "How do you think the child's choice of toys during the session might reflect their emotional state or inner conflicts?" or "Can you elaborate on how this intervention aligns with the therapeutic power of play you are focusing on in session?" Play therapy supervisors may utilize direct questions, considering their supervisees' cognitive preferences (i.e., do they think about cases linearly or from a sensory perspective), or they may utilize expressive techniques aimed at eliciting consciousness-raising. For example, "using the sand and miniatures, illustrate how your child client's play themes, interactions and expressions correspond with your identified theoretical approach."

The inner ability of a supervisee to view cases from an affect-orientation perspective as opposed to solely a theory-based orientation, can be a pivotal place for supervisees to gain insight and release emotions and thoughts that may be interfering with the play therapy process (Axelsson et al., 2023). The experiential process, Dramatic Relief, can facilitate the supervisee's affective experiences and raise emotions related to a particular case (Aten et al., 2008). This could take place in a variety of forms in the supervisory relationship, such as sharing images of content created in play therapy sessions (i.e., sand trays or art projects) while reflecting on the emotions that arise while taking these still images. It could also be reflected in the re-enactment of play scenarios and providing the supervisee with opportunities to choose to respond differently so as to somatically and affectively experience the potency of therapeutic interventions.

As the self-of-play-therapist evolves, it is critical for supervisors to encourage the short- and long-term effects these changes have on themselves, their clients, and the supervisory relationship (Aten et al., 2008). It is well-understood that the accuracy of self-evaluation increases as supervisees gain experience. An additional experiential process is Self-Reevaluation. Play therapy supervisors can support supervisees through the experiential process of Self-Reevaluation. Self-Reevaluation can include expressive and playful techniques such as collaging, writing, sand tray, puppets, and art. Sample supervisory interventions to enhance Self-Reevaluation may include, "pick a puppet that represents an earlier professional self and a puppet that represents your current professional self. Then, have the puppets dialogue about what each puppet observes in the other," or "create a portrait of selves—one self-portrait to represent your past self, one self-portrait to represent your current self, and a third self-portrait to represent your future self." Supervisors can support supervisees in their self-reflection by considering both the short- and long-term effects their changes have had on themselves, their clients, and even the supervisory relationship. Of note, supervisees benefit from supervisors that offer a balance of encouragement and challenge in their self-evaluations (Steward et al., 2001)

Environmental Reevaluations call for reflection and evaluation of how supervisee behaviors (positive or problematic) have affected or are currently affecting their clients, themselves, and their supervisor. Self-reflection, client feedback, and constructive supervisory feedback are excellent sources of environmental reevaluation (Aten et al., 2008). An example of a playful way to integrate Environmental Reevaluations is to use toys and expressive techniques. For example, "go to the play kitchen and create a plate of food that represents the feedback you get from your environment—consider feedback you get (or don't get) from clients, yourself, your supervisor, and peers/colleagues." A rich discussion can include the amount and type of food from each environmental source, its nutritional value, what the supervisor wants to eat versus what they are provided, and the supervisee's assessment of the value and purpose of each source. In addition, consider how important reflections of culture and values can enhance evaluation and perspective-taking.

Like Consciousness Raising, Self-Liberation involves play therapy supervisees attaining increased self-awareness by assuming appropriate responsibility for their choices and actions (Aten et al., 2008). Supervisors may utilize expressive media (art, sand) or other activities (genograms, self-care inventories), or provide direct feedback to support Self-Liberation. An example play therapy supervisory intervention may include creating a sand genogram of messages the supervisee gained from their family-of-origin surrounding work-life balance: "select 3–5 miniatures that represent each of your family's generational attitude towards work-life balance."

Behavioral Processes

The Supervisor Processes for Change (SPC) includes five behavioral processes that enact supervisee behaviors and commitments (Aten et al., 2008; Freyer et al., 2006). Behavioral processes can be used across supervisee development; however, they may be most useful for advanced play therapy supervisees (Aten et al., 2008).

The first behavioral process, Stimulus Control, involves avoiding stimuli that may stall development or elicit problematic behavior (Aten et al., 2008). Shame, anxiety, and fear tend to be stimuli that, when experienced in large amounts, impede a play therapist's ability to provide attuned client care. Worsening situations can occur when supervisees avoid discussing these challenging emotions in supervision, making situations can become exacerbating or overwhelming. Supervisors can mitigate this by normalizing the experiences of difficult emotions, utilizing appropriate self-disclosure, and encouraging supervisees to explore if and when these challenging emotions arise, how they are able to self-soothe, and regulate. Supervisors can facilitate soothing and regulation in supervision to alleviate shame, anxiety, and fear by directly teaching and practicing regulation and soothing through multiple sensory systems in an effort to expand the supervisee's tolerance and understanding of their emotional states. Play therapist supervisors can support supervisees by providing immediate feedback and inquiry into supervisees' regulatory states and practicing behaviors that can enhance attunement and increase supervisee self-efficacy in working through difficult emotions. Another example of supporting stimulus control is caseload monitoring and selection (Watkins & Scaturo, 2013). Careful selection of cases that support supervisee development and promote the development of professional sophistication is a way that supervisors can meet the evolving needs of supervisees (Aten et al., 2008).

Counterconditioning, as an SPC, supports supervisees in exploring and developing alternate ways of thinking, feeling, and interacting with their clients. Traditionally, counterconditioning in supervision can include watching recorded sessions and providing live supervision or co-therapy (Aten et al., 2008; Watkins & Scaturo, 2013). Play therapy supervisors can enhance the counterconditioning processes following watching a recording or conducting live supervision by inviting the play therapist supervisee to engage in expressive modalities that allow the play therapist to identify unhelpful responses, understand the origins and patterns of those unhelpful responses, and then explore alternative responses or ways of thinking to empower change. Imagine a supervisor directing a supervisee to "create a sandtray that describes a time where you regretted something you did or said in a play therapy session."

Next, Contingency Management is meant to help supervisees learn and reward themselves for enacting positive changes (Aten et al., 2008). Play therapy supervision involves the establishment of supervisory goals that focus on desired play therapy competencies and specific areas of growth (APT, 2022). Supporting the supervisee in identifying and utilizing positive reinforcement (i.e., self-kindness, rewards) when they demonstrate their desired behavior or achieve a professional milestone. This supervisory dialogue sets the stage for the development of a play therapist that is better equipped to self-supervise as they gain professional independence in their practice.

Social liberation involves the supervisees' socialization as a play therapy professional (Aten et al., 2008). From the supervisory relationship and consultation to advanced training and attending annual conferences, socialization as a professional supports the evolution of professionals at any stage (Aten et al., 2008; Ellis et al., 2015). Supporting supervisees' exploration and understanding of the variety of roles and environments that play therapists can exist in supports supervisees in maintaining an expansive versus limiting lens of the profession. Additionally, expressive techniques with sand, art, and writing can help supervisees explore their wishes, dreams, and even anticipated barriers to their professional growth and hopes.

Last, and perhaps most importantly, change can be nurtured through the development of a Helping Relationship (Aten et al., 2008; Bernard & Goodyear, 201; Stoltenberg & McNiell, 2010). The safety that is purposefully fostered by competent play therapy supervisors is intended to invite vulnerable expression and exploration of professional issues that are inherent and demanding in the field of play therapy. Without this supportive relationship, supervisees are at risk of feeling "unanchored" or lost, and the risks of burnout and vicarious trauma also dramatically increase. Careful attention, thoughtful feedback, purposeful exploration, and nurturance of the play therapy supervisory relationship ensure that reflection, support, and feedback are ongoing, bidirectional, and meant to help play therapy supervisees grow.

Conclusion

In conclusion, the integration of the therapeutic elements of play within the framework of the Transtheoretical Model of Clinical Supervision (TMCS) offers a valuable approach for enhancing the effectiveness of play therapy supervision. By acknowledging and incorporating the therapeutic powers inherent in play, alongside the change perspective provided by the TMCS, supervisors can create a supportive and individualized framework that nurtures the development of play therapists. Furthermore, the TMCS facilitates a nuanced understanding of supervisee development and their readiness for change, without being bound to any specific theoretical orientation. This combined approach not only enriches the supervision process but also fosters a deeper appreciation of the complexities involved in play therapist development and the therapeutic process itself—preparing competent play therapy professionals to support the growth and development of the future of play therapy.

References

Association for Play Therapy. (2022). Play therapy best practices: Clinical, professional, & ethical issues. https://cdn.ymaws.com/www.a4pt.org/resource/resmgr/publications/best_practices.pdf.

Aten, J. D., Strain, J. D., & Gillespie, R. E. (2008). A transtheoretical model of clinical supervision. *Training and Education in Professional Psychology, 2*, 1–9. http://dx.doi.org/10.1037/1931-3918.2.1.1.

Axelsson, S., Kihlberg, S., Davis, P., & Nystrom, M. B. T. (2023). Psychotherapy students' experiences of supervisee-centered supervision based on deliberate practice, feedback-informed treatment and self-compassion. *Counselling and Psychotherapy Research, 00*, 1–15. https://doi.org/10.1002/capr.12708.

Baker, C. (2023). History and overview of play therapy supervision. In S. L. Born & C. Baker (Eds.), *Play therapy supervision: A practical guide to models and best practices* (pp. 3–8). Routledge.

Bernard, J. M. & Goodyear, R. K. (2014). *Fundamentals of clinical supervision* (5th ed.). Pearson.

Bernard, J. M., & Goodyear, R. K. (2019). *Fundamentals of clinical supervision* (6th ed.). Pearson.

Born, S. L., Timm-Davis, N., & Gislason, E. (2023). Models of clinical supervision in play therapy supervision. In S. L. Born & C. Baker (Eds.), *Play therapy supervision: A practical guide to models and best practices* (pp. 22–56). Routledge.

Ellis, M. V., Hutman, H., & Chapin, J. (2015). Reducing supervisee anxiety: Effects of a role induction intervention for clinical supervision. *Journal of Counseling Psychology, 62*(4), 608–20. http://dx.doi.org/10.1037/cou0000099.

Falender, C. A. (2018). Clinical supervision – The missing ingredient. *American Psychologist, 73*(9), 1240–50. https://doi.org/10.1037/amp0000385.

Freyer, J., Bott, K., Riedel, J., Wedler, B., Meyer, C., Rumpf, H., et al. (2006). Psychometric properties of the 'Processes of Change' scale for alcohol misuse and its short form (POC-20). *Addictive Behaviors, 31*, 821–32. https://doi.org/10.1016/j.addbeh.2005.06.007.

Gilbert, M., & Evans, K. (2001). *Psychotherapy supervision: An integrative-relational approach.* Open University Press.

Hudspeth, E. F. (2015). Clinical supervision in play therapy: Research, practice, and application. *International Journal of Play Therapy, 24*(2), 55–8, https://doi.org/10.1037/pla0000011.

Lehrman-Waterman, D., & Ladany, N. (2001). Development and validation of the evaluation process within supervision inventory. *Journal of Counseling Psychology, 48*, 168–77. https://doi.org/10.1037//0022-0167.48.2.168.

Longest, C. (2023). Best practices and ethical considerations in play therapy supervision. In S. L. Born & C. Baker (Eds.), *Play therapy supervision: A practical guide to models and best practices* (pp. 57–68). Routledge.

Peabody, M. A., & Schaefer, C. E. (2016). Towards semantic clarity in play therapy. *International Journal of Play Therapy, 25*, 197–202. https://doi.org/10.1037/ pla0000025.

Peabody, M. A., & Schaefer, C. E. (2019, September). The therapeutic powers of play: The heart and soul of play therapy. *Play Therapy Magazine.*

Pearson, Q. M. (2004). Getting the most out of clinical supervision: Strategies for mental health. *Journal of Mental Health Counseling, 26*, 361–73. https://doi.org/10.17744/mehc.26.4.tttju8539ke8xuq6.

Prochaska, J. O., & DiClemente, C. C. (1983). Stages and processes of self-change of smoking: Toward an integrative model of change. *Journal of Consulting and Clinical Psychology, 51*(3), 390–95. https://doi.org/10.1037//0022-006x.51.3.390.

Prochaska, J. O., & DiClemente, C. C. (1986). The transtheoretical approach. In J. C. Norcross (Ed.), *Handbook of eclectic counselor* (pp. 163–99). Routledge.

Prochaska, J. O., & Norcross, J. C. (2007). *Systems of psychotherapy: A transtheoretical analysis* (6th ed.). Wadsworth.

Prochaska, J. O., Crimi, P., Lapsanski, D., Martel, L., & Reid, P. (1982). Self-change processes, self-efficacy and self-concept in relapse and maintenance of cessation of smoking. *Psychological Reports, 51*(3), 983–90. https://doi.org/10.2466/pr0.1982.51.3.983.

Schaefer, C. E., & Drewes, A. A. (Eds.). (2014). *The therapeutic powers of play: 20 core agents of change* (2nd ed.). Wiley.

Steward, R. J., Breland, A., & Neil, D. M. (2001). Novice supervisees' self-evaluations and their perceptions of supervisory style. *Counselor Education and Supervision, 41*, 131–41. https://doi.org/10.1002/j.1556 6978.2001.tb01277.x.

Stoltenberg, C. D., & McNeill, B. W. (2010). *IDM supervision: An integrative developmental model for supervising counselors and therapists* (3rd ed.). Taylor & Francis.

Turnbull, J. (2000). The transtheoretical model of change: Examples of stammering. *Counseling Psychology Quarterly, 13*, 13–22. https://doi.org/10.1080/09515070050011033.

Watkins, C. E., & Scaturo, D. J. (2013). Toward an integrative, learning-based model of psychotherapy supervision: Supervisory alliance, educational interventions, and supervisee learning/relearning. *Journal of Psychotherapy Integration, 23*(1), 75–95. https://doi.org/10.1037/a0031330.

Part II

Comparing Theoretical Approaches through the Lens of the Therapeutic Powers of Play

1

Psychoanalytic Play Therapy

The Power of the Creative Force to Unlock the Unconscious

Dana Wyss and Athena A. Drewes

Chapter Outline

"Children use play to communicate at their own level and at their own pace, without feeling interrogated or threatened"—Anna Freud (1965)

Introduction

In nearly 100 years of using play therapeutically, psychoanalytic approaches to play therapy have evolved substantially. Although most students are taught outmoded psychoanalytic theory, psychoanalysis actively continues to address a wide range of current issues, such as individual alienation, identity and diversity, marginalization and exclusion, and emerging cultural realities (Levy, 2011).

"Psychoanalytic therapy" has dramatically evolved since Freud first coined the term in the early 1900s. The use of play to treat children, in a non-directive and child-led way, however, dates back to the 1930s with Hermione Hug Hellmuth, Anna Freud, and Melanie Klein. Shortly after, play therapy based on psychoanalytic theory was established and has been an essential part of the work through the years (Punnett, 2016). Contemporary analytic theorists and clinicians have extended these views to the neurobiological spheres. Advances include Jungian analysis, psychodynamic psychotherapies, developmental psychology, attachment theory, and object relations theory, which all underline the importance of early relationships, family dynamics, and attachment patterns in shaping personality and psychological makeup (Tarzian, Ndrio & Fakoya, 2023). This chapter will explore the origins and foundation of psychoanalytic play therapy, its theoretical basis, and the therapeutic powers of play employed.

Important Contributors

Sigismund Shlomo "Sigmund" Freud

Sigmund Freud laid the foundation for psychodynamic play therapy. Although he clinically focused on adults, his informal analyses of his own children, most notably Anna Freud, and treatment of Little Hans, a five-year-old boy with a horse phobia (1930), set the stage for the logical next step of treating children (Bromfield, 2003). Freud stated "every child at play behaves like a creative writer, in that he creates a world of his own or rather, re-arranges the things of his world in a new way which pleases him" (pp. 141–154). Freud recognized that play involves a suspension rather than a denial of reality (Freud, 1930; Levy, 2011).

At the core, Freud's work propelled therapy into a new realm, including the use of art and play to explore and unlock the inner world. "Art is a vehicle for psychical conflicts, and that creativity is a form of sublimation" (Freud & Kul-Want, 2010). Freud's curiosity about the unconscious desire and the death drive and their relation to the psyche's predilection for pleasure also led to advances in trauma work through his observations of soldiers returning from the First World War (Freud, 1920).

Hermine von Hug-Hellmuth

Hermine von Hug-Hellmuth, a teacher in Vienna, became the first child psychoanalyst to formally treat children with talk and play, using and interpreting children's spontaneous play and working with parents as needed, preceding Anna Freud and Melanie Klein by several years (Bromfield, 2003; Punnett, 2016). She initially treated her young clients in their own homes, appreciating the influence of family and saw the child's difficulties rooted in their parents' unresolved troubles (Bromfield, 2003).

Not only did she understand the importance of the child's spontaneous play and its themes and interpretations, but she also found it equally important to share this with the parents. Hug-Hellmuth believed the child would experience a better upbringing, including education and development through that didactic work. She (1920) wrote that "[t]he analysis both of the child and of the adult has the same end and object; namely, the restoration of the psyche to health and equilibrium which have been endangered through influences known and unknown" (p. 287). She also believed that conscious insight was not necessary for a child to find relief and help in play (Bromfield, 2003). Due to her premature death and the fact that she is often not given credit in future research, little is known about her life or work (Plastow, 2011; Punnett, 2016).

Anna Freud

Anna Freud, daughter of Sigmund Freud, is considered one of the major founders and mothers of child psychoanalysis, and is most cited regarding child therapy. She opened the Hampstead Child-Therapy Clinic in 1947. Her goal of treatment was to help children come to consciously understand why they thought, felt, and behaved as they did, and that insight invited change (Bromfield, 2003). Her theory was based on the psychosexual stages developed by Sigmund Freud, but she expanded it to include the relationship between normal development and formation of psychopathology due to the child's significant attachment to others from birth to adolescence. Blockages in the progression of development were the underlying cause of psychopathology and the goal of treatment was removal of these blockages so natural, healthy development could occur. She respected the child's behavior and defenses as ways to cope with anxieties, traumas, life experiences and growing up. She also considered factors such as the child's health, living conditions, cognitive ability, as well as promoting parent guidance and school consultation, as important aspects of child therapy (Bromfield, 2003).

Anna Freud viewed child analysis as having the aim of increasing ego control by expanding consciousness. However, she diverged from Melanie Klein in that she believed that children were not capable of forming the transference neurosis which was central to adult analysis because their primary objects (parents) were still actively alive in their lives and prevented transposing neurotic conflicts onto the analyst, and that child analysts cannot be neutral to their clients (Freud, 1965). The child analyst could not be a blank screen whereby the child projects their internal dynamics (Levy, 2011). She felt that because of the analyst's dependence and close work with the child's parent and others in their environment, made the analyst a real object to the child, and prevented the development of a transference neurosis.

While not seeing play as equivalent to free association, as did Klein, Anna Freud did see interpretation as central to child analysis. Interpretation was seen as a means to help children become aware of the defenses they employed. She also used verbalization and clarification of preconscious material, suggestion and reassurance (Levy, 2011).

Anna Freud elaborated on her father's psychosexual stages to include the gradual evolution of attachments to others outside of the immediate family. She further explored and expanded on the continuum of what is considered normal development versus the formation of psychopathology (Punnett, 2016; Freud, 1965). She believed that the goal of the work was to remove blockages that lead to psychopathology to allow for healthy development. Moreover, consistent contact with the parents and a detailed life history of the client were necessary to gain a further understanding of the child's daily life (Punnett, 2016).

Melanie Klein

Melanie Klein (1955) saw the child's play in therapy as the equivalent of the adult's free associations and that play was the vehicle to making interpretations directly even to very young children's unconscious (Bromfield, 2003). Klein focused on the young child's experiences of abandonment, envy and rage, especially around the relationship with the mother, the primary object relationship.

She developed a theory which describes the importance of playing for ego development and the interplay between internal and external reality (1955). According to Klein (1955), children's object relations begin almost at birth, and arise with the first breastfeeding experience (Ramires, 2016). The way the child experiences the external world is constantly being influenced by the internal world which is being developed. Ego development occurs on the basis of intense drives and conflicts.

Klein saw play as where the child is able to symbolize, or displace, emotions, fantasies, fears, anger, guilt and anxieties onto other objects in the external world, that are not the primary objects (parents, caregivers) (Klein, 1955). The role of the analyst would be to interpret the fantasies and anxieties underlying the play (Ramires, 2016).

For Klein (1955), the child's formation of transference neurosis with the therapist allowed for interpretation and analysis of play, to discern the roots of the conflict. Child analysis, therefore, required the interpretation of feelings, anxieties, and expressions through the play (Levy, 2011). Interpretation was crucial as it facilitated contact with the unconscious of the child and removed repression of intrapsychic material (Levy, 2011). Thus, play was seen as a vehicle for interpretation of deeply unconscious fantasies rather than a therapeutic vehicle (Levy, 2011).

D. W. Winnicott

Winnicott (1971) followed Klein's objects relations approach but furthered the understanding of play. He saw play as a thing in and of itself, overcoming the concept of sublimation (Ramires, 2016). Winnicott (1971) saw play as "a reflection of the child's capacity to occupy a space between psychic and external reality in which the child uses elements from both domains" (p.15). Thus, allowing the child to internalize their relationships with their caretakers, and with the therapist, cocreate representations of new and more successful ways of experiencing self and others, and of relating (Levy, 2011). Winnicott used interpretation judiciously, for the purpose of shifting unconscious transference, and presented interpretations in a nondogmatic manner, so that children were free to accept or reject them (Levy, 2011). For Winnicott (1971), play was inherently therapeutic because it opened potential space in the therapeutic relationship, and within this metaphorical space, the child could symbolically destroy, differentiate from and use the analyst (Levy, 2011). He believed it was possible to do deep psychotherapy through play without interpretation as the pleasurable component of play was the blending of intrapsychic reality with the control of actual objects, such as the therapist.

In addition to the above major contributors to analytical psychology, are Margaret Lowenfeld, Dora Maria Kalff and Carl Jung. Space does not allow expounding on these theorists, and readers are directed to chapters within this volume that cover them more extensively.

Underlying Philosophy

The foundations of psychoanalytic theory highlight the importance of exploring unconscious information and emotional conflicts and developing a strong sense of self. Our core primary attachments and experiences shape our feelings and way of being in the world, and these experiences build our belief systems. The core emergence of self occurs developmentally before language, ergo these experiences and imprints become encoded within us (Spiel et al., 2019).

Early child analysts viewed play as a route into the unconscious minds of children, much as dreams are used therapeutically for adults (Levy, 2011). Play was also recognized as a useful medium as children were unable to use the traditional method of lying on the couch and engaging in free association. By creating a setting that allowed the child to relax and loosen the ego's control, material would be revealed to consciousness in a symbolic, disguised form (Levy, 2011). This setting would be congruent with the child's developmental level, so that fears, wishes and needs would be expressed naturally. And thus, the therapist would be able to observe, interpret and engage children therapeutically (Levy, 2011). Consequently, play became the primary route for child analysis as it served to develop a sense of mastery, allowed for wish fulfillment, permitted assimilation of powerful experiences, transformed experiences of the individual from passive to active, was a route for fantasizing about internalized representations of important people, and became a vehicle for gaining distance from the demands of reality and the superego (Levy, 2011).

Access to the Unconscious

Early analysts saw that unconscious conflicts were pressing for expression but the ego controlled expression. Consequently, the therapist became "archeologists of the mind," unearthing the fragments of childhood conflicts that lay hidden beneath the surface of the unconscious (Levy, 2011). Freud wrote of insight, facilitated by the therapist's interpretations and analysis of transference (Schaefer, 1993), as the key component toward curing a client in psychoanalysis.

Sigmund Freud (1920) defined "dream work" as the mental processes that transform unacceptable, unconscious wishes and impulses into acceptable, if often undecipherable, conscious dream images. This dream work is adaptive because it allows people to sleep undisturbed by thoughts and impulses which, if known, would awaken them and cause distress.

According to Elkind (1981), "play work" is a parallel mental process and serves as the royal road to the child's unconscious. Interpretation by the play therapist is often needed to decipher the hidden meaning and give insight into unconscious mental processes. In both play work and dream work, one primarily bypasses the censorship of the superego by the defense mechanisms of projection, displacement, and symbolization, sublimation, and fantasy compensation (Drewes & Schaefer, 2016).

Just as Freud discusses that dreams are a pathway to the unconscious and the way to unlock these truths, similarly, one could assert that play is a pathway to the unconscious. Through the analysis of symbolic meaning, these truths and deeper psychological conflicts and motivations are revealed. (Klein, 1955; Punnett, & Green, 2019). Metaphors are a higher form of cognition and play an important role in affect regulation and the development of self-complexity (Levy, 2011).

A key task of psychoanalysis is overcoming resistance and gaining self-awareness. Thus use of art and play offers a less threatening means than direct discussion and contact with the material (Searle & Streng, 2001).

Transference

Psychoanalytic therapy is deeply rooted in exploring the experience of transference, countertransference, and projective identity. By exploring these experiences and past relationships that have shaped the individual, and by being understood, healing can occur. Klein offered interpretations very early in the analysis, believing children established an immediate transference. The success of the analysis came from the delivery of a correct interpretation and not from any preparation or from being sensitive to the child's milieu. She interpreted the child's behavior from the onset and bypassed the defenses, striking directly at the unconscious symbolic meanings of the child's play in the session; thus, the main focus was on defenses. In contrast, Anna Freud believed it important to prepare children for interpretation and to be sensitive to the milieu in which the child resides

(Punnett, 2016). Her method involved having a preparatory phase consolidating the working relationship between child and therapist, then careful interpretation of defenses and later the drives as the repressed became more and more conscious. Her main focus was the ego (Punnett, 2016).

Consistent supervision to address these experiences is pivotal to fully understanding the treatment dynamics (Punnett, 2016).

Projection is a process in which one attributes unacceptable parts of oneself, that is, thoughts, feelings, impulses, to individuals or play objects. This can be done in either a conscious or unconscious manner. It is a way of believing that certain characteristics belong to someone or something else rather than taking responsibility for them. The individual projects feelings and experiences about their current and past attachment figures and significant experiences onto the therapist and the space (Drewes & Schaefer, 2016; Schaefer, 1993). This may happen through the relationship, through interactions inside or outside of the therapy room, or through the play and art created in sessions. Transference can be positive, wherein feelings of love, admiration, or idealization are expressed. Alternatively, negative transference can occur where the individual reacts with anger, resentment, or mistrust from unresolved conflicts experienced in the past (Freud, 1912).

Countertransference is the therapist's emotional reactions and responses to the child and their projections, which can, in turn, either inform or negatively impact the therapeutic relationship. Sometimes what we feel in response tells us more about ourselves and our own issues, some of which are unresolved and need to be kept out of the child's way. At other times, it can help us understand what is going on in the child and the treatment (Bromfield, 2003).

Projective identification is when the individual projects parts of themselves onto objects or figures in the play scenario, seeing themselves in a similar way.

Model of Psychopathology

Sigmund Freud conceptualized mental illness not as a single traumatic event, but rather as a condition that developed over time and was linked to the person's life history (Punnett, 2016). These unconscious contents cause anxiety and pressure to be released into the conscious mind. The mind is always under pressure, for the expression of two instinctual drives, sexuality and aggression. And their expression went against social mores and needed to fit in socially. These unacceptable thoughts and wishes are kept out of our awareness and are repressed, and then expressed only symbolically (Punnett, 2016).

Psychopathology occurs when the client experiences regression in times of stress, which is related to a strong preference or fixation for one instinct. Blockages in the development stunt the ability to flourish and lead to maladaptive defensive behaviors. "In psychoanalytic psychology, problems are viewed as disturbances when regulating impulses between the id, ego, superego. The ego fails at regulating the demands of the id, the superego, and the external reality" (Punnett & Green, 2019, p. 46). When these components are in conflict, defenses arise to deal with the conflict, with some defenses more primitive than others, such as denial versus projection. Sigmund Freud used the term neurosis when a conflict between the id and superego occurs, and the ego is unable to resolve this conflict or becomes overwhelmed by depression or anxiety. When this occurs, the child might regress to an earlier stage of development or become fixated at the stage of development where the conflict or trauma occurred. Once the individual can rely more on the Ego than the Id, balance leads to growth in healthy relationships and logical decisions, and the individual functions optimally, being able to tolerate frustration and cope with conflict (Punnett, 2016).

The Structure of Personality

Id: The id consists of raw instinctual activity and psychic energy (Punnett, 2016). It is the most primitive and operational part, based on the pleasure of immediate gratification of desires and needs. These instinctual drives are unconscious.

Ego: This develops from the Id and Superego and is the relative principle that mediates the Id's desires with the external world and what is socially acceptable. It is the mind's central organizing agency (Punnett, 2016).

Super-ego: This is the intrapsychic structure that represents learned cultural standards (Punnett, 2016). It is the internalized social contract and moral values acquired from caregivers and culture. It works to suppress the Id and increase morally acceptable behavior.

When these components are in conflict, the use of defense mechanisms comes into play in order to allow the individual to continue to function or defend against perceived threats, whether they are real or might be imagined (Punnett, 2016).

Freud's Understanding of Child Development

Sigmund Freud proposed an understanding of development through the lens of psychosexual stages of development. These centered on the core desires of each stage, which were related to different areas of the body and centered around the need to satisfy these desires. If someone experiences too little or too much gratification during any stage, they could experience fixation. This becomes an unresolved conflict, leading to issues related to the corresponding stage, and has the potential to lead to regression in times of stress (Freud, 1919; Punnett, 2016).

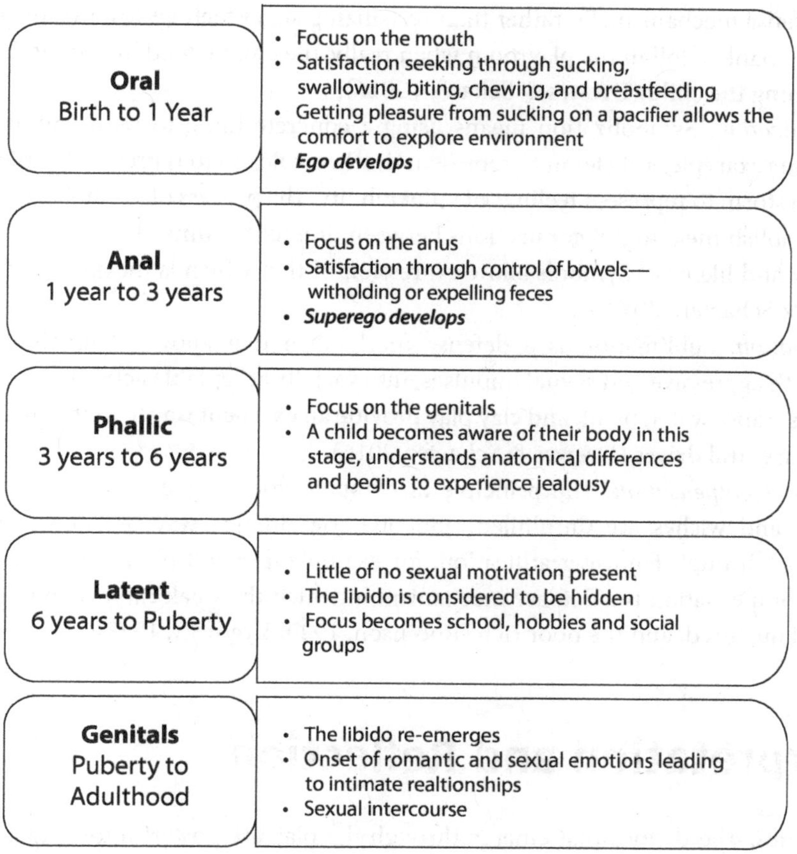

Figure 1.1 Psychosexual Stages of Development

Psychoanalytic Play Therapy Theory

Through observation of child-led symbolic play and free play, the therapist can analyze recurring themes, interpret transference, and use the playroom as a projective space. This therapeutic space becomes a holding environment for the child to act out and explore. The therapist utilizes the relationship instead of any specific directive or tool to create this opportunity. The toys and art materials then become a catalyst for the unconscious, allowing the child to express and work through underlying conflicts and anxieties. As the therapist observes this experience, they can interpret the symbolic representations to gain insight into the child's inner world (Bromfield, 2003; Punnett & Green, 2019).

Key Components

Displacement in the play room involves taking out frustrations, feelings, and impulses on play objects that are less threatening. Displacement of aggression is a common example of this defense mechanism. So rather than verbalizing angry feelings towards the mother, a child may spank a doll in the playroom when really, the child would like to hit the mother for punishing the child (Drewes & Schaefer, 2016).

Symbolization. Symbolization means using a concrete thing to represent an abstract concept, for example, a skeleton to represent death, a volcano to represent hostile feelings, a boat in a storm to represent feelings of vulnerability. The process of symbolization enables one to establish meaningful connections between different realms of experience based on proximity and likeness. Symbols allow expression of that which is inexpressible in words (Drewes & Schaefer, 2016).

Sublimation. Sublimation is a defense mechanism that allows channeling libidinal drives, both aggressive and sexual impulses, into socially acceptable activities, for example, art, sports. Sand, water, paint, and clay play provide an excellent way to gratify unconscious anal and urethral drives (Drewes & Schaefer, 2016).

Fantasy Compensation. The principle of compensatory activity is when one's needs, impulses, and wishes are unfulfilled, and one tries in one way or another to obtain satisfaction through fantasy gratification, for example, pretend play, movies, and books. Fantasy compensation is a defense mechanism in which the weak can become strong, the neglected nurtured, and the poor rich (Robinson, 1920; Vygotsky, 1978).

Interpretation and Reflection

Play themes: The themes that emerge through the play are powerful tools that assist the therapist in understanding the child's inner world. They can allow a window into their emotional and psychological states. Symbolization and unconscious communication themes may include fighting, building, knocking down, and nurturing. These can all serve as symbolic representations of internal conflicts and desires (Winnicott, 1971).

Separation and individuation: The child may leave things behind, hide things in the office, or exhibit anxiety about separating from an attachment figure (Drewes & Schaefer, 2016).

Aggression and control: At times when a client feels scared, powerless, or helpless, feelings of frustration, rivalry, or the need to control may manifest in the playroom (Drewes & Schaefer, 2016).

Attachment and Rejection: Nurturing, caregiving, and dependency, as well as fears of rejection, often play out in the therapeutic space. Attachment theory is essential in understanding how early relationships influence current behavior (Drewes & Schaefer, 2016).

Fantasy and Wish Fulfillment: Fantasy is paramount to the development of the psyche. Play allows children to express wishes and desires. They can experience power, success, and control when they may have felt powerless (Drewes & Schaefer, 2016).

Trauma and Healing: Whether the trauma is physical, emotional, sexual, or psychological, play offers a powerful means for children to work through their experiences. The child may repeat play about injury, rescue, or survival while the therapist observes and interprets the meaning to facilitate healing (Drewes & Schaefer, 2016).

Conceptualizing Goals of Treatment

The goal of psychoanalytic therapy is to help the id, ego, and superego come into balance, and allow the different instinctual forces, at the developmental level, to resolve. By lowering defenses, through nondirective, child-led play, the child is able to access perceived threats, whether real or imagined, and bring them into consciousness through symbolic play and therapist interpretation. Regression, in service of the ego, may occur to access earlier stages that have become fixated or unresolved in order to bring to consciousness and ultimately free up psychic energy and move development forward.

Anna Freud (1965) viewed interpretation as central to child analysis. The role of interpretation was a means to help children become aware of the defenses they employed because they were more rigid than those of adults. The analyst uses interpretation judiciously and balances between internal and external elements of the case (Levy, 2011).

Analytic play therapy is not simply about the uncovering and analysis of the wound. By following the internal productions of these images and symbols through the child's play and expression, the therapist can understand the core psychological issues and wounds, usually by assisting in the production of symbol-making. In treatment, the child's ego becomes stronger and more flexible, and in turn the family also becomes more understanding and flexible (Punnett, 2016).

Treatment Stages. The treatment stages are the *initial phase*, the *working phase*, and the *end phase*. The *initial phase* is an introduction and orientation to therapy (intake, treatment goals with parents and child, understanding the freedom of the therapy space). The focus of the initial phase of treatment seeks to induce an ego state conducive to perceiving inner conflicts via the interpretation of defenses (Levy, 2011).

The *working phase* includes chaos, struggle, reparation, and resolution, whereby the child's negative thoughts, feelings, and struggles are experienced and projected upon the therapist. Testing of limits will occur both with the therapist and the larger context of the child's family and social life. Specific trauma may be divulged, toys used symbolically in disclosure of fantasies, fears, worries, and past events, with the goal to transform these affects in such a way as to serve the child. Progress is cyclical, with regression in ways that serve the child, then progression, until the child has acquired sufficient ego strength to maintain the gains.

The *end phase* is when termination of treatment occurs, determined by the therapist, seeing that the child has made sufficient gains. The frequency of sessions is reduced, and the child has some control over the termination, and prepares for it (Punnett, 2016).

The goal of analytic child play therapy is to recover mental health, to reestablish a balance of the psyche that has been disturbed by impressions both known and unknown. The use of play in all its forms and the use of symbolic material that arises from this constitutes the psychodynamic approach. The goal for growth and maturation is to develop and to keep pace with chronological and mental abilities, to free the flow of energy so it is not to be inhibited by the use of defense mechanisms and to help the child develop a unique identity and experiences such that the child can adapt in spite of particular life circumstances to meet the demands of family, school and society (Punnett, 2016).

Role of the Therapist

The therapist and their way of being are the therapy in psychoanalysis. The inquisitive, genuine, authentic, and empathic response and acceptance of the child are paramount. The therapist strives to create an atmosphere of safety and acceptance, of genuine positive regard for the child. The play therapist's empathic and inquisitive posture toward the child, experience, and self-expression are essential (Bromfield, 2003). As psychoanalysis is a self-inquiry, it is essential that the therapist respects the child's thoughts, feelings, behaviors, and play (Bromfield, 2003). We aim to create the conditions in which a child will be most willing to risk the pain and humiliation of looking in the "mirror" of reality (Bromfield, 2003). The therapist works with the child in a nondirective and child-led way, allowing the child to select the toys and ways to utilize them, while observing the play and assessing the underlying symbolic meaning being presented.

The child analyst's role is primarily seen as that of bringing unconscious conflicts into conscious awareness and strengthening ego control over the child's life. This often is accomplished through the development and interpretation of transference material that emerged through the child's play, reflecting back what the child has produced. Early child analysts tried to minimize the impact of their own participation in the play setting to avoid contaminating the material with their own presence.

Contemporary psychoanalytic child therapists treat play mainly as a vehicle for the expression and interpretation of preconscious and unconscious material, and the engagement of the therapist with the child directly through play itself is therapeutic (Levy, 2011). The therapist is an observer and also a participant, while maintaining the ability to think analytically about what is transpiring in the interaction and in the room, including what is happening verbally, nonverbally, and symbolically in the play (Allan, 1997; Punnett, 2016). The play therapist also must accept a measure of uncertainty due to the relative ambiguity of the meaning of the child's play. The child therapist needs to cultivate patience and let the therapeutic relationship emerge and evolve (Levy, 2011).

The therapist uses their own ego to assess feeling states, emotions, and fantasies from within, to analyze the play, and then to make appropriate interventions using these insights to understand the unconscious processes in the child. At any point in time, the therapist will consider an intervention based on these factors and make a decision to: (a) observe,

(b) reflect on feelings and thoughts, (c) ask for clarifications or amplification of the symbol, or (d) use interpretation to link feelings and thoughts to the past or present, to help an issue become clearer or more understandable, or to assist in resolving a current relationship problem (Punnett, 2016).

The therapeutic relationship is paramount. Depending on which roots of psychoanalytic theory you follow as a modern psychoanalytic play therapist, will determine how soon you move into the interpretation of the material. Construction of a therapeutic, psychoanalytic relationship permits a sense of security to develop. This relationship allows unacceptable psychically dangerous feelings to emerge and be addressed in more productive ways (Levy, 2011).

The importance of the therapeutic relationship is stressed by Stern's (1985, p. 2) investigation of the "now moments" as that "all the events that regulate the feelings of attachment, physical proximity, and security are mutually created experiences . . . they cannot exist as a part of known self-experience without an *other*." Neuroscience research further underscores that having face-to-face contact has the potential for rewiring brain patterns previously established at the neurophysiological level and through psychotherapy this interactive repair, or as Anna Freud wrote, the "corrective emotional experience" with the therapist in the therapeutic relationship aids in the resilience of the patient to cope with life's ups and downs (Punnett, 2016).

The therapeutic alliance is especially complicated in psychoanalytic child treatment since the therapist must maintain working alliances with the child's caretakers, teachers, school-based mental health professionals, and others. Child therapists must develop working alliances with other adults while also keeping the needs and subjectivity of their child patients central and alive (Levy, 2011).

Many play therapists make use of analytic techniques such as symbolic play, interpretation, and sand tray work. Training is a necessary component, being first and foremost a qualified and licensed mental health professional and having achieved foundational competence in play therapy (Punnett, 2016) through academic training and clinical supervision in the use of analytical techniques. To be a child analyst, one must also complete their own personal analyses to gain perspectives on their own childhood conflicts so as to be able to tolerate issues that may be raised by children or parents (Punnett, 2016). In addition, the child analyst must also have a capacity for introspection, maturity, be able to play and be in touch with the inner child that exists in all of us, and a willingness to be open, as well as the ability to be empathic without overidentifying with or being repulsed by the child's behavior (Punnett, 2016).

Roles of Caregivers and Collaterals

Hug-Hellmuth worked with the parents as needed to continue to work with the child.

Sigmund Freud worked directly with the parents and did not have direct contact with the child client. Anna Freud saw parents as collaterals, meeting on a regular basis, necessary in obtaining family history and background information along with current functioning, and consulting with them as needed. Anna Freud thought it important to keep in close contact with the child's parents, to work from a detailed life history of the child, and to gain an understanding of the child's daily life experiences. She did not work directly with the parents on the resolution of their contributing issues; rather, she referred them for their own analysis (Punnett, 2016). Melanie Klein preferred minimal contact with the parents, as it would interfere with the transference with the child and the analytic work.

In modern psychoanalysis, parents are considered collaterals and are not brought directly into the therapy of the child. However, parents are the primary source of information about the child and the home. Parents can tell us their perceptions of the child's behaviors at home, getting along with peers or siblings, and at school (Bromfield, 2003). Their participation in giving historical and current information, along with consultation to support the child's development, is a critical component. Parents, along with the child, are included in treatment planning, and meeting them where they are, whatever their lifestyle, so that the parent will be willing and trusting to speak candidly and fully (Bromfield, 2003).

School and collaterals are involved as necessary for follow-up with behavioral interventions and to increase support for the child's challenges as needed (through direct teacher or school counselor contact) as well as through empowering parents to follow through with acquiring necessary services for their child. During this time, rapport is established and the therapeutic alliance is built (Punnett, 2016).

The therapeutic alliance, considered paramount as an initial stage and throughout treatment, is especially complicated in psychoanalytic child treatments since the therapist must maintain working alliances with the child's caretakers, teachers, school-based mental health professionals, and others. The therapist then must respond to multiple demands that emanate beyond the child and embrace this state of affairs, balancing one's approach with multiple inputs. The child therapist must develop working alliances with other adults while also keeping the needs and subjectivity of their child clients central and foremost (Levy, 2011).

Research/Empirical Support

The empirical study of psychoanalytic play therapy has been sparse and weak. The vast majority of research has been in the form of the case study, the in-depth and subjective analyses of a single child's treatment. For many decades, the *Psychoanalytic Study of the Child*, an annual volume, presented many studies and theoretical essays by the world's foremost analytic clinicians (Bromfield, 2003). *Psychoanalytic Psychology* has also occasionally published detailed reports of individual child treatment.

Until recently, few studies have cited the benefits of long-term, depth therapies. In fact, such therapies were considered outmoded, not cost-effective and of little benefit (Punnett, 2016). In addition, the methods of psychoanalytic play therapy (e.g., interpretations, empathic listening) cannot be standardized the way a cognitive-behavioral intervention can be. As well as many of the goals and experiences of psychoanalytic therapy (ego growth, self-awareness) are not that easy to define and assess quantitatively. Further, psychoanalytic therapy is as much art as science (Bromfield, 2003). However, the current research in attachment by Alan Schore (2003), neuroscience, and research by others (Roesler, 2013) have led to renewed interest in long-term therapies (Punnett, 2016). Shedler (2010) provided empirical evidence for the efficacy of psychodynamic therapy with clients maintaining therapeutic gains and improvement after treatment concluded. Current research underscores the importance of early childhood and the development of attachment, which affects what happens in the therapeutic relationship in longer-term therapies.

Based on more recent infant research, the psychopathology of the child is thought to reside within the inter- and intra-subjective relationships of the parents/caregivers and is enriched by the intergenerational transmission of conflicts (history of the parents and grandparents). This research has validated the use of long-term therapies, psychoanalytic and analytic psychotherapy, to effect change. Psychoanalytic and analytical play therapy as treatments for children are important because play therapists are integrating a multimodal approach that encompasses visual, tactile, auditory, and sensory modalities, and over time, this can affect brain patterns, especially as these relate to emotions (Punnett, 2016).

Case Study through the Lens of the Therapeutic Powers of Play

Therapeutic Powers of Play Employed

Facilitates Communication

While most adults can plunge into their unconscious through words and dialogue, children often struggle to articulate deep needs, emotions, and experiences in words. Therefore, play and art are tools to access these complex feelings and thoughts (Bromfield, 2003).

Play, while lacking the precision of language, allows certain advantages as it is the child's natural form of expression and it provides both clients and therapists "plausible deniability" (p. 50) concerning troubling material. That is, it permits both parties to suspend and, if necessary, to disavow its reality. After all, it is "only" a game (Levy, 2011)! Play, therefore, frees the participants to express and explore these issues in ways that would be far more difficult if verbal means of communication were exclusively used (Levy, 2011).

Access to the Unconscious

Fantasy compensation: This healing power is a major change mechanism in psychoanalytic play therapy. It is best applied when unresolved conflicts from earlier in life are negatively impacting the client's current functioning. A broad range of fantasy techniques can be used to access the unconscious, such as through use of play therapy toys and materials, sand play, puppet play, and the directed daydream. Interpretations by therapists can help the client gain insight into the meaning of unconscious expressions (Drewes & Schaefer, 2016).

Symbolic play and interpretation: The objects, behaviors, and themes observed in the playroom represent a window into the deeper meaning of the individual's internal world. Focusing on anxieties, defenses, and fantasies can help the therapist understand the underlying concerns of the presenting symptom(s). Techniques used include parallel, conjoint, and directed play, emphasizing the symbolic meaning and therapeutic relationship. (Klein, 1955; Freud, 1965).

Free association: This process is fundamental to connecting with the unconscious. The patient shares verbally, through art, play, or writing. They are asked to express their thoughts and feelings without censoring themselves. Also, it allows the free state and listens without interrupting or imposing any ideas or thoughts into the process. There is some criticism that this process is subjective and that different therapists may interpret the material differently (Tarzain et al., 2023). Other research supports the importance of free association in supporting creativity, the release of blocked material, and tapping into the unconscious (Awuzie, 2018; Farber, 2005).

Self-Expression

Free play. Like free association, free play is the creation of a holding space that allows spontaneous creative expression, such as play, drawing, storytelling, or movement. This allows the unconscious material to be uncovered and the ability to work through thoughts, emotions, and conflicts, all within the experience of the play. Winnicott (1971) proposed that this process allows individuals to explore their world, emotions, and conflicts safely and symbolically. These symbolic objects, actions, drawings, and experiences assist the therapist in interpreting the unconscious and can be a guide for the therapy (Klein, 1955).

Fosters Emotional Wellness

Catharsis

Cathartic release is intended for situations and regression, where stress has triggered strong negative affect, which the client has been unable or unwilling to express and release (fixation). Catharsis involves the release of pent-up negative affect, such as anger or sadness, which has a strong healing effect. It is regarded by many as a major mechanism of change in psychotherapy (Drewes & Schaefer, 2016).

Catharsis is believed to produce therapeutic change by not only discharging deeply felt emotions that are stored up, but by increasing one's conscious awareness and control of them. By deliberately expressing a strong emotion, the child is likely to experience power over it. A shift from an external locus to an internal locus of control can then occur (Drewes & Schaefer, 2016).

Also, catharsis allows one the satisfaction of completing some or all of a previously restrained or interrupted sequence of self-expression and development (fixation). In the safety of the playroom, the child can verbally or physically express that which would have occurred as a natural reaction to some upsetting experience had the expression not been thwarted at the moment (Nichols & Efran, 1985). This termination of "unfinished business" prevents future emotional arousal (Drewes & Schaefer, 2016).

The Role of Play. Play contributes to the effectiveness of catharsis in several ways: (1) the playroom provides a safe and supportive environment to vent negative affect; (2) symbolic play expression provides a sufficient psychological distance from experiencing painful affect. Physical play activities such as pounding clay allow the release of both physical tension and negative affect; (3) the positive feelings aroused in play (power, fun) help to balance the negative emotions that are released (Drewes & Schaefer, 2016).

Abreaction

Abreaction, a psychoanalytic term, is defined as a mental process in which repressed memories of a traumatic event are brought to consciousness, and re-experienced with an appropriate release of negative affect. The basic psychoanalytic premise is that we have a basic need to assimilate emotionally significant experiences into a unified, coherent conceptual system. Unassimilated experiences will keep reemerging into consciousness so as to accomplish assimilation. Abreaction in the playroom offers an opportunity for a "corrective emotional experience" which can be obtained from the acceptance and empathic response of the therapist to the child's painful re-experience (Drewes & Schaefer, 2016).

The Role of Play. The abreaction goals of cognitive assimilation and emotional release are achieved in play therapy through three main mechanisms: (1) miniaturization of experiences. The small toys used to re-create the trauma experiences give children a sense of power over the event; (2) active control and mastery whereby children actively control the playing out of a trauma event which had been experienced passively. They can change the ending of the re-experiencing to one of mastery of the trauma, which results in a cognitive restructuring of the experience; (3) Piecemeal Assimilation by Repetition. Children will typically reenact the trauma over and over again in their play, so that there is a slow healing process by repetition. Sigmund Freud termed this process of habituation—the repetition compulsion. By playing out the trauma in the form of a story, the child can form a coherent narrative from the often-fragmented memories elicited by the trauma and place it within a larger context. The concrete play materials facilitate the remembrance of vivid sensory details of the trauma, which tend to be stored in the right hemisphere of the brain (Drewes & Schaefer, 2016).

Positive Emotion

Through the use of nondirective play, the child is able to release negative emotions, thereby allowing for positive emotions to be accessed and emerge or to be newly created.

Enhances Social Relationships

Attachment

All analytic therapists recognize that their relationships with their child clients are essential components of therapy. The concept of the therapeutic alliance has evolved with contemporary psychoanalysts incorporating new developments in child development, neurobiology, family dynamics, and in psychoanalysis itself (Levy, 2011). Construction of a therapeutic, psychoanalytic relationship permits a sense of security to develop, which allows unacceptable, psychically dangerous feelings to emerge and be addressed in more productive ways (Levy, 2011). Initial deficits in early childhood attachment can be replaced with the corrective positive experience of a secondary attachment with the therapist.

Increases Personal Strength

Resiliency

Through the resolution of id and superego conflicts, the child develops their sense of self, and the ego is strengthened allowing for resiliency to develop.

Accelerated Psychological Development

Past traumas and experiences, and psychic conflicts, lead to a point of fixation whereby psychological and emotional development can become stuck and stagnant. Through therapy, the release of repressed memories and feelings occurs, and a freeing of psychic, emotional energy, occurs which results in an acceleration in psychological development bringing the child to function at their current chronological age.

Self-regulation

Metaphors are higher forms of cognition and play an important role in affect regulation and development of self-complexity (Levy, 2011).

Play itself is seen as providing a crucial vehicle for children to develop affect regulation, and self-awareness in the process of containing, regulating, and repairing the treatment relationship, allowing for experimentation and promoting the experience of new self-states through play (Levy, 2011).

Self-esteem

The simultaneous emergence of unconscious symbolic material helps in the broadening consciousness of the child and facilitates individual strengths and assists the child in coping with all life has to offer (Punnett, 2016). Play becomes the primary route in child analysis in that it serves to develop a sense of mastery; permits assimilation of overpowering experiences; transforms the child's experience from passivity to activity and allows for wish fulfilment (Levy, 2011), which builds the child's self-esteem.

Cultural, Diversity, and Inclusion Considerations

One primary consideration is access. Psychoanalysis can often include multiple sessions a week over long periods. While this can be valuable to many clients, it can also be time-consuming and costly. Many people, especially marginalized populations, may not have the transportation, financial means or time to fully access the benefits (Barkai, Altman, Rubin & Drasin, 2023).

During intake and the initial assessment, the therapist needs to explore and be open to, without judgment, the caregivers'/parents' current life style, issues, and multi-generational issues that impact the child's functioning.

Given the non-directive and nonjudgmental approach of analytical play therapy, the child is free to explore, play out, and bring up through metaphor and symbolic play any cultural or gender identity feelings, thoughts, or behaviors. The play and the safety of the therapeutic space and alliance allow freedom to explore gender roles, identity, self-concept, and autonomy. With the tools in the room, children can negotiate societal norms and their own feelings and experiences. A child may dress up as a superhero of a different gender or play with toys that they have been told are for the opposite gender. This allows them to engage in role play that explores all possibilities without fear of rejection or ridicule (Drewes & Schaefer, 2016).

Case Formulation and Application

From a psychoanalytic perspective, Herman's (see Appendix for case study of Herman being referenced) issues stem back to his birth and poor object relations connection to his mother. He had no ability to bond with his mother while in the NICU and touch and contact were withheld by caregivers around him. His multiple placements further prevented him from establishing a secure attachment with his caregiver. His grandmother, while a more stable person in his initial life, was emotionally unavailable due to her own domestic violence abuse and alcohol abuse, as well as her negative interactions with Herman, who was a fussy and demanding infant. His multiple foster care placements and sexual abuse further underscored his inability to form healthy attachments and added to his internal world view of a lack of trust and not having any personal power to change his external world. Herman's negative interactions and defenses were utilized in a self-protective manner to avoid further abandonment and hurt, from constantly changing therapists, home placements, bullying, and multiple caregivers, which would only reactivate his past repressed experiences. He was fixated at a primal oral phase, seeking out food as nurturance, and his development was fixated due to his traumas and past experiences. There was no psychical energy to learn academically or to modulate his strong negative id impulses. Herman's ego self was confused and poorly formed, struggling to know his place in his world and within his sexual identity.

Herman was assigned to a seasoned psychoanalytically trained play therapist who was able to commit to long-term treatment. It was essential that he be able to have a constant "other" with which to begin to form a therapeutic alliance from which he could work on his repressed and unconscious experiences. After all the preliminary evaluations, school contacts, interviews with his current caregiver and obtaining past assessments, the therapist was able to begin the initial stage of treatment. This was a lengthy process, allowing Herman to lead the sessions, utilizing the toys and therapist as he felt necessary. Herman's affect was unmodulated, with lots of testing of limits by throwing toys, trying to destroy them, jumping up on tables, and having no boundaries between himself and the therapist. The therapist set limits on his behaviors of trying to destroy the toys or hurt the therapist, by remaining in a neutral position, sitting in a central location within the room, and responding with a neutral but firm tone of setting limits. The play therapist saw Herman three times a week at a low-cost clinic near his school. The therapist was able to get Herman from school at the end of the day and bring him to therapy, thereby lessening the time constraints on the foster family. After seven months of testing limits, Herman's behaviors began to settle down, and affect regulation was established. He was able to sit in the chair and play with the toys in an appropriate manner without trying to break them.

Within the working phase, which took almost 1.5 years, of three times a week therapy, Herman's unconscious issues of abandonment and the physical pain of withdrawal at birth, his grandparents' physical abuse, and his sexual abuse, emerged in his metaphorical, abreaction play. He was able to cathartically play out his rage and anger by displacing these strong negative feelings in hanging male figures under scalding water and having them "burn up" and be punished. Over many months, there was regression (in service of the ego) to infancy in wanting to talk baby talk during therapy and have a baby bottle to suck on in therapy, and eventually a pacifier. Herman would ask his therapist to sit close to him, and to rock him in the rocking chair as he snuggled up with a blanket and bottle. Through many sessions, he would close his eyes, not speak, and fall asleep as he was rocked. Metaphorical play included owning a store where the therapist got to buy lots of food and even a baby, who had been left there by another lady, and which the therapist would take home and care for. Direct interpretations dealt with his wishful fantasy of having his therapist be his mother and give him the care he didn't have growing up. Herman eventually moved from the oral stage, into the anal stage, using finger paint, messing up clay and throwing it (as feces), and pouring water into the sand tray. Within a short period of time his development progressed through the stages to his current age-appropriate level.

Herman's lack of control over his internal world, as well as the external world, manifested in the use of the sand tray where he set up battles between himself and his therapist. He gave himself magical powers and could bring his figures back to life, protect them with invisible bubbles, and ultimately always destroyed his own and his opposing adversaries, which his therapist managed, so that no one would win at the end of the battle. All was lost, and there was no way out. As his unconscious memories surfaced and related feelings, Herman was slowly able to allow his opposition to stay alive or come back to life as well. By the end of the second year, he was able to allow the two sides to become friends and find other, less lethal, ways to let out their anger. During this time, his therapist was able to offer interpretations to his negative affect and play, bringing into consciousness the anger, impotence, and fear he felt from past object abandonment.

The therapist utilized supervision throughout treatment as many of Herman's negative behaviors, that he especially targeted her with, were upsetting and evoked counter-transference feelings of anger, and fantasies of abandoning the treatment. The supervision was crucial in helping the therapist maintain a neutral reaction to the negative cathartic and unmodulated expressions of anger, rage, loss, abandonment and pain that were emerging from Herman's unconscious and into consciousness.

During this time, the foster parents and school reported that Herman's behaviors were subsiding. He was no longer taking risks with wild behaviors, showing aggression toward peers or themselves and his academic abilities were dramatically improving. He was able to sit in his seat and participate in learning and doing assignments.

After over two and a half years of therapy, three times per week, the therapist began to lessen therapy to twice a week, for a period of several months, as his gains were consolidated. The therapist then went to weekly, and eventually to biweekly sessions as termination was discussed. After a total of three years in therapy, Herman was able to begin the process of termination. He had made significant improvement in affect regulation and his sense of self, and he had a strong ego that was resilient and able to appropriately deal with his external world.

Challenges in Implementation

Treatment frequency can range from five days a week to several times a week, to weekly, biweekly, or monthly, depending on the needs of the child and family. More traditional analytic work will usually continue over a period of a year to several years. Some psychodynamic variations allow for a narrower treatment focus, which could be completed in a shorter period of time (Punnett, 2016). Consequently, this intensive treatment will require a more lengthy time and a costly financial commitment by the parent and child. Not all insurances will allow for longer-term treatment. And, the time to travel and schedule multiple sessions within a week may create a burden on the family.

Also, for the child therapist, learning and mastering psychoanalytic play therapy can be demanding, both intellectually and emotionally. Training and supervision needs, along with personal therapy, will have to be factored in for the therapist in order to maintain objectivity and flexibility in dealing with transference and counter-transference issues.

Conclusion

While it is argued that Freud is highly controversial as he placed too much focus on sexuality and there is a significant lack of empirical evidence, this work remains foundational as it has led to several advances and has greatly influenced the psychotherapy world. Psychoanalytically informed play therapy can be a powerful form of treatment, although it can be lengthy, costly, hard, and painful for both children and their parents (Bromfield, 2003).

Psychoanalytic play therapy has value, although a long-term child-led treatment approach, in light of recent infant research that has validated the use of long-term therapies, psychoanalytic and analytic psychotherapy, to effect change. This treatment approach helps children recover mental health, re-establish the balance of the psyche that has been disturbed by impressions and past events, broken attachments, and fixations in development. The nurturing therapeutic relationship and simultaneous emergence of unconscious symbolic material help in the broadening consciousness of the child and facilitate individual strengths and assist the child in coping with all life has to offer (Punnett, 2016).

Through the interactive, dynamic interchange of play in psychoanalytic play therapy, whereby repair abounds, children are able to develop a greater capacity for awareness of self and other, for better affect regulation, and for participating in social relationships in more satisfying ways (Levy, 2011).

References

Awuzie, S. (2018). Creative writing as psychotherapy. *Biomedical Journal, 1*, 3.

Barkai, A. R., Anonymous, Altman, N., Rubin, C., & Drasin, R. (2023). Taking outside in, turning inside out: Exploring social dimensions and psychotherapeutic process in the play therapy of a young girl in foster care. *The International Journal of Psychoanalysis, 104*(2), 281–300. https://doi.org/10.1080/00207578.2022.2158091.

Bromfield, R. N. (2003). Psychoanalytic play therapy. In C. E. Schaefer (Ed.), *Foundations of play therapy* (pp. 1–13). Wiley & Sons.

Drewes, A. A., & Schaefer, C. E. (2016). The therapeutic powers of play. In K. J. O'Connor, C. E. Schaefer, & L. D. Braverman (Eds.), *Handbook of play therapy* (2nd ed., pp. 35–60). Wiley & Son.

Elkind, D. (1981). *The hurried child.* Addison-Wesley.

Farber, S. K. (2005). Free association reconsidered: The talking cure, the writing cure. *Journal of the American Academy of Psychoanalysis and Dynamic Psychiatry, 33*(2), 249–73.

Freud, S. (1912). *Three essays on the theory of sexuality*. Standard Edition, Vol. 7. Hogarth Press.

Freud, S. (1920). *Introductory lectures on psychoanalysis*. Standard Edition, Vol. 15–16. Hogarth Press.

Freud, S. (1930). *Civilization and its discontents*. London Hogarth Press.

Freud, A. (1965). *The ego and the mechanisms of defense*. International Universities Press.

Freud, S., & Kul-Want, C. (2010). Beyond the pleasure principle. Leonardo da Vinci and a memory of his childhood. In C. Kul-Want (Ed.), *Philosophers on art from Kant to the postmodernists* (pp. 74–96). Columbia University Press.

Hug-Hellmuth, Hermine von. (1920). On the technique of child-analysis. *International Journal of Psycho-Analysis, 2*, 287–305.

Klein, M. (1955). *The psychoanalysis of children*. Free Press.

Levy, A. J. (2011). Psychoanalytic approaches to play therapy. In C. E. Schaefer (Ed.), *Foundations of play therapy* (2nd ed., pp. 43–59).

Nichols, M. P. & Efran, J. S. (1985). Catharsis in psychotherapy: A new perspective. Psychotherapy: *Theory, research, practice, training, 22*(1), 46.

Plastow, M. (2011). Hermine Hug-Hellmuth, the first child psychoanalyst: Legacy and dilemmas. *Australasian Psychiatry, 19*(3), 206–10.

Punnett, A. F. (2016). Psychoanalytic and Jungian play therapy. In K. J. O'Connor, C. E. Schaefer, & L. D. Braverman (Eds.), *Handbook of play therapy* (2nd ed., pp. 61–92). Wiley & Son.

Punnett, A., & Green, E. J. (2019). Psychoanalytic play therapy. *Play Therapy, 14*(3), 46–8.

Ramires, V. R. (2016). The intersubjective nature of play development and its role in child psychoanalytic psychotherapy. *Frontiers in Psychology, 7*, 1–3.

Roesler, C. (2013). Evidence for the effectiveness of Jungian psychotherapy: A review of empirical studies. *Behavioural Sciences, 3*, 562–75.

Robinson, E. S. (1920). The compensatory function of make-believe play. *Psychological Review, 27*(60), 429–39.

Schaefer, C. E. (1993). *The therapeutic powers of play*. Aronson.

Schore, A. N. (2003). *Affect regulation and the repair of the self*. Norton.

Searle, Y., & Streng, I. (2001). *Where analysis meets the arts: The integration of the arts therapies with psychoanalytic theory*. Taylor & Francis Group, *ProQuest Ebook Central*. https://ebookcentral.proquest.com/lib/lmu/detail.action?docID=690268.

Shedler, J. (2010). The efficacy of psychodynamic psychotherapy. *American Psychologist, 65*(2), 98–109.

Spiel, S., Lombardi, K., & DeRubeis-Byrne, L. (2019). Treating traumatized children: Somatic memories and play therapy. *Journal of Infant, Child, and Adolescent Psychotherapy, 18*(1), 1–12. https://doi.org/10.1080/15289168.2019.1566974.

Stern, D. N. (1985). *The interpersonal world of the infant*. Basic Books.

Tarzian, M., Ndrio, M., & Fakoya, A. O. (2023). An introduction and brief overview of psychoanalysis. *Cureus, 15*(9), e45171.

Vygotsky, L. (1978). *Mind in society*. Harvard University Press.

Winnicott, D. W. (1971). *Playing and reality*. Routledge.

2

Child-Centered Play Therapy

Kristi Perryman

Chapter Outline

Introduction

CCPT is recognized by the Association for Play Therapy (APT, 2024, Ray & Landreth, 2019) as one of the seven seminal play therapy theories that are foundational for all training to ensure best practice. Additionally, Filial Therapy, which is a play therapy approach that teaches parents CCPT skills, is also one of the two seminal historically significant approaches highlighted (APT, 2024; Scuka & Guerney, 2019). CCPT is a non-directive approach that embraces the attitude that children are capable of self-direction as they naturally work toward self-actualization.

Landreth (2023) described CCPT as, "an encompassing philosophy for living one's life in relationships with children-not a cloak of techniques the play therapist puts on upon entering the playroom and takes off when leaving, but a philosophy resulting in attitudes and behaviors for living one's life in relationships with children" (p. 53). CCPT is unique from other play therapy theoretical perspectives due to its focus on the relationship with the child as the healing intervention empowering children to fully express and develop themselves rather than on activities with the goal of changing a behavior or resolving a problem.

Underlying Philosophy

CCPT is based on the work of Carl Rogers and the Person-Centered theory he developed (1961). According to Person-Centered theory, the counselor-client relationship offers the impetus for change, and all human beings have an innate tendency to grow. Rogers offered the core conditions that are the necessary foundation of the therapeutic relationship. The therapist must demonstrate empathy, genuineness, and unconditional positive regard toward their client, and this acceptance enables them to better accept themselves, thus allowing for change.

Virginia Axline (1947) was a student of Rogers and adapted the Person-Centered theory for working with children through play as "the child's natural medium of self-expression" (p. 16). She described CCPT and the relationship with a child by offering readers a glimpse into her groundbreaking work, describing each play session in detail in her book, *Dibs: In Search of Self* (1964).

CCPT is focused on the relationship with the child and being present with them and focuses on the child rather than the behavior, creating an accepting and safe environment for growth and change. Axline's work with children through play was further developed by Guerney (1964) and Landreth (2023). Landreth was co-founder of the Association for Play Therapy and founder of the Center for Play Therapy at the University of North Texas, authoring many books and research articles that have added to the understanding of CCPT.

Louise and Bernard Guerney trained parents in CCPT to utilize the language of play with their own children and enhance the parent-child relationship, which was the origin of Filial therapy. This approach will be described more in depth in the Roles of Caregivers and Collaterals section of this chapter.

CCPT is a seminal theory that has profoundly impacted play therapy. The focus on the relationship and inherent belief in the child to self-actualize radically differs from directive approaches that focus on changing the child. Additionally, it is the foundation for Filial, Child Parent Relationship Therapy (CPRT), and Teacher Child Relationship Therapy (TCRT), which foster the relationship of the child with other significant adults in a child's life to enhance the understanding of their motivations, thoughts, and feelings through the therapeutic language of play.

Personality Theory

CCPT is a counseling theory based on Carl Rogers' self-actualization theory of personality development (1961). Personality theory serves as a way of conceptualizing human nature and development throughout the lifespan. Rogers' theory was first called non-directive or client-centered and later, person-centered therapy to ensure focus on the person as a human rather than as a client. Rogers posited that comprehending one's personality could only truly be understood from an individual's own view and reality, with a focus therefore on the present rather than the past.

Embracing person-centered theory of personality, Landreth (2023) described the person, the phenomenal field, and the self as crucial foundations of personality theory. The person is described as the thoughts, feelings, behaviors, and physical being of the child, with one aspect changing the others as they strive toward self-actualization, emphasizing that behavior is purposeful (Landreth, 2023).

The phenomenal field includes all things the child has experienced and serves as their lens for viewing their world, encompassing the thoughts, feelings, behaviors, and the actual physical being of the child (Landreth, 2023). Similarly, the self emerges from interaction with the phenomenal field and occurs as the child experiences the reactions of those around them. These evaluative interactions leave a child with the sense that they are good or bad based on these experiences (Landreth, 2023). Rogers (1961) emphasized the natural tendency to strive to become or maintain self-actualization and the role of the relationship and unconditional positive regard in empowering another to also view themselves in a positive light. Only when one accepts themselves can they change. The unconditional positive regard and accepting attitudes of those within the child's phenomenal field empower them to also accept themselves and thus change.

Model of Psychopathology

Psychopathology according to person-centered theory arises due to incongruence between the idealized self and the literal self-concept (Rogers, 1961). Human beings naturally seek congruence, feeling, behaving, and experiencing in ways consistent with their view of self. Higher self-worth is thus consistent with more congruence. If our perceived behaviors, thoughts, and feelings are not congruent with this view, incongruence occurs, creating maladjustment and behaviors for coping. Person-centered and CCPT emphasize that this drive toward self-actualization is an inherent basic need that all humans constantly strive to attain (Rogers, 1961; Landreth, 2023).

Maladjustment results in behaviors that serve as coping mechanisms as one seeks congruence. These behaviors are not an attempt to be bad or maladjusted, but are self-protective. Therefore, a true person-centered view of maladjustment or psychopathology necessitates the need to view the associated behaviors as emerging due to a need to protect the self rather than as misbehavior, dysfunctional behavior, maladjustment, or psychopathology. It is crucial that the CCPT therapist strives to see the world through the eyes of the child and to understand their view of self and the experiences that have led to the observed self-protective behaviors.

Conceptualizing Goals of Treatment

In CCPT, the child leads the session, rather than the therapist, with the child viewed as a person rather than a problem to be fixed. Ray and Landreth (2019) stressed that, therefore, goals in the traditional sense, created by a therapist, are inconsistent with the CCPT philosophy. Because of this, novice play therapists may fear they cannot practice as a child-centered play therapist since goals are required for managed care. It is crucial that this misconception and feelings of incongruence be clarified so that the needs of children can be met through the developmentally appropriate lens of CCPT. A child-centered play therapist is not simply applying relational techniques but instead wholly lives this approach as a way of being and thus cannot genuinely be any other way. As Landreth (2023) pointed out, CCPT, "is a way of being rather than doing" (p. 66).

The CCPT therapist, working within the confines of managed care, must ethically formulate treatment goals. This can be difficult and bring about feelings of incongruence. However, with the focus on helping the child, the therapist must make some adaptations to achieve this goal. Goals can be easily conceptualized by reviewing the required therapeutic conditions, the view of human nature, CCPT objectives, and knowledge of the research regarding the benefits of CCPT. Goals can also exist in the form of therapeutic conditions for growth (Landreth, 2023) based on Rogers (1961) core conditions. These include being real or genuine, having a warm, caring acceptance and having a sensitive understanding. The primary therapeutic goal is the relationship, met through the presence of the therapeutic conditions.

The CCPT therapist has a core belief in a child's natural tendency and ability to individuate, mature, and grow, given the core conditions posited by Rogers (1961). These are provided through the therapeutic conditions for growth listed above. By facilitating an environment of acceptance and safety, the child learns that their feelings are acceptable, has self-respect, responsibly expresses their feelings, takes self-responsibility, solves problems, exercises self-control and self-acceptance, and makes choices and the responsibility for them (Landreth, 2023). A crucial goal of the therapist is therefore to create the environment that facilitates the child's natural tendency for growth as they cope with issues that have occurred or are occurring in their world.

Landreth developed what he referred to as "broad therapeutic objectives of CCPT" (2013, p. 92), intended to help a child. The following objectives serve to offer a broad framework for comprehending the characteristics that the CCPT therapist strives to facilitate and the benefits for children:

1. Develop a more positive self-concept.
2. Assume greater self-responsibility.
3. Become more self-directing.
4. Become more self-accepting.
5. Become more self-reliant.
6. Engage in self-determined decision making.
7. Experience a feeling of control.
8. Become sensitive to the process of coping.
9. Develop an internal source of evaluation.
10. Become more trusting of himself. (Landreth, 2012, pp. 84–5)

The CCPT therapist embraces the belief that these objectives coincide with the child's natural drive toward self-actualization, and therefore there is no need to direct or teach the child, as they will naturally grow in these areas if provided with the core conditions within the relationship to do so. The objectives, though never directly taught, can serve as treatment goals, understanding that the therapist is focused on the child as a person, not a goal to achieve.

Ray & Landreth (2019) also pointed out that research on CCPT supports externalized and internalized behavior change, self-concept, teacher relationships, and academic achievement, noting that though behavioral goals are not used, this positive view of human nature denotes that given a safe and accepting environment, the child will innately move forward in positive ways. CCPT studies with positive outcomes include increases in self-esteem, expressive language in students with speech delay, academic achievement, and adaptive, as well as overall, behaviors (Blanco & Ray, 2011; Blanco et al., 2012; Blanco et al., 2017; Danger & Landreth, 2005; Kot et al., 1998; Perryman & Bowers, 2018; Massengale & Perryman, 2021; Post et al., 2020). Knowledge of the proven benefits of CCPT is a helpful component in therapist congruence in terms of the necessary goal setting for billing purposes.

Guerney (1983) posited stages of CCPT that were later adapted (Nordling & Guerney, 1999) which can also contribute to treatment planning and goal setting. The first stage is *warm-up* in which the relationship is established, the *aggressive* stage where the child works on resolving issues in their world by demonstrating a need for control. Next is the *regressive* stage with the child exploring attachment and nurturance, demonstrating play often younger than expected for their age and development. Finally, during the *mastery* stage, the child works on mastery and confidence, integrating growth from previous stages, signaling readiness for termination (Nordling & Guerney, [1999]). Aggressive and regressive stages are frequently interwoven and viewed as the *working stage* where the child is doing their deep therapeutic work (Cochran et al., [2010]). With these stages in mind, the CCPT therapist can create goals associated with each stage.

Goals are an ethical and needed requirement part of treatment planning for managed care to ensure best practices when working with children but should only be established through one's theoretical lens. The child-centered play therapist views the accomplishment of goals as a byproduct of the therapeutic relationship in which a child discovers their internal strengths. The child is neither encouraged nor precluded from working toward goals or solutions to problems by the therapist. The child is viewed as the professional in resolving their problems, resulting in an internal locus of control rather than fostering a dependence on the therapist as the authority.

The CCPT therapist holds the inherent belief that the child will naturally grow and move forward, given the presence of the therapeutic conditions and thus meet the broad objectives of play therapy. Examples of therapeutic goals from a CCPT perspective could include those focused on building a therapeutic relationship, expression of feelings, demonstration of self-control, problem solving, responsibility for choices, and self-acceptance, and so on as defined by the objectives of play therapy. Using the stages of CCPT (Nordling & Guerney, 1999), goals may also include expressing aggression, exploring attachment, gaining self-confidence, and resolving issues inhibiting their growth. Specific behavioral concerns easily fall under the umbrella of these areas and would emerge if the stated conditions are present based on the CCPT view of human nature. This core belief and the incorporation of the needed components can allow for congruence in the necessary goal setting for the child-centered therapist.

Role of the Therapist

The CCPT therapist, equipped with the ability to create therapeutic conditions and embracing the person-centered view of human nature, has a deep faith in the child and their ability to be self-directing as they strive for growth (Landreth, 2023). The CCPT therapist is focused on seeing the world through the child's eyes, creating a safe environment that facilitates growth and utilizing play as the language. They must convey a positive unconditional regard for the child with an abiding belief in their ability to self-actualize. The CCPT therapist is not evaluative of the child as they strive to support them in learning to trust their own internal locus of control. This is crucial as the child develops their sense of self through the constructs of the person, the self, and the phenomenal field (Rogers, 1961). Because the child therefore views themselves through the lens of how others respond to them, it is imperative that the therapist's attitudes toward the child reflect their belief in their ability to self-direct and grow.

Play is the medium for the child to express their thoughts, feelings, and view of their world. The therapist does not choose the play, nor is the child required to play. They are free to choose how their time is spent in the playroom. Play serves as the language for them to express themselves as they naturally seek relationships, ways to problem solve, and to regulate their emotions (Ray & Landreth, 2019). In this process, they gain a positive self-concept, self-control, confidence, and resilience, seeing themselves as capable and worthy. Axline (1964) described *Eight Basic Principles*, which serve as a foundation for therapeutic relationships with children and Landreth (2012) later revised them below:

1. The therapist is genuinely interested in the child and develops a warm, caring relationship.
2. The therapist experiences unqualified acceptance of the child and does not wish that the child was different.
3. The therapist creates a feeling of safety and permissiveness in the relationship, so the child feels free to explore and express himself completely.
4. The therapist is always sensitive to the child's feelings and gently reflects those feelings in such a manner that the child develops self-understanding.
5. The therapist believes deeply in the child's capacity to act responsibly, unwaveringly respects the child's ability to solve personal problems, and allows the child to do so.
6. The therapist trusts the child's inner direction, allows the child to lead in all areas of the relationship, and resists any urge to direct the child's play or conversation.
7. The therapist appreciates the gradual nature of the therapeutic process and does not attempt to hurry the process.
8. The therapist establishes only those therapeutic limits necessary to anchor the session to reality and which help the child accept personal and appropriate relationship responsibility (p. 80).

The CCPT therapist maintains a focus on the child, rather than the problem(s), embracing the basic principles, utilizing both verbal and non-verbal skills in a playroom specifically created and organized with therapeutic toys. Selected toys should enhance the therapeutic process. Landreth (2012) identified the types of toys needed as real-life toys, acting out aggressive-release toys, and toys for creative expression and emotional release. Toys are placed on shelves according to theme or, in the case of a tote bag playroom, placed in plastic bags or storage containers. A list of therapeutic toys suggested by Landreth, (2012, p. 167–9) are included in the Appendix.

Child-centered play therapists also provide services in schools, homes, and other locations that lack a specific playroom. A tote bag playroom can be utilized with the toys placed on a tablecloth on the floor by theme as they typically would be on shelves. Options for a tote, as suggested by Landreth (2012, pp. 166–7) are listed in the Appendix.

The child-centered play therapist uses the identified toys as their tools for communication, speaking the natural language of the child rather than expecting them to verbalize on an adult level. Toys are not labeled by the therapist to maintain focus on the child's world, where they decide what the toys are and label them as they choose (Landreth, 2023).

Using the toys, the child will express themselves, communicating their inner world in their own developmentally appropriate way. The therapist uses tracking, reflection of content, reflection of feelings, and facilitative responses to respond to the child with understanding, sensitivity, and acceptance, conveying responsibility but also freedom (Landreth, 2023). Facilitative responses include those that encourage decision making, creativity, and personalization/relationship, including those that return responsibility and esteem building (Landreth, 2012). Responses should not include those that question, evaluate, or praise. Examples of tracking, reflection of feeling and content, and facilitative responses will be addressed in this chapter's case example.

Also, responses should be brief and interactive, not interrupting or directing the child's play but helping the child continue (Landreth, 2023). The therapist should match the child's energy and affect, both in their responses and their facial expressions. Sensitivity to the child is required to gauge the frequency needed. An example would be a child that acts silly to keep the therapist's attention or to entertain them. Initially, the therapist reflects, "You are smiling, you think that's funny." Or "You think that's silly." Upon recognition that the child is overly focused on pleasing or entertaining, the attuned therapist offers fewer content and feeling reflections while still conveying presence as they lean in and focus their energy on the child. They may convey that they are paying attention through tracking play in a calm, engaged, but soft and non-evaluative tone, allowing the child to co-regulate and focus their play internally rather than relying on the therapist.

One of the most important roles of the CCPT therapist is the ability to set firm and consistent limits in a non-reactive way. In this relationship, as with all others, limits are a necessity. Limits make a child feel safe and that the relationship is trustworthy. Without this, little will be accomplished as the child's ability to explore and express themselves will be inhibited. The therapist consistently and non-punitively ensures the safety of the child, the therapist, and the playroom through limit setting. Within the play therapy relationship, limits are not reviewed as classroom rules but instead set only as needed. The CCPT therapist accepts the child but does not accept all behaviors. Limits are crucial to a healthy therapeutic relationship, as they enable the child to learn self-control, trust, and experience the safety in which to explore, grow, and learn. This is not possible without a competent therapist, capable of setting and enforcing firm and consistent limits.

Landreth (2023) emphasized that limits should be "minimal and enforceable" (Landreth, 2023, p. 304). Limits are introduced as needed to protect the child, the therapist, the playroom, and toys' safety. They may also be needed to minimize behaviors that interrupt the therapeutic process. Examples would be frequently leaving the room, socially inappropriate behaviors such as undressing or inappropriate attempts to gain affection like sitting on the therapist's lap or kissing, or attempting to take toys (Landreth, 2023). Limits are important to maintain the here-and-now focus of therapy, ensure safety, and ground the child in reality (Landreth, 2020).

A model for limit setting was developed by Landreth (2012). This model Acknowledges the child's desire, Communicates the limit, and Targets an acceptable alternative (ACT). **A**cknowledging the feelings and desires of the child verbally is the first step in limit setting. This step is crucial as often it is the only one needed. Most often adults simply tell the child to stop unwanted behavior, with no acknowledgment that their behavior is the way they express what they are feeling. Skipping this step leaves the child frustrated and even angry as they continue to feel misunderstood. Acknowledging the feeling also elicits mirror neurons as this step acknowledges a desire or feeling and conveys understanding.

Communicating the limit is the next step in the ACT model. The way the limit is communicated is especially important as the therapist must do it in a firm but also not evaluative or angry manner. The choice, after all, still belongs to the child to decide what to do next. The limit should also be communicated in a non-personal way to avoid judgment on the person of the child. Stating, for example, "The glue is not for the sand," clearly conveys the limit in a non-evaluative manner rather than "Don't pour glue in the sand."

The next step in the ACT model is to Target acceptable behavior. Using the previous example, the statement, "The glue is for the paper," offers an acceptable way of using the glue, again in a non-evaluative way.

The last step in ACT is to State the final choice after going through the earlier steps at least three times (Landreth, 2023). A child may choose through their behavior to not play with a toy for the rest of the play session. Again, it is crucial that the final limit be stated with a calm but clear demeanor so that the child recognizes it is their choice and that the therapist is still accepting them, but not the behavior. If the child chooses not to have access to that toy for this session, it is removed or put out of their access for the remainder of the session. However, the toy is there when they return for their next visit so that they can learn from their choices.

During limit setting, the therapist must respond rather than react. They need to have the self-awareness to know behaviors that may be a trigger for them. The answer I give to new play therapists when they ask about a specific limit is almost always, "It depends." Not all situations are the same and, thus, require the therapist to be aware and sensitively respond to the child. For example, one child may throw sand from the sandbox to seek attention from the therapist. The therapist should set a limit but also ensure they are giving attention in appropriate ways through their responses and body language. Another child may be overly organized and clean, and one day shovel sand outside the sandbox with such intense emotional energy that the therapist allows it to continue, reflecting feelings and content, recognizing this as some cathartic need to express something previously buried in the child. When struggling with whether to set a limit, the CCPT therapist should ask themselves three questions: What message do I send if I set a limit? What message do I send if I do not set a limit right now? Is setting this limit my need or the child's? I find that answering these questions clarifies even the most confounding situations that may arise.

Finally, the therapist must also be able to recognize themes in the child's play. Themes may include power and control, aggression, helplessness, mastery, safety and security, nurturing, death/loss, and sexualized (Bratton & Homeyer, 2002). Themes are identified by observing what the child chooses to play with and how the toys are used. Thematic play is repetitive with intensity and emotional energy (Landreth & Bratton, 2019). It is the recognition of themes that allows the therapist to understand a child's internal struggles and needs and to provide suggestions to parents, teachers, and other adults in a child's life. Themes will be revisited in the Case formulation and Application section of this chapter.

Roles of Caregivers and Collaterals

This section will review the roles of caregivers and collaterals in CCPT. The term "parents" in this section will refer to any caregiver, whether biological, foster, or adoptive parent or guardian. Collaterals in a child's life most often include teachers and school counselors, though at times they may also include guardians ad litem, juvenile workers, court-appointed child advocates, and others.

The CCPT therapist regards the parent as the professional on their child. The therapist has skills that can enhance the parent-child relationship but never loses sight of the crucial role of the parent in the child's world. From a CCPT perspective, the parent may be involved by directly conducting play sessions with their child using a Filial approach or as partners in the therapeutic process, providing needed information and working with the therapist to incorporate feedback.

As previously discussed, Filial Therapy is an approach based on CCPT. It includes small group instruction for parents over twenty weeks in which CCPT skills are taught and practiced with the therapist. The therapist then supervises the parents working with their child in the home. This was the first approach of its kind as it was unheard of to teach parents therapeutic skills rather than leaving this role to mental health professionals (Scuka & Guerney, 2019). The Guerneys emphasized the role of the parent as the primary adult in a child's life, believing in their ability to develop the needed skills to better understand the feelings and behaviors of their child.

Landreth and Bratton (2005, 2019) further adapted Filial therapy to a ten-session model, entitled Child-Parent Relationship Therapy. This model is taught through small ten-week psychoeducational groups, limiting the number of parents to six. Parents serve as a support for one another as they learn and practice CCPT skills to incorporate with their child at home. They review recorded play sessions with their child for feedback and suggestions from one another and the group facilitator/teacher. Research has demonstrated the effectiveness of CPRT, and it is an evidence-based approach. An overview of this research will be addressed in the research section of this chapter.

As partners in the therapeutic process, the CCPT therapist engages the parents from the first meeting and employs empathy, genuineness, warmth, and unconditional positive regard to build a trusting partnership. The CCPT therapist views human nature the same for adults as they do for children, as doing otherwise would be incongruent. Working with parents can be difficult for some therapists, and they may blame them for the child's difficulties. It is important to view them from the same person-centered perspective, as doing the best they can while they attempt to grow and to move forward. They too have developed protective behaviors because of their own life experiences. Helping the child often means empathically assisting the parents to gain insight into the impact on their relationship with their child. It is often in these early meetings or later ones that the therapist encourages the parents to seek their own therapy and makes the necessary referrals.

The initial meeting takes place without the child present so that the parent feels free to express their feelings and concerns. The child should never be present at meetings in which they are spoken about. The parents hold a powerful position in the phenomenal field of the child, and their view of themselves is therefore greatly impacted by interactions with them. Parents also need to feel free to express their concerns about their child with the therapist in the privacy of their office. Adults in a child's life may assume the child is not listening or does not care what is being said. The CCPT therapist frequently must remind parents, teachers, and other collaterals of the importance of keeping these conversations private. A therapist would never bring in an adult partner and discuss their client in front of them as though they were not there or allow them to make disparaging comments that could negatively impact not only the self-concept of the client but also impair trust with the therapist. Children deserve the same respect.

In the initial meeting with the parents, the therapist collects information about the child's birth, development, and any potential family concerns. Landreth (2023) pointed out that this exchange may elicit empathy toward the child from the therapist but can also influence perception in negative ways, in which the reported problems become the focus. The CCPT therapist strives to bracket this information as it should not change their treatment or how they interact with the child. Those working in school settings must be diligent in this regard as information is often discussed openly about students.

In this session, parents are educated about the therapy process, confidentiality, and expectations for the relationship with the parents, the child, and treatment are also reviewed. The process is explained in terms of play being the child's language and toys, their words due to cognitive development, and the parents can see the playroom and ask questions. Frequently, questions arise about the number of sessions that will be needed. The CCPT therapist informs the parents of the research regarding the average number of sessions to see improvement, explaining that this can vary depending on the severity and duration of the issues.

To support the child in the therapeutic process, parents and others should avoid asking the child about their sessions. If they feel they need to report to parents or other adults in their lives, the message is quickly received that the sessions are not theirs and success will be limited. Parents are informed that if something important comes up, they will be contacted sooner to ensure trust in the therapist. Likewise, the parent should not praise artwork created in play therapy as this can build a reliance on pleasing them rather than doing their own work in the playroom.

Teachers have a vital role in the lives of children. This includes teaching various topics such as reading and math, as well as social-emotional skills as a child learns to navigate peer relationships. Landreth and Bratton (2005; 2019) created a version of CPRT for teachers to utilize with their students, teacher-child relationship therapy (CTRT). Post, et al. (2020) conducted a study on the impact of the CTRT training on the attitudes of teachers toward classroom behaviors and found that CTRT had a positive impact on those teacher attitudes that are consistent with CCPT, as well as those related to trauma-informed care and the ability to conduct CCPT skills in their classroom.

Play therapy can be explained the same way to other collaterals in the child's world in terms of how they developmentally communicate through the language of play. This understanding is crucial to trusting the therapist, the play therapy process, and supporting the child. The adults in a child's life hold the power. Therefore, the therapist will be limited in their ability to help the child without the support of the collaterals involved. The CCPT therapist works diligently to maintain trusting partnerships with the important collaterals in the child's life to help the child.

Research/Empirical Support

CCPT is established as an evidence-based approach for working with children three to twelve with social emotional issues, developmental delays, and relational and behavioral issues (Ray, 2015). It is also the most comprehensively researched type of play therapy, with eighty years of research to support its effectiveness in clinical and school settings with numerous populations (Lin & Bratton, 2015; Post et al., 2020; Ray et al., 2022; Schoonover & Perryman, 2023).

CCPT is an evidence-based approach, given a scientific rating of three out of five for promising research evidence by the California Evidence-Based Clearinghouse for Child Welfare (CEBC, 2024). They report research evidence for children three to ten years of age who are struggling with anxiety, disruptive behaviors, and those exposed to domestic/intimate partner violence. It is also listed on the Title IV-E Prevention Services Clearinghouse as Promising for child well-being in the areas of behavioral and emotional functioning, social functioning, educational achievement, and attainment.

Positive changes have been shown in as few as 12–16 CCPT sessions lasting thirty minutes. These research studies included two to three weekly sessions (Lin et al., 2015; Ray et al., 2015). CCPT studies with positive outcomes have demonstrated increases in self-esteem, expressive language in students with speech delay, academic achievement, and adaptive as well as overall behaviors (Blanco & Ray, 2011; Blanco et al., 2017; Blanco et al., 2012; Danger & Landreth, 2005; Kot, Landreth, & Giordano, 1998; Perryman & Bowers, 2018; Massengale & Perryman, 2021; Post, McAllister, Sheely, Hess, & Flowers, 2004).

Research also supports CCPT with diverse populations that include minoritized children and those from various cultural backgrounds as well as those with disabilities for externalizing and internalizing behaviors (Bratton & Lin, 2015; Cebellos et al., 2021; Lin & Bratton, 2015; Massengale & Perryman, 2021; Robinson et al., 2017; Schottelkorb et al., 2020; Taylor & Ray, 2021). CCPT is a culturally appropriate approach for working with diverse and minoritized children, as it focuses on seeing the world through their eyes.

CCPT also has a great deal of research with children who have experienced trauma and the protective behaviors associated with abuse (Gutermann et al., 2016; Haas, 2017; Humble et al., 2019; Kram, 2019; Perryman, et al., 2020; Ray et al., 2022; Schoonover et al., 2022) and has shown positive results. Conroy and Perryman (2022) posited that CCPT is effective for addressing ACEs with children as the relationship is emphasized by safety and engagement.

CCPT has one of the longest histories in the field of intervention research, dating back to the 1940s (Baggerly et al., 2010) demonstrating effectiveness with various populations and for a variety of issues. It is an evidence-based approach for working with children. Knowledge about research is crucial for therapists working in the twenty-first century and beyond. Without the ability to educate those in a child's life and advocate for appropriate services by articulating the research, a therapist may soon be deemed irrelevant.

Case Study through the Lens of the Therapeutic Powers of Play

Therapeutic Powers of Play Employed

Play therapy facilitates communication, enhances social relationships, fosters emotional wellness, and increases personal strengths through twenty core agents (Schafer & Drewes, 2014). The CCPT therapist believes these agents of change naturally occur within the safety of the therapeutic relationship as the child uses their natural language of play to express their deepest feelings and experiences in the world. Therefore, the therapeutic powers are not gained through direct activities or teaching on behalf of the therapist but instead, are met by the child's self-direction. Equipped with the eight Basic Principles (Axline, 1947; Landreth, 2012), the CCPT therapist will therefore create a psychologically, physically, and culturally safe environment for Herman (see Appendix for the case study of Herman being referenced) to explore previously hidden aspects of himself and find solutions to his problems. This aligns with the *warm-up* stage of CCPT according to Nordling and Guerney, (1999), in which the relationship is established by facilitating communication through play.

The *aggressive* stage in which the child demonstrates deep therapeutic work and exhibits a need for control as the medium of play fosters emotional wellness in these moments. During the *regressive* stage, social relationships are enhanced through play as the child explores attachment and nurturance. During the final stage of *mastery*, the child works on mastery and confidence, integrating growth from previous stages, signaling readiness for termination and exhibiting personal strengths through their play.

The unconditional positive regard, genuineness, and warmth conveyed by the therapist will allow Herman to view himself in a positive and competent way. The relationship with the therapist will naturally extend to those outside the playroom as Herman develops an internal locus of control through his play to resolve issues within the safety of the therapeutic relationship. He will learn to approach the world with a new self-confidence, self-control, self-acceptance, self-reliance, and resiliency gained in the CCPT process. Accepting himself allows him to better accept others and develop healthy attachments with the new relational neuropathways developed in the therapeutic relationship with the therapist.

The CCPT therapist, therefore, would never directly teach or create learning opportunities through the therapeutic powers but inherently believes in Herman's ability to direct himself in his own time and own way. The following case study will offer a view into the CCPT process with Herman, employing the therapeutic powers of play.

Cultural, Diversity, Inclusion Considerations

Embracing cultural humility in work with clients is foundational to the relationship in which there is a felt mutual respect and curiosity about the other, creating trust. The CCPT therapist therefore recognizes their own biases and works to confront them and" honors the reality that there are a multiplicity of truths and experiences based on a person's identities, background, and experiences" (Ray et al., 2022, p. 15).

Herman is culturally diverse, with his mother identifying as Caucasian, his grandfather as Hispanic, and grandmother as African American. Additionally, Herman has reported not liking being a boy and preferring clothes that are non-gender specific and painting his nails. The CCPT therapist conveys their genuine interest in the child, including acknowledging his identities as well as existing limitations due to differences. Asking Herman about preferred pronouns would be important for conveying acceptance and respect on behalf of the therapist.

The CCPT therapist must broach with the family as often as needed, beginning in the initial session, and attend to what Ogawa et al., (2022) refers to as "cultural opportunities" (p. 29) as they present themselves in the playroom. The CCPT therapist considers the child's developmental age in broaching and when addressing culturally related issues in the playroom. The CCPT therapist would reflect the underlying feelings and implore relational responses. They must continually work to respond rather than react and thoughtfully approach cultural opportunities in a warm, genuine, and caring manner.

While Herman is chronologically ten years old, his behaviors reflect a child who is developmentally much younger, and the therapist would be sensitive to responding in ways that match his language and play accordingly. The CCPT therapist continually self-reflects on their work with Herman outside the playroom to strive for cultural humility. The CCPT therapist must embrace the core conditions and work to fully understand their own culture and identities as they simultaneously work to also understand fully those of the client.

A multicultural playroom was described by Ray et al., (2022, p. 287) as, "intentionally designed to facilitate a child's free expression and exploration of self, including all cultural aspects of self," which includes culturally appropriate toys. The CCPT therapist can gain an understanding of what aspects of his cultural identities are most salient for Herman and ensure the playroom is appropriately equipped with a variety of toys that reflect African American and Latinx culture. Due to Herman's sensory-seeking behaviors, the inclusion of a weighted blanket, water beads, a small trampoline, kinetic sand, and fidget toys may also be helpful for expression, self-soothing, and self-nurturing as they provide sensory stimulation (Swan & Schottelkorb, 2022).

In addition to the toys mentioned above, there are others that could be helpful in self-regulation due to the complex trauma that Herman has endured. The CCPT therapist will work to see the world through Herman's eyes, aware that he will have trauma responses during play therapy and work to be responsive rather than reactive. A yoga ball can be helpful for sensory integration as well as self-regulation through rhythmic movement as it is large and strong enough for a child to lie on it and rock. It can also be a relational tool as it is rolled back and forth to the therapist, and so on, as the child seeks relational experiences and co-regulation. While the bop bag is also often used by children to lie on, punch, and so on, the yoga ball offers a different sensory experience because of the shape and maneuverability.

Case Formulation and Application

Child development is a primary consideration in case formulation and application. Herman is chronologically ten years old. According to Ojiambo and Taylor (2006), this age is characterized by an increase in attention, regulation and self-control, and comprehension of social rules. They can think more logically and react appropriately to social rules. They typically find comfort in relationships with friends, parents, teachers, and others.

Due to Herman's experiences prior to and after birth, he does not meet the criteria of a typical ten-year-old. He has angry and aggressive outbursts, acts in dangerous ways, struggles with attention and sitting still for instruction, and lacks friends. He has been aggressive toward peers as well as teachers. This impulsivity and aggression are common for children who experienced drug use in utero and have had significant trauma since.

These behaviors will present themselves in the playroom as play therapy mirrors events in his environment. In these situations, it will be crucial that the CCPT therapist remains calm and consistently and firmly sets and enforces limits using the ACT model. For example, "I see that you are angry, but I am not for hitting. The bop bag is for hitting if you choose to." It is likely that the aggression will present itself through play that requires the therapist to remove a toy for the rest of the session. For example, Herman may repeatedly shoot the therapist with the dart gun. In this case, stating the final choice will be required: "I see you decided not to play with the dart gun today." The CCPT therapist would, however, have the gun in the following session so that Herman would have the opportunity to self-direct in a responsible way. Due to the trauma he has endured, it may take several sessions for him to trust the therapist to follow through, so consistency is crucial. The CCPT therapist continues to have unconditional positive regard and demonstrates warmth and genuineness toward the child, always accepting them, even when they cannot accept the behavior. The therapeutic powers of play are evident as Herman expresses his feelings and needs (both conscious and unconscious) through his play and experiences catharsis as he gains power over his fears.

As a diverse child, Herman is also likely to have a beginning awareness of his racial identity development and is starting to have thoughts about his cultural identity (Ojiambo & Taylor, 2006). Since Herman is biracial, with his mother identifying as Caucasian, his grandfather as Hispanic, and grandmother as African American, his cultural development will be apparent in his play as he explores his own identity. The CCPT therapist will acknowledge these occurrences as they track and reflect on content and/or feelings. They may also include relational responses. For example, if Herman were to make a derogatory comment about a Black person, the Black therapist could say, "You think Black women are stupid. I am a Black woman" in a calm and accepting tone. This could provide an opportunity to connect with Herman in a genuine and congruent way, offering him the opportunity to process either verbally or through his play his own identity development, facilitating communication through play.

At 10 years old, boys are physically developing more muscle and thus gross motor skills and beginning to have more body hair. At this age, Herman is likely to express more curiosity about sexual development. Since Herman has expressed that he does not like being a boy and chooses non-gendered clothing and wears nail polish and eyeliner, he is already exploring his gender identity, and this will be apparent in his play as he continues to explore his own gender identity. During these moments, the CCPT therapist conveys warmth and positive regard. For example, Herman picks up the tiara and asks if he can wear it. The CCPT therapist reflects, "You are wondering if it's ok to wear that . . . In here, you can choose the things you wear." This unconditional acceptance will allow Herman to freely play out his feelings and desires without fear of judgment, allowing for self-expression through play.

Due to maternal drug use that resulted in Herman having withdrawal symptoms at birth, lack of bonding with a significant adult, sexual abuse, and exposure to domestic abuse in the home, he has a high Adverse Childhood Experiences (ACEs) score, and this should be considered in therapy. The ACEs are exposures to trauma before age 18 and result in negative social, emotional, and health outcomes throughout the lifespan, without intervention. These include exposure to emotional and physical neglect, emotional and physical abuse, as well as sexual abuse, domestic violence, loss of a parent, and having a family member with addiction, depression, mental illness, or incarcerated (Felitti et al., 1998).

Trauma results in physiological responses of fight, flight, or freeze, designed to achieve safety (Levine, 2015; Porges, 2009; Van der Kolk, 1994). Of these responses, Herman has a fight response in which he becomes aggressive and volatile at times with no provocation. Due to his traumatic experiences, he responds to situations, fighting to survive, unable to distinguish danger. Due to the trauma Herman has endured, he will undoubtedly express some of these events through play as he attempts to make sense of and reconcile them. At the same time, Herman seems to seek out dangerous situations, which indicate sensory-seeking behavior along with impulsivity. These symptoms are due to the maternal drug use while he was in utero that prevented optimal brain development. Additionally, intimacy may be interpreted as a threat (Perry et al., 2016) since he has been sexually abused by an older child. Herman's experiences have not always indicated that adults are a source of safety, so he will not trust easily. This will be demonstrated through what may seem like endless limit testing, seeking a trusting relationship. He is likely to engage in sexualized play and attempt to sit on the therapist's lap or ask her to touch him inappropriately. Should this occur, the therapist would respond again using the ACT model, sensitively but firmly setting limits. The CCPT therapist would never want the child to feel shame due to these behaviors. "You want me to touch you, but your body is not for me to touch," or "You want to sit in my lap with the blanket. You can sit on the cushion with the blanket." Herman will seek to enhance social relationships through his play as he explores attachment and appropriate ways to connect.

Post-traumatic play for children often includes repetition of aspects associated with the event as children attempt to reconcile the trauma. Common themes for Herman will include conflict and aggression along with those that are sexual until he has been able to fully express these experiences. Complex trauma appears in the playroom with messiness and intensity with the various mediums rather than organized and free, so the unconditional acceptance of the therapist is needed. Of course, limits may be set as needed to protect the playroom. "You want to pour the glue in the sand, but the glue is for the paper." These instances allow an increase in personal strengths through play as the child has opportunities to creatively problem-solve and self-regulate.

Landreth (2023) also pointed out that these children are more likely to have emotional blocks in play therapy or play disruptions (Perry et al., 2016). They may need to distance themselves from the play when it feels too threatening. The child may be immersed in intense play and then suddenly stop, go to another area of the room, and pick up a different toy. This is like the adult in therapy who feels overwhelmed as they share with the therapist and changes the subject to talk about the weather to distance themselves emotionally. If this occurs, the therapist will offer a facilitative decision-making response: "You worked hard on that. It looks like you decided to do something else," acknowledging rather than praising their effort and decision to do something else.

Challenges in Implementation

There are many challenges for the CCPT therapist as they work with Herman, as he has behaviors not conducive to a healthy relationship. First, the CCPT therapist will have to bracket the intake information regarding Herman's behaviors and abuse. While this information is likely to elicit empathy on the part of the therapist, it may also create preconceived notions about what he will look like in the playroom and take away from the experience of being with the child. The therapist may approach Herman with hypervigilance because of reading about him, sending the message that he is not trustworthy and that the therapist is more concerned with protecting themselves than getting to know the person he is.

Herman is likely to be physically aggressive with the therapist, which can also create hypervigilance. It will be important that the therapist trusts in his ability to make responsible decisions and continues to provide opportunities for him to do so, conveying belief in him. Sending the message of acceptance of Herman, but not his behaviors, can be challenging but also necessary. It is easy to take such behaviors personally. Being purposely injured by Herman or derogatory comments made toward the therapist can be difficult to deal with and to maintain the eight basic principles. The skilled CCPT therapist does not take these behaviors personally but sees them as protective in nature and continues to utilize the core conditions to seek a relationship with Herman, setting boundaries only as needed.

Sexualized behaviors can also be difficult for the CCPT therapist, and they frequently happen with no warning, requiring regulation and quick thinking to ensure safety and that no messages of shame are relayed in the tone as limits are set. The CCPT therapist views these behaviors as an attempt to connect with the therapist in ways they have learned previously to do so with adults or to play out their experiences. Warmth and positive regard in setting these limits maintain the relationship and convey acceptance of the child and not the behavior.

Finally, Herman will require great patience and perseverance on the part of the CCPT therapist. Herman will not be present as a child seeking a relationship due to the abuse he has endured. However, Dhaese and Gaskill (2024) described the role of the relationship as "the most powerful therapeutic impact play therapists can create" (p. 5). They also encouraged an understanding of what rewards the child in therapy, emphasizing that the human brain naturally gravitates toward feeling safe, nurtured, and supported. The CCPT therapist must maintain their belief in the relationship to heal and persevere because a great deal of repetition is required. Dhaese and Gaskill (2024) pointed out that the need for repetition through recurring somatosensory stimulation rather than relying on verbal modalities is necessary. Because Herman experienced much trauma prior to and soon after his birth, the lower brain region was compromised and resulted in disorganization. This part of the brain does not learn through verbal language and is stored implicitly. Through CCPT, Herman will play, naturally engaging in somatosensory stimulation. In this process of playing out his experiences and feelings, he will gain control and regulate as he creates new endings and emotional resolution. The CCPT therapist, equipped with the basic principles and belief in the child, will persevere, never giving up on the child, remaining as a guest on their journey as they repeat the play as necessary for healing.

Working with children with complex trauma takes an emotional toll. Therapists will be impacted by the trauma being played out before them or with them. They must seek places to process this secondary trauma if they are to be able to continue the work. They should seek their own therapy and have trusted colleagues to share their own reactions with. Self-care must be established prior to needing it; otherwise, it becomes an added stressor. Therefore, the CCPT therapist must show themselves the same warmth, genuineness, and unconditional positive regard that they show their clients to be congruent.

Conclusion

Panksepp and Bevin (2012) referred to the attuned relationship that creates synchrony of bodily functions such as hormones, brain waves, and heart rates, creating opportunities to learn from the other. The CCPT relationship offers an opportunity for children to have this co-regulatory relationship with a therapist who has created the psychological, physical, emotional, and cultural safety for them to heal and grow. In CCPT, children develop the skills needed to self-regulate and the necessary neural pathways to build and maintain trusting relationships beyond the confines of the playroom.

Equipped with their belief in the child to naturally strive to resolve his past trauma and gravitate toward self-actualization, the CCPT therapist perseveres, abiding by the eight basic principles and unwavering belief in the child. They fully embrace the therapeutic powers of play, viewing play as the healing component for change.

Appendix

Playroom Toys

Balls	Egg cartons	Refrigerator (wood)
Band-aids	Empty fruit and vegetable cans	Rope
Barbie doll	Erasable nontoxic markers	Rubber snake, alligator
Bendable doll family	Flashlight	Sandbox, large spoon
Blunt scissors	Gumby (Bendable nondescript figure)	School bus
Bop Bag	Hand puppets (doctor, nurse, police officer, mother, father, sister, brother, baby, alligator, wolf)	Soap, brush, comb
Broom, dustpan	Handcuffs	Spider and other insects
Building blocks (various shapes and sizes)	Hats: firefighter, police officer, tiara, crown	Sponge, towel
Cereal boxes	Lone Ranger-type mask and other masks	Stove
Chalkboard, chalk	Medical kit	Stuffed animals (two or three)
Colored chalk, eraser	Medical mask	Telephone (two)
Construction paper (several colors)	Nursing bottle (plastic)	Tinker toys
Crayons, pencils, paper	Pacifier	Tissues
Cymbals	Paints, easel, newsprint, brushes	Tongue depressors, popsicle sticks
Dart Guns	Pitcher	Toy soldiers and army equipment
Dinosaurs, shark	Plastic Knives	Toy watch
Dishes	Play Camera	Transparent tape, nontoxic glue
Dishpan	Play money and cash register	Truck, car, airplane, tractor, boat, ambulance
Doll bed, clothes blanket	Pots, pans, silverware	Watercolor paints
Doll furniture (sturdy wood)	Pounding bench and hammer	Xylophone
Dollhouse (open on floor type that child can lean into)	Puppet theater	Zoo animal and farm animal families
Dress up clothes	Purse and jewelry	
Drum	Rags or old towels	

Tote Bag Playroom

Aggressive hand puppet (alligator, wolf, or dragon)	Dollhouse (may use a box that holds reams of paper, box lid can serve as dollhouse, draw lines on inside of lid to mark rooms; box doubles as storage container for toys)	Popsicle sticks
Band-aids	Dollhouse furniture (at least bedroom, kitchen, and bathroom)	Play dough
Bendable doll family	Handcuffs	Small airplane
Bendable Gumby (nondescript figure)	Lone Ranger-type mask	Small car
Blunt scissors	Medical mask	Spoons
Costume jewelry	Nerf ball	Telephone (two)
Cotton rope	Newsprint	Toy soldiers (20-count is sufficient)
Crayons (eight-count box)	Nursing bottle (plastic)	Transparent tape
Dart Guns	Pipe cleaners	Two play dishes and cups
Doll	Plastic knife	

References

Association for Play Therapy. Retrieved April 19, 2024, from Member Publications https://www.a4pt.org/general/custom.asp?page=Publications.

Axline, V. (1947). *Play therapy: The inner dynamics of childhood.* Read Books Ltd.

Axline, V. (1964). *Dibs in search of self: Personality development in play therapy.* Houghton Mifflin.

Baggerly, J. N., Ray, D.C. & Bratton, S. C. (Eds.). (2010). *Child-centered play therapy research: The evidence base for effective practices.* John Wiley & Sons.

Blanco, P. J., & Ray, D. C. (2011). Play therapy in elementary schools: A best practice for improving academic achievement. *Journal of Counseling & Development*, *89*, 235–43. http://dx.doi.org/10.1002/j.1556-6678.2011.tb00083.x.

Blanco, P. J., Ray, D. C., & Holliman, R. (2012). Long-term child centered play therapy and academic achievement of children: A follow-up study. *International Journal of PlayTherapy*, *21*, 1–13. http://dx.doi.org/10.1037/a0026932.

Blanco, P. J., Holliman, R. P., Muro, J. H., Toland, S., & Farnam, J. L. (2017). Longterm child centered play therapy effects on academic achievement with normal functioning children. *Journal of Child and Family Studies*, *26*,1915–22. http:// dx.doi.org/10.1007/s10826-017-0701-0.

Bratton, S., & Homeyer, L. (2002). *Play therapy session summary.* University of North Texas-Department of Counseling, Development and Higher Education Counseling Program Clinical Services.

Bratton, S., & Lin, Y. (2015). A meta-analytic review of child-centered play therapy approaches. *Journal of Counseling & Development, 93*(1), 45–58.

California Evidence-Based Clearing House for Child Welfare (CEBC) (2024). Child-centered play therapy. https://www.cebc4cw.org/program/child-centered-play-therapy-ccpt/.

Ceballos, P. L., Post, P., & Rodríguez, M. (2021). Practicing child-centered play therapy from a multicultural and social justice framework. In E. Gil & A. A. Drewes (Eds.), *Cultural issues in play therapy* (2nd ed., pp. 13–31). The Guilford Press.

Cochran, J., Cochran, N., Nordling, W., McAdam, A., & Miller, D. (2010). Monitoring two boys' processes through the stages of child-centered play therapy. *International Journal of Play Therapy, 19*(2), 106–16.

Conroy, J., & Perryman, K. (2022). SECURE: A neuro-informed Lens for treating trauma with child centered play therapy. *International Journal of Play Therapy, 31*(3), 143–52. https://doi.org/10.1037/pla0000172.

Danger, S., & Landreth, G. (2005). Child-centered group play therapy with children with speech difficulties. *International Journal of Play Therapy, 14*, 81–102. http://dx.doi.org/10.1037/h0088897.

Dhaese, M. J. & Gaskill, R. L. (2024) Helping depressed, dissociative and withdrawn children: Integrating holistic expressive play therapy and polyvagal theory. *Polyvagal Power in the Playroom*, 150–65.

Felitti, V. J., Anda, R. F., Nordenberg, D., Williamson, D. F., Spitz, A. M., Edwards, V. & Marks, J. S. (1998). Relationship of childhood abuse and household dysfunction to many of the leading causes of death in adults: The Adverse Childhood Experiences (ACE) Study. *American Journal of Preventive Medicine, 14*(14), 245–58.

Guerney, B. (1964). Filial therapy: Description and rationale. *Journal of Consulting Psychology, 28*(4), 304–10.

Guerney, L. F. (1983). Client-centered (nondirective) play therapy. In C. Schaefer & K. O'Connor (Eds.), *Handbook of play therapy* (pp. 21–64). Wiley.

Gutermann, J., Schreiber, F., Matulis, S., Schwartzkopff, L., Deppe, J., & Steil, R. (2016). Psychological treatments for symptoms of posttraumatic stress disorder in children, adolescents, and young adults: A meta-analysis. *Clinical Child and Family Psychology Review, 19*(2), 77–93.

Haas, S. (2017). *Child-centered play therapy with children affected by adverse childhood experiences: A single case design.* [Unpublished doctoral dissertation]. University of North Texas.

Humble, J. J., Summers, N. L., Villarreal, V., Styck, K. M., Sullivan, J. R., Hechler, J. M., & Warren, B. S. (2019). Child-centered play therapy for youths who have experienced trauma: A systematic literature review. *Journal of Child & Adolescent Trauma, 12*(3), 365–75.

Kot, S., Landreth, G. L., & Giordano, M. (1998). Intensive child-centered play therapy with child witnesses of domestic violence. *International Journal of PlayTherapy, 7*, 17–36. http://dx.doi .org/10.1037/h0089421.

Kram, K. (2019). *Child-centered play therapy and adverse childhood experiences: Effectiveness of impulsivity and inattention.* [Unpublished doctoral dissertation]. University of North Texas.

Landreth, G. (2012). *Play therapy: The art of the relationship*. Routledge.

Landreth, G. (2023). *Play therapy: The art of the relationship* (4th ed.). Routledge.

Landreth, G., & Bratton, S. (2019). *Child- parent relationship therapy (CPRT): An evidence-based 10 session filial therapy model* 2nd ed. Routledge.

Levine, P. (2015). *Trauma and memroy: Brain and body in a search for the living past: A practical guide for understanding and working with traumatic memory*. North Atlantic Books.

Lin, Y. W., & Bratton, S. C. (2015). A meta-analytic review of child-centered play therapy approaches. *Journal of Counseling & Development, 93*(1), 45–58.

Massengale, B. & Perryman, K. (2021). Child-centered play therapy's impact on academic achievement: A longitudinal examination in at-risk elementary school students. *International Journal of Play Therapy, 30*(2), 98.

Nordling, W. J., & Guerney, L. (1999). Typical stages in the child-centered play therapy process. *The Journal for the Professional Counselor, 14*(1), 17–23.

Ogawa, Y., Cheng, Y., & Ray, D., (2022). Cultural opportunities and comfort in play therapy. In D. Ray, Y. Ogawa, & Y. Cheng (Eds.*), Multicultural play therapy: Making the most of cultural opportunities with children* (pp. 13–28). Taylor & Francis.

Ojiambo, D., & Taylor, L. (2006). The extraordinary 10-year-old. In D. Ray (Ed.), *A therapists guide to child development: The extraordinary years* (pp. 136–51). Routledge.

Panksepp, J. & Bevin, L. (2012). *The archeology of the mind: Neuroevolutionary origins of human emotions*. Norton.

Perry, B. D., Hambrick, E.& Perry, R. D. (2016). *A neurodevelopmental perspective and clinical challenges. In Transracial and intercountry adoptions: Cultural guidance for professions* (pp. 126–153). Columbia University Press.

Perryman, K. L. & Bowers, L. (2018). Turning the focus to behavioral, emotional and social well-being: The impact of child-centered play therapy. *International Journal of Play Therapy, 27*(4), 227.

Porges, S. W. (2009). The polyvagal theory: New insights into adaptive reactions of the autonomic nervous system. *Cleveland Clinic journal of medicine*, 76(Suppl 2), S86.

Post, P., Grybush, A., Flowers, C., & Elmadani, A. (2020). Impact of child-teacher relationship training on teacher attitudes and classroom behaviors. *International Journal of Play Therapy, 29*(3), 119–30. https://doi.org/10.1037/pla0000118.

Ray, D., & Landreth, G. (2019, September). Child-centered play therapy. *Play Therapy Magazine, 14*(3), 18–19. www.a4pt.org.

Ray, D., Armstrong, S., Balkin, R., & Jayne, K. (2015). Child-centered play therapy in the schools: Review and meta-analysis. *Psychology in the Schools, 52*(2), 107–23.

Ray, D., Ogawa, Y., & Cheng, Y. (2022). Cultural humility and the play therapist. In D. Ray, Y. Ogawa, & Y. Cheng (Eds.), *Multicultural play therapy: Making the most of cultural opportunities with children* (pp. 13–28). Taylor & Francis.

Ray, D., Chung, R., Turner, K., & Aguilar, E. (2022). The multicultural playroom. In D. Ray, Y. Ogawa, & Y. Cheng (Eds.), *Multicultural play therapy: Making the most of cultural opportunities with children* (pp. 13–28). Taylor & Francis.

Robinson, A., Simpson, C., & Hott, B. L. (2017). The effects of child-centered play therapy on the behavioral performance of three first grade students with ADHD. *International Journal of Play Therapy, 26*(2), 73–83. https://doi.org/10.1037/pla0000047.

Rogers, C. R. (1961). *On becoming a person: A therapist's view of psychotherapy*. Houghton Mifflin.

Schaefer, C. E., & Drewes, A. A. (Eds.). (2014). *The therapeutic powers of play: 20 core agents of change* (2nd ed.). Wiley.

Schoonover, T. J., & Perryman, K. (2023). Child-Centered play therapy and adverse childhood experiences: A single-case research design. *Journal of Child and Adolescent Counseling, 9*(1), 1–20. https://doi.org/10.1080/23727810.2022.2138045.

Schottelkorb, A., Swan, K., & Ogawa, Y. (2020). Intensive child-entered play therapy for children on the autism spectrum: A pilot study. *Journal of Counseling & Development, 98*(1), 63–73.

Scuka, R., & Guerney, L. (2019, September). Filial therapy. *Play Therapy, 14*(3), 20–22. www.a4pt.

Swan, K. & Schottelkorb, A. A. (2022). *Cultural opportunities with children with disabilities. In Multicultural play therapy* (pp. 109–127). Routledge.

Taylor, L. & Ray, D. (2021). Child-centered play therapy and social-emotional competencies of African American children: A randomized controlled trial. *International Journal of Play Therapy, 30*(2), 74.

Title IV-E Prevention Services Clearinghouse (2024). Child centered play therapy. https://preventionservices.acf.hhs.gov/.

Van der Kolk, B. A. (1994). The body keeps the score: Memory and evolving psychobiology of post-traumatic stress. *Harvard review of psychiatry, 1*(5), 253–265.

3

Gestalt Play Therapy

Embodied Play

Renee Turner

Chapter Outline

Introduction

Gestalt therapy is a relational, experiential, and process-oriented therapy focused on whole-person integration. Developed by Frederick (Fritz) and Laura Perls in the 1940s, gestalt therapy was later translated to therapeutic work with children by Violet Oaklander. In her seminal text, *Windows to Our Children* (Oaklander, 1978, 2015), Oaklander described the application of gestalt therapy using play therapy with children.

Aligned with existential-humanism, gestalt play therapists believe children are self-regulating and growth-oriented (Blom, 2006). Gestalt therapy posits that "awareness (including owning, choice, and responsibility) and contact bring natural and spontaneous change" (Yontef, 1993, p. 142). In the context of play therapy, awareness is generated through creative strategies such as fantasy, metaphor, storytelling, enactments, movement, and so on. From this awareness, children (in tandem with their caregiver system) move toward a unified whole.

Though recognized as a seminal/historically significant theory by the Association for Play Therapy, literature on gestalt play therapy (GPT) is minimal. As a result, GPT is less understood than some of its play therapy theory counterparts. Consequently, play therapists interested in GPT often struggle to identify the theoretical framework needed to conceptualize and apply play therapy through a GPT lens. This chapter highlights the central theoretical tenets of GPT with children and families using the therapeutic powers of play.

Underlying Philosophy

I-Thou Relating

The most foundational theoretical tenet emphasizes the importance of authentic relating. Laura Perls, the mother of gestalt therapy, transformed gestalt therapy when she integrated the work of existential philosopher Martin Buber, specifically the philosophical concept of *I-Thou* versus *I-It* relating (Yontef, 1993). Buber (1958) asserted that I-Thou relating prioritizes presence, authenticity, connectedness, and inclusion in interpersonal encounters. In an I-Thou relationship, individuals encounter each other as whole persons rather than as objects or transactions. In this stance, the flow between the client(s) and therapist is free from objectification and recognizes the mutual relational impact of authentic relating. When adopting an I-Thou stance, the focus becomes the relationship *between* the client and therapist rather than solely focusing on the client. Consequently, gestalt therapy is relational, with space for the therapist to "be" more fully in session with the client, including self-disclosure and therapeutic inquiry. This encounter is transformative and enriching for all parties involved.

Phenomenology and Holism

The phenomenological approach focuses on the immediacy, or here-and-now, of the child's experiences. The client's experience or behavior is not interpreted but instead met with curiosity as a vehicle to promote awareness (Joyce & Sills, 2018). Through this lens, gestalt play therapists explore the *what* and *how* of behavior instead of why (Oaklander, 2001). Attending to here-and-now experiences increases perception and expands awareness, which serves as a foundation for change and integration. Understanding the child's unique perception lends contextual data and moves beyond a behavioral focus. The phenomenological approach also asserts that individuals have unique perceptions and lived experiences.

The child's perception is influenced by their *phenomenological field*, or the total history of one's experiences (Mann, 2020). Everything that has ever happened to the client, including generational and cultural factors, is embedded in one's phenomenological experience. Gestalt therapy draws on *field theory* to provide a framework for understanding contextual influences on the client's experience. Joyce and Sills (2018) describe three clinical fields: (1) the *experiential field,* which encompasses the person's awareness and perceptions of their experiences, (2) the *relational field*, which centers on the "mutual influencing" within the therapeutic relationship, and (3) the *larger field*, which is comprised of social, cultural, and historical influences (p. 29). This frame is important when conceptualizing children's lived experiences and their perception, which often differs from the perceptions of their caregivers. Gestalt play therapists honor and respect the child's experience of the world and understand that all behavior serves a purpose. Understanding the child and system holistically is the cornerstone of gestalt therapy.

Phenomenology and holism are inextricable. The term "holistic" is a popular term among mental health clinicians, which generally indicates the integration of mind, body, and spirit. Without question, gestalt therapy integrates all aspects of the client (intellect, sensation, body, emotion, energy); however, holism extends beyond just the individual client. Holism from a gestalt lens centers on the inseparable nature of the person (organism) from their environment or field. The organism is environment-dependent and is in a constant dance to self-regulate and meet its individual needs and the environment's needs, all within the context of countless seen and unseen contextual factors. From this perspective, behavior must be understood in the context of the organism's environment. When considered through this dynamic lens, meeting needs is complicated and can result in the frequent presenting problems described later in this chapter. Gestalt play therapists seek to understand the child's behavior within its context and increase individual and system awareness of barriers that prevent the child from making contact and meeting needs.

Contact and Resistance

At the most basic level, contact is "the ability to be fully present in a particular situation with all aspects of the organism—senses, body, emotional expression, intellect—ready and available for use" (Oaklander, 2015, p. 22). The goal is to expand the child's ability and capacity to make contact. However, working with contact should be a gentle process, slowly stretching the child's capacity. The play therapist must remain attuned to the child's experience to recognize and honor resistance.

Resistance is self-protecting and expected in the therapeutic process (Oaklander, 2023). Oaklander (2015) stated that "resistance is the child's ally; it is the way [they] take care of [themselves]" (p. 23). Resistance is an indication of a child's level of contact and contact boundaries. The contact boundary is "where [children] meet and withdraw from [their] environment" (Mann, 2020, p. 34). Awareness of one's contact boundaries facilitates differentiation and the child identifying "me" and "not me" from the environment (Zinker, 2008). Related to contact boundaries are contact boundary disturbances, or creative adjustments, that influence the child's sense of self.

Personality Theory

Gestalt therapy posits that personality or the "self" does "not exist independently within a field or context" (Wheeler, 1997, p. 116). Instead, the "self" "is created in the process of making contact with the environment" (Mann, 2020, p. 18) as it attempts to fulfill needs and self-regulate. Environmental factors influence how children fulfill or block their needs, resulting in contact boundary disturbances or creative adjustments.

Creative Adjustments

Creative adjustments (originally known as resistances) are adaptations made in relation to an environment or system. All creative adjustments are functional within a given environment, field, or family system. When the environment, field, or system lacks support, a "child may creatively adjust by compensating for what is lacking in the environment" (Mann, 2020, p. 8). For example, a grieving child may avoid making contact with their sadness about a sibling's death when doing so disrupts their caregiver's ability to remain emotionally regulated. Instead, the child may creatively adjust by adopting caregiving or pleasing patterns to support the family system. Creative adjustments include but are not limited to desensitization, introjection, projection, retroflection, and confluence. See Blom (2006) for a comprehensive discussion of creative adjustments in the context of play therapy.

Model of Psychopathology

Formal diagnostic labels are controversial among gestalt therapists. Diagnostic labels are fixed and objectifying, violate phenomenological principles by positioning the therapist as an expert, and deny the uniqueness of individuals (Joyce & Sills, 2018). Despite this, assessment and diagnosis are necessary aspects of play therapy in a world driven by managed care and other stakeholders. When diagnoses are required, gestalt play therapists must adopt a relational frame to view psychopathology that is inclusive of the child's phenomenology and diversity. Play therapists are also cautioned against placing great stock in outside assessments as doing so can "contribute to unfounded interpretations" (Blom, 2006, p. 56).

Mann (2020) states that all "behavior has a function and we can only begin to understand its function if we consider it within the context of the person's whole situation (p. 86)." This statement is especially true when working with children and families, as behavioral problems are the most common presenting concern. From a gestalt perspective, "behavioral problems" occur as a result of contact boundaries and creative adjustments to the child's environment. The creative adjustments made by the child are self-preserving and largely out of the child's awareness. Blom (2006) asserts that "children with contact boundary disturbances are incapable of being aware of their needs and healthy contact with the environment. These children's integrated holistic functioning of the senses, body, emotions and intellect is fragmented by using contact boundary disturbances, which negatively affect the natural process of organismic self-regulation" (p. 30).

One behavior that is frequently pathologized by caregivers and stakeholders is anger. Aggressive energy is natural and necessary to negotiate the environment and does not necessarily indicate pathology. From a gestalt lens, anger is a protective, healthy response to a boundary violation (e.g., emotional, contractual, physical, spiritual, or need-based). The energy facilitated by aggression provides the energy to renegotiate boundaries. Some practitioners are uncomfortable working with and promoting the cathartic release of big feelings, especially anger, out of fear of losing control in the playroom. Through a gestalt lens, the goal is to make contact and experience what arises.

Conceptualizing Goals of Treatment

The overarching goal of gestalt therapy is integration through awareness. Gestalt play therapists utilize expressive interventions to achieve the same goals as talk-based gestalt therapists. Using expressive art, music, projections, movement, sound, fantasy, storytelling, and, of course, play, gestalt play therapists remain focused on embodied awareness regardless of the goal or subgoal. Primary subgoals include increasing sense of self, identifying and establishing boundaries, promoting self-regulation, and increasing self-nurturing and self-support (Oaklander, 2023). Addressing healthy aggressive energy and integrating polarities (extreme opposites) are also common goals in GPT. Finally, from a family perspective, the overarching goal is to improve system and individual needs fulfillment and organismic self-regulation.

Gestalt therapists are reminded to hold the relationship in mind when identifying and addressing goals and adopting a stance of *creative indifference*. Creative indifference does not indicate a lack of concern; rather, it reflects a lack of agenda and trust in the client. Mann (2020) describes creative indifference as "being open to each unfolding moment in the therapy session without the need to rescue, pre-plan, or hide behind a bunch of techniques" (p. 60). Oaklander (2015) suggested that the gestalt play therapy process follows these general phases: (1) building the relationship, (2) addressing contact, (3) strengthening the self, (4) emotional expression, (5) self-nurturing, (6) addressing persistent problems, and (7) closing and termination. While the GPT process is flexible, goals should generally align with the scaffolded approach outlined by Oaklander, paired with the spirit of creative indifference.

Role of the Therapist

Oaklander (2022) emphasized that "nothing happens in therapy without at least a thread of a relationship" (p. 20). Therefore, being fully present and embodied, maintaining attuned contact, and prioritizing curiosity over agenda (Turner, 2023) is essential. Following the I-Thou philosophy, gestalt play therapists often develop relationships with children before engaging in more directive play therapy. As such, less directive play therapy is commonly utilized in the beginning phase as the therapist observes how the child interacts and makes contact with the environment, including the therapist. As the relationship progresses, gestalt play therapists utilize non-directive and directive approaches.

The overall level of directiveness can be described as semi-directive, based on the therapeutic relationship and the child's capacity and awareness. Some sessions are less directive; some are more directive. Regardless of the level of directiveness, the therapist is an active co-participant in the play therapy session, providing reflections, naming curiosity, and offering the child experiments. Experiments are an active way to promote awareness and integration. There are countless possible experiments in GPT, limited only by the play therapist's imagination (Mann, 2020). Common experiments (illustrated in the chapter case study) include *exaggeration* (saying or doing something louder or bigger), *repetition* (saying or doing something multiple times), *giving voice* (narrating a thing or person), and *becoming* (embodying a person or thing) (Naranjo, 1993). Above all else, experiments should be playful and, when possible, fun!

Oaklander (2015) provides countless examples of experiments in her seminal text, *Windows to Our Children*. However, readers are encouraged to interpret Oaklander's experiments as inspirational ideas rather than steps. Experiments are individualized, graded, and purposeful; the gestalt play therapist generally does not follow a protocol or predetermined steps when applying experiments. Ideally, "experiments develop naturally, moving forward with its own momentum, the [child] engaged and energized by what is emerging" (Joyce & Sills, 2018, p. 115).

Invitations to experiment should be personal and grounded in the here-and-now. Also, note that invitations to experiment are only invitations. The phrase "there is no such thing as a failed experiment" is commonly used among gestalt therapists. This means that, regardless of the response, the therapist and client learn from the process. The therapist gains awareness of the client's contact and resistance; the client gains awareness of their boundary and sense of self in the environment. The child maintains autonomy in their participation in experiments at all times. Forcing experiments is imposing an agenda on the child, which can cause long-term damage to the therapeutic relationship. This is one reason why play therapists must be theoretically integrated rather than pulling techniques without consideration for the theoretical application.

Beyond the relationship, Oaklander (2001) summarized the role of the therapist in the following ten points:

"**1.** To evaluate those aspects of children that have been lost, restricted, inhibited, or blocked and thus interfere with natural, healthy growth and development.
2. To provide materials for children that are appropriate to their age level as needed in the therapeutic process.
3. To enhance experience required to strengthen the sense of self and promote emotional expression within a safe environment.
4. To honor and accept children as they present themselves.
5. To maintain good contact with children—to be fully involved—and to be sensitive to children's energy level, which may signal a breaking of children's own contact.
6. To avoid interpretation, and to gently guide children into the self-ownership of their projections.
7. To be willing to engage with children in play.

8. To be respectful of the therapist's own limits and boundaries—to set clear boundaries for children as needed.
9. To be congruent, authentic, and nonmanipulative.
10. To communicate with, educate, and involve the parents as much as possible."

(p. 52–53)

Roles of Caregivers and Collaterals

Although the child is most often the identified client in GPT, working within the child's field and family/caregiver system is essential. Thus, caregiver work is integrated into all stages of the gestalt play therapy process. Starting with the intake, the gestalt play therapist explores the child's field; however, exploring the field is a dynamic and ongoing process. Early caregiver-child sessions are necessary for the therapist to observe family/caregiver dynamics and *how* the child engages with their environment.

During family/caregiver play therapy, the therapist is curious about attunement, contact, and presence quality between members of the child's system. Good *family/caregiver contact* requires caregivers to be aware of self, others, the system, and the interplay between. In family/caregiver play therapy sessions, the gestalt play therapist evaluates:

- What examples of I-Thou and I-It relationships are observed?
- When and how is good contact made? Who is available for contact?
- What are the barriers to good contact within the system?
- How do the child and family/caregivers experience here-and-now relating?
- What feelings are the individual and family unit aware of and openly discussing?

The therapist also notices how the child and family/caregiver system addresses and meets individual and relational needs, noting creative adjustments.

- What needs are being expressed indirectly?
- Which feelings are being expressed indirectly?
- How does the child engage with their environment differently based on who is present in the family/caregiver play session?

Given the importance of the field and field conditions on the child, caregiver consultations occur frequently to continue to explore the field with caregivers. Zinker (2008) emphasized the importance of boundaries, intimacy (connection), and flexibility within a healthy system. In the initial phase, consultations address contact and contact boundaries, individual and relational needs, creative adjustments, and system dynamics (Zinker, 2008), often through reframing the child's behavior or presenting concern. Gestalt play therapists also provide education on the importance of presence, attunement, and attachment, providing experiential engagements when possible to strengthen the field. Later sessions may include the caregiver addressing persistent system issues.

Case Study through the Lens of the Therapeutic Powers of Play

Therapeutic Powers of Play Employed

Gestalt Play Therapy consistently employs the therapeutic powers of play. The case study (see Appendix for case study of Herman being referenced) below highlights the following therapeutic powers of play outlined by Schaefer and Drewes (2014): (a) self-expression, (b) direct teaching, (c) indirect teaching, (d) catharsis, (e) abreaction, (f) therapeutic relationship, (g) empathy, (h) creative problem solving, and (i) self-regulation.

Self-Expression

Self-expression is inherent to play therapy. However, while self-expression is inherent to the general play therapy process, self-expression is foundational to gestalt's theory of change. Self-expression found through play therapy promotes the expression of unexpressed parts and polarities, or extreme opposites. One common experiment in gestalt therapy is "becoming." For example, children may spontaneously or by invitation "become" a puppet. Becoming involves embodying, giving voice to, and acting as the item. In the following case illustration, Herman "becomes" Hulk, which helped him make contact with the range of emotions connected to his anger.

Indirect Teaching

Indirect teaching is another natural function of GPT as it relies on projection, metaphor, and experiential learning to promote integration and change. Taylor de Faoite (2014) suggests that the use of metaphor allows children to tell stories parallel to their lives and gain control by altering stories and changing endings. Through a gestalt lens, play allows children to make contact indirectly and move toward ownership and responsibility (Blom, 2006; Oaklander, 2023). Due to Herman's complex trauma history, indirect teaching is a valuable tool for awareness that supports his natural pace of healing. Examples of indirect teaching used in the case of Herman include body scanning and body mapping, guided imagery, sensory play, and projective drawings.

Direct Teaching

Directive techniques can facilitate direct learning in GPT. Direct learning content commonly addresses basic psychoeducation, emotional literacy, somatic/body awareness, differentiation, and needs exploration. Herman received direct teaching about the "good," "bad," and neutral aspects of anger, his general emotions, and somatic awareness. The volume of direct teaching will vary depending on the child, the presenting problem, and the therapist's style; however, direct teaching will be present in some fashion throughout GPT.

Abreaction

Often associated with trauma, abreaction through a GPT lens represents a contact boundary or contact disturbance. However, through a GPT lens, children demonstrate a range of abreaction encounters during play therapy sessions beyond a trauma response. When viewed through the lens of breaking contact, we can observe abreaction during frenetic and chaotic play (difficulty making or sustaining contact), children turning their backs to the therapist, or changing play modalities/materials after a poignant reflection that causes contact too quickly. The key task for gestalt play therapists is to manage and respect the protective resistance of abreaction as it arises. Herman's case illustrates the myriad ways contact boundaries/disturbances show up in the playroom.

Catharsis

Catharsis is the release, purging, or cleansing of emotions. The gestalt therapy process utilizes experiments designed to elicit contact with unexpressed parts and is strongly associated with catharsis. Unfortunately, misgivings exist about the application of cathartic release, as Fritz Perls often promoted cathartic release without discernible consideration of the therapeutic relationship. It is important to note that contemporary gestalt practitioners, including gestalt play therapists, emphasize the importance of cathartic release only within the context of a safe relationship guided by trauma-informed principles. Gestalt play therapists utilize expressive interventions to achieve the same goals as talk-based gestalt therapists. Anger, sadness, and shame are the most common emotions expressed during cathartic release, but any emotion or experience can become "stuck."

Hitting the bop bag, sword battles, and destructive play are all examples of common play behaviors associated with "big feelings." Pounding and molding clay is another GPT technique frequently modeled by Violet Oaklander. These interventions promote a full-body cathartic release of strong energetic feelings like anger. Some practitioners are uncomfortable working with and promoting the cathartic release of big feelings, especially anger, out of fear of losing control in the playroom. Through a gestalt lens, the goal is to make contact and experience what arises.

Expressive activities also promote catharsis depending on how the therapeutic experience is processed. For example, the act of art-making can evoke spontaneous catharsis as clients make contact with unconscious or unexpressed emotions. However, gestalt play therapists can also invite catharsis by pairing movement, sound, and dialoguing with expressive creations. These activities promote a safe and playful way of achieving the same goals as Fritz Perls, while respecting the therapeutic relationship.

Therapeutic Relationship

As indicated, the I-Thou principle informs all aspects of GPT. Gestalt play therapy not only permits but encourages the therapeutic use of self in play therapy sessions to satisfy the spirit of I-Thou. As a result, emotional transparency and self-disclosure are central to the relationship. This therapeutic power of play also pertains to the value of co-creation in the GPT relationship. In the case of Herman, the therapist illustrated instances of "feeling with" the client and reflecting the feeling outward for the client to experience relationally.

Empathy

Empathy is related to self-nurturing work and is essential to integration in GPT. The goal of self-nurturing work is to "help children be more accepting, caring, and actively nurturing to themselves" (Oaklander, 2023, p. 43), especially those with trauma histories. Oaklander (2023) encourages children to "talk" to the self-critical and fragmented parts to increase compassion. Blom (2006) outlines three phases of self-nurturing work: (1) make contact with an unacceptable part, (2) nurture the unacceptable part, and (3) engage in "homework" activities that support nurturing the previously unaccepted part (p. 117–119). In the case study, Herman makes contact with aspects of his anger through the Hulk figures and then slowly embodies and verbalizes empathy and understanding.

Creative Problem Solving

Play therapy promotes "out of the box" thinking or divergent thinking (Russ & Wallace, 2014). GPT relies on creative problem solving to enhance children's sense of self. The act of creative problem solving allows a child to experience mastery and teaches them how to deal with frustration while maintaining power and control over their choices (Oaklander, 2023). From a GPT perspective, contacting and expressing one's aggressive energy and setting boundaries is also associated with creative problem solving as the child renegotiates their contact boundaries.

Herman's case illustrates creative problem solving through creating and building with non-traditional toys (obstacle course), which also lends a sense of power, control, and safety during early sessions. The case illustration also highlights the importance of aggressive energy in using creative problem solving to sharpen Herman's sense of self.

Self-Regulation

A unique aspect of gestalt therapy is the theoretical emphasis on sensation and the body. Joseph Zinker (2008) suggests that "experiencing the here-and-now begins with sensation" (pg. 94). Using play and expressive strategies, gestalt play therapists help children identify sensations and facilitate moving energy or emotion from the bottom up. In addition to basic tracking and reflection of feelings, gestalt play therapists guide the child into greater awareness of their sensations and emotions through somatic reflections. *Somatic reflections* provide the client with data about observable (breath, posture, gestures), which facilitates *embodied awareness*.

From a gestalt perspective, embodied awareness is a pathway to organismic self-regulation. For example, the bob bag, found in many play therapy rooms, is one item that invites aggressive release and is categorized as aggressive play. However, from a GPT perspective, aggressive release is also self-regulating. Herman's case illustrates many forms of regulation, including down-regulating (relaxing) and up-regulating (releasing).

Cultural, Diversity, and Inclusion Considerations

Gestalt therapy is rooted in social activism (Melnick & Lukensmeyer, 2022) and has the potential for holistically integrating culture and diversity. Several critical aspects of the theory align with inclusion. For example, field theory centers on broadening awareness of the ground and "awareness of multiple frames of reference in experiencing and understanding our world" (Tucker, 2023, p. 63), including diversity. Additionally, the phenomenological frame underscores the importance of the client's lived experience. Overall, gestalt therapy provides a sensitive and flexible framework to include diversity and cultural components while still focusing on the individual's unique experience and personal growth.

Unfortunately, the application of gestalt therapy is also subject to an individualistic viewpoint. It is crucial to acknowledge that gestalt therapy exists within an environment or field shaped by a middle-class, white culture that is steeped in a colonized, westernized medical model (Joyce & Sills, 2018). Applied through a "therapist knows best" lens, gestalt therapy techniques can place the play therapist in a position of power that jeopardizes the therapeutic relationship. Some theoretical aspects (focusing on the body/sensation, using direct language, inviting aggression, directive experiments) can be employed in a manner that ignores cultural and diversity factors unique to the client. There is no one-size-fits-all approach in gestalt therapy. The potential held within gestalt therapy may not be realized if the clinician is not intentional in their practice.

Challenges in Implementation

Practically speaking, GPT is underrepresented, with limited literature and empirical research. As a result, play therapists may struggle to find training and supervision to enhance their knowledge and skills. The lack of empirical research is a direct reflection of resistance within the gestalt community to manualize and structure the therapy. Research methods used in empirical research are largely incongruent with the philosophy embedded in gestalt therapy.

GPT is unstructured and not outcome-driven, which can be challenging for those who work best with clear steps. Instead, experiments are spontaneous and emerge from the field or play therapy process, often based on the therapist's intuition and creativity (Joyce & Sills, 2018; Naranjo, 1993). Returning to the lack of empirical research, intuition is not scientific or measurable. Consequently, the play therapist must hone their self-awareness.

Self-awareness is underscored in gestalt therapy, so much so that Oaklander (2023) describes GPT therapy as a *way of being* in the playroom. As such, therapists must remain intentional about exploring their personal processes, including, but not limited to, awareness, contact patterns and boundaries, and their own embodiment. In short, gestalt therapists are engaged in a parallel process similar to that of their clients. Thus, it is essential that gestalt play therapists remain committed to personal growth and awareness through an ongoing personal growth process, including personal therapy.

Case Formulation and Application

Intake Session

The first step as a gestalt play therapist is to explore the client's field and phenomenology. I remained curious about how Herman *experiences* his life rather than focusing on behaviors and behavioral changes. During the intake with Herman's foster parents, I inquired about a few key aspects to understand his life and presenting concerns. His foster parents appeared motivated to support Herman's ADHD diagnosis but could not easily identify his regulation needs or patterns of activation.

Sessions 1–2

In the first session, I focused on building an authentic relationship with Herman and attuning to his needs without an agenda. As is typical with GPT, the first session with the child is generally less directive, to observe the child's level of contact, embodiment, creative adjustments, and energy flow. In other words, how does Herman experience himself in relation to his environment? In this exploratory session, I observed that Herman made little contact with me but appeared very curious about the playroom and the toys, making contact with nearly every toy and play item in the playroom. His play was disorganized and slightly chaotic, with relatively few moments of sustained attention. Despite a formal assessment of ADHD, my sense of Herman was that his presentation aligned more consistently with symptoms related to trauma. Also, though he appeared to make contact with the playroom and the toys, he was not very connected to his own embodied experience.

The second session was a family observation session, which was essential to gauge the family's contact patterns, level of attunement, presence quality, and awareness. I had a few guiding questions in my mind: (1) how does Herman get his needs met, (2) how does he show up in the family system, (3) what are his patterns of making and sustaining contact, and (4) how does resistance show up in the family system? In this session, I observed that Herman's foster mother managed many of his behaviors non-verbally by giving him disapproving looks. I observed several creative adjustments during this session.

Sessions 3–6

Herman appeared to be activated in the waiting room (jumping up and down) and intentionally bumped and crashed into walls as we walked to the playroom. When we entered the playroom, I asked if Herman knew what an obstacle course was and if he would like to build one together. He looked at me with a big smile and immediately started planning everything we could build. I took off my shoes (which I commonly do in play therapy sessions), and Herman followed. I used the opportunity to talk about my feet and how good it felt to rub them on the carpet and feel myself connect to the ground (*indirect teaching*). Together, we pulled the cushions off the couch to use as crash/landing pads, used painter's tape to create paths on the floor, and set up a "boxing" station with the bop bag. Once the obstacles were built, I followed Herman's lead through the course. I provided emotional and sensory reflections of my own experience (*indirect teaching*), occasionally asking, "I wonder how it feels in your body?" inviting him to check in with his inner experience. Herman appeared to check in but did not verbally respond to these queries. Near the end of the session, without saying a word, Herman walked over to the dollhouse, placed two dolls in a bed, and walked away (*abreaction*). He punched the bop bag and yelled for a few minutes (*catharsis*), then said, "I'm ready to leave."

When Herman entered the playroom in session four, he explored the room and the toys. I noted to myself how much more connected and grounded Herman appeared than in the initial session. He was excited to go to the playroom and told me everything he wanted to build on the way to the playroom. He kicked his shoes off and started planning and constructing the obstacle course (*creative problem solving*). I asked if I could add some challenges to the course, and with his consent, I placed cards from a yoga/posture game at various parts of the obstacle course for "bonus points." (It is essential to build in choice-making when using GPT.) When the yoga/posture game was selected, I modeled and taught Herman body scanning to increase awareness of his sensations and embodied experience (*direct teaching*). At the end of the obstacle course, Herman returned to the dollhouse, added the two dolls to the bed again, and then punched the bop bag. He returned to the dollhouse again, adding a few more items, then repeatedly punched the bop bag, repeating this cycle three times. I remained quiet at the dollhouse, only providing somatic reflections to increase bodily awareness through Herman's aggressive work. He ended the session by picking up a baby doll and tossing it to the ground (*abreaction*). Herman left the session quietly, in a low mood.

Sessions 7–9

In this session, he gravitated toward the Hulk figures, especially the largest of the figures (approximately 14" tall). He told me about watching superhero movies with his foster dad, and I noted the polarity between Hulk and Bruce Banner. I invited Herman to make contact with each polarity by "becoming" both Hulk and Bruce Banner to embody their respective energy and personalities. After playing with intentional *exaggeration* and *amplification*,

Herman became the Hulk, yelling "Hulk smash, Hulk smash!" as he hit the bop bag and destroyed the dollhouse. He laughed and used the playroom mirror to make silly faces with aggressive poses. I reflected to Herman that "sometimes anger can feel silly." I also noted that Herman did not make contact with Bruce Banner.

In the next session, Herman was goal-directed and planned a battle between the large (14") and small (5") Hulk figures. Herman described how "bad" Hulk (the larger toy) would destroy the town. He placed the two Hulk figures across from one another, with the larger of the two figures in an aggressive stance. I reflected on the contrast between the small and large Hulk figures, spontaneously prompting Herman to describe the difference between "big anger" and "little anger." I provided Herman with an embodied reflection, "I can really tell the difference between those two in my body," using movement and gestures to exaggerate the embodied feeling. Herman responded by mirroring my movements and deepened his contact with the two parts by playing with the facial expressions and voices of each corresponding Hulk figure. I offered Herman an experiment to create a dialogue between the two parts, to which he agreed. Herman primarily gave the smaller figure a voice, telling the larger figure, "You mess up everything! Why won't you stop it!!" The larger Hulk grunted in return, and I observed Herman's mood shift (eyes pointing to the ground, furrowed brow). Matching his energy, I whispered, "I wonder what that Hulk (motioning to the larger figure) needs?" Herman spoke quietly, "Probably for someone to love him" (*empathy*). Herman ended the session by punching the bop bag. I observed tears form in his eyes and said, "I see the tears in your eyes. I feel sad with you" (*therapeutic relationship*).

Shame was prominent in these sessions as Herman made contact with these parts. When Herman made contact with shame, he either hid in the play tent (*abreaction*) or engaged in cathartic release. After Herman went into the play tent for the second time, I wondered aloud if he wanted to play with some ways to help his body feel calm (*self-regulation*). Herman said, "maybe," so I showed him how to hug himself with a blanket, use different breathing patterns, and how to use a finger labyrinth. In later sessions, he opted to take markers and paper inside the play tent and drew quietly (*self-regulation*). Herman reported that he did not have a space to regulate like this at home.

Sessions 10–17

Over the next few sessions, the Hulk play was repeated. We explored the energy of Hulk's anger and his remorse after he loses control. We explored the usefulness of anger and the importance of naming feelings out loud (*direct teaching*). Rescue play emerged during this time. In later sessions, Herman would intermittently provide nurturing and care to the larger Hulk. I observed aggressive themes reduce and nurturing themes increase as sessions progressed. Herman also spent longer segments at the dollhouse. During this time, his play shifted to "monsters" attacking the dollhouse.

Initially, the "monsters" were in the dollhouse's bedroom closet. Together, Herman and I devised plans to protect the house and attack the monsters. Our play was small (isolated to the figures, whispers). After the second iteration of Herman "spooking" the monsters, I invited him to find the power in his body by linking his prior play themes. I said, "I wonder how it would be if he had the power of Hulk to 'spook' the monster." Herman grinned and transitioned his play to big, powerful play, with an offer to experiment by exaggerating and repeating sounds and motions to embody his experience more deeply. I playfully mirrored his movements and engaged in active play with Herman.

Until that point, the monsters had been invisible; however, Herman chose an oversized snake to become the monster and attack the dollhouse. Herman, with the power of Hulk, rescued this family inside the dollhouse and killed the snake. This play theme occurred over several sessions. Each time, he killed the snake differently (buried alive in the sand, drowned in a pot of water, "cut up" with the sword). After Herman "cut up" the snake, I offered an experiment to draw the snake and tear up the paper. He drew a crude snake, ripped it up, and hid the portions of the snake all over the playroom. After the snake's death, Herman would check in on the dollhouse family, sometimes setting up a meal in the kitchen, and other times "tucking" them in bed.

Sessions 18–26

In this series of sessions, we continued recursive work related to making contact, identifying, and satisfying needs. I invited more directive experiments to increase awareness and self-nurturing. Herman and I experimented with taking ownership of his projections by making "I" statements and facilitating responsibility for his emotions. It is important to note that in gestalt play therapy, "responsibility" for one's emotions does not indicate that Herman is responsible for the experiences that caused his trauma and anger, nor does it indicate that he is responsible for getting his needs met by an outside party (his foster parents). Responsibility in this context refers to the organism's sharpened sense of self that identifies a need and makes healthy and full contact with the need, ultimately moving toward need fulfillment. Clearly, this process requires a combination of individual and family/caregiver therapy to support Herman's growth. Unfortunately, a child cannot outheal systems that are unwilling or unable to meet the child's needs.

Conclusion

Gestalt Play Therapy is a dynamic existential-humanistic, relational, and experiential model of play therapy. Utilizing expressive therapy in the context of relational embodiment, GPT increases awareness of the total organism, including system and relational needs. Gestalt play therapy prioritizes the co-created relationship to increase relational and somatic awareness in the here-and-now. The case of Herman highlights the primary therapeutic powers of play associated with gestalt play therapy.

References

Blom, R. (2006). *The handbook of gestalt therapy: Practical guidelines for child therapists.* Jessica Kingsley Publishers.

Buber, M. (1958). *I and thou.* Scribner.

Joyce, P., & Sills, C. (2018). *Skills in gestalt counselling and psychotherapy* (4th ed.). Sage.

Mann, D. (2020). *Gestalt therapy: 100 key points and techniques.* Routledge.

Melnick, G. N., & Lukensmeyer, C. J. (2022). Gestalt roots and social activism: An interview with Carolyn J. Lukensmeyer. *Gestalt Review, 26*(2), 200–28. https://doi.org/10.5325/gestaltreview.26.2.0200.

Naranjo, C. (1993). *Gestalt therapy: The attitude and practice of an atheoretical experientialism.* Crown House Publishing.

Oaklander, V. (1978). *Windows to our children.* Gestalt Press.

Oaklander, V. (2001). Gestalt play therapy. *International Journal of Play Therapy, 10(*2), 45–55. https://doi.org/10.1037/h0089479.

Oaklander, V. (2015). *Windows to our children* (2nd ed.). Gestalt Press.

Russ, S. W., & Wallace, C. E. (2014). Creative problem solving. In C. E. Schaefer & A. A. Drewes (Eds.), *The therapeutic powers of play: 20 core agents of change* (pp. 213–23). Wiley.

Schaefer, C. E., & Drewes, A. D. (2014). *The therapeutic powers of play: 20 core agents of change.* Wiley.

Taylor de Faoite, A. (2014). Indirect teaching. In C. E. Schaefer & A. A. Drewes (Eds.), *The therapeutic powers of play: 20 core agents of change* (pp. 51–67). Wiley.

Tucker, P. (2023). Enhancing dialogue about cultural difference through Gestalt group work theory and practice. *Gestalt Review, 27*(1), 56–78. https://doi.org/10.5325/gestaltreview.27.1.0056.

Turner, R. (2023). The embodied process in gestalt sandtray. *World Journal for Sand Therapy Practice®, 1*(11). https://doi.org/10.58997/wjstp.v1i11.60.

Wheeler. G. (1997). Self and shame: A gestalt approach. *Gestalt Review, 1*(3), 221–44. https://doi.org/10.2307/44394019.

Yontef, G. M. (1993). *Awareness, dialogue, and process: Essays on gestalt therapy.* The Gestalt Journal Press.

Zinker, J. C. (2008). *In search of good form: Gestalt therapy with couples and families.* GIC Press.

4

Attachment Theory, Theraplay, and the Therapeutic Powers of Play

Gloria M. Cockerill

Chapter Outline

Introduction

Beginning one's journey as a play therapist, one is guided to think critically about the underlying theory and framework from which to base the assessment of the client and client system and how to conceptualize the treatment process overall. While theory provides the framework and guides the initial phases of a play therapist's work, this is only the beginning. Recognizing and developing one's understanding of the catalysts for change within the therapeutic process, The Therapeutic Powers of Play, allows for a deeper understanding of what is happening in the playroom and how to more effectively implement the tools in one's toolbox. Peabody and Schaeffer (2019) highlight in their article in the APT Play Therapy Magazine the critical importance for practitioners to understand both child development and possess a clear grounding in how and why a child's thoughts, feelings and behaviors change in the playroom. Play Therapy and its many approaches tend to be oversimplified and misunderstood, making it crucial for practitioners to not only grasp the underlying concepts at play but also be able to explain to caregivers the significance of our work and the positive impact on children, parents, and families at large.

As a professional trained in both directive and non-directive approaches to play therapy, there is a time and place for incorporating the varying tools to effectively meet the needs of clients on their journey to healing. While working in foster care early in my career, I was faced with the profound emotional and developmental impact of trauma and early attachment disruptions in children, their ability to engage in a therapeutic relationship, and their capacity to engage in the playroom at all. I was confronted with the fact that while I thought I was ready to provide a sanctuary for change in my small playroom, they seemed frozen in time. They had clearly missed out on so many critical childhood experiences that would allow them to trust themselves, others, and the world around them. Attachment theory, as one of the most widely researched theories of child development, provided a lens to begin to comprehend the underlying needs of my clients and Theraplay®[1] became a fundamental component of treatment. This chapter will review fundamental concepts of attachment theory. Utilizing the case of Herman, the reader will be oriented to Theraplay, a seminal approach to play therapy focused on addressing the fundamental building blocks of relationship and will consider The Therapeutic Powers of Play that are typically at work throughout the Theraplay Treatment Process.

Underlying Philosophy

The work of John Bowlby and the development of our understanding of the attachment behavioral system are foundational to the later work of others that include Mary Ainsworth and Mary Main (Yip et al., 2015). On a simplistic level, attachment theory posits that the infant's innate drive to secure proximity to their caregiver allows the infant to experience a safe space from which to explore their environment and access support in moments of distress, leading to a stronger capacity for survival (Benoit, 2004). Bowlby's work and the developing body of research take this further, noting that this innate drive and need for an infant to engage in behaviors that allow for proximity to their caregiver not only provides a sense of safety but also the organizing responses that foster healthy brain development and emotional regulation (Buckwalter, 2018). Throughout the first year of life, the early repetitive interactions and patterns of relationship established between the child and the primary caregiver ideally provide experiences of co-regulation during episodes of distress that allow the infant to develop internal representations of self or an inner working model (IWM) in which they view themselves as lovable/valued, others as dependable, and the world as a generally safe place. They also begin to develop their capacity for affect regulation, developing templates for how to manage future challenging situations (Schore & Schore, 2007). As cited in Buckwalter (2018), Schore's work also notes the importance of

[1]A registered service mark of The Theraplay® Institute, Evanston, IL, USA.

right brain to right brain interactions between the primary caregiver and the child during this critical phase of development. The relational dance developed between the infant and caregiver, coupled with considerations such as a child's genetics, including temperament, approach to parenting, and environmental stressors, work together to provide strong indicators for social-emotional success across the life span (Howe et al., 1999).

Theraplay

The Theraplay Model, fundamentally grounded in Bowlby's attachment theory, is a dyadic approach typically utilized to address attachment-related issues with its primary focus on the enhancement of the parent-child relationship (Booth & Jernberg, 2010). Developed in the late 1960s by Ann Jernberg and Phyllis Booth, Theraplay aims to recreate the early parent-child relationship through the provision of practitioner-planned play sequences that provide repetitive, rhythmic, developmentally appropriate, relational, rewarding, and respectful experiences for the child and caregiver (Booth & Jernberg, 2010). It is through these interactions that the practitioner aims to provide the child and their caregiver with an experience of felt safety, active, co-regulating moments with one another, and ultimately repetitive positive, joyful experiences to reorganize the inner working models of both members of the dyad (Norris & Lender 2020).

In consideration of the significance of the infant-parent relationship, Theraplay has separated aspects of the interactions in the infant-parent relationship into four dimensions: Structure, Engagement, Nurture and Challenge (Lindaman et al., 2018). Each of these constructs focuses on a different critical aspect of the typical infant-parent relationship (Booth & Jernberg, 2010). These dimensions create the foundation from which practitioners develop and adjust treatment and session plans focused on providing each dyad with a sense of safety and attunement during experiences that allow for coregulation and joyful moments of connection in the here and now (Norris & Lender, 2020).

In the Theraplay text, Booth and Jernberg (2010) define and highlight the key aspects of each dimension, which are summarized below:

Structure refers to the practitioner and the parents' leadership role in ensuring a sense of safety through organized and regulated experiences in which the child can explore their world, learn about themselves, and develop an ability to self-regulate.

Engagement encompasses the attuned responses utilized by the therapist and then the parent to entice their infant into moments of joyful connection in which the child experiences themselves as seen and heard. Equally as important is the parent's response to the infant's negative affective states, reinforcing that they are not alone and are valued despite challenging feelings.

Nurture focuses on the typical caretaking behaviors like feeding, holding, and rocking that provide the infant with comfort, reassurance, and down regulation. These interactions further highlight the infant's sense of self as lovable.

Challenge highlights the parent's role in providing developmentally appropriate risks while supporting the infant's ability to manage the tension created by the risk, which leads to an increased sense of mastery and efficacy for the infant or young child.

While each dimension can be operationalized into a distinct area of focus, it is critical to recognize that, as in the infant-parent dance, each dimension is often less discrete and blends together during their day-to-day interactions. The organic nature in which an adult organizes, attunes, provides care, and supports the child as they draw them out of their comfort zone toward growth and development will create ebb and flow in how each dimension is incorporated.

Personality Theory

The American Psychological Association defines personality as "the enduring characteristics and behavior that comprise a person's unique adjustment to life, including major traits, interests, drives, values, self-concept, abilities, and emotional patterns," and further notes the impact personality has on one's behavior (apa.org, n.d.). Attachment theory and its focus on the nature and quality of one's earliest relationships and interactions provide a window into a child's identity development and personality formation (Howe et al., 1999). It is in the context of connection and the quality of our first relationships that the facets of personality begin to take shape in the formation of implicit and explicit representations of themselves, others, and the world around them, referred to as one's inner working model (Howe et al., 1999). As we grow, we rely on these internal representations to serve as guides for our behavior and interactions with the world, allowing us to strive toward individuation, which Hoffman et al. (2011) highlighted as a primary goal for a child. For example, a child whose early patterns of caregiving are generally positive develops a healthy sense of self as worthy of care, and adult caregivers as trustworthy, will likely come to view the world as typically a safe place, and their capacity to make friends and trust their schoolteacher, and so on, will be higher. On the flip side, a child with inconsistent caregiving, who doubts they are worthy of care and has not experienced their caregivers as dependable and trustworthy, will likely view the world with a sense of fear, with heightened survival and protective instincts that will negatively impact their ability to enter healthy relationships.

Model of Psychopathology

Attachment theory and Theraplay's view of psychopathology are in the context of the impact of the strengths and/or challenges within the early infant caregiver relationship. Howe et al., (1999) recognize that while attachment theory and early relational experiences are only a piece of the puzzle, ongoing research continues to highlight the critical impact the nature of these experiences have on a child's emotional development, social development, and on their capacity for sustaining relationships across the lifespan. Cassidy et al., (2013) cite Bowlby's 1944 article in which he highlights and describes his initial understanding that poor early childhood experiences serve as antecedents to emotional dysfunction. Specifically, interactions between a young child and their caregiver in which the child experienced separation, isolation, neglect, harsh, and/or inconsistent patterns within the relationship are emphasized. Throughout the treatment process, the Theraplay practitioner is less focused on a specific diagnosis but rather guiding the interactions between the child and caregiver to meet the child's underlying needs, strengthening the caregiver's capacity to mentalize for their child and provide attuned, responsive caregiving. Through these experiences, the practitioner assists the caregiver in reorganizing the child's sense of self, others, and the world.

While this framework may not pay specific attention to psychopathology, it is not to say that we do not notice when progress is marked by a reduction in symptoms that are contributing factors to a diagnosis. In addition, it is critical to recognize the impact the presence of psychopathology will have on the safety of the treatment process for the caregiver, child, or both and consideration must be paid to the possible adjustments, delays, or an alternative approach to working with a dyad based upon contraindications. These contraindications include: a caregiver with their own untreated mental illness and/or addiction, non-compliance with their mental health treatment, current issues of domestic violence in the home, and diagnosed personality disorders that will likely interfere with the caregiver's capacity to recognize the impact of their own behavior on others, including their child (Norris & Lender, 2020). In addition, Booth & Jernberg (2010) note that the practitioner will need to consider the appropriateness of Theraplay as the modality of choice when a child may be actively experiencing a psychotic episode, when the acuteness of the trauma is too great, when it may be too challenging to manage a child's physically aggressive patterns of behavior, (i.e., when a primary focus on containment may be needed), and/or when a child has experienced sexual trauma. While all these children may at some point benefit from Theraplay, additional work may need to precede engaging in the protocol with a focus on safety for the child, caregiver, practitioner, and with thoughts toward the accommodations/adaptation required to ensure the underlying needs of clients are first and foremost.

Conceptualizing Goals of Treatment

Whelan and Stewart (2014) describe the goal of play-based, attachment-focused treatment as the reorganization of the child's IWM through experiences that are "attuned and responsive." At its core, Theraplay's overarching goals throughout the treatment process are to enhance both the child and caregivers' sense of internal safety, create positive shifts in the inner working models of each participant, and enhance the attachment relationship (Lindaman et al., 2018). Following a complete assessment, goals for treatment are individualized based upon the needs and strengths of the child and their caregivers.

The assessment process begins with an interview with the caregiver(s) focusing on exploring and obtaining information related to the reason the family is seeking services, a review of the child's developmental history, and consideration of all family relationships and dynamics. Questions specific to understanding how structure, engagement, nurture, and challenge are currently implemented in their family are beneficial as well. Throughout the process, consultation with additional key adults may be warranted to provide support to the child across environments. The next part of the assessment phase will include the administration of the Marschak Interaction Method (MIM), a clinical observational tool that provides the practitioner with an opportunity to assess the interactions and relational dynamics of a caregiver and child through the lens of each dimension (Lindaman et al., 2018). The MIM utilizes a standard series of play-based tasks, targeting each of Theraplay's four dimensions to assess both the parent's capacity to provide their child with aspects of each of the dimensions, as well as the child's capacity to accept the caregivers' efforts (Norris & Lender, 2020). This process concludes with a strengths-based parent feedback session with caregivers and the development of a treatment plan to address presenting problems framed from the perspective of each of the dimensions and with the strengths and needs of the dyad as paramount. Developing the appropriate balance in focus regarding needs in the four dimensions identified through the assessment process is key. As a result, while the overarching goals to shift the inner working models or relational blueprint that has been established by the child-caregiver dance will remain consistent across families, the short- and long-term treatment goals will vary greatly.

Role of the Therapist

Following the assessment and in collaboration with the caregivers, the Theraplay practitioner initiates the treatment protocol, beginning with a parent demonstration session. This session serves multiple purposes, including preparing the caregiver for their role in the treatment process, providing an opportunity for the caregiver to directly experience what their child will experience, engaging the caregiver to begin to enhance their capacity to mentalize for their child, and providing an additional opportunity for ongoing assessment for the therapist. The therapist will be able to assess the caregiver's readiness to engage in the treatment protocol straight away or if clinical adjustments will need to be made to ensure safety and overall success of treatment. Once the protocol begins, the practitioner guides and directs here-and-now interactive play experiences to support both the caregiver and the child in engaging in the activities that simulate the interactions of a parent with their infant, often providing the corrective, reparative connections that foster an improved sense of self for both individuals. Often in the Theraplay experience, the practitioner is considered an attachment figure for the caregiver to facilitate the caregiver being available to the child as their attachment figure. The practitioner, from the start, serves as the leader and, over the course of treatment, aims to shift leadership to the caregiver; the adult consistently provides for the overall structure and sense of felt safety for all participants in the session.

The focus of caregiver sessions allows the play therapist to continue to understand and empathize with the caregivers' experience of the child across environments and support the caregiver in enhancing their understanding of the child's underlying needs and motivation. Parent sessions also focus on the integration of Theraplay principles into the caregivers overall parenting approach outside the playroom. While the incorporation of specific session-based activities into a family's daily routines may be encouraged, it is more about enhancing the caregivers' underlying understanding of the dimensions and how to obtain session-like responses throughout the mundane day-to-day experiences. For example, supporting parents in developing routines (structure) that will ease the stress and reduce resistance to getting ready for school or bed.

Roles of Caregivers and Collaterals

The Theraplay approach, as an attachment-focused treatment, recognizes and values the significance of partnering with a child's caregivers. Historically, as a modality, Theraplay began with several sessions with the child and practitioner, independent of the caregiver's engagement. As the modality has continued to develop, the focus shifted to including the caregiver from the first session and beginning to transition leadership as clinically appropriate to the caregiver. For example, the caregiver who demonstrates a strong capacity and understanding of structure will be guided by the play therapist to lead activities where the primary focus is structure. On the other hand, if a caregiver struggles with providing down-regulating nurture in a way that serves the child's regulatory needs, the practitioner will likely provide these to the child, role modeling and easing the caregiver toward providing these experiences over time to ensure that any historically negative dyadic interactions are not replicated in session. Typical Theraplay practice will focus on the dyadic relationship between the child and each caregiver or the primary attachment relational needs of the client. Once stability in the primary relationships has been established, it may be beneficial to consider the inclusion of additional members of the family system, supporting the family in integrating the experience across relationships and dynamics (Norris & Lender, 2020).

While ideally the therapeutic work is being facilitated by the play therapist with the primary caregiver for the child, it is important to note that this may not be the biological parent and could include, but is not limited to, foster parent, grandparent, extended relatives, or identified caregivers in a residential program. In Doing Play Therapy, Meany-Walen and Kottman (2018) also note the importance of collaborating with other important members of the child's system, which may include teachers, extended family, and other professionals connected to the child and/or family. In addition, it may be relevant to refer and support families in seeking appropriate additional supportive services, which may include speech therapy, occupational therapy, physical therapy, and so on, to address other aspects of the child's experience.

Research/Empirical Support

Over the course of the last fifty plus years, a growing body of research has continued to bolster the support for Theraplay implementation, marked by the California Evidence—

Based Clearinghouse for Child Welfare recognizing the model in 2009 as a promising practice for infant and toddler mental health. In 2014, the United States Substance Abuse and Mental Health Services Administration listed the model in The National Registry of Evidence—Based Programs and Practices, recognizing the model as evidenced based (Hong, 2023). Specifically, Theraplay has been acknowledged as effective for addressing problems associated with internalizing patterns of behavior and promising for working with children presenting with symptoms on the autism spectrum (Norris & Lender, 2020). While Theraplay is grounded in attachment theory, it is important to highlight that, as cited on page ninety-five of Booth, Lindaman, and Cockerill (2018): "Researchers and clinicians in the fields of affect regulation (Schore, 1994); interpersonal neurobiology (Siegel, 1999); the emotional circuitry of the brain, including PLAY circuits (Pansksepp, 1998; Panksepp & Biven, 2012); and polyvagal theory, arousal regulation and the Social Engagement System (Porges, 2011, 2015) have further enriched the practice by identifying key elements of early interaction and how it affects the developing brain of the child. A greater understanding of the mechanisms and impact of early trauma (Schore, 2003; Van der Kolk, 1994; Perry, 1994) helps fine-tune our approach to meet the individual needs of each child and parent," lending these other fields support and guidance that have led to adaptation and strengthening the implementation and approach of the Theraplay model. In addition to the growing body of empirical support for Theraplay, practitioners across the globe provide anecdotal evidence bearing witness to the shifting parent-child dynamics and overall growth, development, and capacity for relationships their clients demonstrate over the course of the treatment protocol.

Case Study through the Lens of the Therapeutic Powers of Play

Therapeutic Powers of Play Employed

In the case of Herman (see Appendix for the case study of Herman being referenced), that follows, Theraplay will provide opportunities to enhance all aspects of social relationships (therapeutic relationship, attachment, social competence, and empathy) (Schaefer & Drewes, 2014). In addition, Theraplay treatment will aim to foster emotional well-being through experiences of positive emotions, creating new positive experiences that will serve as a corrective and counterconditioning experience to fears, as well as experientially providing for increased stress inoculation and management. Lastly, the direct nature of Theraplay as a model will foster healthier patterns of communication. Each of these core agents of change will be addressed below in the case formulation and application.

Cultural, Diversity, Inclusion Considerations

Theraplay as a therapeutic approach has been adapted for application across the globe (Norris & Lender, 2020). Often utilized with children in foster care and adoptive families to facilitate the development of a primary attachment, Theraplay has also been implemented successfully with biological families in which the behaviors of a child or caregiver have created stress, negatively impacting the attachment relationship. It is important to note that due to the ability of practitioners to easily adapt the model to meet varying developmental needs and cultural values, practitioners have long provided anecdotal evidence that the model can be utilized with a broad range of issues in which relational dynamics have been stressed. Norris and Lender (2020) guide practitioners not to mute the significance of cultural norms on all levels, encouraging attention to where the general tenets of a Western-based philosophical approach to the importance of attachment and the attachment relationship intersect and/or conflict with familial or local norms. All aspects of what may be viewed as Theraplay's relationship recipe (Structure, Engagement, Nurture, and Challenge) are considered present across cultures, but how they present or the goal of the relational shift through treatment will look distinct through the lens of each individual child, family, culture/community (Norris & Lender, 2020).

Case Formulation and Application

Herman's in utero and early childhood experiences draw into focus a need to primarily address the impact of the inconsistencies and general lack of attuned responsive caregiving needed during the critical phase of early childhood development. Currently residing in a stable placement with his therapeutic foster parents, engaging Herman and his foster parents using Theraplay would be beneficial and likely increase the positive prognosis related to a transition to a pre-adoptive home when identified. For a Theraplay practitioner, Herman and his foster parents would be ideal candidates for beginning therapy using the model. It is likely that many of the previous attempts to engage Herman in therapeutic services and the limited reports of progress were impacted by his early childhood experiences, and fundamentally Herman's attachment and relationship needs should be met first.

Enhances Social Relationships

Regardless of the modality, the therapeutic relationship/alliance is viewed as a cornerstone of the underlying process. Cited in Stewart & Echterling (2014), they note that Bordin identified three aspects that encapsulate the therapeutic relationship: a common focus, a sense of safety in the therapeutic process, and a connection to the therapist. The therapeutic alliance is a building block for Herman and will contribute positively overall to the enhancement of social relationships. For Herman, relationships have been marked by neglect, abuse, numerous abrupt changes at critical phases of development, and transitions, including therapeutic relationships with interns, which tend to be finite in nature, impacting the limited progress to date. The primary goal of implementing Theraplay as an approach will be to help foster his connection and sense of safety with his play therapist grounded in the reorganization of how he is viewed and experienced by the therapist. This will be critical as they also work toward treatment goals that will foster attachment with his foster parents, developing a new schema for relationships from the ground up.

Nash (2014) defines social competence as the combination of having the required social skills and being able to apply them to applicable scenarios. Early on, these skills are experientially developed through various forms of play, including rough-and-tumble play, role play, fantasy play, and game play (Nash, 2014). For Herman, one can clinically gather that attention to these facets of development was not central to his early experiences with caregivers. Theraplay, by nature returns to the basics of reciprocal game play, including peek-a-boo, making faces, playing Superman or airplane, and other rough-and-tumble play approaches. Based on his age, adaptations to these types of interactions will be made to increase his comfort with the overall activity while still providing for some of the younger missed opportunities in face-to-face primary intersubjective moments with others, establishing a sense of safety, connection, and positive joy that will increase his capacity to seek and accept similar interactions from others.

Empathy is a complicated process experienced and developed within the context of a relationship. Gaskill (2014) cites the work of Perry and others, noting the development of empathy as a treatment goal for children like Herman, who have been impacted by abuse and neglect. Booth and Jernberg (2010) highlight that the development of empathy stems from the infant-parent interactions in which the parent can attune to and mirror the affective state of the child, supporting the child in developing not only an understanding of their own emotions but also the emotions and intentions of others. Theraplay treatment will guide Herman's foster parents in providing consistent experiences in which his affective states are mirrored back for Herman, enhancing his own understanding of his emotions, which will lay the groundwork for increased capacity to engage empathically with others. In addition, it will support his foster parents in understanding what lies beneath his behavior and intentions, especially as it relates to what has been presented as unprovoked aggressive patterns.

Fosters Emotional Well-Being

Kottman (2014) cites Teach and Lyubomirsky's work, noting the impact of positive emotions as a counterbalance to negative emotions. Among the strategies that Kottman (2014) notes as critical to the promotion of positive emotions in play therapy sessions, she includes creating a safe space, a focus on having fun and being fun, role modeling the expression of positive emotions, and working with parents. Theraplay historically and consistently relies on three frequently unspoken rules: no hurts (focus on safety of all present), stick together (focus on being present and responsive, ensuring interactions are positive, and when ruptures or moments of misattunement occur, they will be repaired), and have fun (focused on the power of play and reciprocal enjoyment and engagement) (Norris & Lender, 2020). Herman has likely not experienced significant moments of shared joy and connection prior to moving to his current placement. The inconsistencies in his experiences have likely led to his misreading cues and/or having his own cues misunderstood. The repetitive, experiential nature of Theraplay sessions will support him in experiencing positive emotions, feeling joy, and sharing positive experiences with others, his therapist, and foster parents.

Herman's life experiences have been filled with fear and heightened stress, likely resulting in both periods of overactivation and underactivation of his attachment system to have his needs met (Norris & Lender, 2020). It is also likely that his skilled foster parents' attempts to provide care result in reactions from Herman that vary in range from acceptance to resistance and outright rejection, potentially impacting their ongoing efforts to connect with him. Theraplay's interactive and experiential nature will provide direct here-and-now play sequences that will offer implicit learning opportunities, combining playful, matter-of-fact engagement that will counter condition Herman's tendency toward a fear response. Van Hollander (2014) notes the challenge of experiencing joy and fear simultaneously and weakening the fear response by partnering it with an experience that is in direct opposition to fear. One specific area of focus will be related to Herman's experience of nurturing touch, which has been negatively impacted by his experiences with neglect and sexual abuse.

By its nature, the attachment relationship and the development of the IWM serve a function to support stress inoculation and management. Herman's early experiences have included in utero exposure to danger and violence, multiple transitions in primary caregivers, primary caregivers who were not able to prioritize his safety and protection, violence in the home environment, and periods of heightened fear and anxiety without the benefit of a schema from which to manage these stressful experiences. Cavett (2014) notes that a review of current research brings attention to the benefits of therapeutic approaches in which a child can experience stress-inducing moments coupled with an experience that will bring them back within their window of tolerance or state of regulation. In addition, play, in and of itself, serves to reduce the experience of stress and enhance one's ability to regulate their emotions overall (Jernberg & Booth, 2010). Theraplay, by its nature, will provide healthy opportunities for Herman to experience minor stressors within and potentially mildly outside his window of tolerance while simultaneously guiding and supporting him in gaining mastery over managing the experiences. The use of this playful approach will also provide stress reduction, creating space for the experience of shared joy and connection.

Facilitates Communication

Theraplay fosters and facilitates the development of improved communication between the caregiver and child as well as for the child in other environments, using primarily direct approaches to teaching within dyadic, familial/group, or caregiver only sessions. In sessions, the practitioner is guiding, role modeling, and engaging the participants in active practice and repetition of the experience. Additionally, in caregiver-specific treatment sessions, direct teaching addresses practicing, role modeling, and considering both how to incorporate specific activities/interactions into the family's daily routines as well as considering the more global application of Theraplay principles (e.g., increasing structure in the home by establishing a consistent routine for managing transitions). Fraser (2014) highlights the significant impact on learning and integrating skills that occurs when clients engage actively and directly in play-based interventions with others. In addition, the use of metaphor and indirect approaches to supporting and enhancing the caregiver's ability to mentalize for the child in their care can further augment the treatment process. In the case of Herman, working closely with his foster parents and teachers to consider contributing factors to his dysregulated behavior, engaging in role modeling and practicing how to provide Herman with the needed structure, engagement, and nurturing will allow Herman to experience periods of co-regulation, building toward self-regulation.

Increases Personal Strengths

Norris and Lender (2020) highlight the development of self-regulation in response to the attuned responsive caregiving of a child during the early years of life. Repeated experiences of the infant accessing their adult to serve as a co-regulating other, in which the adult attends to, notices, and responds accordingly to their physiological needs and emotional states, establish moments of affective synchrony (Schore & Schore, 2008). It is important to note that the caregiver is not required to achieve affective synchrony or "get it right" 100% of the time, but it is more so critical that in moments of misattunement, the caregiver strives to repair and reconnect with the child, further enhancing the sense of self as worthy of care (Schore & Schore, 2008). For Herman, his ability to self-regulate was negatively impacted by his in-utero exposure to substances. Theraplay treatment will focus on engaging Herman and his foster parents in experiences in which Herman can access and receive co-regulating, specifically down-regulating experiences, which provide comfort and allow him to remain socially engaged. Collaborating with teachers to incorporate approaches that are working in session and in the home to support Herman in regulating himself will support the potential to positively impact his school experience socially and academically.

A primary component of the IWM developed through the attachment relationship is one's view of self (self-esteem). Herman's early caregiving experiences, of limited physical contact beginning with his stay in the NICU, persisted while in the care of his grandmother. As an infant who was not the recipient of consistent, attuned responsive caregiving, attachment theory guides the practitioner to recognize that Herman began to view himself as not worthy of care, unimportant, and unlovable. This template has served as a guiding force in relationships as he transitioned from foster home to foster home and in his development of peer relationships. Through Theraplay experiences, the practitioner will engage Herman in activities in which the therapist and foster parents can and will genuinely delight in him, attend to his regulatory needs to both cope with a range of experiences and moments within his window of tolerance while also aiming to expand his capacity to tolerate new and exciting moments while remaining in a state of regulation. Experiencing and tolerating success around mild, developmentally appropriate risk-taking while the practitioner and caregivers revel in his success and celebrate him will also strengthen his sense of self and mastery.

Challenges in Implementation

Based on Herman's history, his current age, and the impact his life experiences have had on his developmental presentation, treatment will likely be longer than typical. His experiences as a child who faced both deprivation of touch and sexual abuse will need to be considered and adapted carefully as nurturing aspects of the Theraplay model are implemented. While it will be critical for Herman, as it is for all people, to experience positive, healthy, stress-reducing, down-regulating experiences where physical touch is utilized, it is also likely that these experiences will not be congruent with what he has learned about touch, requiring careful attention and attunement by both the provider and his foster parents. Herman's aggressive patterns of behavior that appear unprovoked have potentially created moments in his interactions that initiate a fear response from his foster parents, impacting their ability to attune to his needs. Providing additional support to his foster parents around increasing their own understanding and mentalization of his behaviors, as well as Herman's underlying developmental needs, will be critical to the success of the intervention. It is also important to note that while Theraplay will begin to address and support Herman's attachment needs and thus likely have a positive impact on his ability to engage in relationships with his foster parents, teachers, and peers, the long-term nature of the traumatic experiences he has endured will require additional treatment to more effectively process these events. Consideration should be given to models of trauma treatment that have been positively integrated with Theraplay, such as Eye Movement Desensitization Reprocessing (EMDR), Dyadic Developmental Psychotherapy, Cognitive Behavioral Play Therapy (CBPT), and/or integrating Bruce Perry's Neurosequential Model of Therapeutics (Hong & Coleman, 2023). Once a pre-adoptive home has been identified, it would also be encouraged to integrate them into the Theraplay sessions.

Conclusion

Attachment theory and Theraplay, as a play-based attachment intervention, provide a framework from which to consider the therapeutic needs of Herman. Engaging Herman and his foster parents from this perspective, the play therapist will begin to unlock change agents that will enhance social relationships, foster emotional wellness, facilitate communication, increase one's personal strengths, and will focus on addressing the developmental impact of his early attachment experiences.

References

American Psychological Association. (n.d.). Personality. Retrieved April 15, 2024, from https://www.apa.org/topics/personality.

Benoit, D. (2004). Infant-parent attachment: Definition, types, antecedents, measurement and outcome. Paediatrics & Child Health, 9(8), 541–5. PMID: 19680481; PMCID: PMC2724160. https://doi.org/10.1093/pch/9.8.541.

Booth, P. B., & Jernberg, A. M. (2010). *Theraplay helping parents and children build better relationships through attachment-based play* (3rd ed.). Jossey-Bass.

Buckwalter, K. D. (2018). Overview of attachment theory and clinical application. In K. D. Buckwalter & D. Reed (Eds.), *Attachment theory in action* (pp. 3–16). Rowan & Littlefield.

Cassidy, J., Jones, J. D., & Shaver, P. R. (2013). Contributions of attachment theory and research: A framework for future research, translation and policy. *Development and Psychopathology*, *25*(402), 1415–34. https://doi.org/10.1017/S0954579413000692.

Cavett, A. M. (2014). Attachment. In C. E. Schaefer & A. A. Drewes (Eds.), *The therapeutic powers of play 20 core agents of change* (2nd ed., pp. 131–41). Wiley.

Fraser, T. (2014). Direct teaching. In C. E. Schaefer & A. A. Drewes (Eds.), *The therapeutic powers of play 20 core agents of change* (2nd ed., pp. 39–50). Wiley.

Gaskill, R. (2014). Empathy. In C. E. Schaefer & A. A. Drewes (Eds.), *The therapeutic powers of play 20 core agents of change* (2nd ed., pp. 195–209). Wiley.

Hoffman, K., Powell, B., & Benton, C. M. (2011). *Raising a secure child.* The Guilford Press.

Hong, R. (2023) Overview of theraplay integration with other therapeutic models. In R. Hong & A. R. Coleman (Eds.), *Theraplay innovations and integration* (pp 23–8). Jessica Kingsley Publishers.

Hong, R., & Coleman, A. R. (Eds.). (2023). *Theraplay innovations and integration* (pp 23–8). Jessica Kingsley Publishers.

Howe, D., Brandon, M., & Hinings, D. (1999). *Attachment theory, child maltreatment and family support: A practice and assessment model.* Macmillan.

Kottman, T. (2014). Positive emotions. In C. E. Schaefer & A. A. Drewes (Eds.), *The therapeutic powers of play 20 core agents of change* (2nd ed., pp. 103–20). Wiley.

Kottman, T., & Meany-Walen, K. K. (2018). *Doing play therapy.* The Guilford Press.

Lindaman, S., Booth, P., & Cockerill, G. M. (2018). Theraplay: Creating felt safety, emotional connection and social joy in relationships. In K. D. Buckwalter & D. Reed (Eds.), *Attachment theory in action* (pp. 3–16). Rowan & Littlefield.

Nash, J. B. (2014). Social competence. In C. E. Schaefer & A. A. Drewes (Eds.), *The therapeutic powers of play 20 core agents of change* (2nd ed., pp. 185–93). Wiley.

Norris, V., & Lender, D. (2020). *Theraplay the practitioner's giode.* Jessica Kingsley Publishers.

Panksepp, J. (1998). *Affective neuroscience: The foundations of human and animal emotions.* Oxford University Press.

Peabody, M. A., & Schaefer, C. E. (2019, September). The therapeutic powers of play: The heart and soul of play therapy. *Play Therapy*, *14*(3), 4–6.

Perry, B. D. (1994). *Neurobiological sequelae of childhood trauma: PTSD in children. In M. M. Murburg* (Ed.), Catecholamine function in posttraumatic stress disorder: Emerging concepts (pp. 233–255). American Psychiatric Association.

Porges, S. W. (2011). *The polyvagal theory: Neurophysiological foundations of emotions, attachment, communication, and self-regulation.* W. W. Norton & Company.

Porges S. W. (2015). Making the world safe for our children: Down-regulating defence and up-regulating social engagement to 'optimise' the human experience. *Children Australia*, *40*(2), 1965. doi.org/10.1017/cha.2015.12.

Schore, A. N. (1994). *Affect regulation and the origin of the self: The neurobiology of emotional development.* Lawrence Erlbaum Associates, Inc.

Schore, A. N. (2003). *Early relational trauma, disorganized attachment, and the development of a predisposition to violence.* In D. Siegel & M. Solomon (Eds.), Healing trauma: Attachment, mind, body, and brain (pp. 101–167). Norton.

Schore, J. R., & Schore, A. N. (2008). Modern attachment theory: The central role of affect regulation in development and treatment. *Clinical Social Work Journal*, *36*(1), 9–20. https://doi.org/10.1007/s10615-007-0111-7

Schaefer, C. E., & Drewes, A. A. (Eds.). (2014). *The therapeutic powers of play: 20 core agents of change* (2nd ed.). Wiley.

Siegel, D. J. (1999). *The developing mind: Toward a neurobiology of interpersonal experience* (1st ed.). Guilford Press.

Stewart A. L., & Echterling, L. G. (2014). Therapeutic relationship. In C. E. Schaefer & A. A. Drewes (Eds.), *The therapeutic powers of play 20 core agents of change* (2nd ed., pp. 157–69). Wiley.

Van der Kolk, B. A. (1994). The body keeps the score: Memory and the evolving psychobiology of posttraumatic stress. *Harvard Review of Psychiatry, 1*(5), 253–265. doi: 10.3109/10673229409017088. PMID: 9384857.

Van Hollander, T. (2014). Therapeutic relationship. In C. E. Schaefer & A. A. Drewes (Eds.), *The therapeutic powers of play 20 core agents of change* (2nd ed., pp. 121–30). Wiley.

Whelan,W. F., & Stewart A. L. (2014). Attachment. In C. E. Schaefer & A. A. Drewes (Eds.), *The therapeutic powers of play 20 core agents of change* (2nd ed., pp. 171–83). Wiley.

Yip, J., Ehrhardt, K., Black, H., & Walker, D. O. (2015). Attachment theory at work: A review and directions for future research. *Journal of Organizational Behavior*, *39*(2), 185–98. https://doi.org/10.1002/job.2204/.

5

Jungian Analytical Play Therapy

JP Lilly[1] *and Rachel McRoberts*

Chapter Outline

Introduction

Jungian Analytical Play Therapy (JAPT) can be considered both one of the earliest and yet most elusive theories. C. G. Jung (1875–1961) pioneered our underlying assumptions, including a non-directive, creative, collaborative approach valuing the symbolic language

[1]Sadly, JP Lilly passed away on June 20, 2024. This was his final chapter submitted prior to his untimely death. We are honored that we are able to include this chapter, which highlights his lifetime of clinical work, teaching, and training, in Jungian Analytical Play Therapy.

of the unconscious, integrating spirit and science, embodied with a unique vocabulary; he worked prolifically, yet never with children. However, he personally mentored the development of Sandplay Therapy (Kalff, 1966/2020), analyzed the childhood dreams of adult clients (Jung, 1936–1940/2008), and encouraged lifelong personal and professional development of clinicians, with multicultural and creative sensibilities. Jung's students uniquely identified the power of the parent-child dyad, especially the child's ability to perceive and symbolically act out the unconscious projections of their parents, and thereby overtly encouraged parents to do their own work as well (Wickes, 1927). Jung also inspired the developmental model identifying the Self and individuation process in childhood (Fordham, 1976, 1985, & 1994). Through these steps, we can trace our lineage as JAPTs. The careful reader can also see that Jung sowed the seeds for the therapeutic value of contemporary concepts such as intergenerational trauma, inner-child work, creative expression, and identity formation. Jung did not leave us so much with a formula, but a philosophical framework on which to continue building. Training as a Jungian has historically been inaccessible to many, being mentor-based, requiring extensive reading, reflection, and writing in addition to specific clinical training. Through the following brief description and case conceptualization, two leaders in the JAPT community will concisely describe the underlying philosophy and basic tenets that guide our current attention, research, and practice.

Underlying Philosophy

The underlying philosophy of Jungian Analytical Play Therapy (JAPT) is based on the theory of C. G. Jung, including the structure and function of the psyche. The psyche includes all aspects of our human psychology, known and unknown, conscious and unconscious, personal and collective (CW 8). The *collective unconscious* is vast, encompassing all the lives ever lived, all the art and inventions, and stories ever told in human history, around the world; the typical organized patterns of these universal phenomena are called *archetypes*, and they speak a symbolic language. The *personal unconscious* is connected to the collective but is also more unique to us and our direct experience with the World, our interpretations of what those experiences mean about ourselves and others, and our emotional responses. The psyche is an archetype, but we all have one as well.

The psyche has four main functions: symbolic, religious, reflective, and transcendent. The symbolic function includes our ability to "get" other people and move through the World with ease, nearly automatically, by having access to our unconscious: this includes an intuitive knowledge of what facial expressions mean, the ability to empathize, the capacity to "read the room," and to quickly and deeply gauge what is going on and how we are expected to behave. It also includes the building blocks for developing and utilizing language, the use of objects as toys to represent our internal and external worlds, and an appreciation of beauty and meaning in the world. The *religious function* (CW 11) not only includes the human propensity to organize these symbols into large meaningful patterns, such as the major world religions and personalized spiritual practices, but also the need for humans to be able to trust, predict, and delight in the world; this encompasses the many routines and rituals we all engage in for self, family, and community care: from sleep/wake cycles to holiday celebrations, we are creatures of habit. We also tend to divide the world into relatable opposites: up and down, yes and no, good and bad. We do this unconsciously in order to be able to quickly make decisions, but such duality can also be difficult to manage. There are many nuances in life. The religious function can help us explain why we crave both a sense of order as well as mystery; it also appreciates that *numinous experiences* are a common phenomenon (Jung, CW 8; Lönneker & Maercker, 2021; Otto, 1917/1923). Numinous experiences are likened to spiritual, strangely curious, synchronistic events that may seem like messages from beyond. They grab our attention and can kick-start or validate a change. A change toward healing is an experience of the *transcendent function*. The transcendent function (Jung, CW 8) allows us to go beyond the binary; to withstand and hold conflicting ideas, which we call the *tension of the opposites* (Jung, CW 7), even accepting and integrating them with wisdom. It is still unknown what makes change "click" in the psyche. It may be an unconscious acceptance of a numinous encounter, but something allows the ego to feel safe enough to make the once hidden unconscious material more conscious. The *reflective function* (Jung, CW 8, CW 12) is what many other therapies solely depend on, but it is one of the most conscious; basically, it's our ability to stop and think. Without an unconscious or intuitive and automatic knowledge of symbology, we cannot hope to consciously reflect on or make sense of what raw data might mean, whether that data comes from within us or from the environment.

JAPT considers the child's mythic arc: how their story changes over time, their character development, and our perceptions of them as we journey with them. In short, JAPT's aim is to create space and mitigate conditions so that the psyche may safely make the unconscious more conscious. Children do this largely through play and co-regulation with loving, understanding caregivers who are validating and safe guides. Through this process, we become more aligned within ourselves and at peace with the World.

Personality Theory

JAPT conceptualizes each person as being on a path of individuation. Individuation may be understood as the lifelong process of coming to know and embodying our true Self (Jung, CW 7). Ideally, this occurs through the healthy development and alignment of the ego-Self axis (Ediger, 1972). Being ourselves radiates from the Self but is always informed by and negotiated with the World. In order to accommodate the demands of the World and interact with it, we develop an ego, or little "s" sense of self. This is often painful and leaves one at odds (Jung, CW 17 & 18). We have to wrangle and reckon with many of these dualities or tensions of the opposites. That's the ego's big job.

The ego, though, adapts to changing conditions and growth by cultivating and pruning; we refer to this nature as being *compensatory*. These acts can be conceptualized as structures in the psyche with an archetypal core that often become fragmented: *complexes* and *personae*. While the common use of the word "complex" mostly has negative connotations today, Jung developed and used the term more broadly (CW 2, CW 8). Our constellated thoughts, feelings, felt sense, and mental images about any person, place, thing, event, or aspect of the World, often summed up in one "trigger word," can be considered a complex. Complexes have an emotional tone and are attached to an archetypal core. They can act as a catalyst for the expression of a strong emotion, acting out, or numbing. Jung (CW 8) said that even our idea of ego, the "I am" or "me" we refer to, is a complex, subject to being made more conscious and transcended through greater alignment with the Self. Other common complexes arise from our earliest experiences and closest relationships: Mother, Father, etc. They also form out of perceived expectations or patternings, such as what it means to be a Child; depending on how we were treated as a child, what was accepted and rejected, and how conscious of that experience we are shapes what we believe about children, how we expect children to behave to be treated, and what they deserve. In this way, complexes hold clues to how we react or what can be considered symptomology.

> *For behind every individual father there stands the primordial image of the Father, and behind the fleeting personal mother the magical figure of the Magna Mater. These archetypes of the collective psyche, whose power is magnified in immortal works of art and in the fiery tenets of religion, are the dominants that rule the preconscious soul of the child and, when projected upon the human parents, lend them a fascination which often assumes monstrous proportions. From that there arises the false aetiology of neurosis.* (Jung, as cited in Wickes, 1927, p. xxi)

For example, if we are triggered into feeling like a Child because a person in authority is speaking to us sternly, we may react out of our Child complex. The archetype of the Child has many aspects between its Divine and Orphaned duality, but our complex of what to do when we are a child is based on our psyche's experience and knowledge. We may fawn, become silent, or cry if we learned that being submissive, repentant, and vulnerable is safest. Conversely, we may become indignant, challenge, and even fight. We project these complexes onto others as well. In this scenario, a Father complex may have been projected onto a teacher or boss.

To develop sets of specialty skills, or roles within specific contexts, we develop *persona*. As children we may develop persona around being a Sibling, Student, Athlete, Musician, Dancer, or Warrior within certain contexts; later in life, our roles as Parent, Teacher, Mechanic, Cleric, Therapist, and so on. Ideally, our complexes and personae are well aligned with the ego-Self axis, healthy, and useful. When they are misaligned, unconscious, or overly compensatory, we are more likely to call them "symptomatic".

Model of Psychopathology

JAPT tends to not pathologize behaviors or people. We see all the functions of the psyche as an attempt to self-regulate, though there is a developmental nature to the process of individuation. However, when the ego is not well aligned with the Self, and unconscious material demands to be felt, a phenomenon typically referred to as psychopathology emerges. Jung challenged Freud's famous assumption that dreams are the "royal road to the unconscious," favoring the complex instead. To Jung, the complex is

> *The architect of dreams and symptoms.*
>
> *Nor is this via so very "royal," either, since the way pointed out by the complex is more like a rough and uncommonly devious footpath that often loses itself in the undergrowth and generally leads not into the heart of the unconscious but past it* (CW 8, p. 142, § 210).

Complexes in and of themselves are normal, but they are assumptions filled with bias and prejudice based on our unique intersectional lens of culture and experience, and they can be overly so. But if we dig deep enough, they always make sense. They are compensatory in that they attempt to offset the confusion, pain, and rejection of parts of the ego. They are the psyche's army, attempting at once to keep the peace while fighting battles. "Because I am alone in the world, I must fight for survival"; we might call this the Lone Wolf or a Warrior complex, deriving a theme from World myths, which may serve Herman as an *alter-ego*. Jung (CW 8) taught that if we touch upon a complex that is pushed very far into the unconscious, it will evoke an "I don't know" response. This explains why a child may give this response if asked why they became so upset, did the thing, or what they think about a tragic event. This is also an explanation for why creative expression as a means of dialoguing with the unconscious, or play therapy, is preferable for children and those who have experienced trauma.

Unmet needs and adverse childhood experiences (ACEs) often interfere with healthy development: physically, psychologically, and socially. From a Jungian perspective, this is too much for the developing ego to bear. Material has been pushed into the unconscious, and complexes have formed that seem to have been generalized. Rejected aspects of the ego are pushed into a part of the unconscious we call the Shadow; the Shadow may include any thoughts, feelings, or perceptions that may be perceived as being unacceptable. For a small child who experiences neglect, any expressed need that is neglected or punished can be banished to the Shadow. Through building healthy attachments with the Self and others, unconscious material may feel safe to come into the light of consciousness. Developmental theory teaches us that there are three steps: (1) Getting to know the child, (2) Increasing affectionate interactions, (3) Looking deep inside instead of paying attention to surface behaviors (Infant Child Enrichment Services, 2020).

Jung (CW 15, 17) identified that while parents are not solely responsible for who a child is, their multigenerational influence is incontrovertible in light of archetypal, and now intergenerational theory; this includes their trauma history, attachments, complexes, psychological armory, values, symbology, and vital parts of life left unlived. In this case (see Appendix for case study of Herman being referenced), the child does not know who his biological father is but is said to emulate his foster father. Because both males and females have caused him great harm through neglect and abuse, he may be having difficulty internalizing and identifying with feminine and masculine traits and roles.

Jung also acknowledged that what we now commonly call "externalizing" or "acting out" behaviors are really just cues for parents and caregivers to pay attention (Jung &

Ostrowski-Sachs, 1971). "Neurosis is always a substitute for legitimate suffering" (CW 11, para 129), he said, meaning that symptoms arise because the reality of the pain is too great. This pain may also stem from Herman's preconscious felt sense of his mother's and grandmother's pain. Herman has likely missed the developmental task of being seen, heard, and understood, which is necessary for the development of the symbolic and reflective functions. Hebb (1949) first posited the now common knowledge that when it comes to interpersonal neurobiology, what "wires together fires together" (Shatz, 1992) and can be predictive of future learning, behavior, and mental health (Keysers & Gazzola, 2014). But as Jung said in 1931: "Only when mirrored in our picture of the world can we see ourselves in the round. Only in our creative acts do we step forth into the light and see ourselves whole and complete" (Jung, CW 8, p. 491). Herman likely does not see himself reflected in the world as attuned to others, safe, worthy, or whole. His entire life is fragmented, like a broken mirror. It would be our role as JAPTs to create a space for Herman where together we can listen to and resonate with the Self and put the pieces together.

Conceptualizing Goals of Treatment

We might imagine what Herman's foster parents, teachers, and peers may want of him, and their observed behaviors, based on the presented information. But what about Herman? What does he want? What if we ask him? What is he conscious of? What might his psyche want? While other theories may attempt to address the behaviors head-on, we, as JAPTs, look to them for clues. Why does x behavior make perfect sense? How is it compensatory for unmet psychic needs, despite the ongoing consequences? How might we scaffold play therapy interventions while supporting Herman and his family in the practical management of his dysregulated emotions? The JAPT view takes into account our underlying philosophical assumptions, as well as the evidence of the neurosequential model of therapeutics, and the power of a well-attuned play therapy relationship. In this way, our treatment plan may include problem statements for both the "observed" and suggestions for possible "underlying" or unconscious problems; we might also call these "soft interpretations."

Because of his age and experience with therapy, we imagine that Herman may have at least some idea about why he was brought to therapy and some thoughts and feelings about that. Part of building temenos would be hearing that out, talking about how we might spend our time together and what we both think might help. Building collaborative goals with clients is part of ethical practice across mental health disciplines, including play therapy (ACA, 2014; APT, 2022; NASW, 2024).

The treatment plan, then, should be developmentally appropriate, not only in that it is clear, concise, and doable, but that it is understood by the child. We want to keep it simple, but also specific, and aligned with the child, and our Jungian approach (McRoberts, 2024). We may find ourselves adapting our language to contain less jargon (though we are quite attached to our Jungian terminology). The *goals* should ideally be what the child wants, in their own words; this may, however, include what the adults in the child's life are asking of them, or what we think the child means when they're acting out, in which case it may be reworded so that a child might feel more empowered and buy-in. *Objectives* are what the child or caregiver will do; ideally, these are things the child agrees to, but they may also be a hope that we communicate to the child. We want to check in with the child with our statement to at least see if it resonates; if it doesn't, we may need to take a smaller step to be more in tune with what they're willing to do. Sometimes this is just showing up and participating in play therapy sessions. Objectives include words like: *engage, attend, develop, practice,* as well as *consider* and *continue,* to reflect our value of building on strengths. What the play therapist plans to do in those sessions are the *interventions.* Intervention words may include: *reflect, explore, support, co-develop/interpret, provide, assist,* and *follow up.*

Here are some possible treatment plan components, where we are imagining what Herman might say, as well as how we might co-create and explain the plan to him and his caregivers.

#1. Observed Problem: Internalized and externalized behaviors, including ADHD symptoms, emotional dysregulation, and aggression (per report).

Underlying Problem/Soft Interpretation: Developmental trauma and lack of co-regulation may have contributed to rapid and ongoing dysregulation and disconnection from self and others.

Goal (Client's own words, verbally/symbolically): "I don't want to get in trouble all the time." (What we might sense, or what Herman might say after initial defensiveness and remorse, which may take a few sessions, as well as us broaching a conversation about why he's been brought to therapy. We might have to let him know that we know he's been getting into trouble. This may be more conscious to him than the nuances of his specific feelings as a result of trauma.) Build trust, empathy, and self-awareness through co-regulation.

Objectives (What the Client/Caregiver Will Do)

1. Herman and his caregivers will practice using feeling identification and reflection in a variety of situations. *"Let's practice using feelings words everyday. ALL the feelings! Not just the tough ones."*
2. Caregivers will intervene and provide Herman with real-time kindness and support when he is acting out, using connection, reflective listening, and amplification to help shine a light on what Herman is trying to say. "*We know when you act-out, you're really trying to tell us something from deep down inside. We're all going to work together to help you know what that is and tell us in ways that don't get you in trouble.*"

Interventions (What the Play Therapist Will Do)

1. Play therapist will co-create a safe, permissive environment (*temenos*), where Herman may express himself freely. "*You won't get in trouble in here.*"

2. Play therapist will assist and co-interpret expressed feelings in the playroom. *"I'll do a lot of guessing out loud about how I think you might feel in here. You can always tell me if I'm wrong."*

#2. Observed Problem: Hoarding food (per report).
Underlying Problem/Soft Interpretation: Infant neglect may have led to a deep fear of continued scarcity and mistrust of adults to meet his needs. His cries went unanswered, and he's tired of asking. He does not trust adults to meet even his basic needs, and in turn, himself. The food may be a tangible symbol of Herman's great need for nurturing, the internalization of the good-enough mother. *"Sometimes kids who don't get enough food are afraid there won't be enough."*
Goal (Client's own words, verbally/symbolically): "I don't want to have to wait or ask for food all the time."

Objectives (What the Client/Caregivers Will Do)

1. Foster parents and Herman will co-construct a snack basket to be kept and replenished in Herman's room, which he may access without restriction. *"We'll work together to keep a snack basket in your room."*
2. Herman will work with caregivers and play therapists to identify body cues and communicate his feelings of hunger, fear of scarcity, and when the snack basket needs refilling. *"Your part will be practicing looking for and using feeling-words more."*

Interventions (What the Play Therapist Will Do)

1. Play therapist will provide initial and ongoing emotional support, psychoeducation, and accountability for the child and family in creating and maintaining the snack basket (physically and symbolically) while building a trusting relationship.
2. Play therapists will reflect and amplify feelings and meaning frequently throughout each play therapy session (non/verbal interactions, art/play activities, charts, cards, etc.).

Role of the Therapist

JAPTs trust that the child knows where they need to go emotionally and psychologically in order to heal. Through developing an attuned relationship with the child, the JAPT therapist does not so much evaluate but aims to encourage the development of, and communication with, the symbolic language of the child. Through the JAPT valuing and understanding the language of the unconscious, the child is safe and free to make this material more conscious.

JAPTs look to the child's symptoms as clues to the unconscious material that is attempting to emerge. We honor symptoms as attempts by the ego to self-regulate. Symptoms often serve a compensatory function, "acting out" the wishes or symbolic resolution to Shadow material. They are also our roadmap, showing us the way both to the heart of the pain and the escape route. Instead of attempting to extinguish the symptom, we aim to accept it, join with it, empathize with it, slowly bringing greater awareness and subsequent healing as the child's ego strengthens. Children cannot develop healthy egos without adults seeing them and offering their own ego strength to borrow. We refer to the integration of the safe and protected space (Kalff, 1966/2020), literally and figuratively, by Jung's (1935/1977) use of the Greek term *temenos*, the root of the word "temple," meaning a sacred place; the creation of temenos depends upon qualities and interpretations of the playroom, the JAPT's reverence for the child and trust in the psyche, as well as the therapeutic relationship. Temenos is an agreed-upon place, a reverence, a felt sense, and a practice. While it involves the active participation of the child, it is the JAPT's responsibility to mindfully tend it.

The JAPT, along with the play, assists the child in three distinct ways: serving as a container, witness, and co-interpreter (Lilly, 2015). We often use non-directive, child-centered play therapy (CCPT) interventions such as reflecting feelings and content (Landreth, 1991/2025), but we tend to take greater liberties with the active use of silence, expansion of meaning, and the use of the therapist; JAPT uniquely includes co-interpretation and experiential participation. That experiential participation may sound more directive, as we analyze what a child's unconscious may be brewing, but it needs an attuned caregiver to accept, contain, and help them understand. Jung teaches us that translating emotion into image leads to greater integration; while the spontaneous image from the child is preferred, it may also arise from the well-attuned JAPT. We might wonder aloud, staying with the topic as introduced by the child, or suggesting an activity such as: "I wonder what it looks like to feel hungry," or even asking a question, in service of the child's fuller expression like: "Can you show me in the sand?" or "Would you like to paint or draw a picture of that?" We might also elaborate on a metaphor or story that the child has suggested, by saying that it reminds us of a fairy tale and asking if the child would like to hear it (Mills & Crowley, 2014; von Franz, 1996). As containers in the playroom, we may psychically hold the tension of the opposites for the child, their story, our perceptions of the Self, along with *soft interpretations*; this containment may also be more tangible in the creation and maintenance of the temenos. While joining with, matching, and going with the child's energy is a primary aim, a highly dysregulated child may also need the JAPT to set limits on the pacing of unconscious material being discharged. Analytical witnessing of the play may involve verbalizing our soft interpretations or hunches; beyond a mere expansion of meaning, we aim to assist with the integration of unconscious material more consciously (Lilly, as cited in Kottman & Meany-Walen, 2018). In this way, we model and encourage the use of ego strength, providing both physical and emotional safety. We act as guardians of the child's psyche, helping to support the ego while assisting with the pacing of unconscious material becoming more conscious. This also extends to the therapist taking an advocacy role for the client with their support system.

JAPT may also borrow techniques and interventions from a variety of modalities as needed, which may, at first glance, appear to be prescriptive or eclectic. However, we are always working from a strong Jungian foundation and follow the child's lead as we dance with their conscious and unconscious. The active use of the relationship, including the client's transference and our countertransference in the playroom, is sacred. It's an additional responsibility for the JAPT to do their own deep work to be aware of and manage our own complexes, symbolic associations, and capacity to hold the child's projections. This may look like taking on the role of the Good Mother, the Wise Old Man, or the Trickster, as a child may indicate, to safely and symbolically play out a complex or experiment with their developing ego strength.

Roles of Caregivers and Collaterals

Herman has been abandoned by his caregivers and therapists again and again. We can imagine that there are subsequent layers of fear, anger, grief, and mistrust built up in Herman to protect his psyche from further pain. Without a great deal of empathy and the co-construction of meaningful, predictable rituals, Herman will likely continue to be on the defensive.

While several people report that the child's outbursts seem to come out of nowhere, all manifestations from the psyche are attempts by the unconscious to become more aware of an inner conflict (CW 9ii); these spontaneous acts of flooding the conscious mind with unconscious material can be frightening and strange (CW 7). It sounds like this may be the case for both Herman, his caregivers, and his peers. It would be important to build enough trust and gain enough buy in from the caregivers to try to see past their disturbance of Herman's behavior and try to see the whole child in the round: his whole personhood, his inherent value, his feelings, and what he is trying to say. They will need to be symbolic detectives, too, attempting to meet the needs he might not be aware he's expressing. Herman needs the adults in his life to psychically hold and literally protect him. This includes being bullied and assisting with real-time self-regulation at school.

Herman's care team could take the initiative in the collection of artifacts, photos, and history to assist in the co-creation of a life book. Life books are likened to scrapbooks that tell the story of the life of the child in care (AdoptUSKids, 2020). The current history provided to us about Herman is lacking in a hopeful, loving narrative for him to integrate. Children need to know, understand, and integrate their story to be able to tell it cohesively and act as the hero within it. Stories can access the Self-Healer. Even in families where there is significant trauma and abuse, there is also love, strength, and attempts at connection. It is the elders' responsibility to reframe Herman's creation story and journey to them, where he is the beloved child and the hero, supported by them.

The creation of healthy familial routines and rituals supports psychosocial development that resonates deeply in the body. Like with a newborn baby, supporting healthy, calm, delightful routines, especially around eating and sleeping, is vital. Being with him and responding to him as caregivers may be needed more than generally considered necessary because he missed these milestones. The psyche needs safety reinforced. This may look like setting up a snack basket in his room, so he never has to "steal" food. It may look like an extended bedtime routine with stories he loves, lying beside him, running to him to tuck him back in, and singing him to sleep after a nightmare.

The neurosequential model of therapeutics (Perry, 2006) teaches us about the need for "bottom-up" processing, especially when a child is dysregulated. The "bottom" of the brain (brainstem), in charge of automatic responses, including trauma, needs to be soothed before emotional (limbic system) and cognitive processing (cortex), or conscious control of one's actions, can come online further up in the brain. This is an intuitive process in healthy child development (think about how we might reason with a tantruming toddler) but needs to be practiced intentionally with older children. All adults in Herman's life might be encouraged to take this three-step approach to interacting with Herman (and others!) when strong emotions are noticed:

1. Validate: Let the child know we acknowledge and value their feelings. Note the feeling. Name it. A word is a symbol that can contain the abstract. Withhold judgment of it being "good" or "bad." All feelings are valid. Ex: "You look tired . . . ", "It seems like you're angry."
2. Empathize: Stay with the feeling. Feel it with the child. Let them know we're there with them. "Yes . . . that's hard"; "I know that's not what you wanted . . . "; "It hurts so bad."
3. Offering Support: Children need the grown-ups in their lives to help, especially if they've experienced developmental trauma. This is the time to responsively step in, but also empower them to choose. The psyche is likely in a repressed state, meaning the child is acting younger than their chronological age. Be gentle. Ex: "Is there anything I can do to help?"; "Would it help if I. . . ?" Offer basic comforts. Expect verbal rejection. Placing comforting items (blankets, toys, etc.) or sitting near the child may also offer consolation.

Research/Empirical Support

With the increase in neuroscientific research on attachment and early childhood trauma comes greater acknowledgment of Jung's theories from the early 1900s. The importance of the development of the symbolic function (though known by slightly different terms across disciplines) through healthy attachments and play as a foundation of healthy brain architecture is now well known (Center on the Developing Child at Harvard University, 2011; Quinn et al., 2018; Siegel, 2007 & 2020). This includes the ability to read facial expressions, language development, empathize with others, as well as understanding social norms and accepting one's self. Without this foundation, we lack cognitive awareness and control of our behavior. Intergenerational trauma is evidenced through our knowledge not only of ACEs but interpersonal neurobiology and archetype theory (CDC, 2023; Gaskill & Perry, 2014;

Kestly, 2014; Panksepp & Biven, 2012; Perry, 2006; Roesler, 2024; Yehuda & Lehrner, 2018). Cross disciplinary research has demonstrated that empathy and kindness extended toward an entire system can lead to individual and collective healing (Lucero, 2018). Preserving and creating stable, predictable relationships and healthy attachments throughout cultures and time have been held together with personal and collective routines and rituals, now also recognized as empirically significant interventions (Blaustein & Kinniburgh, 2019), which Jungians call the *religious function*. Meaningful engagement of the reflective function may assist those who have experienced childhood abuse, like Herman, and are therefore at higher risk for identity diffusion and treatment-resistant symptomatology (Horváth at al., 2023; Penner et al., 2019). Ego and spiritual transcendence are ongoing areas of study, especially in their psychospiritual relationship to resilience (Hanfstingl, 2013).

Jung's original conceptualizations of the importance of engaging and navigating both associative and analytic processes for healthy emotional and cognitive functioning (CW 5, 8, 9i), or what we call *mode-shifting* in JAPT (McRoberts, 2024; Pringle & Swoden, 2017), has now been validated by several studies across disciplines, most of which do not credit Jung, and some of which are Nobel-worthy (Kahneman, 2011). Social, creative engagement is known to be good for us emotionally, physically, and spiritually, across cultures and ages, and is supported by the World Health Organization (Fancourt & Finn, 2019). We now have compelling neurobiological evidence of archetypal patterning, supporting Jungian concepts of the personal and collective, the cultural significance of the unconscious, as well as the functions and language of the psyche (Alcaro et al., 2017; Panksepp & Bieven, 2012).

Nondirective sandplay therapy, which may be a component of JAPT or a stand-alone Jungian-oriented intervention, now has two meta-analyses (Lee & Jang, 2015; Wiersma et al., 2022), hearty neurobiological research (Akimoto et al., 2018; Foo & Pratiwi, 2021) is gaining attention as an "official" evidence-based treatment (Freedle, 2022). Jungian psychotherapies have always been more popular in the United Kingdom, where research continues, but less defensively than in America (Roesler, 2018). However, we'd like to acknowledge that *evidence-based practice* is both a policy movement and a dynamic, collaborative process that includes "the integration of the best available research with clinical expertise in the context of patient characteristics, culture and preferences" (APA, 2008). As JAPTs, we acknowledge that our work needs to be forever curious, humble, and responsive. Like the neurosequential model of therapeutics (Perry, 2006), which has been adapted for and applied by Jungians (Freedle, 2019), and the therapeutic powers of play, JAPT is less of a specific collection of techniques or interventions but an integrative model with a theoretically rooted framework.

Case Study through the Lens of the Therapeutic Powers of Play

The therapeutic powers of play, as identified by Schaefer & Drews (2014), includes twenty core areas across four domains: (I) Facilitates Communication (A. self-expression, B.

access to the unconscious, C. direct teaching, D. indirect teaching); (II) Fosters Emotional Wellness (A. Catharsis, B. Abreaction, C. Positive Emotions, D. Counterconditioning Fears, E. Stress Inoculation, F. Stress Management); (III) Enhances Social Relationships (A. Therapeutic Relationship, B. Attachment, C. Social Competence, D. Empathy); (IV) Increases Personal Strengths (A. Creative Problem Solving, B. Resiliency, C. Moral Development, D. Accelerated Psychological Development, E. Self-Regulation, F. Self-Esteem). The main principle of the therapeutic powers of play is that play itself is the change agent; it is not a method, medium, or catalyst for change.

Herman's developmental and current play behavior is unknown (see Appendix for case study of Herman). However, neglected children often do not experience the building blocks of healthy play, which in turn builds a trusting, collaborative relationship with the World, because they miss the basics (Winnicott, 1971): the songs and games that are supposed to happen in a loving caregiver's lap. Ideally, these developmental games engage the symbolic and religious function by accessing the unconscious (Schaefer & Drewes, 2014, I.B.), forming the relational foundation of wellness (II); through playing early, collaboratively, and often, children and caregivers co-create sacred space and trust in a loving World: building healthy attachments (III.B.), communication skills (I.), subsequent co- and self-regulation (IV. E.), and sufficient ego strength (IV.). We might think of the archetype of the Divine Child as a part of Herman's Self that was pushed into Shadow; he was not delighted in and nurtured as he deserved; he was not free, safe, and lifted up. His "acting out" behaviors may be seen as a larger, amplified kind of babyish play, attempting to compensate for countless times he was ignored: throwing things, hitting, kicking, climbing up to high places both as a sense of mastery over his body and the World, but also to see if people think, or care, if it's safe.

Therapeutic Powers of Play Employed

In the playroom, building the therapeutic relationship (III.A) as well as inviting and communicating with the unconscious (I.B.) is of utmost importance to the JAPT. The therapist and child are collaborators in the exploration and creativity of the process. Jung identified that material may be communicated visually, audio-verbally, and/or kinetically, with some people favoring one means of expression over another (CW 8, § 170—171). In JAPT, the child leads, and together with the well-attuned therapist, co-contains and co-interprets the material that arises from the unconscious to help make sense of it. The trust starts with the JAPT's belief in, value of, and healing capacity of the unconscious. The transformational space was called *the vas* by Jung (CW 13, CW 16); we can imagine this space as a delicate container such as the womb, a baptismal font, a sacred circle, or a vessel used by chemists to combine, heat, and distill base materials. The therapist's attitude, including our value of the whole child, the personal and collective unconscious, the trust that the psyche self-heals, and engagement with unconscious material all matter.

There is a dance that occurs between the child and the therapist, their unconscious material, and creative problem-solving. As the child grows more comfortable and confident

(II, IV). with the therapist, in the space, and with the process, their self-expression (A.I) and creative problem solving (IV), involving both direct and indirect teaching (A. C. & D) occur. The unconscious is the main teacher, but it is also the process of mode-shifting, or shuffling material back and forth between the unconscious and the conscious, the thinking and the feeling, the child and therapist, through play, that encourages creative cognition (McRoberts, 2024). Throughout the therapeutic process, the psyche is *de-integrating*, unpacking old patterns of understanding and enacting, and *re-integrating* with new ways of imagining, organizing, and meaning making (Fordham, 1973; Lilly, 2015).

While being open to his unique expression in play, we would also be on the lookout for archetypal patterns of *wounding* and *healing* (Mitchell & Friedman, 1994 & 2017); wounding themes may include the creation of chaos, being split, confined, isolated, injured, or hidden, while healing themes are transformational, referencing the Self through centering, integrating, birthing, journeying, or bridging. We might expect archetypes of Wounded Child, The Warrior, Elders/the Sage, and the Lovers to emerge from this child through play. His psychic wounds need tending, and through the use of *soft interpretations*, we would try to see and respond to them appropriately, with empathy. His Warrior self is to be respected; he fights for his survival but is in need of mentorship and training from trusted Elders.

As the child develops their ability to communicate with their own unconscious (I.B), counterconditioning (II.D); the tension of the opposites is resolved through symbolic re-enactment, re-telling, and re-imagining. In this way, symbols may be counterconditioning (II.D). As their confidence in themselves (IV.F), the therapeutic relationship (III.A), and their ability to self-regulate (IV.E) grows, so does attachment (III.B) with primary caregivers, empathy for others in general (III.D), overall emotional wellness (II), as well as moral and psychological development (IV.C & D.).

Cultural Considerations

Each child comes into the world with a history, both recent and ancient, personal and collective. JAPT acknowledges that there are archetypes and symbols that may have particular cultural significance to each child and family. We see it as our responsibility to be ongoing students of the world, learning the customs, traditions, rituals, and symbols that are known to humans, especially in this digital age. We cannot assume that we know what a symbol means to a child. We are called to be curious and try to understand.

Herman is disconnected from his biological family, which has been described as a diverse and not fully known blend of cultures. This influence on the psyche should not be ignored. While over-identification with any particular trait or group can become inflated and problematic (This Jungian Life, 2023), it is normal to seek and find a safe and comfortable place to land and feel at home; this is the religious function at work.

His reports that he "does not like being a boy" and has been experimenting with make-up may or may not be indicative of the popular cultural phenomenon of the increased categorization of children as a gender or sexual minority (Marino et al., 2023). This may be a child's desperate wish to reject the entire ego and all the tangible pains of this earthly body, to more greatly identify with the anima or the spiritual Self. It may also be an attempt to more fully embody aspects of the feminine, holding the tension of the opposites, to internalize the archetypal Mother; in this child's current story, the Mother has been largely neglectful and destructive; however, the Mother is also life-giving and loving. Through the work of exploring masculine and feminine archetypal symbols, both through play and through discussing cultural identity, in the playroom and at home, these attempts to reject parts of the self may become more integrated.

The elders in the community, both male and female, traditionally pass down the traditions and rituals, that give structure and meaning to life, through storytelling and embodied, collective engagement. He may be re-enacting familial patterns based on the stories being told about them. The current "case history," Herman's [Current] Story, is one of tragedy, disconnection, and pain with no resolution; he is at best the Wounded Child, the Orphan, and at worst the Villain. Herman's story must have deeper threads of meaning and hope in order to be a historical narrative he can build on.

JAPT looks for clues from the unconscious for ancestral guidance. We are trained to continually seek out personal and collective multicultural meanings of symbol and ritual, expressions of the archetypes. Caregivers may assist in this process as well. More concretely, perhaps Herman is experiencing discrimination at school or feeling left out in his identity as a child of mixed race. Are the family having conversations about race, color, and identity? Have they been intentional about exploring aspects of African American and Hispanic cultures and looking for resonance in this child? While it is unfortunately understandable that we might not ever know the exact details of Herman's ancestral lineage, there are boundless opportunities to value and explore the stories, foods, art, clothing styles, dances, family, and religious traditions across Africa, North and South America, the Caribbean Islands, and Spain. Active engagement in meaningful cultural activities may also assist with spiritual well-being and decreased symptomology (Smith et al., 2013).

Case Formulation and Application

Before Herman was born, his mother experienced great suffering. Based on Herman's abuse experienced in his maternal grandmother's home, and the lack of information we have about the maternal grandfather, we might assume the home was less than ideal. We do know that they came from mixed heritages and have experienced specific hardships and prejudices from others for generations. Herman's mother invested in relationships with several men and endured domestic violence that left her with chronic pain, both physically and emotionally. Herman was conceived and born through that reverberating pain. Likely out of a sense of overwhelm, shame, and an innate love for a child she knew on some level she could not care for, she stayed away. Herman was rejected by both his mother and his unknown father. He has been left alone in his pain, both physically and emotionally.

Herman experienced birth trauma. These effects run deep into his unconscious mind. While it was necessary for him to be in the NICU for medical care, it was neglectful in that it was bright, overcrowded, and he was not held. Babies need to be held and soothed, especially those who are born experiencing withdrawals from opioids and have lost their mothers. After he left the hospital, the neglect continued and was amplified by further abuse. His world was chaotic, lonely, and frightening. Without loving and attentive caregivers, children first frantically fight to get their needs met, then numb to conserve resources and prepare for death. Herman's will to live is strong but is at odds with his distrust of the World. He attempts to conquer it and his unmet needs to be soothed into feeling good by thrill seeking, dopamine and cortisol-releasing behaviors.

Herman missed the connection needed in order to fully develop a healthy ego. While he may "know better," in that he has been told the rules in the classroom and at home, unconsciously he does not trust the World enough, with good reason. He needed to get his needs met, and it failed him time and time again. Now he feels he is on his own. This is disturbing for everyone involved: his teachers, peers, and caregivers, but most importantly to the JAPT: him.

Imagining what his behavior might mean symbolically gives us some clues about where this reported "out of nowhere" behavior comes from. For example, the simple experience of "quiet," often a part of a normally functioning classroom or bedtime, may be one of the most overwhelming triggers for him; "quiet" is when he finally stopped screaming out of sheer exhaustion as a baby in pain; "quiet" means the adults in the house are creeping around or have gotten so high they've passed out.

His sleep disturbance is likely an underdeveloped symbolic and religious function, but may be medical as well. Medications often disturb children's sleep, and the problem is likely rooted much deeper. Because he was never soothed to sleep, he doesn't know how to do it on his own. It makes perfect sense that he might wake up hungry and go seek out and "sneak" food, so as not to not upset any potentially highly dysregulated adult that might "catch him."

We can see, too, that he's craving connection. He admires his foster father and is exploring aspects of both the masculine and the feminine, trying to know them both more fully.

Challenges in Implementation

The deep lack of information about the specifics of how Herman tries to connect, and how his caregivers demonstrate their tender care and delight in him is demonstrative of how the system has over-pathologized him. He has likely missed developmental milestones, as well as the freedom to play in the presence of well-attuned caregivers and develop his symbolic function. A child who has not been encouraged to play is less likely to spontaneously do so, especially on the cusp of adolescence; this may be why CCPT has not been effective. As

JAPTs, we are aware that Herman's ego may be heavily defended, and we'd be prepared with patience, curiosity, and plenty of materials for him to choose from.

Conclusion

The human spirit is remarkably resilient, but we're designed to do so with deeply rooted connections. Mental health treatment, along with many aspects of our contemporary life, demands quick, easy, formulaic answers. Jung warned that this time was coming years ago, and that we'd suffer for it. JAPT is not, and will likely never be the most popular modality. Jung hoped that his theory would help uphold the seemingly disconnected evidence of humanity as it emerged across disciplines. He famously said, "Thank God, I'm Jung, and not a Jungian!" (Hannah, 1976, p. 78). It's a lot of work to continue to stay grounded, curious, and discern which is the right way to turn in the middle of a storm. We trust, as Jung did, that his legacy will continue to attract a small but significant minority of practitioners and clients who want a more spiritual, integrative, relational, creative approach.

References

AdoptUSKids. (2020). Life books 1010: Tops from an adoption worker. https://professionals.adoptuskids.org/life-books-101-tips-from-an-adoption-worker/.

Akimoto, M., Furukawa, K., & Ito, J. (2018). Exploring the sandplayer's brain: A single case study. *Archives of Sandplay Therapy, 30*(3), 73–84.

Alcaro, A., Carta, S., & Panksepp, J. (2017). The affective core of the Self: A neuro-archetypical perspective on the foundations of human (and animal) subjectivity. *Frontiers in Psychology, 8*(1424), 1–13. https://doi.org/10.3389/fpsyg.2017.01424.

American Counseling Association. (2014). 2014 ACA code of ethics. https://www.counseling.org/docs/default-source/default-document-library/ethics/2014-aca-code-of-ethics.pdf

American Psychological Association (APA). (2008). Evidence-based practice in psychology. https://www.apa.org/practice/resources/evidence#:~:text=Evidence%2Dbased%20practice%20is%20the,at%20their%20August%202005%20meeting.

Association for Play Therapy (APT). (2022). Play therapy best practices: Clinical, professional, and ethical issues. https://cdn.ymaws.com/www.a4pt.org/resource/resmgr/publications/best_practices.pdf.

Blaustein, M., & Kinniburgh, K. (2019). *Treating traumatic stress in children and adolescents: How to foster resilience through attachment, self regulation, and competency.* The Guilford Press.

Center on the Developing Child at Harvard University. (2011). Serve & return interaction shapes brain circuitry [Video]. YouTube. https://youtu.be/m_5u8-QSh6A.

Edinger, E. F. (1972). *Ego and archetype: Individuation and the religious function of the psyche.* Shambhala Publications.

Fancourt, D., & Finn, S. (2019). *What is the evidence on the role of the arts in improving health and well-being?* A scoping review. World Health Organization.

Foo, M., & Pratiwi, A. (2021). The effectiveness of sandplay therapy in treating patients with generalized anxiety disorder and childhood trauma using magnetic resonance spectroscopy to examine choline level in the dorsolateral prefrontal cortex and centrum semiovale. *International Journal of Play Therapy, 30*(3), 177–86. https://doi.org/10.1037/pla0000162.

Fordham, M. (1976). *The self and autism.* Academic Press.

Fordham, M. (1985). *Explorations into the self.* Academic Press.

Fordham, M. (1994). *Children as individuals.* Free Association Books.

Freedle, L. R. (2019). Making connections: Sandplay therapy and the neurosequential model of therapeutics. *Journal of Sandplay Therapy, 28*(1), 91–109. https://www.sandplay.org/journal/abstracts/.

Freedle, L. R. (2022). Sandplay therapy: An evidence based treatment. *Journal of Sandplay Therapy, 31*(1), 3–9. https://www.sandplay.org/journal/abstracts/volume-31-number-1-2022/freedle-lorraine-razzi-sandplay-therapy-an-evidenced-based-treatment/.

Gaskill, R., & Perry, B. P. (2014). The neurobiological power of play: Using the neurosequential model of therapeutics to guide play in the healing process. In C. A. Malchiodi & D. A. Crenshaw (Eds.), *Creative arts and play therapy for attachment problems* (pp. 178–94). The Guilford Press.

Jung, C. G. (1935/1977). *The Tavistock lectures.* In H. Read, M. Fordham, G. Adler & W. McGuire (Eds.), R. F. C. Hull(Trans.), The collected works of C. G. Jung, volume 18: The symbolic life. Routledge & Kegan Paul.

Jung, C. G. (2008). *Children's dreams: Notes from the seminar given 1936–1940* (L. Jung & M. Meyer-Grass, Eds.; E. Faizieder & T. Woolfson, Trans.). Princeton University Press.

Jung, C. G., & Ostrowski-Sachs, M. (1971). *From conversations with C. G. Jung.* Juris Druck.

Hanfstingl, B. (2013). Ego and spiritual transcendence: Relevance to psychological resilience and the role of age. *Evidence-Based Complementary and Alternative Medicine, 949838*, 1–9. https://doi.org/10.1155/2013/949838.

Hannah, B. (1976). *Jung, his life and work: A biographical memoir.* Putnam Adult.

Hebb, D. (1949). *The organisation of behaviour.* John Wiley and Sons

Horváth, Z., Demetrovics, O., Paksi, B., Unoka, Z., & Demetrovics, Z. (2023). The reflective functioning questionnaire-revised- 7 (RFQ-R-7): A new measurement model assessing hypomentalization. *PLoS One, 18*(2), e0282000. https://doi.org/10.1371/journal.pone.0282000.

Infant Child Enrichment Services. (2020). Strategies for building attachment. https://icesagency.org/strategies-for-building-attachment/.

Kahneman, D. (2011). *Thinking, fast and slow.* Farrar, Strauss and Giroux.

Kalff, D. M. (2020). *Sandplay: A psychotherapeutic approach to the psyche* (B. L. Matthews, Trans). Analytical Psychology Press: Sandplay Editions (Original work published 1966).

Kestly, T. A. (2014). *The interpersonal neurobiology of play: Brain-building interventions for emotional well-being.* Norton.

Keysers, C., & Gazzola, V. (2014). Hebbian learning and predictive mirror neurons for actions, sensations and emotions. *Philosophical Transactions of the Royal Society of London. Series B. Biological Sciences, 369*(1644), 20130175. https://doi.org/10.1098/rstb.2013.0175.

Kottman, T., & Meany-Walen, K. K. (2018). *Doing play therapy: From building the relationship to facilitating change.* The Guilford Press.

Landreth, G. (2024). *Play therapy: The art of the relationship* (4th ed.). Routledge (Original work published 1991).

Lee, J.-S., & Jang, D.-H. (2015). The effectiveness of sand play treatment meta-analysis. *Korean Journal of Child Psychological Therapy, 10*(1), 1–26.

Lilly, JP. (2015). Jungian analytical play therapy. In D. A. Crenshaw & A. L. Stewart (Eds.), *Play therapy: A comprehensive guide to theory and practice* (pp. 48–65). The Guilford Press.

Lönneker, C., & Maercker, A. (2021). The numinous experience in the context of psychopathology and traumatic stress studies. *Culture & Psychology, 27*(3), 392–416. https://doi.org/10.1177/1354067X20922139.

Lucero, I. (2018). Written in the body?: Healing the epigenetic molecular wounds of complex trauma through empathy and kindness. *Journal of Child & Adolescent Trauma, 11*(4), 443–55. https://doi.org/10.1007/s40653-

Marino, J. L., Lin, A., Davies, C., Kang, M., Bista, S., & Skinner, S. R. (2023). Childhood and adolescence gender role nonconformity and gender and sexuality diversity in young adulthood. *JAMA Pediatrics, 177*(11), 1176–86. https://doi.org/10.1001/jamapediatrics.2023.3873.

McRoberts, R. (2024). *Jungian counseling & play therapy: Classical theory for the digital age.* [Manuscript submitted for publication]. Routledge Press.

Mitchell, R. R., & Friedman, H. S. (1994). *Sandplay past, present & future.* Routledge Press.

Mitchell, R. R., & Friedman, H. S. (2017). Archetypal themes in the sandplay process. *Journal of Sandplay Therapy, 26*(1). https://www.sandplay.org/journal/abstracts/volume-26-number-1/rogers-mitchell-rie-and-friedman-harriet-s-archetypal-themes-in-the-sandplay-process/.

Mills, J. C., & Crowley, R. J. (2014). *Therapeutic metaphors for children and the child within.* Routledge Press.

National Association of Social Workers. (2024). Social workers' ethical responsibilities to clients. https://www.socialworkers.org/About/Ethics/Code-of-Ethics/Code-of-Ethics-English/Social-Workers-Ethical-Responsibilities-to-Clients.

National Center for Injury Prevention and Control, Division of Violence Prevention. (2023, June 29). Center for Disease Control (CDC). https://www.cdc.gov/violenceprevention/aces/index.html.

Otto, R. (1917). *Das heilige: Über das irrationale in der idee des göttlichen und sein verhältnis zum rationalenb* (English translation, 1923). Oxford University Press.

Panksepp, J., & Biven, L. (2012). *The archaeology of mind: Neuroevolutionary origins of human emotion.* W. W. Norton & Company.

Penner, F., Gambin, M., & Sharp, C. (2019). Childhood maltreatment and identity diffusion among inpatient adolescents: The role of the reflective function. *Journal of Adolescence, 76*, 65–74. https://doi.org/10.1016/j.adolescence.2019.08.002.

Perry, B. D. (2006). Applying principles of neurodevelopment to clinical work with maltreated and traumatized children: The neurosequential model of therapeutics. In N. B. Webb (Ed.), *Working with traumatized youth in child welfare* (pp. 27–52). The Guilford Press.

Pringle, A., & Sowden, P. T. (2017). The Mode Shifting Index (MSI): A new measure of the creative thinking skill of shifting between associative and analytic thinking. *Thinking Skills and Creativity, 23*, 17–28. https://dx.doi.org/10.1016/j.tsc.2016.10.010.

Quinn, S., Donnelly, S., & Kidd, E. (2018). The relationship between symbolic play and language acquisition: A meta-analytic review. *Developmental Review*, 1–15. https://doi.org/10.1016/j.dr.2018.05.005.

Roesler, C. (2018). *Research in analytical psychology: Empirical research*. Routledge

Roesler, C. (2024). *Deconstructing archetype theory: A critical analysis of Jungian ideas*. Routledge.

Schaefer, C. E., & Drewes, A. A. (Eds.). (2014). *The therapeutic powers of play: 20 core agents of change* (2nd ed.). https://cdn.ymaws.com/www.a4pt.org/resource/resmgr/education_&_training/therapeutic_powers_of_play_2.pdf.

Shatz, C. J. (1992). The developing brain. *Scientific American, 267*, 60–7. https://doi.org/10.1038/scientificamerican0992-60.

Siegel, D. (2007). *The mindful brain*. Norton.

Siegel, D. J. (2020). *The developing mind: How relationships and the brain interact to shape who we are* (3rd ed.). The Guilford Press (Original work published 1999).

Smith, L., Webber, R., & DeFrain, J. (2013). Spiritual well-being and its relationship to resilience in young people: A mixed methods case study. *Sage Open, 3*(2), 1–16. https://doi.org/10.1177/2158244013485582.

This Jungian Life. (2023, December 13). Yascha Mounk: Why society crumbles when we obsess over identity. https://youtu.be/z_5YEztSQ28?si=5nOqA_zg0uy8cAYu.

von Franz, M.-L. (1996). *The interpretation of fairy tales* (Rev. ed.). Shambhala Publications.

Wickes, F. G. (1927). *The inner world of childhood: A study in analytical psychology*. Appleton.

Wiersma, J. K., Freedle, L. R., McRoberts, R., & Solberg, K. B. (2022). A meta-analysis of sandplay therapy treatment outcomes. *International Journal of Play Therapy, 31*(4), 197–215. https://doi.org/10.1037/pla0000180.

Winnicott, D. W. (1971). *Playing and reality*. Basic Books.

Yehuda, R., & Lehrner, A. (2018). Intergenerational transmission of trauma effects: Putative role of epigenetic mechanisms. *World Psychiatry, 17*(3), 243–57. https://doi.org/10.1002/wps.20568.

6

Using the Therapeutic Powers of Play in Adlerian Play Therapy

Terry Kottman and Sherri Cauthen

Chapter Outline

Introduction

In Adlerian play therapy (AdPT) (Kottman, 1993; Kottman & Meany-Walen, 2016, 2018), therapists use the concepts of Alfred Adler's Individual Psychology (Adler, 1927/1998) to conceptualize children and their caregivers while using toys; art activities; therapeutic metaphors and storytelling; sand trays; dance, movement, and music; adventure therapy; and structured play experiences to communicate with clients. The process of AdPT unfolds in four interconnected and overlapping phases: (a) building a relationship with clients; (b) exploring clients' "lifestyles" (how they view themselves, others, and the world, which influences their patterns of thinking, feeling, and behaving); (c) helping clients gain insight into their lifestyles; and (d) reorientating and reeducating clients through facilitating changes in their patterns of intrapersonal and interpersonal dynamics.

During the first phase, the play therapist begins building an egalitarian partnership with the child (Kottman, 2014; Schaefer & Drewes, 2014). While the therapist works on maintaining the relationship with the child throughout the play therapy process, the intense focus on building the relationship varies in length, depending on the child's willingness to "let the therapist in." This phase can last anywhere from a single session to twenty-four sessions but will usually take about two to four sessions.

In the second phase, the play therapist explores the child's lifestyle, gathering information from the child through watching the child's play and asking questions about what happens in the child's life. The therapist might ask the child to draw or paint, tell stories, do puppet shows, dance, make sand trays, create collages, or participate in other playful therapeutic strategies as a way to use the child's natural language (play) to get information about the child's lifestyle. This exploration is a vehicle for helping the therapist understand how the child (a) perceives self, the world, and others; (b) solves problems; (c) forms relationships; (d) gains a sense of belonging and significance; and so forth. This phase can last anywhere from three or four sessions to ten to twelve sessions, depending on how open the child is and how complex the child's issues are.

In the third phase, the play therapist helps the child gain a better understanding of their lifestyle and guides the child to consider making changes in patterns of thinking, feeling, and behaving. This phase (which can last from three or four sessions to twenty-four sessions, with the usual length being between eight to twelve sessions) generally involves some free play, with the therapist using metacommunication to highlight hypotheses about the child's lifestyle themes. Metacommunication involves commenting on what is happening in the session and (sometimes) making guesses about what it means (Kottman & Meany-Walen, 2016). The therapist often uses more directive strategies, such as art techniques, active games, movement activities, directed sand trays, and therapeutic storytelling, to communicate their understanding of the child's lifestyle patterns in a process designed to help the child gain insight.

The fourth phase can last from a single session to between twelve and sixteen sessions, with an average of about eight sessions. During this phase, the therapist invites the child and the significant adults in their life to explore different, more constructive attitudes and perceptions, helping them put these changes into place in their relationships with others and make shifts in their outlooks on the world. The therapist uses play skills and techniques to teach new skills needed for gaining significance, interacting with others, and solving problems.

Underlying Philosophy

The underlying philosophy of Adlerian play therapy is based on Adler's assertion that (a) people are socially embedded and need to belong; (b) all behavior is goal-directed; (c) people perceive reality subjectively; (d) individuals are self-determining and creative; and (e) people have a tendency toward feeling inferior to others (Adler 1927/1954, 1931/1958; Ansbacher & Ansbacher, 1956; Carlson & Englar-Carlson, 2017; Dufrene & Clark, 2022; Kottman & Meany-Walen, 2016; Maniacci & Sackett-Maniacci, 2019; Sweeney, 2019). These five principles are the foundation of the theory and practice of Individual Psychology.

People are socially embedded. Adlerians believe that people are socially embedded, which means that they have a need to belong (Ansbacher & Ansbacher, 1956; Kottman & Meany-Walen, 2016; Maniacci & Sackett-Maniacci, 2019; Sweeney, 2019). By observing the reactions of others to their behavior, children decide on a way for themselves to gain significance and fit into different groups. Adlerians spend time observing children in the context of their families and gathering information about family dynamics because the family is the first group to which children belong. If children do not experience success in their attempts to find a place in their family or in other groups of people in prosocial, constructive ways, they begin striving to belong in negative, self-destructive ways. In Adlerian play therapy, the therapist continually assesses how the child makes connections and gains a sense of significance in his or her family, school, and community, with an eye to helping the child improve his or her ability to positively connect with others.

All behavior is goal-directed. Behavior is purposive (Dreikurs & Soltz, 1964; Kottman & Meany-Walen, 2016; 2018). Adlerians believe that all behavior is goal-directed—that each person has a purpose for every choice they make and every action they take (Maniacci & Sackett-Maniacci, 2019; Sweeney, 2019). However, the goals of behavior are often out of the individual's awareness—while there is a purpose for the behavior, they may not know what it is. In Adlerian play therapy, part of the therapist's job is to help clients begin to recognize the goals of their misbehavior and shift toward working to get their needs met through more appropriate behaviors.

People perceive reality subjectively. Adlerian theory is based on a phenomenological perspective, in which individuals make life choices based on their subjective interpretation of events, rather than on the "facts" of the experience (Adler, 1927/1954; Eckstein & Kern, 2009; Sweeney, 2019). Adlerian play therapists pay attention to what clients believe about what happens to them, rather than what actually ("factually") happens to them. Children come to conclusions about self, others, and the world through observing themselves, the people around them, their interactions with others, and the reactions of themselves and others to various situations in life. Children's behavior organically grows from their perceptions and the conclusions based on these perceptions. Children "act as if" these perceptions and conclusions are true and real. Sometimes children's perceptions and the conclusions they draw about themselves and others, about how life and relationships work, are faulty. While children possess keen observation skills, they often lack the sophistication and experience to be able to accurately evaluate and interpret situations and relationships. It is the job of the Adlerian play therapist to ferret out children's perceptions and conclusions in order to help them more realistically evaluate and interpret what has happened to them and to reframe any self-defeating patterns of thinking, feeling, and behaving that they may have developed.

People are self-determining and creative (Adler, 1927/1998; Kottman & Meany-Walen, 2016, 2018). They constantly make choices about their behaviors, thoughts, feelings, and attitudes. All individuals are unique, special, and different from all other individuals. The Adlerian play therapist believes that, while affected by the environment and heredity, individuals are not determined by either of them. In Adlerian play therapy, the therapist emphasizes that clients have free will and that they can move toward being more intentional in the choices they make and the impact they have on their own lives and the lives of others. By focusing on clients' assets and encouraging clients to exercise consciously their self-determination and their ability to make new choices and interpretations, the Adlerian play therapist can help clients change their interpretations and perceptions; increase their social interest; and learn new ways of thinking, feeling, and behaving.

Human beings have a tendency to feel inferior to others. Adlerians believe that there is almost always a discrepancy between a person's self-perception and their self-ideal. Because of this discrepancy, people experience feelings of inferiority (Ansbacher & Ansbacher, 1956; Kottman & Meany-Walen, 2016, 2018; Maniacci & Sackett-Maniacci, 2019; Sweeney, 2019). Responses to these feelings of inferiority tend to fall along a continuum ranging from discouragement to inspiration. Those who respond to their feelings of inferiority with discouragement usually give up and become despairing, unwilling or unable to act in constructive, positive ways. Another route taken by people who feel discouraged by their feelings of inferiority is the path of overcompensation. These individuals "frequently develop a 'superiority complex.' They spend most of their time and energy trying to counter their own feelings of inferiority by proving that they are 'in fact' not inferior to others—they are better than others" (Kottman & Meany-Walen, 2016, p. 25). People who choose to be inspired, rather than discouraged, by their feelings of inferiority use the gap between where they want to be and where they perceive they are as a positive motivator. They work to improve themselves, their relationships, and their behaviors as a way to move closer to their self-ideal. With children who have developed either of the two discouraged modes of reacting to their feelings of inferiority, the play therapist works to help them shift to the more positive, inspired way of dealing with feelings of inferiority.

Personality Theory

In Adlerian theory, personality is referred to as lifestyle, which is "the person's basic orientation to life, a set of patterns or themes that runs through the person's existence" (Carlson & Slavik, 1997, p. xii). Lifestyle is the way a person sees self, others, and the world and the behavior based on those perceptions. It is a person's characteristic pattern of movement predicated on a unique method of perceiving, conceptualizing, behaving, and striving toward a subjectively determined goal for belonging and gaining significance. There are many elements in lifestyle (family constellation, family atmosphere, assets, Crucial Cs, personality priorities, goals of misbehavior, lifestyle convictions, and mistaken beliefs) that are important in conceptualizing clients in Adlerian play therapy.

Family Constellation

"In Adlerian theory, the family constellation contributes greatly to the child's lifestyle because the family configuration during the child's formative years influences the child's fundamental attitudes and approach to life" (Kottman & Meany-Walen, 2016, p. 175). Family constellation is made up of the psychological birth order of the children, the gender of the children, the personality traits of each family member, the emotional connections between family members, age differences among the children, the size of the family, sibling subsets, and the dominance or submission of family members (Eckstein & Kern, 2009; Kottman & Meany-Walen, 2016; Maniacci & Sackett-Maniacci, 2019; Sweeney, 2019). It may also be influenced by differential treatment of children based on gender, children who are developmentally delayed or have other challenges, and the time gap between the birth of children.

Family Atmosphere

Family atmosphere is the affective tone of the family, which can have a major impact on the development of a child's personality (Eckstein & Kern, 2009; Kottman & Meany-Walen, 2016; Maniacci & Sackett-Maniacci, 2019; Sweeney, 2019). A child's perception of the atmosphere in the family will influence the child's beliefs about self, others, and the world; beliefs about how problems are solved; beliefs about values; beliefs about how people communicate; and beliefs about how relationships work. In AdPT, the therapist observes the child's play and verbalization in any form of family play; asks questions about family interactions; and uses art, storytelling, and sand tray play activities that might relate to family functioning to explore the family atmosphere and family constellation.

Assets

Another factor in an Adlerian play therapist's assessment of lifestyle is the personal and interpersonal assets and strengths demonstrated by the child. Sometimes these assets are obvious (e.g., Greg is very intelligent; Dashia is mechanically gifted and can fix anything; Chika is assertive and compassionate), and sometimes the play therapist has to look deeply to find strengths buried in the child's behavior (e.g., Shul, a child who is exceptional at pushing other people's buttons, is perceptive about their nonverbal reactions; Faith, a child who uses "inappropriate words and phrases," is creative with language).

Crucial Cs

Resilient children have four beliefs that serve as unconscious behavioral guides (Kottman & Meany-Walen, 2016; Lew & Bettner, 1998, 2000). They (a) feel connected to others; (b) believe they are capable and can take care of themselves; (c) know that they count, that they are valued by others, and they make a positive contribution; and (d) have courage and are willing to try behaviors without a guarantee of success. Based on these factors, Lew and Bettner (1998, 2000) developed the Crucial Cs (Connect, Capable, Count, and Courage). In Adlerian play therapy, the therapist observes the child's free play; observes interactions between the child and other family members or classmates; asks the child, parents/caregivers, or teachers questions; solicits drawings or other forms of artistic expression;

invites the child to do sand trays; and engages the child in storytelling, puppet shows, doll play, and so on, as a way of assessing which of these factors can be considered strengths for the child and which present challenges. Based on this assessment, the therapist plans strategies for fostering the Crucial Cs that the child has not incorporated into their belief system.

Personality Priorities

A person's personality priority is a pattern of behavior and reactions stemming from their convictions about how they attain a sense of belonging, significance, and mastery (Kfir, 1981; Kottman & Meany-Walen, 2016). Individuals use personality priorities as their usual mode of thinking about and reacting to situations and relationships with others and as a way to cope with stressful situations in their lives. There are four personality priorities that manifest themselves in children: pleasing; comfort; control (with two subcategories, those who strive for control of themselves and those who strive for control of everything and everyone); and superiority (with two subcategories, achievers and outdoers). Using the skills of Phase 2, the Adlerian play therapist gathers information (Kottman & Meany-Walen, 2016) as a way to discover whether the child is working toward ways to belong, gain significance, and establish a sense of mastery through pleasing, comfort, control, or superiority. The therapist assesses the child's primary and secondary personality priorities and evaluates the child's level of functioning on the continuum of "healthy" to "unhealthy" patterns within that aspect of their lifestyle.

Goals of Misbehavior

Adlerians believe all behavior is purposive, though the purpose of a person's behavior may often be out of his or her awareness (Kottman & Meany-Walen, 2016). While Adlerians consider the purposes of all behavior in the therapeutic process, it is often helpful to focus on the goals of a child's misbehavior, the patterns of destructive behaviors that have led to a referral to therapy. The goals of misbehavior are attention, power, revenge, and proving inadequacy (Dreikurs & Soltz, 1964). To understand the goal of a particular misbehavior, the play therapist gathers information about the child's feelings and patterns of behavior, the need the child is meeting through the misbehavior, the feelings and reactions of the primary adults who interact with the child, and the child's responses when they are corrected or punished. Because each of these factors is specific to one of the four goals of misbehavior, the therapist can usually pinpoint the child's usual goal of misbehavior.

Lifestyle Convictions and Mistaken Beliefs

The primary purpose of AdPT for gathering all of this information is to facilitate the therapist's understanding of the child's lifestyle (Kottman & Meany-Walen, 2016). As the foundational structure for conceptualizing lifestyle, the therapist considers the child's lifestyle convictions and mistaken beliefs.

Lifestyle convictions can be formulated through the therapist completing the following sentence stems as they believe the child would complete them:

I am . . .

Others are . . .

The world is . . .

Life is . . .

Based on these convictions, my behavior must/should be . . .

These convictions (usually out of the child's awareness) constitute the phenomenological perspective through which everything that happens to the child is filtered. Children usually form their lifestyles before they are eight years old—children are good observers, but poor interpreters. As Adlerian therapists explore clients' lifestyles, they look for self-defeating beliefs based on distorted interpretations that clients are "acting as if" they are true even when those interpretations do not serve them in positive ways—these are often called "mistaken beliefs" or self-defeating beliefs. After going through and examining which of these convictions are mistaken, the therapist can plan strategies for helping the child reexamine their convictions during Phase 3 and 4, perhaps making shifts in how they view self, others, and the world.

Model of Psychopathology

Adlerian play therapists tend to define psychopathology as discouragement (Kottman & Meany-Walen, 2016; Sweeney, 2019). Discouragement can be created through an impaired sense of connectedness to other people and belonging in a community. Discouragement can result when people are overwhelmed by or overcompensating for their feelings of inferiority (Eckstein & Kern, 2009). Finally, clients may experience maladjustment because of mistaken beliefs about self, others, and the world or private logic that undermines their capacity for functioning in healthy ways. The goal in AdPT is for the therapist to understand enough about the client's lifestyle as a precursor to enhancing the client's self-understanding and shifting their lifestyle beliefs and behaviors through encouragement as a means of diminishing the client's discouragement.

Conceptualizing Goals of Treatment

The goals of AdPT follow the phases of the play therapy process (Kottman & Meany-Walen, 2016). The initial goal (which corresponds to the first phase) is for the therapist to develop relationships with the child and (if possible) the significant adults in the child's life, working together as a team to create the best possible atmosphere for helping the child.

The second goal, parallel to the second phase of therapy, is for the play therapist to acquire information about the child's lifestyle (and the parents'/caregivers' and teachers' lifestyles). The therapist then uses this information as the raw material for formulating a comprehensive set of hypotheses about views on self, others, and the world and the connection between these beliefs and the child's attitudes, feelings, and behavior. The treatment plan for the remainder of the therapeutic work with the child is based on this conceptualization.

The primary goal in the third phase of AdPT is for the therapist to help the child begin to gain insight into their lifestyle, mistaken beliefs, behavioral and attitudinal patterns, and personal assets, along with increased awareness of the impact of their family constellation and family atmosphere, their functioning at the life tasks, their progress toward mastery of the Crucial Cs, their shifting toward the more positive qualities of their personality priorities, and the goals of their misbehavior. As a bridge to the fourth phase of play therapy, the therapist guides the child to evaluate whether they wish to make emotional, attitudinal, and behavioral changes.

In the fourth phase of the AdPT process, the goal is to teach the child skills necessary to effect changes outside the playroom. The therapist's goal is to help the child (a) learn the cognitive, affective, and behavioral patterns necessary for a shift from destructive goals and misbehavior toward constructive goals and appropriate behavior; (b) enhance his or her mastery of each of the Crucial Cs; (c) increase feelings of social interest and positive connection to others; (d) adjust self-defeating perceptions in their beliefs about self, others, and the world; (e) reduce discouragement; and (f) help them to understand and "own" their personal assets (Kottman & Meany-Walen, 2016).

Role of the Therapist

The role of the Adlerian play therapist changes depending on the phase of counseling (Kottman & Meany-Walen, 2016). As the play therapist builds a connection with the child during the first phase of therapy, the therapist is a partner and encourager. In this phase, the therapist is usually relatively nondirective, making sure that the child leads the action most of the time. By sharing power with the child in play sessions, creating a sense of teamwork and cooperation in the playroom, the play therapist encourages the child to trust the process, to trust the therapist, and to trust themselves. The therapist uses tracking, restating content, reflecting feelings, returning responsibility to the child, encouragement, limiting, answering questions, asking questions, and cleaning the room together to build an egalitarian and collaborative relationship.

In the second phase, the therapist is an active, directive explorer, collaborating with the child and the significant adults in the child's life to learn more about the child's intrapersonal and interpersonal dynamics. The therapist uses strategies designed to gather information about the child's attitudes, perceptions, thinking processes, feelings, goals of behavior, feelings of inferiority, Crucial Cs, family constellation, family atmosphere, and so forth. In this phase, the therapist might use puppet play, dollhouse play, art techniques, questioning strategies, active games, movement exercises, storytelling, sand tray play therapy techniques, observation of play patterns, and solicitation of early recollections. The intervention strategies in Phase 3 and Phase 4 spring from the therapist's conceptualization of the lifestyles of the child and significant adults in the child's life, so actively engaging in the process of gathering the essential information is critical during this phase.

In the third phase, the Adlerian play therapist is an active guide, using metacommunication, metaphor design, "spitting in the soup," directed sand trays, dance and movement, active games, and art techniques to hold up a mirror to help clients gain insight into their lifestyles, mistaken beliefs, goals of misbehavior, Crucial Cs, assets, and so forth. At times, the play therapist is nondirective and empathically supportive, especially when trying gently to move the child to a new understanding of intrapersonal patterns, situations, and relationships. Other times, the therapist will be rather directive and confrontational, especially when trying to help clients make major shifts in attitudes, perceptions, or behaviors. This often involves directly challenging clients' long-held self-defeating beliefs about self, others, and the world; confronting discrepancies between what is said and what is done; asking clients to try out new, more constructive attitudes outside the session; and so forth.

In the fourth phase (reorientation/reeducation), the Adlerian play therapist is an active teacher and encourager. The therapist can use an assortment of indirect and direct teaching techniques grounded in play to help the child learn and practice new skills and adopt more positive attitudes and perceptions. During sessions, the therapist uses brainstorming, direct and metaphoric instruction, and play-based practice to teach communication skills, social skills, assertiveness skills, negotiation skills, problem-solving skills, and other strategies for positively interacting with others and coping with situations and relationships.

Role of Caregivers and Collaterals

In AdPT, consultation with parents is usually an integral part of the process with children who are struggling with issues connected to family, home, and everyday social functioning (Kottman & Meany-Walen, 2016). With children whose issues are affecting school behavior and/or school performance, the Adlerian play therapist may also decide to consult with their teachers.

During the first phase of the consultation, the therapist works to build a relationship with the significant adults in the child's life—usually parents/caregivers, sometimes grandparents, and/or teachers. In many cases, the primary function of the therapist in this first phase with adults is to let them describe their perception of their relationship with the child and the history of the evolution of the presenting problem and any attempts to alleviate the problem. It is also helpful to get a developmental history of the child. The therapist mainly listens unconditionally to the parents/caregivers (and teachers), asking a few questions, reflecting feelings, paraphrasing, and summarizing.

During the second phase, the therapist uses questioning strategies, art techniques, sand tray play therapy techniques, and/or observation to explore parents' lifestyles in relation to their parenting practices and parents' perceptions of the child's lifestyle. During this phase, the therapist expects that the parents will answer questions about the child's lifestyle, the parents' family-of-origin, the marital relationship, family values, parenting strategies, and so forth. If the child struggles in school, the play therapist will use these same methods for gathering information about the child's teacher's perception of the child's lifestyle, their classroom management style, the teacher's lifestyle, and the interaction between the teacher's lifestyle and the child's lifestyle. At the end of the second phase, the Adlerian play therapist may develop a conceptualization and treatment plan for the significant adults in the child's life if they need help with their own personal issues or with child management or classroom discipline.

During the third phase, the therapist's goal is to work with the significant adults in the child's life to help them gain a better understanding of the child's lifestyle and a different perspective on the child's behavior and motivations. It is also helpful to explore the possibility that their own lifestyle patterns might be preventing them from them being as effective and constructive as they would wish to be in their interactions with the child. In this phase, there is an expectation that parents/caregivers and/or teachers will gain insight into their own lifestyles and the lifestyle of the child and begin shifting their thinking, feeling, and behaving patterns and their attitudes toward themselves, the child, and the world in preparation for the fourth phase, reorientation/reeducation.

Working with the adults in the client's life during the reorientation/reeducation phase, the therapist often teaches parents/caregivers child-rearing skills (such as setting consequences, providing encouragement, recognizing goals of misbehavior) or works with parents/caregivers on issues that might be getting in the way of their application of parenting skills. One of the primary goals is to teach Adlerian child-rearing strategies. Later consultation sessions with parents/caregivers and teachers are spent practicing these new skills with the play therapist so that they can be used in interactions and experiences outside therapy sessions. The play therapist uses teaching techniques (such as brainstorming, modeling, sand tray activities, art experiences, sharing metaphors, role-playing, didactic teaching, and playing games) and encourages skills to reinforce the improvement and effort of the adults. The therapist might also use Familial Encouraging Connection Therapy (FECT), a program designed to teach parents/caregivers to use non-directive play therapy skills to build relationships with their children and to apply Adlerian child-rearing skills (Kottman, 2023).

Research/Empirical Support

The National Registry of Evidence-based Programs and Practices (NREPP) of the Substance Abuse and Mental Health Services Administration (SAMHSA) determined that Adlerian play therapy was "evidence-based" for helping children with externalizing behavior problems and a promising treatment for children's self-concept. This was later affirmed by the Penn State Social Science Research Institute. In the last decade, studies have provided support for the efficacy of Adlerian play therapy (e.g., Akay & Bratton, 2017; Dillman Taylor et al., 2019; Jamaludin et al., 2018; Meany-Walen et al., 2014; Meany-Walen & Teeling, 2016; Mirzaie et al., 2019; Stutey et al., 2017). Recently, Dillman Taylor and Kottman (2019) did a research study designed to establish interrater reliability for the Adlerian Play Skills Checklist, and Dillman Taylor, Thompson, and Kottman (2022) produced a measurement model that will increase the credibility of research into Adlerian play therapy. These two studies were intended to facilitate future research into the efficacy of Adlerian play therapy.

Case Study of Herman

Therapeutic Powers of Play Employed

During the first phase, the Adlerian play therapist builds an egalitarian partnership with the child—using the therapeutic powers of *Therapeutic Relationship* and *Positive Emotions* (Kottman, 2014; Schaefer & Drewes, 2014). During this first phase, the play therapist will also work to foster the therapeutic powers of *Social Competence, Empathy,* and *Self-Expression* (Schaefer & Drewes, 2014). During the second phase, the play therapist will continue to cultivate the therapeutic powers of play, including *Therapeutic Relationship, Positive Emotions, Social Competence, Empathy,* and *Self-Expression,* as well as providing space for the therapeutic powers of play, *Catharsis, Abreaction,* and *Access to the Unconscious.* While continuing to incorporate the powers of play present in the first and second phases of the play therapy process, in the third phase, there is a shift to emphasize *Moral Development, Self-Regulation, Resiliency, Accelerated Psychological Development,* and *Indirect Teaching.* By the fourth phase, there is often an addition of the therapeutic powers of *Direct Teaching, Stress Management, Stress Inoculation, Creative Problem Solving,* and *Counterconditioning Fears* (Schaefer & Drewes, 2014).

Cultural Considerations

Herman (see Appendix for case study of Herman being referenced) may be confused about his cultural identity, especially in the area of race and ethnicity, given that his mother, maternal grandmother, and maternal grandfather all come from different racial and ethnic groups. He does not know the cultural background of his father. The lack of knowledge about his culture may be contributing to his difficulties in finding a place where he can feel that he belongs and can create positive ways of gaining significance.

Adlerian Case Formulation of Herman's Lifestyle

Herman's complex background and early life experiences have significantly impacted his development. Adlerian theory suggests that feelings of inferiority stem from early childhood experiences and can drive individuals to compensate in ways that might be maladaptive. Herman's early exposure to substance misuse, neglect, and abuse has likely contributed to profound feelings of inferiority and insecurity. His struggles with identity, expressed through non-gender-specific dressing and using makeup, may be attempts to find a sense of self and belonging in a world that has been chaotic and unsupportive.

Impact of Family Constellation and Family Atmosphere

Herman appears to be an only child with no known biological siblings. The transitions from his biological mother to his maternal grandmother, and then into foster care, have created a pattern of instability and insecurity. Herman's relationships with his biological caregivers were marked by neglect, abuse, and a lack of nurturing, which have deeply impacted his sense of self and his behavior. The current foster home provides a stark contrast to his early experiences, offering the potential for positive change through consistent and nurturing care.

Herman's early life experiences and the lack of stable, nurturing relationships have likely contributed to deep-seated feelings of inferiority. His aggressive and risk-seeking behaviors can be understood as maladaptive attempts to compensate for these feelings and to assert control in his life. The positive relationship with his foster parents, especially his foster father, highlights Herman's need for acceptance, belonging, and positive role models. The lack of interaction with his foster siblings and difficulties in school settings suggest ongoing challenges with developing social interest and feeling connected to a community.

The family atmosphere with Herman's biological mother was likely chaotic and unstable due to her opioid addiction and transient lifestyle. The mother's addiction and inability to provide stable care would have created an environment lacking in consistent nurturing and emotional support. Herman experienced neglect and a lack of secure attachment, contributing to feelings of abandonment and insecurity. The early foster care placements were also unstable and traumatic, especially given the behavioral issues that led to his movement between homes and the sexual abuse he suffered. The lack of consistent and nurturing caregivers in these placements contributed to a sense of unpredictability and mistrust in adults. These experiences likely intensified Herman's feelings of being unwanted and unworthy of care, reinforcing his maladaptive behaviors as a way to seek attention and assert control.

The current home is described as stable, nurturing, and loving. The foster parents are highly skilled, patient, and provide a supportive environment. The foster parents value consistency, understanding, and positive reinforcement. They offer a sense of security and acceptance. Despite the challenging behaviors, this positive atmosphere has given Herman a chance to form healthier attachments, particularly with his foster father. This environment offers the potential for healing and the development of a more positive self-concept.

Crucial Cs

Herman seems to be struggling with all four of the Crucial Cs. Herman's early attempts to *connect* were severely disrupted. His mother was unable to form a nurturing bond due to her addiction and unstable lifestyle. His maternal grandmother also provided a hostile environment filled with domestic violence and neglect. Herman experienced further disconnection with multiple foster placements, instability, and abuse, compounding his feelings of isolation. In his current therapeutic foster home, Herman has begun to develop a sense of connection with his foster parents, particularly his foster father. However, he still struggles with peer relationships, especially with his foster siblings, who avoid him.

Herman's early environment did not foster a sense of *capable*. Neglect and lack of nurturing likely led to a lack of opportunities to develop basic skills and self-efficacy. Herman's learning disabilities in reading and math, combined with his ADHD, further impair his sense of capable. His disruptive behaviors and inability to sit still in class contribute to his academic struggles and feelings of inadequacy. Despite the support from his foster parents, Herman's continued behavioral challenges and academic difficulties in school undermine his sense of competence. The frequent changes in therapy and ineffective medications have also likely contributed to feelings of frustration and helplessness.

Herman's early experiences of neglect and abuse likely led him to feel that he did not matter; he did not *count*. His mother's addiction and the unstable environments would have given him little sense of being valued. The abuse he suffered and the repeated moves due to behavioral issues likely reinforced feelings of worthlessness and being unwanted. In his current home, Herman has begun to feel valued by his foster parents, who show patience and love. However, his frequent suspensions from school and difficulties with peers continue to challenge his belief that he counts and that his contributions are valued.

Herman's early traumatic experiences likely undermined his ability to feel *courage*. The consistent instability and lack of supportive relationships would have made it difficult for him to develop resilience. His aggressive and risky behaviors can be seen as maladaptive attempts to assert control and cope with his fear and insecurity. These behaviors indicate a struggle to face challenges in healthy ways. While his current foster home provides a more supportive environment, Herman's ongoing behavioral issues and nightmares indicate that he still struggles with fear and insecurity.

Personality Priority

Herman's personality priority can be understood in the context of his early life experiences: early life was marked by neglect, instability, and abuse. These experiences likely left him feeling powerless and vulnerable, leading to a deep-seated need to regain control over his environment and his life. The multiple changes in caregivers and living situations have reinforced his need to assert control. Each new environment likely presented new challenges and uncertainties, prompting Herman to use control as a coping mechanism. The absence of stable, nurturing relationships in his early years would have prevented Herman from developing a sense of security and trust in others. As a result, he may feel the need to rely on himself and assert control to protect himself from further hurt and abandonment.

Goal of Misbehavior

Based on Herman's case study, it appears that his primary goal of misbehavior is power. This goal manifests in several ways:

Power through Aggression: Herman often becomes angry and aggressive with little provocation. This can be seen as a way to assert control over his environment and to ensure that he is not seen as weak or vulnerable.

Risk-Seeking Actions: His behavior of climbing out of windows and engaging in dangerous activities indicates a desire to control his own actions and to push boundaries in an attempt to feel powerful and in control of his life.

Disruptive Actions in School: Herman's inability to sit still, running around the classroom, and disruptive behavior can be interpreted as attempts to control the attention of those around him. By acting out, he ensures that he is noticed, even if the attention is negative.

Dressing in Non-Gender Specific Ways: His choice of clothing and use of nail polish and eyeliner can be seen as a way to assert his identity and control how he is perceived by others.

Difficulty with Rules and Boundaries: Herman's frequent suspensions from school and conflicts with peers and teachers indicate a resistance to external power and authority. This resistance can be a way to assert his independence and avoid feeling dominated by others.

Lifestyle Conviction and Mistaken Beliefs

The following are some examples of Herman's lifestyle convictions. The ones marked with asterisks are mistaken beliefs. (Remember that mistaken beliefs may be based on factual information or personal experiences—they are not necessarily inaccurate; they are self-defeating for clients who are living as if their beliefs are always true in all relationships.)

I am unlovable.* I am unimportant.* I am a bad person.* I am stupid and can't do school work.* I am so different from anyone else, I will never fit in anywhere.*

Others are dangerous.* Others are untrustworthy.* Others are unreliable.*

Others are out to hurt me.* Others are more likely to get love than I am.* Others are trying to control me.* Others will hurt me if I let myself be vulnerable or let them get close to me.*

The world is scary, dangerous, unpredictable, unstable, crazy, awful, never safe.*

Life is out of control, scary, dangerous, unpredictable, unstable, crazy, awful, unsafe.*

Based on these convictions, my behavior must/should be show others they can't control me, designed to push others away so I am not vulnerable, unpredictable so I can keep others off-balance so they can't hurt me.*

Challenges in Implementation—Treatment Plan for Herman

Because Adlerian play therapy always proceeds through the four phases, the description of challenges in implementation will be arranged according to each of the phases. The twenty therapeutic powers of play align closely with each phase of Adlerian Play Therapy, offering specific tools for both the child and therapist to foster emotional growth, insight, and behavioral change. From building rapport and gaining insight into the child's inner world to reorienting the child's behavior in healthier directions, these powers support a child's journey through each phase of AdPT. As such, they offer a holistic and comprehensive approach to therapy that respects the child's developmental needs and emotional landscape.

The therapeutic powers of play, as identified by Schaefer and Drewes (2014), includes twenty core areas across four domains:

- **II.** *Fosters Emotional Wellness:* A. Catharsis, B. Abreaction, C. Positive Emotions, D. Counterconditioning Fears, E. Stress Inoculation, F. Stress Management;
- **I.** *Facilitates Communication:* A. self-expression, B. access to the unconscious, C. direct teaching, D. indirect teaching;
- **III.** *Enhances Social Relationships:* A. Therapeutic Relationship, B. Attachment, C. Social Competence, D. Empathy; and
- **IV.** *Increases Personal Strengths:* A. Creative Problem Solving, B. Resiliency, C. Moral Development, D. Accelerated Psychological Development, E. Self-Regulation, F. Self-Esteem.

Phase 1

Phase 1 of Adlerian play therapy would focus on establishing a strong therapeutic relationship (**III.A.**) and creating an environment of trust and safety with Herman. This would allow him to feel more safe, secure, and understood (**I.A.**). Because of his history, this phase would be both challenging and foundational. It would be imperative for the therapist to establish an egalitarian relationship, with clear and consistent boundaries in a gentle manner (**III.A., II.C.**). This could help Herman feel safe and understand the structure and limits within the therapeutic setting (**IV.E.**). The atmosphere of the playroom should be welcoming and filled with a variety of play materials (toys, art supplies, games, costumes) that can appeal to Herman's interests and encourage him to express himself (**I.A.**). Sessions should be regular and consistent to help Herman feel secure and know what to expect (**I.D.**), reducing his anxiety (**II.F.**) and building trust (**III.A.**). The therapist would show genuine interest and empathy toward Herman by reflecting his feelings and validating his experiences without judgment (**III.D.**). In Phase 1, the therapist would participate in play activities that Herman initiates, allowing him to choose how he wants to play without directing or controlling the activities (**IV.**). This would show respect for his autonomy and interests as well as help him feel in control (**IV.**) and safe in the therapeutic space (**IV.F.**). The therapist would pay close attention to the themes and patterns that emerge in Herman's play, as they can provide insights into his internal world (**I**.B.) and struggles. The therapist would use metacommunication to reflect Herman's emotions and experiences expressed through play, using encouragement to increase the expression of his thoughts and feelings (**I**.A., **II**.C.) through play and verbal communication (**IV**.D., **III**.C.). The therapist could also use open-ended questions to facilitate deeper exploration (**I**.B.). The therapist would reinforce Herman's efforts (**III**.C.) and participation in therapy and use empowerment by giving him choices (**IV**.E.) and involving him in decisions about the therapeutic process (**III**.C.). The therapist would also identify and acknowledge Herman's strengths and assets during play, to help him see his own value and capabilities and help build his self-esteem (**IV**.F.) and sense of competence (**III**.C.).

Phase 2

In Phase 2 of Adlerian play therapy, the therapist would work to understand Herman's unique way of interacting with the world, his self-perceptions, and how his early experiences have shaped his current behavior and beliefs. The therapist would use the information gathered to formulate hypotheses about Herman's lifestyle, including family constellation, family atmosphere, assets, Crucial Cs, personality priorities, and goals of misbehavior. Based on the observations and interpretations from Herman's play, the therapist can formulate hypotheses about his lifestyle convictions (**IV**.F.) and mistaken beliefs (**IV**.D.). Understanding these underlying patterns can help the therapist develop targeted interventions to address Herman's specific needs and challenges (**II**.F.)

In Phase 2, the therapist would continue to carefully observe Herman's play choices, themes, and patterns. It is important to note how he interacts with different toys, characters, and scenarios. The therapist would look for recurring themes in Herman's play that might reflect his internal world (**I**.B.), such as themes of control, power, vulnerability, fear, and identity (**IV**.A., **IV**.B.). Some ways of exploring lifestyle include discussion of feelings, using metaphors and stories, and the use of drawing and art. During the play, the therapist would metacommunicate or ask open-ended questions about Herman's feelings, behavior, and thoughts (**I**.B., **II**.F., **II**.E., **II**.D., **III**.D.). The therapist could use art or movement activities to help Herman express emotions that might be difficult to articulate verbally (**I**.A.). This could include asking Herman to draw pictures or develop movements or stories related to his family, feelings, or experiences (**I**.A.). These drawings, stories, and movements could then be used to help him gain insights into his beliefs and patterns of thinking, feeling, and behaving (**I**.B., **IV**.D.).

Phase 3

Phase 3 of Adlerian play therapy focuses on helping the client gain insight (**I**.B., **IV**.D.). In this phase, the therapist helps the child understand and make sense of their behaviors, feelings, and beliefs (**II**.). For Herman, this would involve guiding him to recognize how his past experiences and current lifestyle convictions influence his actions and emotions (**III**.). The therapist would work with Herman to connect his play behaviors to his real-life experiences and emotions, helping him to see patterns and understand the motivations behind his actions (**II**.A., **I**.B.). For example, if he often plays out scenarios of characters being abandoned, the therapist might metacommunicate about how this might relate to his feelings about being in foster care. One intervention would be to introduce scenarios in play that gently challenge Herman's mistaken beliefs. For example, the therapist could tell a story about a situation where a character makes a mistake but is still loved and accepted (**I**.D., **III**.A., **II**.D., **II**.E.). Other ways of helping Herman gain insight would be to use play to explore the consequences of different actions and help Herman understand the impact of his behaviors and how his play behavior reflects his lifestyle conviction (**IV**.A.). For instance, if he frequently engages in aggressive play, it might indicate a conviction that he needs to be powerful to be safe (**III**.A., **II**.D., **II**.E.). The therapist can use metacommunication to share a tentative hypothesis about the purpose of this behavior. The therapist could also use metaphors and stories (**I**.D.) to help Herman express complex feelings and beliefs (**I**.A.). For example, a story about a brave but misunderstood hero can mirror Herman's own experiences (**I**.D.). It would also be important to encourage Herman to explore different outcomes in his stories. This can help him see that there are multiple ways to view and manage situations (**IV**.A.).

The therapist's role in Phase 3 would be to gently challenge Herman's mistaken beliefs and use play scenarios to show alternative ways of thinking and acting (**IV**.B.). For instance, show a character achieving safety through cooperation rather than aggression (**I**.D., **IV**.E., **IV**.D.). The use of metaphors, stories, symbolic play, and art (**I**.D) can also help Herman gain insight into his experiences. The use of metaphors (**I**.D.) could be used to create situations that mirror Herman's experiences and explore deeper issues of how they relate to real-life thoughts and feelings.

Specific interventions such as role playing (**I**.D.) and art could be used to help him gain insights into his own life (**I**.B., **IV**.B). By guiding Herman to gain insights into his behaviors and beliefs during Phase 3 of Adlerian play therapy, it helps him understand the connections between his past experiences and current actions, paving the way for meaningful and lasting change (**I**.B.). Another goal for Herman in Phase 3 would be to help him identify different feelings to promote emotional awareness (**I**.A.). Herman's emotional vocabulary could be expanded to assist in articulating his emotions more clearly (**I**.A.), by labeling and understanding his emotions.

Phase 4

Phase 4 of Adlerian play therapy focuses on reorientation and reeducation (**I**.D., **I**.C.), and the therapist would work on guiding Herman to adopt new, healthier ways of thinking and behaving. For Herman, this phase would involve encouraging him to adopt positive beliefs (**II**.C.), develop better coping strategies (**II**.F.), and build more adaptive behaviors based on the insights gained in the previous phase (**IV**.A.). The goal is to foster resilience (**IV**.B) self-esteem (**IV**.F.), and social interest (**III**.C.).

The role of the therapist in Phase 4 is to encourage positive change and collaborate with Herman to set achievable and meaningful goals that focus on improving his behavior (**II**.F.), emotional regulation (**II**.C., **IV**.E.), and social interactions (**III**.C.). Empowering

Herman to set and achieve goals enhances his self-esteem (**IV**.F.) and encourages a sense of mastery and agency over his life (**IV**.)

Improving Herman's social skills and empathy can lead to better relationships with family and peers, fostering a sense of belonging and support (**III**.D.). The therapist would use play to foster empathy and understanding of other perspectives. This would include promoting cooperation, teamwork, and sharing (**III**.C., **I**.C., **IV**.B.). The therapist can help Herman work on social skills so that he can build better relationships with peers by using play to practice communication, conflict resolution, and making friends through play (**I**.D., **I**.C., **III**.C.). The therapist would teach and introduce ways of coping such as deep breathing, mindfulness, etc. (**II**.F., **II**.E., **II**.D.). By developing effective coping strategies and positive beliefs, Herman would become more resilient (**IV**.B.) in the face of future challenges.

In Phase 4, the therapist would help Herman apply the insights and skills he has learned in therapy to real-life situations, ensuring that changes are sustainable (**II**.C., **IV**.E., **IV**.D). In this stage, the therapist would help Herman reframe negative, mistaken beliefs into positive empowering ones (**IV**.). For example, practicing changing beliefs like "I must be aggressive to be safe" to "I can feel safe by asking for help and using my words" would be extremely useful to Herman.

Working with Herman's Foster Parents and Teachers

It would be imperative to involve Herman's foster parents and teachers in all four phases of therapy to reinforce the new behaviors and beliefs at home/school (**III**.C., **IV**.B.). Caregivers should be provided guidance on how they can support Herman's growth (**III**.A). By reinforcing these new patterns and celebrating his progress, Herman can develop the resilience (**IV**.B.) and self-confidence (**IV**.F.) needed to navigate his world more effectively.

Conclusion

Although Herman's case is extremely complex, there are many ways an Adlerian play therapist could use the therapeutic powers of play to help him. Throughout the play therapy process, the therapist would use the therapeutic powers of *Therapeutic Relationship* and *Positive Emotions, Social Competence, Empathy, Self-Expression, Catharsis, Abreaction, Access to the Unconscious, Moral Development, Self-Regulation, Resiliency, Accelerated Psychological Development, Indirect Teaching, Direct Teaching, Stress Management, Stress Inoculation, Creative Problem Solving*, and *Counterconditioning Fears* (Schaefer & Drewes, 2014).

References

Adler, A. (1954). *Understanding human nature* (W. B. Wolf, Trans.). Fawcett Premier (Original work published 1927).

Adler, A. (1958). *What life should mean to you.* Capricorn. (Original work published 1931)

Adler, A. (1998). *Understanding human nature.* Oneworld Oxford. (Original work published in 1927).

Akay, S., & Bratton, S. (2017). The effects of Adlerian play therapy on maladaptive perfectionism and anxiety in children: A single case design. *International Journal of Play Therapy, 26*(2), 96–110. https://doi.org/org/10.1037/pla0000043.

Ansbacher, H., & Ansbacher, R. (Eds.). (1956). *The individual psychology of Alfred Adler: A systemic presentation in selections from his writings.* Harper & Row.

Carlson, J., & Englar-Carson, M. (2017). *Adlerian psychotherapy.* American Psychological Association.

Carlson, J., & Slavik, S. (Eds.). (1997). *Techniques in Adlerian psychology.* Accelerated Development.

Dillman Taylor, D., & Kottman, T. (2019). Assessing the utility and fidelity of the Adlerian play therapy skills checklist using qualitative content analysis. *International Journal of Play Therapy, 28*(1), 13–21. https://doi.org/org/10.1037/pla0000082.

Dillman Taylor, D., Meany-Walen, K. K., Nelson, K. M., & Gungor, A. (2019). Investigating group Adlerian play therapy for children with disruptive behaviors: A single-case research design. *International Journal of Play Therapy, 28*(3), 168–82. https://doi.org/org/10.1037/pla0000094.

Dillman Taylor, D., Thompson, K., & Kottman, T. (2022). Strengthening the efficacy of Adlerian play therapy through the measurement model. *International Journal of Play Therapy, 31*(3), 164–73. https://doi.org/org/10.1037/pla0000176.

Dreikurs, R., & Soltz, V. (1964). *Children: The challenge.* Hawthorn Books.

Dufrene, R., & Clark, L. B. (2022). Adlerian theory. In D. Capuzzi & M. Stauffer (Eds.), *Counseling and psychotherapy: Theories and interventions* (7th ed., pp. 95–116). American Counseling Association.

Eckstein, D., & Kern, R. (2009). *Psychological fingerprints* (6th ed.). Kendall/Hunt.

Jamaludin, L., Johari, K. S. K., Amat, S., & Lee, G. M. (2018). The effectiveness of Adlerian group play therapy-based counseling intervention on the holistic wellness of neglected children. *International Journal of Academic Research in Business and Social Sciences, 8*(4), 1221–32. https://doi.org/10.6007/ijarpedv9-i1/6975.

Kfir, N. (1981). Impasse/priority therapy. In R. Corsini (Ed.), *Handbook of innovative psychotherapies* (pp. 400–15). Wiley.

Kottman, T. (1993). The king of rock and roll. In T. Kottman & C. Schaefer (Eds.), *Play therapy in action: A casebook for practitioners* (pp. 133–67). Jason Aronson.

Kottman, T. (2014). Positive emotions. In C. Schaefer & A. Drewes (Eds.), *The therapeutic powers of play* (2nd ed., pp. 103–21). Wiley.

Kottman, T. (2023). *Facilitating Familial Encouraging Connection Therapy* (FECT). Encouragement Zone.

Kottman, T., & Meany-Walen, K. (2016). *Partners in play: An Adlerian approach to play therapy* (3rd ed.). American Counseling Association.

Kottman, T., & Meany-Walen, K. (2018). *Doing play therapy: From building the relationship to facilitating change.* Guilford.

Lew, A., & Bettner, B. L. (1998). *Responsibility in the classroom: A teacher's guide to understanding and motivating students.* Connexions Press.

Lew, A., & Bettner, B. L. (2000). *A parent's guide to motivating children.* Connexions Press.

Maniacci, M., & Sackett-Maniacci, L. (2019). Adlerian psychotherapy. In D. Wedding & R. Corsini (Eds.), *Current psychotherapies* (11th ed., pp. 59–100). Cengage.

Meany-Walen, K. K., & Teeling, S. (2016). Adlerian play therapy with children with externalizing behaviors and poor social skills. *International Journal of Play Therapy, 25*(2), 64–77. https://doi.org/org/10.1037/pla0000022.

Meany-Walen, K. K., Bratton, S. C., & Kottman, T. (2014). Effects of Adlerian play therapy on reducing students' disruptive behaviors. *Journal of Counseling and Development, 92*, 47–56. https://doi.org/org/10.1002/j.1556-6676.2014.00129.x.

Mirzaie, H., Mehraban, A. H., Hosseini, S. A., Fard, F. G., & Oori, M. J. (2019). Comparison of the effect of Filial and Adlerian play therapy on attention and hyperactivity of children with attention deficit hyperactivity disorder: A randomized clinical trial. *Iranian Rehabilitation Journal, 17*(4), 341–50. https://doi.org/10.32598/irj.17.4.341.

Schaefer, C., & Drewes, A. (Eds.). (2014). *The therapeutic powers of play* (2nd ed.). Wiley.

Stutey, D. M., Dunn, M., Shelnut, J., & Ryan, J. B. (2017). Impact of Adlerian play therapy on externalizing behaviors of at-risk preschoolers. *International Journal of Play Therapy, 26*(4), 196–206. https://doi.org/10.1037/pla0000055.

Sweeney, T. (2019). *Adlerian counseling and psychotherapy: A practitioner's wellness approach* (6th ed.). Routledge.

7

Cognitive Behavioral Play Therapy

Lisa Remey

Chapter Outline

Introduction

Cognitive Behavior Therapy (CBT), a well-established therapeutic approach, has been the focus of research for several decades. However, in 1993, Susan Knell introduced Cognitive Behavioral Play Therapy (CBPT), a novel application of CBT specifically tailored for working with children. This chapter delves into the foundations of CBT and CBPT, explores their application in harnessing the therapeutic powers of play, and illustrates effectiveness through the case of Herman (see Appendix for case study of Herman being referenced). As you navigate this chapter, consider the unique interplay between the client's natural language of play and the therapeutic powers of play within the structure of CBPT play sessions. This includes examining how the collaboration of client-led and therapist-led interactions works toward treatment goals, with the child, caregivers, and therapist all as active participants.

Underlying Philosophy

Cognitive Behavioral Therapy (CBT) was developed in the 1960s by Aaron Beck and was initially called cognitive therapy. This approach was originally applied to address depression. Beck (1964) explains, in the simplest form, how people feel and react is based on the way they interpret the situations around them, reflecting their perceptions rather than the actual events. CBT aims to understand a client's current ways of thinking and behaving and then equips individuals with the tools to change any maladaptive cognitive and behavioral patterns. CBT has been extensively researched and shown to effectively treat a wide range of disorders and clients (Hadler & Mahato, 2019). CBT can be applied to diverse populations, including varied educational levels, socioeconomic levels, cultures, and ages, from young children to older adults (Beck, 2021; Hadler & Mahato, 2019). In addition, it can be utilized in schools, vocational programs, clinics, hospitals, and other settings, as well as individually, in groups, and in family formats.

The foundation of CBT treatment lies in the understanding that thoughts, feelings, and behaviors directly influence a client's underlying beliefs and patterns of behavior. Clinicians and clients work together to uncover and identify these cognitive formulations and conceptualizations. These are unique to each individual client and characterize their specific disorder or area of concern. This individual case conceptualization serves as a guide for the CBT therapist in selecting therapeutic interventions tailored to the client's underlying beliefs, values, behaviors, and desired outcomes (Beck, 2021).

Cognitive Behavior Play Therapy (CBPT) is an evidence-based theoretical approach based on the CBT model that uses children's natural language of play and play-based interventions to help children with their thoughts, feelings, and behaviors through age-appropriate interactions and interventions (Knell, 2022; Shrinivasa et al., 2018). CBPT utilizes the concepts and theoretical framework of CBT, adapting them to work with children and incorporating the therapeutic power of play. In a CBPT session, both the therapist and the client collaborate, using both structured and unstructured activities in a blend of client-led and therapist-led interactions (Knell, 2015). CBPT is structured yet flexible, allowing the therapist to meet the client where they are during the session while focusing on shared goals between caregivers, the client, and therapist. The framework includes both directive and nondirective play, reaching various aspects of the therapeutic powers of play, including the client's own play and therapist-selected interventions. For example, a therapist-selected activity like a feeling toss game focusing on self-expression and communication.

Personality Theory

The role of personality within cognitive behavioral therapy is based on the interactions of situations, behaviors, cognitions, mood states, and conditions (Merrill and Strauman, 2004). These interactions, combined with an individual's past and current experiences, shape their perspective of the world, themselves, and others. These unique factors integrated within the individual serve to predict behaviors and vary from person to person. Merrill and Strauman (2004) point out that research within the context of CBT and personality studies has mainly focused on maladaptive personality, with limited exploration of adaptive personality processes. Consideration of individual personality helps the therapist see particular characteristics that can assist in formulating a case conceptualization. Personality disorders within the framework of Cognitive Behavioral Therapy (CBT) are seen as stemming from an individual's interpretation of events, core beliefs, and dysfunctional behavior, including their assumptions about themselves and others (Beck, 2021). When these interpretations are disordered and persistent, they can lead to reactions from others that further validate these distorted experiences and perceptions.

There are several aspects that can affect personality and responses. The interplay of temperament and disposition with the social environment plays a role in how an individual responds (Lautieri, 2019). Temperament is the behavioral style of responding to the world. Disposition relates to character traits and an innate tendency to act in a certain way. Temperament and disposition impact a child's behavior, influencing how emotions are managed, the ability to regulate, and adaptation to new situations. The interaction between disposition and temperament affects how children respond to their environment, shaping their personality. Lautieri (2019) expands on the idea that social learning and personality development work together to establish an individual's core beliefs. For children, a CBPT therapist can intervene to shift core beliefs, preventing maladaptive beliefs from being embedded during development.

Model of Psychopathology

Within the Cognitive Behavioral Therapy (CBT) model, it is believed that psychopathology arises as a product of faulty processing of information that manifests itself in maladaptive and dysfunctional thinking patterns, leading to negative emotions and dysfunctional behaviors (Gaudiano, 2008). The CBPT therapist helps the client to identify, modify, and shift actions, cognitions, and feelings to produce increased functioning toward identified treatment goals.

Psychopathology in the CBT model believes that faulty information processing arises due to distorted and faulty informational thinking, which directly affects clients' experiences of negative emotions and maladaptive behaviors (Gaudiano, 2008; Drewes & Cavett, 2019). A CBPT therapist needs to have a knowledge base of child development. The understanding of developmental and developmental play is foundational to understanding the potential developmental impact of experiences and the ability to meet clients where they are developmentally (Fuggle et al., 2013). In turn, the CBPT therapist can identify processing patterns through play. The therapist helps the client to identify, evaluate, and modify maladaptive cognitions to produce more realistic and adaptive behaviors and feelings. Play therapists use the powers of play to model adaptive patterns through interventions such as bibliotherapy, puppet storytelling, and play scenarios.

Conceptualizing Goals of Treatment

Case conceptualization is the cornerstone of CBT, which develops a framework for treatment (Beck, 2021). The process begins with initial contact and evolves throughout therapeutic sessions. Information gathered from the caregivers, client, and the therapist assessment and observations is included (Knell, 2015). The therapist gains insight into the client's strengths, difficulties, aspirations, and challenges in building an understanding of the client. The CBT framework utilizes the formulation to comprehend the development of core beliefs and automatic thoughts that contribute to client difficulties and how an individual's thoughts, feelings, and behaviors interact (Beck, 2021). This serves as a tool to understand the client's current way of thinking and behaving to move toward shifting cognitive and behavioral patterns. With this understanding of client and family information and consideration of individual values, culture, and treatment goals for seeking treatment, a plan is collaboratively formed and adjusted as needed.

The goals of cognitive behavioral play therapy are to reduce symptoms and improve functioning while considering each child's unique needs (Cavett, 2015). The therapist and caregivers collaborate to identify these goals during the initial intake, where caregivers share their concerns and areas they would like to see change. However, the process does not end there. The cognitive behavioral play therapist includes the child client in the process, inviting them to share their goals and become active participants. This collaborative approach continues throughout the play therapy sessions, allowing the therapist to learn from and about the child client (Cavett, 2015). Case conceptualization is an ongoing process that helps therapists, caregivers, and clients work together to define problems and set treatment goals. It also guides the therapist in selecting interventions and structuring sessions for each client's needs.

Role of the Therapist

The therapeutic relationship is crucial to the effectiveness of CBPT, just like in other therapeutic models. While the relationship itself is not the primary driver of change, it plays a key role in establishing rapport, genuineness, understanding, and empathy (Cavett, 2015; Fenn & Byrne, 2013). This support and relationship pave the way for feedback and facilitate cognitive and behavioral change. When working with minors, it is essential to have a positive relationship with not only the client but also with the caregivers. This positive relationship creates a safe environment for exploring experiences, associated feelings, and thoughts, and addressing concerns and difficulties (Cavett, 2015. Strategies and interventions can be explored to improve functioning within the relationship and the powers of play. The therapist involves the child in treatment by listening and observing the child's experiences and communication through play (Knell, 2011; Drewes, 2009). Based on this, the therapist can provide personalized strategies and interventions to develop adaptive thoughts and behaviors that match the client's needs.

A CBPT therapist alternates between structured and unstructured play to develop and model skills (Knell, 2022). This balance of structured and unstructured aspects of a CBPT session allows the therapist to work collaboratively with the client. The therapist selects and introduces developmentally appropriate interventions to address client goals as part of the session structure. Additionally, the client brings spontaneous material to the sessions, and the therapist responds accordingly, integrating modeling and facilitative responses utilizing the therapeutic power of play to foster accelerated psychological development and emotional wellness during both structured and unstructured elements. Knell (2022) discusses interweaving play prompts into unstructured play. For example, a therapist may utilize the TPoP of direct and indirect teaching by selecting a children's book addressing anger and reading it in session, followed by a play prompt for a puppet story with a theme of feeling mad. The client may, in turn, include situations where a character is coping with anger in play. The alternation between counselor prompts and client spontaneous play provides the groundwork for collaborative sessions and enrichment of content to address treatment goals.

Roles of Caregivers and Collaterals

Caregivers are an integral part of the CBPT framework and are involved in the treatment process from intake to termination. The level of involvement will depend on the client's age, individual circumstances, and specific needs. It is essential to consider the level of support needed to facilitate interactions with child clients and implement strategies outside of sessions (Knell, 2015). Initial information is gathered from caregivers seeking the services and provides the client's history of concerns and family and client experiences. This information builds an understanding of the client and directs treatment goals and client sessions. Collaboration between the therapist, caregivers, and collaterals is important for building rapport, working toward treatment goals, engaging in the therapeutic process, and extending the benefits of play therapy sessions into external environments.

Caregiver sessions are an important aspect of treatment to provide feedback, monitor progress, and offer psychoeducation (Knell, 2015). During these sessions, the therapist gives an overview of the client's sessions, including themes, learned strategies, and observed progress. Caregivers also share any changes they have noticed outside of the session. This feedback can lead to modifications in treatment goals if necessary. Psychoeducation, another TPoP of direct teaching, is a key component, helping caregivers expand their knowledge of child development and explore parenting strategies to support the family and client. The involvement of caretakers is an important part of the process (Hadler & Mahato, 2019).

The integrated approach of alternating client and caregiver sessions supports the collaborative aspect of CBPT, considering case conceptualization as an ongoing process to meet clients where they are and move together to meet identified goals. The skill-building aspect extends beyond sessions to bring the benefits of therapy into other aspects of the client's life. One aspect of CBPT is to help maintain adaptive behaviors in the natural environment after play therapy sessions. Additionally, research shows that CBT can have lasting effects beyond therapy sessions (Knell, 2015).

Involving collateral contacts with other adults involved in the client's life, such as teachers, school personnel, or medical practitioners, enriches the depth of case conceptualization and service collaboration. School is a primary part of a child's life; therefore, understanding a client's experience in school, both regarding learning and relationships, is important. Parallels and discrepancies between home and school provide the CBPT therapist with valuable information to understand the client's difficulties and experiences (Fuggle et al., 2013). This in-depth understanding is needed to bring about change to maladaptive cognitions and behaviors. Hadler and Mahato (2019) state that when teachers are involved in the therapy process and with active involvement, there is an improved outcome of change. Integrating caregiver support and collaborating with others increases not only the therapist's understanding but also the ability to effect change across multiple settings.

Research/Empirical Support

Cognitive behavioral therapy (CBT) is a well-researched, evidence-based, empirically validated approach (Drewes & Cavett, 2019). Guadiano (2008) expands this statement to describe CBT as one of the most dominant psychotherapy modalities. CBT, paired with play therapy, utilizes play-based activities to treat many different disorders, applying developmental strategies to children (Knell, 2011; Drewes & Cavett, 2019). CBPT's focus is to help clients make changes, increasing their ability to handle problems faced (Ab Razak et al., 2018). The Association for Play Therapy considers Cognitive Behavioral Therapy as one of the major historical theories that underpin play therapy practice.

The focus of CBPT sessions is to improve behaviors and shift maladaptive thinking, supporting clients through structured and unstructured developmental activities (Knell, 2022). The shift helps to strengthen adaptive thoughts and behaviors, building connections between behaviors, feelings, and views of self and others. By establishing a positive therapeutic relationship, providing a supportive and safe environment, and communicating through play and fantasy, child clients can play out and deal with emotional and behavioral issues (Ab Razak et al., 2018; Schaefer & Drewes, 2009).

CBPT is widely used, but it has not been as extensively studied and researched as CBT. However, there is emerging research going on in Italy, Pakistan, Iran, and Africa, as well as the United States. Knell (2022) noted that CBPT has been discussed in various case studies, demonstrating its application to a wide range of presenting concerns and reporting its effectiveness. One aspect to differentiate is the importance of researchers correctly utilizing the CBPT term versus referencing child therapy that utilizes play. Knell (2022) reported increased international studies that demonstrated client improvement after receiving

CBPT. Unfortunately, currently, many are inaccessible in English and difficult to obtain. Further research is needed to build empirical support for the use of CBPT.

Case Study through the Lens of the Therapeutic Powers of Play

Employing Therapeutic Powers of Play

The therapeutic powers of play (TPoP) are an integral part of play therapy, focusing on play as the natural language of children (Schaefer & Drewes, 2009). Being grounded in the knowledge of TPoP supports the play therapist in the individual assessment of clients and equips them in the application of recognizing needed focus areas of TPoP. In conjunction with theory, this knowledge base is used to bring about change (Peabody & Schaefer, 2019). TPoP within CBPT sessions is observed in structured and unstructured play. A cognitive behavioral play therapist skillfully navigates between client-led and therapist-led portions of sessions while also providing and processing aspects of TPoP. As the natural powers of play are utilized in sessions, a CBPT therapist enhances aspects through verbal and nonverbal communication, whether introducing an intervention/activity, tracking client play, or through facilitative responses. The four primary areas of TPoP (fostering emotional wellness, increasing personal strengths, enhancing social relationships, and facilitating communication) are interwoven throughout sessions, with aspects intentionally focused on during specific phases of treatment to best meet client needs.

Let us look at the case example of working with Herman. During the initial sessions, the focus on the TPoP of enhancing social relationships centered around building a therapeutic relationship, assessing attachment to identify others in Herman's life with whom he feels connected, and gaining knowledge regarding his social relationships. Recognizing and increasing personal strengths is inquired about during intake with caregivers and is a focus during play therapy sessions, with strengths identified during conversations and structured and unstructured play activities.

When considering the current concerns that Herman and his caregivers are experiencing and the added factor of having had multiple therapists over the last three years without significant change, it is essential to check in on Herman's view of the problem and past therapy sessions. This first step with Herman correlates with the CBPT collaboration and client participation process. That said, the focus of TPoP during initial sessions is to facilitate communication, enhance social relationships, and increase personal strengths. This includes building a therapeutic relationship with Herman and his foster parents, providing opportunities for self-expression in understanding aspects of the problem, and identifying areas of desired change.

As the therapeutic process continues, additional aspects will be included, such as a focus on shifting dysregulation, using both directive and indirective teaching to identify and apply self-regulation skills, creative problem-solving, and increasing the client's sense of self as client strengths are identified and applied.

Additional treatment goals may be identified later and collaboratively defined. This may occur during the working phase of sessions to address aspects of the client's history and where maladaptive patterns began developing to address how they currently affect the here and now. For example, to address adverse experiences from early childhood that affect the neurodevelopment of building healthy attachments and social-emotional learning, the TPoP may focus on accelerated psychological development, attachment, and social competence both during direct and nondirective play. As Herman brings attachment-related play into sessions, facilitative responses focus on changing relationships, having personal needs met, and relating to others. An example of how spontaneous client-initiated play occurs in session is when Herman selected "restaurant" kitchen play, taking my order, cooking, and serving food, utilizing TPoP of social competence and attachment. A play prompt is given to reverse roles to meet the needs of Herman as a customer. This type of play activates the TPoP of accelerated psychological development to address developmental aspects of attachment and social competence (also TPOP).

Cultural, Diversity, and Inclusion Considerations

Fuggle et al. (2013) emphasize the importance of a child therapist not only understanding home and family circumstances but also client and family cultural groups, parenting practices, and how these relate to caretakers' varied expectations of children based on age and gender. When considering Herman's background, I am mindful of the potential impact of his exposure to and experiences in diverse environments, cultures, ethnicities, and situations. As play therapy progresses, Herman's past experiences may become evident, leading to increased awareness of his perspectives and the impact of those experiences. Herman's having several different caretakers and homes would impact not only his view of the world and social-emotional perceptions but also aspects of culture, socioeconomics, and diversity.

Herman's developmental stage is at age ten, which, for some, is considered the beginning stage of puberty. Children at this age experience developmental aspects of change, including physical, social, emotional, cognitive, and self-exploration (Davies & Troy, 2020). At this developmental stage, it would be common for Herman to explore his sense of identity, including his gender, ethnicity, and relationships with others. Research shows that racial identity begins to emerge during preadolescence, which lays the foundation for adulthood (Ray, 2015). These elements may be brought into the play therapy sessions as Herman explores relationships and how he views himself and the world. A developmental play-based prompt involves creating a scene or town (on the floor or in the sand tray) that includes different types of families using miniatures such as houses, buildings, and a culturally diverse selection of people figures. An additional prompt of adding to the town, helping figures such as teachers or neighbors to show that support can come from beyond those in the household. This prompt focuses on the TPoP of accelerated development and access to the unconscious, providing an opportunity to explore types of relationships and identity awareness. As a CBPT therapist, my awareness of developmental stages informs me of possible spontaneous information that may be brought into sessions within both nondirective play and directive play prompts.

This child-focused approach during CBPT sessions brings balance to the collaboration of treatment goals, allowing new goals to be formulated. It is difficult to say in what ways Herman's experiences have impacted his identity. However, the collaborative relationship is what brings forth the opportunity to explore and support Herman at his own pace. His development and past experiences, together with the typical growth and development during pre-adolescence, are aspects to consider.

Case Formulation and Application

Case conceptualization informs the CBPT therapist's work and selection of interventions. As previously stated, within the theoretical framework of CBPT, treatment goals will be established collaboratively with the caregivers during the intake session to understand current struggles. The therapist will aspire to understand past experiences, consider how they relate to current concerns, and begin formulating a case conceptualization. As I review Herman's case, right away, there are concerns that stand out as areas that directly impact Herman. His early experiences, beginning with neonatal care, consist of trauma, separation, and abandonment. It is also common for children in foster care to experience incomplete and ambiguous loss, which adds additional layers of difficulties (Howard et al., 2024). These early developmental experiences will affect attachment, neurobiological development, social-emotional development, and his ability to regulate (Davies & Troy, 2020). His experiences also impact the development of his internal belief system regarding himself, others, and the world around him. Child development, attachment, and neurobiological development directly impact how the world and self are viewed and the development of adaptive or maladaptive cognitions (Fuggle et al., 2013). Herman experienced difficult attachments beginning with his neonatal care and beyond. These experiences affect his maladaptive cognitions and current social engagement and nervous system, which will, therefore, be considered in selecting interventions. As a CBPT therapist, I continue to consider all aspects from a child development perspective and keep a child focus during sessions to meet Herman where he is currently. Awareness of these areas keeps the therapist in tune with client readiness and concerns presented in sessions.

The initial focus is on treatment goals, which brought Herman to play therapy. The initial sessions aim to help Herman and his caregivers find success and relief from problematic behaviors, initiate change, and alleviate current negative experiences. In turn, this will also bring continued engagement and involvement from Herman and his foster parents during treatment. My overall case conceptualization will keep past experiences and development in mind so that I can understand and work with Herman. As therapy progresses, I will keep the child focused and follow Herman's lead to address concerns as he is ready. At that time, I will select interweaving interventions to address needs. Part of the CBPT conceptualization is a continuation and collaborative awareness of overall needs and areas of concern that necessitate cognitive restructuring during treatment.

Treatment goals will also be determined collaboratively with the client in their first session. The initial session with Herman focuses on establishing a therapeutic relationship, understanding his perspective of the world around him, setting the tone and structure for sessions, and collaborating to identify treatment goals. I began by sharing the therapy process and learning about Herman's previous experiences, inquiring about what he viewed as helpful and unhelpful. He shared that he enjoyed activities such as games when meeting with previous counselors. Herman also expressed that he did not like meeting with caregivers because he felt he was in trouble. Herman appreciated being included in choosing the activities and goals he would like to work on. His goals included avoiding trouble at school, having more freedom to make choices, and wishing he could have a say in establishing the rules. I explained how we could work together to understand the available options and generate ideas to help him in the classroom. He was open to the idea of identifying choices that would help him avoid negative consequences. I also informed him that each session would begin with a check-in, exploring the positive and negative decisions made during the week. It was emphasized that the goal is to understand his experiences, his feelings, and difficult situations from the week and explore together to build what options work best for him and not to reprimand him. Following the check-in each week, a session plan is created together consisting of counselor-led and client-led activities.

The case conceptualization focuses on building adaptive functioning in the here and now to support Herman in shifting behaviors, identifying and expressing feelings in developmentally accepted ways, and utilizing/applying coping skills to reduce negative consequences. It is important to consider how Herman's history of changes in caregivers, prenatal drug exposure, and disruptive behaviors impacts developmental aspects such as neurodevelopment, regulation development, and social development. Early adverse experiences disrupt neurodevelopment, affecting the ability to self-regulate, reciprocity, cognitive processes such as attention and language, as well as executive functioning (Gaskill & Perry, 2014; Smith & Pollak, 2020). The utilization of TPoP within the CBPT framework of both directive and nondirective play activities enhances development. Maintaining a client-focused approach to meet clients at their current developmental stage is crucial for the TPoP, accelerating psychological development. Herman, for example, chooses to play in the house area and take care of the baby dolls with a theme of nurturing. Integrating the TPoP and CBPT, my facilitative responses reflect the caring for, supporting, and nurturing of the baby dolls. To build self-esteem and empathy, which are also components of TPoP, I reflect on Herman's ability to care for and comfort while meeting the dolls' needs. Additional benefits of TPoP that are a part of Herman's nurturing play include empathy, experiencing positive emotions, abreaction, and accelerated psychological development relating to his own needs for nurturing and caring. I enhance meaning through facilitative responses reflecting the needs of babies and expanding to children in general and wondering who else supports and helps meet needs, such as teachers and others.

With that said, Herman has an additional diagnosis of ADHD. It is recognized that children with ADHD might be two to three years behind their peers in maturity and skill development. Individuals may also struggle with cognitive inhibition, cognitive flexibility, and working memory. Berger et al. (2013) state that it is common for a one to three-year delay in cognitive performance, maturation of brain development, development of attentional function, and executive functioning skills, with behaviors resembling the typical development of a younger child. With this knowledge, a therapist can consider Herman's development and difficulty with attention and body control through a developmental lens correlating to a younger age. His playfulness in sessions, at times, reflects younger developmental play. Herman navigates to the floor play using scenes, puppets, and the house/kitchen area. Meeting him where he is developmentally provides the opportunity to enhance skills through therapist and client-led play. This TPoP of accelerated development goes together with the role play and rehearsal of skills through play interactions. In addition, the repetition of adaptive interactions, communications, and play activities within adult-to-child interactions supports neurodevelopmental development (Gaskill & Perry, 2014).

Specific areas of focus centered on treatment goals of decreasing outbursts and increasing coping strategies will consist of recognizing creative problem solving as navigating tasks within play, such as completing a difficult task, accepting limits given, and transitioning activities. During sessions, it is common for clients to become frustrated when attempting to complete a task. When this occurs, reflecting an observed coping strategy within play reflects the TPoP of stress management, self-regulation, and indirect teaching. For example, Herman repeatedly missed the target when playing a soft dart-throwing game. As Herman continued attempts, I reflected, "That can be frustrating to keep missing; I noticed you took a deep breath, stayed calm, and kept trying." This reflection brings awareness to positive choices made by building on skills and strategies. An additional CBPT activity that increases the TPoP of personal strength and emotional wellness is gameplay. Gameplay involves making decisions, practicing reciprocity, self-regulation, cooperation, and following rules while having fun and enjoying the experience. During a therapy session, a facilitative response might involve the therapist observing a client's actions and providing positive feedback. For example, the therapist could say, "I noticed you started to reach for the dice to start your turn and paused. Nice job catching yourself and waiting for your turn." These responses facilitate the TPoP of indirect teaching, self-regulation, and self-esteem.

The structuring of CBPT sessions emphasizes opportunities for TPoP of indirect teaching, practicing self-regulation, and stress management. For instance, as Herman follows the session structure of check-in, transitioning between counselor-led and client-led activities, adaptive skills are practiced and internalized and can then be bridged outside of sessions with an increased ability to self-regulate and apply coping self-talk. During check-in, we will review Herman's week and focus on the times when he was able to "pause and think" before making choices that reflect the TPoP of direct teaching. To continue enhancing Herman's ability to pause and think, the concept is integrated and reflected both during directive and nondirective play. During Herman's nondirective play, I intentionally look for and reflect on instances when he appears to think before taking action, such as in kitchen play, pausing after placing food items in a pan and looking at utensils, stating,

"Looks like you are pausing and thinking about what you need next." This type of intentional facilitative response utilizes the TPoP of indirect teaching. A direct teaching aspect of TPoP is selecting activities such as Simon Says, in which pause and thinking are part of the game itself. I additionally focus on reflecting any shifts in pause and thinking or shifts in behaviors observed in sessions, which inherently enhance the TPoP of self-esteem and self-efficacy, building a foundation for adaptive behaviors and skills to navigate experiences.

TPoP employed consists of exploring through directive and nondirective play and activities. Facilitative responses will focus on building awareness, exploring the effects of behavioral responses, and building an understanding of self. For example, as Herman plays with the vehicles and becomes frustrated with setting up details, he pauses and then tries again. I reflect this by stating, "That was frustrating when it did not work the way you wanted. However, you stayed calm, paused, and tried again." The initial focus of supporting Herman's identified goal of reducing consequences will be increasing awareness of actions, decreasing dysregulation, and developing the ability to pause and think to move toward change collaboratively.

The focus of play activities includes direct and indirect teaching, facilitating communication while increasing personal strengths, and exploring self-regulation strategies. The ebb and flow between structured and unstructured portions of the play therapy session build emotional wellness, providing Herman with opportunities to express thoughts and feelings in a variety of ways, such as exploring his current experiences with others at home and school, with a focus on catharsis and abreaction regarding the effects of choices made, combined with facilitative responses and collaborative activities that offer opportunities to identify positive emotions and stress management strategies.

During sessions, Herman experiences the TPoP of catharsis as expressing himself in different ways, through both emotional expression and movement. The play therapy room provides an environment to express strong emotions in a way that self-understanding can occur and helpful strategies can be identified. Self-regulation skills are also practiced during sessions. For example, Herman may express anger by hitting a bop bag of air and verbally sharing anger toward teachers and schoolwork, leading to the cathartic release of feelings in the safety of the play therapy session.

Table 7.1 Transcript example of what might be said when Herman is expressing anger by hitting a bop bag.

Transcript	Analysis
H: *(hitting bop bag)* "School is annoying, the teachers don't like me. I never get to do anything I want."	Spontaneous play and release physically and verbally of feelings and experiences.
T: "You feel mad at school and wish you had more choices."	Reflecting and normalizing feelings.
H: "Yeah, I'm always in trouble" *(hitting bop bag harder)*	TPoP of self-expression, catharsis, therapeutic relationship

To increase awareness, the CBPT therapist reflects on his feelings and observations of body movement. After releasing emotions using the bop bag of air, the therapist prompts Herman to feel his heart and notice his breath. Then, the therapist provides direct teaching of calming breaths, prompting him to notice how his body changes once more. This direct and indirect teaching supports overall session goals through the therapeutic powers of play.

CBPT sessions can also be fun, and through the TPoP of the therapeutic relationship in which both positive and negative experiences are shared, spontaneous moments within the sessions of play and laughter continue to build a positive therapeutic relationship and genuine acceptance. This acceptance may be unique for Herman due to his past experiences both at home and school. Due to his early adverse experiences, Herman developed automatic negative thoughts and core beliefs of feeling unaccepted. When utilizing TPoP to enhance social relationships not only will the therapeutic relationship benefit, but areas of attachment, social competence, and empathy will also be shifted and developed, beginning to form adaptive beliefs regarding acceptance and attachment.

Knowing that one can do well and achieve tasks increases the ability to move forward and try new things. With a positive therapeutic relationship, Herman moves toward reduced fears of failing and continues to collaboratively explore action plans that work for him. Part of the ongoing feedback of CBPT is exploring aspects of success with Herman and efforts to reinforce progress and use new strategies. At the start of each session, Herman shares both positive and negative experiences from his week. The purpose of this check-in is to provide positive reinforcement and feedback, facilitate responses focusing on feelings, normalize feelings and experiences, review the action plan from the week, and explore problem-solving and coping strategies (Remey, 2024).

During sessions, Herman naturally has opportunities to utilize self-control in many ways, such as taking turns during gameplay or handling frustration (ending a session, completing a difficult task, losing a game, following a limit, such as hitting a bag of air vs. a wall).

Herman often is dysregulated in the classroom and noncompliant with teacher expectations, movement around the classroom, and behaviors that disrupt the class and hurt himself and the staff. A core aspect will be working toward gaining an understanding of self, understanding the range of emotions, and building self-regulation skills. Herman's role as an active participant is key to success. To teach regulation and practice self-control, a new game is introduced. The Action Reaction Game employs the TPoP of facilitating communication, self-regulation, and increasing personal strengths to build Herman's skills of compliance, body awareness, and self-control.

Given the dysregulation occurring during Herman's day, a primary focus of CBPT sessions will utilize direct and indirect teaching to inform and explore his experiences. The ebb and flow between direct and non-direct portions of sessions provide TPoP opportunities for catharsis and abreaction. The prompts and facilitative responses of the CBPT therapist are essential ingredients of sessions. Building the therapeutic relationship is another crucial piece of the beginning phases and initial sessions. Building this relationship is a key factor in the trust and acceptance of clients to express themselves in the safety of the play therapy sessions. Facilitative responses during the working phases will include navigating negative choices and behaviors to understand the client; a strong working alliance is needed for success, enabling the client to share challenges and mistakes and guide the therapist with any misunderstandings regarding the client's thoughts, feelings, and actions. Genuine sharing and exploration are requirements as both are active participants.

The therapist also seeks to gain an understanding of any changes Herman would like to see in his life so that he can work toward identifying treatment goals collaboratively to engage him in the process. Herman's buy-in and engagement are crucial to working toward change. Caregivers' and school staff's goals focus on behaviors and the ability to function in the classroom and comply with classroom expectations. Herman's viewpoint is primarily centered more on his desire not to be in trouble and the ability to do as he wants. Working together in session to identify goals and his parts of the problems marks a beginning point to shift behaviors to work toward adaptive behaviors.

In the early stages of CBPT sessions, it is important to acknowledge and understand feelings and desires. The focus is on recognizing behavioral choices as helpful or unhelpful and understanding their impact on the problem at hand. Therapists use selected interventions and facilitative responses to achieve this. As the sessions progress, it is important for Herman to return for feedback on the effectiveness of the tools being used and to develop skills that will help him change his actions and gain insight into his own feelings and perspectives. This includes considering the perspectives of others, such as teachers and peers. Collaboration with caregivers and school staff, especially teachers, is crucial in developing a behavioral plan. Once Herman shows interest in trying different strategies, the therapist will work with him to create a doable plan. Herman can begin to meet the classroom standards and make positive changes.

Table 7.2 Transcript example of what might be said when playing the Action Reaction Game with Herman.

Transcript	Analysis
T: "I have a new game to play today. As you hit the bag of air, I will say pause, fast, or slow. When I do, I want you to do that action. Ready?"	The game goal is to practice self-control and increase body awareness and self-regulation.
H: "OK"	Body paused and looked at the therapist for direction.
T: "I can tell you are ready, your body is still, and you are looking at me for the action. Great, let's go . . . FAST."	Facilitative response to build self-awareness and positive affirmation to increase desired behavior.
H: *(actively participates in game)*	Demonstrating and practicing compliance, body control, and self-regulation.
T: "Pause"	Next directive
H: (*stops body movements*)	Demonstrating compliance, body control, and self-regulation
T: "Nice self-control, you paused your body quick!" "Now, slow"	Detailed positive reinforcement and continued practice of skill

Challenges in Implementation

Challenges regarding progress toward treatment goals consist of the longevity of issues beginning prenatally until now. Each experience has contributed to Herman's physical, neurobiological, and emotional development and affected his view of himself, others, and the world around him. The negative experiences of sexual abuse, removal from several foster homes, and being identified as a behavioral concern by caregivers and school personnel have contributed to a core negative view of self and the world. The CBPT's focus on making changes in the current situation can support shifting cognitions and internalized beliefs; however, due to the longevity of experiences, it will take time for core beliefs to alter. The focus on building adaptive behaviors will begin the process of setting the foundation. It is the belief in the framework of CBPT that once shifts in core thoughts and beliefs start, they can then be built upon with positive reinforcement. Over time, additional areas of concern can emerge from Herman's past that affected perspectives, feelings, and behaviors. A bridge to this portion of improving personal relationships will focus on helping Herman explore experiences where he has received support and care from others. This will help him build awareness of positive attachments and recognize his own resiliency. As a result of TPoP, both in direct and nondirective play, Herman will continue to develop a more adaptable perspective of self, others, and the world.

Conclusion

This chapter explored how Cognitive Behavioral Play Therapy (CBPT) is used to support a case. Using the case of Herman as an example, case conceptualization demonstrates how CBPT play therapists build therapeutic relationships and collaborate with caregivers and the client to identify and achieve treatment goals. The collaborative approach of CBPT involves therapist-led and client-led activities, which lead to improved behaviors and adaptive cognitions, enhancing relationships and shifting views of self and others. Throughout the text, examples from sessions are provided to illustrate how play therapy techniques, both structured and unstructured, are used to bring about the desired change using the therapeutic powers of play.

References

Beck, A. T. (1964). Thinking and depression. II. Theory and therapy. *Archives of General Psychiatry, 10*, 561–71. https://doi.org/10.1001/archpsyc.1964.01720240015003.

Beck, J. S. (2021). *Cognitive behavior therapy: Basics and beyond*. The Guilford Press.

Berger, I., Slobodin, O., Aboud, M., Melamed, J., & Cassuto, H. (2013). Maturational delay in ADHD: Evidence from CPT. *Frontiers in Human Neuroscience, 25*(7), 691. https://doi.org/10.3389/fnhum.2013.

Cavett, A. M. (2015). Cognitive-behavioral play therapy. In D. A. Crenshaw & A. L. Stewart (Eds.), *Play therapy: A comprehensive guide to theory and practice* (pp. 83–98). The Guilford Press.

Davies, D., & Troy, M. F. (2020). *Child development: A practitioner's guide* (4th ed.). Guilford.

Drewes, A. A. (2009). *Blending play therapy with cognitive behavioral therapy: Evidence-based and other effective treatments and techniques.* John Wiley & Sons.

Drewes, A., & Cavett, A. A. (2019, September). Cognitive behavioral play therapy. *Play Therapy Magazine, 14*(3), 24–6.

Fenn, K., & Byrne, M. (2013). The key principles of cognitive behavioural therapy. *InnovAiT Education and Inspiration for General Practice, 6*(9), 579–85. https://doi.org/10.1177/1755738012471029.

Fuggle, P., Dunsmuir, S., & Curry, V. (2013). *CBT with children, young people and families.* SAGE Publications.

Gaskill, R. L., & Perry, B. D. (2014). The neurobiological power of play: Using the neurosequential model of therapeutics to guide play in the healing process. In C. A. Malchiodi & D. A. Crenshaw (Eds.), *Creative arts and play therapy for attachment problems* (pp. 178–94). The Guilford Press.

Gaudiano, B. A. (2008). Cognitive-behavioural therapies: Achievements and challenges. *Evidence-Based Mental Health, 11*(1), 5–7. https://doi.org/10.1136/ebmh.11.1.5.

Halder, S., & Mahato, A. K. (2019). Cognitive behavior therapy for children and adolescents: Challenges and gaps in practice. *Indian Journal of Psychological Medicine, 41*(3), 279–83. https://doi.org/10.4103/IJPSYM.IJPSYM_470_18.

Howard, C., Lascano, D., & Watkins, K. (2024, June). Recognizing and responding to grief and loss in Foster care and adoption. *Play Therapy Magazine, 19*(2), 4–7.

Knell, S. M. (2011). Cognitive-behavioral play therapy. In C. E. Schaefer (Ed.), *Foundations of play therapy* (pp. 313–28). essay, J. Wiley.

Knell, S. M. (2015). Cognitive-behavioral play therapy. In *Handbook of play therapy* (pp. 119–33). https://doi.org/10.1002/9781119140467.ch6.

Knell, S. M. (2022). Cognitive behavioral play therapy. In R. D. Friedberg & E. V. Rozmid (Eds.), *Creative CBT with youth.* Springer.

Lautieri, A. (2019, March 19). *Cognitive-behavioral theory of personality disorders.* Mentalhelp.net; admin. https://www.mentalhelp.net/personality-disorders/cognitive-behavioral-theory/.

Merrill, K. A., & Strauman, T. J. (2004). The role of personality in cognitive-behavioral therapies. *Behavior Therapy, 35*(1), 131–46. https://doi.org/10.1016/s0005-7894(04)80008-x.

Peabody, M. A., & Schaefer, C. (2019, September). The therapeutic powers of play: The heart and soul of play therapy. *Play Therapy Magazine, 14*(3), 4–6.

Ray, D. C. (2015). *A therapist's guide to child development: The extraordinarily normal years.* Routledge.

Razak, N. H. A., Johari, K. S. K., Mahmud, M. I., Zubir, N. M., & Johan, S. (2018). General review on cognitive behavior play therapy on childrens' psychology development. *International Journal of Academic Research in Progressive Education and Development, 7*(4). https://doi.org/10.6007/ijarped/v7-i4/4842.

Remey, L (2024). ADHD and COVID-19: Cognitive behavioral play therapy with an African American Child. In J. Baggerly & A. A. Drewes (Eds.), *Contemporary case studies in clinical mental health for children and adolescents* (pp. 61–75). Rowman & Littlefield.

Schaefer, C. E., & Drewes, A. A. (2009). The therapeutic powers of play and play therapy. In A. A. Drewes (Ed.), *Blending play therapy with cognitive behavioral therapy: Evidence-based and other effective treatments and techniques* (pp. 3–15). John Wiley & Sons, Inc.

Shrinivasa, B., Bukhari, M., Ragesh, G., & Hamza, A. (2018). Therapeutic intervention for children through play: An overview. *Archives of Mental Health, 19*(2), 82. https://doi.org/10.4103/amh.amh_34_18.

Smith, K. E., & Pollak, S. D. (2020). Early life stress and development: Potential mechanisms for adverse outcomes. *Journal of Neurodevelopmental Disorders, 12*, 34. https://doi.org/10.1186/s11689-020-09337-y.

8

Solution-Focused Play Therapy Using Therapeutic Powers of Play to Help Children Succeed

Elizabeth Kjellstrand Hartwig

Chapter Outline

Introduction

In a world that often focuses on problems and challenges that children present, solution-focused play therapy (SFPT) is a strengths-based play therapy theory that emphasizes children's assets and abilities. SFPT helps children develop solutions to problems by building on both internal and external strengths and resources (Hartwig, 2021). This theoretical approach meets children at their developmental level by applying nondirective skills for younger or less verbal clients and more directive activities and techniques for children who are older or more interested in engaging in verbal and directive interventions in the playroom. This chapter will review the underlying philosophy, theoretical basis, model of psychopathology, conceptualization of treatment goals, role of the therapist and other stakeholders, and empirical support of SFPT. The chapter culminates with the application of SFPT to a case study of a 10-year-old child, Herman, through the lens of the therapeutic powers of play (TPoP; Schaefer & Drewes, 2014).

Underlying Philosophy

SFPT is based on the philosophy, key concepts, skills, and techniques of solution-focused therapy (SFT), which was founded in the late 1970s by Insoo Kim Berg and Steve de Shazer. SFPT is a postmodern play therapy approach that is grounded in social construction theory (Hartwig, 2021), which maintains that people make meaning of their world through social interactions. For children, these social interactions occur at home, at school, in the playroom, and in their interactions with significant others in their lives. This theoretical approach was historically developed within the context of the family systems framework, which contends that individuals interact with multiple systems throughout their lives, and these systems can often contribute to and maintain the problem. SFPT differentiates itself from other family systems models through the solution-building process—the focus on creating systemic change by concentrating on strengths, resources, past successes, and future hopes (Franklin et al., 2019).

Personality Theory

Personality theory aims to define what makes people similar or different, in terms of their unique thoughts, behaviors, feelings, and traits. SFPT is not based on personality theory, but rather on constructivist theory, which emphasizes the subjective experience of how people interact and make meaning with others and their environment. In play therapy, children make meaning of their world through the language of play and the interaction between the child, the toys, and the play therapist. Children express themselves in both verbal and nonverbal ways by interacting with toys and engaging in play. As children play, the practitioner uses collaborative communication to help children identify their abilities and successes.

The SFPT approach integrates eight key concepts, developed by de Shazer et al. (2007), that underlie this theory. These tenets are: 1) if it's not broken, don't fix it; 2) if it works, do more of it; 3) if it's not working, do something different; 4) small steps lead to big changes; 5) the solution is not necessarily related to the problem; 6) solution-building language is different from problem talk; 7) no problem happens all the time; and 8) the future is both created and negotiable. These concepts guide play therapists in helping children try new solutions, do more of what's working, work on smaller goals first, focus on capabilities, find exceptions to problems, and create a preferred future. These tenets do not highlight aspects of a child's personality, but rather emphasize how children make meaning through their experiences in the playroom.

Model of Psychopathology/Resiliency

As a postmodern theory, SFPT offers children, caregivers, and practitioners a new way to consider psychopathology and mental illness. Psychopathology is the study of symptoms, causes, and classifications of mental disorders. Traditional psychotherapy approaches focus on the past, dysfunction, causes of problems, and diagnoses of mental disorders. SFPT, on the other hand, does not see clients through the lens of mental illness or dysfunction. Instead, SFPT is grounded in a model of resiliency that focuses on learning how clients bounce back from adversity and unveil the power within. Through this model of resiliency, SFPT uses the solution-building process to define the presenting problem and then identify goals to help children move toward a more preferred future. De Jong and Berg (2013) outline the solution-building process through the following five stages: (1) describing the problem, (2) developing well-formed goals, (3) exploring exceptions, (4) end-of-session feedback, and (5) evaluating client progress. Rather than focusing on problems or symptoms, the solution-building process empowers children to find solutions to problems that brought them to play therapy. This process will be elucidated later in the chapter with an applied example in the case formation and application section.

The first stage of the solution-building process is identifying and understanding the presenting problem. Play therapists can do this through several means: gathering information in the intake paperwork, facilitating a caregiver consultation, and learning about the problem from the child in play therapy. In the intake paperwork, SFPT practitioners ask questions for caregivers to complete prior to meeting with the caregiver that explore the presenting problem. These questions provide a starting place for understanding the presenting problem, identifying what the caregivers and child have already tried to address the problem, what strengths, interests, and abilities the child has, and how the caregivers hope that play therapy can help. As the practitioner meets with the child's caregiver and later works with the child in play therapy, the practitioner will get a richer description of the problem and, more importantly, an understanding of a preferred future and goals for therapy.

Conceptualizing Goals of Treatment

The next stage of solution-building is developing well-formed goals. Berg and Miller (1992) presented seven qualities of well-formed goals as: (1) important to the client; (2) small and achievable; (3) concrete and behavioral; (4) phrased to describe the presence of something versus its absence (e.g., "increasing regulation skills" rather than "not being anxious"); (5) representing a beginning step rather than a final result; (6) realistic within the context of the client's life; and (7) a challenge to the client. In the initial caregiver consultation, the practitioner will discuss the presenting problem and potential goals with the caregiver. Questions such as "How will you know when play therapy has been successful?" or "What would your child be doing different that would let you know that play therapy was helpful?" can be an excellent way to begin goal setting with caregivers. One of the most iconic solution-focused techniques that is used in goal formation is the miracle question. Play therapists could use the following wording to pose the miracle question to caregivers: "If a miracle happened tonight and the presenting problem was magically resolved, what would your child be doing different tomorrow that would let you know that the miracle happened?" Practitioners can then partner with caregivers to identify positive behavioral changes that the child could work toward during the course of play therapy.

Children also have ways of expressing potential goals and envisioning a future in which the problem is less of a problem. Children may express this nonverbally through play or verbally through SFPT interventions. Hartwig and Taylor (2022) recommend several creative interventions for setting goals with children through play-based expressive art, sand tray, and puppet activities. For children, play therapists can use the Magic Wand activity (Hartwig, 2021; Wells & McCaig, 2016). This activity begins with an expressive art intervention in which the therapist and child create magic wands using wooden dowels, paper stars, ribbons, sequins, and other art materials. After creating their wands, the therapist can ask the child the following question: "Imagine that this is a magic wand, and by waving your wand, you could make the problems or challenges in your life disappear. What will be different in your world?" The child can choose to respond or not to the question; however, just thinking about what might be different in their world can create the context for positive change. The Magic Wand activity invites children to be creative and consider potential goals.

Role of the Therapist

The role of the therapist in SFPT is to collaborate with the child to identify strengths and resources and support the child in taking small steps toward clinical goals in play therapy. This can be achieved through the next two stages of the solution-building process: exploring for exceptions, also called "Searching for Solutions" (Hartwig, 2021), and end-of-session feedback. In SFPT, the practitioner can search for solutions by using the twelve basic skills and SFPT techniques. Basic skills are foundational skills for all mental health practitioners. The SFPT basic skills are similar to skills from other play therapy approaches. Hartwig (2021) derived the twelve basic skills from De Jong and Berg's (2013) twenty Skills for Not Knowing. The SFPT twelve basic skills are divided into four categories: nonverbal skills, content skills, encouragement skills, and interviewing skills. These skills are presented in Table 8.1 with a description of each skill.

Table 8.1 SFPT Basic Skills

Skill	Description
Nonverbal Skills	
1. Practitioners' nonverbal behavior	Leaning forward, using open arms and posture, matching facial expression and tone of voice to child's affect, and believing in the child's capabilities
2. Empathy	Communicating care, respect, and positive regard to the child
3. Reflecting behavior	Observing and stating what the child is doing, noticing who and what are important to child based on their play behaviors
Content Skills	
4. Reflecting content	Paraphrasing what the child is saying, noticing who and what are important to child based on what they say, incorporating child's key words
5. Reflecting feeling	Observing and stating what the child is feeling, noticing who and what are important to child based on what feelings they express
6. Summarizing	Providing a summary of the child's behaviors, statements, or feelings
Encouragement Skills	
7. Complimenting	Recognizing client strengths and abilities through direct and indirect compliments, acknowledging the child's self-compliments
8. Amplifying solution talk	Noticing times when the child is doing something well or better and exploring how the child was successful in making this change
9. Returning focus to the client	Helping the child focus on how they see themselves as a part of the solution; allowing the child to make choices in the playroom (e.g., "You can decide what that is.")
Interviewing Skills	
10. Open-ended questions	Primarily using questions that begin with "what" or "how" and allowing the child to respond in a variety of ways
11. Relationship questions	Using questions that invite the child to consider possibilities from another person's perspective
12. Exploring client meaning	Getting a clearer understanding of what the child says or does and how the child makes meaning about past successes and future possibilities

The SFPT twelve basic skills should be used according to a child's developmental level. Young children between the ages of three and five, and sometimes children who have experienced trauma, tend to use play as a means of communication rather than verbal dialogue. Therefore, SFPT practitioners use more of the nondirective skills, such as reflecting behavior, content, and feelings, with younger or less verbal clients. For older children and adolescents, ages six to eighteen, practitioners can use nondirective or directive skills, depending on the child's language and cognitive development and interest in participating in more directive activities or responding to questions in the playroom. Directive SFPT skills used with older children include amplifying solution talk, open-ended questions, relationship questions, and exploring the child's meaning. SFPT practitioners value the concept of "leading from one step behind" (Cantwell & Holmes, 1994, p. 20). This means that SFPT practitioners take their cue from children in recognizing

Table 8.2 SFPT Techniques

Technique	Description
Finding exceptions	Identifying times when the problem does not exist or is less of a problem
Coping questions	Asking the child to share how they have managed to work through challenges, even when they have faced adversity
Scaling	Asking the child to self-assess their progress on a scale of 0 to 10, recognize what they have already done to make progress, and identify next steps in working toward their goal
Solution mission	Tasking the child or caregiver with a between-session activity that will help the child make progress toward the goal or help the caregiver support the child in making progress
End-of-session feedback	Providing a summary of the session, strengths the child demonstrated, and plans for between-session activities to work toward the goal

when children need to lead in the play, make choices in the playroom, and not be directed in certain activities, as well as when to invite the child to participate in directive activities and respond to strengths-based questions.

SFPT also uses several techniques to help children identify strengths and past successes. One example of an SFPT technique that was previously described is the miracle question, which can be asked verbally to caregivers and through expressive means with children (e.g., Magic Wand activity). Table 8.2 provides a list and description of several SFPT techniques.

These techniques empower children to identify exceptions to problems, examine how they cope with challenges, self-assess their progress, and review what they have accomplished in sessions.

Roles of Caregivers and Collaterals

Caregivers, family members, and other significant people in the child's life are an important part of SFPT. As an approach based on family systems, SFPT practitioners recognize the importance of partnering with parents, stepparents, guardians, grandparents, siblings, teachers, school counselors, coaches, youth leaders, band directors, pediatricians, psychiatrists, and others to help the child succeed. This is accomplished through three types of integrated services: caregiver consultations, family play therapy, and systemic consultations. Caregiver consultations are an important component of SFPT because they provide a means for developing a collaborative relationship with the caregiver (e.g., parent, stepparent, and guardian) and checking in with the caregiver on a regular basis to assess progress. The initial caregiver consultation is scheduled with one or more caregivers prior to the first session with the child, without the child present for this initial meeting. During the caregiver consultation, the practitioner will provide a tour of the playroom, discuss the purpose and process of play therapy, describe the theoretical foundations of SFPT, and review informed consent (Hartwig, 2021). The practitioner then provides a space for the caregiver to share their concerns about their child and their hopes for how play therapy can help their child make positive changes. The practitioner and caregiver work together to identify potential goals for the child in play therapy.

Practitioners continue to meet with caregivers on a regular basis to assess progress toward goals. For the final stage in the solution-building process, evaluating client progress, practitioners enlist children in play therapy and their caregivers in assessing how the child has made progress and when the child is getting closer to ending play therapy sessions. A typical structure for SFPT sessions includes the following: session one—initial caregiver consultation, sessions two to four—play therapy sessions with the child, session five—check-in caregiver consultation to acknowledge the strengths and efforts of the caregiver and child and assess the progress of the child, sessions six and beyond—continuation of play therapy with three to four sessions of play therapy followed by a caregiver consultation, and celebration session—the final play therapy session when the child, caregivers, and practitioner acknowledge that sufficient progress has been made. Practitioners engage caregivers in regular consultations to enlist the caregiver in being a part of the solution and to assess the child's progress toward their goal.

Family play therapy sessions can also be used as an adjunct to individual play therapy to involve caregivers and/or other members of the child's family in the play therapy process. Gil (2015) identified several benefits of family play therapy: nurturing the attachment between caregiver and child, increasing play, creativity, and laughter between family members, changing negative patterns of interaction, and presenting solutions that might not have emerged through caregiver consultations or individual play therapy. In family play therapy, goals shift from an individual goal to a family goal, such that all family members become a part of creating change for the family, not just the individual child. Hartwig (2021) provided several solution-focused family play therapy interventions that can be used to work with families in play therapy.

Lastly, consulting with other members of the system can engage more people in helping the child to be successful in play therapy and beyond. Ensuring that the practitioner has acquired a signed release of information form, the practitioner can reach out and consult with the child's teacher, school counselor, pediatrician, and other significant people in the child's life. In these consultation calls or meetings, the practitioner can share the goals that the child is working on in play therapy and learn from the other person how the child is struggling (e.g., describing the problem), when the presenting problem is not happening (e.g., exploring for exceptions), and what progress the child is making, even if it's a small amount of progress (e.g., evaluating progress). The practitioner can encourage the consultant to look for small steps of progress in the child and let the child know when they notice this progress. These consultations let others know that many people are working together to help the child find solutions.

Research/Empirical Support

SFT has a strong evidence base in demonstrating efficacy with a variety of presenting issues, cultures, and age groups. In 2017, Macdonald identified over 2,800 published

SFT studies. These studies included 7 systematic reviews, 10 meta-analyses, and 143 randomized controlled trials (RCTs), of which 92 RCTs demonstrated positive and significant outcomes compared to other approaches. Kim et al. (2019) asserted that SFT was recognized as a promising intervention by the Substance Abuse and Mental Health Services Administration (SAMHSA) National Registry of Evidence-Based Programs and Policies. SFPT is a culturally affirming approach with an emphasis on building a collaborative therapist/client relationship and embracing diversity by recognizing clients as the experts of their own lives. The therapeutic benefits of SFT with African American, Asian, Hispanic and Latinx, Iranian, Lithuanian, and Native American clients and communities have been elucidated in a myriad of studies (Brogan et al., 2020; Catipon, 2017; Cepukiene et al., 2018; Himmelberger et al., 2022; Hogan et al., 2017; Johnson & Williams, 2015; Kim et al., 2015; Liu et al., 2015; Maldonado, 2018; Meyer & Cottone, 2013; Reddy et al., 2022; Suitt et al., 2016; Tehee et al., 2021; Watkins & Kurtz, 2001). Authors have also described how to use SFT as an affirming approach for queer clients (Handley et al., 2021; Ouer, 2016).

A number of studies have identified positive outcomes in employing SFT with children. Literature has highlighted the effectiveness of SFT with children who are bullied, experience anxiety and depression, struggle with academic concerns, and exhibit disruptive behaviors (Copur & Kubilay, 2022; Corcoran, 2008; Daki & Savage, 2010; Hartwig, 2017; Karababa, 2023; Kvarme et al., 2013; Moosa et al., 2017; Schmit et al., 2016). Hsu et al. (2021) reported small to medium effect sizes on internalizing and externalizing behaviors for SFT involving children and their families. Similarly, researchers have indicated effective and positive outcomes for SFT with children in group therapy and participating together with their parents or caregivers (Carr et al., 2017; Gong & Hsu, 2017). SFT researchers continue to develop and facilitate studies to explore the efficacy of SFPT with children.

Case Study through the Lens of the Therapeutic Powers of Play

In this section, the case study of Herman (see Appendix for case study of Herman being referenced), a ten-year-old child, will be applied to SFPT through the lens of the therapeutic powers of play. This section includes a description of how the powers of play are employed with SFPT, diversity and inclusion considerations, and case formulation and application. This section culminates with an assessment of the challenges of implementation.

Therapeutic Powers of Play Employed

The therapeutic powers of play are the mechanisms of play that produce change in the playroom (Schaefer & Peabody, 2016). These powers of play provide a foundation for how play creates change. Schaefer and Drewes (2014) identified twenty powers of play as core agents of change, which were categorized into four sections: facilitating communication,

Table 8.3 Therapeutic Powers of Play Applied with SFPT

Power of Play	SFPT-Applied Example
Positive emotions	Herman engages in play as an enjoyable activity, which stimulates mood, playfulness, and his sense of wellbeing.
Social competence	Herman learns and practices social skills through play to build competence in interacting with others.
Creative problem solving	Herman engages in nondirective and directive play to develop solutions to his problems.
Resiliency	Herman identifies and experiences competence through play by trying things out, practicing skills, and learning about his capabilities.
Self-esteem	Herman experiences acceptance and recognizes his abilities and competencies through play.
Self-expression	Herman expresses his feelings, beliefs about family and relationships, and exploration of gender in the playroom.

fostering emotional wellness, enhancing social relationships, and increasing personal strengths. Hartwig (2021) elucidated how all twenty powers of play are applied in SFPT. While each power of play can be an agent of change in SFPT, some powers of play are most relevant to the key concepts and philosophical foundations of SFPT. These six powers of play hail from all four categories and include the following: positive emotions, social competence, creative problem solving, resilience, self-esteem, and self-expression. Table 8.3 presents how each TPoP is generally applied with SFPT to Herman in the playroom.

In the case formation and application section, the Exploring Exceptions/Searching for Solutions stage of the solution-building process offers examples of how the TPoP are applied to Herman's case.

Cultural, Diversity, and Inclusion Considerations

There are several diversity and inclusion factors that should be considered in this case study (see Appendix for case study of Herman being referenced). The first is Herman's ethnicity. Herman's biological maternal family members identify as Caucasian, Hispanic, and African American, with no known ethnicity of his biological father. Herman has been placed in a foster family, and it is unclear what the foster parents' ethnicity is. It would be important for the practitioner to explore how the foster parents recognize and embrace Herman's ethnicity, how Herman chooses to identify, and what awareness Herman and his foster parents have about potential microaggressions and racism that Herman has or could experience at home and in school, whether intentional or not. Other aspects of Herman's culture can also be gathered and explored in play therapy.

Another aspect of Herman's culture and a consideration in play therapy is gender expression. Herman has expressed to his foster parents that he does not like being a boy and wants to dress in non-gender-specific ways. Embracing diversity starts with the practitioner. SFPT practitioners should seek to learn from and understand their clients' cultures, including their gender expression and gender identity. Being knowledgeable about queer identities, the use of various pronouns, and affirming practices in play therapy is part of being a competent practitioner. In the case presentation below, the author uses he/him pronouns; however, if Herman chose to use other pronouns in the playroom, the practitioner would use different pronouns to match Herman's gender identity. In the playroom, practitioners should have multiple resources and toys that allow children to explore their gender and express themselves in gender-specific or nonbinary ways. Examples of queer-affirmative playroom resources include the following: gender-specific and gender-neutral dress-ups (e.g., princess dresses, butterfly wings, police uniform, tool belt, capes, career-related outfits), rainbow figures (e.g., pride flag, rainbow bridge), bisexual and transgender figures (e.g., heart figure with transgender colors), multiple individual brides and grooms with different skin tones, and gender-neutral toys (e.g., blocks, medical kit). SFPT practitioners can also use bibliotherapy to facilitate thought or discussion with a child about their gender expression or identity. Recommendations can be found online for LGBTQIA+ books for children (Reading Rockets, 2024; The New York Times, 2024). The Trevor Project also has multiple resources for caregivers of children exploring gender expression (Trevor Project, 2024).

Another consideration is Herman's health and disabilities. Herman had fetal exposure to opioids, was in the Neonatal Intensive Care Unit (NICU) for over a month, and was not held often during his time in the NICU. These experiences as a newborn may have severely impacted Herman's development and attachment style. Wilkinson et al. (2023) found that prenatal opioid exposure was linked to multiple developmental delays, behavioral health conditions, and learning disorders. This finding may explain some of Herman's behavioral challenges and learning disabilities. Some of these symptoms may be treated with medication; however, it appears that the psychiatrist has not found the right medications or dosages to best address Herman's symptoms. The SFPT practitioner can best support Herman in play therapy by using toys and interventions that support neurodiversity, such as sensory toys, weighted blankets, expressive art materials, and sand therapy. Additionally, collaborating with Herman's school can ensure that his Individualized Education Program (IEP) includes strategies and resources that support neurodiversity and learning challenges.

A final consideration is Herman's trauma history. Herman experienced multiple traumas as a child, including a lack of attachment with his mother as a newborn, intimate partner violence, neglect, and substance abuse in his grandmother's house, removal from his grandmother's house, sexual abuse by another foster child for multiple months, and bullying at school. All of these adverse childhood experiences may contribute to Herman's developmental and behavioral challenges. SFPT practitioners can integrate trauma-informed practices in the playroom by creating a safe environment, building a therapeutic alliance, using nondirective skills as needed by allowing children to lead in the play, and offering a variety of expressive tools for children to express themselves.

Case Formulation and Application

For this section, the author will utilize the five-stage solution-building process to describe how an SFPT practitioner would conceptualize and work with Herman in play therapy.

Describing the Problem

SFPT begins with the first phone call to the caregiver, which in Herman's case is one of his foster parents. The SFPT practitioner, Eve, schedules an initial caregiver consultation with both foster parents. Eve sends paperwork to the caregivers to complete and sign, including the SFPT Client Information form (Hartwig, 2021) that asks several questions about the presenting problem and the child's strengths and resources that can be followed up on in the caregiver consultation. In the caregiver consultation, Eve introduces the caregivers to the playroom, discusses SFPT and the process of play therapy, and reviews informed consent. To understand Herman's presenting problems and potential resources, Eve explores the following questions with the caregivers from Hartwig (2021, pp. 189–190): (1) "What is the presenting problem or concern you have regarding your child?" (2) "How are you hoping I can help your child?" (3) "What have you tried with your child to address this problem?" (4) "What has your child tried to address this problem?" (5) "What goal or goals would you like your child to work on in therapy?" (6) "What are your child's strengths, hobbies, and activities they enjoy?" (7) "Who or what are sources of support for your child (e.g., friends, pets, family members, neighbors, spirituality)?" and (8) "What questions do you or your child have that I can answer during our initial consultation?" Discussing the caregivers' responses to these questions provides a foundation for understanding their presenting concerns and some of Herman's sources of support. In this initial caregiver consultation, Eve emphasizes the importance of the practitioner, caregivers, child, and other members of the child's system (e.g., teacher, school counselor, psychiatrist) collaborating to help the child be successful in working toward goals.

Developing Well-formed Goals

Based on the information provided by the caregivers in the initial consultation, it is evident that there are numerous goals that Herman could work on in play therapy. The caregivers identify an initial goal that seems most relevant to how Herman is being challenged at home and in school currently. This goal is to increase anger management skills by developing three skills for managing anger.

Eve asks the caregivers to share what they and the school are already doing to support Herman in managing his anger. The foster mother shares that they give consequences when the other boys at home bother him by tapping his head while he's playing games. They also share that they support Herman by giving him art supplies so he can paint and create art when he needs time to himself. Eve also asks the caregivers to describe what it would look like if Herman had achieved this goal. The foster father shares that Herman would first recognize what causes him to get angry and notice when he is getting angry. He states that Herman would take some calming breaths and acknowledge verbally that he is feeling angry. Herman would use several skills for managing his anger, such as walking away, listening to music, petting their family dog, using the punching bag in the basement, or going outside to play basketball. When ready, Herman would be able to come back and discuss what caused his anger and what he or the other person could do different to change this in future situations like this. Eve thanks the caregivers for taking the time to build a collaborative relationship with her, share helpful information about Herman's challenges, strengths, and resources, and develop potential therapeutic goals for Herman.

Exploring Exceptions/Searching for Solutions

In the first session with Herman, Eve invites him back to the playroom and shares with him that he can choose what he'd like to play with first. Herman says, "I don't know what to play. What games do you have?" Since he is ten years old and more verbal than younger clients, Eve asks Herman if he would like to play a directive rapport-building activity so they can learn more about each other. She offers him two options: Thumball™—a soccer-style ball that has prompts on each panel (Talicor, 2018)—and Totika—a wood-stacking game that comes with cards that have questions to answer with each turn (Open Spaces, LLC, 2019). Herman chooses Thumball™. Eve explains that when Herman catches the ball, he will look to see where his thumbs land on the ball and will respond to one of the prompts on the ball where his thumbs touch. Herman catches the ball and responds to the prompt "Favorite food." In the dialogue below, the author will point out the SFPT basic skills used by the practitioner in building a relationship with the client.

Herman: "My favorite food is pizza."
Eve: "What's your favorite kind of pizza?" (open-ended question)
Herman: "Pepperoni, for sure!"
Eve: "You like pepperoni pizza the most." (reflecting content) "My favorite kind of pizza is called Hawaiian pizza, and it has bacon and pineapple on it. What do you think of that?" (open-ended question)
Herman: "That sounds weird, but I would try it because I really like bacon!"
Eve: "Wow—you're willing to try something new, even if you're not sure how it tastes." (complimenting)

Herman and Eve continue playing with the Thumball™ and learning more about each other for 10 minutes. After they are done playing with the ball, Herman asks Eve a question. In this exchange, the author will point out some SFPT techniques and apply TPoP so you can see both at work in this part of the play therapy session.

Herman: "Why am I here?"
Eve: "You're curious about why your mom brought you here today. What did she tell you about why she brought you?"
Herman: "She told me that she wants me to not be angry anymore."
Eve: "That might be hard to never get angry. Are there times when you're not angry at home or school?" (SFPT—finding exceptions)
Herman: "Yeah, lots of times. I'm really happy when I play games or eat dinner!" (TPoP—positive emotions) "But I do get mad a lot at school because of the way people treat me."
Eve: "So there are times when you aren't angry, like when you're eating or playing games. You mentioned you get mad with how people treat you at school. How do they treat you?"
Herman: "They make fun of my makeup and clothes. I like how I look, but some people don't." (TPoP—self-esteem)
Eve: "You think the way you dress and do your makeup looks good, but your peers make fun of you. When they make fun of you, what do you do?"

Herman: "Sometimes I throw chairs at them because I'm so mad. Other times I run out into the hall to get away from them."

Eve: "Going out into the hall is one way you've found to take a break and get away from them. How else have you coped with your anger when they make fun of you?" (SFPT—coping question)

Herman: "Sometimes I don't say anything. I just keep my anger inside, so I don't get in trouble." (TPoP—resiliency, social competence)

Eve: "Oh, so sometimes you cope by keeping your anger inside so you can get along with others, but you still feel really angry. That must be hard to have all that anger inside. Here in play therapy, there are lots of ways you can express your anger and other feelings you have." (TPoP—self-expression)

Herman: "I think that would help."

Eve: (*showing Herman the sandtray and figures*) "This is a sandtray and you can see that there are lots of figures grouped into different categories, such as people, animals, vehicles, and fantasy figures. Let's pretend that a miracle happened tonight, and you got a special superpower that allowed you to manage all the anger you feel, so that when people did things that made you angry, you knew what to do to cope with the anger and express it in ways that didn't get you in trouble. I'd like you to create a scene of what your world would be like if a miracle happened, and you had that superpower." (SFPT—miracle question)

Herman creates a scene in the sand where a rainbow fairy would fly over dragons, schools, and homes and sprinkle "kindness glitter" over everything (TPoP—creative problem solving).

After they process the sand tray, Herman and Eve discuss setting a goal of identifying times when Herman gets angry and exploring different ways to manage or express his anger. This goal matches what the caregivers had identified as a potential goal for Herman.

End-of-Session Feedback

In the last few minutes of the session, Eve takes time to provide end-of-session feedback to Herman.

Eve: "Herman, today you did a lot of things in play therapy. We played with the Thumball™ and got to learn some things about each other. I learned that you really like pepperoni pizza and playing video games. Then you asked about why you're here, and we discussed some things that are challenging you at home and school, such as getting angry with people who make fun of you. You shared that sometimes you know how to cope with feeling mad, like going out into the hall at school to take a break or playing games at home. Next, I asked you to create a scene in the sand of what your world would be like if you had a superpower to manage your anger. In the scene you created, a rainbow fairy sprinkled kindness glitter over lots of things to help other people to be kind. You did a lot of things today in play therapy."

Herman: "It was fun."

Eve: "Herman, I have a mission for you. Would you be willing to try something out this week before I see you again next week?"

Herman: "Sure. What?"

Eve: "I'd like you to think about how people could be kinder to you and also how you could be kinder to others. You don't have to do anything different, just think about how you and other people could be kinder. Would you be willing to try that and then come back and tell me next week?"

Herman: "OK, I'll try it. Next time, can we play that Totika game?"

Eve: "Yes, I'd love to play that with you. OK, let's go out into the waiting room now, because our session is over. I'm looking forward to playing with you next week!"

Herman: "Me, too!"

Eve takes Herman out to the waiting room and schedules another session with him for the next week.

Evaluating Client Progress

In working with Herman and his caregivers, Eve uses several strategies for evaluating client progress. One strategy that Eve uses is asking Herman at the beginning of the session, "What's something different or better since I saw you last week?" Eve can also check in with Herman on the Solution Mission by asking, "Last week I asked you to think about ways that you or others could be kinder. What are some ways that you thought about over the past week?" Another strategy that Eve uses is the scaling technique. Table 8.4 describes the steps to effective scaling (Hartwig & Taylor, 2024) and an example of how Eve would facilitate this technique with Herman.

Another way to assess progress is to meet every few weeks with the caregivers for a caregiver consultation (Hartwig, 2021). In these meetings, Eve can explore with the caregivers how Herman has made progress toward his goal of increasing anger management skills. Eve can use scaling to assess this or ask questions to learn more about how progress was made. Eve would ask what Herman is doing different to make this progress and what the caregivers are doing different to notice his progress or help him make progress. In the caregiver consultation, Eve can also learn more about how Herman is still being challenged at home or school and explore ideas for what might help Herman cope with these challenges.

One recommendation Eve has for exploring challenges at home is to have a family play therapy session with Herman, both foster parents, and the two foster boys. In this session, Eve facilitates the Family Zoo technique (Hartwig, 2021) in which each person in the family chooses and creates or colors an animal and then places their animal in a family habitat. Eve observes the family as they create the Family Zoo, notices the interactions between Herman and other members of the family, and uses processing questions to explore family strengths and resources. The family play therapy session engages all members of the family in having fun together and doing more of what's working to help Herman succeed.

Challenges in Implementation

Some potential challenges in implementation of SFPT with Herman include participation, limits needed in the playroom, and collaboration with others. The first possible challenge involves Herman's willingness to participate in play therapy. Given that he has worked

Table 8.4 Steps to Effective Scaling

Step	Description	Example
1. Defining the scale	The scale should be from 0 (not 1) to 10 with 10 as the desired position.	With a goal of "increasing anger management skills" the scale would be 0 = no anger management skills and 10 = lots of anger management skills
2. Describing each end of the scale	Asking the child to describe what they would be doing different at a 10 and what they would be doing (or not doing) at a 0.	"Herman, what I heard you say is that if you were at a 10 then you would have lots of anger management skills, such as using stress balls or fidgets, petting the dog, and taking a break. If you were at a 0, you would not have any anger management to use and may be really angry and wanting to fight someone or throw something."
3. Choosing a number on the scale	Asking the child to choose what number they are on the scale at this time.	"Herman, I'd like you to use the hopscotch rug to jump to what number you are on the scale right now. OK, I see you jumped to a 3!"
4. Getting to that number	Asking the child what they did to get to that number. This is the most important part of scaling. The practitioner asks, "What else?" several times to get a rich description of what the child is doing.	"Herman, what are you doing to get to a 3?" [Herman shares that he's squeezing stress balls in class to try and ignore peers who are making fun of him.] "You're using stress balls in class to help you manage your anger. What else?"
5. Identifying next steps	Asking the child to identify what it would take to get just a little higher on the scale.	"Herman, what would it take for you to get to a 3.1 on your anger management scale?" [Herman shares that he could ask the teacher if he could take a break when students say mean things to him.] "Ok, so if you were able to take more breaks in school, that would help you get a little higher on the scale. Would you be willing to ask your teacher about that this week?"

with various therapists in the past using different play therapy modalities, he may not be willing to engage in play therapy again. Taking time to build a relationship with Herman is paramount. As the therapeutic alliance is developed and nurtured, Herman may be willing to trust Eve and be open to participating in play therapy sessions.

Another challenge to implementation is potential limits that need to be set. At school, Herman has resorted to fighting, throwing chairs, and kicking his teachers when he is angry or dysregulated. In the playroom, Eve will create a safe and consistent environment by using the twelve basic skills, building rapport with Herman, and providing toys and materials for him to express himself in a variety of different ways. Even with these skills and tools in place, Eve may need to set limits with Herman if he gets angry or chooses to express himself in aggressive ways in the playroom, such as throwing toys across the room, stomping on sand tray figures, or ripping dress-ups that don't fit. Eve would use limit-setting skills (Landreth, 2024) if these behaviors were to occur and would assess how to best support Herman in the playroom to help him express himself in ways that are safe and don't hurt himself, the therapist, or the toys.

The last challenge to implementation is collaborating with others. In SFPT, working with other members of the system, such as teachers or doctors, can help to create more systemic change for the client. Sometimes, however, members of the system may be part of maintaining the problem. For example, if the teacher yells at Herman every time he fidgets or gets up from his desk, this creates an ongoing process in which Herman continues to get in trouble, even when he's trying to manage his symptoms or feelings. With consent, Eve can have consultation meetings with the teacher to identify how Eve can support Herman in play therapy and explore small changes that the teacher could make to support Herman in class. While all these challenges to implementation may feel daunting at times, an SFPT practitioner, like Eve, will find what's working and help Herman and others do more of it and look to make small steps that can create big changes.

Conclusion

SFPT is a strengths-based theoretical approach that uses the therapeutic powers of play as agents of change in helping children reach their clinical goals. SFPT is guided by eight key concepts that ground the approach and five stages of solution building that outline a process for working with clients. Through both nondirective and directive interventions, SFPT practitioners can match the twelve basic skills and strengths-based techniques of this approach to the developmental needs of each child. In Herman's case, Eve used several elements of SFPT to support Herman in working toward an initial goal of developing anger management skills. These include collaboration with caregivers and the school, relationship-building and expressive interventions, recognition of Herman's strengths and abilities, and affirmation of Herman's culture, neurodiversity, and gender expression. SFPT builds on the therapeutic powers of play to promote change and growth in children and their families.

References

Berg, I. K., & Miller, S. D. (1992). *Working with the problem drinker: A solution-focused approach*. W.W. Norton.

Brogan, J., Bloomdahl, S. C., Rowlett, W. H., & Dunham, M. (2020). Using SFBC group techniques to increase Latino academic self-esteem. *Journal of School Counseling, 18*(10–18), 1–37.

Cantwell, P., & Holmes, S. (1994). Social construction: A paradigm shift for systemic therapy and training. *Australian and New Zealand Journal of Family Therapy, 15*, 17–26.

Carr, A., Hartnett, D., Brosnan, E., & Sharry, J. (2017). Parents plus systemic, solution-focused parent training programs: Description, review of the evidence base, & meta-analysis. *Family Process, 56*(3), 652–68. https://doi.org/10.1111/famp.12225.

Catipon, M. A. A. D. (2017). Solution-focused play therapy: Working with children in the Philippines. In D. Hogan, J. Tuomola, & A. K. L. Yeo (Eds.), *Solution-focused practice in Asia* (pp. 62–6). Routledge.

Cepukiene, V., Pakrosnis, R., & Ulinskaite, G. (2018). Outcome of the solution-focused self-efficacy enhancement group intervention for adolescents in foster care setting. *Child and Youth Services Review, 88*, 81–7. https://doi.org/10.1016/j.childyouth.2018.03.004.

Copur, E. O., & Kubilay, G. (2022). The effect of solution-focused brief therapy approaches on adolescents' peer bullying skills: A quasi-experimental study. *Journal of Child and Adolescent Psychiatric Nursing, 35*(1), 45–51. https://10.1111/jcap/.12348.

Corcoran, J. (2008). A comparison group study of solution-focused therapy versus "treatment as usual" for behavior problems in children. *Journal of Social Service Research, 33*, 69–81. https://doi.org/10.1300/J079v33n01_07.

Daki, J., & Savage, R. (2010). Solution-focused brief therapy: Impacts on academic and emotional difficulties. *The Journal of Educational Research, 103*, 468–74. https://doi.org/10.1080/00220670903383127.

De Jong, P., & Berg, I. K. (2013). *Interviewing for solutions* (4th ed.). Brooks/Cole.

de Shazer, S., Dolan, Y., Korman, H., Trepper, T, McCollum, E., & Berg, I. K. (2007). *More than miracles: The state of the art of solution-focused brief therapy*. Taylor & Francis.

Franklin, C., Bolton, K. W., & Guz, S. (2019). Solution-focused brief family therapy. In B. H. Fiese, M. Celano, K. Deater-Deckard, E. N. Jouriles, & M. A. Whisman (Eds.), *APA handbook of contemporary family psychology: Family therapy and training, Vol. 3*. (pp. 139–53). American Psychological Association. https://doi.org/10.1037/0000101-009.

Gil, E. (2015). *Play in family therapy* (2nd ed.). The Guilford Press.

Gong, H., & Hsu, W. (2017). The effectiveness of solution-focused group therapy in ethnic Chinese school settings: A meta-analysis. *International Journal of Group Psychotherapy, 67*, 383–409. https://doi.org/10.1080/00207284.2016.1240588.

Handley, V., Jordan, S., Fife, S., & Turns, B. (2021). Using solution-focused brief therapy and animal-assisted therapy with sexual minorities: A pilot microanalysis study. *Journal of Systemic Therapies, 40*(4), 67–87. https://doi.org/10.1521/jsyt.2021.40.4.67.

Hartwig, E. K. (2017). Building solutions in youth: Evaluation of the human-animal resilience therapy intervention. *Journal of Creativity in Mental Health, 12*(4), 468–81. https://doi.org/10.1080/15401383.2017.1283281.

Hartwig, E. K. (2021). *Solution-focused play therapy: A strengths-based clinical approach to play therapy*. Routledge. https://doi.org/10.4324/9780429354984.

Hartwig, E. K., & Taylor, E. R. (2024). Solution-focused play therapy: The magic of strengths-based play. *Journal of Systemic Therapies, 42*(3), 22–42. https://doi.org/10.1521/jsyt.2023.42.3.22.

Hartwig, E. K., & Taylor, E. R. (2022). Small steps lead to big changes: Goal setting in schools using solution-focused play therapy. *International Journal of Play Therapy, 31*(3), 131–42. https://doi.org/110.1037/pla0000179.

Himmelberger, K., Ikonomopoulos, J., & Vela, J. C. (2022). Evaluating the impact of solution-focused brief therapy on hope and clinical symptoms with Latine clients. *The Professional Counselor, 12*(3), 198–216. https://doi.org/10.15241/kh.12.3.198.

Hogan, D., Hogan, D., Tuomola, J., & Yeo, A. (Eds.). (2017). *Solution-focused practice in Asia*. Routledge.

Hsu, K. S., Eads, R., Lee, M. Y., & Wen, Z. (2021). Solution-focused brief therapy for behavior problems in children and adolescents: A meta-analysis of treatment effectiveness and family involvement. *Children and Youth Services, 120*. https://doi.org/10.1016/j.childyouth.2020.105620.

Johnson, S. D., & Williams, S. L. (2015). Solution-focused strategies for effective sexual health communication among African American parents and their adolescents. *Health & Social Work, 40*(4), 267–74. https://doi.org/10.1093/hsw/hlv056.

Karababa, A. (2024). A meta-analysis of solution-focused brief therapy for school-related problems in adolescents. *Research on Social Work Practice, 34*(2), 169–81. https://doi.org/10.1177/10497315231170865.

Kim, J. S., Franklin, C., Zhang, Y., Liu, X., Qu, Y., & Chen, H. (2015). Solution-focused brief therapy in China: A meta-analysis. *Journal of Ethnic & Cultural Diversity in Social Work: Innovation in Theory, Research & Practice, 24*(3), 187–201. https://doi.org/10.1080/15313204.2014.991983.

Kim, J., Jordan, S. S., Franklin, C., & Froerer, A. (2019). Is solution-focused brief therapy evidence-based? An update 10 years later. *Families in Society: Journal of Contemporary Social Services, 100*(2), 127–38. https://doi.org/10.1177/1044389419841688.

Kvarme, L. G., Aabø, L. S., & Sæteren, B. (2013). "I feel I mean something to someone": Solution-focused brief therapy support groups for bullied schoolchildren. *Educational Psychology in Practice, 29*(4), 416–31. https://dx.doi.orga/10.1080/02667363.2013.859569.

Landreth, G. L. (2024). *Play therapy: The art of the relationship* (4th ed.). Routledge.

Liu, X., Zhang, Y. P., Franklin, C., Qu, Y., Chen, H., & Kim, J. S. (2015). The practice of solution-focused brief therapy in mainland China. *Health & Social Work, 40*(2), 84–90. https://doi.org/10.1093/hsw/hlv013.

MacDonald, A. (2017). SFBT evaluation list. *European Brief Therapy Association*. https://solutionsdoc.co.uk/sfbt-evaluation-list/.

Maldonado, M. D. (2018). *Integrating solution-focused brief therapy with child-centered play therapy to facilitate trauma resolution resulting from parental deportation in Latino children*. [Doctoral dissertation, Mississippi College]. ProQuest Information & Learning.

Meyer, D. D., & Cottone, R. R. (2013). Solution-focused therapy as a culturally acknowledging approach with American Indians. *Journal of Multicultural Counseling & Development, 41*(1), 47–55. https://doi.org/10.1002/j.2161-1912.2013.00026.x.

Moosa, A., Koorankot, J., & K., Nigesh, K. (2017). Solution focused art therapy among refugee children. *Indian Journal of Health and Well-Being, 8*(8), 811–16. www.iahrw.com/index.php/home/journal_detail/19#list.

Open Spaces, LLC. (2019). *Totika self-esteem game*. https://www.therapygames.net/.

Ouer, R. (2016). *Solution-focused brief therapy with the LGBT community: Creating futures through hope and resilience*. Routledge. https://doi.org/10.4324/9781315744360.

Reading Rockets. (2024). *LGBTQ books for kids*. https://www.readingrockets.org/books-and-authors/booklists/me-and-my-life/lgbtq-books-kids.

Reddy, S. M., Naseh, M., Panisch, L. S., Rafieifar, M., O'Gara, J. L., & Cervantez, C. (2022). Solution-focused brief therapy in Iran: A scoping review of the outcome literature. *Journal of Evidence-Based Social Work, 19*(4), 493–508. https://doi.org/10.1080/26408066.2022.2083923.

Schaefer, C. E., & Drewes, A. A. (2014). *The therapeutic powers of play: 20 core agents of change*. Wiley.

Schaefer, C. E., & Peabody, M. A. (2016, June). Glossary of play therapy terms. *Play Therapy, 11*(2), 20–4.

Schmit, E. L., Schmit, M. K., & Lenz, A. S. (2016). Meta-analysis of solution-focused brief therapy for treating symptoms of internalizing disorders. *Counseling Outcome Research and Evaluation, 7*(1), 21–39. https://doi.org/10.1177.2150137815623836.

Suitt, K. G., Franklin, C., & Kim, J. (2016). Solution-focused brief therapy with Latinos: A systematic review. *Journal of Ethnic & Cultural Diversity in Social Work: Innovation in Theory, Research & Practice, 25*(1), 50–67. https://doi.org/10.1080/15313204.2015.1131651.

Talicor. (2018). *Thumball™*. https://talicor.com/product-category/toys-slash-play-sets/thumball/.

Tehee, M., Killgore, R., Mack, S., Isaacs, D. S., & Ficklin, E. (2021). When justice does not work: A solution focused approach to violence against Native women in Indian country. *Wisconsin Journal of Law, Gender & Society, 36*(1), 33–58.

The New York Times. (2024, June 27). *15 LGBTQ books for kids and teens recommended by queer librarians, educators, and independent booksellers.* https://www.nytimes.com/wirecutter/reviews/15-lgbtq-books-for-kids-and-teens/.

Trevor Project. (2024). *Resource center.* https://www.thetrevorproject.org/resources/.

Watkins, A. M., & Kurtz, P. D. (2001). Using solution-focused intervention to address African American male overrepresentation in special education: A case study. *Children & Schools, 23*(4), 223–34.

Wells, K. B., & McCaig, M. (2016). The magic wand question and recovery-focused practice in child and adolescent mental health services. *Journal of Child & Adolescent Psychiatric Nursing, 29*(4), 164–70. https://doi.org/10.1111/jcap.12159.

Wilkinson, A., Rackers, H. S., & Harmon, T. M. (2023). Developmental implications of prenatal opioid exposure among school-aged children: A mixed methods and community-initiated analysis. *BMC Public Health, 23*(1), 1–9. https://doi.org/10.1186/s12889-023-16702-8.

Part III

Integrative Approaches and Applications

1

Prescriptive Play Therapy

Athena A. Drewes

Chapter Outline

Introduction

Prescriptive psychotherapy is an approach, and it is not new (Dimond, Havens & Jones, 1978; Goldstein & Stein, 1976; Kaduson, Schaefer & Cangelosi, 2020). Over the years, it has gained popularity in the field of psychotherapy and has now mushroomed in popularity and use within the field of play therapy (Drewes & Seymour, 2019). However, *Prescriptive*

Play Therapy is *not* actually a theory at all, although it is frequently listed under Theories of Play Therapy by the Association for Play Therapy, and should be considered instead a seminal "school of psychotherapy." Prescriptive play therapy is a *therapeutic approach* that incorporates a variety of theories and techniques in order to customize the play intervention to meet the specific and diverse needs of individual clients. Thus, Prescriptive Play Therapy, foremost, is a way of conceptualizing how to conduct treatment (Schaefer & Drewes, 2016).

The prescriptive play therapist "seeks to answer the age-old long-standing question: What treatment procedures administered by which therapist to which client with which specific problems are predicted to yield the best outcome" (Schaefer, 2011, p. 365). The client × therapist × treatment interaction view of effective psychotherapy is at the heart of the prescriptive approach. The task of the prescriptive therapist is to co-develop with the client a set of achievable goals, a coherent problem formulation (an explanation based on a thorough assessment of why the presenting problem exists or what is causing it), and a treatment plan tailored to the individual client's specific problem and situation. The focus is to resolve the specific problem(s) that brought the client into therapy, not to enhance the client's general psychological well-being or personal development (Schaefer & Drewes, 2016).

Underlying Philosophy

Basic Tenets

There are six basic tenets or beliefs that are the cornerstone of prescriptive play therapy.

Tenet 1: Individualized Treatment

Most importantly, the central aim of prescriptive play therapy is to *tailor* it and make it an individualized intervention that addresses the specific needs of the client. The answer to Gordon Paul's (1967, p. 11) question "*What* treatment, by *whom*, is most effective for *this* individual with that *specific* problem, under which set of circumstances, and how does it come about?" must always be at the forefront. Treatment is not a "one size fits all" approach applicable to most or all types of client problems, and there is no research or evidence showing that there is just one theoretical school or treatment approach that has proven strong enough to produce optimal change across the many different and complex psychological disorders to date. Because each person comes in with their history, causation of the problem, strengths, weaknesses, along with familial, developmental, environmental, cultural, and diversity factors, the play therapist must tailor the intervention not just to the disorder or symptoms but also to the personal characteristics and situation of the client (Norcross & Wampold, 2011; Schaefer & Drewes, 2016). What works for one client in one situation may not, and usually will not, work for another client without consideration of the above factors.

Tenet 2: Differential Therapeutics

Differential therapeutics has as its core premise that some play interventions are more effective than others for certain disorders and rejects the view that all major forms of psychotherapy are equally effective for specific disorders (Schaefer, 2011). Play therapists must assess which play interventions are more effective than others for certain disorders and recognize that a client who does poorly with one type of play therapy may do well with another. Meta-analytic studies (Shrinivasa, Bukhari, G., & Hamza, 2018; Stevens, Hyman & Allen, 2000; Cuijpers et al., 2023; Peris et al., 2021) have shown that specific interventions work better for specific disorders or syndromes so that the strength of specific treatment effects is seen, with mean effect sizes of specific factors consistently surpassing those of common factors.

Tenet 3: Transtheoretical Approach

Being prescriptive requires a transtheoretical or eclectic way of thinking and working. It requires selecting from different theories' therapies and techniques and formulating a therapeutic intervention that is considered best for a particular client. According to John Norcross (2005) "two or more therapies are integrated in the hope that the result will be better than the constituent therapies alone . . . [the] emphasis is on integrating the underlying theories of psychotherapy along with the integration of therapy techniques from each (p. 8)." Consequently, it requires a more flexible way of thinking and treating clients. It is a needs-based and developmental approach in its conceptualization, with consideration of the child's personality and developmental stage (Gil & Shaw, 2009).

A three-fold criterion of empirical evidence, clinical experience, and the desires of the client drives the selection of different theories and techniques for the best therapeutic change agents or healing powers of play for a particular client (Norcross, 1987; Schaefer & Drewes, 2014). Selection is made, of what is most valid or useful, from a wide therapeutic spectrum, taking on a flexible and pluralistic approach. Thus, the more "tools in your toolbox," coupled with the knowledge about how to differentially apply them, the more effective you will be across the large variety of presenting problems and symptoms one encounters in play therapy clinical practice (Schaefer, 2011).

The prescriptive play therapist needs to utilize "synthetic eclecticism" (Norcross, 1987), whereby there is an intentional and thought-out combining of various theories into one coordinated treatment intervention. Not an atheoretical treatment approach in which the clinician throws together various techniques learned or applies a treatment approach from various schools of thought in a manner that ignores the theory underlying them. Play therapists are warned against using techniques or treatment approaches (taking a little from here and a little from there, learned at conferences or in workshops) and applying them in a haphazard way, which will be ineffective at best and may, in fact, be harmful to some clients (Norcross, 1987; Barlow, 2010).

Learning one theory well, as your original lens and way of thinking and formulating cases, having supervision and clinical experience, and then learning a second theoretical or treatment approach and learning how to blend them within or across therapy sessions, through supervision, clinical experience, reading research, and attending conferences, will lead to a far better and more secure sense of how to work more effectively.

Most clinicians eventually learn that we cannot function effectively without moving outside of the theoretical model which we had been originally trained, recognizing the strength of another orientation may, at times, synergistically complement, and exponentially improve, the limitations of our own approach (Schaefer, 2011).

Tenet 4: Integrative Psychotherapy

Can you just be prescriptive or do you need to also be integrative? Well, you can be both, but one does often lead to the other. Since you are not confined to one single-school theory or approach, you do wind up combining different theories and techniques to strengthen an intervention and broaden the scope of your practice. The play therapist utilizes elements from a range of theories and/or techniques. The aim is to establish an intervention tailored to a particular client's situation and characteristics (Kaduson, Schaefer & Cangelosi, 2020). Prescriptive play therapy is flexible and is a multifaceted approach allowing the therapist to select the method that has proven most effective in resolving a client's problems (Kaduson, Schaefer & Cangelosi, 2020). Goldfried (2001, p. 229) stated, "most of us as therapists eventually learn that we cannot function effectively without moving outside of the theoretical model which we had originally been trained, recognizing that the strength of another orientation may at times synergistically complement the limitations of our own approach."

The term *Integrative Psychotherapy* is used to describe any multimodal approach that combines *two or* more theories (Schaefer & Drewes, 2016; Drewes & Seymour, 2019). Thus, individual, group and family play therapy strategies may be integrated to treat a particular case, or non-directive, psychodynamic, and humanistic play theories may be combined within treatment with more directive, cognitive-behavioral, or Adlerian approaches.

An integrated, multicomponent intervention reflects the complex and multidimensional nature of most disorders, which arise from the fact that they are caused by an interaction and synergistic (multiplying) effect of biological, psychological, social, cultural, and environmental factors. Consequently, given this multidetermined underpinning, an integrated, multifaceted approach becomes crucial in order to be effective.

As an example, children with ADHD—attention deficit/hyperactivity disorder—may require a multidimensional treatment approach utilizing psychotropic medication, parent management training, social skills development and playgroups, and individual therapy to work on executive functioning skill building. And ADHD may also be a comorbid psychological disorder that may be linked with trauma and may need additional integrative components as well.

The field of play therapy has seen a growing movement toward integration (Drewes, Bratton & Schaefer, 2011; Drewes & Seymour, 2019). Play therapists are becoming "assimilative integrative" (Norcross, 2005), assimilating other theories and blending theory and techniques into their work. Theoretical integration cannot be hurried, as it requires in-depth knowledge of each theory, taking classes or reading research, training, supervision, and practical experience in several theoretical orientations (Schaefer & Drewes, 2016).

However, there may be times when the therapist will implement a single theory (such as humanistic, nondirective approaches) which would be most effective prescriptively for a child's particular disorder (Kaduson, Cangelosi, & Schaefer, 2020).

Tenet 5: Prescriptive Matching

Because differential rates of improvement are found among different treatment procedures, prescriptive play therapists seek to "match" the most effective play intervention to a specific disorder (Norcross, 1991; Schaefer & Drewes, 2016; Shrinivasa, Bukhari, G., & Hamza, 2018). Typically, a theory of psychotherapy is matched rather than a higher level of direct matching of a change agent to the cause of the disorder. For example, in formulating the treatment plan, the prescriptive play therapist selects a therapeutic power of play change agent designed to reduce or eliminate the *cause* of the problem. By treating not only the symptoms but also the underlying cause(s), this approach will help assure that the problem is less likely to reoccur in the future (Kaduson, Schaefer & Cangelosi, 2020). For example, Theraplay (Munns, 2009), an attachment-oriented play intervention, would be a logical match for a child presenting with an attachment disorder. Similarly, abreaction/reenactment play therapy (Prendiville, 2014) is a trauma-focused intervention intended for children who have experienced recent trauma or a stressor. And, cognitive behavioral play therapy would then focus on changing the dysfunctional thoughts triggering anxiety and depression in the child.

In evidence-informed matching (Bohart, 2005; Shrinivasa, Bukhari, G., & Hamza, 2018), an intervention is tailored to a client by considering three main factors: (1) empirically supported treatment for a specific disorder, (2) client needs and preferences, and (3) therapist variables that include clinical judgment and practical experience (working within one's level of competence and scope of practice). Evidence-based practice is, therefore, a combination of these three factors and is not just about applying the best research evidence for treating client disorders (Schaefer & Drewes, 2016). Client-therapist matching differs from the above in that it involves matching the personal qualities of the client to those of the therapist, such as similar personalities, values, backgrounds, cultural and/or racial backgrounds, gender identities, etc.

Ethically, if the therapist does not feel competent or comfortable in implementing the intervention that is best suited for treating a client's problem, it is imperative that the therapist recommends a referral to qualified professionals who could provide the necessary treatment. Play therapists are bound by the ethics of their licensing profession and must adhere to not working outside their scope of practice—which includes competence, training, experience, and personal abilities.

Tenet 6: Comprehensive Assessment

Play therapy practitioners are under time and financial constraints to get treatment started and progressing. Comprehensive assessments cut into the ability to begin the initial treatment plan because they can be time consuming (and should ideally take up to three sessions to obtain all the necessary facets of assessing the child and family), be hampered by agency protocols and practices, and parental eagerness to get the problem resolved quickly. But a comprehensive assessment is critical to obtaining an in-depth understanding of the child, the family, and the origins of the child's presenting difficulties. It enables the clinician to pinpoint the underlying cause of the disorder so that the therapist can then select a therapeutic power of play most likely to repair this causal factor (Kaduson, Schaefer & Cangelosi, 2020). Thus, the therapist would customize the treatment to the individual needs, strengths, and problems of the client. Assessment is cost-effective overall because it reduces the duration of treatment by enabling the therapist to focus on the likely cause of the problem and have the best treatment option.

Multiple sources and methods of assessment (developmental history, objective measures: rating scales, behavioral checklists, interviews, projective techniques, strengths and weaknesses inventories, as well as subjective measures: including drawings, play observations, and family interactions) must be used to gather data from multiple perspectives and opportunities.

The assessment needs to consider:

The Problem

- Nature of the problem
- History of previous therapy
- Parents' treatment preferences/expectations
- Child and family's readiness and motivation to change
- Empirically based guidelines for treating the presenting problem

The Client

- Developmental history (include questions about in utero drug/alcohol exposure, birth history, parental stressors, and traumas during and after pregnancy, etc.)
- Family history (include questions about drug/alcohol use past and present, mental illness history, separations, deaths, domestic violence, etc.)
- Client strengths

The goal of assessment is not just to determine a diagnosis, but to also remember that it is a holistic view of the personal variables. And, that we are treating the whole person, including the system surrounding the client who has a disorder, and not specifically just a disorder.

Personality Theory

Prescriptive Play Therapy is "a term used for approaches that attempt to tailor the application of psychological interventions to individual clients" (Schaefer, 2011, p. 365). It does not explain certain aspects of human thoughts, behaviors, emotions, and predictability about future behavioral events, nor does it address personality factors, the nature and origin of psychopathology, and so on, in a formally testable and generalizable way, which a theory would do. Therefore, there is no separate personality theory. However, the theories that serve as the clinician's lens and on which the interventions are based, such as humanistic, cognitive-behavioral, or psychoanalytic, do have their own personality theories that clinicians would use in thinking about their cases.

Model of Psychopathology

Causal therapy—therapy designed to eliminate the cause of the problem, would be the highest form of prescriptive matching. But it is not always possible to identify the pathological process underlying the problem, or the precipitating cause may no longer be occurring. In such cases, the prescriptive play therapist must then must turn to other bases for matching treatment to the client, such as evidence-informed matching and client-therapist matching.

A comprehensive assessment aids the play therapist in being able to create an effective treatment plan. One of the goals of a comprehensive assessment prior to treatment selection is to pinpoint the underlying cause of the disorder so that the therapist can then select a change agent (therapeutic power of play) (Schaefer & Drewes, 2014) that is most likely to remedy the cause or causal factor.

Conceptualizing Goals of Treatment

Before therapy begins, using information gathered, an individualized case formulation is created. The case formulation is descriptive and explanatory, summarizing the client's most important strengths, issues, and problems and the probable cause(s) or contributory factors. It is shared with the parents/caregivers and child/teen, and, as needed with collateral parties such as teachers, school counselors, and significant family members or religious leaders. Within the case formulation, the treatment goals and strategies, predicted obstacles to the treatment, and means of evaluating progress are delineated (Kaduson, Schaefer & Cangelosi, 2020). The object of the thorough assessment, along with the case formulation, is the creation of a clear and specific individualized intervention geared toward specific presenting problem(s) and the unique characteristics of the client. Thus, a clearly delineated treatment plan becomes the roadmap to termination.

Treatment plans need to be: SMART: *simple*: what do I want to accomplish; *measurable:* how will I know when it is accomplished; *achievable:* how can the goal be accomplished; *relevant*: does this seem worthwhile; and *time-bound:* when can I accomplish this goal. In this way, the client and therapist can have reasonable expectations of how long therapy may take, points along the way where the goals are reviewed and modified or crossed off as accomplished, and a view of what a successful outcome will look like. Treatment plans should be collaborative with input from the parents/caregivers and child/teen, so there is "buy in" to the treatment process. There are many useful play-based techniques that you can use to help make the treatment planning more playful and invitational (Drewes & Cavett, 2012).

Then the individualized, tailored intervention is formulated as an outgrowth of the comprehensive assessment and case formulation in order to reduce symptoms and presenting problems. And as treatment proceeds, the prescriptive play therapist collects periodic assessment data to evaluate treatment progress and revise the intervention as needed.

Role of the Therapist

To be a prescriptive play therapist, you must become familiar with the major theories of play and play therapy. Play therapists should develop a clear understanding of play and the way it has been integrated into play therapy, as well as the way play behavior changes with development. Play therapists need to critically assess the many play materials and techniques now available, and whether these materials and techniques are culturally and gender-appropriate and sensitive for specific client populations.

The role of the play therapist in the prescriptive approach varies depending on the particular play approach that is tailored to the case. For example, the therapist would be directive and structured when implementing a behavioral strategy but nondirective when following a child-centered orientation. The approach chosen will also depend on the degree of support, insight, or instruction available (Schaefer & Drewes, 2016).

Thus, the prescriptive play therapist is required to know and be competent in more than one theory and technique of play therapy. First, you must become competent in one theory, which becomes your lens for viewing the case, understanding symptom causation, and its treatment approach. Supervision, clinical experience, training, and knowledge help to secure a solid baseline and way of working. It can be a non-directive or directive theory and approach that you start with. Then learn another theory and approach, preferably building your "arsenal" with one non-directive and one directive theory and approach, as most complex trauma and treatment cases will require the use of one or the other or both together at some point in treatment. For example, learning a humanistic or child-led theory and approach is always an excellent way to start as it offers a solid foundation in order to be able to sit in silence when a child or teen chooses not to talk and to understand and decipher the use of metaphor and fantasy in the play. Then add to it something that is directive, such as cognitive-behavioral play therapy or Adlerian play therapy, which are much more therapist-led and directive. But the play therapist may also need to add on an Attachment theory and approach (such as Theraplay or Filial Therapy) to work with parents who will need to be partners in the treatment process. Thus, the prescriptive play therapy approach is best suited to therapists who are open, *flexible*, and pragmatic, as well as skillful in adapting a particular treatment protocol to their own personal style and the needs of the client (Schaefer & Drewes, 2016).

Play therapists need to also select treatment approaches that are evidence-based and empirically based. Treatment selection must be based on (1) empirically supported and/or evidence-based treatments for the disorder, (2) client needs and preferences, and (3) therapist variables. Therapist variables include therapist expertise, comfort level, and clinical judgment (Kaduson, Schaefer & Cangelosi, 2020). Consequently, the onus is on the clinician to keep up to date on latest research and treatment trends by reading journal articles and attending training workshops and conferences in order to offer the most effective treatment. Supervision and consultation are critical components that are lifelong when working as a clinician, but especially as a prescriptive and integrative play therapist to ensure you are not working outside the scope of your license and missing crucial aspects of transference and treatment effectiveness.

Roles of Caregivers and Collaterals

Caregivers and collaterals are critical components to creating a comprehensive treatment plan and assessing the progress of the treatment method(s) being used. In conducting an initial intake and assessment, multiple informants, such as parents, teachers, the child, and community and religious supports, are necessary in order to obtain a complete picture of the child's and family's strengths and needs. Ongoing contact about the child's functioning in multiple settings is needed, as well as periodic treatment plan reviews for modifying the treatment plan.

As treatment progresses, caregivers and collaterals become critical informants in monitoring change in the client's presenting problem(s) and helping the therapist assess how the treatment is working and the client's progress or lack thereof. This feedback is crucial in deciding whether to maintain or adjust the treatment plan, which helps in the prevention of premature termination and will enhance the likelihood of treatment success (Kaduson, Schaefer & Cangelosi, 2020). Research shows that weekly monitoring of symptom change throughout all phases of treatment is most effective (Schaefer & Gilbert, 2015).

Individual meetings before or after the session, school observations and the use of standardized formal and informal measures may need to be conducted at various points, which aid in determining when termination should be planned or whether a referral to another clinician may be necessary. This continuous monitoring of symptoms helps ensure tailored treatment and allows for changes and modifications to the treatment plan where there may have been negligible or negative results (Kaduson, Schaefer & Cangelosi, 2020).

Considerations for Practice

- Be flexible.
- Learn one theory first, and learn it well, in-depth, through training, supervision, experience, reading up on research, and attending workshops and conferences. Have it as your solid base and lens for formulating your case plan and treatment plans.
- Learn a second theory that is different and compatible, such as first being nondirective and child-led, while the second is directive and more therapist-led. Become immersed

in the theory and its application, and obtain supervision for using it within and across sessions for specific treatment disorders.

- Remember, learning is lifelong, and supervision/consultation (be it paid supervision or peer supervision) should be as well, especially as you learn how to be prescriptive and integrative.
- Carefully think about matching your theoretical and treatment approaches. Do not throw things together without rationale and solid theory; understand the benefits and how to apply the therapeutic powers of play.
- Resist utilizing unfounded treatment approaches that may seem alluring, innovative, and offer credentials but do not have a solid theoretical basis or may have minimal empirical research showing effectiveness.

Research/Empirical Support

While there is research existing using an integrative play therapy approach for the treatment of various disorders in children, there is no empirical research on just using a prescriptive approach. However, there is research on trying to identify the core agent of change in psychotherapy for specific disorders (Norcross & Wampold, 2011; Shrinivasa, Bukhar, G., & Hamza, 2018). Since prescriptive play therapy is not a theory, in and of itself, and has no underlying view regarding personality disorders, research cannot really be conducted. However, researchers might consider, through the lens of prescriptive play therapy, how they will integrate treatment approaches or theoretical approaches to base their research.

Therapeutic Powers of Play and Prescriptive Play Therapy

The healing powers of play have been written about (Schaefer & Drewes, 2014) and studied. Schaefer (Schaefer & Drewes, 2014) considered the therapeutic powers of play the heart and soul of play therapy. These are the basic mechanisms, essential ingredients in play, of therapeutic change; that is, healing forces that produce therapeutic change. They are not tied to any specific theory or model (Beutler & Harwood, 2000; Schaefer & Drewes, 2014; Kaduson, Schaefer & Cangelosi, 2020), but rather are descriptions of observed relationships. They are more general than techniques, and they are more specific than theories, yet are not theories. Instead, they try to answer the question of what are the therapeutic forces that produce the desired change in a client's behavior (Schaefer & Drewes, 2014). Once the active ingredients in a play intervention have been identified, the inert factors can be eliminated, and a more time-efficient and cost-effective intervention can be developed.

Therefore, the prescriptive play therapist looks not only to outcome research but also to the process or *component analysis* research to identify the specific therapeutic change mechanisms that underlie effective outcomes (Norcross & Wampold, 2011; Schaefer & Drewes, 2014). Plus, we should be continually searching for the mediator and moderator variables that can help us understand the relationships between a specific play treatment and outcome. The most well-known powers of play are its *communication powers* (children express themselves non-verbally and through the metaphor of play better than with words), its *teaching power* (children learn and remember better when instruction is made fun and enjoyable), its *ego-boosting powers* (children gain a sense of power, control, and competency through play), and its *self-actualization power* (children, teens, and adults have the freedom to be completely themselves in play).

Prescriptive play therapists are continually seeking to acquire a deeper understanding of all the therapeutic powers of play and try to determine the best application of these change mechanisms for specific disorders. Based on the understanding of the therapeutic powers of play, a prescriptive matching of these remedies/interventions and approaches to the causes or determinants of a disorder occurs. For example, directive teaching would be indicated for a child who has difficulty making friends due to a lack of social skills or anger control skills. The therapist would use a directive approach utilizing puppets, bibliotherapy, and role modeling that might fall under Cognitive Behavioral Play Therapy. Or stress inoculation might be matched up for a child experiencing medical-related fear or anxiety about an upcoming surgery. The play therapist again might utilize a more directive, Cognitive Behavioral Play Therapy theoretical approach, with desensitization and gradual exposure along with the use of puppets and bibliotherapy therapeutic interventions.

Further, in working with a child having an insecure attachment, an attachment-oriented and trained play therapist would be the best clinician to work with this child. A mismatch of therapist or change agents can, on the other hand, result in the worsening of symptoms or a significant lack of improvement in the treatment process (Kearney & Silverman, 1999; Schaefer & Drewes, 2014). By incorporating most or all of these curative powers of play into their repertoire, prescriptive play therapists are able to offer specific treatment for a wide range of psychological disorders.

Case Study through the Lens of the Therapeutic Powers of Play

Therapeutic powers of play considered

The case study of Herman (see Appendix for case study of Herman being referenced) will utilize child-led psychodynamic play therapy and cognitive-behavioral play therapy, as well as systems theory in working with collaterals (school, parents/home). All the areas of the therapeutic powers of play will be utilized: *Facilitates Communication*: self-expression/understanding, conscious thoughts and feelings, access to the unconscious, direct teaching, and indirect teaching. Also, *Foster Emotional Wellness* through abreaction, catharsis, positive emotions, and stress management. The nondirective, child-led portion is chosen specifically for *Enhancing Social Relationships* through the need to create a therapeutic relationship, attachment (often the therapist becomes a secondary attachment figure), social competence, and empathy (both from the therapist and enhancing the skill in the client); and finally *Increases Personal Strengths* through more directive means of creative problem-solving, increasing resiliency, helping to accelerate psychological development (through removal of past traumatic issues that result in developmental and emotional arrest), self-regulation, and improved self-esteem (Schaefer & Drewes, 2014).

The case study will more specifically delineate the presenting problems, the treatment approach and techniques, and the progression toward healing.

Cultural, Diversity, Inclusion Considerations

Herman comes from a mixed heritage, but it is unclear how he identifies himself or which ethnicity he sees himself as. It would be important to explore with Herman his ethnic background and whether he has a particular preference or identity with any of them. At that point, if he does select a particular ethnicity, it would be important for his foster parents to be able to celebrate and honor that heritage through food, holidays, cultural events, and contact with children and families of the same background. Further, it is noted that Herman has expressed not liking to be a boy, using nail polish and eyeliner and dressing in non-gender-specific ways. It would be important to be affirming of his emerging sexual identity, any preference in the use of personal pronouns, and use of play materials. Discussion will be important in working with the foster parents to spend time allowing for discussion regarding their personal views of Herman's emerging sexual identity. The therapist would want to help them in their attempts to form a closer relationship and level of trust and offer psychoeducation around any areas regarding helping Herman with his emerging sexual identity.

Case Formulation

Herman has experienced complex trauma starting from in utero. His mother's substance misuse while he was conceived and in utero significantly impacted his neurological development, compounded by the mother's physical trauma of falling down stairs and relational violence. His mother's lack of resources, financial and emotional, while carrying Herman added to her stress level, resulting in the significant impact of cortisol on the developing fetus. Upon birth, Herman suffered from the trauma of withdrawal as well as physical withdrawal from his mother, and lack of physical contact in the NICU further exacerbated poor neurological and emotional connections. He then again experienced separation and abandonment while placed with his maternal grandmother. Although his first three years were in one household, his grandmother and her paramour further added to his trauma through experiencing domestic violence and an unstable, chaotic household. Herman had little support in being able to regulate his physiological and emotional states, and his lack of physical contact further negatively impacted his ability to form a trusting relationship and feel nurtured. After removal from his grandmother, the systems surrounding him failed him as well. He was placed twice in different foster homes due to his behaviors, and then compounding his already heavy load of trauma (and ACEs), he experienced repeated sexual abuse at age six that went undetected for a long period of time. Having intern therapists rotating out and no one stable secondary attachment figure further exacerbated Herman's ability to form interpersonal attachments. All of these ruptures in relationships caused by moves, lack of interpersonal connection, and personal violation have further exacerbated Herman's lack of trust of others and have resulted in poorly regulated affect, behavior, and neurology. Now, as a pre-teen, Herman is beginning to feel emerging personal and sexual identity issues as his physiology and hormonal changes occur, adding yet another layer of stress onto a poorly developed core structure.

At first glance, it is a strength that Herman is able to connect to his foster father, seeing him as a positive role model whom he admires. He has skilled foster parents who are attentive to his needs and knowledgeable in how to work with complex trauma and special needs. He sees them as a support and is slowly beginning to develop a relationship, testing out his trust in them.

Areas to think about include first having a stable, long-term therapist committed to working with Herman, his foster parents, and the surrounding system. Next, looking at how Herman's neurology is impacting his development. A thorough multi-pronged assessment, through formal (e.g., Child Behavior Checklist, Child and Adolescent Needs and Strengths, trauma assessments; sensory integration evaluation) and informal assessments (e.g., play observation, classroom observation, foster parents and child play observation) is necessary. In addition, a neurosequential assessment utilizing Perry's (2005) neurosequential model of therapeutics would aid in identifying areas of strength and underdevelopment. Sensory integration issues also need to be assessed, given Herman's risk-taking behaviors, which may be due to a need for overstimulation. Affect regulation would need to be a beginning point in helping to soothe the amygdala through a combination of relaxation techniques and ways to safely discharge anxiety and energy in a safe, trusting setting, before any play therapy could begin. Work with the foster parents, through consultation, psychoeducation about neonatal abstinence syndrome (NAS) and subsequent behaviors, dyadic sessions with Herman, and even the use of filial therapy will help to bolster limit setting, create positive time together, and further attachment. Looking systemically beyond the home, the school and teachers would also need to receive psychoeducation about NAS and its impact academically and behaviorally in children, how it changes with development, as well as a better understanding of complex trauma and its impact academically, behaviorally, and emotionally. His Individual Education Plan (IEP) will need to be reviewed in light of testing results to see if he is in the right-sized classroom and receiving all the support services he is eligible for. Teachers would also be involved in helping to offer random positive reinforcement (catch Herman while he is being "good") to increase on-task behaviors, utilize cognitive-behavioral techniques, and appropriate limit setting (use of ACT), and to work together with the therapist, family, and child on a collaborative treatment plan. Psychiatric input would help to assess for proper medication matching after a DNA profile is obtained. The treatment plan would be reviewed every four to six months to assess progress and prescriptively change any approaches.

Treatment would need to be a prescriptively delineated approach building first from addressing affect regulation and safety in the therapy room, to a non-directive, child-led approach in individual and dyadic therapy, with foster parent(s), to bringing directive approaches through psychoeducation, attachment, and cognitive-behavioral play therapy to address behaviors, neurological, sensory, and trauma issues, as well as issues of trust and attachment, and negative worldviews. Simultaneously, treatment would need to work on collaborative treatment planning to include the school, teachers, foster parents, and any outside collateral sources, and psychiatric input for medication management.

Case Application

After obtaining the necessary signed consents for assessment and counseling from social services, the play therapist spent various times throughout the school week sitting in Herman's classroom. The purpose of the observations was to make a functional behavioral analysis, seeing at what times trouble spots occurred, as well as learning more about the classroom environment and teaching approach, and to observe strengths. Herman was referred for a full neuropsychological and academic evaluation to further assess his learning difficulties. The play therapist conducted a neurosequential analysis of Herman's areas of strength and weaknesses, a sensory integration evaluation, as well as other formal and informal assessments. Results from his NAS evaluation and psychiatric medication management were obtained.

Herman's opioid exposure in utero significantly impaired neural networks, affect regulation, and self-soothing, compounded by traumatic exposure to domestic violence, maternal opioid addiction, and multiple attachment breaks with removal from the grandmother's home and placement in three different foster homes. Herman needed a multidisciplinary treatment approach that also included a pediatric consultation for documentation of neonatal abstinence syndrome (NAS), its impact on his development, and possible medication considerations. The treatment environment included a safe space and a secondary attachment figure, willing to work long term, to begin affect regulation, social reconnection, and development of problem-solving skills. A collaborative and play-based treatment plan was formulated with Herman, along with his teacher, foster parents, and other members of the multidisciplinary team. Medication management was to include the use of Guanfacine, to address attention and impulsivity, and continued use of Risperidone, which should also help deal with affect regulation and attention and concentration.

Herman initially had a period of child-led sessions that enabled him to build trust and a sense of safety while slowly reducing his dysregulation (*Enhances Social Relationships:* therapeutic relationship; attachment; *Fosters Emotional Wellness:* stress management; *Increases Personal Strengths:* Self-regulation). In the sessions, he could release his energy in a safe, non-threatening way through throwing balls, games of Nerf basketball, use of a jump rope, rocking chair, and stomping his feet (*Fosters Emotional Wellness:* catharsis, abreaction, positive emotions; *Increases Personal Strengths:* self-regulation). Then treatment prescriptively moved into an integrative approach, with part of the session focusing on skill building for the first fifteen minutes (*Facilitates Communication:* direct teaching, indirect teaching) and trauma-focused cognitive-behavioral components (feelings identification and expression, identifying the relationship between thoughts, feelings, and behaviors, affect regulation). (*Facilitates Communication:* self-expression, direct teaching, indirect teaching; *Increases Personal Strengths:* creative problem solving, self-regulation). Sensory integration techniques and neurosequential approaches for affect regulation and calming the amygdala were utilized (such as jumping rope, jumping safely off a table, stomping feet), and then switching to child-led, nondirective psychodynamic play therapy, enabling Herman to express himself autonomously for twenty to thirty minutes (*Facilitates Communication:* access to the unconscious, self-expression; *Fosters Emotional Wellness:* catharsis, abreaction, positive emotions, stress management). Finally, a five-minute closing with deep breathing and mindfulness exercises to assist in transitioning from the session and techniques he could teach his foster parents and utilize at home and in school (*Facilitates Communication*: direct teaching; *Increases Personal Strengths*: self-regulation; self-esteem, resiliency, creative problem solving).

The Gingerbread Person Feelings Map (Drewes, 2001) template was brought out for Herman to add some feelings and select the colors he wanted to shade in the body where he felt them. This "ice breaker" assessed the extent of his "feelings" vocabulary and level of awareness of any physical reactions he felt when angry or upset (*Facilitates Communication*: direct teaching).

During the child-led portion of the session (about twenty minutes), Herman chose to explore the sand tray, touching the sand, burying his hand and arm in it, and occasionally picking several miniatures to play with and bury in the sand (*Facilitates Communication*: self-expression, access to the unconscious; *Fosters Emotional Wellness*: stress management, positive emotions).

Working together to clean up the room and having Herman learn "hills and valleys" deep breathing, tracing his fingers and breathing in, pausing, and out as he went up and down the five fingers on his hand occurred during the last few minutes of the session (*Facilitates Communication:* direct teaching; *Increases Personal Strengths*: self-regulation).

Over the next three sessions, Herman slowly began to build a therapeutic relationship with this play therapist, trusting her authentic and transparent responses and beginning to invite her into his play, but he also tentatively tested limits to see what would happen. The balance of empathy, unconditional positive regard, and limit setting by the therapist helped Herman learn to make choices and see the natural consequences of his actions (*Enhances Social Relationships*: therapeutic relationship, attachment, social competence, empathy; *Increases Personal Strengths*: resiliency, moral development, self-esteem). The use of pre-frontal cognitive behavioral techniques to address his ADHD and lack of concentration aided in his focus and problem-solving skill development (*Facilitates Communication*: direct teaching; *Increases Personal Strengths*: creative problem solving, self-regulation). He slowly began to develop self-control. Throughout the remainder of therapy, the therapist used various trauma-informed Cognitive Behavioral Play Therapy and Attachment-based, play-based, techniques that dealt with feelings identification and expression, anger management, problem solving, and role-playing responses, using puppets, expressive arts, and sand tray (*Facilitates Communication*: self-expression, direct teaching; *Fosters Emotional Wellness:* stress management, catharsis; *Increases Personal Strengths*: creative problem solving, moral development, self-regulation). In addition, Herman practiced, in school and at home when upset, the various calming techniques learned and practiced at the end of the session whenever he began to feel upset. Herman learned ways to self-talk, telling himself that he was not stupid, that he could pass the test or do the assignment, and that there were other things he was good at to help calm him down and get through the task, which added to feelings of self-competence and resilience. He often used his self-talk while utilizing deep breathing exercises and techniques, creating various mantras (e.g., I can do it; I am smart and capable) (*Facilitates Communication:* direct teaching; *Fosters Emotional Wellness*: stress management; *Increases Personal Strengths*: creative problem solving, resiliency, self-regulation, self-esteem).

Herman's non-directive play became more enlivened with fierce battles and catastrophes, loss and abandonment themes, in the sand tray as well as enacted with the puppets in which he was always the victor over his opponents (*Facilitates Communication*: self-expression, access to the unconscious; *Fosters Emotional Wellness*: catharsis, abreaction, positive emotions). He often put this therapist into the position of feeling frustrated, helpless, and hopeless, as well as angry, because no matter what was tried, Herman would turn the situation to his advantage to win. This therapist began to have insight into the play situation and the daily frustration, anger, and underlying rage that occurred as a parallel process. This resulted in empathic reflective statements by the therapist that validated Herman's experiences and innermost feelings and began to impact and transform Herman's anger, feelings of loss, and abandonment. By the mid-therapy point (twelve sessions), there was a significant lessening of negative behaviors in the classroom and in the foster home (*Enhances Social Relationships:* therapeutic relationship, attachment, empathy).

This play therapist also worked systemically with the school to make sure that Herman's IEP was being followed and that he had the accommodations of extra time, being able to go to a quiet space when distressed, a support person during high-stress times, like transitions and testing, and counseling. The classroom teacher was supported and helped throughout the school year to become aware of sensory integration needs and how to create a more positive classroom environment. The play therapist shared observations from the behavioral analysis, sensory integration assessment, neurosequential assessment, and what the communicative purpose of Herman's misbehavior was. Insights into the possible chain of events and triggers that led to the escalation of his behavior, along with the times when he was enjoying what he was learning, helped the teacher modify her reactions to Herman's behaviors. The teacher received strategies to increase the rate of teacher-delivered praise and positive recognition for constructive classroom behavior. She was given strategies for "catching Herman being good," and encouraged random specific positive verbal reinforcement for the behaviors she wanted to see more of and the ignoring of the negative behaviors she wanted to see decreased.

The teacher helped to create a quiet space for Herman and the other students who may need it, where he could sit in a comfortable corner, on a bean bag, and put on headphones with soft music playing for a short break whenever he felt stressed. He could look at a book for a limited time, practice using some mindfulness or deep breathing exercises, and then return to his seat in a calm and quiet manner. Soon his teacher and principal began to see the positive results.

Assessment and psychological testing results were shared with the teacher to create a more individualized learning approach for Herman. Testing showed that he was of average intelligence, with difficulties with auditorily presented material, and a preference for visually based learning. As a result, she started to break down directions into shorter components, giving them one at a time, rather than overloading him with multiple directions at once. She used posters and pictures in the classroom that helped to support her verbal teaching. She also set up a system with Herman that when she asked a question that she knew he could answer, she would approach his desk slowly, giving him time to think of an answer, and then she would call on him. When she knew he would not know the answer, or it was too hard, she would not go near his desk, helping to lessen his anxiety about not having the right answer and being embarrassed. This was a secret "code" between them, which the other children were unaware. Over time, Herman began to feel more confident, spontaneously raising his hand to answer questions, and peers stopped teasing him about not knowing his work (*Increases Personal Strengths*: creative problem solving, resiliency, self-esteem).

Concomitantly, the play therapist worked with both foster parents, meeting at the end of the session and monthly individual parent sessions and phone calls. Information was shared about what was being done in the sessions (*Facilitates Communication*: direct teaching). They learned some of the calming deep breathing strategies to utilize at home with Herman to help reinforce through practice and were encouraged to have positive communication by reinforcing the behaviors they wanted rather than negatively and punitively responding to unwanted behaviors. Each foster parent chose a specific evening as their special time with Herman (as well as with each of the other foster children) to increase attachment and positive interactions. As time progressed, the foster parents began to see a positive shift in Herman's behavior and interactions with each of them and the other foster children, thereby lessening the emotional stress and increasing positive time together. Finally, enrollment in an after-school Tae Kwon Do class helped Herman feel competent, have an avenue for physical release, and form more positive social relationships (*Facilitates Communication*: self-expression; *Enhances Social Relationships:* social competence, empathy; *Increases Personal Strengths*: resiliency, accelerated psychological development; self-regulation and self-esteem).

Challenges in Implementation

A weakness suggested of prescriptive play therapy is its lack of investment in theory generation. Indeed, prescriptive play therapists are not interested in the development of single theories, but rather in the identification of change mechanisms underlying successful psychotherapy of all types and in the development of prescriptive matching of change mechanisms to the underlying determinants of the disorder (Schaefer, 2011). Consequently, the clinician needs to be competent in more than one therapeutic orientation, and so a second challenge is having the necessary training and supervision in one or two major schools of psychotherapy. A lifelong learning approach is needed to help facilitate acquiring knowledge, competence, and skills in several schools of play therapy, such as humanistic, psychodynamic, and cognitive-behavioral, as well as in the major modalities of individual, group and family play therapy (Schaefer, 2011). A third challenge with the prescriptive approach is that flexibility can deteriorate into just arbitrarily combining and using various approaches without sound theoretical bases, along with not having proper training and supervision. It can become a hodgepodge of therapies if a rational, systematic procedure for prescriptive matching of treatment approach to disorder does not occur.

In the case study of Herman, it is critical that careful thought is given to treatment approaches and sequencing for a successful outcome. Further, training and supervision/consultation should underpin the treatment process to manage transference issues as well as assure the best treatment methods and approach are being utilized.

Conclusion

This chapter contains an overview of the basic premises and core practices of the prescriptive approach to play therapy. Prescriptive play therapists draw from a number of therapeutic approaches to have a wealth of change agents at their disposal. They then tailor their therapeutic interventions to the needs of the individual client by utilizing four sources of information: empirical and evidence-based research, clinical experience/expertise, client preferences/context, and the likely cause(s) of the presenting problem, followed up with supervision, training, and experiential knowledge.

Most play therapists are becoming increasingly prescriptive in their practice. Growth in the field is due to the realization that we cannot remain purists, or strictly dogmatic, or that only one way of working is the "true" way. We need to be transtheoretical, eclectic, integrative, and evidence-informed (Schaefer & Drewes, 2016; Drewes & Seymour, 2019).

References

Barlow, D. H. (2010). Negative effects from psychological treatments. A perspective. *American Psychologist, 65*(1), 13–20.

Beutler, L. E., & Harwood, T. M. (2000). *Prescriptive psychotherapy: A practical guide to systematic treatment selection.* Oxford University Press.

Bohart, H. C. (2005). Evidence-based psychotherapy means evidence-informed, not evidence-driven. *Journal of Contemporary Psychotherapy, 35*(1), 39–53.

Cuijpers, P., Miguel, C., Harrer, M., Plessen, C. Y., Ciharova, M., Papola, D., Ebert, D., & Karyotaki, E. (2023). Psychological treatment of depression: A systematic overview of a meta-analytic research domain. *Journal of Affective Disorders*, 335, 141–151. https://doi.org/10.1016/j.jad.2023.05.011

Dimond, R., Havens, R., & Jones, A. (1978). A conceptual framework for the practice of prescriptive eclecticism in psychotherapy. *American Psychologist, 33*, 239–48.

Drewes, A. A. (2001). The gingerbread person feelings map. In C. E. Schaefer & H. Kaduson (Eds.), *101 more play therapy techniques* (pp. 92–7). Aronson.

Drewes, A. A., Bratton, S. C., & Schaefer, C. E. (2011). *Integrative play therapy*. Wiley.

Drewes, A. A., & Cavett, A. (2012). Play applications of trauma-specific TF-CBT components for young children. In J. Cohen, T. Mannarino, & E. Deblinger (Eds.), *Trauma-focused CBT for children and adolescents: Treatment applications*. Guilford Press.

Drewes, A. A., & Seymour, J. W. (2019). Integrative psychotherapy with children. In J. C. Norcross & M. R. Goldfried (Eds.), *Handbook of psychotherapy integration* (3rd ed., pp. 341–56). Oxford University Press.

Gil, E., & Shaw, J. P. (2009). Prescriptive play therapy. In K. O'Connor & L. M. Braverman (Eds.), *Play therapy theory and practice: Comparing theories and techniques* (pp. 451–88). Wiley.

Goldfried, M. R. (2001). *How therapists change: Personal and professional reflections*. American Psychological Association.

Goldstein, A. P., & Stein, N. (1976). *Prescriptive psychotherapies*. Pergamon Press.

Kaduson, H., Cangelosi, D., & Schaefer, C. (2020). *Prescriptive play therapy: Tailoring interventions for specific childhood problems*. Guilford.

Kearney, C., & Silverman, W. (1999). Functionally based prescriptive and nonprescriptive treatment for children and adolescents with school refusal behavior. *Behavior Therapy, 30*, 673–95.

Munns, E. (Ed.). (2009). *Application of family and group theraplay*. Rowman & Littlefield.

Norcross, J. C. (1987). *Casebook of eclectic psychotherapy*. Brunner/Mazel.

Norcross, J. C. (1991). Prescriptive matching in psychotherapy: An introduction. *Psychology, 28*, 439–43.

Norcross, J. C. (2005). A primer on psychotherapy integration. In J. C. Norcross & M. R. Goldfried (Eds.), *Handbook of psychotherapy integration* (2nd ed.). Oxford University Press.

Norcross, J. C., & Wampold, B. (2011). What works for whom: Tailoring psychotherapy to the person. *Journal of Clinical Psychology in Session, 67*(2), 127–32.

Paul, G. (1967). Strategy of outcome research in psychotherapy. *Journal of Consulting Psychology, 31*, 109–19.

Peris, T. S., Thamrin, H., & Rozenman, M. S. (2021). Family intervention for child and adolescent anxiety: A meta-analytic review of therapy targets, techniques, and outcomes. *Journal of Affective Disorders, 286*, 282–95.

Perry, B. D. (2005). Applying principles of neurodevelopment to clinical work with maltreated and traumatized children: The neurosequential model of therapeutics. In N. Boyd (Ed.), *Working with traumatized youth in child welfare* (pp. 27–52). Guilford.

Prendiville, E. (2014). Abreaction. In C. E. Schaefer & A. Drewes (Eds.), *The therapeutic powers of play* (2nd ed., pp. 83–98). Wiley.

Schaefer, C. E. (Ed.). (2011). *Foundations of play therapy* (2nd ed.). Wiley.

Schaefer, C. E., & Drewes, A. A. (2014). *The therapeutic powers of play: 20 core agents of change* (2nd ed.). Wiley.

Schaefer, C., & Gilbert, J. (2015). How to assess a child's progress in play therapy. *Play Therapy, 12*(3), 16–19.

Schaefer, C. E., & Drewes, A. A. (2016). Prescriptive play therapy (pp. 227–40). In K. J. O'Connor, C. E. Schaefer & L. D. Braverman (Eds.), *Handbook of play therapy* (2nd ed.). Wiley.

Shrinivasa, B., Bukhari, G. R., & Hamza, A. (2018). Therapeutic intervention for children through play: An overview. *Archives of Mental Health, 19*(2), 82–9.

Stevens, S. E., Hyman, M. T., & Allen, M. (2000). A meta-analysis of common and specific treatment effects across the outcome domain of the phase model of psychotherapy. *Clinical Psychology: Science and Practice, 7*, 275–90.

2

AutPlay Therapy

Play Therapy through a Neurodiversity Affirming Lens

Robert Jason Grant and Sarah Moran

Chapter Outline

Introduction

This chapter will highlight case conceptualization through a neurodiversity-affirming lens. The AutPlay Therapy framework will be discussed and utilized to understand neurodiversity-affirming play therapy. A case study example (Herman) will be mentioned throughout the chapter to better conceptualize the therapy planning. Herman is identified as a ten-year-old male with several presenting issues. He is also identified as being neurodivergent—ADHD, learning differences, and fetal alcohol syndrome. This complex case indicates therapy needs revolving around trauma, multiple attachment disruptions, and exploration of gender and identity. This chapter seeks to demonstrate that a neurodiversity-affirming approach is foundational to working with any neurodivergent child, regardless of therapy goals.

Underlying Philosophy

The Neurodiversity Paradigm

Neurodiversity has always existed, and neurodivergent people have existed since the beginning of humanity. There has not always been formal language for this culture of people, but that has changed dramatically within the last few decades. With the emergence (mostly led by neurodivergent individuals) of concepts such as neurodiversity and neurodivergence, this type of identity and culture is being better understood. Walker (2021) defined the following constructs related to neurodiversity:

1. Neurotypical (neuronormative)—Having a style of neurocognitive functioning that falls within the dominant societal standards of what that society considers "normal" or "correct."
2. Neurodivergent—Having a brain (neurotype) that functions in ways that diverge from the dominant societal standards of "normal" and "correct."
3. The Neurodiversity Movement—A social justice movement that seeks civil rights, equality, respect, and full societal inclusion for the neurodivergent.
4. The neurodiversity paradigm—a specific perspective on neurodiversity—a perspective or approach that boils down to these fundamental principles:

   – Neurodiversity is a natural and valuable form of human diversity.
   – The idea that there is one "normal" or "healthy" type of brain or mind, or one "right" style of neurocognitive functioning, is a culturally constructed fiction, no more valid (and no more conducive to a healthy society or to the overall well-being of humanity) than the idea that there is one "normal" or "right" ethnicity, gender, or culture.
   – The social dynamics that manifest in regard to neurodiversity are similar to the social dynamics that manifest in regard to other forms of human diversity (e.g., diversity of ethnicity, gender, or culture). These dynamics include the dynamics of social power inequalities, and also the dynamics by which diversity, when embraced, acts as a source of creative potential. (pp. 34–46)

Neurodiversity refers to the broad diversity that exists in human neurobiology. There are countless ways in which the human brain and mind can develop, both structurally and functionally. Many of these fall within a range that can be considered as "typical" neurodevelopment, while some fall outside of that range and can be considered to "diverge" from the norm (Ecker et al., 2015; Pellicano & den Houting, 2022). Robinson (2013) proposed that neurodiversity is the idea that neurological differences like attention-deficit hyperactivity disorder (ADHD) and autism are the result of normal, natural variation in the human genome. Science suggests that conditions like autism have a stable prevalence in human society as far back as we can measure. There is awareness that ADHD, sensory differences, autism, and other manifestations emerge through a combination of genetic predisposition and environmental interaction; they are not the result of disease or injury. This represents a new and fundamentally different way of looking at neurodivergence that was traditionally pathologized. Long (2023) recognized that neurodivergence in our systems means differences in our systems. This can mean differences in communication, thought, perception, approach, social navigation, and so on. The differences are not deficits to be changed or "fixed." The valuing of differences is essential for creating richer stories and better services for neurodivergent children and adults.

AutPlay Therapy Framework

AutPlay Therapy is not a theory or approach. It is a guide or framework for implementing neurodiversity-affirming play therapy and utilizing the therapeutic powers of play to address the mental health needs of neurodivergent children (Grant, 2023). Neurodivergent children can include autistic, ADHD, sensory differences, learning differences, developmental disabilities, and any child whose neurotype diverges from the societal norm. The foundation of AutPlay is the neurodiversity paradigm and neurodiversity-affirming concepts. An individualized (prescriptive and/or integrative therapy) approach to working with each child is promoted; thereby choosing and/or integrating play therapy theory for the best fit for each child.

The AutPlay Therapy framework encourages affirming application of the twenty core agents of change of the therapeutic powers of play, which can materialize in a number of different ways (Grant, 2023). The AutPlay framework presents the implementation of non-directed play and/or structured play therapy interventions that are specifically chosen or created for the individual neurodivergent child. Therapeutic play processes and play interventions are mindfully chosen with input from both the parent and the child. Each intervention could embody one or more of the twenty core agents of change depending on the child's assessed needs. Due to the variance in the spectrum of presentation with neurodivergent children, it is likely that the therapist will experience a variety of the therapeutic powers of play, although children may benefit from a focus on specifically identified agents of change. Thus, it becomes important for the therapist to have a grounded knowledge of the therapeutic powers of play. The intersection between the therapeutic powers of play and the therapist's understanding of the neurodiversity paradigm creates the most beneficial, safe, and healthy environment for neurodivergent children to address their mental health needs through play therapy.

Although the AutPlay framework considers any mental health need a child may be experiencing, there are three overarching goals in working with neurodivergent children through a play therapy process.

Self-worth (strengths). Neurodivergent children can spend a significant amount of time navigating various environments that are not affirming of their neuro differences. Consider an ADHD child who is consistently getting into trouble at school for fidgeting too much, talking too much, not staying focused long enough, moving their body in distracting ways, or simply preferring to bounce on a ball while completing a worksheet instead of sitting in a chair. The constant messages from the adults in authority that the way the child is, their neurodivergent self, is wrong, bad, needs to change, and so on, batter the self-worth of the child. Imagine being a certain person of color and all day long at school being told your skin was not right, not appropriate, bad, disrespectful, and so forth. Something you cannot change and is a part of who you are is being villainized by those who have identity development power over you. This is not going to support healthy self-worth. Therapy goals should always include strengthening the child's self-worth regardless of other therapy goals. Self-worth can be a standalone goal or something the therapist consistently affirms throughout therapy.

Identity awareness (self-concept). A neurodivergent person will be a neurodivergent person for the totality of their life. What they believe and how they feel about being neurodivergent will have a large impact on their overall mental health. Throughout therapy, there should be a focus on understanding and growing in affirming acceptance of a person's neurodivergence. This should be something that is implemented age-appropriately and progress in knowledge and understanding as the child grows and develops. When a neurodivergent person can understand their internal system and how their brain works, this can be empowering information, especially if it is processed as affirming and not as a deficit. This becomes critical information to help the individual learn strategies, techniques, and ideas for helping them navigate and advocate.

Self-advocacy. Advocacy is an essential piece of learning for most neurodivergent individuals. It is likely that therapy will involve advocacy discussion and implementation. Many neurodivergent children will be experiencing environments that do not affirm their neurodivergence and are not adequately meeting their support needs. This will likely continue throughout their life and requires learning self-advocacy skills. Self-advocacy becomes an essential goal for neurodivergent individuals to ultimately participate in processes and navigate their wants and needs successfully.

Grant (2023) proposed that being neurodiversity affirming is a philosophy, approach, and choice to work with clients through a neurodiversity lens, especially neurodivergent clients. Being mindful that processes, theories, approaches, and techniques are free of ableism, and working to build up the client's individual identity instead of trying to change them to a neurotypical standard. At its very basic level, the AutPlay framework is about diversity, specifically neurodiversity, and relies upon an understanding of the neurodiversity paradigm and neurodiversity affirming concepts when implementing play therapy approaches to address the mental health needs of neurodivergent children.

Personality Theory

Humanistic psychology focuses on humans as unique individual, with free will (personal agency), and an innate drive to achieve their full potential (Mcleod, 2023). Humanistic psychology rejects psychodynamic views of individuals as being driven by their unconscious and regards behaviorism as dehumanizing, due to the reinforcement of stimulus-response behavior and the focus on animal research to explain human behavior. A humanistic approach in therapy focuses on formulating a complete view of the individual using a client-centered approach and unconditional positive regard, within the context of their social environment (Mcleod, 2023).

Humanism considers that for individuals to be healthy and whole, it is important to foster social support within their communities (Cherry, 2022). Some goals that support an individual in achieving self-actualization include discovering strengths, identifying beliefs and values, pursuing experiences that bring joy, developing skills, learn to accept yourself and others, focusing on things you are passionate about, and maintaining a positive outlook (Cherry, 2022). At the play therapy level, theories influenced by humanistic constructs, such as child-centered play therapy, engage the child in one-on-one therapy to create a safe and supportive environment for the child to meet these goals.

Many of the goals found in humanistic psychology and in play therapy approaches derived from humanistic influence are in line with the core beliefs of the AutPlay Therapy framework. The framework supports a client-centered approach using a neurodiversity-affirming lens. The meshing of humanistic and neurodiversity-affirming philosophy promotes the development of a strong sense of identity and self-worth around the uniqueness of a client's brain, interests, and preferences within the social context of the client's community.

Model of Psychopathology

The Sociocultural Model

The sociocultural model of psychology draws from the work of Lev Vygotsky and various intellectual traditions and theoretical perspectives. It is influenced by several key figures and movements in psychology and related disciplines. The sociocultural perspective looks at a person, their behaviors, and their needs in the context of their culture and background. It considers how behavior and thinking differ from culture to culture and from one situation to another (Chirkov, 2020). This perspective includes neurodiversity. For example, a child who is neurodivergent would experience life as a neurodivergent person and often as a specific neuro minority (autistic, ADHD child, etc.). This exists as an identity, a culture within the greater neuronormative culture. How might a therapist's neuronormative influence and conditioning affect their views of the neurodivergent child? How might the therapy process be affected by not valuing neurodiversity?

As society becomes increasingly diverse, therapists must develop cultural humility, which means they must understand and address issues of not only race, culture, and gender, but also neurotype. Diversity-informed therapy aims to offer both a helping role and a process that uses modalities and defines goals consistent with the life experiences and cultural manifestations of clients. It strives to recognize client identities to include individual, group, and universal dimensions, advocates the use of universal and culture-specific strategies and roles in the healing process, and balances the importance of individualism and collectivism in the assessment, diagnosis, and treatment of clients and client systems (Sue, 2001). Stewart et al. (2012) proposed that this therapeutic perspective integrates the impact of cultural and social norms, starting at the beginning of therapy. Therapists who use this perspective work with clients to obtain and integrate information about their cultural patterns into an individualized therapy approach based on their particular situation. The sociocultural model of psychology is a theoretical framework that emphasizes the influence of social and cultural factors on human behavior and mental processes. This model suggests that individuals cannot be fully understood in isolation from their social and cultural contexts. Instead, it posits that these contexts significantly shape individuals' thoughts, feelings, and behaviors. The following key concepts are conceptualized from various thoughts on sociocultural theory and adapted to include neurodiversity implications:

Culture. Shared beliefs, values, norms, customs, traditions, and practices that characterize a particular group of people. It encompasses everything from language, caregiver and peer influences, community influences, gender norms, societal norms, family, personal, and/or religious values, power dynamics, to mainstream media and social media. Neuronormative culture has often collided with neurodivergent culture, with neuronormative held concepts overpowering and denying neurodivergent culture.

Socialization. The process through which individuals learn and internalize the norms, values, and behaviors of their culture. It occurs through various means, including family, peers, media, education, and religious institutions. "Appropriate" or accepted socialization has often meant that neurodivergence is relegated to a mistake, a disorder, or something that is not right. This can leave the neurodivergent person struggling to "fit in" with the socialization dynamics of their culture while simultaneously having their identity denied.

Social Identity. Refers to the part of an individual's self-concept that is derived from their membership in various social groups, such as gender, ethnicity, nationality, neurotype, religion, or socioeconomic status. These social identities influence how individuals perceive themselves and others, as well as how they behave in different social contexts. Neurodivergent identity has historically been pathologized, demeaned, and treated as something that needs to be fixed to "look" like the correct social identity presentation. Socialization processes that deny neurodivergent identity often create disabling processes and overall poor mental health.

Cultural Bias. The tendency to interpret and judge behavior from the perspective of one's own culture, leading to misunderstandings or misinterpretations of individuals from different cultural backgrounds. Cultural bias is similar to the double empathy theory in neurodiversity work. *Acculturation.* The process through which individuals and groups adapt to and adopt the cultural practices and norms of a dominant or host culture while retaining elements of their own cultural identity. This process can have significant psychological implications, including changes in identity, values, and interpersonal relationships. For neurodivergent individuals, acculturation demands can lead to the devaluation and pathologizing of their neurotype, which leads to masking, poor self-worth, and internalized ableism.

The Social Model of Disability

Neurodiversity and more specifically neurodivergence through the sociocultural model can best be understood through the social model of disability. Olkin (2022) stated that disability within the social model is seen as one aspect of a person's identity, much like race/ethnicity, gender, and so on. From this perspective, disability is believed to result from a mismatch between the disabled person and the environment (both physical and social). It is this environment (society and/or culture) that creates the handicaps and barriers, not the disability (Olkin, 2022; Pantazakos & Vanaken, 2023). From this perspective, the way to address disability is to change the environment and society, rather than people with disabilities. Ableism, negative stereotypes, discrimination, and oppression serve as barriers to environmental change and full inclusion.

Buder and Perry (2021) shared that the social model of disability suggests that if societies were set up and constructed in a way that was accessible for people with disabilities (which includes neurodivergence), those individuals would not be restricted from full participation in the world around them. In other words, the social model of disability views the origins of disability as the mental attitudes and physical structures of society rather than a medical condition faced by an individual. Essentially, the social model says that individual limitations are not the cause of disability. Rather, it is society's failure to provide appropriate services and adequately ensure that the needs of disabled and/or neurodivergent people are taken into account in societal organization. Inclusion London (2021) stated that a lack of affirming presence and barriers create exclusion, discrimination, and disadvantage for people who differ from the societal created standard of "normal." The social model, in highlighting the barriers, can often simultaneously identify solutions. Inclusion London highlighted three types of barriers common within the social model of disability:

1. Attitudinal barriers—The social and cultural attitudes and assumptions about people who are neurodivergent or have a disability that explain, justify, and perpetuate prejudice, discrimination, and exclusion in society; for example, assumptions that certain people can't work, can't be independent, can't have sex, shouldn't have children, need protecting, are "child-like," are " dangerous," and should not be seen in public situations because they are upsetting, are unpredictable, and so on.
2. Physical barriers—These are barriers linked to the physical and system environments and cover a huge range of barriers that prevent equal access, such as stairs, narrow corridors and doorways, curbs, inaccessible toilets, inaccessible housing, poor lighting, poor seating, broken elevators, or poorly managed streets and public spaces. As well as rigid, non-inclusive, controlling, inflexible, closed-minded, conforming, and dismissive environmental systems.
3. Information/Communication Barriers—The barriers linked to information and communication, such as lack of sign language interpreters for deaf people, lack

> of provision of hearing induction loops, lack of sensory accommodations, and lack of understanding that there are more ways to communicate than verbally, dismissiveness of learning differences, lack of awareness or care for neurotype and nervous system needs, and ignoring of self-advocacy initiatives
>
> (para. 15–17).

Goering (2015) stated that the social model of disability focuses attention on the attitudinal obstacles faced by people with nonnormative presentations. Other people's expectations about quality of life for a disabled and/or neurodivergent person not only affect the ways in which physical structures and institutional norms are made and sustained (based on presumptions about inability to perform), but also can create additional disability by making it harder for such individuals to feel good about themselves. The social model of disability reminds us to be careful about what we presume to be irremediable through social change and to question the ways in which we currently understand neurodiversity. Challenging standard definitions of normality and impairment will require listening carefully to the experiences of neurodivergent people and thinking creatively about possibilities for inclusion, accommodation, and accessibility.

The central idea of the social model of disability is that needs and differences (no matter how difficult or distressing) do not make neurodivergent individuals any less worthy of access to society than others. This model fits nicely within the context of the sociocultural model and helps inform and understand neurodivergence and other disabilities as an identity and culture. Neurodivergent individuals may have needs such as attachment disruptions, executive dysfunction, regulation struggles, trauma responses, depression, and sensory differences. There is no treatment approach or "cure" for neurodivergence, but a neurodivergent individual may need accommodations or therapies for issues they are struggling with. The social model promotes a society where neurodivergent needs (supports) are accommodated and where neurodivergent people can maintain their identity and enjoy full access to society.

Role of the Therapist

Grant (2023) stated that regarding play therapy, there seem to be two fundamental questions and possible issues for therapists working with neurodivergent children. (1) Does the therapist understand the therapeutic powers and importance of play, or do they view it as frivolous? (2) If the therapist does believe in the therapeutic powers and importance of play, does the therapist believe that neurodivergent children play, or do they believe that play, and its therapeutic powers, are somehow lost on neurodivergent children? To be neurodiversity-informed and affirming means the therapist will recognize and value the play preferences and style of neurodivergent children and understand that play therapy theory and the therapeutic powers of play hold many benefits for neurodivergent children.

Marschall (2022) stated that when a therapist is neurodiversity affirming, they recognize that neurodivergence by itself is not a flaw or illness that needs to be "fixed" or corrected.

They recognize that neurodivergence can come with its own set of strengths that can be fostered. Neurodiversity affirming therapy is not a specific set of interventions or things the therapist says or does in their sessions. Rather, it is an approach to therapy and an overarching philosophy that impacts how the therapist views their client and the client's experience. At the same time, a neurodiversity affirming therapist acknowledges and affirms that neurodivergence can accompany support needs. If someone insists that neurodivergence is always a strength with no support needs, they are falling into the trap of toxic positivity and not honoring the full experience of neurodivergent people. A neurodiversity affirming approach requires therapists to examine the individualized nature of therapy approaches when working with neurodivergent clients. Indeed, neurodiversity argues that all children should and could benefit from neurodiversity affirming practices.

Grant (2023) defined several neurodiversity-affirming play therapy constructs that the therapist can implement within any play therapy theory or approach to ensure a non-ableist and affirming presence in the theory or model.

1. Recognize that neurodiversity means there is no such thing as a "normal" brain. Variation in neurology is natural, and none is more right or wrong than another.
2. Understand that neurodivergent children (autistic, sensory differences, ADHD, learning differences, etc.) are not in play therapy because they are neurodivergent. They are in therapy because they have needs such as anxiety, regulation challenges, trauma issues, social needs, and parent/child relationship issues, and so on. Being neurodivergent is understood as awareness of the child, which may require different methods of implementing play therapy to match the child's neurotype. Navigate from the perspective—"I'm not going to work with you on changing who you are, I'm going to work with you on how to help you get what you want or need."
3. Honor the child's play preferences and special interests. All neurodivergent children play, and there are multiple types and ways to play. Each child's play preferences should be respected, and Neurodivergent children should not be forced to play in a specific way.
4. Encourage children's voices to be heard and valued in deciding on processes, needs, and goals. Children should have a say in what needs they want to address.
5. Avoid play interventions that promote masking and camouflaging. Instead, focus on strengths and help children recognize what they already do well; assist them utilize their strengths to address their needs.
6. Respect body autonomy and presume competence.
7. Value and allow for multiple methods of communication.
8. Recognize that different is okay; different is not bad, wrong, or a problem. Navigating differently is supported. The focus is never on trying to change a neurodivergent child to "look" like a neurotypical standard.
9. Value relationship development as a core process in Play Therapy. The therapeutic relationship is key to working with neurodivergent children and their families and should begin with first contact and continue until termination.

10. Understand that play is the natural language of children. The therapeutic powers of play are a grounding principle in play therapy. Play is the change agent and not a manipulative tool to get to a change. Play is not withheld or used as a reward to gain compliance.
11. Realize the play therapy process will involve advocating for inclusion, addressing self-worth, understanding identity, awareness of the social model of disability, the double empathy problem, ableism, and self-advocacy development.
12. Conceptualize that the play therapy process may involve non-directive methods, directive methods, or an integrative or prescriptive approach. The therapy approach and process should be individualized to the unique neurotype of each child, understanding their neurodivergent spectrum of presentation (pp. 80–84).

Play therapists working through the AutPlay Therapy framework with neurodivergent children should take care to meet the child where they are and not attempt to make a neurodivergent child conform to the experiences they may have with neurotypical children. Therapists should enter the neurodivergent child's world (build relationship) and try to see things from their point of view. The play therapist is essentially the person who stands in the gap between a play therapy theory or approach that may have ableist or non-affirming components and the neurodivergent child. It is the responsibility of the therapist to ensure that when a theory or approach reaches the child, it has been filtered of ableist ideas and addresses the child in a neurodiversity-affirming manner.

Conceptualizing Goals of Therapy

The medical model, which therapists are trained under and encouraged to use in the American medical system, tends to focus on diagnosis and treatment. The medical model can be alienating and counterproductive to neurodivergent people, as it fails to understand neurodivergence and does not use affirming language (Long, 2023; Pantazakos, & Vanaken, 2023). This creates a challenge for clinicians when developing a therapy plan. Typical therapy goals tend to use ableist language by assuming there is a "normal" to be measured against. Confronting and reframing ableist language is part of the work in AutPlay Therapy when working directly with the child, when formulating goals for therapy, and when talking about the child to caregivers.

Grant (2024) proposed that when a neurodivergent child or adolescent is entering therapy, the first affirming step that the therapist should take is to ask, "What are the mental health needs?" "Why is the neurodivergent child coming to therapy?" A neurodivergent child does not need any therapy simply because they are neurodivergent. It is critical that the goals of therapy be neurodiversity-affirming in nature. Approaches focused on reducing neurodivergent "symptoms" are not only unlikely to solve the problem but can be counterproductive, as mental health is positively correlated with positive self-concept and perceived social support (Dallman et al., 2022; Pantazakos & Vanaken, 2023).

Neurodiversity affirming goals and interventions "do not seek to reduce, alter, or replace behaviors simply because they are considered autistic" (Dallman et al., 2022, p. 6). Instead, behaviors are framed through the lens of curiosity, consideration of the person's ability to communicate their wants/needs, sensory preferences, and environmental barriers. Therapists need to be considerate of their own goals and expectations for therapy, and be mindful that their approaches are free of ableism when working with neurodivergent clients to successfully promote the "all the time goals" of the AutPlay Therapy framework: self-worth, identity awareness, and self-advocacy (Grant, 2023). The therapist should ensure that these goals are being addressed in the therapeutic process, in addition to any other identified therapy needs. Additional mental health goals may also be addressed, such as attachment, trauma, anxiety, depression, and so on. As additional goals are addressed, it is critical to continuously build up the client's self-worth and identity awareness. It is also essential to think about what the best way is to address the additional goals for this neurodivergent child based on their neurodivergent spectrum of presentation.

Roles of Caregivers and Collaterals

Research agrees that systemic approaches and techniques are well suited to working with neurodivergent children and families (Grant, 2024; Long, 2023). The majority of seminal theories of play therapy involve some level of parent engagement as part of the therapeutic process. Parents and caregivers engage in the therapeutic process through the initiation of therapy, ensuring the child is in attendance, implementation of homework (if part of the treatment plan), and by setting the stage for expectations regarding the effectiveness of therapy (Grant, 2024).

AutPlay Therapy offers a great deal of flexibility when working with parents/caregivers and the parent partnering (training) component. In AutPlay, the therapist considers the parent to be a partner in the process. This means the parent is considered an equal and important member of the therapy process. Grant (2023) stated that the parent's voice, opinions, and concerns are valued. The parent is considered the most influential and important relationship in the child's life. As such, the therapist will actively pursue the parent's insight and expertise on their child and family. Grant (2023) furthered that the therapeutic powers of play and the benefits of play in family work exist for all members of the family, not just the children. Ariel (2005) proposed that

> Play provides an opportunity to experience what has been denied or ignored, in the safe, benign, fun world of pretend. The play experience lives in the twilight zone between cognition and emotion, where the defenses are not on alert. (p. 6–7)

There are several reasons why the involvement of family members in a child's play is important and healthy for both the child and parent. Not only is formal family play therapy valuable, but supporting play in the home setting can be important for neurodivergent children's self-worth, social, emotional, regulatory, and cognitive development.

Case Study through the Lens of the Therapeutic Powers of Play

Therapeutic Powers of Play Employed

Under the umbrella of play therapy, the therapeutic powers of play can be recognized throughout various theories and approaches. Some powers may be more evident or primary in some theories versus others, but certainly, the therapeutic powers of play serve as a unifying component in the vast world of play therapy. This chapter does not capture all the play therapy theories, approaches, and therapeutic powers of play that exist, but it does provide a snapshot of the variety that integrates and influences neurodiversity affirming concepts (Grant, 2023).

Historically, Schaefer (1993) identified fourteen therapeutic powers of play based on a review of the literature and play therapists' clinical experiences. Later, the list was expanded and revised to include twenty core therapeutic powers of play (Schaefer & Drewes, 2014). Based on similarity of therapy goals, the twenty powers were classified into the following four categories: facilitates communication, fosters emotional wellness, enhances social relationships, and increases personal strengths (Schaefer & Drewes, 2014).

Our case example focuses on Herman (see Appendix for case study of Herman being referenced), a multiple neurodivergent child (ADHD, learning differences, and fetal syndrome). For our purposes, this conceptualization will focus on neurodiversity-affirming philosophy and the therapeutic powers of play, categories of increased personal strengths, and facilitate communication. The twenty core powers of play aligned with these categories will include self-expression, direct teaching, self-regulation, and self-esteem. Direct teaching is chosen to address goals of improving self-expression, self-esteem, and self-regulation.

Self-Expression. In the AutPlay Therapy framework and neurodiversity affirming philosophy, we would conceptualize it as self-advocacy. This includes the child's ability to be themselves, operate within their neurotype, and not be exposed to devaluing or degrading ideas about how their brain works. A direct teaching example would include the AutPlay intervention *I Can Use My Voice* (Grant, 2024, p. 210). In this directive, the practitioner provides a toy or real microphone for the child. The practitioner explains they are going to practice and/or role-play advocating for themselves. The practitioner and child create a few scenarios where the child may need to advocate. The practitioner may need to explain the concept of advocacy and provide some examples. The child can think of scenarios, but the practitioner will likely need to assist. Once the scenarios have been established, the child uses the microphone and practices standing up and advocating. This may involve asking for help from a teacher, telling a child they do not like what they are doing, or telling an adult that something is bothering their senses. Advocacy does not have to be verbal. Other methods of communicating advocacy can also be explored and practiced. As the child displays advocacy, the practitioner should respond with encouragement to the child. The practitioner and child can continue this intervention until they have practiced all their scenarios.

Self Esteem. The AutPlay therapy framework and neurodiversity affirming philosophy conceptualize self-worth (self-esteem) as an "all-the-time goal" that neurodivergent children need. Many neurodivergent children, like Herman navigate multiple systems, experiences, and people that devalue their self-worth. For any therapy to be successfully addressed, it is critical to build up and accomplish a healthy self-worth in neurodivergent children. A direct teaching example would include the AutPlay intervention *Paint Swatch Pieces of Me* (Grant, 2024, p. 188). In this intervention, the child chooses a paint swatch that has several shades of color (they can choose whatever colors they like) to represent things about themselves. The practitioner explains that they are going to write on each color of the paint swatch something the child thinks is a strength they have, something positive about themselves, or something they like about themselves. The child should think of as many things as they can (they can use multiple paint swatches if needed). The practitioner can also help the child identify positive things. Once the child has finished writing their ideas, the practitioner and child talk about each one and how it contributes an important piece to the child's identity. The practitioner can further the intervention by asking the child to rank the things identified from the most important part of their identity to the least important. The practitioner and child can then discuss the child's rankings. The child is encouraged to keep the paint swatch as a visual reminder of the important parts of their identity.

Self-Regulation. This area is a common therapy goal highlighted in the AutPlay Therapy framework as many neurodivergent children struggle with regulation/dysregulation. Often, this is due to environmental reasons such as sensory needs, social anxiety, confusion, new places and people, and lack of support, which can create dysregulation in a neurodivergent child's system. A direct teaching example would include the AutPlay intervention *Feelings Field Trip* (Grant, 2024, p. 80). In this intervention, the practitioner instructs the child to choose a color of construction paper that they associate with an anxious or worried feeling. The practitioner explains to the child that they are going on a "feelings field trip." The practitioner instructs the child to write on the construction paper all the things that they can think of that make them feel anxious or worried. The practitioner can help the child by adding things to the list and verifying with the child that what the practitioner added is relevant for the child. The practitioner and child read through the list, making sure everything that is relevant is listed. The practitioner instructs the child to rip the paper into pieces and think about getting rid of all the worried and anxious feelings while they are ripping up the paper. The child gathers up all the ripped-up pieces, and the practitioner and child take their "field trip" to an outside trash can, throwing all the pieces into the trash can. As the pieces are thrown away, the practitioner helps the child connect with releasing the anxiety, worry, and dysregulated feelings. This intervention can be repeated in future sessions anytime the child needs to take "a feelings field trip."

Cultural, Diversity, Inclusion Considerations

The case example "Herman" is of mixed heritage, including Hispanic and African American backgrounds, though his father's ethnicity is unknown. Cultural considerations for this case should include beliefs and family values of African American and Latino family systems, as both pertain to his mother's upbringing and view of the world. Specific focus on African American cultural context is indicated as Herman's grandmother was his primary caregiver until the age of three.

Latino and African American families both value the individual within the context of the collective welfare of the family system (Garcia-Preto, 2005; Hines & Boyd-Franklin, 2005). It is common practice in Latino and African American families for children to be cared for by extended members of the family, especially in times of crisis. Some African American families may experience difficulty when their efforts to help extended family members leave them feeling depleted emotionally, physically, and/or financially (Hines & Boyd-Franklin, 2005). This is apparent in our case study, as Herman's relationship with his grandmother was reportedly strained due to her resentment for having to care for him, which led to physical and emotional neglect in her care of him, and ultimately removal from her care.

Latino families view going outside of the family for help only as a last resort (Garcia-Preto, 2005). African Americans assume that therapists will operate in the same way professionals in other agencies do, by telling them what they can and cannot do; for some, turning toward family therapy is perceived as turning toward "the system" that has negatively influenced African American wellbeing (Hines & Boyd-Franklin, 2005). Some children and families feel that they have been forced into therapy, particularly if the child was referred by school, social welfare department, court, or the police, and as a result, they can be ambivalent about the therapeutic process (Hines & Boyd-Franklin, 2005). Listening to and validating stories around environmental and social contexts that led to the referral to therapy is crucial to gaining buy-in from BIPOC families (Garcia-Preto, 2005; Hines & Boyd-Franklin, 2005).

Mallipeddi and VanDaalen (2022) defined intersectionality as the different social influences that make up an individual's experiences, such as gender and sexism, ethnicity and racism, and disability and ableism. The intersectional framework supports the understanding of social oppression and its ramifications through the integration of multiple contextual factors (Mallipeddi & VanDaalen, 2022). Therapists seeking to better understand their clients' lived experience and serve the neurodivergent communities that might otherwise be ignored must consider the overlap between intersectionality and neurodiversity-affirming care. Herman's exploration of gender is an important aspect of his intersectionality and would be an appropriate goal for therapy later, after the neurodiversity-affirming work has been conducted with the child and family.

Zeng (2022) noted that boys with learning disabilities often demonstrate more disruptive behaviors at school, calling attention to them. This is true for our case study, Herman, whose psychological and academic testing for ADHD appeared to have been conducted due to the exhibited behaviors at school. The high referral rate of African American children to special education programs and IEP accommodations can be stigmatizing, emotionally damaging, increase the risk of misdiagnosis, and/or can impact the child from receiving the support they need (Zeng, 2022). Looking at Herman's case through the lens of an intersectional, trauma-informed, and neurodiversity-affirming framework, any accommodations in the form of an IEP must be considerate of Herman's racial identity and complex trauma history, not just the externalized behaviors that warranted referral from the teacher for evaluation.

Case Formulation and Application

Herman's case indicates multiple therapy needs—attachment work, possible Child-Parent Relationship Therapy (CPRT) with his foster parents, trauma processing, gender exploration, and challenges at school in relation to both academic and social dynamics.

Neurodiversity affirming goals are first and foremost to build rapport with the client and to highlight the client's individual identity and strengths. Our case study, Herman, presents a complex case with the intersectionality of neurodivergence, mixed race, and gender non-conforming identities. The additional presenting challenges of fetal syndrome, multiple attachment breaks, and trauma indicate that goals for therapy need to be scaffolded so as not to be overwhelming for the child.

Challenges in Implementation

Maintaining neurodivergent affirming language throughout the work with this child and family is crucial to upholding the values of the AutPlay Therapy framework. The initial challenge would be to gain buy-in from the child/family, due to their past experiences of therapy involving frequent therapist turnover and multiple approaches, with limited outcomes or felt support. The family would likely ask that therapy goals focus on the presenting needs of attachment and trauma, and psychoeducation with the family would be indicated to help them understand the complexity of addressing trauma needs with a neurodivergent brain. Ongoing parent support in addition to individual work with the child will encourage buy-in from caregivers and strengthen the therapeutic trust with the therapist. To gain buy-in from the child, a neurodiversity affirming approach and prioritizing therapy goals is indicated so as not to overwhelm the child and to scaffold successes over time.

Conclusion

A neurodivergent affirming lens can allow therapists to move between different models of therapy to meet the child/family where they are. A neurodivergent affirming therapist would be able to use a variety of play therapy modalities with this case, and Autplay

Therapy specifically is designed to highlight the collaboration between the therapist, child, and family using the therapeutic powers of play through a neurodivergent affirming lens.

References

Buder, S., & Perry, R. (2021, November 5). *The social model of disability explained.* Social Creatures. https://www.thesocialcreatures.org/thecreaturetimes/the-social-model-of-disability#:~:text=In%20July%201990%2C%20the%20landmark,other%20areas%20of%20public%20life.

Cherry, K. (2022). What is humanistic psychology?: A psychology perspective influenced by humanism. *Verywellmind.* https://www.verywellmind.com/what-is-humanistic-psychology-2795242.

Chirkov, V. (2020). An introduction to the theory of sociocultural models. *Asian Journal of Social Psychology, 23*(2), 143–62.

Dallman, A. R., Williams, K. L., & Villa, L. (2022). Neurodiversity-affirming practices are a moral imperative for occupational therapy. *The Open Journal of Occupational Therapy, 10*(2), 1–9. https://doi.org/10.15453/2168–6408.193.

Ecker, C., Bookheimer, S. Y., & Murphy, D. G. M. (2015). Neuroimaging in autism spectrum disorder: Brain structure and function across the lifespan. *The Lancet Neurology, 14*, 1121–34.

Garcia-Preto, N. (2005). Latino families. In M. McGoldrick, N. A. Garcia-Preto, & J. Giordano (Eds.), *Ethnicity and family therapy* (3rd ed., pp. 153–65). Guilford Publications.

Goering, S. (2015). Rethinking disability: The social model of disability and chronic disease. *Current Reviews in Musculoskeletal Medicine, 8*(2), 134–8. https://doi.org/10.1007/s12178-015-9273-z.

Grant, R. J. (2023). *The AutPlay therapy handbook: Integrative family play therapy with neurodivergent children.* Routledge.

Grant, R. J. (2024). *Play interventions for neurodivergent children and adolescents: Promoting growth, empowerment, and affirming practices* (2nd ed.). Routledge.

Hines, P. M., & Boyd-Franklin, N. (2005). African American families. In M. McGoldrick, N. A. Garcia-Preto, & J. Giordano (Eds.), *Ethnicity and family therapy,* (3rd ed., pp. 87–100). Guilford Publications.

Inclusion London. (2021). The social model of disability. https://www.inclusionlondon.org.uk/disability-in-london/social-model/the-social-model-of-disability-and-the-cultural-model-of-deafness/.

Long, É. (2023). "Difference which makes a difference" (Bateson, 1972): How the neurodiversity paradigm and systemic approaches can support individuals and organizations to facilitate more helpful conversations about autism. *Journal of Social Work Practice, 37*(1), 109–18. https://doi.org/10.1080/02650533.2022.2142768.

Mallipeddi, N. V., & VanDaalen, R. A. (2022). Intersectionality within critical autism studies: A narrative review. *Autism in Adulthood: Challenges and Management, 4*(4), 281–9. https://doi.org/10.1089/aut.2021.0014.

Marschall, A. (2022, November 29). What does it mean for a therapist to be neurodiversity affirming? *Verywellmind.* https://www.verywellmind.com/what-does-it-mean-for-a-therapist-to-be-neurodiversity-affirming-6829954.

Mcleod, S. (2023). Humanistic approach in psychology (humanism): Definition & examples. *SimplyPsychology*. https://www.simplypsychology.org/humanistic.html.

Olkin, R. (2022, March 29). *Conceptualizing disability*: Three models of disability. https://www.apa.org/ed/precollege/psychology-teacher-network/introductory-psychology/disability-models

Pantazakos, T., & Vanaken, G. (2023). Addressing the autism mental health crisis: the potential of phenomenology in neurodiversity-affirming clinical practices. *Frontiers in Psychology, 14*. https://doi.org/10.3389/fpsyg.2023.1225152.

Pellicano, E., & den Houting, J. (2022). Annual research review: Shifting from 'normal science' to neurodiversity in autism science. *Journal of Child Psychology and Psychiatry, 63*(4), 381–96.

Robinson, J. E. (2013). What is neurodiversity? Neurodiversity means many things to people. Here's my first-person definition. *Psychology Today*. https://www.psychologytoday.com/us/blog/my-life-aspergers/201310/what-is-neurodiversity.

Schaefer, C. E. (1993) *The therapeutic powers of play*. Rowman & Littlefield Publishers.

Schaefer, C. E., & Drewes, A. A. (2014). *The therapeutic powers of play: 20 core change agents* (2nd ed.). John Wiley & Sons.

Stewart, S. M., Simmons, A., & Habibpour, E. (2012). Treatment of culturally diverse children and adolescents with depression. *Journal of Child and Adolescent Psychopharmacology, 22*(1), 72–9. https://doi.org/10.1089/cap.2011.0051.

Sue, D. W. (2001). Multidimensional facets of cultural competence. *The Counseling Psychologist, 29*(6), 790–821. https://doi.org/10.1177/0011000001296002.

Walker, N. (2021). *Neuroqueer heresies: Notes on the neurodiversity paradigm, autistic empowerment, and postnormal possibilities*. Autonomous Press.

Zeng, S. (2022). Intersectionality of equality in educational settings through the lens of gender, race, and disability. *Proceedings of the 2022 International Conference on Sport Science, Education and Social Development (SSESD 2022)*, 402–8. https://doi.org/10.2991/978-2-494069-13-8_48.

3

FirstPlay® Therapy

Janet A. Courtney

Chapter Outline

Introduction: FirstPlay® Therapy Model Background

In this section, I (this chapter author) introduce how and why FirstPlay® Therapy evolved from the seminal play therapy theory of Developmental Play Therapy (DPT). My first introduction to DPT and founder, Viola Brody, was in 1993 when I attended the Association for Play Therapy annual conference. I had a background working in adoption and foster care and was intrigued by the uniqueness of DPT as a healing approach with its emphasis on nurturing touch and developmental games to support the attachment relationship—all without the use of play materials. Soon after the conference, I attended several intensive DPT training courses and eventually arranged for training in my local area. When I chose to complete a dissertation on DPT, I was thrilled when Dr. Brody agreed to be on my dissertation committee, but then deeply saddened when she died before its completion. It was an honor to be invited to give the Tribute to Vi Brody at the 2003 Annual APT General Assembly. After her death, I carried on the teachings of DPT, among other practitioners (e.g., Derapelian, 2023; Schwartzenberger, 2020; Stammers, 2017) to a new generation of play therapists.

However, I and the participants in my workshops always raised one nagging concern: the issue of practitioners *touching* children. In the early years of Brody's teaching and practice, the topic of (caringly) touching children was not a major apprehension among professionals. Consequently, Brody's recommendations regarding ethical considerations involving touch were sparse. However, as the heartbreaking revelations of abuse of children by adults in positions of responsibility came to the forefront in the 1980's and "90's, concerns of professional liability regarding the touch of children heightened (Courtney & Nolan, 2017). The need to address ethical considerations regarding touch and children became paramount (See APT Paper on Touch, 2022). In my effort to effectively address professional considerations of touch with children, I examined this topic through several means including my doctoral research in DPT (Courtney & Gray, 2011, 2014); and through extensive post-doctoral training and research (see Courtney & Nolan, 2017; Courtney & Siu, 2018). Through deep reflection, it became apparent I needed to evolve my approach to working with infants and children (Courtney, 2020b). Since touch is so crucial to child development and healing, I pondered the question: Who does the touching? The simple answer is that we can empower *the parents and caregivers* to be guided and supported to provide that caring touch delivered through the joyful developmental games that Brody advanced. FirstPlay® also incorporates therapeutic storytelling, which will be elaborated on in the foundations in the next section.

Underlying Philosophy: FirstPlay® Therapy Foundations

FirstPlay® Therapy is a newer manualized infant play therapy model (Courtney, 2020b) that has evolved over the past two decades that is intentionally designed to address two different developmental levels. The first level is conceived for infants ages birth to thirty-six months and is titled FirstPlay® Infant Play Therapy. The second developmental level is conceived for ages three to twelve years and is named FirstPlay® Somatic Storytelling. Both interventions share the same foundations that synthesize several different theoretical models including Developmental Play Therapy (Brody, 1997b), Filial play therapy (Guerney, 2015), Attachment Theory (Bowlby, 1988; Schore & Schore, 2012), Ericksonian play therapy (Courtney & Mills, 2016), and the research into touch (Field, 2014) and infant mental health. Additionally, the schools in massage programs (Palmer & Barlow, 2017) have informed the older children's level. Each of the FirstPlay® foundations will now be reviewed in more detail in the following sections (refer to Figure 3.1).

Developmental Play Therapy

Developmental Play Therapy (DPT) was created by psychologist, Viola Brody, and is considered a seminal and historically significant theory in the field of play therapy. Brody (1997a, 1997b) advocated that children need caring touch for healthy emotional and psychological growth and development—a fact that modern research now supports (Field,

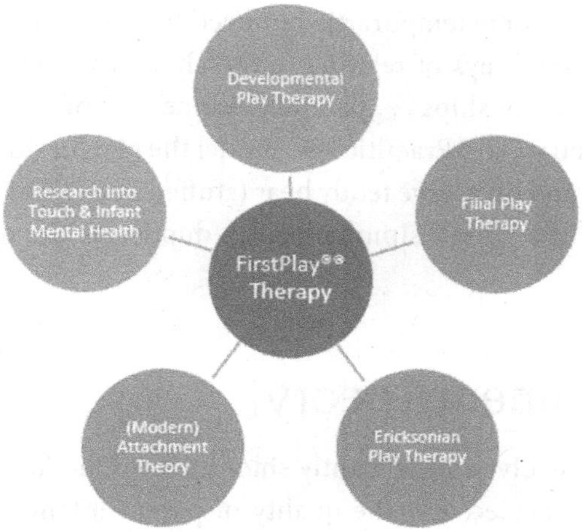

Figure 3.1 FirstPlay® Therapy Foundations.

2014; Jackson & McGlone, 2020). In her groundbreaking book, "The Dialogue of Touch," she wrote that touch is our first communication (Brody, 1997b). She taught that through the playful relationship of nurturing touch by an attuned adult, children gained a "felt sense of self," or a bodily awareness that helped them develop a "centering place within" (Brody 1996, 1997a, 1997b). Brody emphasized that the development of an inner "I" or core self needed to happen *first* before a child was ready for higher states of emotional and cognitive development. Children who experience caring touch are then able to develop empathetic attachment relationships with others. They also learn how to better self-regulate their own emotional states. The best way for children to receive caring touch experiences was through the enactment of playful "developmental games" (as Brody called them) implemented by attuned therapists specifically trained in DPT. This pre-symbolic play, or what I call "*first-play*" activities, can be exemplified by those early playful touch games one might observe between a parent and infant, such as patty-cake or peek-a-boo. Brody deemed that the nurturing touch element involved in these playful games was intrinsically healing, and that children who missed those critical experiences of development (through abuse/neglect, for example) can be helped by an attuned therapist to "go back and pick up what they missed" (Brody, 1997b).

Filial Play Therapy (Role of the Therapist and Caregivers)

Filial Play Therapy, as founded by Louise and Bernard Guerney in the 1960's (Guerney, 2015) advocated for parents as "change agents." In Filial play therapy, trained practitioners guide, facilitate, and supervise parents to provide attuned parent training in Client Centered Play Therapy techniques. FirstPlay® has adapted this Filial parent empowerment principle to guide, facilitate, model, and supervise parents in the FirstPlay® nurturing touch activities. Guerney (2015) wrote, "The advantage to assigning a therapeutic role to the parents is that they become temporarily removed from the entanglements of the family dynamics. They learn new ways of relating to the child. They execute new concepts and perceptions of family relationships . . . parents become part of the solution instead of part of the problem" (p. x). FirstPlay® Practitioners model the playful story techniques on a baby doll for the infant level and on a large teddy bear (stuffed animal) or pillow cushion for ages three and older, while the parent simultaneously duplicates the touch-based techniques with their own child.

Modern Attachment Theory

Attachment theory has evolved significantly since its introduction by John Bowlby (1988) in the 1950s, which advocated that the quality of parent-infant bonds sets the stage for healthy emotional and psychological development. Schore and Schore (2012) proposed an expansion of Bowlby's attachment theory constructs to go beyond how attachments are formed (safety, internal working models, a secure base) to include research into brain development. Schore and Schore (2012) therefore reframed attachment theory to be prefaced by the word *modern to* acknowledge the recent advancements in neuroscience. Thus, "*modern* attachment theory" is informed by neuroscience and, from this perspective, Schore and Schore (2012) described secure attachment relationships as "the essential matrix for creating a right brain self that can regulate its own internal states and external relationships" (p. 44). This right brain hemisphere self is accomplished by the sensitivity of the caretaker to cultivate "synchronous, reciprocal, and jointly satisfying mother-infant interactions" (p. 43). Porges (2018) describes the importance of activating the "social engagement system," which is mediated through the parasympathetic branch of the vagus nerve. The social engagement system is stimulated by an attuned caregiver that can provide cues of safety to the infant through face-to-face contact and by responding to the infant's signaling behaviors such as crying, smiles, and cooing.

Ericksonian-based Storytelling

Ericksonian-based storytelling principles are another foundational underpinning of FirstPlay® Therapy. Formulated by psychiatrist, Milton Erickson (Mills & Crowley, 2014) as a hypnotherapy intervention, he would often tell a parallel metaphorical story to a client once they reached an alpha state of being. Embedded within the story were helpful solutions to give unique options to the clients to address the presenting problem. The right brain hemisphere is activated in processing metaphorical types of storytelling, and clients can extract meanings that are relevant to them that can support new responses and ways of relating (Mills & Crowley, 2014). Joyce Mills adapted Erickson's work to develop a resiliency-focused play therapy model called StoryPlay®. It was thus through my training in StoryPlay® (Mills & Crowley, 2014) and also in an adult-focused Ericksonian Hypnotherapy that the roots of Ericksonian metaphorical principles of healing were adapted to the creation of FirstPlay® Stories that also include a somatic or touch-based element (Courtney, 2020a). In FirstPlay® metaphorical stories are created for a child, and then the touch-based techniques are embedded within the story. FirstPlay® Somatic Storytelling Practitioners then demonstrate the therapeutic story techniques to parents via a teddy Bear or a pillow cushion (or with a babydoll for infants) while the parent simultaneously draws the story techniques on the child's back. For this reason, older children engaged in FirstPlay® may know this approach *not* as FirstPlay® Somatic Storytelling, but as a fun and relatable name known as "BACK Stories." For parents with infants ages birth to thirty-six months engaging in the FirstPlay® Infant Play Therapy level, practitioners guide and supervise parents in a story titled, "The Baby Tree Hug©."

Brody (1976) also highlighted the vital role of imaginative storytelling, or what she called *fantasy*, as related to memory, attachment, and touch. She wrote, "Fantasy is essential to successful attachment for it is only through fantasy that one can continue a relationship when the other person is not there" (Brody, 1976, p. 19). In this, she is speaking to the internal memory schemas that we carry within us related to our attachment relationships. Playful storytelling is one way that supports memory building in the attachment relationship between a parent and child. In FirstPlay®, it is through the avenue of caring, respectful touch in combination with therapeutic storytelling that generates our ability to *feel memory*.

The Neurobiology of Touch

Since FirstPlay® practitioners are facilitating caring touch between parents, caregivers, and children and sometimes corrective experiences of touch, it is valuable to understand the current neurobiological research on touch. Part of the responsibilities of practitioners is to provide psychoeducation to parents about the interpersonal, emotional, and social benefits of touch. Over the past thirty years, neuroscience research has led to a deeper understanding of how the neural pathways in our body and brain are connected to memory, touch sensations, emotions, and trauma (Field, 2014; Hudspeth, 2016a; Porges, 2018; Schore, 2019). In this, we have also gained new insights into how touch is related to empathy and interpersonal relationships. Sensory mirror neurons are activated when we watch another person being touched, and these are connected to a network of resonance circuits (Badenoch, 2008). Additionally, emerging research has found that gentle touch triggers the unmyelinated C-tactile afferents (CTs) that are found only on the hairy part of the skin and are connected to the social and emotional part of the brain (Jackson & McGlone, 2020). We know that neurotransmitters, including oxytocin, serotonin, and dopamine, are released when we are provided with certain types of nurturing touch experiences (Schore, 2019). Oxytocin, sometimes called the "love" or the calming and connectivity hormone when released lowers the stress hormone cortisol, resulting in helping children to calm down (Field, 2014). Conversely, (and sadly) high levels of cortisol are released when children are abused and subjected to harsh physical touch, which can lead to diseased neural networks (Durrant & Ensom, 2012).

Infant Massage Promotes Infant Mental Health & Attachment

A portion of the FirstPlay® infant level includes the integration of infant massage techniques as delivered through a playful story to promote infant mental health and parent-child attachment (Baldwin, 2020; Siu, 2023; Zeanah, 2019). Perry (2006) lists "therapeutic massage" as a developmentally appropriate intervention for ages birth to two years as infants need "rhythmic movement" and "patterned sensory input (auditory, tactile, motor)," "simple narrative," and "attuned responsive caregiving and emotional and physical warmth" (p. 41). Additionally, the emotional development of the right-lateralized "human social brain" is, in part, supported by the "tactile-gestural non-verbal communication functions" between parent-infant (Schore & Schore, 2012, p. 257). Research has revealed the qualitative and quantitative positive benefits of infant massage and shows that the massage of the infant not only benefits the baby, but also the caregivers providing the touch (Field, 2014; Pinero-Pinto et al., 2020; Priyadarshi et al., 2022; Siu, 2023). A summary of the benefits for infants include: (a) increased parent-child attachment and bonding by creating nurturing and joyful intimacy, (b) helped infants experience the sensation of relaxation, (c) promoted a deeper and more sound sleep, (d) increased oxygen and nutrient flow to the cells, (e) improved digestion and bowel elimination, (f) initiated the process of teaching babies about caring positive touch and respectful personal boundaries, (g) produced a reduction of stress and distress and better emotional regulation, (h) decreased heart rate, blood pressure, and (i) stimulated the release of oxytocin important for calming and connectivity (Courtney, Velasquez, Bakai Toth, 2017; Field, 2014).

Roles of Caregivers and of FirstPlay® Practitioners

As mentioned in a previous section, FirstPlay® borrows from Filial play therapy to empower the parent as a change agent. However, instead of the Filial model of parents receiving training in Client Centered Play Therapy techniques, FirstPlay® practitioners provide direct instruction to parents to provide the gentle touch storytelling techniques and first-play activities to their child or infant as outlined in the *FirstPlay® Parent Manual©* (2013). This is accomplished by practitioners demonstrating the playful touch-based activities on a baby doll while the parent simultaneously provides the storytelling techniques to their own child. The FirstPlay® practitioner does not touch the child, and it is a modification from DPT, where the playful caring touch and developmental games were provided directly by the therapist. Parents are thus empowered to securely provide attuned and nurturing touch to their infant or child as facilitated by the FirstPlay® practitioner. Thus, as in Filial Therapy, the key factor in FirstPlay® is that the parent-infant/child relationship is seen as the curative factor, and the parent is viewed as the "expert" on themselves. FirstPlay® practitioners engage parents from a resiliency-focused and strength-based perspective to create a sense of safety in a warm welcoming holding environment of empathy and compassion.

Research Support

FirstPlay is informed by the vast research in infant mental health (Zeanah, 2019; Courtney, 2020a & b). Additionally, since FirstPlay® stands on the shoulders of DPT, it's important to acknowledge the past research that was completed on DPT which mainly consisted of case studies exploring the changes in children before and after treatment (Brody, 1992, 1994, 1996, 1997a, 1997b,; 1999; Brody, Fenderson, & Stephenson, 1976; Courtney, 2012; Stammers, 2017). In my dissertation I studied the effects of Developmental Play Therapy training exercises designed to examine practitioners' self-awareness related to experiences of their own attachment relationships and touch (Courtney, 2006; Courtney & Gray, 2011; 2014). Indeed, early on Brody advocated that, "It is just as important to help the adults experience and define their own feelings. . . . In fact, many times, the adult cannot understand the child's feelings until he becomes more aware of his own feelings" (Brody, Fenderson, & Stephenson, 1976, p. 39). Additionally, FirstPlay® is informed by the current research in neuroscience related to infant mental health (Zeanah, 2019), touch, and infant massage (please refer back to the already mentioned research for these topics above).

Research in FirstPlay® is emerging and similarly to DPT, the majority of research consists of qualitative case studies exploring changes in the infant, child, and parental system before, during and after treatment (Baldwin, Velasquez, & Courtney, 2020; Courtney, 2020a; 2023; 2024; (in press); Courtney & Nowakowski-Sims, 2018; Courtney & Nowakowski-Sims, 2019). Excitingly, two pilot studies have been completed in FirstPlay®. One was a dissertation studying the impact of FirstPlay® with adolescent mothers (Baldwin, 2020). The second pilot study was conducted by Siu (2023) from the University of Hong Kong to examine the effects of FirstPlay® related to the enhancement of parent-infant bonding and attachment. The research outcomes indicated that FirstPlay® touch interactions increased the parent's sensitivity and sense of bonding with their infant in the here and now serve-and-return moments of reading infant non-verbal cues (Siu, 2023). The good news is that there are a few more FirstPlay® research studies currently in process. As time moves forward, we hope to see more published research supporting the efficacy of FirstPlay® in action.

Therapeutic Powers of Play

FirstPlay® therapy utilizes the transtheoretical approach of the Therapeutic Powers of Play that was originally conceptualized by Charles Schaefer and later elaborated by Schaefer and Drewes (2014). It highlights four domains of change broken down into twenty subcategories.

- **I.** Facilitates Communication: A. self-expression, B. access to the unconscious, C. direct teaching, D. indirect teaching;
- **II.** Fosters Emotional Wellness: A. Catharsis, B. Abreaction, C. Positive Emotions, D. Counterconditioning Fears E. Stress Inoculation, F. Stress Management;

III. Enhances Social Relationships: A. Therapeutic Relationship, B. Attachment C. SocialCompetence, D. Empathy; and

IV. Increases Personal Strengths: A. Creative Problem Solving, B. Resiliency, C. Moral Development, D. Accelerated Psychological Development, E. Self-Regulation, F. Self-Esteem.

Although FirstPlay can tap into several of these areas, it predominantly draws from the power of Enhancing Social Relationships. Note, the above outline organization will be simplified to identify the therapeutic powers of play in the following sections (i.e., II.C, III.B, IV.A, etc.). In keeping the therapeutic powers of play in mind, we will now consider the case of Herman.

Case Study of Herman through the Lens of the Therapeutic Powers of Play

Conceptualizing Goals of Treatment

It is heartbreaking to read the case of Herman (see Appendix for case study of Herman being referenced) and understand the early developmental trauma beginning with the opioid exposure in utero. If we are going to approach this case utilizing the FirstPlay® infant play therapy level of intervention (birth to three years), let's imagine that there was an opportunity to intervene with Herman's biological mother. With permission to adjust this case scenario, perhaps we could hope that an intervention was initiated immediately after birth when the opioid exposure was revealed as positive, and Herman was placed in the NICU. We will assume that the state department of child and family health was alerted, and a case worker was assigned who met with the biological mother and recommended a voluntary residential substance treatment program for mothers with their infants. We will assume that the biological mother agreed to go into treatment with baby Herman once his withdrawal symptoms were stabilized and he was discharged from the hospital. We will also imagine that there is a practitioner certified in FirstPlay® who is on staff at the substance abuse residential center where the biological mother and infant will reside for at least twelve months. (Note, FirstPlay® has been successfully utilized with a group of mothers in residential substance abuse treatment [refer to Courtney, 2020a, Chapter 10 for a case example].)

Neonatal Abstinence Syndrome (NAS)

When working with infants exposed to opioids, a FirstPlay® practitioner must have some understanding of the symptoms that an infant will experience due to Neonatal Abstinence Syndrome (NAS) and the ensuing Neonatal Drug Withdrawal. When we consider baby Herman with the diagnosis of NAS and Neonatal Drug Withdrawal symptoms we could expect that he experienced frequent high-pitched crying, difficulty sleeping, tremors, poor feeding and nursing, vomiting, abdominal cramping, loose stools, fever, respiratory distress, a stiff and rigid body, muscular pain and emotional suffering (CDCP, 2023). (https://www.cdc.gov/pregnancy/opioids/basics.html). FirstPlay® practitioners will be sensitive to these NAS special needs of baby Herman and to also understand that when guiding the nurturing touch FirstPlay® activities (I. C. Direct teaching) that certain body parts may experience pain such as a foot heel that has often been used to draw blood. Thus, care must be made to be aware of the infants needs (II. F. Stress Management—lowering stress levels to foster emotional and physical wellness for the infant).

Cultural Diversity, Inclusion Considerations

When working with the biological mother and baby Herman, it's important to take into consideration their multi-cultural background, noted as Hispanic and African-American descent. It is possible that the mother may have experienced an array of prejudicial inequities and possible intergenerational historical trauma (Hudspeth, 2016b). The adverse impact of racism can begin within the womb and is present at birth. Because it is vital to acknowledge the effects of racism, a FirstPlay® mission statement for racial equity and cultural humility was created as follows (IV. B. Increases Personal Strengths: Resiliency; IV. F. Self-Esteem):

> As FirstPlay® practitioners we commit ourselves to work with our family systems to acknowledge the realities of the inequalities in society and to formulate a practice of "cultural humility." Practitioners recognize that racist violence, direct aggression and microaggressions, and systemic racism have an impact on early relationships and that intergenerational trauma affects Black, Indigenous, and People of Color from birth. Practitioners acknowledge that they are willing to look at their own personal unconscious or implicit biases and prejudices and to take action to make personal changes as self-awareness grows. FirstPlay® practitioners are committed to ensuring every baby and their families have the opportunity to be valued and loved and to be treated with the highest of respect regardless of their backgrounds. Practitioners desire to make this world a better place for infants and their families. (Courtney, 2014, p. 105)

Assessment

FirstPlay® practitioners are encouraged to obtain training in the Diagnostic Classification of Mental Health and Developmental Disorders of Infancy and Early Childhood: DC:0–5 as the best way to build assessment skills with children ages birth to five years of age (Zero to Three, 2016). We will acknowledge that baby Herman has experienced severe trauma beginning with the exposure to opioids in utero, domestic violence factors, and the subsequent NICU hospitalization, where he was deprived of nurturing touch and a lack of sensitivity to his needs. Beyond this, a thorough intake will be completed with the biological mother to assess for trauma experiences and to complete a genogram to assess for potential intergenerational historical trauma, and experiences of touch (both positive and hurtful), as well as exploring her early attachment relationships. The Circles of Attachment assessment will be implemented with the biological mother (see Appendix

A), along with an attachment drawing asking her to "Draw a picture of a mother and baby" (Courtney, 2011; Gillespie, 1994). This drawing is again completed at the end of treatment, specifically for the parent to compare images to promote self-awareness (IV. B. Increases Personal Strengths: Resiliency).

Steps of FirstPlay® In Action

The *FirstPlay® Therapy Parent Practitioner Manual* (Courtney, 2014) outlines a six-session curriculum that acts as a guiding framework for a suggested treatment plan. Each section of the curriculum sets forth the "steps of implementation" and "tips of facilitation." The curriculum is meant to act as a flexible guiding springboard to use when creating a customized treatment plan. Therefore, it is a suggested outline, and practitioners and parents can modify this as deemed appropriate for each family. For this case example of baby Herman and his biological mother, we will imagine that the FirstPlay® Practitioner was able to follow through with the six-session curriculum with the dyad as set forth below.

Session 1—Assessment and Introduction to FirstPlay®

The purpose of the first session is to gain a detailed assessment of the presenting case situation and to develop a therapeutic relationship of trust and safety with the biological mother (III.A. Enhances the therapeutic relationship). FirstPlay® practitioners will then review the introductory material with the mother found in the first few pages of the *FirstPlay® Parent Manual©* along with the parental consent forms. A complete genogram will be completed along with the Circles of Attachment and the drawing of a parent and infant (III. B. Facilitating maternal attachment self-awareness). The mother is seen without the infant for this first session.

Session 2—Live FirstPlay® Demonstration

In the second session practitioners directly teach parents (I.C. Direct teaching) the FirstPlay® Infant Therapy techniques using the *Baby Tree Hug* story in the FirstPlay® Parent Manual© and video-record the demonstration part of the session for a review at the next planned session. The FirstPlay® practitioner will create a safe holding space with respect for cultural factors to create a therapeutic alliance with the biological mother and baby Herman (III.A. Enhances the therapeutic relationship). The mother is taught three essential concepts:

1) We follow the lead of the baby and consider that baby Herman is in the "driver's seat" (IV. F. Increases personal strengths: Self-Esteem/Empowerment).
2) Baby Herman is to be respected and we therefore guide to ask for his "permission" to engage with the playful activities and touch, and (IV. F. Increases personal strengths: Self-Esteem/Empowerment).

Figure 3.2 Stephanie Crowley tells the *Baby Tree Hug* story to baby Abigail.

3) The biological mother will understand the need to regulate herself first to be in a calm place before we begin the play session. We do this by guiding the mother and infant in a "Calm, Relax and Connect," imagery (IV. E. Increases personal strengths: Self Regulation).

The FirstPlay® practitioner will be tracking for serve and return interactions and encouraging eye contact and prosodic voice to the baby to build attunement and support the attachment relationship (III. B. Facilitating the attachment relationship between mother and infant).

The practitioner will also be asking the mother questions about what she thinks baby Herman is feeling or how he might be experiencing the playful touch activities (III. D. Enhancing maternal empathy). This supports the development of empathic resonance (III. D. Enhancing maternal empathy). The biological mother will be asked to then practice the nurturing touch story with Herman at least once a day on-going (I.C. Direct teaching; III. B. Facilitating the Attachment relationship).

Session 3—FirstPlay® and Video-Recording Review

During this session, selected portions of the video recording completed in the previous FirstPlay® session will be reviewed with the biological mother. Specific suggested questions are asked, such as "What do you think your baby was feeling at this moment?" or "What do you think was your baby's favorite part of the session?" (I. A. Facilitates Communication; Self-expression). The FirstPlay® practitioner will also assess the biological mother's ability to respond to her infant's cues and to reinforce the nurturing touch, playful story activities learned in the first session. (Facilitates Communication; Direct teaching, I. C.;

III. D, Enhancing maternal empathy). The biological mother will also be asked to show the FirstPlay® practitioner what they have practiced with their baby during the week related to the FirstPlay® Parent Manual© (III. C. Enhances Social Competence).

Session 4—Introduce the FirstPlay® activities

In the fourth session, the FirstPlay® practitioner will encourage the biological mother to share more about her early attachment and play experiences and explore with her songs and developmental games that she played or remembers from her childhood (I. A. Facilitates Communication: Self-expression). During this time, we consider any cultural developmental games that might be relevant to the parent (IV. B. Increases Personal Strengths: Resiliency; IV. F. Self-Esteem). The FirstPlay® practitioner will also introduce the biological mother and baby Herman to the other FirstPlay® activities (other than the *Baby Tree Hug* story) found in the FirstPlay® Parent Manual©. These will be played and practiced together in the session (III. B. Facilitating the attachment relationship between mother and infant). The mother will then be asked to practice these new play activities between sessions—including any new developmental games that the mother has shared in session (III. B. Facilitating the attachment relationship between mother and infant).

Session 5—FirstPlay® the Parent Is the Instructor

In session five, parents are empowered to take the lead to guide the practitioner through the *Baby Tree Hug* story (I.C. Communication: Direct teaching; IV. B. Increases Personal Strengths: Resiliency; IV. F. Self-Esteem). Another caregiver can be invited to the session, and parents can demonstrate to that person the FirstPlay® activities and story. That said, let us pretend that the biological mother invited her mother (baby Herman's grandmother) to attend this session. This provides the opportunity to intervene generationally. Once the grandmother understands the purpose of the visit and agrees to participate, the grandmother will be given a babydoll and the biological mother will then guide the grandmother as she implements the story with baby Herman (I.C. Communication: Direct teaching). Note, if there is a significant other caregiver in the infant's life, such as the baby's father, the mother will most likely guide them to provide the story directly to the baby, and the mother might guide on a baby doll in that case.

Session 6—FirstPlay® Putting It All Together

In this final session, the FirstPlay® practitioner will review with the biological mother the full course curriculum, including the *Baby Tree Hug* techniques and first-play activities, and any of the information discussed in the past five sessions (III. B. Facilitating the attachment relationship between mother and infant). The mother will again be asked to

"Draw a picture of a mother and baby" for her to then compare her first drawing with this second drawing to share any insights she might observe between the before and after drawings (III. D. Enhancing maternal empathy; IV. B. Increases Personal Strengths: Resiliency; IV. F. Self-Esteem). Hypothetically, since the mother will still be residing at the substance abuse treatment center, the FirstPlay® practitioner will be having ongoing contact with the mother to support the parent-infant attachment relationship. It is possible that the FirstPlay® practitioner will also be conducting FirstPlay® groups with the other mothers in treatment. That way, the biological mother will be engaging with other mothers who are also striving to change their lives to be substance-free and who desire to grow awareness in their parenting skills. (III. C. Enhances Social Competence).

Challenges in Implementation

Due to intergenerational trauma, many parents might never have received early nurturing touch and play from their own parents. From an attachment theory point of view, a parent may lack an *internal working model* of knowing how to provide nurturing playful activities with their own babies. They may lack the understanding of how to read their baby's behavioral cues for engagement or not. Thus, a FirstPlay® practitioner may need to spend a few extra sessions to work with the parent first from a psychoeducational stance so parents can learn how to be attuned to their infant's cue-based needs and to respond with sensitivity and respect. Parents must also understand their own need for self-regulation prior to having a FirstPlay® session, as self-regulation is the precursor to co-regulation with their infant. This may be challenging for the biological mother in treatment as she will be learning new ways of regulating her emotional states beyond the use of substances.

Conclusion

This chapter presented the underlying foundations of FirstPlay® Therapy including DPT, Filial play therapy, Ericksonian therapeutic storytelling, Attachment Theory, and the research into infant mental health and touch. Utilizing the case study of Herman in infancy, we understood that Herman had been exposed to severe trauma beginning in utero with the opioid exposure and resulting NICU one month hospitalization. Through the lens of the therapeutic powers of play, we imagined a FirstPlay® six-session intervention where the biological mother was guided to provide nurturing and respectful touch to baby Herman through the *Baby Tree Hug* story. The FirstPlay® practitioner established a safe holding space with respect for cultural factors to create a therapeutic alliance with the biological mother and baby Herman. We imagined that the FirstPlay® practitioner helped to support the attachment relationship as the biological mother provided sensitive and attuned care to baby Herman. It is possible that the biological mother may never have experienced these types of early life play activities and may be learning new ways of interrelating for the first time. We hope that the opportunity for early intervention with baby Herman will lead to the breaking of challenging intergenerational patterns of relating, leading to a more secure attachment relationship that supports social, emotional, and psychological wellness. The focus on the reciprocal (serve and return) relationship between the biological mother and baby Herman can help to organize the development of brain neuroplasticity structures of resilience—potentially overcoming the deleterious effects of NAS. As baby Herman grows, the model will be adapted to follow his developmental needs to include the next level of touch-based storytelling interventions found in FirstPlay® Somatic Storytelling designed for ages three to twelve years (Courtney, 2020c).

Appendix A

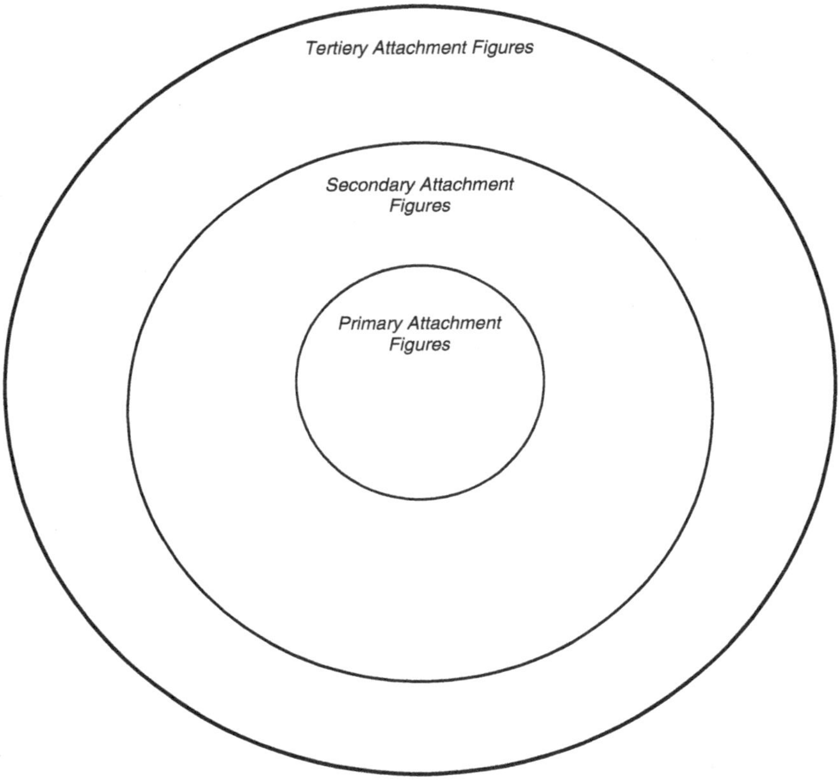

Circles of Attachment

Credit: Janet A. Courtney, PhD, & FirstPlay® Therapy

References

Association for Play Therapy. (2022). *Paper on touch: Clinical, professional, & ethical issues.* https://cdn.ymaws.com/www.a4pt.org/resource/resmgr/resource_center/Paper_on_Touch_2022__-_Final.pdf.

Badenoch, B. (2008). *Being a brain-wise therapist: A practical guide to interpersonal neurobiology.* W. W. Norton & Company.

Baldwin, K. M. (2020). *An examination of adolescent maternal-infant attachment relationship outcomes following a FirstPlay® therapy infant storytelling-massage intervention: A pilot study* (IRB approved, dissertation). Florida Atlantic University.

Baldwin, B., Velasquez, M., & Courtney, J. A. (2020). FirstPlay® therapy strengthens the attachment relationship between a mother with perinatal depression and her infant. In J. Courtney (Ed.), *Infant play therapy: Foundations, models, programs, and practice* (pp. 83–100). Routledge.

Bowlby, J. A. (1988). *Secure base: Parent-child attachment and healthy human development.* Basic Books.

Brody, V. A. (1992). The dialogue of touch: Developmental play therapy. *International Journal of Play Therapy, 1*(1), 21–30.

Brody, V. A. (1994). Developmental play therapy. In B. James (Ed.), *Handbook for treatment of attachment-trauma problems in children* (pp. 234–9). The Free Press.

Brody, V. A. (1996). Play therapy as an intervention for acting-out children. In G. L. Landreth, L. E. Homeyer, G. Glover, & D. S. Sweeney (Eds.), *Play therapyInterventions with children's problems* (pp. 22–4). Jason Aronson Inc.

Brody, V. A. (1997a). Developmental play therapy. In K. J. O'Connor & L. M. Braverman (Eds.), *Play therapy theory and practice: A comparative casebook* (pp. 160–83). John Wiley & Sons.

Brody, V. A. (1997b). *The dialogue of touch: Developmental play therapy* (2nd ed.). Jason Aronson.

Brody, V. A. (1999). Circle time in developmental play therapy. In D. S. Sweeney & L. E. Homeyer (Eds.), *Group play therapy: How to do it, how it works, whom it's best for* (pp. 139–61). Jossey-Bass Publishers.

Brody, V. A., Fenderson, C., & Stephenson, S. (1976). *Sourcebook for developmental play.* State of Florida Department of Education.

Courtney, J. A. (2006). Assessing practitioner experiences of developmental play therapy (Doctoral dissertation). Barry University School of Social Work, Miami Shores, Florida.

Courtney, J. A. (2012). Touching autism through developmental play therapy. In L. Gallo-Lopez & L. C. Rubin (Eds.), *Play-based interventions for children and adolescents with autism spectrum disorders* (pp. 137–57). Routledge.

Courtney, J. A. (2014). *FirstPlay® practitioner manual.* Developmental Play & Attachment Therapies, Inc.

Courtney, J. A. (2020a). *Infant play therapy: Foundations, programs, models and practice.* Routledge.

Courtney, J. A. (2020b). Conceptualizing infant play therapy in the context of infant mentalhealth. In J. A. Courtney (Ed.), *Infant play therapy: Foundations, programs, models, and practice* (pp. 1–17). Routledge.

Courtney, J. A. (2020c). *Healing child and family trauma through expressive and play therapies: Art, nature, storytelling, body, mindfulness*. Norton & Co.

Courtney, J. A. (2023). Touch considerations in infant and early childhood play therapy reflective supervision. In S. Born & C. Baker (Eds.), *Play therapy supervision: A practical guide to models and best practices* (pp. 169–78). Routledge.

Courtney, J. A. (2024a). Reflective supervision in infant play therapy practice. In A. Drewes & J. Mullen (Eds.), *Supervision can be playful. Techniques for child and play therapist supervisors* (2nd ed., pp. 341–53). Rowman and Littlefield.

Courtney, J. A. (2024b). Treatment planning in FirstPlay® infant play therapy. In L. L. Wonders & M. Affee (Eds.), *The play-based and expressive therapies treatment planner: A guide to working with children and adolescents* (pp. 105–12). Routledge.

Courtney, J. A. (in press). Facilitating parental attunement in infant play therapy. In D. Crenshaw (Ed.), *Play therapy: A comprehensive guide to theory and practice*. Guilford.

Courtney, J. A., & Gray, S. W. (2011). Perspectives of a child therapist as revealed through an image illustrated by the therapist. *Art Therapy: Journal of the American Art Therapy Association, 28*(3), 132–9.

Courtney, J. A., & Gray, S. W. (2014). A phenomenological inquiry into practitioner experiences of developmental play therapy: Implications for training in touch. *International Journal of Play Therapy, 23*(2), 114–29.

Courtney, J. A., & Nolan, R. D. (2017). *Touch in child counseling and play therapy: An ethical and clinical guide*. Routledge.

Courtney, J. A., & Nowakowski-Sims, E. (2018). Technology and the threat to secure attachment relationships: What play therapists need to consider. *Play Therapy, 13*(3), 10–14.

Courtney, J. A., & Nowakowski-Sims, E. (2019). Technology's impact on the parent-infant attachment relationship: Intervening through FirstPlay® therapy. *International Journal of Play Therapy, 28*(2), 57–68.

Courtney, J. A., & Siu, A. F. Y. (2018). Practitioner experiences of touch in working with children in play therapy. *International Journal of Play Therapy, 27*(2), 92–102. http://dx.doi.org/10.1037/pla0000064.

Courtney, J. A., Velasquez, M., & Bakai Toth, V. (2017). FirstPlay® infant massage storytelling: Facilitating corrective touch experiences with a teenage mother and her abused infant. In J. A. Courtney & R. D. Nolan (Eds.), *Touch in child counseling and play therapy: An ethical and clinical guide* (pp. 48–62). Routledge.

Derapelian, D. (2023). *Core attachment therapy: Secure attachment for the adopted child* (4th ed.). Kindle Direct Publishing.

Durrant, J., & Ensom, R. (2012). Physical punishment of children: Lessons from 20 years of research. *Canadian Medical Association Journal, 184*(12), 1373–7.

Field, T. (2014). *Touch* (2nd ed.). MIT Press.

Gillespie, J. (1994). *The projective use of mother-and-child drawings: A manual for clinicians*. Brunner/Mazel.

Guerney, L. F. (2015). Foreword. In E. Green, J. N. Baggerly, & A. C. Myrick (Eds.), *Counseling families: Play-based treatment* (pp. ix–xi). Rowman & Littlefield.

Hudspeth, E. F. (2016a). Neuroscience influences. *International Journal of Play Therapy, 25*(1), 1–3. http://dx.doi.org/10.1037/pla0000021.

Hudspeth, E. F. (2016b). Introduction: Play therapy applications with diverse cultures. *International Journal of Play Therapy, 25*(3), 113.

Jackson, E., & McGlone, F. (2020). The impact of play on the developing social brain: Newinsights from the neurobiology of touch. In J. A. Courtney (Ed.), *Infant play therapy: Foundations, models, programs and practice* (pp. 18–36). Routledge.

Mills, J. C., & Crowley, R. J. (2014). *Therapeutic metaphors for children and the child within* (2nd ed.). Routledge.

Palmer, D., & Barlow, J. (2017). Teaching positive touch: A child-to-child massage model for the classroom. In J. A. Courtney & R. D. Nolan (Eds.), *Touch in child counseling and play therapy: An ethical and clinical guide* (pp. 189–201). Routledge.

Perry, B. D. (2006). Applying principles of neurodevelopment to clinical work with maltreated and traumatized children: The neurosequential model of therapeutics. In N. B. Webb (Ed.), *Working with traumatized youth in child welfare* (pp. 27–52). Guilford Press.

Pinero-Pinto, E., Benítez-Lugo, M. L., Chillón-Martínez, R., Rebollo-Salas, M., Bellido-Fernández, L. M., & Jiménez-Rejano, J. J. (2020). Effects of massage therapy on the development of babies born with Down syndrome. *Evidence-based Complementary and Alternative Medicine, 2020*, 1–9.

Priyadarshi, M., Kumar, V., Balachander, B., Gupta, S., & Sankar, M. J. (2022). Effect of whole-body massage on growth and neurodevelopment in term healthy newborns: A systematic review. *Journal of Global Health, 12*, 12005. https://doi.org/10.7189/jogh.12.12005.

Porges, S. (2018). Polyvagal theory: A primer. In S. W. Porges & D. Dana (Eds.), *Clinical applications of polyvagal theory: The emergence of polyvagal-informed therapies* (pp. 50–72). Norton.

Schaefer, C. E., & Drewes, A. A. (2014). *The therapeutic powers of play: 20 core agents of change* (2nd ed.). Wiley.

Schore, A. N. (2019). *Right brain psychotherapy*. Norton & Company.

Schore, A. N., & Schore, J. R. (2012). Modern attachment theory: The central role of affect regulation in development and treatment. In A. N. Schore (Ed.), *The science of the art of psychotherapy* (pp. 27–51). John Wiley & Sons.

Schwartzenberger, K. (2020). *Neurosensory play in the infant-parent dyad. In J. A. Courtney, Infant play therapy*: Foundations, programs, models and practice. Routledge.

Siu, A. (2023). Feasibility and acceptability of using FirstPlay®® to enhance mother–child interaction: A pilot study of mothers' perspectives. *Scandinavian Journal of Child and Adolescent Psychiatry and Psychology, 11*(1), 69–77. https://doi.org/10.2478/sjcapp-2023-0007.

Stammers, L. (2017). The neurobiology of touch: Developmental play therapy with a child diagnosed with sensory processing disorder. In J. A. Courtney & R. D. Nolan (Eds.), *Touch in child counseling and play therapy: An ethical and clinical guide* (pp. 35–47). Routledge.

Zeanah, C. H. (2019). *Handbook of infant mental health* (4th ed.). Guilford Press.

Zero to Three. (2016). *Diagnostic classification of mental health and developmental disorders of infancy and early childhood: DC:0–5*. Author.

4

TraumaPlay™

Paris Goodyear-Brown

Chapter Outline

Introduction

TraumaPlay™ is an attachment-grounded, flexibly sequential play therapy model that provides an umbrella framework of core components for trauma treatment with children and their caregivers (Goodyear-Brown, 2010). Based on best practices in the fields of childhood trauma and play therapy, the components provide a scaffolding that structures moment-to-moment decision-making along a continuum of treatment, with the overarching goal of *following the child's need all along the way*. TraumaPlay™, even as a name, amplifies the often counterintuitive path toward healing: understanding the neurobiology of trauma, the neurobiology of play, and the power of one to heal the other (Goodyear-Brown, 2019a).

The model draws heavily from the fields of Interpersonal Neurobiology and play therapy, attachment theory, polyvagal theory, somatic understandings, and offers several pathways for posttraumatic play and play-based gradual exposure. The Therapeutic Powers of Play (TPoP) (Drewes & Schaefer, 2014), which represents a group of twenty change agents that play provides, will be examined with a view toward which TPoP are used to amplify change effects in each core component of treatment. The ultimate goals of TraumaPlay™ include helping the client leach the emotional toxicity out of the traumatic event(s), increase the child's felt sense of their own goodness while also enhancing an internalized sense of safety and competence, build a family-wide coherent narrative of the hard thing(s) that have happened, and celebrate the resiliencies of the client and their caregivers (see Figure 4.1).

Underlying Philosophy

The TraumaPlay™ Philosophy begins with an understanding of the unspoken contracts and multitude of attachment behaviors that evolve between children and "good enough" caregivers in "good enough" caregiving situations that ultimately lend themselves to healthy developmental trajectories.

We see trauma, and particularly the Adverse Childhood Experiences (ACEs) (Felitti, Anda, Nordenberg, Williamson, Spitz, Edwards, Koss, & Marks, 1998), as interruptions to the healthy conditions for care. As we move through the list of ACEs from neglect to abuse to incarceration of a parent, substance abuse by a parent, mental illness of a parent, divorce, and subsequent separation from one or more parents, what do all of these have in common? The ACEs rob the child of the thousands of repetitions of attuned, responsive caregiving that lead to healthy development.

We work to provide conditions in our play spaces that recapitulate healthy attachment behaviors and facilitate growth in developmental areas that may have been blocked. Bringing back the joy for families in distress is the focal point of change. Therefore, parents and other caregivers (teachers, nannies, kinship care providers) must be included in the treatment process (Dowell et al., 2010; Goodyear-Brown, 2021).

Our emphasis on the inclusion of caregivers is reflected in the assessment phase. TraumaPlay™ clinicians take time to understand the family system and the therapeutic needs from the parent's perspective, the child's perspective, and to get the felt sense of each parent/child dyad in the system prior to co-creating a treatment plan with the caregivers. During training, clinicians are often hesitant to implement the extended assessment phase. Our extended assessment phase is congruent with the core TraumaPlay™ belief that "one size does not fit all" in terms of treatment approaches. We must deeply understand *what the system can hold* prior to crafting a plan with the family. However, once they have begun doing so, they find that families feel highly supported by the intentionality of the "getting to know you" pace.

We view assessment as intervention. During the assessment phase, we are asking various parts of the family system to act in ways they do not typically interact (e.g., we may ask them to tell stories or nurture one another in specific ways). More importantly, during the assessment phase, the TraumaPlay™ therapist embodies a triad of therapist roles: Safe Boss, Nurturer, and Storykeeper. These roles will be elaborated on later in this chapter, and each of these roles seeks to capture many activities of the attuned caregiver. We believe that more is caught than taught, and as the therapeutic use of self is communicated in these three roles, we begin the Cascade of Care—embodying these safe attachment roles for the caregivers first so that they can then become Safe Boss, Nurturer, and Storykeeper for the child in their care. As the system (therapist, child, caregivers) becomes attuned to the needs of the child, areas of development that need enhancement naturally emerge. These needs often include direct work with the caregivers.

TraumaPlay™ offers a whole array of treatment goals specific to helping caregivers shift their parenting paradigms, grow in their co-regulation abilities, play skills, and attunement to the child. Deeper work might include helping parents with their own negative activation during their child's big behaviors, expanding their own reflective capacity and window of

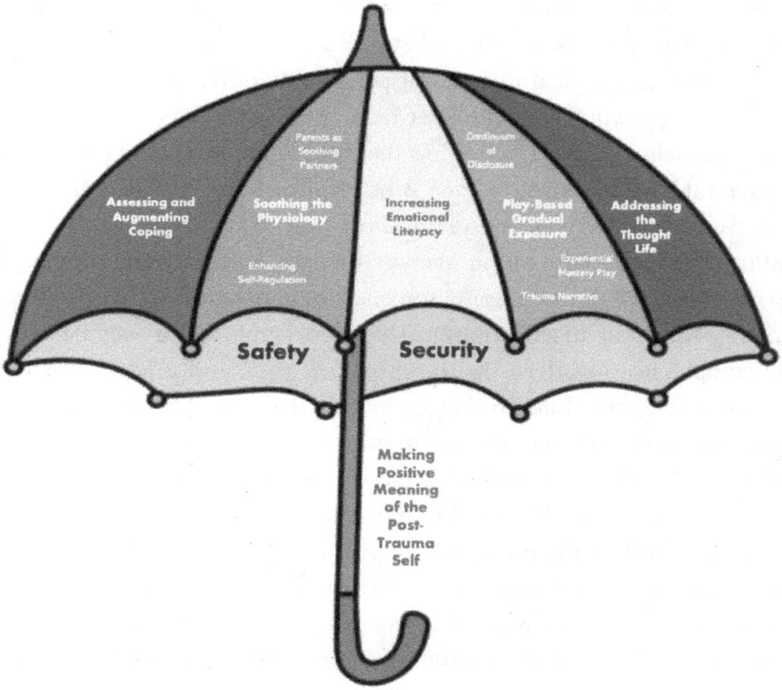

Figure 4.1 TraumaPlay™ Umbrella Framework.

tolerance, and may even require looking back at their own family of origin dynamics (Goodyear-Brown, 2021).

Another piece of our underlying philosophy is that we must *tell the truth to the child* in age-appropriate and developmentally sensitive language. When a child is existing in a vacuum of silence about domestic violence, substance abuse, or mental illness of a parent, their autonomic nervous system is already holding the unspoken story. Children are constantly learning how to language their day-to-day experiences, and their bodies are constantly interpreting their own autonomic nervous system responses in relationship to those around them, so it becomes crazymaking for children when there is a felt sense of panic, terror, grief, anger, and so on, but it is not named by their Safe Bosses. For healing to occur, Storykeeping grown-ups need to translate the story from the big behaviors of the child (sympathetic activation, or immobilization) to the neocortex. In fact, we view this process of *bringing it into the room* as necessary because it is already somatically present in the space. In essence, offering the nuanced narrative to the child invites the neocortex to frame the felt sense of the trauma, ultimately creating a "neocoretext"—a new core story.

Personality Theory

TraumaPlay™ values the entire context, both nurture and nature, of the process of growth and change. Assessment begins with a thorough bio-psycho-social-cultural interview with the caregivers. This initial session encourages the parent to speak freely, and the therapist works to embody Safe Boss, Nurturer, and StoryKeeper for the caregiver.

The five major psychological theories of personality development attempt to explain, understand, and/or predict how humans behave. TraumaPlay™ embraces a *Yes, and* approach to personality theory. Do we view the child or family system through a biological lens? A behavioral lens? A cognitive lens? A humanistic lens? A psychodynamic lens? The TraumaPlay™ answer is yes, yes, yes, yes, and yes (sort of).

TraumaPlay™ leans heavily on humanistic theories and purports that meeting needs bottom up (Maslow, 1943) and offering unconditional positive regard (Rogers, 1957) are pillars of change for traumatized children. This model embraces a deep belief that there is a drive for competence (Watters, 2020) within all of us and offering what we call *the competency surge* (helping children engage in play that enhances their sense of mastery over their environment and themselves) mitigates the approach to trauma content.

The physiological underpinnings of behavior are deeply respected in TraumaPlay™, leading to assessment questions related to in utero injuries such as the mother's ingestion of drugs or alcohol during the pregnancy or the mother being under toxic stressors that lead to the release of massive amounts of cortisol into the developing brainbody of the fetus. Somatic understandings and careful assessment of the child's sensory systems are also required to provide an optimal treatment environment. The goal here is to understand the child's unique exteroception and interoception needs, and to offer tools and experiences that meet these. While many children are sensory seeking or sensory defensive, children with complex trauma often have a complex presentation of both sensory seeking and sensory defensive behaviors. Medical issues, hospitalizations after birth, the meeting of developmental milestones, the baby's overall demeanor during the first year of life (easy-going, colicky, difficult to soothe or slow to warm up) are all part of our initial assessment.

Cognitive theories are also considered, and time is spent understanding how motivation, decision-making, problem-solving, and the ability to complete sub-goals in pursuit of a larger goal all play into the potential difficulties that the child is facing. TraumaPlay™ leans heavily on understandings of polyvagal states and the window of tolerance for distress. Clients—both children and their parents—benefit from cross-hemispheric work where the exploration of their own autonomic nervous system states often is collateral to the caregivers exploring their own movements in and out of the states of hyper and hypo arousal.

Less heavily weighted in the direction of psychodynamic theory, we certainly believe that many of our thoughts, emotions, urges, and memories lie outside of conscious awareness. TraumaPlay™ therapists are likely to help clients and their parents make clear connections between their thoughts, feelings, and actions, and approach any cognitive distortions, problematic behaviors that represent over- or under- responding to emotions, and the actual consequences of their actions over the course of treatment.

Model of Psychopathology

TraumaPlay™, while appropriate for use with children with one discrete traumatic event, was created for children with complex trauma, and for those who present with developmental trauma disorder (van der Kolk, 2005), evidencing developmental impacts in each developmental arena. TraumaPlay™ does not support a model of psychopathology in the traditional sense. The idea that our clients (sometimes also referred to as patients) come to us with a sickness of mind or a series of abnormalities that must be challenged or ameliorated is antithetical to what TraumaPlay seeks to support. If we take each part of the word psychopathology, psycho meaning "mental or of the mind," pathos meaning "suffering", and—othology meaning "study of," we might define psychopathology as the study of mental suffering. The most profound suffering of children occurs when their parents, the ones who have unspoken contracts to mitigate the child's suffering, break their contracts. We view the interruptions to healthy development caused by the ACES as cheating the child out of the titrated doses of distress that attuned, responsive caregivers allow while otherwise comforting and nurturing the child. This suffering often manifests in internalizing symptoms like suicidal ideation and looping intrusive thoughts or as externalizing symptoms like self-harm and aggression toward others. Co-regulation always precedes self-regulation, and children with complex trauma were not co-regulated. The therapist, then, seeks to recapitulate the attachment behaviors of healthy caregiving in a moment-to-moment awareness of the child's unmet needs throughout the course of treatment.

TraumaPlay™ therapists embrace the epigenetic explanation that psychopathology can be communicated to the next generations through changes in DNA (Zhou & Ryan, 2023). Psychopathology can also be engendered by the stories a child is told. *The stories we are told are the stories we become until we learn a new story* is the TraumaPlay™ mantra that guides treatment. Children are likely to encode the negative messages embedded in the story being told and assign blame to the self when stories are not fully explained. Creating coherent narratives that tell a new story by highlighting resiliencies, assigning positive intentionality to both clients and caregivers, countering blame or false responsibility that the client might carry related to the trauma, and supporting healthy connections between the client and their caregivers. Each core component of TraumaPlay™'s umbrella framework represents a treatment goal that mirrors what would have happened in healthy development. We see this umbrella framework as a protective covering for children from the torrential rains of trauma.

Play is the language of children (Landreth, 2012) and is optimal for helping parents and children shift paradigms and storykeep differently. In the next section, each component of TraumaPlay™ will be described and tied to specific Therapeutic Powers of Play. However, we give primacy to delight as the all-encompassing change agent holding and supporting all the rest.

Conceptualizing Goals of Treatment

The TraumaPlay™ therapist holds the idea that each child and their case is unique. Clinical decision-making in terms of which treatment goals to focus on streamlines to two overarching questions the therapist asks in conceptualization: (1) How do we follow the child's need in this moment? and (2) What can the system hold? A flexibly sequential umbrella framework is offered, and integrates non-directive and directive approaches while encouraging the therapist to make nuanced choices that follow the needs of the child (Powell, Cooper, Hoffman, & Marvin, 2013) throughout the continuum of treatment.

Each component defines the specific treatment goal, which then lends to treatment planning, leading to a series and variety of interventions in its delivery, whilst also employing the therapeutic powers of play. The therapist considers (a) sense of safety and security; (b) assessing the client's current coping strategies and the potential need to augment adaptive coping choices for both child and caregivers; (c) ability for self-regulation and having caregivers as soothing partners; (d) gauging emotional literacy; (e) titration of disclosure, mastery and trauma narrative; (f) addressing the thought life; and (g) how positive meaning can be made by the post-trauma self (Goodyear-Brown, 2021).

Enhancing Safety and Security

Enhancing the sense of safety and security of the child in TraumaPlay™ sessions is paramount before any trauma narrative work can be done. One of the ways in which the therapist does this is through the physical setup of the playroom, considering the space (bigness and smallness of), light, color, sound, and the play materials (Goodyear-Brown & Yasenik, (Eds.)). The play objects, which are categories of toys that are selected to invite certain kinds of play, and the physical environment, connect to interoception as well as exteroception of the child's body, offering the experience of felt safety. Once the neuroception of felt safety has been established, exploration and experimentation can take place for the child.

Therapeutic use of self (Goodyear-Brown & Yasenik, (Eds).) is the second pathway for either enhancing or hindering the client's neuroception of safety. Proximity of the child toward or away from the therapist, verbal and non-verbal behaviors of the therapist, including tone, cadence, intonation, which word in a reflection is stressed, and so on, are all important. The self of the therapist is crucial here in creating safety, both in the physical space and in the relationship with the child. From there, the therapist is able to extend support to the child either directly or indirectly, thereby disarming any fear response with felt safety (Dana, 2018; Porges, 2015; Purvis, Cross & Sunshine, 2007; Yasenik & Gardner, 2023).

Therapeutic Powers of Play Employed

As the therapist sets up the playroom purposefully to enhance the sense of safety and security of the child, this allows for the *facilitation of communication*. It expands the capacity for the child for *self-expression* through the use of the play space and play materials.

When the therapist engages with the child, attuning to their needs, this sets up the therapist as the secure base for exploration and support and as a safe haven. The child is able to explore and return for comfort and nurture, hence building secure *attachment* and establishing a positive *therapeutic relationship*. As the therapist continues to exhibit consistent safety and security, be it through the physical or emotional use of self when communicating with the child through play, the *therapeutic relationship* is strengthened.

Assessing and Augmenting Coping

Does the child have an adaptive set of coping strategies in place for the processing of trauma? The therapist offers one or more prop-based play interventions to ascertain the current coping of the child. The prop-based interventions utilized in this treatment goal allow for the therapist to evaluate what coping strategies the child currently has in place, whether they are adaptive or maladaptive, and to identify if the adaptive coping repertoire of the child needs expansion prior to trauma processing. In addition to looking at the current coping responses of the child, the social supports of the child, such as family, school, and peers, are also to be assessed. A plan can then be made for augmenting the positive social supports and mitigating the influences that may put the child at risk

Therapeutic Powers of Play Employed

The assessment and augmentation of coping strategies employ the therapeutic powers of play through *direct and indirect teaching*. The therapist is able to help the child expand their coping tools through these two therapeutic powers. With the child being actively involved in the assessment and augmenting process through playful prop-based interventions, opportunities are available to the therapist to provide instruction and *modellng*. This allows the child to try out and practice new *coping strategies*. In addition, *indirect teaching* through the use of therapeutic stories such as the Worry Wars book (Goodyear-Brown, 2010) enables the therapist to expand the *coping strategies* of the child.

The Copecakes intervention (Goodyear-Brown, 2021) is an example of *direct teaching* where the therapist teaches the child how to cope better. With the use of props such as baking tins and cupcake liners, the child is able to learn the basic ingredients needed for adaptive coping as he or she is physically involved in learning the coping strategies in a playful way.

Soothing the Physiology: Enhancing Self-Regulation and Parents as Soothing Partners

From history-taking to observation of the child in play therapy sessions, the therapist asks how able is the child to soothe their own physiology? Is the child able to move back within the window of tolerance? How able are the caregivers to provide co-regulation for the child?

The therapist pays attention to the arousal state of the child, noticing whether the child has the tendency to shift more into mobilization or immobilization states (Porges, 2011). Techniques to help the child downregulate or upregulate through using tools in the playroom, such as music, craft, or movement, can then be customized in order to attend to the needs of the child in being soothed by a safe other so that self-regulation can be enhanced.

In TraumaPlay™, co-regulation takes place before self-regulation. Caregivers need to be equipped to become soothing partners. Gaining an understanding of the stressors that are currently present in the family system, along with having the caregiver do a dyadic assessment with their child, enables the therapist to determine the parental play skills and co-regulation skills that need enhancing, as well as the psychoeducation required. The reflective capacity and the ability of the caregiver in following the need of the child in discipline (Buckwalter, 2020; Goodyear-Brown, 2021) are also explored, allowing treatment planning to include attunement and delighting-in experiences between caregiver and child (Helle et al., 2022; Salo et al., 2020) which supports caregivers as partners in the therapeutic process. Caregivers benefit from an expanded toolkit that includes not only behavior management strategies but also the SOOTHE strategies, which codify a set of practices for parents and teachers to employ when the child is not in their choosing mind (Goodyear-Brown, 2010, 2021).

Therapeutic Powers of Play Employed

The specific therapeutic power of play that increases the personal strengths of the child at work here is that of *self-regulation*. The play activities that allow a child to either upregulate or downregulate increases the ability of the child to know when to activate or when to calm oneself. Self-regulation techniques can be taught either via *direct or indirect teaching*. Emotional wellness is then fostered with the therapeutic power of play of *stress management* as the child learns how to reduce the emotional stress levels that typically arise from the experience of trauma.

The inclusion of caregivers as soothing partners relates to the enhancement of *social relationships*, particularly with *attachment*, and also in fostering emotional wellness due to the generation of *positive emotions*. The playful delighting-in experiences can promote powerful joy-filled moments between caregiver and child, resulting in attachment repairs and strengthening the attachment relationship whilst in the midst of increased positive emotions.

Enhancing Emotional Literacy

Is the child able to understand and accurately communicate the feeling state he or she is in? How does the child express them? Determining the scope of emotional literacy that a child has, particularly the emotions that usually escalate the child, helps to lay the foundation for trauma narrative work.

The Color-Your-Heart technique is an informal assessment instrument that could provide the therapist with a visual representation of the internal life of the child, along with evaluating if the child is able to form associations between articulated feeling labels and the behaviors and experiences they have. Different play-based and kinesthetic interventions can then be introduced to increase emotional literacy for the child. These may be geared toward enhancing emotional granularity, expanding feelings vocabulary, understanding their interoceptive cues that a certain feeling is present, or pairing feelings with the situations that often engender them.

Therapeutic Powers of Play Employed

For the child who is limited in his or her verbalizations, the play activities enable the *facilitation of communication* through *self-expression* where the child is able to share and tell, along with being able to label the feelings to various experiences.

Continuum of Disclosure, Experiential Mastery Play, and Trauma Narrative

Play-based gradual exposure and posttraumatic play are broken down into these three pathways that children often use to process trauma. First, we consider how the child self-titrates their exposures to trauma-based material along with how it is communicated through the play materials. Being aware of the perpetrator symbols and their containment, the self-objects and how they are nurtured, while also promoting competency surges for the child, may be needed to help the child create a coherent narrative of the trauma history or trauma experience.

Along with the continuum of disclosure, the therapist looks at the various ways in which the child, through prop-based gradual exposure, can begin to work through their fears and anxieties arising from the trauma content. The awareness of the perpetrator's symbols and self-objects for containment from the titration of disclosure can be used by the therapist to facilitate experiences of mastery for the child, allowing for *catharsis* and *abreaction*, and restoring a sense of power and control. While many children begin to play through the trauma using the continuum of disclosure, and others need some mitigators in the approach to hard things (EMP), another group of children is so mired in the avoidance symptoms of PTSD that they require a structured approach to the trauma narrative. In these cases, the therapist shares power with the child regarding the timing and the play mediums used.

Therapeutic Powers of Play Employed

With the play items available, children are able to approach the thoughts, feelings, and bodily sensations associated with the traumatic events, thereby allowing the therapeutic powers of *catharsis* and *abreaction* to take place and fostering emotional wellness. The child is able to emotionally release any *negative emotions* attached to the disclosure and processing. Given the play materials, the child is able to reenact the experiences through play in order to gain a sense of *mastery* over the trauma, thereby increasing *resiliency* during the therapeutic process.

The therapist is able to engage the child in mastery play, which not only leads to the child's ability to experience the big feelings and fears that arise from the aftermath of a traumatic event or from repeated incidents of trauma events, the child is able to, through the play, to overcome the fear. This *counterconditions* the fear they experienced, whilst also reinforcing what is termed in TraumaPlay™ as "competency surges", which enhances *resiliency*. At the same time, the therapeutic powers of *stress management* and *self-regulation* are also applied. From here, various ways of mastery can also be explored, highlighting *creative problem solving*.

The scaffolding from the therapist regarding the use of play-based interventions whilst embodying the role of a nurturer, safe boss and storykeeper, demonstrates acceptance and attunement to the needs of the child at any given moment during this treatment goal. This is significant as through the therapeutic powers of play, within the safety of the therapeutic relationship, the coherence of trauma narrative can be integrated.

Addressing the Thought Life

The therapist sees this work as coming behind the child and sweeping up any cognitive distortions that may have been revealed during trauma processing. These can be negative self-talk the child has about themselves or others, as well as false attributions about the trauma incident. Areas of psychoeducation and cognitive restructuring can be identified, allowing the child to externalize specific thoughts and be able to kinesthetically manipulate them through play-based techniques to the point where the child gains a sense of control over their thought life.

Therapeutic Powers of Play Employed

Indirect teaching through the use of storytelling and therapeutic metaphors can facilitate the learning and positive reinforcement of positive cognitions. It also allows the child to look at their situation differently and from different perspectives. Indirect teaching allows the therapist to help the child examine negative cognitions and, through either direct or indirect teaching or both, teach them new skills and ways of thinking. As the child continues to apply the new skills and ways of thinking in their lives through repetition in the playroom and outside of the therapy sessions, *self-esteem* is greatly improved for the child.

Making Positive Meaning of the Post-Trauma Self

The therapist does a review of treatment goals and looks at the extent in which each of the treatment goals have been met. Celebration and honoring the therapeutic journey of the child and their resiliency with purposeful inclusion of the caregivers helps to make a meaningful goodbye.

Therapeutic Powers of Play Employed

As the child looks forward in his or her journey post-therapy, playing out possible future scenarios and utilizing the therapeutic power of play for *stress inoculation* enhances the healing and positive meaning-making of the posttrauma self. This serves to reduce any anticipatory anxiety as well as empower the child in being able to handle any intense situations he or she might find themselves in. The celebration and honoring of the therapeutic journey is made, for example, through graduation ceremonies, with emphasis placed on the personal strengths of *resiliency* and *self-esteem* that have been increased.

In TraumaPlay™ sessions, the caregivers are often involved in the termination session, which includes playful parent-child celebration activities. This further reinforces secure *attachment* and enhances *social relationships*.

Role of the Therapist

The TraumaPlay™ therapist embodies three roles in therapy—safe boss, storykeeper, and nurturer. These roles align with the bottom-up brain development needs of clients (Perry & Hambrick, 2008). The three parts of the triune brain: the reptilian brain stem, the limbic brain, and the neocortex, lend themselves to three core questions. The brain stem is always asking, *Am I safe?*; the limbic brain is always asking, *Am I loved?*; and only when these two lower brain-region questions are answered with a consistent "yes!" can the thinking brain do its job of asking *What can I learn from this?* (Bailey, 2001). The three embodied roles are overlayed on this triune template and help clinicians (and caregivers) move in and out of caregiving roles (Figure 4.2).

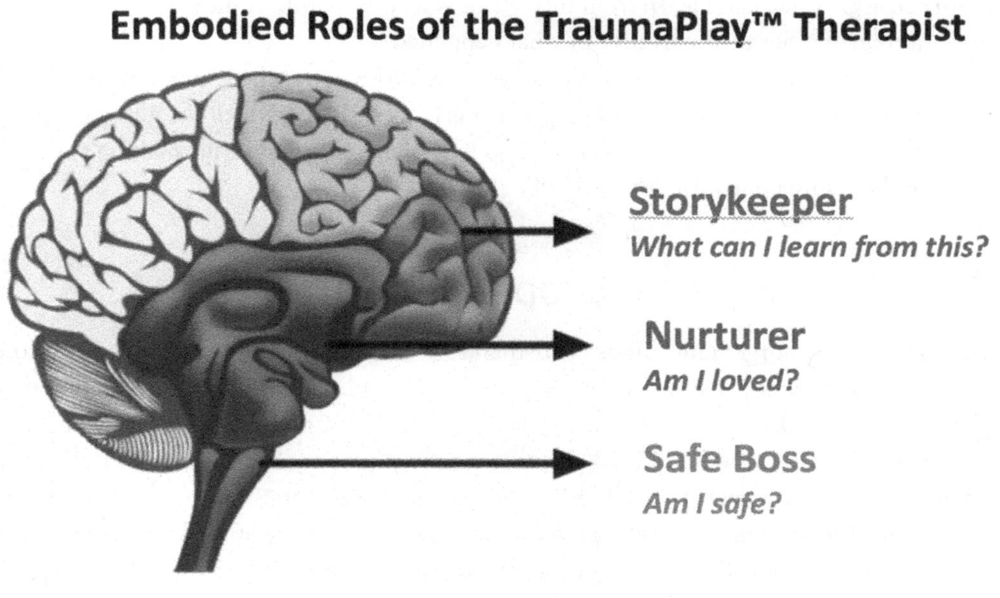

Figure 4.2 Embodied Roles of the TraumaPlay™ Therapist.

Safe Boss

This involves the therapist ensuring that limits are set where needed and sharing power with the child where necessary. There are clear boundaries and a consistent environment for the child. This role aligns with the brain stem and the work of regulation as the brain stem asks, "Am I safe?" When the child is dysregulated, the clinician becomes Safe Boss, setting and maintaining boundaries calmly and kindly while naming and meeting underlying needs (for food, hydration, sensory input, rest, etc.). Safe Boss presence must be established foundationally. All other therapeutic scaffolding begins here.

Nurturer

This role aligns with the limbic brain asking, "Am I loved"? The therapist, in the role of the nurturer, is paying attention to the needs of the child, continuing to meet the needs while delighting in the child and offering nurture in physical and verbal ways. This also enhances secure attachment and regulation.

Storykeeper

Only after a therapist has become Safe Boss and Nurturer to the client will they have earned the right to answer the question that the neocortex begins to ask—"What can I learn from this?" Regulation and connection must precede Storykeeping, and co-regulation always precedes self-regulation.

If the two lower brain region questions are answered in the affirmative, then the thinking brain can ask, "What can I learn from this?" This is where the role of the storykeeper comes in—crafting an integrated narrative of what happened.

The therapist in this role is able to hold the hard stories of the clients in their care. He or she can use the words, images, and somatic experiences, along with all the glimpses of the trauma content that the child has provided, to help create the story while making coherent sense of the trauma narrative for the child.

Research/Empirical Support

TraumaPlay is a burgeoning model and therefore in need of more research. Each core component of the model is supported by a wealth of empirical evidence. As an integrative play therapy model, TraumaPlay is heavily informed by Child-Centered Play Therapy, Theraplay, the ARC model, TF-CBT, and Somatic Experiencing, each of which has a strong body of empirical support. Research unique to this integrative approach is ongoing. Meanwhile, the TraumaPlay umbrella serves as a synthesis of current best practices in the field of trauma work with children and their caregivers. Clinicians and researchers in both non-directive and directive methods will find a place in TraumaPlay.

Case Study through the Lens of the Therapeutic Powers of Play

Cultural, Diversity, Inclusion Considerations

A core principle of TraumaPlay™ is cultural responsiveness (Casey et al., 2022; Coull & Parson, 2024; Landreth, 2023) which begins with cultural humility (Dowtin, 2022; Jaminez-Pride; 2021; Ray et al., 2022). In this case, exploration related to how Herman (see Appendix for case study of Herman being referenced) himself identifies in terms of race, culture, ethnicity, gender, and sexuality will all be important parts of assessment and treatment. The intake will serve to capture how the parents believe the client is identifying in these areas, but support for Herman himself around this question might include the Power Flower (Arnold, Burke, James, & Martin, 1991), directive sand tray prompts related to self-definition in several areas, and permission for various parts of self to be more or less prominent at different developmental levels. Herman was born into several marginalized demographics and has most likely experienced institutional oppression in various forms as a result of this. His sociocultural experiences will need to be heard.

Case Formulation and Application

TraumaPlay™ therapists place a high value on a thorough, multi-pronged assessment phase that allows clinicians to see the needs of the family system through the eyes of the child, the eyes of the caregiver, and through observation of the parent/child dyad as they negotiate tasks together. Clinicians are also welcome to add an additional assessment session that offers a family play therapy prompt and observes the family dynamics as a whole.

Through a TraumaPlay™ lens (Goodyear-Brown, 2024b), assessment begins by threading the needle backwards from Herman's big behaviors to his earliest life experiences. Parents are enlisted as partners during the intake, answering questions in multiple categories. A heavy emphasis is placed on questions related to development in utero and in the first three years of life outside the womb.

The TraumaPlay™ Storykeeping tool (Goodyear-Brown, 2024a) helps to catalogue information in relevant categories, while specific developmental questions are meant to re-open the compassion well for a parent who may be hardened and exhausted to help them reflect on the earliest ACEs the child experienced. Assessment begins with Storykeeping, defined by the TraumaPlay™ model as *threading the needle from the big behavior we are currently seeing all the way back to its earliest origins* (see Figure 4.3).

In the case of Herman, while he scored significantly high for ADHD and externalizing behaviors on the CBCL, it is important to remember that this checklist looks at symptoms and not at causality. It is also important to view the endorsed symptoms through the trauma-informed lens of autonomic nervous system states and the impediments that hyperarousal, hypoarousal, and collapse can cause to learning and academic success.

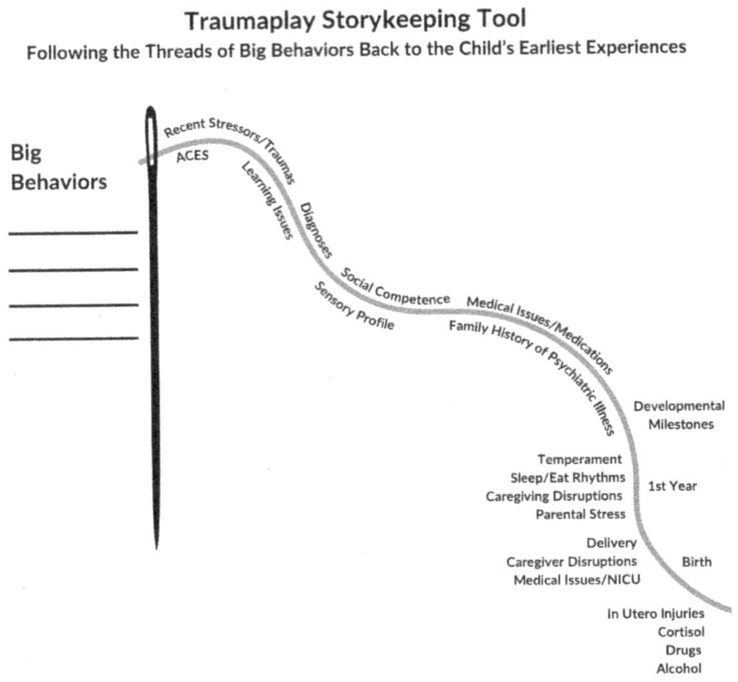

Figure 4.3 TraumaPlay™ Storykeeping Tool: Threading the Needle.

Herman spent a lot of time in his early life alone. From his first days in the NICU, where there were so many babies with needs that Herman only received intermittent and unpredictable attention, through to his three years in his maternal grandmother's care, where he spent inordinately long periods of time in his crib with a bottle and no human interaction, there was little serve-and-return communication, a wasteland devoid of the kinds of experiences that wire our brains and bodies for relational health.

From the most global conceptual view, Herman did not get to be delighted in or have his basic needs met with any predictability or joyful relationship. TraumaPlay™ therapists consider the face, voice, body, and proxemics of the caregiver to be the first experience-rich environment for the newborn. Warm eye gaze, "motherese" or melodic prosody of voice, gentle rocking, or jiggling while being held close to the caregiver, these interactions become the playground for the child with a "good enough" caregiver. Herman was not only robbed of attuned responsive caregiving that would co-regulate him through the transition from his mother's womb to the outside world, but he also had the additional in utero injuries of his mom's illicit drug use. Born addicted to opioids, no amount of co-regulation by a caregiver would have been enough to save him from the painful effects of withdrawal.

I (Paris) have had several cases in which a child has had parental rights terminated in the hospital setting. As I ask foster/adoptive parents what those first weeks in the NICU looked and felt like, these parents described the withdrawal symptoms of their tiny newborn: vomiting, seizures, sweats, chills, inconsolable crying, and rigid bodies. These parents are desperate to provide soothing and comfort to the child, but no matter how much they hold, rock, or croon to their new baby, they cannot take away the pain. The core schema developing for these infants is often something like "I just have to hurt. There is no one who can keep me safe, meet my needs, or help me feel better." This ultimately gives way to a *control foundation* instead of a trust foundation (Erikson, 1950).

Soothing the Physiology

Biological underpinnings cannot be ignored; the in utero injuries of opioid use combined with the high comorbidity rate between alcohol and drug use set up a high potential for Herman's developing neurobiological systems to be deeply dysregulated. The paucity of touch that the client received in the NICU was exacerbated by his placement with his grandmother. In fact, if any associations were made between touch and a felt sense autonomically, the association would likely be that touch equals to pain. This core belief was further enhanced by his sexual abuse in his second placement. An early treatment goal in TraumaPlay™ would be to begin pairing touch with genuine comfort and genuine delight in the child, recapitulating through nurturing games. Herman's in utero injuries (alcohol abuse) may have damaged his reptilian brain stem, causing sensory processing differences. Given all of his adverse childhood experiences, Herman is likely to be not only leaning in the direction of sensory defensiveness or sensory-seeking behaviors, but also have a complex presentation of both. TraumaPlay™ therapists will spend as much time as needed becoming detectives together with the client's current foster care parents to try and understand *which sensory systems in which situations* may need to be coregulated differently.

Grandmother's window-of-tolerance (WOT) for co-regulating Herman through his distress was extremely narrow. Our work will be to expand the WOT for the foster parents, helping them explore cross-hemispherically their own arousal states while working to help them understand and mitigate their negative activation with Herman through breathwork, mindfulness work, parental mantras like "I am bigger, stronger, wiser, kind," and self-care strategies.

Herman's parents are concerned about his increasing anger and aggression. It may be useful to frame this behavior within a polyvagal context (Goodyear-Brown & Yasenik, 2024). Herman spent the first six years of his life necessarily harnessing the most adaptive coping response he could manage, given that he was repeatedly neurocepting life threat. TraumaPlay™ therapists utilize the Polyvagal Zoo to explain to children and their caregivers the autonomic states that can be engendered by the neuroception of safety/danger/life threat. From the beginning of Herman's life, he felt intense pain: the pain of withdrawal without any way to escape or fight back necessitated a dorsal vagal collapse. When he witnessed his grandmother and her paramour hurt each other over and over again, his system responded by dropping into the dorsal vagal shutdown that had been geniusly practiced from his earliest moments of life. Complete with intermittent dissociation, this immobilization response protected him in the NICU and served him well in the war zone that was his grandmother's home.

In his first placement (from ages three to five), he may have begun to experience some felt safety, or at least a reprieve from the neuroception of life threat. When this occurs, it is our natural healing bent to climb up the polyvagal ladder, seeking social engagement. The phrase "upwardly mobile" used in my mother's generation (Paris) for those who were climbing the social ladder can be applied to the polyvagal ladder. It is innately human to move toward social engagement when we are neurocepting safety. However, it is impossible to bypass sympathetic activation (mobilization) when one has been in a state of immobilization. This awareness reminds me of the camp chant, *Going on a Bear Hunt*. The chorus of "You can't go over it. You can't go under it. You can't go around it. You've got to go through it" is poignantly true. In this first placement, hope may have sparked that Herman's three-year-old self had finally arrived at a place that was safe, with people who would connect with him. His autonomic nervous system, responding to this hope, allowed him to *risk* becoming sympathetically activating. This may have involved elopement behaviors (running away from school or home) as well as aggressive behaviors (the fighting bear response).

Parents as Partners

After four years of trying to connect deeply with Herman, they may be suffering from exhaustion and felt hopelessness or helplessness. Affirming their importance as Safe Boss, Nurturer, and Storykeeper will be critically important, as will offering the SOOTHE strategies (*Fosters Emotional Wellness: stress management; Increases Personal Strengths; Self-regulation*) and helping them see themselves as the providers of co-regulation that he never received. Moreover, Herman may need in-vivo delighting-in games with his caregivers in order to deepen attachments and bring back the delight in the relationships prior to trauma processing (*Enhances Social Relationships: attachment).*

Increasing Emotional Literacy

Herman has experienced layers of betrayal, trauma, and grief. The unspoken contract between a parent and child was broken first by his biological mother using meth when pregnant with him. Herman may need lots of time to expand an emotional vocabulary prior to being able to integrate the emotional aspects of his adverse childhood experiences into an integrated narrative (*Facilitates Communication: self-expression; access to the unconscious; Increases Personal Strengths: self-regulation*).

Continuum of Disclosure, Experiential Mastery Play

Discrete traumatic memories may be impossible to delineate, and Herman's first showing or telling of his child sexual abuse may be through glimpses and snapshots of the trauma. Herman may use the tools of the playroom to engage in enactments of implicit memories, including making sexual grunting noises, or manifesting other sensory memories related to the abuse (*Facilitates Communication: self-expression, access to the unconscious; Fosters*

Emotional Wellness: catharsis, abreaction). He may also seek out small challenges to his own strength or abilities in order to experience the competency surge (*Increases Personal Strengths: resiliency, creative problem solving, self-esteem*). These might include choosing a perpetrator symbol for the older boy who sexually abused him and containing it, or choosing a self-object and carefully watching how the therapist nurtures it. There are likely to be other experiences, related to his various caregivers and foster siblings that may be given in glimpses, requiring the therapist to be ready to project "I see what you are showing me and you can show me more (*Facilitates Communication: direct and indirect teaching; Enhances Social Relationships: therapeutic relationship, empathy*)."

Trauma Narrative

If Herman is entrenched in the avoidance symptoms of PTSD, then he may benefit from a more structured invitation to make coherent sense of his multiple caregiver disruptions. Doors of Doubt, a sand tray intervention that was co-created with a client of mine (Paris) who had been in five separate homes, may be useful with Herman (*Facilitates Communication: direct teaching, access to the unconscious*). I would offer him a variety of doors and ask if we could put the doors in the sand to represent each of his transition to each new placement. These doors are spaced at intervals in the sand tray based on how long he felt like he had been in each home. He is then invited to choose symbols for the family members in that home. One completed example is pictured below (Photo 4.1).

If we were to use such an intervention with Herman, we would begin with the hospital NICU, move to his grandmother's (and her paramour's) home, the first placement where he lived from three to five, and the second placement where he lived for only one year, but was sodomized by a sixteen-year-old boy repeatedly, and finally to his current foster home.

Addressing the Thought Life

If we step our way through the core beliefs that may have been generated (or were certainly reinforced) in each "home," we might guess that in the NICU, Herman generated a core belief that "I just have to hurt, no one can help me feel better." In his grandmother's home, he may have learned, "Grown-ups are unpredictable . . . you never know when they are going to get angry. People express anger by hitting each other. I am a burden and a bother. I don't deserve to exist. The grown-ups don't have time for me. I must take care of myself." It may have been most adaptive in his grandmother's home to descend into a dorsal vagal state (using the Polyvagal Zoo animals, this might mean that Herman becomes the sloth [dissociated and numbed] when left in his crib for hours). In moments of intense fighting between his grandmother and her paramour, he might also become the fainting goat, freezing and collapsing (Figure 4.4). In his first foster home, he may have generated the core belief, "I am too much for the grown-ups." In his second placement, he may have learned, "I am never safe. I must stay ready . . . stay awake, because I can be hurt at any moment and no one can help me."

Photo 4.1 Doors Representing Transitions between Homes.

If we think about the thinking, feeling, doing dance that is constantly occurring for all humans, if Herman *thinks* he must stay alert at all times, he may feel anxious, guarded, exhausted, and undefended. He may *be* hypervigilant; he may have engaged in dorsal vagal shutdowns during his sexual abuse (Goodyear-Brown & Kenney-Noziska; 2024; Goodyear-Brown, 2012) and if that did not work, engage in fawning behaviors that sought to please his perpetrator in order to avoid being hurt worse. Herman had a paucity of co-regulation in the NICU and a denuded, neglectful environment in his home with his grandmother. An attuned, responsive caregiver could have paired loving co-regulation and need meeting with touch, deepening the neural pathways toward social engagement with caregivers as an adaptive coping strategy a good idea. However, grandmother's impatience communicated, "you are too much for me" and "it is wrong to need so much from me" instead of communicating I will try to understand the underlying need that has not been met yet and do what I can do to meet it.

Challenges in Implementation

The largest risk in cases like this is always that the caregivers may give up on Herman before he can make substantial shifts in his ANS and become more regulated. The older he

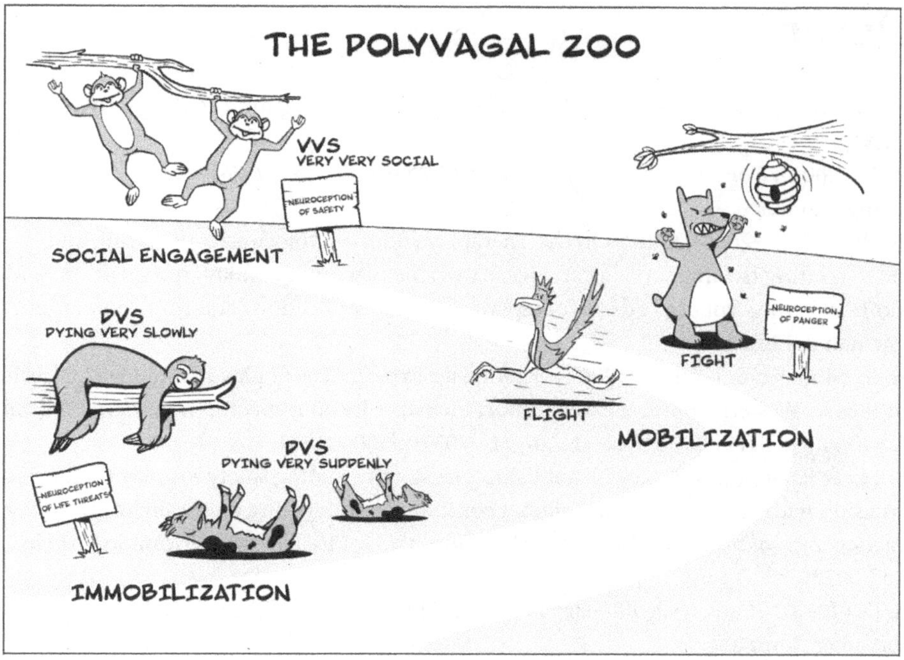

Figure 4.4 The Polyvagal Zoo.

gets, the bigger his physical body becomes, the more damage can be done in his school and home, and the more difficult it becomes for caregivers to see him as a hurt, vulnerable child inside the shell of his tween/teen body. Depending on what part of the country he lives in, his identity formation may also be impeded by his burgeoning identification with groups that continue to be marginalized in our society. Also, while the hope of neuroplasticity guides TraumaPlay™ clinicians, it is possible that there will be limitations to his reflective capacity or to his ability to regulate himself independently of an external regulator, requiring some support for a lifetime.

Conclusion

TraumaPlay™ was created for clients like Herman. The umbrella framework of flexibly sequential treatment components requires a constant reliance on the attachment relationship between the therapist and the client and continual movement in and out of the triad of therapist roles: Safe Boss, Nurturer, and Storykeeper, following the child's need all along the way. As healthy attachment behaviors are recapitulated in the therapeutic context and Herman's foster parents are equipped more fully as partners in this work, they can become more effective Storykeepers—threading the needle backwards from Herman's current big behaviors to his earliest experiences, creating a coherent narrative with his foster family while leaching the emotional toxicity out of the events.

References

Arnold, R., Burke, B., James, C., & Martin, D. (1991). *Educating for a change*. Between The Lines.

Bailey, B. (2001). *Conscious discipline: 7 basic skills for brain smart classroom management*. Loving Guidance.

Buckwalter, K. D. (2020). Ghosts in the Theraplay room—Exploring, considering and understanding the impact of a caregiver's own history on Theraplay treatment. In S. M. Booth & A. M. Jernberg (Eds.), Theraplay®: Theory, applications and implementation. Rowman & Littlefield.

Casey, S., Moss, S., & Wicks, J. (2022). Therapists' experiences of play therapy with Muslim families in Western countries: The importance of cultural respect. *International Journal of Play Therapy, 31*(1), 56. https://doi.org/10.1037/pla0000153.

Coull, H., & Parson, J. A. (2024). Establishing trust and creating safety for play therapy service provision with an Australian aboriginal community: Informing culturally responsive practice. *International Journal of Play Therapy, 33*(3), 140–153. https://doi.org/10.1037/pla0000220

Dana, D. (2018). *The Polyvagal theory in therapy: Engaging the rhythm of regulation*. W. W. Norton & Company.

Dowell, K. A., & Ogles, B. M. (2010). The effects of parent participation on child psychotherapy outcome: A meta-analytic review. *Journal of Clinical Child & Adolescent Psychology, 39*(2), 151–62. https://doi.org/10.1080/15374410903532585.

Dowtin, L. L. (2022). Cultural humility and social justice in play therapy supervision. In K. C. Schafer & D. A. Drewes (Eds.), *Play therapy supervision* (pp. 9–21). Routledge.

Erikson, E. H. (1950). *Childhood and society*. W. W. Norton & Co.

Felitti, V. J., Anda, R. F., Nordenberg, D., Williamson, D. F., Spitz, A. M., Edwards, V., Koss, M. P., & Marks, J. S. (1998). Adverse Childhood Experiences (ACE) study questionnaire. Centers for Disease Control and Prevention.

Goodyear-Brown, P. (2010). *The worry wars: An anxiety workbook for kids and their helpful adults!* Routledge.

Goodyear-Brown, P. (Ed.). (2012). *Handbook of child sexual abuse: Identification, assessment, and treatment*. Wiley.

Goodyear-Brown, P. (2019a). *Trauma and play therapy: Helping children heal*. Routledge.

Goodyear-Brown, P. (2019b). *TraumaPlay™ foundational training* [PowerPoint slides]. TraumaPlay Institute.

Goodyear-Brown, P. (2021). *Parents as partners in child therapy: A clinician's guide*. The Guilford Press.

Goodyear-Brown, P. (2024a). Treatment planning in TraumaPlay: Storykeeping for the family system. In L. L. Wonders & M. Affee (Eds.), *The play-based and expressive therapies treatment planner: A guide to working with children and adolescents*. Routledge.

Goodyear-Brown, P. (2024b). The thread the needle tool. Routledge

Goodyear-Brown, P., & Kenney-Noziska, S. (2024, March). The genius of the disembodied self: Coping with child sexual abuse. In P. Goodyear-Brown & L. Yasenik (Eds.), *Polyvagal power in the playroom: A guide for play therapists*. Routledge.

Goodyear-Brown., P. & Yasenik, L. (Eds.), Polyvagal power in the playroom: A guide for play therapists. RoutledgeAdd this to the reference list: Goodyear-Brown., P. & Yasenik, L. (Eds.), *Polyvagal power in the playroom: A guide for play therapists.* Routledge

Helle, J., Vøllestad, J., Schanche, E., & Hjelen Stige, S. (2022). From seeing difficult behaviour to recognizing legitimate needs: A qualitative study of mothers' experiences of participating in a Circle of Security Parenting program in a public mental health setting. *Psychotherapy Research*, 1–12. https://doi.org/10.1080/10503307.2022.2083291

Jimenez-Pride, C. (2021). Cultural humility in the telemental health playroom. In A. Crenshaw & J. Stewart (Eds.), *Play therapy and telemental health* (pp. 68–83). Routledge.

Landreth, G. L. (2012). *Play therapy: The art of the relationship*. Routledge.

Landreth, G. L. (2023). Being culturally responsive. In G. L. Landreth. *Play therapy: The art of the relationship* (pp. 99–108, 4th ed.). Routledge.

Maslow, A. H. (1943). A theory of human motivation. *Psychological Review, 50*(4), 370–96. https://doi.org/10.1037/h0054346.

Perry, B. D., & Hambrick, E. (2008). The neurosequential model of therapeutics. *Reclaiming Children and Youth, 17*(3), 38–43.

Porges, S. W. (2011). *The polyvagal theory: Neurophysiological foundations of emotions, attachment, communication, and self-regulation*. W. W. Norton & Co.

Porges, S. W. (2015). Play as neural exercise: Insights from the Polyvagal theory. *Mindgains. org*, 3–7.

Powell, B., Cooper, G., Hoffman, K., & Marvin, B. (2013). *The circle of security intervention: Enhancing attachment in early parent-child relationships*. Guilford Press.

Purvis, K. B., Cross, D. R., & Sunshine, W. L. (2007). *The connected child: Bring hope and healing to your adoptive family*. McGraw-Hill.

Ray, D. C., Ogawa, Y., & Cheng, Y. J. (2022). Cultural humility and the play therapist. In *Multicultural play therapy* (pp. 13–28). Routledge.

Rogers, C. R. (1957). The necessary and sufficient conditions of therapeutic personality change. *Journal of Consulting Psychology, 21*(2), 95–103. https://doi.org/10.1037/h0045357.

Salo, S., Flykt, M., Mäkelä, J., Lassenius-Panula, L., Korja, R., Lindaman, S., & Punamäki, R. L. (2020). The impact of Theraplay® therapy on parent-child interaction and child psychiatric symptoms: A pilot study. *International Journal of Play, 9*(3), 331–52. https://doi.org/10.1080/21594937.2020.1823322.

Schaefer, C. E., & Drewes, A. A. (2014). *The therapeutic powers of play: 20 core agents of change*. John Wiley & Sons.

van der Kolk, B. A. (2005). Developmental trauma disorder: Toward a rational diagnosis for children with complex trauma histories. *Psychiatric Annals, 35*(5), 401–8. https://doi.org/10.3928/00485713-20050501-06.

Watters, E. R., & Wojciak, A. S. (2020). Childhood abuse and internalizing symptoms: Exploring mediating & moderating role of attachment, competency, and self-regulation. *Children and Youth Services Review, 117*, 105305.

Yasenik, L., & Gardner, K. (2023). *Play therapy dimensions model: New insights for integrative play therapists*. Jessica Kingsley Publishers.

Zhou, A., & Ryan, J. (2023). Biological embedding of early-life adversity and a scoping review of the evidence for intergenerational epigenetic transmission of stress and trauma in humans. *Genes, 14*(8), 1639.

5

The Therapeutic Powers of Play in Digital Play Therapy™

Jessica Stone

Chapter Outline

Introduction

Charles Schaefer loved to pose questions and pursue answers. He would have a twinkle in his eye as he asked a variety of professionals questions that indicated his ponderings of the time. A prolific writer, he produced over sixty books, along with over one-hundred articles, cofounded the Association for Play Therapy, and founded the International Play Therapy

Study Group (Dignity Memorial, 2020). Dr. Schaefer's work has shaped each generation of play therapists after his, and he has left behind a legacy that the field will carry forward.

One of his foundational contributions was the formulation and organization of the therapeutic powers of play, as is highlighted throughout this book (Schaefer, 1993; Schaefer & Drewes, 2014). Through his posed questions and the pursuit of answers, he worked to define the components of play and then extended this quest to define the differentiations between "just play" and therapeutic play therapy. Ultimately, Schaefer sought to present a "comprehensive account of how play therapy works, and [by] specifically highlight[ing] those elements of the play process likely to be responsible for its most beneficial effects" (p. xi). He believed that "play is not just a medium for applying other interventions such as positive reinforcement or reframing, but that play itself has a number of therapeutic elements that produce behavior change" (p. xi).

These play agents of change can be found within and applied to a variety of play-based therapeutic interactions. One approach is Digital Play Therapy™ (DPT). DPT, established as a distinct modality and approach by Stone in 2020 and further developed in 2022, is founded on key principles: the 5Cs, speaking the client's language, the therapeutic powers of play, and prescriptive play therapy. These principles delineate the therapeutic components and guide the responsible integration of digital tools in therapy sessions. Building on Schaefer's insights regarding fundamental therapeutic agents and the process of change, DPT utilizes play's universal appeal, making therapy relevant across diverse cultural trends and generational interests. The rise of the digital native necessitates the inclusion of digital experiences in therapy and is critical for cultural inclusivity (Cole, 2019; Prensky, 2001; Stone, 2020, 2022). This chapter highlights the application of the therapeutic powers of play as a key cornerstone of DPT.

The Underlying Philosophy of DPT

Digital Play Therapy is an innovative approach that capitalizes on the familiarity, customizability, and engaging nature of digital mediums. The incorporation and inclusion of digital tools into therapy facilitate a therapeutic experience that resonates with many clients, particularly with the digital native generation. This generation includes "individuals born after 1980, who were raised in an environment in which they were surrounded by technology and who possess technological skills different from those possessed by the members of the prior generation" (Cole, 2019, para 2; Palfrey & Gasser, 2016; Prensky, 2001).

Play

Professionals often wonder, and rightfully so, if play that is different from the traditional has general value, and by extension, therapeutic value. To evaluate this, we must have a firm grasp on the meaning of play; however, this is complicated as play is one of those experiences that is easier to recognize than define (Schaefer, 1993). Kaduson and Schaefer

(2021) consulted a number of resources to define play through eight characteristics (Barnett, 1990; Gray, 2011; Schaefer & Drewes, 2014). They posited that play:

1) Is freely chosen
2) Is intrinsically motivated
3) Values means over ends
4) Involves multiple positive affects
5) Is personally directed
6) Includes active involvement
7) Includes nonliterality/pretense
8) Includes flexibility (p. 3)

Play is a fundamental human element across the lifespan and throughout time. Adults and children alike benefit from play (Poyer, 2013; PsychCentral, 2022) around the globe (Lester & Russel, 2010). Mancala-like boards have been found in Neolithic sites, estimated to be between 6,000 and 10,000 years old (Alex, 2020).

Digital Play

> Through digital play, children have multifaceted experiences that contribute to their well-being. (Unicef, 2024, p. 59)

Recent research and writings have identified important positive components of digital play. Digital play has been found to provide optimized learning (Psychgeist, 2024), improved reading efficiency (Pasqualotto et al., 2022), improved memory and attention (Chaarani et al., 2022), improved alerting network efficiency (Wang et al., 2023), reduced medical anxiety (Kitchens, 2024), reduced stress, anxiety, and feelings of isolation (esa, 2023), reduced symptoms of depressive disorders (Ruiz et al., 2022), promoted offline social interactions with friends (Steinsbekk et al., 2024), and improved family co-play happiness (Wang et al., 2018). Purported correlations with aggressive and violent behavior have also been debunked (Johannes et al., 2022; Drummond et al., 2020). As the RITEC-8 Unicef 2024 report found, "In recent years more attention has been given to the potential for digital play and digital games to also make positive contributions to children's development" (p. 4).

Digital play is play—and—play is not a waste of time. It is not merely a passing of time. Friedrich Froebel, a German educator who invented kindergarten (Louis & Powell, 2020), offered the following in 1861:

> It has indeed been stated . . . as a fundamental truth, that the plays and occupations of children should by no means be treated as offering merely means for passing the time (we might say, for consuming time), hence only as outside activity, but rather that by means of such plays and employments the child's innermost nature must be satisfied. (1861/1895, p. 108)

The components within play have purpose. Lowenfeld stated that play "is the expression of the child's relation to the whole of life" (Lowenfeld, 2008, p. 23), and digital play has entered this arena.

Therapeutic Digital Play

Using digital tools in therapeutic environments is actually "about strategically modifying environments to align with therapeutic goals" (Muftau-Lediju, 2024, para 5). In a personal communication, Muftau-Lediju shared:

> I think it's imperative that we as healthcare professionals not shy away from researching the value of tech and videogames especially with mental health, when it is applied as a tool it can have impactful results; It's important to note that as clinicians we make sure we connect the impactful lessons learned to extend outside of the game itself. (personal communication, April 8, 2024)

Drawing from the insights of Ceranoglu (2010), Stone (2019, 2020, 2022, 2023), and Granic et al. (2014), the integration of video games into mental health treatment offers numerous advantages. These include cognitive enhancement, improved strategy, critical thinking, frustration tolerance, motivational growth, emotional regulation, social navigation, prosocial behavior, enhanced problem-solving abilities, creativity, flexibility, adaptation, leadership, and organizational skills.

In therapeutic digital play, clients work toward therapeutic goals through these identified arenas. This can be facilitated through interactions with both non-player characters (NPCs) and/or other human players within the game environment. Changing in-game perspectives, such as altering viewpoints or assuming different characters, offers new insights and problem-solving strategies. Gameplay promotes exploration of personal needs, coping strategies, and problem-solving through trial and error, thereby fostering control and autonomy. Therapeutic gameplay can enhance the player's sense of personal agency, facilitate goal setting and planning, and provide opportunities for mastery development. Digital games and programs can also serve as a safe space for emotional and physical self-care, with opportunities for deep personal insights and self-evaluation. The adaptability of digital games, from 2D to 3D experiences, allows clinicians to tailor the gaming environment to each individual's needs, offering a diverse range of therapeutic opportunities (Stone, 2022).

Digital Play Therapy™

> Digital play therapy is a modality that utilizes highly motivating, immersive activities to incorporate areas of client culture and interest into the play therapy process to deepen relationships, gather information, implement interventions, and advance the treatment plan forward. (Stone, 2022, p. 16)

Digital Play Therapy™ (DPT) is a specialized modality that integrates the use of digital tools and play therapy principles to enhance and support the play therapy process and provide structure to therapeutic digital play. Drawing upon foundational elements such as the therapeutic powers of play, prescriptive play therapy, and the unique DPT framework of the 5Cs (competence, comfort, culture, congruency, and capability), DPT is characterized by its use of digital tools to deepen therapeutic relationships, gather relevant information, implement interventions, and advance treatment plans forward (Stone, 2020, 2022).

DPT offers three distinct levels of therapeutic engagement:

1) inviting and engaging in discussions that include a client's digital interests,
2) incorporating digital tools within the session for content sharing, searching, and exploring,
3) direct use of the digital tool together, i.e., co-playing within digital environments (Stone, 2020, 2022).

These levels aim to have the client feel seen, heard, and valued; integrating their digital cultural context into the therapeutic process. The use of DPT is not merely about incorporating the latest technological trends into therapy, but is anchored in a deep respect for the client's cultural milieu and an adherence to solid, foundational principles. This approach ensures that the digital elements used in therapy are not only engaging and motivational, but also therapeutically grounded. DPT offers versatile and impactful tools to address a wide range of emotional, cognitive, and social needs within the therapeutic setting. For more detailed information, please refer to Stone's 2022 text *Digital Play Therapy, 2nd edition.*

The Efficiency and Effectiveness of Digital Play Therapy™

While Digital Play Therapy™ (DPT) follows the same general principles and timelines as traditional play therapy, it offers unique advantages that can potentially enhance treatment efficiency and effectiveness. The integration of digital tools into the therapeutic process provides opportunities for more engaging, expressive, and tailored interventions.

Accelerated Therapeutic Progress

DPT's use of highly engaging and motivating digital activities can lead to accelerated therapeutic progress. The immersive nature of digital environments allows clients, particularly those from the digital native generation, to express themselves more freely and process emotions more readily. This increased engagement can result in more productive therapy sessions and potentially faster achievement of treatment goals.

Customization and Prescriptive Approach

One of DPT's key strengths lies in its prescriptive approach, which allows for highly customized therapeutic interventions. By identifying important details about the client, including their individual characteristics, treatment goals, and the guiding theoretical frameworks, therapists can tailor digital play experiences to meet specific needs efficiently. This targeted approach ensures that interventions are relevant and impactful, potentially shortening the time required to achieve therapeutic goals.

Cultural Relevance and the 5Cs

The DPT framework, anchored by the 5Cs (Competence, Comfort, Culture, Congruency, and Capability), emphasizes cultural relevance, representation, and inclusivity. By integrating the client's cultural background and interests, particularly their engagement with digital tools, DPT enhances the therapeutic alliance and engagement. This cultural attunement, coupled with the motivational aspects of digital activities, facilitates potentially deeper and quicker therapeutic engagement, thereby contributing to more efficient treatment outcomes.

Flexibility and Adaptability

Digital tools offer unparalleled flexibility in adapting therapeutic activities to the client's evolving needs. Therapists can quickly adjust game settings, choose different digital environments, or switch between various digital tools within a single session. This adaptability allows for real-time responsiveness to the client's emotional state and therapeutic progress, maximizing the effectiveness of each session.

Enhanced Expression and Communication

For many clients, especially those who struggle with verbal expression, digital tools provide alternative means of communication. Through avatars, game characters, or digital art creation, clients can externalize their thoughts and feelings more easily. This enhanced ability to express and process emotions can lead to more rapid insights and breakthroughs in therapy.

While the overall duration of therapy may still vary based on individual client needs and therapeutic goals, DPT's unique attributes offer the potential for more efficient and effective treatment. By capitalizing on the engaging nature of digital tools, customizing interventions, and emphasizing cultural relevance, DPT can create a therapeutic environment that is both highly motivating and deeply attuned to the client's needs, potentially leading to more rapid progress and positive outcomes.

The Underlying Personality Theory of DPT

Before one can properly discuss the underlying personality theory of DPT, clarity must be provided regarding the nature of this particular approach. DPT is a *modality* to be used within the context of a clinician's theoretical foundation (Stone, 2022, 2020). In this case, an attempt to provide a distinction between theory and modality is made, despite a lack of consensus within the field regarding the definitions.

Psychological Theory

A psychological theory is a set of ideas and principles that explain various aspects of human thoughts, behaviors, and emotions. Psychological theories provide a framework for understanding how and why people act in certain ways, as well as what the concepts of pathology and healing are. Theories offer hypotheses that can be tested through research. A theory typically guides the clinician's understanding of a client's concerns and directs the therapeutic approach and interventions used (Reinfeld, n.d.).

Modality

A modality is the method or medium through which therapy is delivered. It can include the techniques and specific interventions used in therapy sessions (Torres, 2024). "It encompasses diverse approaches and techniques that therapists and counselors utilize to address clients' mental health needs" (para 5).

Digital Play Therapy™ (DPT) is not confined to a single psychological theory; instead, it embraces theoretical agnosticism. This approach allows for flexible integration of various therapeutic models to suit the individual needs of clients and the belief systems of the clinician. DPT is a modality—not a theoretical framework. The therapist has the freedom and the responsibility to ascribe the analyses, interpretations, meanings, and paths to change as their foundation provides. For the sake of example, this section will provide a path of application according to the author's primary theoretical foundation.

The Importance of an Underlying Personality Theory

In the application of Digital Play Therapy™ (DPT), the underlying personality theory a therapist chooses to integrate plays a crucial role in shaping the therapeutic process and outcomes. This choice is vital as it influences how therapists perceive and interpret clients' behavior and interactions within the digital play environment. Each personality theory provides a unique lens through which a therapist can understand the underlying motivations, conflicts, and needs of their clients. For instance, a psychodynamic approach might lead the therapist to focus on unconscious processes and early childhood experiences that manifest during digital play sessions. Alternatively, a cognitive-behavioral framework could guide the therapist to prioritize the identification and modification of distorted thinking patterns through digital interactions.

Choosing an appropriate personality theory aids therapists in selecting and implementing interventions that are not only tailored to the specific psychological makeup of the client but also congruent with the therapeutic goals. It allows therapists to utilize the virtual elements of DPT—such as interactive games and simulations—in ways that are theoretically informed and clinically effective. Ultimately, the integration of a well-suited personality theory enriches the therapeutic process, providing deeper insights into the client's behaviors and facilitating meaningful changes in their psychological well-being. Therefore, it is essential for therapists to carefully consider which theoretical foundation they apply in their practice of DPT to maximize the benefit for their clients.

The underlying personality theory holds paramount importance in the application of the therapeutic powers of play, particularly within the framework of Digital Play Therapy™ (DPT). By selecting a specific personality theory, therapists are equipped with a structured lens through which to view and interpret a client's actions, play choices, and interactions within the digital environment. This theoretical grounding not only informs the therapist's understanding of the client's internal world but also guides the selection and implementation of therapeutic interventions that resonate most effectively with the client's needs.

Formulating a Model of Psychopathology Within Digital Play Therapy™

Digital Play Therapy™ (DPT) is not a standalone theoretical model of psychopathology; rather, it serves as a versatile and integrative tool that enhances the therapist's ability to conceptualize the client's experiences and needs within their chosen theoretical framework. DPT provides a dynamic context where various aspects of the client's life and internal world can be explored, understood, and addressed through digital interactions (Stone, 2022, 2023).

Conceptualization of the Client

DPT facilitates a comprehensive understanding of the client by allowing the therapist to observe and interact with the client in a digital environment. This environment can reveal many facets of the client's personality, coping mechanisms, and areas of struggle. Through digital play, clients can express themselves in ways that might be difficult in traditional therapy, providing insights into their inner world, including their:

- *Emotions and Emotional Regulation*: Digital play can highlight how clients manage emotions such as frustration, joy, fear, and anger.
- *Behavioral Patterns*: The way clients engage with digital games can reflect their real-world behaviors, responses, and patterns.
- *Cognitive Processes*: Digital tools can help identify cognitive strengths and weaknesses, such as problem-solving skills and attention span, and reflect their styles, skills, and strategies.

Integrating Systems Involved

DPT acknowledges the influence of various systems on the client's life, including family, social networks, educational institutions, and digital communities. By incorporating these systems into the therapeutic process, DPT allows for a holistic approach to understanding and addressing psychopathology. This includes:

- *Family Dynamics*: Observing interactions within family-based digital activities can reveal relational patterns and attachment styles.
- *Social Relationships*: Multiplayer games and online interactions can shed light on the client's social skills and peer relationships.

Addressing Client Needs

DPT enables therapists to tailor interventions to meet the specific needs of the client. By engaging in digital play, therapists can identify and address:

- *Emotional Needs*: Helping clients process and express emotions in a safe and controlled environment.
- *Behavioral Needs*: Developing strategies to manage behaviors that interfere with daily functioning.
- *Cognitive Needs*: Enhancing cognitive skills through targeted digital activities.

Cultural Sensitivity

DPT allows for the inclusion of culturally relevant content, ensuring that therapy respects and reflects the client's cultural background and personal identity. This cultural sensitivity helps:

- *Affirm Identity*: Incorporating games and activities that resonate with the client's cultural heritage and personal preferences.
- *Facilitate Understanding*: Enabling discussions about cultural values, beliefs, and experiences within the context of digital play.

Exploring Beliefs and Desires

Digital environments offer a unique space to explore the client's beliefs, desires, and aspirations. Through digital play, clients can experiment with different roles and scenarios, providing insights into their:

- *Core Beliefs*: Understanding how the client views themselves, the world, and their place in the world.
- *Desires and Aspirations*: Identifying goals and motivations that drive the client's behavior.

Societal Expectations

DPT also considers the impact of societal expectations and pressures on the client. Digital games often mirror societal norms and challenges, allowing clients to navigate these within a therapeutic setting. This exploration can help clients:

- *Recognize External Pressures*: Identifying societal influences that contribute to stress or conflict.
- *Develop Coping Strategies*: Creating strategies to manage societal expectations and their impact on mental health.

Conceptualizing Pathology within Theoretical Frameworks

While DPT itself does not provide a specific model of psychopathology, it enhances the therapist's ability to conceptualize the client's issues within their theoretical framework. Whether the therapist operates from a psychodynamic, cognitive-behavioral, humanistic, systemic perspective, or otherwise, DPT offers tools and insights that can be integrated into these frameworks. This integration involves:

- *Identifying Underlying Issues*: Using digital play to uncover unconscious conflicts, cognitive distortions, or relational patterns.
- *Formulating Treatment Goals*: Aligning digital interventions with the theoretical goals of therapy, such as increasing insight, modifying behaviors, or improving relational dynamics.
- *Tailoring Interventions*: Adapting digital activities to support specific therapeutic techniques and objectives.

Conceptualizing Treatment Goals in Digital Play Therapy™

The formulation of treatment goals within DPT is a thoughtful process that integrates the core tenets of DPT with a nuanced understanding of each client's specific needs. This process is informed by multiple sources:

1. Information gathered and understood about the client
2. Insights from people in the client's life
3. The therapist's theoretical foundation

Based on these inputs, treatment goals are conceptualized and continually refined throughout the therapeutic process, ensuring they remain tailored to the client's evolving needs.

Foundation of Treatment Goals

The foundation of goal formulation in DPT is deeply rooted in the therapy's central tenets, which emphasize the therapeutic alliance, the power of digital engagement, and the importance of personalization (Stone, 2022). Central to this approach is an appreciation for the client's lived experience, digital literacy, and unique psychological profile. DPT harnesses the potential of digital environments to facilitate therapeutic exploration, expression, and growth, making alignment with client-specific needs paramount (Stone, 2020, 2022, 2023).

Integration of Client Needs

Formulating treatment goals in Digital Play Therapy™ (DPT) involves a comprehensive assessment of the client's psychological well-being, culture, and individual needs. Digital play provides a versatile medium for clients to express complex emotions and thoughts through symbolic play, avatar customization, and role-playing games. Tailored interventions address emotional regulation, coping, and interactive skills, and cognitive development, while culturally relevant digital content ensures inclusivity and respect for the client's background. Continuous adjustments based on progress and feedback allow for a flexible and dynamic approach, creating engaging and relevant goals that resonate with the client's identity and needs.

Therapeutic Powers of Play and Digital Engagement.

DPT extends the principles of the therapeutic powers of play into the digital realm, recognizing that digital play offers unique opportunities for expression, learning, and psychological healing. Treatment goals are conceptualized with an understanding of how digital play can facilitate communication, emotional wellness, social relationships, and personal strengths. Interactions within the play can be identified, recognized, communicated, and/or sought as defined by the structure and concepts provided by the therapeutic powers of play. This also assists in identifying components to include in one's case notes.

The Role of the Therapist in Digital Play Therapy™

The role of the therapist in Digital Play Therapy™ (DPT) is multifaceted, characterized by an aware, open, observant, and accepting approach. This role extends to the digital realm, utilizing the unique opportunities presented by digital gameplay to facilitate therapeutic growth and change. Therapists invite the whole client to be present, vulnerable, and connected within therapeutic interactions, maintaining acute awareness of the dynamics of the digital environment and its impact on the client. They continuously seek to improve their digital literacy to better connect with clients and guide the therapeutic process. Openness to digital tools allows for the exploration of innovative ways to engage clients and address their unique needs.

Observing clients' interactions with digital tools provides valuable insights into their inner world, helping therapists tailor interventions effectively. Acceptance involves validating clients' digital experiences without judgment, fostering a safe environment for exploration and self-expression. Therapists adeptly match clients with digital gameplay by understanding client preferences, assessing therapeutic goals, and leveraging the specific offerings of digital games. Continuous monitoring and adaptation ensure that the therapeutic use of digital tools remains aligned with the client's evolving needs and therapeutic progress.

Roles of Caregivers and Collaterals in DPT

Caregivers and collaterals play a pivotal role in the therapeutic journey of clients engaged in Digital Play Therapy™. Their contributions enrich the therapy process by providing valuable insights, supporting ongoing assessment, and actively participating in treatment when appropriate. During the initial assessment phase, caregivers and collaterals offer critical insights that contribute to a nuanced understanding of the client's history, behaviors, and therapeutic needs. They help identify concerns and goals, share observations that may not be immediately apparent in therapy, and provide crucial information about the client's digital habits and family dynamics. This comprehensive input is invaluable for developing a case conceptualization that informs the therapeutic strategy.

Caregivers are essential for monitoring progress and supporting the generalization of therapeutic gains. Their ongoing feedback highlights changes in the client's functioning across different contexts, allowing for adjustments to the treatment plan. Inclusion in co-play sessions within the DPT framework fosters stronger family relationships, models positive digital engagement strategies, and tailors digital activities to address specific treatment goals. This involvement empowers caregivers to be proactive contributors to the therapeutic process, enhancing the effectiveness and sustainability of therapeutic outcomes.

Narrative Analysis of Herman's Case Study from a Psychodynamic + DPT Perspective

Herman (see Appendix for case study of Herman being referenced), a ten-year-old boy of various heritages, has faced numerous challenges since birth, including prenatal exposure to opioids, early childhood neglect, and significant trauma. This case study explores Herman's therapeutic journey using a combined Psychodynamic and Digital Play Therapy™ (DPT) approach. The analysis will highlight the application of the therapeutic powers of play and the core agents of change activated throughout Herman's therapy. DPT can be utilized with the therapist's theoretical framework. This analysis is written from the author's framework to illustrate how one might apply DPT tenets and a theoretical framework to a client's treatment.

Background

Herman was born to a mother with a history of opioid use and domestic violence. His early life was marked by a lack of nurturing and stable attachments, resulting in a possible insecure attachment style. After being moved through several foster homes and experiencing sexual abuse, Herman currently resides in a therapeutic foster home. Despite a currently stable environment, he exhibits severe behavioral issues, struggles with ADHD, and has learning disabilities.

Through the digital play characteristics identified by Unicef's RITEC-8 report: autonomy, competence, emotions, relationships, creativity, identities, diversity, equity, and inclusion, and safety and security, Herman can be presented with therapeutic digital interventions with significant breadth and depth (Unicef, 2024). When digital games are designed or include key components and experiences, they can allow the player to:

> experience a sense of control and agency, have freedom of choice, experience mastery and feelings of achievement, experience, understand and regulate a range of emotions, feel connected to others and manage those social connections, imagine different possibilities, act on original ideas, make things, and explore, construct and express facets of themselves and others. (p. 59)

Anticipated Clinical Presentation for Herman

In considering Herman's clinical presentation within the context of Digital Play Therapy™ (DPT) and a psychodynamic framework, several key characteristics are expected to manifest. Herman's digital gameplay is likely to exhibit a notable degree of chaos, with characters running erratically and shifting from one activity to another in a disorganized manner. This chaotic behavior mirrors Herman's frequently dysregulated emotional state and his difficulties with frustration tolerance. Consequently, his strategic abilities in digital games are anticipated to be low, reflecting his struggle to plan and approach tasks systematically, as he may have some executive functioning struggles.

At times, Herman might exhibit hyperfocus on specific elements of the game, which could abruptly shift to avoidance behaviors, as he struggles to maintain a balanced engagement with the digital activity. His cognitive challenges, such as difficulty with retention and organization, are anticipated to impact his ability to remember game objectives and maintain an organized approach to gameplay. Additionally, Herman is likely to face significant challenges with multi-sequential tasks, struggling to follow a series of steps or complete tasks that require sustained attention over multiple stages.

Table 5.1 Comparison Table for Digital Play Therapy™ (DPT), Psychodynamic Therapy, and Psychodynamic Digital Play Therapy™ (Psychodynamic DPT)

Aspect	DPT	Psychodynamic	Psychodynamic DPT
Key Tenets	Incorporates digital tools in therapy, leveraging client interests and culture for engagement and therapeutic outcomes	Focuses on unconscious processes, early childhood experiences, and the therapeutic relationship	Combines principles of DPT with psychodynamic focus on unconscious processes and early relationships
Underlying Philosophy	Integration of digital experiences with traditional play therapy principles, balance, and respect for client culture	Based on Freudian theories, emphasizing unconscious mind and early development	Integrates digital tools into psychodynamic framework, respecting client culture and unconscious influences
Personality Theory	Not specific to any one personality theory, uses digital tools to explore and express personality traits and dynamics	Derived from Freud's theory of personality: id, ego, and superego	Uses digital tools to explore personality dynamics within a psychodynamic framework
Model of Psychopathology	Uses digital interactions to understand and address psychological concerns, difficulties, and disorders	Psychopathology arises from unconscious conflicts and early experiences	Combines digital play tools with psychodynamic understanding of psychopathology
Conceptualizing Goals of Treatment	Enhance therapeutic engagement through digital tools, foster self-expression, insight, and emotional regulation	Increase self-awareness, understand unconscious processes, resolve internal conflicts	Utilize digital tools to facilitate psychodynamic goals of self-awareness and resolution of unconscious conflicts
Role of the Therapist	Employ and engage in one or more level of DPT (Level 1, 2, 3), be open to the whole client: culture, needs, desires, interests, etc., curate and present digital resources which facilitate meeting the treatment goals, continually assess for further needs, difficulties, and successes.	Neutral, interpretive, helps uncover unconscious material	Employ and engage in digital interactions at appropriate levels (Level 1, 2, 3), interpretive within the psychodynamic framework, open to the whole client, continually assess for further needs, difficulties, and successes.
Role of Caregivers	Informed and involved in the therapeutic process, support agreed-upon use of digital tools at home and in therapy	Involvement varies, often provides background information and support	Informed about digital tools used, involved in supporting therapeutic goals in alignment with psychodynamic principles
Role of Collateral Contacts	Collaboration with educators, other therapists, and professionals to integrate digital tools and support therapeutic goals	Collaboration as needed for holistic understanding and support	Collaborates to support the integration of digital tools within a psychodynamic framework

Herman's difficulty with nurturing, both in giving and receiving, will probably be evident within the digital play context. His interactions may be inconsistent, fluctuating between moments of genuine connection and apparent indifference, reflecting his underlying attachment issues and emotional insecurities. Understanding these anticipated clinical presentations will enable the therapist to tailor interventions within the DPT framework, addressing Herman's unique needs and promoting therapeutic progress.

Possible Attachment Style Manifestations

Ainsworth et al. (1978) set the foundation that defined the four primary attachment styles we still refer to today: secure, insecure avoidant, ambivalent (insecure-resistant or anxious-ambivalent), and disorganized. Due to his history, Herman may exhibit any of Ainsworth's attachment styles except for secure attachment. This may manifest in various ways within a digital play therapy context.

If Herman exhibits an insecure-avoidant attachment style, he might prefer independence, show little emotional expression, and have a lack of connection to the therapist, the therapist's character, non-player characters (NPCs), and other players within the digital environment. He may also resist progressing through the experience together with others. This apparent detachment might be misinterpreted as a lack of care; however, it is more likely indicative of an intense, yet unexpressed, desire for connection and acceptance. Herman's difficulties with follow-through are expected to surface during gameplay, where he may start various tasks or missions but fail to complete them.

Alternatively, Herman might display behaviors indicative of an ambivalent attachment style. This could include reluctance to explore the game map, incongruent emotional responses, and a strong reluctance to leave the therapist character's side. He may also display intense separation anxiety when momentarily lost and be inconsistent as a caregiver in the game—nurturing and attentive at times, but distant or intrusive at others.

If Herman's attachment style is disorganized, his behavior may appear chaotic and random. He may lack strategies for dealing with stress, leading to confusing, erratic, fearful, and inconsistent behaviors. In gameplay, this could manifest as rapidly changing games, characters, and locations, an inability or unwillingness to connect with others within the play, and an inability to accept comfort or soothing from others.

Therapeutic Powers of Play and Core Agents of Change in Herman's Treatment

Digital play in therapy includes so many possibilities between different types of hardware and the millions of software options (Stone, 2022). With so many ways to play, interact, elicit, and activate the therapeutic powers of play and core agents of change, it is important that we address each of them to explain and/or illustrate how all of them might appear in Herman's experience of Psychodynamic Digital Play Therapy.

Table 5.2 Therapeutic Powers of Play and Core Agents of Change in Herman's Treatment

Therapeutic Power	Description	Examples and Applications in Herman's Treatment
Facilitate Communication	Digital tools enable indirect expression of thoughts and emotions, and symbolic play helps process internal conflicts.	**Self-expression**: Role-playing games, VR, art creation, avatar customization. **Access to the unconscious**: Symbolic play to explore fears and traumas. **Direct and Indirect Teaching**: Games to improve executive functions, attention, and cognitive skills; tasks requiring strategy and planning.
Foster Emotional Wellness	Digital games provide safe outlets for emotions, allow for careful abreaction, and promote positive emotions.	**Catharsis**: Expressing emotions through gameplay without real-world consequences. **Careful abreaction**: Reliving trauma in a controlled manner. **Positive emotions**: Engaging in fun and relaxing digital activities. **Counterconditioning fears**: Safe environment to work through fears. **Stress inoculation and management**: Learning to handle stress and regulate responses through gameplay.
Enhance Social Relationships	Co-play builds rapport and trust, while digital interactions foster social competence and empathy.	**Therapeutic relationship**: Consistent, stable engagement through Level III digital play therapy. **Attachment**: Positive co-play interactions to reinforce healthy attachment patterns. **Social competence**: Practicing social skills through directed techniques or trial and error in gameplay. **Empathy**: Experiencing and practicing empathy in digital scenarios.
Increase Personal Strengths	Digital games enhance problem-solving, resilience, moral development, and self-regulation.	**Creative problem-solving**: Strategy and planning games to develop problem-solving skills. **Resiliency**: Coping with challenges through in-game feedback and therapist support. **Moral development**: Navigating moral dilemmas in narrative-driven games. **Accelerated psychological development**: Tailored digital experiences for focused psychological growth. **Self-regulation**: Practicing self-regulation techniques within and outside of gameplay. **Self-esteem**: Building self-esteem through a stable, long-term therapeutic relationship.

1. Facilitate Communication
   - Self-expression: Digital tools like role-playing games, immersive technologies (i.e., VR), art creation, and more allow Herman to express his thoughts and emotions indirectly. His use of nail polish and eyeliner can be seen as attempts at self-expression and exploring identity. Detailed avatar/character customization facilitates the exploration and representation of a variety of identity components.
   - Access to the unconscious: Through symbolic play in digital environments, Herman can process his internal conflicts, experiences, and traumas. This allows the therapeutic exploration of his fears, anxieties, perceptions, experiences, response patterns, and coping strategies.

- Direct and Indirect Teaching: Digital games can improve Herman's executive functioning abilities, as well as attention and specific cognitive skills. Information and instruction regarding emotional regulation and coping skills can occur within engaging digital gameplay. This can include critically thinking through a task, strategizing, researching, planning, finding tools, teaming up, studying a map, watching YouTube videos, and more.
- Games that could be used include: Roblox, Among Us, Virtual Sandtray App, Plants versus Zombies (original), Procreate, and MultiBrush.

2. Foster Emotional Wellness
   - Catharsis: Playing digital games allows for catharsis without the same "real-world consequences" one might encounter in a physical environment. Herman can express himself however he needs throughout the digital play. This could be expressed through activities such as destroying something, yelling, crying, talking, laughing, creating something, deep breathing, running around, and so on.
   - Careful abreaction: Reliving a past traumatic experience with intensity can happen spontaneously or be elicited intentionally within any play, including digital play. If abreaction is spontaneous, the therapist will guide the client to a more regulated state, either through the digital gameplay or with the game paused. Recognizing which variables were present for Herman that could lead to abreaction will be important as treatment progresses.
   - Positive emotions: Engaging in enjoyable digital activities can help Herman express and process his emotions and provide moments of connection, happiness, fun, and relaxation.
   - Counterconditioning fears: As Herman engages in various digital play experiences, he will most likely encounter situations that induce fear responses. These experiences could be ones he chooses consciously or unconsciously to work through his fears, or the therapist could introduce them. Being able to work through fear responses in a safe environment without real-world consequences can lessen Herman's anxiety and allow him to think through situations more clearly.
   - Stress inoculation and management: These two piggy-back on counterconditioning fears as natural next steps for Herman to learn how to protect himself from stressful situations and moderate his responses to stress. This can also activate direct and indirect teaching from the first section. As situations arise in the digital gameplay, the therapist can assist Herman in learning these regulation skills.
   - Games that could be used include: *Job Simulator*, *Roblox*, *Legend of Zelda: Breath of the Wild*, *Fortnite*, *Wombo Dream AI*, *Thisissand*, and *MultiBrush*.
3. Enhance Social Relationships
   - Therapeutic relationship: The digital play therapist uses co-play in digital games to build rapport and trust with Herman. This involvement is crucial given Herman's history of mistrust and insecurity, and will build with consistency, stability, safety, and predictability. Entering Herman's world and engaging with him in Level III digital play therapy will provide these experiences within and outside of the digital environment.

- Attachment: Herman can learn through experience and modeling, over time, that relationships with other humans have the potential to be safe and trustworthy. He may benefit greatly from positive interactions in co-play sessions with his foster father in particular, due to his strong admiration for him, in the office and at home to reinforce healthy attachment patterns. This can be further extended to the foster mother, and possibly the brothers, over time.
- Social competence: Through interactions with characters, whether a human is controlling the character or not, opportunities for social competence exploration, practice, and skill building abound within digital gameplay. Herman would be able to practice different approaches through directed techniques and/or trial and error. Working through these in a therapeutic setting provides valuable feedback and processing of these experiences, which can then be generalized to Herman's day-to-day interactions.
- Empathy: Children who have endured the difficulties Herman has can have difficulty experiencing, giving, and receiving empathy. Through digital gameplay, Herman will be able to enter into situations that involve empathy at his own pace. The therapist's guidance on which games are to be played, how empathy can be experienced, displayed, provided, and/or accepted will be crucial in Herman's ability to develop healthier reactions in this arena.
- Games that could be used are: Animal Crossing: New Horizons, Bogo, Henry, Roblox, Slither.io, Baba Yaga, and Bubbu.

4. Increase Personal Strengths

- Creative problem-solving: Digital games that require strategy and planning can help Herman develop a more complete personal identity, problem-solving skills, strategic skills, and cognitive flexibility, ultimately helping him work toward mastery and autonomy.
- Resiliency: Through repeated in-game challenges and supportive feedback within the gameplay and from the therapist, Herman can learn to cope with frustrations and setbacks more effectively.
- Moral development: Digital gameplay, particularly those with a narrative backstory, is rife with moral dilemmas that need to be navigated by the player. The therapist and Herman can navigate these with or without verbalizations, depending on the situation and his needs.
- Accelerated psychological development: Compared to many traditional methods, digital gameplay allows for a specific and pointed approach to psychological development. Environments and experiences tailored to Herman's needs can be presented, which allows for an intentional focus on the identified needs within the therapeutic goals.
- Self-regulation: Herman struggles significantly with self-regulation. The therapist can repeatedly provide experiences and environments for Herman to explore, identify, practice, and employ methods of self-regulation. This can be within the gameplay interactions directly, or between the therapist and Herman

outside of the game, incorporating direct or indirect teaching of self-regulation techniques.

- Self-esteem: Due to the difficult experiences in Herman's life so far, it is likely that his self-esteem has not developed according to his chronological age. Abuse, neglect, abandonment, and rejection, particularly at very early ages, disrupt the development of self-esteem significantly. Herman would most likely benefit from a consistent, stable, long-term relationship with one therapist who is his "person," engaging in therapeutic activities (digital and traditional), having fun, working through the difficulties, and maintaining the connection throughout.
- Games that could be used: *Roblox*, *Bogo*, *The Legend of Zelda: Breath of the Wild*, *Don't Starve Together*, *Acron*, *Virtual Sandtray App*, and *Procreate*.

Cultural Diversity and Inclusion

Incorporating DPT into Herman's treatment necessitated a sensitive approach to his cultural background and experiences. Games and digital activities were carefully selected to reflect and respect his heritage and unique personal identity, including his non-gender-specific preferences. This inclusivity in game selection can help affirm Herman's identity, contributing to a more personalized and effective therapeutic experience. Please give some examples.

Digital tools allowed for the inclusion of culturally relevant content and facilitated discussions about identity, representation, and acceptance. Incorporating games and activities that reflect Herman's cultural heritage and interests created a more inclusive and relatable therapeutic environment. This approach not only respected his background but also helped him feel seen, heard, understood, accepted, and valued, fostering a deeper sense of connection and safety within the therapeutic process.

Case Formulation and Application

Case formulation for Herman centered on addressing his trauma history, behavioral issues, and the need for emotional and coping skill development. His therapeutic plan was designed to be comprehensive and multi-faceted, incorporating psychodynamically oriented Digital Play Therapy (DPT) as a core component alongside medication management and special education support to provide a holistic approach to his care.

Trauma History

Herman's early life was marked by significant trauma, including prenatal exposure to opioids, early childhood neglect, multiple foster placements, and sexual abuse. These experiences have likely contributed to his insecure attachment styles and pervasive feelings of instability and insecurity. The psychodynamically oriented DPT approach recognizes the need to create a safe and predictable therapeutic environment where Herman can explore and process his traumatic experiences through metaphoric, symbolic, interactive, and immersive digital play and co-play. By providing a controlled and engaging digital space, Herman can re-experience and work through his trauma in a way that feels safe and more manageable.

Behavioral Issues

Herman has a history of exhibiting severe behavioral issues, including anger, aggression, hyperactivity, and difficulty with self-regulation. The integration of psychodynamically oriented DPT will allow for tailored interventions aimed at improving Herman's emotional regulation and executive functioning. Games designed to enhance problem-solving skills, strategic thinking, and emotional regulation can be incorporated into his treatment plan. These digital tools not only provide immediate outlets for Herman's emotions but also facilitate the development of long-term coping strategies.

Emotional and Social Skill Development

Herman's difficulties with emotional and social skills can be addressed through targeted DPT interventions. Co-play activities with the therapist help build rapport and trust, essential given Herman's history of mistrust and insecurity. Digital games that require collaboration and interaction with non-player characters (NPCs) and other players can be used to enhance Herman's social competence and empathy. These activities provide Herman with opportunities to practice social interactions, receive feedback, and process his experiences in a safe, controlled therapeutic setting.

Medication Management

Alongside DPT, Herman's treatment would include continued medication management to address his ADHD and other needs. Regular consultations with his psychiatrist can ensure that his medication regimen is continuously monitored and adjusted as needed. The use of digital tools in therapy will provide valuable insights into Herman's responses to medication, allowing for more informed adjustments and integrated care.

Special Education Support

Herman's learning disabilities and special education needs are also a critical component of his treatment plan. Collaboration with his special education teachers can help to ensure that his therapeutic interventions align with his educational goals. Digital tools that promote learning and cognitive development can be used both in therapy and at school to support his academic progress.

Continuous Adjustments and Tailoring

Herman's progress should be continuously monitored, and his treatment plan adjusted based on his evolving needs. Regular assessments and feedback from digital play sessions can provide real-time data on his emotional and behavioral responses, allowing for timely and effective adjustments to his interventions. The flexibility of DPT enables the therapist to adapt the therapeutic activities to better suit Herman's state and therapeutic goals.

Implementation Challenges

- **Consistency:** The lack of stable therapeutic relationships (and relationships overall) in the past posed a challenge. Establishing therapeutic rapport and stability for Herman requires a long-term commitment from the therapist to build trust and security. Continuous engagement and consistent interactions are crucial in providing Herman with a sense of reliability and safety.
- **Engagement:** Herman's fluctuating interest and hyperactivity make it difficult to maintain consistent engagement in any play activities. Tailoring interventions to his interests and providing a variety of engaging and stimulating activities can help maintain his focus, interest, and participation.
- **Emotional Regulation:** Herman's tendency to become quickly emotionally dysregulated requires careful monitoring and adaptive interventions. Implementing techniques such as mindfulness and resonant breathing activities within the digital play context, and using games that promote emotional regulation skills, can help manage his dysregulation and improve his ability to cope with stress.

Herman's case study, examined through the lens of the therapeutic powers of play, a psychodynamic approach, and Digital Play Therapy, illustrates the potential of this combination to provide a multifaceted, culturally sensitive approach to treatment. By employing a range of digital games and activities that activate the therapeutic powers of play, significant strides can be made in addressing Herman's complex needs, offering hope for continued growth and healing.

Conclusion

Digital Play Therapy™ (DPT) stands as a versatile and inclusive modality that effectively integrates digital tools within therapeutic practices to address the complex needs of clients.

By utilizing the structure and concepts within the therapeutic powers of play, DPT offers innovative pathways for emotional, cognitive, and social development. This approach not only honors the client's cultural and personal identity but also fosters meaningful therapeutic relationships, ensuring a comprehensive and adaptive treatment process that promotes sustained healing and growth.

Appendix: Getting Started with Apps and Games for Digital Play Therapy™

General Therapeutic Apps

1) Calm
   a) Platform: iOS, Android
   b) Description: A meditation and relaxation app with guided sessions to help manage stress and anxiety
   c) Uses in Therapy: Useful for teaching clients mindfulness and relaxation techniques
   d) Therapeutic Powers of Play: Foster Emotional Wellness, Increase Personal Strengths
2) MoodMission
   a) Platform: iOS, Android
   b) Description: An evidence-based app designed to help individuals manage depression and anxiety by providing coping strategies
   c) Uses in Therapy: Provides clients with practical tools to manage their emotions outside of therapy sessions
   d) Therapeutic Powers of Play: Foster Emotional Wellness, Increase Personal Strengths

Apps for Emotional, Social, and Cognitive Development

3) Journey
   a) Platform: PlayStation, PC
   b) Description: A visually stunning game focusing on exploration and emotional storytelling
   c) Uses in Therapy: Encourages emotional expression and self-reflection through its immersive environment
   d) Therapeutic Powers of Play: Foster Emotional Wellness, Increase Personal Strengths

4) Minecraft
    a) Platform: Multi-platform
    b) Description: A sandbox game that allows players to build and explore virtual worlds
    c) Uses in Therapy: Promotes creativity, problem-solving, and can be used for collaborative play in therapy
    d) Therapeutic Powers of Play: Enhance Social Relationships, Increase Personal Strengths, Facilitate Communication
5) Animal Crossing: New Horizons
    a) Platform: Nintendo Switch
    b) Description: A life simulation game where players create and manage their island paradise and interact with neighbors. The therapist and client can also visit each other's islands.
    c) Uses in Therapy: Facilitates social interaction, relaxation, and facilitates processing of a variety of experiences
    d) Therapeutic Powers of Play: Enhance Social Relationships, Increase Personal Strengths, Facilitate Communication
6) Flower
    a) Platform: PlayStation, iOS
    b) Description: A game where players control the wind and guide petals through lush environments
    c) Uses in Therapy: Provides a calming experience, useful for clients needing stress relief and mindfulness practice
    d) Therapeutic Powers of Play: Foster Emotional Wellness, Increase Personal Strengths
7) Celeste
    a) Platform: Multi-platform
    b) Description: A platformer game that deals with themes of mental health and perseverance
    c) Uses in Therapy: Helps clients explore and discuss challenges related to mental health and resilience
    d) Therapeutic Powers of Play: Foster Emotional Wellness, Increase Personal Strengths

Simple Apps and Programs

8) Bubbles
    a) Description: A simple app where bubbles appear and pop with touch
    b) Uses in Therapy: Provides sensory stimulation and can be used for relaxation and regulation
    c) Therapeutic Powers of Play: Foster Emotional Wellness, Increase Personal Strengths

9) Fluid
   a) Description: A colorful fluid movement app that responds to touch
   b) Uses in Therapy: Offers visual and sensory stimulation for relaxation and creative expression
   c) Therapeutic Powers of Play: Foster Emotional Wellness, Increase Personal Strengths
10) Sand Draw
   a) Description: Various apps that simulate drawing in the sand with different themes
   b) Uses in Therapy: Encourages creative expression and can be used for grounding and relaxation
   c) Therapeutic Powers of Play: Foster Emotional Wellness, Increase Personal Strengths
11) Breathe2Relax
   a) Description: Guides users through breathing exercises and provides stress management information
   b) Uses in Therapy: Teaches clients effective breathing techniques to manage stress and anxiety
   c) Therapeutic Powers of Play: Foster Emotional Wellness, Increase Personal Strengths
12) Google Arts and Culture Suite
   a) Description: Includes programs like Blob Opera and Kandinsky for creative musical and artistic expression
   b) Uses in Therapy: Useful for emotional regulation and creative therapy interventions
   c) Therapeutic Powers of Play: Foster Emotional Wellness, Facilitate Communication, Increase Personal Strengths

Medium Apps and Programs

13) Storybird
   a) Description: An app for creating illustrated stories and poems
   b) Uses in Therapy: Enhances storytelling and creative writing skills, useful for self-expression and narrative therapy
   c) Therapeutic Powers of Play: Facilitate Communication, Increase Personal Strengths
14) Virtual Sandtray®© App and VR Programs
   a) Description: A digital version of sand therapy with extensive confidentiality and customization options
   b) Uses in Therapy: Allows clients to create and interact with their own sand trays, enhancing traditional sand therapies with expansive features
   c) Therapeutic Powers of Play: Facilitate Communication, Foster Emotional Wellness, Increase Personal Strengths

15) Zones of Regulation
    a) Description: An app based on the Zones of Regulation framework to help users categorize feelings and develop coping skills
    b) Uses in Therapy: Teaches emotional regulation and coping strategies
    c) Therapeutic Powers of Play: Facilitate Communication, Foster Emotional Wellness, Increase Personal Strengths
16) Bogo VR
    a) Description: A virtual pet simulator with interactive minigames
    b) Uses in Therapy: Promotes engagement, empathy, and responsibility through virtual pet care
    c) Therapeutic Powers of Play: Enhance Social Relationships, Foster Emotional Wellness, Increase Personal Strengths

More Advanced Apps and Programs

17) Beat Saber
    a) Platform: VR (Oculus, PlayStation VR)
    b) Description: A rhythm game where players slice blocks in time with the music
    c) Uses in Therapy: Encourages physical activity, coordination, and can be used for mood elevation and stress relief
    d) Therapeutic Powers of Play: Foster Emotional Wellness, Increase Personal Strengths
18) Vader Immortal Series
    a) Platform: Oculus
    b) Description: A three-part VR series set in the Star Wars universe, focusing on mastery and power
    c) Uses in Therapy: Offers immersive experiences that can help with emotional regulation, stress relief, and empowerment
    d) Therapeutic Powers of Play: Foster Emotional Wellness, Increase Personal Strengths
19) theBlu
    a) Platform: VR (Wevr)
    b) Description: An underwater VR experience with various interactive scenes
    c) Uses in Therapy: Provides a calming, immersive environment for stress relief and relaxation
    d) Therapeutic Powers of Play: Foster Emotional Wellness, Increase Personal Strengths
20) Wander/Google Earth
    a) Platform: Oculus (Wander), Multi-platform (Google Earth)
    b) Description: Virtual exploration of real-world locations
    c) Uses in Therapy: Can be used for reminiscence therapy, grounding, and exploring personal histories and experiences
    d) Therapeutic Powers of Play: Enhance Social Relationships, Facilitate Communication, Increase Personal Strengths

21) Roblox

  a) Platform: Multi-platform
  b) Description: A platform with a vast collection of user-created games
  c) Uses in Therapy: Encourages creativity, social interaction, and can be tailored to various therapeutic goals
  d) Therapeutic Powers of Play: Enhance Social Relationships, Facilitate Communication, Increase Personal Strengths

References

Ainsworth, M. D. S., Blehar, M. C., Waters, E., & Wall, S. (1978). *Patterns of attachment: A psychological study of the strange situation*. Lawrence Erlbaum Associates. https://mindsplain.com/wp-content/uploads/2021/01/Ainsworth-Patterns-of-Attachment.pdf.

Alex, B. (2020, June 16). The ancient history of board games. *Discover*. https://www.discovermagazine.com/planet-earth/the-ancient-history-of-board-games.

Barnett, L. A. (1990). Developmental benefits of play for children. *Journal of Leisure Research, 22*(2), 138–53.

Ceranoglu, T. A. (2010). Video games in psychotherapy. *Review of General Psychology, APA, 14*(2), 141–6.

Chaarani, B., Ortigara, J., Yuan, D., Loso, H., Potter, A., & Garavan, H. P. (2022). Association of video gaming with cognitive performance among children. *JAMA Network Open, 5*(10), e2235721.

Cole, N. L. (2019). *So what is culture, exactly?* ThoughtCo. https://www.thoughtco.com/culture-definition-4135409.

Dignity Memorial. (2020). Obituary: Charles Schaefer. https://www.dignitymemorial.com/obituaries/scarsdale-ny/charles-schaefer-9370593.

Drummond, A., Sauer, J. D., & Ferguson, C. J. (2020). Do longitudinal studies support long-term relationships between aggressive gameplay and youth aggressive behaviour? A meta-analytic examination. *Royal Society Open Science, 7*, 00373. http://dx.doi.org/10.1098/rsos.200373.

Entertainment Software Association. (2023). *Power of play*. https://www.theesa.com/wp-content/uploads/2023/09/PowerOfPlay2023_Final.pdf.

Froebel, F. (1895). *Pedagogics of early childhood* (J. Jarvis, Trans.). Appleton (Original work published 1861).

Granic, I., Lobel, A., & Engels, R. (2014). The benefits of gaming. *American Psychologist, 69*(1), 66–78.

Gray, P. (2011). The decline of play and the rise of psychopathology in children and adolescents. *American Journal of Play, 3*(4), 443–63.

Johannes, N., Vuorre, M., Magnusson, K., & Przybylski, A. K. (2022). Time spent playing two online shooters has no measurable effect on aggressive affect. *Collabra: Psychology, 8*(1), 34606. https://doi.org/10.1525/collabra.34606.

Kaduson, H. G., & Schaefer, C. E. (2021). Introduction: The therapeutic powers of play. In H. G. Kaduson & C. E. Schaefer (Eds.), *Play therapy with children: Modalities for change* (pp. 3–8). American Psychological Association.

Kitchens, R. (2024). *Health headlines: Video games helping kids with vaccine anxiety.* 7KLPC. https://www-kplctv-com.cdn.ampproject.org/c/s/www.kplctv.com/2024/03/05/health-headlines-video-games-helping-kids-with-vaccine-anxiety/?outputType=amp&fbclid=IwAR0_eU7YggrX4X5CrXYf4WHxsDqQIx6TXRAKKr0qE-RAAolx4XRelBVeElQ.

Lester, S., & Russel, W. (2010). *Children's right to play: An examination of the importance of play in the lives of children worldwide.* Working paper no. 57. Bernard van Leer Foundation. https://www.researchgate.net/publication/263087157_Children%27s_Right_to_Play_An_Examination_of_the_Importance_of_Play_in_the_Lives_of_Children_Worldwide#fullTextFileContent.

Louis, S., & Powell, S. (2020, March). *About Friedrich Froebel, who invented "kindergarten".* Froebel Trust. https://www.froebel.org.uk/about-us/the-power-of-play/about-friedrich-froebel.

Lowenfeld, M. (2008). *Play in childhood.* Liverpool University Press.

Muftau-Lediju, H. (2024, April 2). *Enhancing therapeutic gaming: The role of occupational therapists in manipulating environments for executive functioning.* LinkedIn. https://www.linkedin.com/pulse/enhancing-therapeutic-gaming-role-occupational-hadijat-jokac/?trackingId=ChCT3bL3RAG%2FeAB39DJcNQ%3D%3D.

Palfrey, J., & Gasser, U. (2016). *Born digital: How children grow up in a digital age.* Basic Books.

Pasqualotto, A., Altarelli, I., De Angeli, A., Menestrina, Z., Bavelier, D., & Venuti, P. (2022). Enhancing reading skills through a video game mixing action mechanics and cognitive training. *Nature Human Behaviour 6*, 545–54.

PsychCentral. (2022). The importance of play for adults. https://psychcentral.com/blog/the-importance-of-play-for-adults.

Prensky, M. (2001). *Digital natives, digital immigrants.* https://marcprensky.com/writing/Prensky%20-%20Digital%20Natives,%20Digital%20Immigrants%20-%20Part1.pdf.

Poyer, R. (2013). The well-being of playful adults: Adult playfulness, subjective well-being, physical well-being, and the pursuit of enjoyable activities. *European Journal of Humour Research, 1*(1), 84–98.

Psychgeist. (2024, April 2). Games are ideal learning spaces [Video]. *YouTube.* https://www.youtube.com/shorts/l7GRkuT-mTM.

Reinfeld, J. (n.d.). Psychological theory definition: Concept, role, debate, and limitations. *Mantra Care.* https://mantracare.org/therapy/what-is/psychological-theory-definition/

Ruiz, M., Moreno, M., Girela-Serrano, B., Díaz-Oliván, I., Jiménez Muñoz, L., González-Garrido, C., & Porras-Segovia, A. (2022). Winning the game against depression: A systematic review video games for the treatment of depressive disorders. *Current Psychiatry Reports, 24,* 23–35.

Schaefer, C. (1993). *The therapeutic powers of play.* Aronson.

Schaefer, C. E., & Drewes, A. A. (2014). *The therapeutic powers of play: 20 core agents of change.* John Wiley & Sons.

Steinsbekk, S., Bjørklund, O., Valkenburg, P., Nesi, J., & Wichstrøm, L. (2024). The new social landscape: Relationships among social media use, social skills, and offline friendships from age 10–18 years. *Computers in Human Behavior*, 108235. https://www.sciencedirect.com/science/article/pii/S0747563224001031.

Stone, J. (2019). Digital Games. In J. Stone & C. E. Schaefer (Eds.), *Gameplay* (3rd ed., pp .99–115) Wiley.

Stone, J. (2020). *Digital play therapy: A clinician's guide to comfort and competence* (1st ed). Routledge.

Stone, J. (2022). *Digital play therapy: A clinician's guide to comfort and competence* (2nd ed.). Routledge.

Stone, J. (2023). *Technology in mental health: Foundations of clinical use*. Routledge.

Torres, J. (2024). Exploring modality in psychology: Definitions and applications. *Listenhard.* https://listen-hard.com/psychological-assessment-and-testing/psychology-modality-explained/.

Unicef. (2024, April). *Responsible innovation in technology for children.* https://www.unicef.org/innocenti/media/8056/file/UNICEF-Innocenti-RITEC-P2-report-2024.pdf.pdf.

Wang, B., Taylor, L., & Sun, Q. (2018). Families that play together stay together: Investigating family bonding through video games. *New Media and Society, 20*(11), 4074–94.

Wang, B., Jiang, J., & Guo, W. (2023). Effects of a single bout of mobile action video gameplay on attentional networks. *PeerJ, 11,* e16409.

6

EMDR and Play Therapy Integration

Ann Beckley-Forest and Annie Monaco

Chapter Outline

Introduction

Adapting the EMDR 8-phase model for children and integrating it fully within play therapy ought to be done in a developmentally sensitive manner that also includes parents or caregivers as collaborators in treatment as much as possible. This chapter will focus on treating early attachment wounds and traumatic experiences as the answer for the relief of present-day behavioral and emotional symptoms. We will consider the importance of the integration of the therapeutic powers of play both conceptually and practically with the procedural steps of EMDR processing in order to magnify the treatment effect and make the benefits of EMDR therapy accessible for children. We will also describe how the addition of prescriptive play therapy approaches to a flexible version of the EMDR protocol can support healing in cases of complex trauma and manage the dissociation that often accompanies complex or developmental trauma.

Personality Theory

Francine Shapiro based the clinical practices of EMDR therapy on a learning theory she developed known as Adaptive Information Processing (AIP). At its core, AIP describes a natural healing process of growth through the linkages in the neural network between experiences of distress and adaptive information acquired through other experiences, such as through secure attachment, access to positive affect, and present conditions of safety (Shapiro, 2017). In traumatic experiences, especially those occurring early in life when the range of adaptive information stored may be more limited or compromised by inadequate caregivers, pathogenic memories may be stored implicitly and in fragments of emotion or sensation or in the form of implicitly held beliefs. In this raw and unprocessed state, they continue to be activated by triggers including thoughts, emotions, and somatic sensations that remind the nervous system of the traumatic experiences and trigger a sense of ongoing threat (Hase et al., 2017).

Treatment planning from an AIP perspective involves both accessing the pathogenic memories and linking to more adaptive information for the nervous system, which allows the natural tendency toward healing to proceed. EMDR therapy was developed to facilitate that process, originally for the adult client who can easily use visualization and verbal processing as aspects of the treatment, but can be used with children with the support of play therapy, since play is the language of children. Applying this conceptual model in clinical work with children, there are clear areas of convergence with play therapy models. Most play therapy approaches have some origins in Carl Rogers' person-centered personality theories and Virginia Axline's early application of these with children (Johnson, 2015) that describe an innate drive toward wholeness and integration—even as the models differ in how the play therapist best facilitates or aids this process. Play becomes a substitute for verbally expressed descriptive language about the nature of the distress, and the playroom and its themes serve as a projection of the child's inner world, including offering ways of accessing post-traumatic thoughts, feelings, and body sensations. The play therapy room is also an exceptional space in which children can experiment with adaptive information—including somatic experience—safely and within their ability to tolerate (see also Beckley-Forest et al., 2023). A prescriptive framework for play therapy allows the selection of play therapy approaches and activities tailored to both the individual child and the stage of treatment (Kaduson et al., 2019). In this integrative approach, we also incorporate a theoretical grounding in attachment theory and the necessity of attachment repair and considerations for the child as a member of a wider family system, which can include both former and current caregivers as well as the community. Creative and playful ways of mobilizing these attachment figures can increase the child's access to adaptive experiences in the process of treatment, which is associated with better outcomes in both the play therapy and EMDR literature (Oram, 2000; Gomez, 2012; Silvestre & Tarquino, 2022)

Model of Psychopathology

As described above, a trauma-focused model for psychopathology such as the AIP model focuses on the impact of pathogenic experiences, especially those early in life, such as the ones described by the landmark Adverse Childhood Experience (ACE) study and associated with negative impacts on mental as well as physical health (Sheffler, 2020). This understanding is an expansion of the category of what constitutes the threshold for traumatic experiences sufficient for a pathogenic effect. Especially for EMDR/play therapists who primarily treat children, it is clear that the immature nervous systems of children are ill-equipped to handle or adaptively process upsetting or perceived threatening experiences, particularly those traumatic experiences involving caregivers. When these events occur repeatedly, such as witnessing a parent's intense anger or rage, the long-term impact on the child's arousal systems is well documented (van der Kolk, 2003; Howells et al., 2012; Dye, 2018).

So many of the children impacted by chronic trauma, especially developmental trauma as described by van der Kolk and others (van der Kolk et al., 2009), present in clinical settings due to extreme mood instability and aggressive impulses turned either outward as violence or inward as self-harm. One way to conceptualize these responses is to apply the polyvagal theory of Stephen Porges (Porges & Dana, 2018) to relate these symptoms to limitations of the Social Engagement System of children exposed to chronic early adversity. Porges describes how once the social engagement system contracts in the presence of real or perceived threats (triggers), the child's responses are no longer mediated by the rational thinking centers of the prefrontal cortex and instead unleash a cascade of aroused neurobiological responses in the sympathetic nervous system (so-called fight or flight response). If the perceived threat is persistent enough, there is eventually a parasympathetic contraction of the here-and-now sensation altogether, sometimes called the freeze response or nervous system collapse. In these cases, the ongoing effort of caregivers to assert power and control has often made the problems much worse as the child may be spending less and less time socially engaged and therefore less able to be reached by choice-based discipline approaches, what play therapist Paris Goodyear-Brown aptly describes as being "not in a Choosing Mind" (2009). These concepts have a significant impact on the necessity of prioritizing the development of a repertoire of sensory grounding as part of the treatment plan, a task well supported by the therapeutic powers of play (Porges, 2024, foreword to Goodyear-Brown & *Polyvagal Power in the Playroom*).

Betrayal trauma is a term used to describe harm caused when adults in a supposedly caregiving relationship threaten, abuse, or exploit a child and is particularly disruptive to the flow of adaptive information associated with a sense of safety and worthiness and is especially challenging to treat (Freyd, 1996). The psychological pain of such experiences is so intolerable to the child as to often lead the nervous system toward dissociation, an adaptive response for day-to-day survival. More severe and ongoing experiences can lead to further fragmentation of experience, sensation, and even identity as the fragments can become more rigidly experienced states organized around phobic avoidance of the trauma content or any perceived trigger or threat (Silberg, 2021; Waters, 2016). Recognizing how the dissociative continuum is operating in these children is a necessary precursor to promoting increased internal coherence and communication among these states or "parts" before opening the associated trauma memory networks for processing.

Conceptualizing Goals of Treatment

Models for treating the psychopathology related to adverse experiences agree on the need for memory retrieval and reconsolidation, even as they differ on how best to manage this exposure process (Ecker, 2020). A play therapy-supported approach to EMDR relies on many different kinds of play as the mechanism by which to access or activate memories, co-regulate through the related emotional and somatic distress, and experiment with adaptive information and reconsolidation of these memories through more secure attachment, present conditions of safety, and personal growth and coherent identity formation.

EMDR therapy uses an 8-phase model to structure the treatment process, and this is highly compatible with a prescriptive conceptualization that may use play therapy techniques from different models or along different parts of the continuum from child-centered to therapist-led activities. See Appendix for a phase-by-phase summary of EMDR-based treatment goals and corresponding examples of how play therapy can be used to support each of these goals.

The play therapist creates a safe space for post-traumatic play both at home (by working closely with caregivers to understand the therapeutic power of play) and in the therapy room using child-centered playtime, and begins to identify themes and metaphors that convey the child's fragmented experiences of adversity and threat. Many of these experiences may be held implicitly, and so the parallels to the play are not self-conscious or highly literal, but are often related to the child's own attempts to process intense emotions or explore bodily states through imaginative enactment (Parker et al., 2021). For example, a child who was abused by a caregiver may create stories that involve running from threats or hiding, recreating the somatic experience of flight or freeze responses. Or another child wrestling with feelings of responsibility for the domestic violence he witnessed might repeatedly play out rescue fantasies involving superheroes saving people from bullies. The non-judgmental acceptance and reinforcement through reflecting and noticing the child's chosen play highlight the emotional safety of the play therapy space and can open these memory networks for further exploration.

In EMDR, the first phase of treatment involves developing a systematic inventory of adverse life experiences or "trauma history," which becomes the focus in the later phases, a roadmap of what experiences need to be reprocessed. Of course, in child therapy, the input of the caregivers and information from others, such as case workers, can assist the therapist, but the treatment plan will still require implementing playful or creative ways to start the process of connecting the dots between past experiences and current ones for the child and the family system. The therapist can use storytelling or therapeutic metaphors for this play-based psychoeducation and collaborate on collecting the autobiographical information in a way that the child can tolerate (for one example, see Beckley-Forest & Lavigne, 2020).

In a play therapy-supported EMDR framework, the goals of the Phase 2 preparation phase are many: to work with both the child and the family system to increase connection and collaboration; to reframe problematic behavior from "bad" to defensive or protective responses rooted in the neurobiology of trauma; and to increase the repertoire of grounding and soothing activities that can help manage dissociative episodes and intense emotional states. Essentially, the therapist works prescriptively to position the child for the best possible success with the desensitization and reprocessing phases.

Attachment-focused play therapy, including dyad models of play therapy, is an excellent adjunct during the preparation phase, especially for children whose caregivers were compromised in some way during their early years of growth and development. Often, these dyad approaches, such as Theraplay®, offer a chance for the parent-child dyad to establish new relationship patterns through structuring play that recreates the conditions for healthier attachment experiences. These activities can be easily paired with EMDR installation, the technique of encouraging short and mindful sets of bilateral stimulation (BLS), such as tapping or the butterfly hug (Artigas & Jarero, 2015), to help the child learn to be mindful of how these experiences land in the body. There are a number of examples in the literature of the success of combining Theraplay® and EMDR (Gomez & Jernberg, 2012; Thompson-Lee, 2020; Vincke, 2020). From an AIP perspective, these positive therapeutic attachment experiences add adaptive material to the child's working memory network to access during processing.

Since so many children with early adversity have used dissociation to cope with the terror, horror, and shame of these experiences, the preparation phase also includes the development of playful and creative ways of expressing their internal fragmentation. This allows parts of the self to be seen, heard, and healed by the healthy self, which may be alienated and charged with holding the most intense pain from the child's present awareness. This work of internal connection proceeds better when mirrored by caregivers who are providing safety and acceptance for all the parts of the child, including the defensive self-states. Monaco (2020) describes a playful adaptation of the traditional conference table technique, which relies on playfulness, fantasy, and props to invite the parts of the self to come together through drawing, sand, dolls, puppets, or other creative arts. These techniques are consistent with Gestalt Play Therapy, developed originally by Violet Oaklander, as a framework within play therapy to provide invitations through art and creativity, play, and sand tray, and to ensure that this internal contact with intense emotional states is made gradually and respectfully. Children use creative measures and symbolic representations in the playroom to talk about their experiences from a safer distance, increasing the possibility for self-compassion toward their younger selves in these expressions (Oaklander, 2022; Blom, 2006).

EMDR's Assessment Phase (Phase 3) is focused on retrieving and activating a core experience from the trauma memory network as an entry point to the distressing images, thoughts, feelings, and body sensations experienced at the time which are fragmented and still being re-experienced intrusively or dissociated within the nervous system.

While in adult EMDR, Phase 3 consists of a series of questions and verbal answers, in a play therapy-supported and developmentally sensitive version for children, we may be bridging from post-traumatic play experiences or using storytelling with caregivers to accomplish the goals of this phase. Also, when the history is not clear, we may use clues from the post-traumatic play or the behavioral or somatic cues to flesh out that assessment of potential targeted memories for EMDR processing. The use of parts work along with expressive materials to keep curiosity about "little you": the younger self-states unfolding at a safe distance is one of the most potent powers of play to support preverbal trauma work, even in children with more significant or severe dissociation who would be on the path to develop dissociative identities in adulthood without intervention, or who have hostile parts or states that imitate the perpetrator (many examples described by Waters, 2016; Silberg, 2021). Current caregivers are often enlisted in this activation through the construction of a story with the help of the therapist, a technique first developed by Joan Lovett (1999, 2015) which is in wide use in the EMDR field, and that can be augmented with play therapy storytelling techniques and metaphors (as described by Mills & Crowley 2014), acted out or made tangible with props, animals, sand tray figures, or drawing.

The activation of the memory leads directly into the actual exposure work, which is at the heart of EMDR therapy, and comprises the (Phase 4) desensitization and reprocessing goals: to bring the fragmented adverse experiences into brief conscious awareness while taxing the working memory with highly playful and movement-oriented dual attention stimulation/bilateral stimulation to help the child move step by step toward integration of the experience into autobiographical narrative memory, counter-conditioning the post-trauma affective and somatic reactivity. By keeping the exposure brief and adding playful, physical bilateral movement such as drumming, dancing, and play sword fights to the traditional eye movements and tapping of adult EMDR, the child is able to begin to digest the memory and give the nervous system a chance to re-establish narrative coherence and grounding in the present. It is interesting to note that some of the most current work in EMDR innovations for adults with complex PTSD is actually focused on adding more action to adult EMDR as well through more physically active and more playful dual attention (de Jongh et al., 2023).

In EMDR's Phase 5, the goal is post-traumatic growth of positive core beliefs, which can be enhanced through the involvement of the caregiver as well as playful experiments in the session by being "bigger and stronger" now or with present safety.

Finally, EMDR Phases 6 and 7 are focused on the closure of the desensitization session and scanning the body for distress, while Phase 8 involves the caregivers in helping the therapist determine whether the amount of reprocessing has been sufficient for a positive impact on the current functioning of the child. These phases are also enhanced by the therapeutic powers of play to help the child express through play and creativity what is going on inside. In Phase 8, the Reevaluation phase, the therapist can notice the shifts in the persistence of post-trauma content in the play or the ability of the child to tolerate and sustain healthy attachment activities with the caregivers, peers, and so on.

Role of the Therapist

The complexity of undertaking a prescriptive and integrative approach to intervention suggests a level of sophistication on the part of the therapist, who must maintain flexibility within the models and be alert to ongoing input, both verbal and non-verbal, from the child and their caregivers. Gardener & Yasenik (2012) described a Dimensions Model for integrative work in play therapy that takes into consideration the shifts in priority as the therapist works along the continuum from non-directive to directive roles in play, monitors the child's level of excitation and modulation, and balances invitations to insight with developmental considerations (pp 29–30). In the use of trauma protocols such as EMDR, we are well aware that phobic avoidance of the remnants of the trauma in the nervous system is a symptom of post-traumatic stress. We must balance the need to lead the client to this work despite these fears with an eye to the egalitarian and emotionally safe relationship in the therapy setting, all the more so in child therapy because of the inherent power differential between children and adults. In addition, adding the intersection of cultural humility (Mosher et al., 2017) and an effort to be alert to biases around neurodiversity and the child's unique experience of self and the world (Grant, 2023) add further layers of thoughtfulness and intention in how the therapist uses power in the therapy room, especially in the move toward more directive activities in therapist-led efforts to begin digesting the trauma. This delicate balance is accomplished best by the therapist who is fully trained and grounded in the approaches (EMDR, structural dissociation, different models of play therapy), receiving ongoing consultation or supervision, and sees themselves as an attachment figure within the family system and inclusive of the child's caregivers, conveying a balance of confidence in the treatment plan and the flexibility to make adjustments quickly.

Roles of Caregivers and Collaterals

Play therapists differ widely in their stance on including caregivers in the play therapy activities while agreeing on the need for frequent and robust communication with caregivers and collaterals such as doctors, teachers, and caregivers. In the EMDR therapy literature on children, there are consistent examples of improved outcomes in trauma processing with a family systems lens and caregiver participation in trauma processing as a witness and attachment interweave (Wesselman et al., 2018; Silvestre & Tarquino, 2022). When caregivers are involved experientially in their child's therapeutic activities, they are more likely to have a felt sense of the child's inner wounds and sensitivities, which increases their compassion for the child and can lower their own defensiveness in the face of often bewildering changes and escalations in the child's mood and behavior. The success of caregiver inclusion is based on intentionality and structure, so that the caregiver is prepared with specific information about their role and an understanding of the therapist's plan for the session to avoid derailing that plan. Adequate collateral sessions are needed to establish validation of the caregiver's concerns by the therapist and a collaborative relationship with the caregiver as a "co-therapist" or healing partner in their child's therapy. Especially in complex trauma and early attachment wounds, helping the current caregivers (parents, foster/adoptive parents, grandparents, and even including teachers, daycare providers, etc.) to understand dissociation and how behaviors may be the efforts of the wounded parts of the child to re-establish safety can be very effective in getting out of a cycle of shame and blame for the child and making emotionally safe space for the trauma processing to unfold. An excellent source to assist with this psychoeducation is the Resources section of the International Society for the Study of Trauma and Dissociation website (https://www.isst-d.org/resources/).

Children with significant early trauma and corresponding dysregulation often receive psychopharmacological interventions as well. Their therapist ought to engage in ongoing collaboration with the prescriber, especially in the case conceptualization of the symptoms as trauma-based, as this can lead to alternative choices in how the prescriber might consider the effects of various medications. For example, how medications may impact hyperarousal due to traumatic stress vs. hyperactivity in an ADHD presentation (Spencer et al., 2016).

Research and Empirical Support

There is considerable research supporting the efficacy of EMDR with children over the past twenty years. The very earliest studies, which took place over the first decade of the 2000s, tended to be smaller-scale studies limited to single incident trauma and had a short duration of treatment (summarized in this meta-analysis by Adler-Tapia & Settle, 2009) but nevertheless showed a significant treatment effect. More recent studies with greater research rigor, a wider variety of presenting problems, and clients have upheld the earlier findings and established EMDR as a fully evidence-based treatment for children with PTSD (Morenzo-Alcazar et al., 2017; meta-analysis by Beer, 2018; Manzoni et al., 2021) and including young children ages four to eight (Olivier et al., 2022) and refugees (Lempertz et al., 2020).

Play therapy likewise has strong research support, although some play therapy approaches have been more thoroughly studied than others in the context of trauma. Of the many options available on a prescriptive play therapy approach, child-centered play therapy has specific evidence of the benefits to trauma-exposed children (Ray et al., 2022). Other relevant play therapy approaches appear positive in the literature, such as Synergetic Play Therapy (Townsend et al., 2021), neurobiologically informed play therapy (Hong & Mason, 2016) and even the use of play therapy via telehealth for hard-to-engage foster families (Winder et al., 2023). The strongest argument for the integration of play therapy in trauma treatment protocols may be the fact that it makes the therapist more likely to lead the therapy toward trauma digestion when the child is avoidant (Tener and Silberstein, 2019). With complex and involved cases with significant attachment wounds, it appears likely that an integration of approaches is the most appropriate, such as in a recent study of best practices in adoption and foster care (Vincke, 2020).

There is a disappointing lack of comparison studies focused on specific therapeutic choices in EMDR with children, or differential strategies within the therapy for complex cases. Clinicians would greatly benefit from more studies of the specific ways in which play therapy techniques can be applied to make trauma processing more tolerable, more efficient, and more deeply connected to the positive meaning-making in play. We have a number of good case studies that can point the way for further research, each describing various play approaches in support of EMDR: integrating with play therapy (Banbury, 2016), in child sexual abuse (Swinden, 2018) and focused on including attachment figures (Rathore, 2018; Swimm, 2018).

Case Study through the Lens of the Therapeutic Powers of Play

The therapeutic powers of play, as described by Schaefer & Drewes (2014), includes twenty core areas across four domains, many of which would operate in integrating EMDR and play therapy to help the child in the described case study, Herman (see Appendix for case study of Herman being referenced).

Facilitates Communication: self-expression, access to the unconscious, direct and indirect teaching.

Child-centered and child-responsive post-traumatic play, along with invitations to creative emotional projections, would give Herman and the therapist access to the intensity of emotion and messages about the trauma held in the body that are not easy to verbally describe. The therapist might begin by noticing and reflecting on the stored intensity of feeling and sensation through tracking his play, and move toward prompts and invitations for Herman to gradually get to know the parts of self that had those hard times in the past through the sand tray, art, and so on. Responses in play can also be used to teach and normalize how trauma is stored in the body, which can help reduce the shame and isolation of the child and caregivers and be incorporated into an extended Preparation Phase, preparing him to face his own narrative more directly. In Herman's case the loss of his biological mother, the shock of withdrawal from opioids, and the grief and terror of the "baby self" are being held implicitly in the nervous system and may lead to dissociative rejection of the need for tenderness and connection.

Fosters Emotional Wellness: catharsis, abreaction, positive emotions, counterconditioning fears, stress inoculation, stress management.

This is the domain that is most clearly connected to the processing phases of EMDR—Phase 3 assessment and activation of the target memory and Phase 4 desensitization and reprocessing. Utilizing the safe space of the playroom as a container to face and counter-condition fears and other strong emotional and somatic reactions through play therapy-based reenactment or recollection, while EMDR's bilateral/dual attention stimulation keeps the child in present awareness and orientation. The therapist must strategically use play to keep the intensity within tolerance through the ability to touch positive emotions in physically active play and through the intervention and shared experiences with caregivers as witnesses and collaborators. In addition to the primary attachment wound of rejection by the biological family, Herman also has an explicit traumatic memory of sexual abuse, and impulses to aggression may be connected to strategies for self-protection. His high-risk or suicidal gestures would potentially be a wounded part's attempt to escape from intense emotional pain. Previous attempts to respond cognitively and behaviorally without the somatic and sensory awareness of the role of neurobiology in these responses have only intensified the problems. Herman can be invited to manifest in the playroom through play, story, or symbol the intensity of rage and fear around the sexual abuse and other fearful experiences. The guidance of the therapist and the support of the caregivers interweave a present orientation to safety and validation during EMDR processing, which can help Herman connect with this wounded part and allow an increased awareness of adaptive information about current realities.

Enhances Social Relationships: Therapeutic relationship, attachment, social competence, empathy.

Child-centered and collaborative play opportunities would give the therapist an opportunity to understand Herman's likes, dislikes, triggers, and post-traumatic themes. In this case, we might expect post-traumatic content around an internalized sense of shame and unworthiness from the abandonment and abuse experienced. Using reflections and projective invitations in a Gestalt play therapy manner increases the relationship with Herman's own wounded parts and can lower defensiveness through the adaptive experience of being "seen" in the play. Involving the caregivers increases their empathy as well as Herman's ability to accept support, and they serve as models for the internalized empathy with the wounded parts of the self. Herman's experience of neglect and abuse has likely been held in an isolated memory network and internalized sense of "I am not lovable or worthy of love," and how that felt experience of both rage and shame lives on in the body, triggering reactions.

With Herman, we would use expressive play modalities to come into gradual contact with the parts of self that feel shame and fear—for example, using sand tray worlds or art prompts to explore "the part that's angry about what happened in the past." These expressions are a natural bridge into EMDR processing, provided the therapist manages the dose of the exposure and keeps the duration of this narrative work within tolerance.

In Herman's case, we would also spend time preparing the caregivers to participate in these processing sessions, giving them models and coaching them in attached responses. In the preparation phase, we would experiment with play-based opportunities to connect in a neurosequential way through co-regulation and shared pleasure in games. After practicing playfully in the session, the caregivers would also be able to incorporate some of these rituals at home, keeping in mind the needs of all of the different internal states (little self, defensive self-protector, detached/avoidant, and most grown-up resourceful self) for their own avenues of validation and co-regulation.

We would also be able to use play and fantasy along with the attachment to the therapist and the caregivers to pay attention to his need to increase his positive sense of self. The play therapy aspects of this approach are a laboratory for experimenting with what EMDR calls the installation of positive beliefs (Phase 5), which can then start to give rise to post-traumatic growth in social skills and self-awareness. In Herman's case, the developmental demands of identity formation and emerging relationships with peers will include a need for exploratory space around gender identity and social and emotional implications. Experiments with positive beliefs such as "I am worthy" and "I can give and receive love" will take on new urgency as adolescence approaches.

Increases Personal Strengths: Creative problem solving, resilience, moral development, accelerated psychological development, self-regulation, self-esteem.

Reducing the burden of unprocessed trauma and the corresponding reactivity allows growth and development to get back on track. In Herman's case, due to the severe and prolonged experience of trauma and neglect and the accompanying fragmentation of the sense of self, this work must proceed consistently but also with sensitivity to the ability to tolerate. The protective distance of expressive projection in play and creativity will help Herman to do this work gradually. We would be able to use storytelling with the help of the caregivers to be gently curious about what "little Herman" experienced and how that is echoed in current emotions and body sensations. Keeping the processing titrated and very active would help Herman be able to handle this intensity, such as through very physical and highly distracting bilateral stimulation through movement, such as sword fights with pool noodles and drumming. Inserting playful sensory experiences with the caregivers—scents, making slime, or playing with sand, snacks, and soothing movements such as swinging—would increase trust in co-regulation as they navigate the intensity.

Cultural, Diversity, Inclusion Considerations

The therapist's stance of broaching and welcoming both resources and attention to wounds around cultural differences is associated with positive outcomes in treatment (Day-Vines et al., 2021). In foster and adoptive families in particular, caregivers may minimize the impact of racial/cultural dislocation and be ill-equipped to support their children in navigating experiences of racism/microaggressions. EMDR processing in these playful contexts can also target the experiences of being "other," and this would give Herman a chance to access the support of the foster parents with the guidance of the therapist in processing these experiences, including those related not only to Herman's Hispanic heritage but also emerging gender identity (VanFrussen et al., 2020).

Case Formulation and Application

The case formulation would involve a thorough inventory of Herman's early experience of adversity, as well as consideration of the formation of dissociative parts or fragmentation and their respective protective strategies experienced as problem behaviors. We would use observations and experiences with Herman's chosen activities and themes in the playroom, as well as some prescriptive play activities, to assist in developing an increased interoceptive sense, engage in experiments in soothing and grounding, and bring the caregivers on board in this play. We would apply this formulation to a strategy of using imaginative play and expressive activities to develop a slow relationship with the wounded parts holding intensely painful experiences, both preverbal and explicitly remembered. We would develop a target selection strategy and assess "where to begin" the titrated exposure work using EMDR processing and play together to manage the intensity, recognizing that initially, Herman might initially only tolerate this exposure for a moment or two at a time in the context of a session where we prioritize a sense of safety, fun, and connection with the caregivers. Finally, we would collaborate with the caregivers in an ongoing evaluation of how the processing is and isn't providing relief, increasing Herman's positive self-concept, autonomy, and somatic regulation based on their observations as well as Herman's own self-report.

Challenges in Implementation

The practice of EMDR therapy requires very specific training in the use of the EMDR protocol and the adaptations to the protocol for children, and the therapist needs to be skilled in order to employ the level of intention and minute-to-minute playfulness and flexibility that makes explicit processing of complex trauma possible. The therapist has to be a strong leader in the room and keep the episodes of EMDR processing short and very playful, and involving the current (safe) caregivers is very important. If Herman's caregivers are carrying their own trauma wounds or are inconsistently emotionally available due to the demands of the other children in the home, that would present a very real challenge along with the need for a permanent plan for Herman.

Conclusion

Ultimately, establishing a true play therapy-supported EMDR protocol and seeing EMDR integrated with play therapy, founded upon AIP theory, as a valid play therapy approach in its own right could benefit the multitude of child therapists looking to bridge these healing traditions and provide relief from post-traumatic stress and the opportunity for growth to children such as Herman.

Table 6.1 Integrating Play Therapy with the Eight Phases of EMDR

EMDR Phase	Goals	Integrating Therapeutic Powers of Play
1 History	Initiate a safe, validating relationship	Child's chosen play themes with attunement and neutrality by the therapist
	Gather information about the traumatic experiences and attachment wounds	In depth exploration of current and past caregivers' attachment patterns; consider post-traumatic play themes
	Shared case conceptualization of trauma work	Metaphor and stories or symbols
	Screen for dissociation	Screening, norming of dissociative experiences for the child, invitations to playful projection of emotions/parts with Gestalt play therapy
2 Preparation	Collaborative relationship as a resource	Use of novelty, humor, physically active play, shared enjoyment & installation of these experiences
	Regulating emotional intensity	Movement, sensory play, expressive arts, sand trays
	Familiarity with EMDR tools and process, experimenting with BLS/DAS*	Play with drums, wands, dance, movement EMDR gadgets ("buzzers") paired with noticing the body, mindfulness
	Mobilize and motivate child and family, promote acceptance of internal states or parts	Creative projections of parts including past and future self, meeting the needs of "baby" parts and others through play and fantasy.
3 Assessment	Retrieve/Activate the trauma memory target	Use of storytelling, drawing, props, materials to set the scene; Activation of the images, thoughts, feelings and body sensations by the therapist and/or caregivers in collaboration with the child
4 Desensitization & Reprocessing	Maintain sufficient activation of memory network	Bridges from post-traumatic play; Collaborative storytelling, use of props, metaphors, artwork
	Taxation of the working memory with high level of DAS/BLS	Active and playful movement, novelty and surprise as well as pendulating and out of the trauma memory network in small doses
	Interweaves as needed	Role play, fantasy, attachment repair in play
5 Installation	Increase positive beliefs about the self	Play experiments, for example, in being "bigger and stronger now"
6 Body scan	Focus on remaining distress in the body	Use playful props, "feeling finder" for increased interoception
7 Closure	Contain the processing within the session	Create tangible or fantasy containers for big feelings
8 Re-evaluation	Consider the shifts in current symptoms and reactivity in determining next steps	Ongoing expressive and projective play offers clues regarding unprocessed material in addition to response to caregiver observation

Bilateral Stimulation or Dual Attention Stimulation—visual, tactile, auditory

References

Adler-Tapia, R., & Settle, C. (2009). Evidence of the efficacy of EMDR with children and adolescents in individual psychotherapy: A review of the research published in peer-reviewed journals. *Journal of EMDR Practice & Research*, *3*(4), 232–47.

Artigas, L., Jarero, I., Alcalá, N., & Cano, T. L. (2015). *The EMDR integrative group treatment protocol for children (IGTP).* https://www.emdrfoundation.org/toolkit/igtp-children.pdf

Banbury, N. M. (2016). Case study: Play therapy and eye movement desensitization and reprocessing for pediatric single incident posttraumatic stress disorder and developmental regression. *International Journal of Play Therapy, 25*(3), 166–174. https://doi.org/10.1037/pla0000026.

Beckley-Forest, A., Lyles, M., & Monaco, A. (2023) EMDR therapy and integrative approaches with children. In D. Farrell, S. Schubert, & M. Kiernan (Eds.), *Oxford handbook of EMDR* (online edition Oxford Academic, April 20, 2023). https://doi.org/10.1093/oxfordhb/9780192898357.013.25.

Beckley-Forest, A., & Lavigne, M. (2020). Taking a play-based trauma history. In A. Beckley-Forest & A. Monaco (Eds.), *EMDR with Children in the Play Therapy Room: An Integrated Approach* (pp. 293–99). Springer Publishing.

Beer, R. (2018). Efficacy of EMDR therapy for children with PTSD: A review of the literature. *Journal of EMDR Practice and Research, 12*(4), 177–95. https://doi.org/10.1891/1933-3196.12.4.177.

Blom, R. (2006). *The handbook of Gestalt play therapy: Practical guidelines for child therapists.* Jessica Kingsley Publishers.

Day-Vines, N. L., Cluxton-Keller, F., Agorsor, C., & Gubara, S. (2021). Strategies for broaching the subjects of race, ethnicity, and culture. *Journal of Counseling & Development*, *99*(3), 348–57.

De Jongh, A., & Hafkemeijer, L. C. S. (2023). Trauma-focused treatment of a client with Complex PTSD and comorbid pathology using EMDR therapy. *Journal of Clinical Psychology, 80*(4), 824–35. https://doi.org/10.1002/jclp.23521.

Dye, H. (2018). The impact and long-term effects of childhood trauma. *Journal of Human Behavior in the Social Environment, 28*(3), 381–92. https://doi.org/10.1080/10911359.2018.1435328.

Ecker, B., & Bridges, S. K. (2020). How the science of memory reconsolidation advances the effectiveness and unification of psychotherapy. *Clinical Social Work Journal, 48*(3), 287–300.

Freyd, J. J. (1996). *Betrayal trauma: The logic of forgetting childhood abuse.* Harvard University Press.

Gardner, K., & Yasenik, L. (2012). *Play therapy dimensions model: A decision-making guide for integrative play therapists* (pp. 29–30). Jessica Kingsley Publishers.

Gomez, A., & Jernberg, E. (2012). Using EMDR Therapy and Theraplay. In A. Gomez (Ed.), *EMDR therapy and adjunct approaches with children: Complex trauma, attachment, and dissociation* (pp. 273–321). Springer.

Gomez, A. M. (2012). Healing the caregiving system: Working with parents within a comprehensive EMDR treatment. *Journal of EMDR Practice and Research, 6*(3), 136–44.

Goodyear-Brown, P. (2009). *Play therapy with traumatized children.* John Wiley & Sons.

Grant, R. J. (2023). *Play interventions for neurodivergent children and adolescents: Promoting growth, empowerment, and affirming practices.* Taylor & Francis

Hase, M., Balmaceda, U. M., Ostacoli, L., Liebermann, P., & Hofmann, A. (2017). The AIP model of EMDR therapy and pathogenic memories. *Frontiers in Psychology, 8*, 1578. https://doi.org/10.3389/fpsyg.2017.01578.

Hong, R., & Mason, C. M. (2016). Becoming a neurobiologically-informed play therapist. *International Journal of Play Therapy, 25*(1), 35–44. http://dx.doi.org/10.1037/pla0000020.

Howells, F. M., Stein, D. J., & Russell, V. A. (2012). Childhood trauma is associated with altered cortical arousal: Insights from an EEG study. *Frontiers in Integrative Neuroscience, 6*, 120.

Johnson, J. L. (2015). The history of play therapy. In K. J. O'Connor, C. E. Schaefer, & L. D. Braverman (Eds.), *Handbook of play therapy* (pp. 17–34). Wiley.

Kaduson, H. G., Cangelosi, D., & Schaefer, C. E. (Eds.). (2019). *Prescriptive play therapy: Tailoring interventions for specific childhood problems* (pp. 6–7). Guilford Publications.

Lempertz, D., Wichmann, M., Enderle, E., Stellermann-Strehlow, K., Pawils, S., & Metzner, F. (2020). Pre-post study to assess EMDR-based group therapy for traumatized refugee preschoolers. *Journal of EMDR Practice & Research, 14*(1), 31–45.

Lovett, J. (1999). *Small wonders: Healing childhood trauma with EMDR.* Simon and Schuster

Lovett, J. (2015) *Trauma- attachment tangle: Modifying EMDR to help children resolve trauma and develop loving relationships.* Routledge.

Manzoni, M., Fernandez, I., Bertella, S., Tizzoni, F., Gazzola, E., Molteni, M., & Nobile, M. (2021). Eye movement desensitization and reprocessing: The state of the art of efficacy in children and adolescents with post traumatic stress disorder. *Journal of affective disorders, 282*, 340–7.

Mills, J. C., & Crowley, R. J. (2014). *Therapeutic metaphors for children and the child within* (2nd ed.). Routledge.

Moreno-Alcazar, A., Treen, D., Valiente-Gomez, A., Sio-Erlos, A., Perez, V., Amann, B. L., & Radua, J. (2017). Efficacy of eye movement desensitization and reprocessing in children and adolescents with post-traumatic stress disorder: A meta-analysis of randomized controlled trials. *Frontiers in Psychology, 8*(1750), 1–10. https://doi.org/10.3389/fpsyg.2017.01750.

Mosher, D. K., Hook, J. N., Captari, L. E., Davis, D. E., DeBlaere, C., & Owen, J. (2017). Cultural humility: A therapeutic framework for engaging diverse clients. *Practice Innovations, 2*(4), 221.

Oaklander, V. (2022). *Hidden treasure: A map to the child's inner self* (pp. 66–80). Routledge.

Oram, K. (2000). A transitional space: Involving parents in the play therapy of their children. *Journal of Infant, Child, and Adolescent Psychotherapy, 1*(4), 79–98. https://doi.org/10.1080/15289168.2000.10486377.

Olivier, E., de Roos, C., & Bexkens, A. (2022). Eye movement desensitization and reprocessing in young children (ages 4–8) with posttraumatic stress disorder: A multiple-baseline evaluation. *Child Psychiatry & Human Development, 53*(6), 1391–404. https://doi.org/10.1007/s10578-021-01237-z.

Parker, M. M., Hergenrather, K., Smelser, Q., & Kelly, C. T. (2021). Exploring child-centered play therapy and trauma: A systematic review of literature. *International Journal of Play Therapy, 30*(1), 2–13. https://doi.org/10.1037/pla0000136.

Porges, S. W., & Dana, D. (2018). *Clinical applications of the polyvagal theory: The emergence of polyvagal-informed therapies (Norton series on interpersonal neurobiology).* WW Norton & Company.

Porges, S. W. (2024). Foreword. In P. Goodyear-Brown & L. A. Yasenik (Eds.), *Polyvagal power in the playroom: A guide for play therapists.* (pp. 12–19). Taylor & Francis.

Rathore, H. E. (2018). Trust and attunement-focused EMDR with a child. *Journal of EMDR Practice & Research, 12*(4), 255–68. https://doi-org.ezproxy.fau.edu/10.1891/1933-3196.12.4.255.

Ray, D. C., Burgin, E., Gutierrez, D., Ceballos, P., & Lindo, N. (2022). Child-centered play therapy and adverse childhood experiences: A randomized controlled trial. *Journal of Counseling & Development, 100*(2), 134–145. https://doi.org/10.1002/jcad.12412.

Schaefer, C. E., & Drewes, A. A. (2014). *The therapeutic powers of play: 20 core agents of change* (2nd ed.). Wiley

Shapiro, F. (2017). *Eye movement desensitization and reprocessing (EMDR) therapy: Basic principles, protocols, and procedures.* Guilford Publications.

Sheffler, J. L., Stanley, I., & Sachs-Ericsson, N. (2020). ACEs and mental health outcomes. In *Adverse childhood experiences* (pp. 47–69). Academic Press. https://doi.org/10.1016/B9780128160657.000045.

Silberg, J. L. (2021). *The child survivor: Healing developmental trauma and dissociation.* Routledge.

Silvestre, M., & Tarquinio, C. L. (2022). Systemic family therapy and EMDR therapy: An integrative approach. *European Journal of Trauma & Dissociation, 6*(4), 100291. https://doi.org/10.1016/j.ejtd.2022.100291.

Spencer, A. E., Faraone, S. V., Bogucki, O. E., Pope, A. L., Uchida, M., Milad, M. R., ... & Biederman, J. (2016). Examining the association between posttraumatic stress disorder and attention-deficit/hyperactivity disorder: A systematic review and meta-analysis. *The Journal of clinical psychiatry, 77*(1), 6862.

Swimm, L. (2018) EMDR Intervention for a 17-month-old child to treat attachment trauma: Clinical case presentation. *Journal of EMDR Practice and Research, 12*(4), 269–79. https://doi.org/10.1891/1933-3196.12.4.269.

Swinden, C. (2018) The Child-centered EMDR approach: A case study investigating a young girl's treatment for sexual abuse. *Journal of EMDR Practice and Research, 12*(4), 282–95. https://doi.org/10.1891/1933-3196.12.4.282.

Tener, D., & Silberstein, M. (2019). Therapeutic interventions with child survivors of sibling sexual abuse: The professionals' perspective. *Child Abuse & Neglect, 89*, 192–202. https://doi.org/10.1016/j.chiabu.2019.01.010.

Thompson-Lee, F. (2020). EMDR-Infused Theraplay®. In A. Beckley-Forest & E. Monaco (Eds.), EMDR with children in the play therapy room: An integrated approach (pp. 349–360). Springer Publishing.

Townsend, B. J., Ishman, L., Dion, L., & Carnes-Holt, K. L. (2021). An examination of child-centered play therapy and synergetic play therapy. *Journal of Child and Adolescent Counseling, 7*(3), 193–206.

Van der Kolk, B. A. (2003). The neurobiology of childhood trauma and abuse. *Child and Adolescent Psychiatric Clinics, 12*(2), 293–317.

van der Kolk, B. A., Pynoos, R. S., Cicchetti, D., Cloitre, M., D'Andrea, W., Ford, J. D., & Teicher, M. (2009). Proposal to include a developmental trauma disorder diagnosis for children and adolescents in DSM-V. Unpublished manuscript: Retrieved: https://complextrauma.org/wp-content/uploads/2019/03/Complex-Trauma-Resource-3-Joseph-Spinazzola.pdf.

Vanfraussen, K., Campforts, E., & Imeraj, L. (2020). Eye Movement Desensitization and Reprocessing with body-oriented interventions within the field of adoption: Translating neuroscience into a clinical case study. *International Journal of Psychotherapy*, *24*(1), 15–28.

Vinke, A. J. G. (2020). Intercountry adoption, trauma and dissociation: Combining interventions to enhance integration. *European Journal of Trauma & Dissociation*, *4*(4), 100169.

Waters, F. S. (2016). *Healing the fractured child: Diagnosis and treatment of youth with dissociation*. Springer.

Wesselmann, D., Armstrong, S., Schweitzer, C., Davidson, M., & Potter, A. (2018). An integrative EMDR and family therapy model for treating attachment trauma in children: A case series. *Journal of EMDR Practice and Research*, *12*(4), 196–207.

Winder, S. D. C., Rinner, A. E., & Dickson, A. B. (2023). Playing Away the Trauma: Telehealth Practices with Foster Parents and Young Children. *The Journal of Foster Care*, *4*(1).

7

Attachment Centered Play Therapy

Clair Mellenthin

Chapter Outline

Introduction

Attachment Centered Play Therapy (ACPT; Mellenthin, 2019) is a family systems model of play therapy which offers a systemic and holistic perspective of child emotional and behavioral distress, as it views symptomology within the framework of family system functioning. It is an integrative, prescriptive play therapy model that harnesses the therapeutic powers of play with the original and contemporary theories of attachment theory. ACPT is not a manualized treatment protocol with step-by-step instructions, instead offering the clinician the flexibility needed in treating the family system through a prescriptive play therapy approach.

ACPT often incorporates individual, parent-child dyad, as well as sibling involvement, with the goal of strengthening the bonds of attachment within the entirety of the family system. In addition, the ACPT therapist meets with the parents independently of the play therapy process to help the parent resolve their own attachment injuries that may be impacting their relationship with their child, address parenting challenges and concerns, as well as teach attachment-centered parenting. Nestled within the framework of family systems theory, ACPT recognizes that there are multiple relational dynamics that influence how a family system interacts with one another. Keeney (1983) refers to this as the circularity of systems and subsystems, and "the between and within" is a dance of communication that happens between relationships. So much of family communication lies in the silent, secret hiding parts of the heart. Understanding the nuances and nature of family functioning and attachment seeking behaviors is critical to truly help the family system experience the change and healing so desperately needed.

Understanding the nature of attachment seeking and reciprocal behaviors between parent and child, sibling to sibling, and how the family operates within their global attachment patterns to the outside world is an especially important aspect to ACPT. As Byng-Hall (2008) states, "Attachment is part of family life . . . it is a mutual influence with every other function within the family ecology" (p. 129). The play therapist needs to understand how the family system operates, views their world and others, the series of interactions driven by attachment needs, and how the family responds to one another's seeking out for closeness and connection.

Viewing family relationships in terms of attachment security provides an additional lens to understand the complexity of family interactions. In ACPT, the spectrum of attachment security (Mellenthin, 2019) is a helpful tool in understanding attachment patterns and ways of engaging with one another. Attachment, like humans, tends to be messy and unique to each individual relationship, as well as how the family system functions globally. This is why it is not uncommon in family therapy to discover that one parent may have a more secure attachment to one child but a more ambivalent attachment to another child. Within the sibling relationship, they may exhibit a more anxious attachment. Between parents, there may be a more avoidant style of attachment, as they move away from vulnerability and emotional intimacy and shut down bids of connection. Overall, the family system functions in an insecure attachment, but each individual relationship has its own attachment patterns.

A brief description of the basic attachment patterns will be provided to give a broad context of security and the attachment-seeking behaviors identified in attachment theory. It is important to note the significance of viewing attachment patterns within the scope of a spectrum. Attachment security ebbs and flows throughout the attachment spectrum (Figure 7.1) depending upon developmental stages, the impact of trauma upon the system, as well as the nature and personality characteristics of each individual member of the family (Mellenthin, 2019).

Figure 7.1 Attachment Spectrum.

Securely Attached Parent-Child Relationships

Secure attachment is characterized by the parent's consistent, predictable, attuned caregiving response to their child's attachment-seeking behaviors. When a child feels stressed, scared, or frightened, the parent can offer comfort and protection. The parent is emotionally available and sensitively responsive to the child's needs (Byng-Hall, 2008). Within the relationship, there is permission for exploration, autonomy, and empathy.

Insecure Parent-Child Attachment Relationships

There are four distinct categories of insecure attachment (Ainsworth et al., 1978; Main & Solomon, 1986). *Insecure anxious* attachment is developed via inconsistent caregiving and nurturing, leading the child to live in a chronically anxious state, as they are unsure if their caregivers will meet their emotional and physical needs. There tends to be elevated levels of distress upon separation and reunion between child and parent, and the child is often difficult to soothe. Insecure attachment patterns fail to offer the developmental goals of felt security or affect regulation (Mellenthin, 2019).

Insecure ambivalent is characterized by the parent's intermittent emotional availability (Byng-Hall, 2008). This is often due to the parents' preoccupation with their own past hurt and relational pain. The child learns to cling close to the parent to avoid being abandoned, and the relationship becomes overly enmeshed while also being simultaneously distant. Ambivalence pervades the attachment system, and crisis and chaos are constant companions. There tends to be a reject-reject interaction between parent and child, as attachment needs are difficult to manage and provide for.

Insecure avoidant is characterized by the parents' emotional unavailability as they avoid coping with vulnerable or intimate emotions and experiences (Byng-Hall, 2008). When a child seeks out comfort, the parent reacts in a rejecting manner and tends to be dismissive of the importance of their child's feelings. There is a propensity to shut down the attachment system and an overall preference for positive feelings. This may lead to a child's development of ignoring their own needs for comfort from others, while giving the appearance of being overly self-reliant. The attachment messaging becomes, "I can only count on me to take care of my needs."

Insecure disorganized/disorientated is also commonly referred to as chaotic attachment (Mellenthin, 2019). Trauma tends to be at the root of a disorganized attachment system, as the parent responds to their child's bids for comfort or connection in a frightening manner, thereby activating the child's attachment system. This puts a child into a double bind, as the more activated they become, the more they need their parent or caregiver, who in turn responds to escalating and frightening behaviors, which causes increased stressful interactions between parent and child. This may also occur when the parent has unresolved trauma, which is activated by the child's cries for connection. The parent becomes overwhelmed and unable to moderate their own affective response. Children with disorganized attachment patterns may develop compulsive caregiving or strategies that are very controlling and at times highly disorganized (Byng-Hall, 2008).

Underlying Philosophy

The underlying philosophy of ACPT is that a child's behavioral or emotional dysregulation is directly related to the attachment quality of the family system. A child learns how to seek out attachment in their bids of attention, connection, and proximity seeking. However, the security of the primary attachment relationship plays a direct role in shaping these behaviors.

Secondly, it is proposed that attachment plays a key role in the processes of change in family functioning (Byng-Hall, 2008). As attachment theorists have postulated, the family must develop a secure enough attachment to the therapist to trust the change process. They must feel safe enough to explore new ways of engaging with one another, and this is shaped directly via the therapeutic relationship. It is why it is so crucial to develop a safe haven for each of the family members, not just the identified client. A child (and their parent) cannot experience soothing if they do not experience a felt sense of safety. If we think of this in terms of systemic functioning, the role of the therapeutic relationship across the family system cannot be overstated enough.

Lastly, the therapist must be flexible and adaptive to meet the unique attachment needs of both the individual and the family system involved. Utilizing a prescriptive play therapy approach can help tailor the play therapy treatment to best support the family system and the various dynamics at play.

Personality Theory

Bowlby (1969) theorized that infant attachment has a long-lasting impact on a person's emotional development throughout their lifetime. Through his observations of infant attachment, he found that those babies who were unable to establish a secure attachment to their caregiver were at higher risk for behavioral and emotional difficulties as well as psychiatric disorders. Bowlby believed that the development of affect regulation is linked to the early nonverbal communication that takes place between infant and caregiver (Fuchshuber et al., 2019). In secure attachment, an infant receives consistent, predictable caregiving. Their primary attachment figure can meet and anticipate their core attachment needs and respond in a nurturing manner toward their physiological and emotional needs. Through these interactions, an infant learns how to process and manage their emotional and primary nonverbal emotions. This repeated experience leads to the development of the internal working model (IWM) of self, with an internalized secure base, which allows for the affectual and emotional regulation and management to develop.

Attachment research has found that children with secure attachment tend to be viewed more positively and are deemed more likable, more resilient, and better able to organize their experiences and take on new challenges. They can function in a more independent, functional, and autonomous manner (Fuchshuber et al., 2019). They are also able to form and maintain healthy relationships both with peers as well as caregivers, and in later development, with romantic relationships. Secure attachment leads to a coherent narrative of self and others, with the child able to recognize social and emotional cues of others, express themselves in healthy ways, and ask for help when needed.

In contrast, when a child has experienced a less-than-optimal upbringing, and their early interactions with caregivers resulted in chaotic, unpredictable, and even cruel exchanges, this can lead the child to develop a highly disorganized and untrusting view of self and others. This leads to difficulty in managing emotions, expressing oneself appropriately, and understanding the social and emotional cues of others. These also can lead to a low level of personality organization, which research has found is associated with increased aggression and negative affect (Fuchshuber et al., 2019). Attachment research has found that children with insecure attachment styles are often disliked by their peers, possess low self-esteem, and are prone to lash out at others (Fonagy et al., 2023; Irvine et al., 2023).

Personality, then, is shaped by both nature and nurture. A child who believes they are loved, lovable, and worthy of love and belonging often acts in lovable ways. They are more likely to seek out relationships and better able to tolerate stress. When there are minor ruptures or moments of misattunement, repair is easily accomplished within the relationship. A child who experiences unpredictable caregiving and develops insecure attachment patterns often portrays a sense of neediness and lack of flexibility. There is mistrust that a loved one will genuinely love them back or will stand by them in times of distress. They may need to make their needs "highly apparent," and their attachment behaviors become overactivated when faced with even minor stresses (Byng-Hall, 2008). The child may also develop an avoidance of emotional closeness and shut down the attachment system when under stress. They may appear as overly self-reliant and send a message out to the world of "I don't want to need you and I don't want you to need me."

When a child believes themselves to be *unlovable*, to truly not be worthy or love and belonging, they may often act out in protective measures that push people away, break trust, and engage in self-fulfilling prophecy making, as each time a relationship ruptures, it becomes a reaffirming affirmation that indeed I am unloved and unlovable. This heartbreaking scenario plays out repeatedly, each rupture cementing their negative IWM.

Model of Psychopathology

Attachment theory adheres to the notion that a child's early caregiving experiences shape their sense of worth and belief in their lovability and belonging. Bowlby (1969) referred to this phenomenon as an Internal Working Model (IWM) which helps to create a child's belief about the world and their sense of belonging within the world. These early experiences and attachment relationships are crucial for the acquisition and development of the capacities for affect regulation, stress regulation, attentional control, mentalization, and "for the infant's sense of self-agency" (Lorenzini & Fonagy, 2013, p. 155). When a child is raised with caregivers who are sensitive to their physical, emotional, and attachment-related needs, who can engage in a nurturing, affirming, reciprocal manner, a child is able to build stable representations of self and others. They learn how to manage difficult emotions, express themselves, and build egalitarian relationships with peers as well as other adults. There is permission for outside relationships to develop and a child can grow their support network to help them navigate the world and the challenges that come with later developmental phases.

Research has long documented the impact and importance of secure attachment and the impact it has on a child's physiological, neurological, social, and emotional development (Fitter et al., 2022; Fonagy et al., 2023; White et al., 2023). Recent research (Fonagy et al., 2023) has found that the impact of early attachment goes well beyond infancy and influences the trajectory of a child's lifespan either positively or negatively, depending on the quality of attachment relationships. Attachment theory is one of the most widely researched models of human and relationship development (Fonagy et al., 2023). Contemporary attachment science has confirmed many of Bowlby's original premises about the nature of attachment and the vital role of the parent-child relationship in child development. Neuroscience has also illuminated new information about the role of mirror neurons and how these neural networks inform and develop attachment security—or the lack thereof. Recent research (Fitter et al., 2022) has further identified how maternal responses to their child's distress influence brain development, particularly in the amygdala, thalamus, and white matter.

When faced with unreliable, chaotic, and/or frightening caregiving, a child's IWM develops into opposite messages of their worth and ability to be loved and loveable (Mellenthin, 2019). Mikulincer and Shaver (2012) eloquently describes the impact of this experience. They state, "When a person's attachment figures are not reliably available and supportive, proximity seeking fails to relieve stress, felt security is undermined, negative models of self and others are formed, and the likelihood of later emotional problems and maladjustment increases" (p. 11).

Mikulincer and Shaver (2012) postulate that when a child faces repeated interactions with inconsistent, unreliable, or insensitive attachment figures, this directly interferes with the development of a secure, stable mental foundation. Research finds this has a drastic impact, including a reduced resilience in coping with stressful life events, and predisposes a person to "break down psychologically in times of crisis" (p. 12). There are several research studies that have addressed the connection between insecure attachment styles and the later development of personality disorders (Lorenzini & Fonagy, 2013); mental health disorders, suicide, low self-esteem, and bullying (Farnicka, 2022; Irvine et al., 2023) and psychopathology (Mikulincer & Shaver, 2012; Shabab et al., 2021).

Insecure, avoidant, and disorganized attachment styles have been found to distinctly influence a child's development of externalizing and internalizing behaviors and diminished social competence, which can last throughout adulthood, as well as worsen over time (Fonagy et al., 2023). Children with insecure attachment are more likely to have trouble with regulating affect and emotions, interacting appropriately with peers, and experiencing increased emotional and behavioral problems. There is an increased risk for the development of significant mental disorders, including depression, anxiety, heightened aggression, social anxiety, obsessive-compulsive disorder, marital and relational dissatisfaction, and distress, as well as severe personality disorders and PTSD (Irvine et al., 2023; Mikulincer & Shaver, 2012).

Recent research (Fuchshuber et al., 2019) found that childhood maltreatment, abuse, and neglect significantly impact neurological and emotional development. Affective neuroscience has proposed that there is a framework of interdependently connected structures that bridge the circuitry of basic emotions, personality traits, and higher-order cognitive functions such as mentalization and mindfulness. When childhood trauma occurs that is chronic and unrelenting, there is a significant impact on brain development and functioning. This contributes to deficits in personality organization, the ability to maintain intimate relationships, allow for vulnerability, as well as being able to express and manage emotions as they arise.

However, attachment science also believes in the reparative nature of earned attachment security and repair within the primary relationship. If a child has access to at least one safe and predictable attachment figure, even if it is not the primary caretaker, it may protect them from behavioral, emotional, and relational problems (Fonagy et al., 2023). While the detriments of maltreatment and attachment disorganization can significantly impact a child, access to one relationship of safety and security can offer a buffer and potentially help detour away from a lifetime of future relational hurt and chaos.

Conceptualizing Goals of Treatment

ACPT consists of three main treatment goals: (1) Identifying the attachment needs of the family system; (2) Identify underlying attachment injuries and ruptures; and (3) Repair, rebuild, and create secure attachment. The first goal is to assess the underlying attachment needs and behaviors that are present in the family system and are driving the unwanted behaviors that have led to a clinical referral (Mellenthin, 2019). This involves both an assessment of the parent's attachment history as well as observation of the child and caregiver together. The parent/primary caregiver is given the *Family Development Questionnaire* (Thompson, as cited in Mellenthin, 2019) to fill out prior to play therapy beginning. This questionnaire is a narrative assessment that is based on the Adult Attachment Inventory (AAI) developed by attachment researchers George, Kaplan, and Main (1985). The parent is asked to provide a written narrative of their own developmental attachment experiences in addition to how they perceive their child's behaviors and emotions. This is reviewed with the therapist and parent/caregiver without the child present prior to observation and assessment of parent and child together in conjoint play therapy sessions. The play therapist observes how the child and parent interact in play therapy and if there appear to be secure, insecure, ambivalent, or avoidant tendencies.

Part of this assessment is a longitudinal evaluation, as this is a family systems model. Each subsystem within the system possesses its own unique attachment patterns, in addition to the global patterns of attachment that are present.

The second goal of ACPT is to identify the attachment injuries and ruptures present within the family system (Mellenthin, 2019). In human relationships, it is common for there to be underlying, unresolved attachment injuries present. This is due to the fallacy of humankind. We are prone to disappoint, mis-attune, and misunderstand one another on a regular basis. In secure attachment, when a rupture of this kind exists, repair also exists. A parent can say, "*I am sorry for losing my temper today. I am working on controlling my big feelings just like you are. It is not okay for me to yell, and I am working on expressing myself in better ways.*" When there is a consistent lack of repair, these attachment injuries can build into major attachment ruptures, which tear apart the bonds of connection. In relationships where there has been trauma, abandonment, divorce, prolonged separation, and neglect, the attachment ruptures can be immense and repair is increasingly difficult, as safety and security are scarce.

The third goal of ACPT aims to strengthen, repair, and rebuild (and sometimes create for the first time) a level of secure attachment between child and parent (Mellenthin, 2019). The therapist works with the parent to create safety, predictability, and security in their caregiving capabilities, establishing a secure base between parent and child. The goal is not perfection but rather striving for a "secure enough" relationship (Byng-Hall, 1995). As the parent becomes a resource to their child, homeostasis can occur, and a new ecology of belonging can begin.

Role of the Therapist

Bowlby (1988) believed that the role of the therapist is to act as a secure base for the client to be able to "explore the various unhappy and painful aspects of his life, past and present, many of which he finds difficult or perhaps impossible to think about and reconsider without a trusted companion to provide support, encouragement, sympathy, and on occasion, guidance" (p. 138). The role of the therapist in ACPT is to model secure attachment to all members of the family system and provide attachment-enhancing experiences within the play therapy process. The ACPT therapist needs to be knowledgeable in attachment theory and science, as the nuances of attachment seeking behaviors can be challenging at times to understand and explain. The therapist provides a safe haven and secure base within the therapeutic relationship to both the child as well as their parent/caregiver. We become the lily pad, so to speak. If we imagine that each of our clients is like a cute little frog looking for safety and respite within the pond, the therapeutic relationship is a lily pad waiting for them to rest, refuel, repair, and replenish so they have the power within to make the next leap. Within the therapeutic relationship, we offer safety and security for the family system to land. This includes the parent, as so much of the dynamics of the parental relationship influences the child. Often, we may be the first model of security for each member of the family system.

As the lily pad, our role is also to moderate and manage the environment of the play therapy process. We need to titrate the dose of vulnerability and emotional intimacy involved in family play therapy, ensuring that the family system is emotionally ready for the planned interventions. The goal of each session should be to provide moments of connection and delight in one another, even when working through difficult emotions and challenges. Depending upon the nature of the attachment relationship, play therapy interventions should be appropriate to meet the needs of the relationship. For some families, this may look like high-energy games and playful interventions, while others may need more quiet and calming interventions. This is why prescriptive play therapy can be incredibly effective in family work, as the therapist engages in a flexible, adaptive manner to meet the family system with the approach that is most beneficial to them, instead of a prescribed model or manualized blanket approach.

Being the lily pad also models appropriate secure attachment to the parent involved, as attachment-based parenting is authoritative yet flexible and nurturing. The therapist helps guide the parent/caregiver into becoming a resource to the child, one who is responsive to their needs, and able to moderate their own affective experience (Mellenthin, 2019). This helps the caregiver to become the secure base for their child. Helping the parent learn how to manage their own fears and anxieties allows the child permission to explore the world around them, including the relationships and IWM of self and others.

Roles of Caregivers and Collaterals

Caregivers play a significant role in ACPT, and their involvement throughout the play therapy process is crucial. ACPT postulates that as attachment ruptures are repaired and family relationships are strengthened, attachment security is possible. Attachment theory advocates for the role of relationship repair and corrective emotional experiences since the beginning of Bowlby's initial work. Contemporary neuroscience confirms the importance of repair and earned attachment security, as the impact on neurological and emotional functioning is increased as attachment increases (Fonagy et al., 2023; Fuchshuber et al., 2019). The therapist often works with the parents independently of the child to help them learn attachment-centered parenting skills, as well as help them to resolve their own feelings of guilt, hurt, rejection, and shame. When possible and clinically appropriate, play therapy involves not just the parent-child dyad but also siblings and other family members to promote systemic healing and repairing.

Research/Empirical Support

There is bourgeoning research into the model of ACPT. In the last few years, graduate students at Baylor University researched the positive impact of using ACPT with LGBTQIA+ adolescents and their family members (Rohrbach, 2022). ACPT is also being used as a play therapy model shown to be effective when integrated with Exposure and Response Prevention (ERP) in treating pediatric obsessive-compulsive disorder (Rose & Lambert, 2024). As a resource in attachment science, the book *Attachment Centered Play Therapy* (Mellenthin, 2019) has been cited in over 100 publications, including peer-reviewed journal articles, books, chapters, and professional presentations in recent years (www.academia.edu, 2024).

Case Study through the Lens of the Therapeutic Powers of Play: Therapeutic Powers of Play Employed

As ACPT is a prescriptive, integrative play therapy approach, the therapeutic powers of play are continuously engaged and utilized throughout the therapy process. Within each of the identified therapeutic powers, Herman (see Appendix for case study of Herman being referenced) would be exposed to multiple play powers as he begins to heal and create a new narrative of his worth, his belonging, and his relationships with others.

Facilitates Communication

Schaefer and Drewes (2014) state, "Play, the natural language of the child, is often the easiest way for children to express troubling thoughts and feelings that are both conscious and unconscious" (p. 9). Self-expression, access to the unconscious, and direct and indirect teaching are therapeutic play powers that can enhance and facilitate communication. In ACPT and attachment theory in general, facilitating communication is an important aspect of building a connection and a secure relationship. Part of being truly seen by another involves communication of self and affirmation of self through a positive, reciprocal relationship. In Herman's life, his use of eyeliner and nail polish may be one way that Herman is both trying to be seen as well as express himself. His outbursts and big behaviors may be ways he is attempting to communicate his attachment needs, however, ineffective this may be. In play therapy, these four play powers can be enhanced between Herman and his caregivers through the use of dress-ups, expressive arts, puppet play, storytelling, and imagination games. As an example, the intervention *Stars and Dots* (Mellenthin, 2020) could be a wonderful way to build upon the foundation of connection while fostering communication between Herman and his foster parents. In the intervention *Stars and Dots*, the caregiver or therapist read the story *You Are Special* (Lucado, 1997). This involves both direct and indirect teaching. Through storytelling (indirect teaching), the child is able to *see themselves* in the story, allowing for personal insight and understanding to grow. The child is taught (direct teaching) ways in which their bids for connection and attention may be pushing people away, as well as the importance of loving and accepting themselves while allowing others to love and accept them (attachment). After the story is read, the child draws their own stars (the positive aspects of self; positive emotions) and dots (negative aspects of self) onto a doll (self-expression, access to the unconscious). They are then invited to share with their caregiver and therapist each of the identified stars or dots. The caregiver helps to reframe negative beliefs with their child, helping them improve their confidence and self-worth. This helps the child to feel accepted, seen, and important.

Fosters Emotional Wellness

Catharsis, abreaction, positive emotions, counterconditioning fears, stress inoculation, and stress management are the therapeutic play powers identified for fostering emotional wellness. As Herman has experienced multiple traumas throughout his young life, these play powers are especially important to incorporate into his play therapy work. Often, where there are big behaviors, there are underlying big emotions, which are important to acknowledge and bring to the playroom. This allows the child to gain mastery over their emotions, leading to self-regulation and the ability to think through stressful situations.

In attachment science, co-regulation is crucial for safety and soothing to take place. By engaging with Herman and his foster parents, we can offer the predictability needed to encourage and influence "safe" relationship exchanges. Normalizing big emotions and increasing the ability to communicate their feelings also enhances emotional wellness. The intervention, *The Family Self-Esteem Game* (Mellenthin, 2019), further demonstrates how the play therapist can utilize the therapeutic powers of play in an integrative approach.

In this intervention, Herman and his foster family will be invited to attend an initial family-based play therapy session. The family will be given six balloons to blow up. Each person will be asked to write one of the following questions per balloon:

1. What is something you are proud you can do?
2. Tell about a time you were able to do something difficult
3. Tell about a time you felt proud of yourself
4. Tell about a time you were nice to someone
5. Tell about a time that you helped yourself feel better
6. Say Something nice to someone else in the room

The "game" then begins. The family chooses two balloons to play with initially. The goal is to keep the balloons bouncing up in the air while standing in a circle. As the family plays together with "great big play," a natural playfulness enters, lowering stress, and creating these moments of delight as the family experiences catharsis, positive emotions, regulation, and decreasing stressful interactions. As one balloon drops to the floor, the game stops, the question is read, and everyone takes turns answering the prompt on the balloon. Following this, the game resumes until all of the questions have been read and answered. The pacing, modeling of communication, and moments of spontaneity help to improve emotional wellness via the incorporation of several simultaneous therapeutic powers of play.

Enhances Social Relationships

Brown (2009; as cited in Stewart & Echterling, 2014) postulates that "play is the cornerstone of all personal relationships and has its roots in the child's first love relationship with his parents" (p. 157). Play becomes the vehicle for love, connection, and delight in a parent-child relationship. In Herman's short life, his previous caregivers were inadequate at best, and he lacked these crucial moments, milestones, and areas of development. Play has healing properties, and playing *with* his safe adults can help to create a safe and secure relationship.

The therapeutic relationship, attachment, social competence, and empathy are the core therapeutic play powers in this section of Schaefer and Drewes (2014) table, Stewart and Echterling (2014) state, "The therapeutic alliance garners its healing power in the way that it embodies the characteristics of a healthy parent-child relationship, namely, that there exists a shared goal or purpose to the relationship, an attuned and known way to engage with one another, and a positive affective connections" (p. 158). Attachment theory strongly encourages the development of a secure base in the therapeutic relationship to facilitate growth and safety in the client family's relationship (Whelan & Stewart, 2014). By creating a safe haven and secure base, the therapist becomes the lily pad for both Herman and his foster parents. It is unknown the attachment patterns between Herman and his caregivers, other than Herman tends to feel safe enough and secure enough to refer to them as Mommy and Daddy. However, his foster parents may not be feeling similarly toward Herman due to his explosive and unpredictable behaviors. This would be an important assessment and avenue for a treatment plan.

By utilizing a prescriptive play therapy approach, the play therapist would assess the differing attachment needs of the family system and utilize specific interventions that would best facilitate the development and repair of the parent-child relationship. Helping both parents and child increase their capacity for empathy by creating moments of emotional intimacy and shared communication is also an important element in strengthening the attachment system. By incorporating predictable, joyful, positive, and consistent play, this can also lead to fostering earned security. Children feel most safe when adults interact with them in developmentally compatible and appropriate ways (Stewart & Echterling, 2014). By helping Herman's foster parents learn about to engage in playful, sensitively attuned ways, the security of the overall attachment dynamics has the potential to develop.

The intervention *Two Hands* (Mellenthin, 2019) could help to enhance this experience and expression of relationship as well as positive emotions. In this intervention, each person is given a piece of blank paper. The parent traces the child's hands on one paper, and the child traces their parent's hands on another. They are then invited to cut out the hands and fill up one another's hands with images, words, symbols, or color to express all of the positive attributes of that person. Once the artwork is completed, the therapist and family explore the hands, how this makes each person feel, and where they feel these feelings in their own body. The hands are then glued to a piece of cardstock and framed for the family to take home to remember the positive parts of self on a daily basis.

Increases Personal Strengths

Schaefer and Drewes (2014) identify creative problem solving, resiliency, moral development, accelerated psychological development, self-regulation, and self-esteem as the specific change agents in this section. As Herman's internal working model of self improves and he begins to view himself as not just loved but lovable and worthy of love and belonging, his self-efficacy, self-esteem, and core view of his inherent value improve. This enhances his resiliency, increases creative problem solving, and moderates affect and self-regulation. In individual and family-based play therapy sessions, helping Herman to identify his strengths is an important tool in helping to change how he sees himself in his narrative.

Using superhero dress-ups can be a playful way to enhance Herman's recognition of his personal strengths, as well as teach healthy coping skills needed to improve his decision-making processes. *The Superhero in the Mirror Technique* (Mellenthin, 2018) is a fun, playful intervention where the child identifies specific "superhero powers" they possess as they begin to get dressed up in superhero clothes. Some powers may be "I can run super-fast," "I am kind," "I love myself," or "I can use my bubble breathing when I am mad." The child then stands in front of the mirror and practices various power poses, yelling out their superhero strengths.

Cultural, Diversity, Inclusion Considerations

The foster parents' cultural and ethnic background is unknown at this point. However, Herman has been identified as being of "mixed heritage" and comes from Caucasian, Black, and Latinx origins. It will also be important to acknowledge and address the many different areas of intersectionality that Herman occupies, including gender, sexuality, religion, neurodivergence, as well as areas of intersectionality within his foster family system. Research (Thompson, 2021) has found that the level of security within attachment is considered an adaptation to different conditions of care, sensitivity, and acceptance. Having items in the playroom that are representative of his ethnic background, in addition to having gender fluid toys, dress-ups, and permission for full acceptance for Herman to be who he is in the playroom, is a critical aspect to developing a secure relationship with his therapist and caregivers.

There are cultural considerations in terms of attachment theory itself that the ACPT therapist needs to be mindful of. Attachment theory has predominantly viewed relationships through the lens of WEIRD (Western, Educated, Industrialized, Rich, and Democratic) samples (Sakman & Sumer, 2024) with the focus on a Westernized view of individualization as the capstone of adulthood. In collectivistic communities, interdependence is much more normalized, and dependence on caregivers is a valued cultural quality. Research has found that the goal of caretaking would be to encourage mutual aid rather than self-reliance (Brown et al., 2014). Depending upon many factors, it is important for the therapist to tailor their interventions to be culturally sensitive and relevant. In ACPT, there are seven core attachment needs identified: Physical touch, emotional closeness, acceptance, unconditional love, safety, security, and play. Play therapy interventions should include these core components while also being very mindful about the depth of trauma Herman has experienced.

Case Formulation and Application

Herman's current behaviors would be viewed in terms of an insecure avoidant/disorganized attachment pattern resulting from the complex, chronic trauma he has experienced in his young life. As his current caregivers, his long-term foster parents would play an integral part in developing earned security within the parent-child relationship. Part of his explosive behaviors may also manifest as part of his bids for connection and for attachment security, as Herman is likely well aware that his foster parents are currently struggling with his behaviors and potentially questioning if they can keep him in their home for much longer. As Herman has already developed a close relationship with his foster parents, their involvement is warranted.

The ACPT therapist would first meet with the foster parents to explore their perception of Herman, as well as explore their own attachment histories and view of their relationships in general and with significant others. The therapist would explore how they respond to Herman's outbursts and ways in which repair occurs after a meltdown. As Herman has lived in their home for several years and refers to them as Mommy and Daddy, this level of emotional intimacy would also be explored to determine if it is reciprocal within the family system.

Assuming his long-term foster parents were agreeable to their involvement, ACPT would then pivot to relationship building with Herman and begin the initial stages of family systems play therapy. A child who has experienced complex, chronic trauma needs to have safe adults in their world who can provide safety and emotional security. Herman's foster parents already play a role in providing consistency, nurture, and are his primary attachment figures. Due to Herman's history of becoming easily dysregulated, the ACPT therapist will be mindful of the importance of neurobiological informed play therapy interventions. Play therapy interventions that focus on building moments of connection and positivity will be introduced, with incremental steps in developing emotional intimacy and literacy employed.

Challenges in Implementation

Building a therapeutic relationship and alliance will most likely take a long time due to the intensity of the trauma Herman has experienced and the multiple caregivers and therapists with whom he has experienced a ruptured attachment. His current foster parents need to be committed to his long-term therapeutic and placement needs for him to experience reparative attachment experiences to create security and emotional safety. Herman's attachment patterns may take considerable time to shift into a more secure attachment relationship. It is vulnerable work to be engaged in long-term therapeutic services where the focus is on the attachment needs of the family system instead of the acting-out child. Due to the current escalation of distress in the system, weekly individual and/or family therapy sessions would be recommended. Over time, as homeostasis within the family system is created, the therapy sessions would begin to taper to meet the needs of both Herman and his foster family.

Conclusion

Attachment Centered Play Therapy is a powerful and effective family systems model of play therapy that engages both caregiver and child. Teaching the caregiver how to truly delight in the child and fully accept them is a beautiful reparative dance that takes place in the magic of the play therapy process. We cannot expect the least powerful, most vulnerable member of the family system to be the change agent. We need to involve the adult caregiver in the play therapy process to allow for long-term change and healing to commence.

References

Ainsworth, M. D. S., Blehar, M. C., Waters, E., & Wall, S. (1978). *Patterns of attachment.* Erlbaum.

Academia.edu. (2024). [website] https://www.academia.edu/mentions?from_navbar=true&trigger=nav.

Bowlby, J. (1969). *Attachment and loss, vol.1: Attachment.* Hogart Press/Institute of Psychoanalysis.

Bowlby, J. (1988). *A secure base: Parent-child attachment and healthy human development.* Basic Books

Brown, D., Rodger, Y. H., & Kapadia, K. (2014). Multicultural considerations for the application of attachment theory. *American Journal of Psychotherapy, 62*(4), 353–63.

Brown, S. (2009). *Play: How it sharpens the mind, opens the imagination, and invigorates the soul.* Bantam Books

Byng-Hall, J. (1995). *Rewriting family scripts: Improvisation and systems change.* Guilford Press.

Byng-Hall, J. (2008). The crucial roles of attachment in family therapy. *Journal of Family Therapy, 30*, 129–46.

Farnicka, M. (2022). Emotional regulation and social support as conditions for aggressor and victim experience in early and late adolescence- developmental psychopathology lenses. *International Journal of Education and Practice, 10*(4), 250–70.

Fitter, M. H., Stern, J. A., Straske, M. D., Allard, T., Cassidy, J., & Riggins, T. (2022). Mothers' attachment representations and children's brain structure. *Frontiers in Human Neuroscience, 16*, 740195.

Fonagy, P., Campbell, C., & Luyten, P. (2023). Attachment, mentalization, and trauma: Then (1992) and now (2022). *Brain Sciences, 13*, 459.

Fuchshuber, J., Heibler-Ragger, M., Kresse, A., Kapfhammer, H., & Unterrainer, H. F. (2019). The influence of attachment styles and personality organization on emotional functioning after childhood trauma. *Frontiers in Psychiatry, 10*, 643.

George, C., Main, M., & Kaplan, N. (1985). *Adult Attachment Interview (AAI)* [Database record]. APA PsycTests.

Irvine, T. J., Aults, C. D., & Menon, M. (2023). Self-esteem moderates the relationship between secure attachment and internalizing and externalizing problems in preadolescence. *Psychological Reports, 126*(2), 758–74.

Keeney, B. P. (1983). *Aesthetics of change.* Gilford.

Lucado, M. (1997). *You are special.* Crossway.

Lorenzini, N., & Fonagy, P. (2013). Attachment and personality disorders: A short review. *Focus, 11*(2), 155–66.

Main, M., & Solomon, J. (1986). Discovery of an insecure-disorganized/disorientated attachment pattern: Procedures, findings, and implications for the classification of behavior. In T. B. Brazelton & M. W. Yogman (Eds.), *Affective development in infancy* (pp. 95–134). Ablex.

Mellenthin, C. (2018). *Play therapy: Engaging and powerful techniques for the treatment of childhood disorders.* PESI Publishing.

Mellenthin, C. (2019). *Attachment centered play therapy.* Routledge.

Mellenthin, C. (2020). *Healing wounded hearts: Understanding attachment disruptions in childhood using attachment centered play therapy.* https://clairmellenthin.com/jjwp/wp-content/uploads/2020/09/Healing-Wounded-Hearts-3-hr-ACPT.pdf

Mikulincer, M., & Shaver, P. R. (2012). An attachment perspective on psychopathology. *World Psychiatry, 11*, 11–15.

Rohrbach, L. (2022). *Attachment-centered play therapy with gender expansive preadolescents and their caregivers in a therapeutic setting* [PowerPoint presentation]. Diana R. Garland School of Social Work at Baylor University.

Rose, R., & Lambert, A. (2024). *How to train your dragon: Using attachment centered play therapy and ERP to treat pediatric OCD* [PowerPoint presentation]. Association for Play Therapy Utah Chapter, 7 June, webinar.

Sakman, E., & Sumer, N. (2024). Cultural correlates of adult attachment dimensions: Comparing the US and Turkey. *Cross-Cultural Research, 58*(2–3), 208–37.

Schaefer, C. E., & Drewes, A. A. (2014). *The therapeutic powers of play: 20 core agents of change* (2nd ed.). Wiley.

Shahab, M. K., Ridder, J. A., Spinhoven, P., Pennix, B. W. J. H., Mook-Kanamori, D. O., & Elzinga, B. M. (2021). A tangled start: The link between childhood maltreatment, psychopathology, and relationships in adulthood. *Child Abuse & Neglect, 121*, 105228, 1–14.

Stewart, A. L., & Echterling, L. G. Therapeutic relationship. In C. E. Schaefer & A. A. Drewes (Eds.), *The therapeutic powers of play* (2nd ed., pp. 157–70). Wiley.

Thompson, R. A. (2021). Eyes to see and ears to hear: Sensitivity in research on attachment and culture. *Attachment & Human Development, 23*(2), 222–30.

Whelan, W. F., & Stewart, A. L. Attachment. In C. E. Schaefer & A. A. Drewes (Eds.), *The therapeutic powers of play* (2nd ed., pp. 171–84). Wiley.

White, L., Kungl, M., & Vrticka, P. (2023). Charting the social neuroscience of human attachment. *Attachment & Human Development, 25*(1), 1–18.

Part IV

Closing Thoughts

Practical Use of the Text

Closing Notes
Practical Use of the Text

Edward Franc Hudspeth

Chapter Outline

In 1982, Charles Schaefer and Kevin O'Connor founded the Association for Play Therapy (APT). From an initial small group of members to 8000 members in October 2024 (APT, 2024d), the play therapy community has grown. This membership growth demonstrates that play therapy training is desired, respected, and valued. Of the current membership of APT, 5374 individuals hold either the Registered Play Therapist (RPT™) (2024a), School-Based Registered Play Therapist (SB-RPT™) (2023a), or Registered Play Therapist-Supervisor (RPT-S™) credential (APT, 2024b). Whether a credentialed play therapist or play therapist-in-training all are held accountable to be competent, skilled, and ethical members of the play therapy community.

The Association for Play Therapy (APT, 2023b, pp. 1–2; 2024, pp. 13–14; Turner et al., 2020) identifies specific areas of competencies as essential to the competent practice of play therapy. These competencies should be woven throughout the training, practice, and supervision of play therapists-in-training, credentialed play therapists, play therapy supervisors, and play therapy trainers and educators. The play therapy competencies are developmental in nature, moving from knowledge to skills and application to maintenance. They are as follows:

Competency 1: Knowledge and Understanding of Play Therapy

The play therapist will:

1a. Demonstrate knowledge of the history of play therapy
1b. Demonstrate understanding of the therapeutic powers of play

1c. Demonstrate knowledge of the therapeutic relationship in play therapy
1d. Demonstrate knowledge of seminal/historically significant play therapy theories and models
1e. Apply theories and stages of childhood development in play therapy
1f. Identify and apply ethical practices in play therapy
1g. Demonstrate an understanding of the play therapy treatment process (e.g., treatment goals and plans, documentation, intake/termination, and tracking of treatment progress)
1h. Demonstrate knowledge of family & systemic theories in play therapy
1i. Demonstrate knowledge of childhood-related problems and mental health diagnosis/disorders
1j. Demonstrate an understanding of the diverse impacts of childhood trauma (e.g., neurobiological, systemic, social) and the implications in play therapy
1k. Demonstrate knowledge of assessment in play therapy

Competency 2: Clinical Play Therapy Skills

The play therapist will:

2a. Apply and articulate the therapeutic powers of play
2b. Demonstrate relationship and rapport building skills (e.g., empathy, safety, unconditional positive regard) by utilizing "self" in relationships with children, caregivers, stakeholders in play therapy
2c. Apply assessments that highlight various aspects of the child and/or system and the play therapy process (e.g., conceptualization, diagnosis, family dynamics, treatment suitability and effectiveness, termination)
2d. Articulate and explain the play therapy process
2e. Demonstrate basic play therapy skills (e.g., tracking, reflection of feeling, limit setting, pacing with the client)
2f. Identify play dynamics (e.g., types of play, themes, and stages) and incorporate clinical considerations in treatment
2g. Develop play therapy treatment goals and plans congruent with theoretical orientation
2h. Demonstrate understanding of own cultural and social identity and its influence in the play therapy process
2i. Exhibit multicultural orientation to diversity, equity, and inclusion through a culturally and socially diverse playroom and play therapy process
2j. Demonstrate play therapy treatment skills congruent with theoretical orientation (e.g., conceptualization and interventions)

Competency 3: Professional Engagement in Play Therapy

The play therapist will:

3a. Maintain play therapy credentials and involvement in professional play therapy organizations
3b. Consistently evaluate and adjust play therapy practices to meet state and discipline ethical guidelines and codes
3c. Apply ongoing integration of APT's guidelines within the Best Practices and Paper on Touch
3d. Recognize and adhere to the limits of professional scope of competence in play therapy
3e. Seek and integrate play therapy-specific continued education, research, and literature
3f. Seek and integrate play therapy-specific supervision and consultation
3g. Practice self-care to maintain quality play therapy services
3h. Seek and integrate ongoing knowledge regarding cultural and social diversity in play therapy

Though many credentialed play therapists were trained long before the play therapy competencies, all should be familiar with them. They are not solely important for play therapists-in-training, but also for those who are credentialed, those who train play therapists, and those who supervise. Also, the competencies are important for the maintenance of our play therapy credential as we seek to remain up to date and ethical practitioners. As such, this text provides an opportunity to revisit and update our understanding of the TPoP and seminal play therapy theories. In the sections below, suggestions are made for how this text may be used across all practitioner levels.

Pre-Credentialed, Play Therapists-in-Training

Whether one is at the beginning, middle, or end of their training to become a play therapist, a routine effort should be made to thoroughly conceptualize each client, decide the best play therapy course of action, and implement a well-developed plan. While being trained to be a play therapist, it is important to recognize and embrace the fact that play-based therapy or play in therapy are not equivalent to play therapy. Play therapy is distinct from them in two areas (a) play therapy has a theoretical thread running throughout all of its facets (Hudspeth, 2021) and (b) play therapy relies on the TPoP as core change agents (Schaefer & Drewes, 2014). With this in mind, this text provides an opportunity to read and experience most seminal play therapy theories and models as well burgeoning theories and models when applied to a hypothetical client case. Though the application is to a single client case, the results provide an example that can be the foundation for application across all clients. As a play therapist-in-training, this text provides:

1. A better understanding of child development theory.
2. An introduction to the TPoP.
3. An introduction to seminal play therapy theories and burgeoning play therapy theories/models.
4. A foundation in play therapy techniques.
5. The ability to conceptualize treatment when linking TPoP and theoretical underpinnings.
6. An understanding of cultural diversity and individual client needs.

During the educational component of play therapy training, play therapy competencies in the category *Competency 1: Knowledge & Understanding of Play Therapy* provide play therapists-in-training with their foundation. As they gain basic knowledge and skills to apply play therapy and move into their initial clinical practice, play therapy competencies in the category *Competency 2: Clinical Play Therapy Skills* become important. For a suggested alignment of these competencies to chapters of this text, see Appendix. For more information related to become a credentialed play therapist as well as play therapy best practices see:

1. **Credentialing standards for the Registered Play Therapist™: APT professional credentialing program.**
   https://cdn.ymaws.com/www.a4pt.org/resource/resmgr/credentials/standards_&_applications/rpt_standards.pdf
2. **Credentialing standards for the School-Based Registered Play Therapist™: APT professional credentialing program.**
   https://cdn.ymaws.com/www.a4pt.org/resource/resmgr/credentials/standards_&_applications/sb-rpt_guide.pdf
3. **Credentialing standards for the Registered Play Therapist-Supervisor ™: APT professional credentialing program.**
   https://cdn.ymaws.com/www.a4pt.org/resource/resmgr/credentials/standards_&_applications/rpt-s_standards.pdf
4. **Play therapy competencies: APT professional credentialing program.**
   https://cdn.ymaws.com/www.a4pt.org/resource/resmgr/credentials/play_therapy_competencies.pdf
5. **Play therapy best practices: Clinical, professional, & ethical issues.**
   https://cdn.ymaws.com/www.a4pt.org/resource/resmgr/publications/best_practices.pdf

Credentialed Play Therapists

Credentialed play therapists already have a strong foundational knowledge about the many aspects of play therapy. However, depending on their training, they may have had limited exposure to multiple seminal play therapy theories, the role of the TPoP, or how these two work together to provide a golden thread running from initial conceptualization to termination. Though many of the offerings noted in the section above also apply to credentialed play therapists, in addition, this text provides credentialed play therapists:

1. Access to updated knowledge, new techniques, and perspectives.
2. Opportunities to refine their existing skills, which helps them stay current by address emerging challenges and potentially improving their knowledge base further.
3. A better understanding of the seminal and burgeoning theoretical frameworks when considered with the TPoP.
4. An opportunity to see a case scenario to practice applying different play therapy theories to various client situations.
5. Enhanced ability to select and implement play therapy approach for each child.
6. Critical thinking skills to analyze and interpret children's play behaviors through a theoretical and TPoP lens.

As a credentialed play therapist, all three categories of the play therapy competencies are important; however, there should be a focus on continued professional growth and remaining up to date. With this in mind, play therapy competencies in the category *Competency 3: Professional Engagement in Play Therapy* are important. For a suggested alignment of these competencies to chapters of this text, see Appendix.

Play Therapy Supervisors

As a play therapy supervisor, it can be reasonably assumed that individuals have a strong foundation in all aspects of play therapy as well as specialized training to supervise play therapists-in training. Play therapy supervisors may also be providing consultation to credentialed play therapist. Thus, this text offers everything noted in the two sections above as well as:

1. A deeper understanding of the TPoP and theoretical frameworks underpinning play therapy allowing them to better guide play therapists-in-training.
2. An opportunity to help play therapists-in-training identify therapeutic goals based on case conceptualization to develop treatment plans grounded in the TPoP and play therapy theory(ies).
3. An ability to provide targeted feedback to supervisees based on their chosen theoretical approach and the child's specific needs.
4. Guide play therapists-in-training in analyzing and interpreting a child's play patterns to create a comprehensive understanding of their presenting issues.

As a play therapy supervisor, all three categories of the play therapy competencies are important. As a supervisor there is a shift in focus and a need to balance one's efforts. In essence, a supervisor is trying to remain up to date while helping play therapists-in-training gain knowledge, skills, and clinical experience using play therapy. For a suggested alignment of these competencies to chapters of this text, see Appendix.

Play Therapy Trainers and Educators

Most likely, play therapy trainers and educators are seasoned play therapy practitioner and competent supervisors. As was mentioned in the section above, they "are trying to remain up to date while helping play therapists-in-training gain knowledge, skills, and clinical experience using play therapy." In addition to being skilled play therapist and competent supervisors, play therapy trainers and educators know how to train others through didactic and experiential methods. As an educator at a university, APT (n.d.) offers syllabi resources, which include:

1. **Sample syllabus: Advanced graduate play therapy course.** https://cdn.ymaws.com/www.a4pt.org/resource/resmgr/education_&_training/sample_advanced_play_therapy.pdf
2. **Sample syllabus: Introductory graduate play therapy course university education (APT, 2024c).** https://cdn.ymaws.com/www.a4pt.org/resource/resmgr/education_&_training/Sample_Play_Therapy_Course_S.pdf

For play therapy trainers and educators, this text offers a comprehensive opportunity to:

1. Deepen understanding of the TPoP and theoretical frameworks underpinning play therapy allowing them to better train play therapists.
2. Use the text's case study approach to guide play therapists-in-training to practice applying different play therapy theories to various client situations.
3. Help play therapists-in-training develop critical thinking skills and comprehensive case conceptualization skills.

As a play therapy trainer or educator, all three categories of the play therapy competencies are important; however, there should be a focus on continued professional growth and remaining up to date. With this in mind, play therapy competencies in all the categories *Competency 1: Knowledge & Understanding of Play Therapy*, *Competency 2: Clinical Play Therapy Skills*, and *Competency 3: Professional Engagement in Play Therapy* are important. For a suggested alignment of these competencies to chapters of this text, see Appendix.

Summary

In this final chapter of the text, we provide suggestions for utilization of the text across all levels of play therapy training and competency. As the text is utilized, other practical ways will likely surface. No text can do everything or provide all one would need to become a

Table 1 Text Chapters and Play Therapy Compentencies Alignment

Text Chapters and Play Therapy Competencies Alignment			
	Competency 1: Knowledge & Understanding of Play Therapy	**Competency 2: Clinical Play Therapy Skills**	**Competency 3: Professional Engagement in Play Therapy**
Part 1: Understanding the Therapeutic Powers of Play			
Chapter 1; What Is a Therapeutic Power of Play	1a, 1b	2a, 2b, 2f	3a, 3b, 3c, 3e
Chapter 2: The Therapeutic Powers of Play: Overview	1a, 1b	2a, 2b, 2f	3a, 3b, 3c, 3e
Chapter 3: Definition of a Theory and Selection	1a, 1d, 1h	2a, 2b, 2e, 2f	3a, 3b, 3c, 3d, 3e
Chapter 4: The Neuroscience of Theories and Therapeutic Powers of Play	1e, 1e, 1j,	2a, 2b, 2f	3e
Chapter 5: Play Therapy Dimensions Model: Theories and Therapeutic Powers of Play Lens	1a, 1b, 1c, 1d, 1h	2a, 2b, 2e, 2f	3a, 3b, 3c, 3d, 3e
Chapter 6: Cases: Conceptualization from a Theoretical and Therapeutic Powers of Play Lens	1b, 1c, 1d, 1e, 1g, 1h, 1i, 1j, 1k	2a, 2b, 2e, 2f, 2g, 2h, 2i, 2j	3a, 3b, 3c, 3e, 3h
Chapter 7: Research and Empirical Support	1g, 1j, 1k	2c, 2g, 2j	3e
Chapter 8: Transtheoretical Model of Supervision	1f	2h, 2i	3a, 3b, 3c, 3d, 3e, 3f, 3g, 3h
Part II: Comparing Theoretical Approaches through the Lens of the Therapeutic Powers of Play			
Part III: Contemporary Models and Integrative Approaches and Applications			
Introduction	1a	2b, 2j	3a, 3b, 3c, 3d, 3e, 3f, 3h
Underlying Philosophy	1d	2d, 2e, 2f, 2j	3a, 3b, 3c, 3d, 3e, 3f, 3h
Personality Theory	1d	2d, 2e, 2f, 2j	3a, 3b, 3c, 3d, 3e, 3f, 3h
Model of Psychopathology	1d	2d, 2e, 2f, 2j	3a, 3b, 3c, 3d, 3e, 3f, 3h
Conceptualizing Goals of Treatment	1d, 1e, 1g	2a, 2c, 2g	3b, 3c, 3d, 3e, 3h
Role of the Therapist	1c, 1d	2a, 2b, 2c, 2d, 2e, 2f, 2g, 2h, 2i, 2j	3a, 3b, 3c, 3d, 3e, 3f, 3g, 3h
Roles of Caregivers and Collaterals	1h	2b, 2e	3b, 3c, 3d, 3e, 3f, 3h
Research/Empirical Support	1b, 1c, 1d, 1f	2c, 2d, 2f, 2g, 2j	3b, 3c, 3d, 3e, 3f, 3g, 3h
Case Study through the Lens of the Therapeutic Powers of Play:			
Therapeutic Powers of Play Employed	1b	2a, 2d, 2g	3b, 3c, 3e, 3h
Cultural, diversity, inclusion considerations	1h, 1j	2h, 2i	3c, 3f, 3h
Case Formulation and Application	1e, 1g, 1i, 1j, 1k	2a, 2c, 2d, 2e, 2f, 2g	3b, 3c, 3d, 3e, 3h
Challenges in Implementation	1f	2h, 2i	3a, 3b, 3c, 3d, 3e, 3f, 3g, 3h

play therapist, supervisor, or trainer. However, this text fills a gap that has existed since play therapy was first conceptualized and used. If we were to ponder the potential magnitude of this text, what comes to mind? What if Freud had this text when working with Little Hans (Freud, 1946, 1963), Jung had it when writing about Anna (Jung, 1969), and/or if Axline had it when conceptualizing and writing *Dibs:In Search of Self* (Axline, 1964)?

Without overstating the importance of this text, we can say that the writing of this text was driven by need, and this need links directly to the growth and importance of play, TPoP, play therapy theories, and the field of play therapy.

References

Association for Play Therapy. (2024a). *Credentialing standards for the Registered Play Therapist™: APT professional credentialing program*. https://cdn.ymaws.com/www.a4pt.org/resource/resmgr/credentials/standards_&_applications/rpt_standards.pdf.

Association for Play Therapy. (2024b). *Credentialing standards for the Registered Play Therapist-Supervisor ™: APT professional credentialing program*. https://cdn.ymaws.com/www.a4pt.org/resource/resmgr/credentials/standards_&_applications/rpt-s_standards.pdf.

Association for Play Therapy. (2023a). *Credentialing standards for the School-Based Registered Play Therapist™: APT professional credentialing program*. https://cdn.ymaws.com/www.a4pt.org/resource/resmgr/credentials/standards_&_applications/sb-rpt_guide.pdf.

Association for Play Therapy. (2023b). *Play therapy competencies: APT professional credentialing program*. https://cdn.ymaws.com/www.a4pt.org/resource/resmgr/credentials/play_therapy_competencies.pdf.

Association for Play Therapy. (2024c). *Sample syllabus: Introductory graduate play therapy course university education*. https://cdn.ymaws.com/www.a4pt.org/resource/resmgr/education_&_training/Sample_Play_Therapy_Course_S.pdf.

Association for Play Therapy. (2024d, October 28). 2024 Year-in-review [video]. *YouTube*. https://youtu.be/LxwAYSJFCA8.

Association for Play Therapy. (n.d.). *Sample syllabus: Advanced graduate play therapy course*. https://cdn.ymaws.com/www.a4pt.org/resource/resmgr/education_&_training/sample_advanced_play_therapy.pdf.

Axline, V. M. (1964). *Dibs: In search of self*. Houghton Mifflin.

Freud, A. (1946). *The psychoanalytic treatment of children*. Imago Publishing Co., Ltd.

Freud, S. (1963). Notes upon a case of obsessional neurosis. In P. Rieff (Ed.), *Three case histories* (pp. 1–57). Macmillan Publishing Company (Original work published 1909).

Hudspeth, E. F. (2021). Play therapy versus a play-based therapy. *Play Therapy, 16*(2), 14. https://cdn.ymaws.com/www.a4pt.org/resource/resmgr/magazine_articles/Play_Therapy_vs_Play-Based_T.pdf.

Jung, C. G. (1969). Two essays on analytical psychology. In H. Read, M. Fordham, G. Adler, & W. McGuire (Eds.), *The collected works of C. G. Jung* (Vol. 7, pp. 9–18). Princeton University.

Schaefer, C. E., & Drewes, A. A. (Eds.). (2014). *The therapeutic powers of play: 20 core agents of change* (2nd ed.). Wiley

Turner, R., Schoeneberg, C., Ray, D., & Lin, Y. (2020). Establishing play therapy competencies: A Delphi study. *International Journal of Play Therapy, 29*(4), 177–90. https://doi.org/10.1037/pla0000138.

Appendix
Case Study—Herman

The following is a composite case study, based on several actual cases, with the names and specifics altered for confidentiality. This case study was utilized by each chapter author for analysis, treatment planning and discussion in Part II and Part III.

Herman is ten years old and of mixed heritage. His mother identifies as Caucasian. But his maternal grandfather was Hispanic and his maternal grandmother was African American. Herman had fetal exposure to prenatal substance misuse involving opioids. His mother was twenty-four years old when she gave birth to Herman and had used opioids since the age of eighteen. She was prescribed opioids for pain after suffering a significant fall down a flight of stairs, having been pushed by her boyfriend. This fall resulted in chronic back pain that was not successfully treated. Herman's mother received her high school diploma, worked at odd jobs for brief periods of time at local stores, and lived with a variety of boyfriends. At the time of her pregnancy, she did not know who the father was.

Herman experienced withdrawal at birth and remained in the NICU for over a month. His mother did not see him or get to hold Herman after his birth. During his stay in the NICU he was not held often and was in a brightly lit space with many other children crying and needing attention. After the NICU, Herman went to live with his maternal grandmother and her paramour until he was almost three years old, when he was removed again due to domestic violence, which entailed hitting each other, yelling, and shouting, along with alcohol abuse by both. His relationship with his grandmother was often strained due to her resenting having to care for him, and Herman's fussiness and difficulties being fed and held. He was often left in his crib for long periods of time with a bottle and had little physical interaction.

After removal from his grandmother, Herman entered into foster care and has been moved twice since age three due to behavioral issues at age five and again at age six after he had been sexually abused. Herman was sodomized by a sixteen-year-old foster boy in his last home over a period of several months while they shared the same room. The abuse was only discovered during a pediatric examination, which noticed some anal fold changes and swelling in the rectum and reports of bowel accidents. Herman has been in his current therapeutic foster home for the past four years. His foster parents appear to be highly skilled, patient, and loving. Herman has a good relationship with his foster parents and calls them Mommy and Daddy. He appears to especially admire and respect his foster father. While parental rights have been terminated and there is no contact with his maternal grandmother, no adoptive family has come forward due to Herman's behavioral issues.

There are two other older foster boys in the home who are on the autism spectrum and avoid interacting with Herman.

When Herman came to live with his foster parents, he was underweight, very quiet, withdrawn, and fearful. He expressed that he did not like being a boy and tried to dress in non-gender-specific ways. Although he liked to use nail polish to paint his nails with different colors and used eyeliner to accentuate his eyes, Herman's behaviors became increasingly difficult to manage, even for his experienced foster parents. They reported that he often became angry and aggressive with little provocation. He seemed to seek out and crave dangerous situations, climbing out of the window to go on the roof. He had difficulty falling asleep, at times getting only an hour or two of sleep at night and spending the rest of the night playing games on his iPad or wandering the house, getting food and hiding it in his room. On many occasions, the foster mother found food wrappers, old half-eaten sandwiches, and juice containers under his bed. When Herman finally did fall asleep, he often had nightmares about monsters and vampires.

The school conducted psychological and academic testing, administered the Child Behavior Checklist (CBCL) and the Conners to assess for ADHD. Herman was found to be of average intelligence with learning disabilities in reading and math. He scored significantly high for ADHD and externalizing behaviors. Although Herman is in a special education class for children with emotional and behavioral issues and has an IEP, he learns very little because of difficulty attending to his classwork and not being able to sit through a full class period or even sit still for more than a few minutes at a time. Herman is constantly getting up, running around the room, fidgeting in his seat, jumping on chairs and tables, and banging against the walls while the teacher is giving a lesson. These episodes appear to have no known precipitants. Herman often appears angry and sullen, but this can quickly become explosive. Peers often tease him about how he looks because of his wearing nail polish and occasionally black eyeliner and try to provoke him into misbehaving. Herman has been suspended several times from school for throwing chairs and desks and fighting with peers. He has even hit or kicked his teachers on several occasions.

Herman was on a variety of medications prescribed by a psychiatrist that, while they worked initially, slowly seemed to lose effectiveness over short spans of time. He was on Ritalin, Adderall, Dexedrine, Lithium, Haldol, and currently is on Guanfacine and Risperdal. Consequently, Herman cycles through medications and dosages. He was in therapy over the past three years with four different therapists. Several were interns who only stayed for a year at a time. These therapists used behavioral modification, CBT, and playing games. He was in individual non-directive play therapy over the past year which does not seem to have made any substantial changes.

Index